Professional
SQL Server™ Analysis
Services 2005 with MDX

Professional
SQL Server™ Analysis Services 2005 with MDX

Sivakumar Harinath

Stephen R. Quinn

Wiley Publishing, Inc.

Professional SQL Server™ Analysis Services 2005 with MDX

Published by
Wiley Publishing, Inc.
10475 Crosspoint Boulevard
Indianapolis, IN 46256
www.wiley.com

Copyright© 2006 by Wiley Publishing, Inc., Indianapolis, Indiana

Published by Wiley Publishing, Inc., Indianapolis, Indiana

Published simultaneously in Canada

ISBN-13: 978-0-7645-7918-9
ISBN-10: 0-7645-7918-5

Manufactured in the United States of America

10 9 8 7 6 5 4 3 2 1

1MA/RW/QV/QW/IN

Library of Congress control number: 2005032272

About the Authors

Sivakumar Harinath

Sivakumar Harinath was born in Chennai, India. Siva has a Ph.D. in Computer Science from the University of Illinois at Chicago. His thesis title was: "Data Management Support for Distributed Data Mining of Large Datasets over High Speed Wide Area Networks." Siva has worked for Newgen Software Technologies (P) Ltd., IBM Toronto Labs, Canada, and has been at Microsoft since February of 2002. Siva started as a Software Design Engineer in Test (SDET) in the Analysis Services Performance Team and is currently an SDET Lead for Analysis Services 2005. Siva's other interests include high performance computing, distributed systems and high speed networking. Siva is married to Shreepriya and had twins Praveen and Divya during the course of writing this book. His personal interests include travel, games/sports (in particular, Chess, Carrom, Racquet Ball, Board games) and Cooking. You can reach Siva at sivakumar.harinath@microsoft.com

Stephen Quinn

Stephen Quinn was born in San Luis Obispo, California. Stephen has a Masters degree (1988) in Cognitive Psychology from California State University, Chico and is scheduled to receive his Masters of Business Administration (MBA) from the University of Washington, Seattle, in June 2006. Stephen is married to Katherine and is raising his daughter, Anastasia. He has been in most roles common to the R&D environment i.e., software developer, technical writer, technical support specialist and several quality assurance roles. Stephen has published some 20 articles in the magazines Byte, InfoWorld and Datamation. With 15+ years of software experience; Stephen has worked the last 8 years at Microsoft; most recently as a Technical Writer in SQL User Education and before that, for several years as Test Manager in the SQL Business Intelligence Unit. You can reach Stephen at srq@portfolioeffect.com

Credits

I dedicate this book in the grandest possible manner to my dear wife Shreepriya who has been fully supportive and put up with me disappearing from home and the late nights when I worked on this book. It is also dedicated to my two month old twins Praveen and Divya who do not know what a book is yet. I wish their cute photographs could be on the cover page. I dedicate this book in memory of my father Harinath Govindarajalu who passed away in 1999 who I am sure would have been proud of this great achievement and to my mother Sundara Bai. Finally, dedicate the book to my inlaws Sundaravathanem Sanjeevi and Geethalakshmi Sanjeevi who have been very supportive and helping during the last six months.

Sivakumar Harinath

I dedicate my contribution to this book to the woman who was most supportive and encouraging about the project. That would be my wife, Kyung Eun (Katherine) Quinn. Also, I would like to dedicate this to my kid, Anastasia who would have preferred I spent much of that writing time with her. To my mother, Roselma Quinn who tolerated incessant last minute changes of plan due to book-related work. And my father, Stephen Thomas Quinn, who tolerated my whining about how much work this book was to produce. Finally, to my MBA study team, thanks to everyone on the team; Jim Braun, Liz Younger, Michael Styles, Kevin Heath, Eduardo Alvarez-Godinez, and Dave Lovely for being understanding about what I was going through.

Stephen R. Quinn

In memory of all those who have been devastated due to the natural calamities in the last two years such as the South Asian Tsunami, Storms Katrina and Rita in the United States and earthquakes in India and Pakistan.

Acknowledgments

Wow!!! It has been an amazing two-year journey, almost to the day, from when we decided to partner in writing this book. It all started when Siva jokingly mentioned to his wife the idea of writing a book on SQL Server Analysis Services 2005. She took it seriously and motivated him to start working on the idea in October of 2003. As always, there are so many people who deserve mentioning that we're afraid we'll miss someone. If you are among those missed, please accept our humblest apologies. We first need to thank Amir Netz, our then Product Unit Manager, who not only granted us the permission to moonlight while working at Microsoft, but also provided constant encouragement and support. It is apropos that it is called moonlighting because we saw a lot of moonlight while working on this book - multiple all nighters took place. We thank Zhaohui Tang, who helped us get in touch with the right publishing people. Our sincerest thanks go to Wiley Publishing for giving us this opportunity and placing their trust in first-time authors like us. They provided immense help, constant feedback, and expert support. We would especially like to thank our editors, Bob Elliot and Adaobi Obi Tulton, who didn't so much as support us as prod us along -- which is exactly what we needed at the time.

We would like to thank our technical reviewers, Leah Etienne and Dylan Huang, who graciously offered us their assistance. Dylan also contributed to the technical content in chapters 9, 11 and 13. We thank all our colleagues in the Analysis Services product team (including Developers, Program Managers, and Testers) who helped us in accomplishing the immense feat of writing a book on a developing product. From the Analysis Services team, special thanks go to Akshai Mirchandani, Richard Tkachuk, Mosha Pasumansky, Marius Dumitru, T.K. Anand, Sasha Berger, Paul Sanders, Thierry D'Hers, Matt Carroll, Andrew Garbuzov, Zhaohui Tang, Artur Pop, and Rob Zare for patiently answering our questions. We also thank our Analysis Services documentation colleagues Dennis Kennedy and Tom Mathews for their helpful input.

Most importantly, we owe our deepest thanks to our wonderful families. Without their support and sacrifice, this book would have become one of those many projects that one begins and never finishes. Our families were the ones who truly took the brunt of it and sacrificed shared leisure time, all in support of our literary pursuit. We especially want to thank them for their patience with us, and the grace it took not killing us during some of the longer work binges. During this long journey life did not stand still: Siva's wife gave birth to twins, Praveen and Divya, and Stephen finished the first year (plus part of the second) of MBA studies at the University of Washington, Seattle. Finally to Siva's wife, Shreepriya, and to Stephen's wife, Katherine, none of this would have been possible without your support.

Contents

Contents

Contents

Contents

Contents

Introduction

We decided to write this book because we sensed the power and excitement associated with Analysis Services 2005 early on in its development, especially in relation to improvements over Analysis Services 2000. We also sensed that with minimal effort you could probably re-configure the user interface elements to pilot a nuclear submarine. Our recommendation, however, is to use Analysis Services 2005 to build, process, and deploy top of the line business intelligence applications. Ok, so we are not shy about admitting to the apparent complexity of the product when faced with the user interface, which happens to be embedded in the Microsoft Visual Studio shell. This is great for you, especially if you are already familiar with the Visual Studio development environment.

With this book, we want to show that not only will you overcome any possible initial shock regarding the user interface, you will come to see it as your friend. It turns out there are many wizards to accomplish common tasks, or you can design the analytic infrastructure from the ground up, it is up to you. This formidable, yet friendly user interface will empower you to implement business analytics of a caliber formerly reserved for academicians writing up government grant proposals or Ph.D. dissertations. More importantly, this power to turn data into information, and we mean, real usable business-related decision making information, can impact the bottom line of your company in terms of dollars earned and dollars saved. And that is what data warehousing, ultimately, is all about. Put another way, the purpose of all this data warehousing is simple; it is about generating actionable information from the data stores created by a company's sales, inventory, and other data sources. In sum, it is all about decision support.

Who This Book Is For

What was the impetus for you to pick up this book? Perhaps you are passionate about extracting information from reams of raw data; or perhaps you have some very specific challenges on the job right now that you think might be amenable to a business analysis based solution. Then, there is always the lure of fame and fortune. Please be aware that attaining expert status in data warehousing can lead to lucrative consulting and salaried opportunities. However, it won't likely make you as rich as becoming a purveyor of nothing-down real estate courses. If your desire is to leave the infomercial career path to others and get really serious about data warehousing in general and business intelligence in particular, you have just the book in your hands to start or continue on your path to subject mastery.

The obvious question now is what are the pre-requisites for reading and understanding the content of this book? You certainly do not have to already know the intricacies of data warehousing, you will learn that here as you go. If you have only the foggiest notion of what a relational database is; well, this book is going to challenge you at best and bury you at worst. If you are not intimidated by what you just read, this book is for you. If you have worked on data warehouses using non-Microsoft products and want to learn how Microsoft can do it better, this book is for you. If you are a database administrator, MIS Professional or application developer interested in exploiting the power of business intelligence then this book is definitely for you!

What This Book Covers

Analysis Services 2005 is the premier multi-dimensional database from Microsoft. This is the most recent of three releases from Microsoft to date. In this release, the tools and server provided have been designed for use as an enterprise-class Business Intelligence Server and we think Microsoft has been successful. Analysis Services 2005 provides you with powerful tools to design, build, test and deploy your multi-dimensional databases. By integrating the tools within Visual Studio you really get the feel of building a BI project. Similar to any application you build within VS; you build your BI projects and deploy them to Analysis Services instance. Due to the new product design and enhanced features you definitely have to know how to create cubes, dimensions and many other objects, maintain them, and support your BI users. Similar to its well-liked predecessors, Analysis Services 2005 supports the MDX language by which you can query data. MDX is for querying multi-dimensional databases much like SQL is for query of relational databases. The MDX language is a component of the OLE DB for OLAP specification and is supported by other BI vendors. Microsoft's Analysis Services 2005 provides certain extensions that help you to achieve more from your multi-dimensional databases.

This book walks you through the entire product and the important features of the product with the help of step by step instructions on building multi-dimensional databases. Within each chapter you will not only learn how to use the features but also learn more about the features at a user level and what happens behind the scenes to make things work. We believe this will provide you additional insight into how features really work and hence provide insight into how they are best exploited. It will also enhance your ability to debug problems which you might not have been able to otherwise. This behind the scenes view is often surfaced through exposure of the XML for Analysis XML/A created by the product based on user interface settings. It works like this; Analysis Services 2005 uses the XML/A specification to communicate between client and server --The Analysis Services 2005 tools communicate to the server using XML/A. Once you have designed your multi-dimensional database using the tools you need to send the definition to the server. At that time the tools use XML/A to send the definitions. You will learn these definitions so that you have the ability to design a custom application which interacts with an Analysis Services instance.

MDX is the language used for data retrieval from Analysis Services. You will get an introduction to the MDX language with basic concepts and the various MDX functions in this book. When you are browsing data using Analysis Services tools; those tools send appropriate MDX to the instance of Analysis Services which contains the target data. By learning the MDX sent to the server for the various desired operations you will begin to understand the intricacies of MDX and thereby improve your own MDX coding skills by extension.

One of the key value-adds found in this book, which we think is worth the price of admission by itself, is that through the chapters you will begin to understand what design trade offs are involved in BI application development. Further, the book will help you in do better BI design for your company in the face of those trade off decisions– especially with the help of a few scenarios. And there are many scenarios discussed in this book. The scenarios are geared towards some of the common business problems that are currently faced by existing Analysis Services customers. While there is no pretension that this book will teach you business per se, it is a book on BI and we did take the liberty of explaining certain business concepts which you are sure to run into eventually. For example, the often misunderstood concept of depreciation is explained in some detail. Again, this aspect of the book is shallow, but we hope what pure business concepts are covered will provide you a more informed basis from which to work. If you know the concepts already, well, why not read about the ideas again? There might be some new information in there for you.

Finally, this book covers integration of Analysis Services with other SQL Server 2005 components – Data Mining, Integrations Services and Reporting Services. These chapters will help you go beyond just a passing level of understanding of Analysis Services 2005; it is really integration of these disparate components which ship in the box with SQL Server which allow you to build start to finish BI solutions which are scalable, maintainable, have good performance characteristics, and highlight the right information. Do not skip the chapters which do not at first seem crucial to understanding Analysis Services 2005 itself; it is the whole picture that brings the real value. Get that whole picture for stellar success and return on your investment of time, and energy.

How This Book Is Structured

The authors of books in the Wrox Professional series attempt to make each chapter as stand alone as possible. This book is no exception. However, owing to the sophistication of the subject matter and the manner in which certain concepts are necessarily tied to others has somewhat undermined this most noble intention. In fact, unless you are a seasoned data warehousing professional; or otherwise have experience with earlier versions of Analysis Services, it is advised you take a serial approach to reading chapters. Work through the first three chapters in order as they will collectively provide you some architectural context, a good first look at the product and an introduction to MDX. Just to remind you, in the simplest terms, MDX is to Analysis Services what SQL is to SQL Server. Ok, that was just too simple an analogy; but let's not get ahead of ourselves! As for the actual layout of the book, we have divided the book into roughly four major sections.

In Part 1 we introduce the basic concepts and then get you kick started using Analysis Services with most of the common operations that you need to design your databases. You will become familiarized with the product if you aren't already and hopefully it will provide you some sense of achievement which will certainly help motivate you to go beyond the simple stuff and move to the advanced.

Part 2 contains chapters that prepare you for the more advanced topics concerning the creation of multidimensional databases. You will learn about the calculation model in Analysis Services 2005 and enhance your dimensions and cube designs using Business Intelligence Development Studio Further you will learn more about the new features in the product such as multiple measure groups, business intelligence wizards, key performance indicators, and actions.

In Part 3 of the book, we include some of the common scenarios used in BI spread across four chapters (all with specific learning agendas of their own). The idea here is for you to get comfortable solving business problems and start you on your way to thinking about how to build larger scale BI databases. We also, we focus on real world business aspects of product usage. Like budgeting and forecasting and to be particularly real world, we have a whole chapter on the use of Office analysis components.

Finally, in Part 4, we cover the integration of Analysis Services with other SQL Server 2005 components that help you build solutions and provide the best support possible to your administrators and BI users. Both Integration and Administration along with Performance are absolutely key to get the maximum out of the system after initial design. This is also the section where you will find Data Mining.

Together, these four sections, that is to say, this book, will provide you a full blown BI learning experience. Since BI and BI applications constitute such an incredibly complex and massive field of endeavor, no one book can possibly cover it all. In terms of BI though the eyes of SQL Server Analysis Services 2005, we hope this book has got it covered!

We also encourage you to take a look at Appendix A; it is the complete MDX Reference as obtained from the Wiley Publishing book, *MDX Solutions, 2nd Edition*. The authors would like to thank George Spofford and Wiley Publishing for allowing use of that reference; it should come in handy for you.

What You Need to Use This Book

You need a computer running some version of the Windows operating system, like Windows XP Professional for example, and a copy of SQL Server 2005 installed on that system. Please see the appropriate documentation from Microsoft for the hardware requirements needed to support the particular version of Windows you own.

Conventions

To help you get the most from the text and keep track of what's happening, we've used a number of conventions throughout the book.

> **Boxes like this one hold important, not-to-be forgotten information that is directly relevant to the surrounding text.**

Tips, hints, tricks, and asides to the current discussion are offset and placed in italics like this.

As for styles in the text:

❑   We *highlight* new terms and important words when we introduce them.

❑   We show keyboard strokes like this: Ctrl+A.

❑   We show file names, URLs, and code within the text like so: `persistence.properties`.

❑   We present code in two different ways:

```
In code examples we highlight new and important code with a gray background.
```

```
The gray highlighting is not used for code that's less important in the present
context, or has been shown before.
```

Source Code

As you work through the examples in this book, you may choose either to type in all the code manually or to use the source code files that accompany the book. All of the source code used in this book is available for download at `http://www.wrox.com`. Once at the site, simply locate the book's title (either by using the Search box or by using one of the title lists) and click the Download Code link on the book's detail page to obtain all the source code for the book.

Because many books have similar titles, you may find it easiest to search by ISBN; for this book the ISBN is 0-764-579185

Once you download the code, just decompress it with your favorite compression tool. Alternately, you can go to the main Wrox code download page at http://www.wrox.com/dynamic/books/download .aspx to see the code available for this book and all other Wrox books.

Errata

We make every effort to ensure that there are no errors in the text or in the code. However, no one is perfect, and mistakes do occur. If you find an error in one of our books, like a spelling mistake or faulty piece of code, we would be very grateful for your feedback. By sending in errata you may save another reader hours of frustration and at the same time you will be helping us provide even higher quality information.

To find the errata page for this book, go to http://www.wrox.com and locate the title using the Search box or one of the title lists. Then, on the book details page, click the Book Errata link. On this page you can view all errata that has been submitted for this book and posted by Wrox editors. A complete book list including links to each's book's errata is also available at www.wrox.com/misc-pages/booklist .shtml.

If you don't spot "your" error on the Book Errata page, go to www.wrox.com/contact/techsupport .shtml and complete the form there to send us the error you have found. We'll check the information and, if appropriate, post a message to the book's errata page and fix the problem in subsequent editions of the book.

p2p.wrox.com

For author and peer discussion, join the P2P forums at p2p.wrox.com. The forums are a Web-based system for you to post messages relating to Wrox books and related technologies and interact with other readers and technology users. The forums offer a subscription feature to e-mail you topics of interest of your choosing when new posts are made to the forums. Wrox authors, editors, other industry experts, and your fellow readers are present on these forums.

At http://p2p.wrox.com you will find a number of different forums that will help you not only as you read this book, but also as you develop your own applications. To join the forums, just follow these steps:

1. Go to p2p.wrox.com and click the Register link.
2. Read the terms of use and click Agree.
3. Complete the required information to join as well as any optional information you wish to provide and click Submit.
4. You will receive an e-mail with information describing how to verify your account and complete the joining process.

   You can read messages in the forums without joining P2P but in order to post your own messages, you must join.

Once you join, you can post new messages and respond to messages other users post. You can read messages at any time on the Web. If you would like to have new messages from a particular forum e-mailed to you, click the Subscribe to this Forum icon by the forum name in the forum listing.

For more information about how to use the Wrox P2P, be sure to read the P2P FAQs for answers to questions about how the forum software works as well as many common questions specific to P2P and Wrox books. To read the FAQs, click the FAQ link on any P2P page.

Professional
SQL Server™ Analysis Services 2005 with MDX

Part I

Introduction

Introduction to Data Warehousing and Analysis Services 2005

A data warehouse is a system that takes data from a company's databases and other data sources and transforms it into a structure conducive to business analysis. Mathematical operations are often performed on the newly structured or organized data to further its usefulness for making business decisions. Finally, the data is made available to the end user for querying and analysis. If the data warehouse is well architected then queries to the data warehouse will return query results quickly (in a matter of seconds). The business decision-maker will have a powerful tool that could never have been effectively used directly from the company's daily operational systems. We consider data analysis to be of two forms. The first requires a person to investigate the data for trends. This method is called On Line Analytical Processing (OLAP). The second form utilizes algorithms to scour the data looking for trends. This method is called Data Mining. Analysis Services 2005 is a business intelligence platform that enables you to use OLAP and Data Mining. Now that you have the big picture of data warehousing, let us look at what you will learn in this chapter.

In this chapter you learn what data warehousing really is and how it relates to business intelligence. This information comes wrapped in a whole load of new concepts, and you get a look at the best known approaches to warehousing with the introduction of those concepts. We explain data warehousing in several different ways and we are sure you will understand it. You will finally see how Analysis Services 2005 puts it all together in terms of architecture—at both client and server levels—based on a new data abstraction layer called Unified Dimensional Model (UDM).

A Closer Look at Data Warehousing

In the book *Building the Data Warehouse*, Bill Inmon described the data warehouse as "a *subject oriented, integrated, non-volatile,* and *time variant* collection of data in support of management's decisions." According to Inmon, the subject orientation of a data warehouse differs from the operational orientation seen in *On-Line Transaction Processing* (OLTP) systems; so a subject seen in a data warehouse might relate to customers, whereas an operation in an OLTP system might relate to a specific application like sales processing and all that goes with it.

The word *integrated* means that throughout the enterprise, data points should be defined consistently or there should be some integration methodology to force consistency at the data warehouse level. One example would be how to represent the entity Microsoft. If Microsoft were represented in different databases as MSFT, MS, Microsoft, and MSoft, it would be difficult to meaningfully merge these in a data warehouse. The best-case solution is to have all databases in the enterprise refer to Microsoft as, say, MSFT, thereby making the merger of this data seamless. A less desirable, but equally workable, solution is to force all the variants into one during the process of moving data from the operational system to the data warehouse.

A data warehouse is referred to as non-volatile since it differs from operational systems, which are often transactional in nature and updated regularly. The data warehouse is generally loaded at some preset interval, which may be measured in weeks or even months. This is not to say it is never measured in days; but even if updates do occur daily, that is still a sparse schedule compared to the constant changes being made to transactional systems.

The final element in this definition regards time variance, which is a sophisticated way of saying how far back the stored data in the system reaches. In the case of operational systems, the time period is quite short, perhaps days, weeks, or months. In the case of the warehouse, it is quite long — typically on the order of years. This last item might strike you as fairly self-evident because you would have a hard time analyzing business trends if your data didn't date back further than two months. So, there you have it, the classic definition that no good book on data warehousing should be without.

Taking the analysis one step closer to the nuts and bolts of working systems, consider that a relational database can be represented graphically as an *Entity-Relationship Diagram* (ERD) in a case tool or in SQL Server 2005 itself (see Figure 1-1 for an example). Not only will you see the objects in the database shown in the diagram, but you will also see many join connections which represent the relationships between the objects. Data warehouses can be formed from relational databases or multi-dimensional databases. When your data warehouse is modeled after the relational database model then data is stored in two-dimensional tables and analytical or business queries are normally very slow. When one refers to a data warehouse it is typically OLAP that is being referred to. In the case of OLAP you have a multi-dimensional database with data stored in such a way that business users can view it and efficiently answer business questions — all with fast query response times. There is more to come in this chapter on the differences between relational and OLAP databases.

Data warehousing is the process by which data starting from an OLTP database is transformed and stored so as to facilitate the extraction of business-relevant information from the source data. An OLTP database, like a point-of-sale (POS) database is transaction-based and typically normalized (well opti-mized for storage) to reduce the amount of redundant data storage generated. The result makes for fast updates, but this speed of update capability is offset by a reduction in speed of information retrieval at query time. For speed of information retrieval, especially for the purpose of business analytics, an OLAP database is called for. An OLAP database is highly denormalized (not well optimized for storage) and therefore has rows of data that may be redundant. This makes for very fast query responses because rel-atively few joins are involved. And fast responses are what you want while doing business intelligence work. Figure 1-2 shows information extracted from transactional databases and consolidated into multi-dimensional databases; then stored in data marts or data warehouses. Data marts can be thought of as mini–data warehouses and quite often act as part of a larger warehouse. Data marts are subject-oriented data stores for well-manicured (cleaned) data. Examples include a sales data mart, an inventory data mart, or basically any subject rooted at the departmental level. A data warehouse on the other hand, functions at the enterprise level and typically handles data across the entire organization.

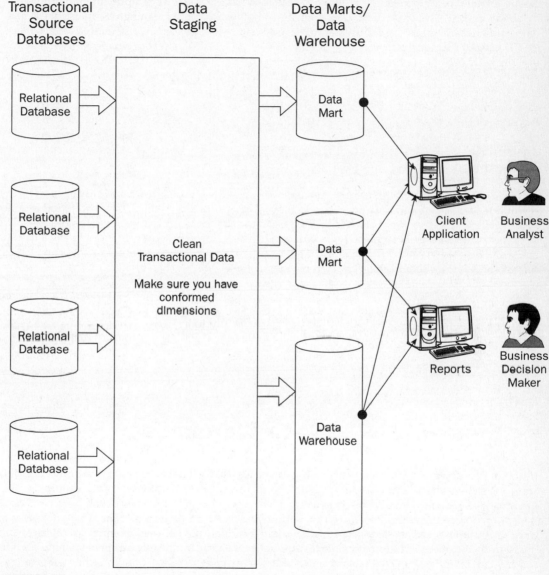

Figure 1-1

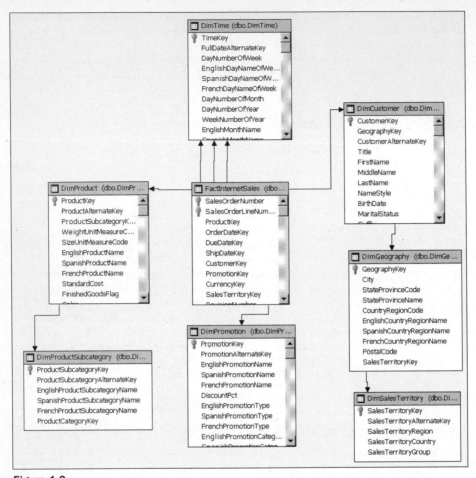

Figure 1-2

Key Elements of a Data Warehouse

Learning the elements of a data warehouse or data mart is, in part, about building a new vocabulary; the vocabulary associated with data warehousing can be less than intuitive, but once you get it, it all makes sense. The challenge, of course, is understanding it in the first place. Two kinds of tables form a data warehouse: fact tables and dimension tables.

Figure 1-3 shows a fact and a dimension table and the relationship between them. A fact table typically contains the business fact data such as sales amount, sales quantity, the number of customers, and the foreign keys to dimension tables. A *foreign key* is a field in a relational table that matches the primary key column of another table. Foreign keys provide a level of indirection between tables that enable you to cross-reference them. One important use of foreign keys is to maintain referential integrity (data integrity) within your database. Dimension tables contain detailed information relevant to specific attributes of the fact data, such as details of the product, customer attributes, store information, and so on. In Figure 1-3, the dimension table Product contains the information Product SKU and Product Name. The following sections go into more detail about fact and dimension tables.

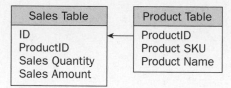

Figure 1-3

Fact Tables

With the end goal of extracting crucial business insights from your data, you will have to structure your data initially in such a way as to facilitate later numeric manipulation. Leaving the data embedded in some normalized database will never do! Your business data, often called detail data or fact data, goes in a de-normalized table called the fact table. Don't let the term "facts" throw you; it literally refers to the facts. In business, the facts are things such as number of products sold and amount received for products sold. Yet another way to describe this type of data is to call them *measures*. Calling the data measures versus detail data is not an important point. What is important is that this type of data is often numeric (though it could be of type string) and the values are quite often subject to aggregation (pre-calculating roll-ups of data over hierarchies, which subsequently yield improved query results). A fact table often contains columns like the ones shown in the following table:

Product ID	Date ID	State ID	Number of Cases	Sales Amount
1	07/01/2005	6	3244	$90,842
1	07/01/2005	33	6439	$184,000
1	07/01/2005	42	4784	$98,399
1	08/01/2005	31	6784	$176,384
1	08/01/2005	6	2097	$59,136
1	08/01/2005	33	7326	$8,635
1	08/01/2005	42	4925	$100,962
1	09/01/2005	31	8548	$176,384
1	09/01/2005	6	945	$26,649
1	09/01/2005	33	8635	$246,961
1	09/01/2005	42	4935	$101,165
1	10/01/2005	31	9284	$257,631
1	10/01/2005	33	9754	$278,965
1	10/01/2005	42	4987	$102,733
...	...	...	...	...

This table shows the sales of different varieties of beer between the months of July and October 2005 in four different states. The product id, date id, and state ids together form the primary key of the fact table. The number of cases of beer sold and the sales amount are facts. The product id, date id, and state id are foreign keys that join to the products, date, and state tables. In this table the state ids 6, 31, 33, and 42 refer to the states MA, CA, OR, and WA, respectively, and represent the order in which these states joined the United States. Building the fact table is an important step towards building your data warehouse.

Dimension Tables

The fact table typically holds quantitative data; for example, transaction data that shows number of units sold per sale and amount charged to the customer for the unit sold. To provide reference to higher-level roll-ups based on things like time, a complementary table can be added that provides linkage to those higher levels through the magic of the join (how you link one table to another). In the case of time, the fact table might only show the date on which some number of cases of beer was sold; to do business analysis at the monthly, quarterly, or yearly level, a time dimension is required. The following table shows what a beer products dimension table would minimally contain. The product id is the primary key in this table. The product id of the fact table shown previously is a foreign key that joins to the product id in the following table:

Product ID	Product SKU	Product Name
1	SBF767	SuperMicro Ale
2	SBH543	SuperMicro Lager
3	SBZ136	SuperMicro Pilsner
4	SBK345	SuperMicro Hefeweizen
...	...	...

For illustrative purposes, assume that you have a dimension table for time that contains monthly, quarterly, and yearly values. There must be a unique key for each value; these unique key values are called *primary keys*. Meanwhile, back in the fact table you have a column of keys with values mapping to the primary keys in the dimension table. These keys in the fact table are called *foreign keys*. For now it is enough if you get the idea that dimension tables connect to fact tables and this connectivity provides you with the ability to extend the usefulness of your low-level facts resident in the fact table.

A multi-dimensional database is created from fact and dimension tables to form objects called dimensions and cubes. Dimensions are objects that are created mostly from dimension tables. Some examples of dimensions are time, geography, and employee which would typically contain additional information about those objects by which users can analyze the fact data. The cube is an object that contains fact data as well as dimensions so that data analysis can be performed by slicing or dicing dimensions. For example, you could view the sales information for the year 2005 in the state of Washington. Each of those slices of information is a dimension.

Dimensions

To make sense of a cube, which is at the heart of business analysis and discussed in the next section, you must first understand the nature of dimensions. We say that OLAP is based on multidimensional databases because it quite literally is. You do business analysis by observing the relationships between dimensions like Time, Sales, Products, Customers, Employees, Geography, and Accounts. Dimensions are most often made up of several hierarchies. Hierarchies are logical entities by which a business user might want to analyze fact data. Each hierarchy can have one or more levels. A hierarchy in the geography dimension, for example, might have the following levels: Country, State, County, and City.

A hierarchy like the one in the geography dimension would provide a completely balanced hierarchy for the United States. *Completely balanced hierarchy* means that all leaf (end) nodes for cities would be an equal distance from the top level. Some hierarchies in dimensions can have an unbalanced distribution of leaf nodes relative to the top level. Such hierarchies are called *unbalanced hierarchies*. An organization chart is an obvious example of an unbalanced hierarchy. There are different depths to the chain of supervisor to employee; that is, the leaf nodes are different distances from the top-level node. For example, a general manager might have unit managers and an administrative assistant. A unit manager might have additional direct reports such as a dev and a test manager, while the administrative assistant would not have any direct reports. Some hierarchies are typically balanced but are missing a unique characteristic of some members in a level. Such hierarchies are called *ragged hierarchies*. An example of a ragged hierarchy is a geography hierarchy that contains the levels Country, State, and City. Within the Country USA you have State Washington and City Seattle. If you were to add the Country Greece and City Athens to this hierarchy, you would add them to the Country and City levels. However, there are no states in the Country Greece and hence member Athens is directly related to the Country Greece. A hierarchy in which the members descend to members in the lowest level with different paths is referred to as a ragged hierarchy. Figure 1-4 shows an example of a Time dimension with the hierarchy Time. In this example, Year, Quarter, Month, and Date are the levels of the hierarchy. The values 2005 and 2006 are members of the Year level. When a particular level is expanded (indicated by minus sign in the figure) you can see the members of the next level in the hierarchy chain.

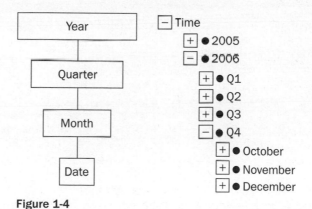

Figure 1-4

To sum up, a dimension is a hierarchical structure that has levels that may or may not be balanced. It has a subject matter of interest and is used as the basis for detailed business analysis.

Cubes

The *cube* is a multidimensional data structure from which you can query for business information. You build cubes out of your fact data and the dimensions. A cube can contain fact data from one or more fact tables and often contains a few dimensions. Any given cube usually has a dominant subject under analysis associated with it. For example, you might build a Sales cube with which you analyze sales by region, or a Call Processing cube with which you analyze length of call by problem category reported. These cubes are what you will be making available to your users for analysis.

Figure 1-5 shows a Beer Sales cube that was created from the fact table data shown previously. Consider the front face of the cube that shows numbers. This cube has three dimensions: Time, Product Line, and State where the product was sold. Each block of the cube is called a *cell* and is uniquely identified by a member in each dimension. For example, analyze the bottom-left corner cell that has the values 4,784 and $98,399. The values indicate the number of sales and the sales amount. This cell refers to the sales of Beer type Ale in the state of Washington (WA) for July 2005. This is represented as [WA, Ale, Jul '05]. Notice that some cells do not have any value; this is because no facts are available for those cells in the fact table.

The whole point of making these cubes involves reducing the query response time for the information worker to extract knowledge from the data. To make that happen, cubes typically contain pre-calculated summary data called *aggregations*. Querying existing aggregated data is close to instantaneous compared to doing cold (no cache) queries with no pre-calculated summaries in place. This is really at the heart of business intelligence, the ability to query data with possibly gigabytes or terabytes of pre-summarized data behind it and yet get an instant response from the server. It is quite the thrill when you realize you have accomplished this feat!

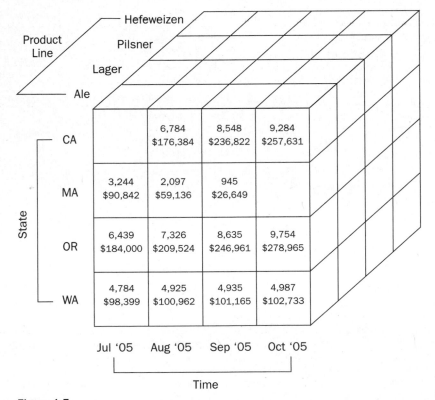

Figure 1-5

You learned about how cubes provide the infrastructure for storing multidimensional data. Well, it doesn't just store multidimensional data from fact tables; it also stores something called *aggregations* of that data. A typical aggregation would be the summing of values up a hierarchy of a dimension. For example, summing of sales figures up from stores level, to district level, to regional level; when querying for those numbers you would get an instant response because the calculations would have already been done when the aggregations were formed. The fact data does not necessarily need to be aggregated as sum of the specific fact data. You can have other ways of aggregating the data such as counting the number of products sold. Again, this count would typically roll up through the hierarchy of a dimension.

The Star Schema

The entity relationship diagram representation of a relational database shows you a different animal altogether as compared to the OLAP (multidimensional) database. It is so different in fact, that there is a name for the types of schemas used to build OLAP databases: the star schema and the snowflake schema. The latter is largely a variation on the first. The main point of difference is the complexity of the schema; the OLTP schema tends to be dramatically more complex than the OLAP schema. Now that you know the infrastructure that goes into forming fact tables, dimension tables, and cubes, the concept of a star schema should offer little resistance. That is because when you configure a fact table with foreign key relationships to one or more of a dimension table's primary keys, as shown in Figure 1-6, you have a star schema. Looks a little like a star, right?

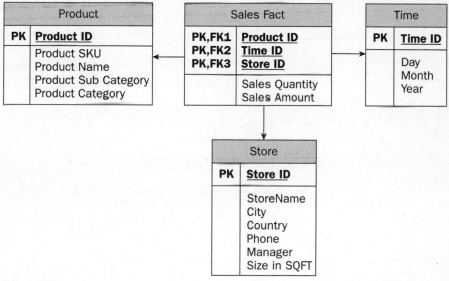

Figure 1-6

The star schema provides you with an illustration of the relationships between business entities in a clear and easy-to-understand fashion. Further, it enables number crunching of the measures in the fact table to progress at amazing speeds.

The Snowflake Schema

If you think the star schema is nifty, and it is, there is an extension of the concept called the snowflake schema. The snowflake schema is useful when one of your dimension tables starts looking as detailed as the fact table it is connected to. With the snowflake, a level is forked off from one of the dimension tables, so it is separated by one or more tables from the fact table. In Figure 1-7 the Product dimension has yielded a Product Category level. The Product Sub Category level is hence one table removed from the sales fact table. In turn, the Product Sub Category level yields a final level called the Product Category — which has two tables of separation between it and the sales fact table. These levels, which can be used to form a hierarchy in the dimension, do not make for faster processing or query response times, but they can keep a schema sensible.

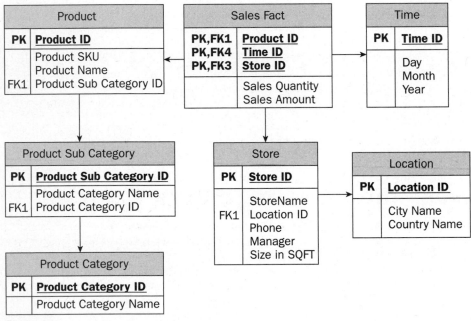

Figure 1-7

You have so far learned the fundamental elements of a data warehouse. The biggest challenge is to understand these well and design and implement your data warehouse to cater to your end-users. There are two main design techniques for implementing data warehouses. These are the Inmon approach and the Kimball approach.

Inmon Versus Kimball
Different Approaches

In data warehousing there are two commonly acknowledged approaches to building a decision support infrastructure, and both can be implemented using the tools available in SQL Server 2005 with Analysis Services 2005. It is worth understanding these two approaches and the often-cited difference of views that result. These views are expressed most overtly in two seminal works: *The Data Warehouse Lifecycle Toolkit* by Ralph Kimball, Laura Reeves, Margy Ross, and Warren Thornthwaite, and *Corporate Information Factory* by Bill Inmon, Claudia Imhoff, and Ryan Sousa.

Kimball identified early on the problem of the stovepipe. A stovepipe is what you get when several independent systems in the enterprise go about identifying and storing data in different ways. Trying to connect these systems or use their data in a warehouse results in something resembling a Rube-Goldberg device. To address this problem, Kimball advocates the use of conformed dimensions. *Conformed* refers to the idea that dimensions of interest — sales, for example — should have the same attributes and roll-ups (covered in the "Aggregations" section earlier in this chapter) in one data mart as another. Or at least one should be a subset of the other. In this way, a warehouse can be formed from data marts. The real gist of Kimball's approach is that the data warehouse contains dimensional databases for ease of analysis and that the user queries the warehouse directly.

The Inmon approach has the warehouse laid out in third normal form (not dimensional) and the users query data marts, not the warehouse. In this approach the data marts are dimensional in nature. However, they may or may not have conformed dimensions in the sense Kimball talks about.

Happily it is not necessary to become a card-carrying member of either school of thought in order to do work in this field. In fact, this book is not strictly aligned to either approach. What you will find as you work through this book is that by using the product in the ways in which it was meant to be used and are shown here, certain best practices and effective methodologies will naturally emerge.

Business Intelligence Is Data Analysis

Having designed a data warehouse the next step is to understand and make business decisions from your data warehouse. Business intelligence is nothing but analyzing your data. An example of business analytics is shown through the analysis of results from a product placed on sale at a discounted price, as commonly seen in any retail store. If a product is put on sale for a special discounted price, there is an expected outcome: increased sales volume. This is often the case, but whether or not it worked in the company's favor isn't obvious. That is where business analytics come into play. We can use Analysis Services 2005 to find out if the net effect of the special sale was to sell more product units. Suppose you are selling organic honey from genetically unaltered bees; you put the 8-ounce jars on special — two for one — and leave the 10- and 12-ounce jars at regular price. At the end of the special you can calculate the *lift* provided by the special sale — the difference in total sales between a week of sales with no special versus a week of sales with the special. How is it you could sell more 8-ounce jars on special that week, yet realize no lift? It's simple — the customers stopped buying your 10- and 12-ounce jars in favor of the two-for-one deal; and you didn't attract enough new business to cover the difference for a net increase in sales.

You can surface that information using Analysis Services 2005 by creating a Sales cube that has three dimensions: Product, Promotion, and Time. For the sake of simplicity, assume you have only three product sizes for the organic honey (8-ounce, 10-ounce, and 12-ounce) and two promotion states ("no promotion" and a "two-for-one promotion for the 8-ounce jars"). Further, assume the Time dimension contains different levels for Year, Month, Week, and Day. The cube itself contains two measures, "count of products sold" and the "sales amount." By analyzing the sales results each week across the three product sizes you could easily find out that there was an increase in the count of 8-ounce jars of honey sold, but perhaps the total sales across all sizes did not increase due to the promotion. By slicing on the Promotion dimension you would be able to confirm that there was a promotion during the week that caused an increase in number of 8-ounce jars sold. When looking at the comparison of total sales for that week (promotion week) to the earlier (non-promotion) weeks, lift or lack of lift is seen quite clearly. Business analytics are often easier described than implemented, however.

Analysis Services 2005

Analysis Services 2005 is part of Microsoft's product SQL Server 2005. SQL Server 2005 is the latest SQL Server release from Microsoft in November of 2005. In addition to Analysis Services 2005, SQL Server 2005 contains other services such as Integrations Services, Reporting Services, and Notification Services among other things. Integration Services, Analysis Services, and Reporting Services together form the core of business intelligence platform with SQL Server as the backend. Analysis Services 2005 not only provides you the ability to build dimensions and cubes for data analysis but also supports several data mining algorithms which can provide business insight into your data that are not intuitive. Analysis Services is part of a greater Business Intelligence platform, which leverages not only the rest of SQL Server 2005, but the .NET Framework (Common Language Runtime) and Visual Studio development environment as well. Next you will learn about the overall architecture of Analysis Services 2005 followed by the concept of Unified Dimensional Model (UDM) which helps you to have a unified view of your entire data warehouse.

SQL Server Analysis Services 2005 has been re-architected as both scalable and reliable enterprise class software that provides fine-grain security. So, not only is it quite manageable; but also protects your data from malicious attacks. The architecture of Analysis Services 2005 provides efficient scalability in terms of scale-out and scale-up features. Several instances of Analysis Services 2005 can be integrated together to provide an efficient scale-out solution. On the other hand, the service has been architected with efficient algorithms to handle large dimensions and cubes on a single instance. Analysis Services 2005 provides a rich set of tools for creating OLAP databases; efficient and easy manageability, as well as profiling capabilities.

The *Business Intelligence Development Studio* (BIDS) integrated within Visual Studio is the development tool shipped with Analysis Services 2005 used for creating and updating cubes, dimensions, and Data Mining models. The *SQL Server Management Studio* (SSMS) provides an integrated environment for managing SQL Server, Analysis Services, Integration Services, and Reporting Services. SQL Profiler in the SQL Server 2005 releases supports profiling Analysis Services 2005, which helps in analyzing the types of commands and queries sent from different users or clients to Analysis Services 2005. You learn more about BIDS and SSMS in Chapter 2 with the help of a tutorial. You learn about profiling an instance of Analysis Services using SQL Profiler in Chapter 12. In addition to the above-mentioned tools, Analysis Services 2005 provides two more tools: the Migration Wizard and the Deployment Wizard. The Migration Wizard helps in migrating Analysis Services 2000 databases to Analysis Services 2005. The Deployment Wizard helps in deploying the database files created using BIDS to Analysis Services 2005.

The SSMS provides efficient, enterprise-class manageability features for Analysis Services. Key aspects of an enterprise class service are availability and reliability. Analysis Services 2005 supports fail-over clustering on Windows clusters through an easy setup scheme and fail-over clustering certainly helps provide high availability. In addition, Analysis Services 2005 has the capability of efficiently recovering from failures. You can set up fine-grain security so that you can provide administrative access to an entire service or administrative access to specific databases, process permissions to specific databases, and read-only access to metadata and data. In addition to this, certain features are turned off by default so that the Service is protected from hacker attacks.

Analysis Services 2005 natively supports XML for Analysis specification defined by the XML/A Advisory Council. What this means is that the communication interface to Analysis Services from a client is XML. This facilitates ease of interoperability between different clients and Analysis Services 2005. The architecture of SQL Server Analysis Services 2005 includes various modes of communication to the service as shown in Figure 1-8. Analysis Server 2005 provides three main client connectivity components to communicate to the server. The Analysis Management Objects (AMO) is a new object model that helps you manage Analysis Server 2005 and the databases resident on it. The OLE DB 9.0 is the client connectivity component used to interact with analysis services 2005 instances s for queries that conforms to the OLE DB standard. The ADOMD.Net is dot Net object model support for querying data from Analysis Services 2005. In addition to the three main client connectivity components, two other components are provided by Analysis Services 2005. They are DSO 9.0 (Decision Support Object) and HTTP connectivity through a data pump. DSO 8.0 is the extension of the management object of Analysis Server 2000 so that legacy applications can interact with migrated Analysis Server 2000 databases on Analysis Server 2005. The data pump is a component that is set up with *IIS* (Internet Information System) to provide connection to Analysis Services 2005 over *HTTP* (Hypertext Transfer Protocol).

Even though XML/A helps in interoperability between different clients to Analysis Server, it comes with a cost on performance. If the responses from the server are large, transmission of XML data across the wire may take a long time depending on the type of network connection. Typically slow wide area networks might suffer from performance due to large XML responses. In order to combat this, Analysis Services 2005 supports the options for compression and binary XML so that the XML responses from the server could be reduced. These are optional features supported by Analysis Services 2005 that can be enabled or disabled on the Server.

Analysis Services 2005 stores metadata information of databases in the form of XML. Analysis Services 2005 provides you with the option of storing the data or aggregated data efficiently in a proprietary format on Analysis Services instance or storing them in the relational database. If you choose the data and/or aggregated data to be stored in the proprietary format you can expect better query performance than the case where the data is being retrieved from the relational database.. This proprietary format helps Analysis Services 2005 to retrieve the data efficiently and thereby improves the query performance. Based on where the data and/or aggregated fact data is stored you can classify the storage types as MOLAP (Multi-dimensional OLAP), ROLAP (Relational OLAP), or HOLAP (Hybrid OLAP).

MOLAP is the storage mode in which the data and aggregated data are both stored in proprietary format on the Analysis Services instance. This is the default and recommended storage mode for Analysis Services databases since you get better query performance as compared to the other storage types. The key advantages of this storage mode is fast data retrieval while analyzing sections of data and therefore provides good query performance and the ability to handle complex calculations. Two potential disadvantages of MOLAP mode are storage needed for large databases and the inability to see new data entering your data warehouse.

ROLAP is the storage mode in which the data is left in the relational database. Aggregated or summary data is also stored in the relational database. Queries against the Analysis Services are appropriately changed to queries to the relational database to retrieve the right section of data requested. The key advantage of this mode is that the ability to handle large cubes is limited by the relational backend only. The most important disadvantage of the ROLAP storage mode are slow query performance. You will encounter slower query performance in ROLAP mode due to the fact that each query to the Analysis Services is translated into one or more queries to the relational backend.

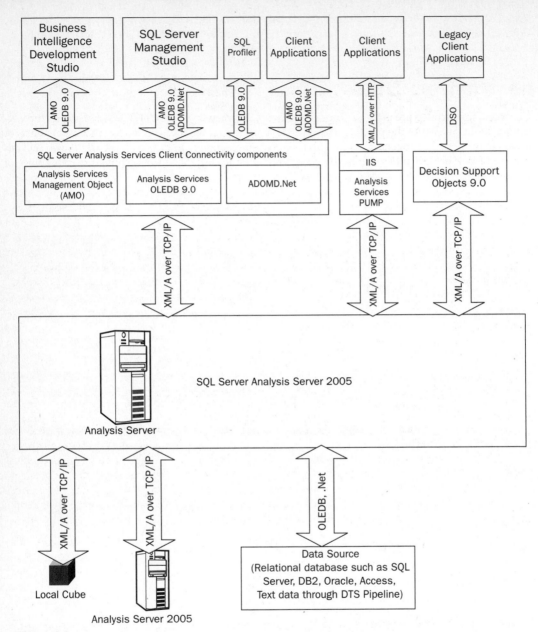

Figure 1-8

The HOLAP storage mode combines the best of MOLAP and ROLAP modes. The data in the relational database is not touched while the aggregated or summary data is stored on the Analysis Services instance in a proprietary format. If the queries to Analysis Services request aggregated data, they are retrieved from the summary data stored on the Analysis Services instance and they would be faster than data being retrieved from the relational backend. If the queries request detailed data, appropriate queries are sent to the relational backend and these queries can take a long time based on the relational backend.

Based on your requirements and maintainability costs you need to choose the storage mode that is appropriate for your business. Analysis Services 2005 supports all three storage modes.

The Unified Dimensional Model

Central to the architecture is the concept of the Unified Dimensional Model (UDM) which, by the way, is unique to this release of the product. UDM, as the name suggests, provides you with a way to encapsulate access to multiple heterogeneous data sources into a single model. In fact, with the UDM, you will be buffered from the difficulties previously presented by multiple data sources. Those difficulties were often associated with cross–data-source calculations and queries—so, do not be daunted by projects with lots of disparate data sources. The UDM can handle it! The UDM itself is more than a multiple data-source cube on steroids; it actually defines the relational schema upon which your cubes and dimensions are built. Think of the UDM as providing you with the best of the OLAP and relational worlds. UDM provides you with the rich metadata needed for analyzing and exploring data along with the functionality like the complex calculations and aggregations of the OLAP world. It supports complex schemas, and is capable of supporting ad-hoc queries that are needed for reporting in the relational world. Unlike the traditional OLAP world that allows you to define a single fact table within a cube, the UDM allows you to have multiple fact tables. The UDM is your friend and helps you have a single model that will support all your business needs. Figure 1-9 shows a UDM within Analysis Services 2005 that retrieves data from heterogeneous data sources and serves various types of clients.

Key elements of the UDM are as follows:

❏ **Heterogeneous data access support:** UDM helps you to integrate and encapsulate data from heterogeneous data sources. It helps you combine various schemas into a single unified model that gives end users the capability of sending queries to a single model.

❏ **Real-time data access with high performance:** The UDM provides end users with real-time data access. The UDM creates a MOLAP cache of the underlying data. Whenever there are changes in the underlying relational database, a new MOLAP cache is built. When users query the model, it provides the results from the MOLAP cache. During the time the cache is being built, results are retrieved from the relational database. UDM helps in providing real-time data access with the speed of an OLAP database due to the MOLAP cache. This feature is called proactive caching. You learn more about proactive caching in Chapter 17.

❏ **Rich metadata, ease of use for exploration, and navigation of data:** UDM provides a consolidated view of the underlying data sources with the richness of metadata provided by the OLAP world. Due to rich metadata supported by OLAP, end users are able to exploit this metadata to navigate and explore data in support of making business decisions. UDM also provides you with the ability to view specific sections of the unified model based on your business analysis needs.

❏ **Rich analytics support:** In addition to the rich metadata support, the UDM provides you with the ability to specify complex calculations to be applied to the underlying data; in this way you can embed business logic. You can specify the complex calculations by a script-based calculation model using the language called MDX (Multi-Dimensional eXpressions). UDM provides rich analytics such as Key Performance Indicators and Actions that help in understanding your business with ease and automatically take appropriate actions based on changes in data.

❏ **Model for Reporting and Analysis:** The UDM provides the best functionality for relating to both relational and OLAP worlds. UDM provides you with the capability of not only querying the aggregated data that are typically used for analysis, but also has the ability to provide for detailed reporting up to the transaction level across multiple heterogeneous data sources.

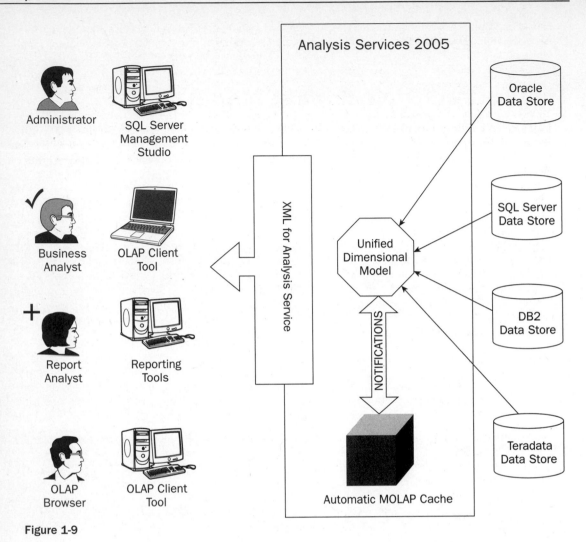

Figure 1-9

Another handy aspect of using the UDM is the storage of foreign language translations for both data and metadata. This is handled seamlessly by the UDM such that a connecting user gets the metadata and data of interest customized to his or her locale. Of course, somebody has to enter those translations into the UDM in the first place; it is not actually a foreign language translation system.

Summary

Reading this chapter may have felt like the linguistic equivalent of drinking from a fire hose; it is good you hung in there because now you have a foundation from which to build as you work through the rest of the book. Now you know data warehousing is all about structuring data for decision support. The data is consumed by the business analyst and business decision-maker and can be analyzed through OLAP and Data Mining techniques.

OLAP is a multidimensional database format that is a world apart in form and function when compared to an OLTP relational database system. You saw how OLAP uses a structure called a cube, which in turn relies on fact tables (which are populated with data called facts) and dimension tables. These dimension tables can be configured around one or more fact tables to create a star schema. If a dimension table is deconstructed to point to a chain of sub-dimension tables, the schema is called a snowflake schema.

By choosing Analysis Services 2005 you have chosen a business intelligence platform with awesome innovations built right in; like the UDM. Also, there is an advantage that Analysis Services 2005 offers — it comes from a particularly strong and reliable company that had the highest market share with its earlier product, Analysis Services 2000. The rest of this book illustrates the power of the platform quite clearly.

In the unlikely event that you didn't read the introduction, mention was made that you should read at least the first three chapters serially before attempting to tackle the rest of the book. So, please do not skip Chapter 2, an introduction to Analysis Services and Chapter 3, an introduction to the technology behind the most famous acronym in business analytics, MDX.

2

First Look at Analysis Services 2005

In Chapter 1 you learned general data warehousing concepts, including some key elements that go into successful warehouse projects, the different approaches taken to build warehouses, and how the warehouses are subsequently mined for information. This chapter introduces you to Analysis Services 2005 and includes an introduction to SQL Server Analysis Services 2005 Tools. These are the very tools, resident in two different environments, which you'll need to develop and manage Analysis Services databases. This chapter also covers some of the differences between Analysis Services 2000 and Analysis Services 2005.

You familiarize yourself with the development environment and interface by working through a tutorial based on a sample database that ships with SQL Server Analysis Services 2005, called *Adventure Works DW*. This tutorial covers many basic concepts and takes you through the Cube Wizard to build and then browse a cube. The tutorial will guide you through using the tools and provide you insights into what the product is doing behind the scenes.

In the management environment you learn the basic operations associated with manageability of Analysis Services 2005. Further, you learn about the constituent objects that make up an Analysis Services 2005 database and what management actions can be taken against them in the management environment. Finally, you are introduced to the MDX Query Editor for querying data from the cubes.

MDX, which stands for Multi-Dimensional eXpressions, is the language through which you retrieve data from multi-dimensional databases.

By the end of this chapter you will be familiar with key components that constitute the Analysis Services Tools, the process of building Analysis Services databases, and how to use MDX to retrieve data from Analysis Services databases. So, snap on your seatbelt and get started!

Differences between Analysis Services 2000 and Analysis Services 2005

Analysis Services 2005 is not just an evolutionary step up from Analysis Services 2000, but a quantum leap forward in functionality, scalability, and manageability. Relational databases provide a simple, flexible, manageable schema; they provide access of data to the end user easily congealed into information-rich reports. On the other hand, OLAP databases are typically used for high-end performance by the user who needs rich analytics and exploration capabilities. Analysis Services 2005 merges the capabilities of relational and OLAP worlds, thereby providing a unified view of the data to the end user. This unified model is called the *Unified Dimensional Model* (UDM). In sum, Analysis Services 2005 is a powerful, enterprise-class product and one that you can use to build large-scale OLAP databases and implement strategic business analysis against those databases. You learn more about the UDM and the advanced analytics capabilities of Analysis Services 2005 in chapters 6, 9 and 18. This chapter gives you hands-on experience with both the development and management tools environments.

Development, Administrative, and Client Tools

If you have used Analysis Services 2000, you have used the Analysis Manager. The Analysis Manager, which is shipped with that version, is implemented as a snap-in to the *Microsoft Management Console* (MMC). The Analysis Manager is a development environment for building Analysis Services databases as well as a management environment to manage multi-dimensional databases. Analysis Services 2000 provided limited functionality with respect to client tools. Customers were able to browse data within the Analysis Manager. A sample application called *MDX Sample* that was shipped along with the product provided you with the capability to build and send queries against Analysis Services databases and view the results.

Analysis Services 2005 has separate environments for development and management. The development environment is called *Business Intelligence Development Studio* (BIDS) and is integrated with Microsoft Visual Studio. Similar to a developer building a Visual Basic or C++ project, you will be able to build a Business Intelligence project. The management environment is called *SQL Server Management Studio* (SSMS). SSMS is one complete integrated management environment for several services (including SQL Server itself, Analysis Services, Reporting Services, Integration Services and SQL Server Mobile) released in SQL Server 2005. The SSMS was built to provide ease of use and manageability for all the database administrators in one single environment. The client tools available to analyze or retrieve data from Analysis Services 2005 are integrated within BIDS as well as SMSS. You can browse data from both of these environments as well. In SSMS you are provided with a query builder to retrieve data from Analysis Services. The query builder replaces the MDX Sample application that came with Analysis Services 2000. In addition the query builder provides intellisense support providing an array of options for you to access MDX language reference including auto completion of key words.

If you have used Microsoft SQL Server 2000 you might also be familiar with SQL Profiler. In the SQL Server 2005 release the capability of tracing, or profiling, queries run against Analysis Services has been integrated into SQL Profiler. Analysis Services Profiler information can be utilized to analyze and improve performance. You learn more about the Profiler in Chapter 12.

Analysis Services Version Differences

Analysis Services 2000 provided a rich feature set that helped in building solid data warehouses. The features combined with the MDX query language provided rich analytics for the customers. As with any software package, though, Analysis Services 2000 had limitations. Some of the limitations of Analysis Services 2000:

❑ Even though Analysis Services 2000 had a rich feature set, modeling certain scenarios either resulted in significant performance degradation or simply could not be accomplished.

❑ There were size limitations on various objects such as dimensions, levels and measures within a specific database.

❑ Analysis Services 2000 loaded all the databases at startup. If there were a large number of databases and/or a very large database, this resulted in long server startup time.

❑ Analysis Services 2000 had a thick client model that helped in achieving very good query performance, but did not scale very well in 3-tier applications (for example, Web scenarios).

❑ The metadata information of the databases was either stored in an access database or a SQL Server database. Therefore maintenance of data and metadata had to be done carefully.

❑ The backup format used to back up Analysis Services databases limited the file size to 2GB.

Analysis Services 2005, in addition to providing the best of the relational and OLAP worlds, overcomes most of the limitations of Analysis Services 2000. Following are some of the benefits of using the Analysis Services 2005:

❑ Two fundamental changes in Analysis Services 2005 are the thin client architecture that helps in scalability of 2-tier or 3-tier applications and the support of the native XML/A (XML for Analysis) protocol for communication between client and server.

❑ Several new features added to Analysis Services 2005 facilitate optimal design of data warehouses to form UDMs. Parts II and III of this book introduce these new features.

❑ Most of the size limitations on various objects have been greatly extended; or for all practical purposes, removed.

❑ Analysis Services 2005 provides better manageability, scalability, fine-grain security, and higher reliability by supporting fail-over clustering.

❑ Analysis Services 2005 natively supports Common Language Runtime (CLR) stored procedures with appropriate security permissions.

❑ Metadata information is represented as XML and resides along with the data. This allows for easier maintainability and control over the service.

❑ Analysis Services 2005 uses a different backup format (you learn about backup in Chapter 12) than the one used in Analysis Services 2000. Therefore, the 2GB backup file limit in Analysis Services 2000 has been eliminated.

Overall, Analysis Services 2005 provides you with a great combination of functionality and ease of use that enables you to analyze your data and make strategic business decisions. You will see these capabilities emerge step by step as you advance through this book.

Upgrading to Analysis Services 2005

If you currently do not have a requirement of upgrading your Analysis Services 2000 to Analysis Services 2005 or you are a first time user of Analysis Services then you can jump to the next section. The upgrade process in general is not a seamless process, and not without its share of gotchas. This is especially true when much of the product has been redesigned, such as you are faced with going from Analysis Services 2000 to Analysis Services 2005. Fortunately, Analysis Services 2005 provides you with a tool called Upgrade Advisor to prepare you to upgrade databases from Analysis Services 2000. Upgrade Advisor is available as a redistributable package with SQL Server 2005. You need to install Upgrade Advisor from the Servers\ redist\Upgrade Advisor folder on your CD/DVD. When you run Upgrade Advisor on your existing Analysis Services 2000 instance, Upgrade Advisor informs you whether your database(s) will be upgraded successfully without any known issues. Warnings are provided by Upgrade Advisor in cases where there might be changes in the names of the dimensions or cubes due to the Analysis Services 2005 architecture. Once you have reviewed all the information from Upgrade Advisor, you are ready to start the upgrade. Follow the steps below to use Upgrade Advisor for analyzing the effects of upgrading your Analysis Services 2000 to Analysis Services 2005.

1. Go to "Program Files\Microsoft SQL Server 2005 Upgrade Advisor" folder on your machine and click the UpgradeAdvisorWizard.exe file to start the wizard. The welcome screen appears, as shown in Figure 2-1. Click the Next button to continue.

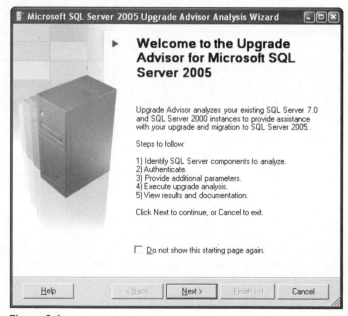

Figure 2-1

2. In the SQL Server 2000 Component selection page, shown in Figure 2-2, enter the name of a machine that contains SQL Server 2000 products. If you click the Detect button then Upgrade Advisor will populate the SQL Server Components page with the services running on the server name provided. If you know the services available on the server machine you can enable the check boxes corresponding to the services available in this page. Select Analysis Services and click Next.

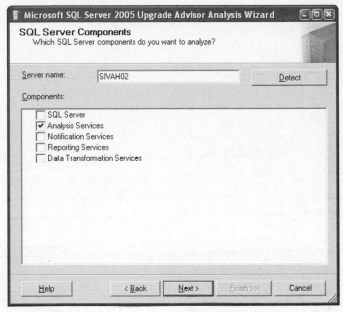

Figure 2-2

3. In the Confirm Upgrade Advisor Settings page, as shown in Figure 2-3, you can review your selections. If your selections are not correct, go back to the previous page and make the appropriate changes. Click the Run button for upgrade analysis.

   In the next screen you see the Upgrade Advisor analyzing the databases on your Analysis Services 2000 server. At the end of the analysis you see the errors and warnings reported by the Upgrade Advisor, as shown in Figure 2-4.

4. Click the Launch Report button to see the detailed report of the analysis and the actions you need to take for a smooth migration of your databases, as shown in Figure 2-5.

We strongly recommend that you run the Upgrade Advisor utility, analyze all the errors and warnings reported, and take the necessary actions. In certain cases you might have to perform some operations on your existing Analysis Services 2000 database. For example, if you have a writeback partition in Analysis Services 2000 that contains data, the recommended approach is to convert the writeback partition to a MOLAP partition, upgrade the database to Analysis Services 2005, reprocess the partition, and then re-create a new writeback partition. Similarly, you might have to perform several steps either before or after the upgrade on your Analysis Services database to ensure your existing applications will work correctly.

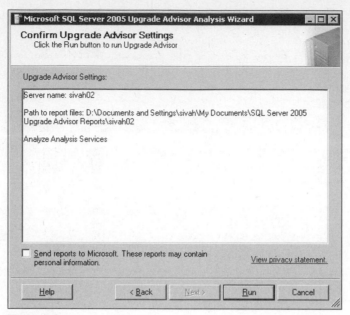

Figure 2-3

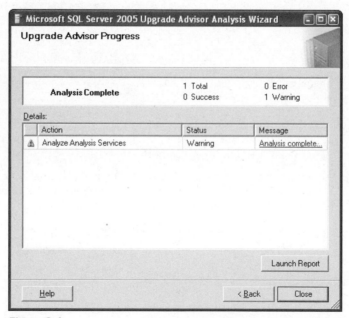

Figure 2-4

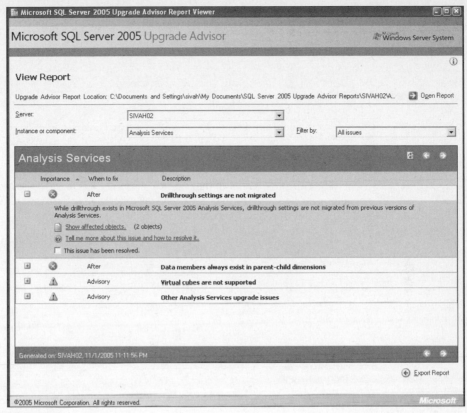

Figure 2-5

Once you have analyzed the Upgrade Advisor report on your Analysis Services 2000 databases you are ready for upgrade. Install the product and select the option to upgrade your Analysis Services 2000 OLAP databases. Analysis Services 2005 only upgrades the metadata of your OLAP databases. So, you will need your relational data source available so that source data can be populated once again into your cubes. You need to process all the databases that have been upgraded from your Analysis Services 2000 installation as well. Once this is completed, all your cubes and dimensions will be available for querying. If warnings in Upgrade Advisor indicate that names of dimensions or hierarchies would be changed and if you have invested a lot in building applications, then your applications might also have to be updated accordingly. Please plan to spend time to ensure all your applications are working for your customers after the upgrade process. We also have an experienced-based general recommendation—test the entire upgrade process on a test machine. In this way, you can verify if your existing applications are working as expected using the Analysis Services 2005 instance. Finally, with confidence you can perform the upgrade on your production machine.

If you do not have a test machine we recommend the following approach: Install Analysis Services 2005 as a named instance. Analysis Services 2005 provides you with a wizard to migrate your databases from an Analysis Services 2000 server to an Analysis Services 2005 instance. Analysis Services 2005 provides you with an integrated environment to manage all SQL Server 2005 products using SQL Server Management Studio (SSMS). SSMS is the newer version of the famous Query Analyzer, which is available in SQL Server 2000.

In the following short tutorial, we will reference Foodmart2000 as a sample database and you can use your own databases where appropriate. To migrate your Analysis Services 2000 databases to an Analysis Services 2005 instance, follow these steps:

1. Launch SQL Server Management Studio, which comes with Analysis Services 2005, by choosing from the Start Menu⇨ All Programs⇨Microsoft SQL Server2005⇨SQL Server Management Studio. Connect to the Analysis Services 2005 instance using SQL Server Management Studio's Object Explorer. Right-click the server name and select Migrate Database as shown in Figure 2-6. This takes you to the welcome screen of the wizard. If someone else had used this wizard and disabled the welcome page you might not see the welcome page. If you are in the welcome page click the next button to proceed to step 2.

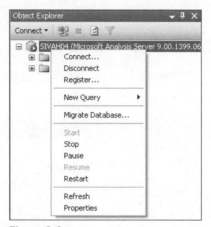

Figure 2-6

2. In the Specify Source and Destination page, the wizard pre-populates the name of your Analysis Services 2005 instance. Enter the machine name of your Analysis Services 2000 as shown in Figure 2-7 and click the Next button.

3. In the Select Databases to Migrate pages you will see the list of databases on your Analysis Services 2000 itemized and pre-selected for migration as shown in Figure 2-8. A column on the right side provides you with the name of the database on your Analysis Services 2005 instance. You have the option of selecting all the databases or just a few databases on your Analysis Services 2000 to migrate. Deselect all the databases and select the Foodmart 2000 database; this is the sample database that is shipped with Analysis Services 2000.

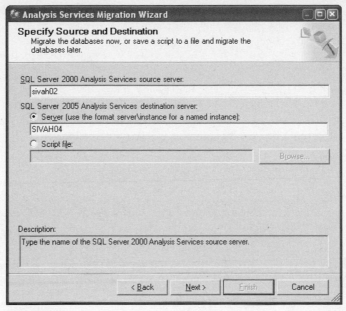

Figure 2-7

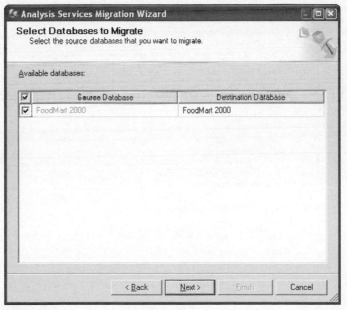

Figure 2-8

4. The Migration Wizard now validates the selected databases for migration. As the Migration Wizard validates the objects within a database for migration, it provides you a report including warnings of objects that will be changed during the migration process, as shown in Figure 2-9. You can save the logs to a file for future reference. Once you have analyzed the entire report, click Next to deploy the migrated database to your Analysis Services 2005 instance.

5. The Migration Wizard now sends the metadata of the migrated database to the Analysis Services 2005 instance. The new database with migrated objects is created on your Analysis Services 2005 instance and the Migration Wizard reports the status, as shown in Figure 2-10. Once the migration process is complete, click the Next button.

6. In the completion page the Migration Wizard shows the new databases that have been migrated in a tree view. Click Finish to complete the migration.

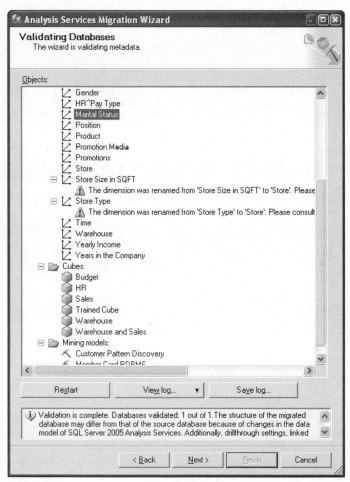

Figure 2-9

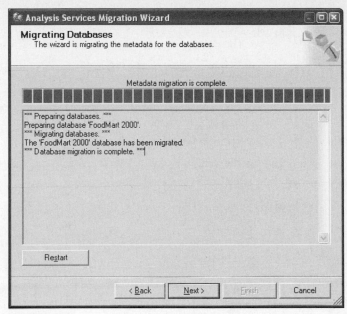

Figure 2-10

You should be aware that the migration wizard will only migrate the metadata of an Analysis Services database and not the data. Hence the migrated cubes and dimensions are not accessible for querying unless you reprocess the databases. Process all the databases that have been migrated, and test your applications against the migrated databases on your Analysis Services 2005 instance. You need to direct your applications to hit the new Analysis Services 2005 instance name. Once you have verified that all applications are working as expected, you can uninstall Analysis Services 2000 and then re-name your Analysis Services 2005 named instance to the default instance using the instance rename utility ASInstanceRename.exe that can be found in the directory \Program Files\Microsoft SQL Server\90\Tools\Binn\VSShell\ Common7\IDE.

Using the Business Intelligence Development Studio

The Business Intelligence Development Studio is the development platform for designing your Analysis Services databases. To start Business Intelligence Development Studio, click the windows Start button and go to Programs⇨ Microsoft SQL Server⇨Business Intelligence Development Studio. If you're familiar with Visual Studio you might be thinking that the Business Intelligence Development Studio (BIDS) looks a lot like the Visual Studio environment. You're right; in Analysis Services 2005 you create Analysis Services projects in an environment that is essentially an augmented Visual Studio project environment. Working in the Visual Studio environment offers many benefits, such as easy access to source control and having many projects within the same Visual Studio solution (a solution within Visual Studio is a collection of projects such as Analysis Services project, C# project, Integration Services project or Reporting Services project).

Creating a Project in the Business Intelligence Development Studio

To design your Analysis Services database you need to create a project using BIDS. Typically you will design your database within BIDS, make appropriate design changes, and finally send the designed databases to your Analysis Services instance. Each project within BIDS becomes a database on an Analysis Services instance when all the definitions within the project are sent to the server. BIDS also provides you the option to directly connect to an Analysis Services database and make refinements to the database. Follow the steps below to create a new project.

To start BIDS, click the Start button and go to Programs⇨Microsoft SQL Server⇨Business Intelligence Development Studio. When BIDS launches, select File⇨New⇨Project.

In the BIDS select File⇨New⇨Project. You will see the Business Intelligence Project templates as shown in Figure 2-11. Click the Analysis Services project template. Type **AnalysisServices2005Tutorial** as the project name and select the directory in which you want to create this project. Click OK to complete the window.

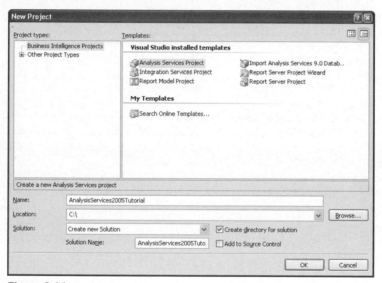

Figure 2-11

You are now in an Analysis Services project, as shown in Figure 2-12.

When you create a Business Intelligence project with a specific name, the project is automatically created under a solution with the same name. A solution will typically contain a collection of related projects. When you create a new project you have the option of adding the project to the existing solution or creating a new solution in the New Project dialog as shown in Figure 2-11. BIDS contains several panes; of most concern here are the Solution Explorer, Properties, and Output panes.

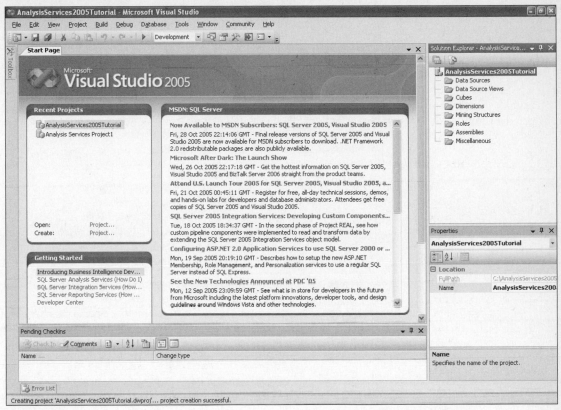

Figure 2-12

Solution Explorer Pane

The Solution Explorer pane in Figure 2-12 shows eight folders, each of which is described here:

- ❑ **Data Sources.** Your data warehouse is likely made up of disparate data sources such as Microsoft SQL Server, Oracle, DB2, and so forth. Analysis Services 2005 can easily deal with retrieving relational data from such configurations. Data sources are objects that contain details of a connection to a data source which include server name, login, password, etc. You establish connections to the relational servers by creating a data source for each one.

- ❑ **Data Source Views.** When working with a large operational data store you don't always want to see all the tables in the database; particularly while building an OLAP database using Analysis Services 2005. With Data Source Views (DSVs) you can limit the number of visible tables by including only the tables that are relevant to your analysis. DSVs help in creating a logical data model upon which you build your Unified Dimensional Model. A DSV can contain tables from one or more data sources, and one of these data sources is called a primary data source. Data sources and DSVs are discussed in Chapter 4.

- ❑ **Cubes.** Cubes are the foundation for analysis. A collection of *measure groups* (discussed later in this chapter) and a collection of dimensions form a cube. Each measure group is formed by a set of *measures*. Because cubes can have more than three dimensions, they are mathematical constructs and not necessarily three-dimensional cubes you can visually represent. You learn more about cubes later in this chapter and in Parts II and III.

❏ **Dimensions.** Dimensions are the categories by which you slice to view specific data of interest. Each dimension contains one or more *hierarchies*. Two types of hierarchies exist: the attribute hierarchy and user hierarchy. In this book, attribute hierarchies are referred to as attributes and user or multi-level hierarchies are referred to as hierarchies. Attributes correspond to columns of a dimension table, and hierarchies are formed by grouping several attributes. For example, most cubes have a Time dimension. A Time dimension typically contains the attributes Year, Month, Date, and Day and a hierarchy for Year-Month-Date. Sales cubes in particular often contain Geography dimensions, Customer dimensions, and Product dimensions. You learn about dimensions in Chapter 5.

❏ **Mining Models.** Data mining (covered in Chapter 13) is the process of analyzing raw data using algorithms that help discover interesting patterns not typically found by ad-hoc analysis. Mining Models are objects that hold information about a dataset after analysis by a specific algorithm which can be used for analyzing the patterns or predicting new data sets. Knowing these patterns can help companies make their business processes more powerful. For example, the book recommendation feature on Amazon.com relies on data mining.

❏ **Roles.** Roles are objects in a database that are used to control access permissions to the database objects (read, write, read/write, process) for users. If you want to provide only read access to a set of users you could create a single role that has read access and add all the users to this role. There can be several roles within a database. If a user is a member of several roles of a database, the user inherits the permissions of those roles. If there is a conflict in permissions, Analysis Services provides the most liberal access to the user. You learn more about roles in Chapters 12 and 19.

❏ **Assemblies.** Assemblies are user-defined functions that can be created by using a CLR language such as Visual Basic.NET, Visual C# .NET, or through languages such as Microsoft Visual Basic or Microsoft C++ that form Component Object Model (COM) binaries. These are typically used for custom operations that are needed for specific business logic and are executed on the server for efficiency and performance. Assemblies can be added at the server instance level or within a specific database. The scope of an assembly is limited to the object to which the assembly has been added. For example, if an assembly is added to the server, that assembly can be accessed within each database on the Server. On the other hand, if an assembly has been added within a specific database it can only be accessed within the context of that database. Within BIDS you can only add dot Net assembly references. You learn more about assemblies in Chapter 10.

❏ **Miscellaneous.** This object is used for adding any miscellaneous objects (design or meeting notes, queries, temporary deleted objects, and so on) that are relevant to the database project. These objects are stored in the project and are not sent to the Analysis Services instance when the database definition is created as a database on the Analysis Services instance.

Properties Pane

If you click an object in the Solution Explorer, the properties for that object appear in the Properties pane. Items that cannot be edited are grayed out. If you click a particular property, the description of that property appears in the Description pane at the bottom of the Properties pane.

Output Pane

The Output pane (to be seen later in this chapter) is used to report warnings and errors during builds. When a project is deployed to the server, progress reporting and error messages are displayed in this pane.

Creating an Analysis Services Database Using the Business Intelligence Development Studio

You are now ready to create a cube. The cube you create in this chapter is based on the relational database Adventure Works DW that ships with Microsoft SQL Server 2005. If SQL Server 2005 is installed on your machine with the sample databases, you will find the Adventure Works DW database on your machine. If you don't have SQL Server sample databases installed on your machine you can restore the database files (AdventureWorksDW.mdb, AdventureWorksDW.ldb). The Adventure Works DW files can be downloaded from the companion web site for this book.

Adventure Works DW contains sales information on a bicycle company. Figure 2-13 shows the structure of the data warehouse you build in this chapter, which consists of two fact tables and eight dimension tables. The fact table is highlighted at the top in the color yellow, and the dimension tables are highlighted in the color blue. The FactInternetSales and FactResellerSales are the fact tables. They contain several measures and foreign keys to the dimension tables. Both fact tables contain three dimension keys, ShipDateKey, OrderDateKey, and DueDateKey, that are joined to the dimension table DimTime. The FactInternetSales and the FactResellerSales fact tables join to the appropriate dimension tables by a single key as shown in Figure 2-13. The ParentEmployeeKey in the Employee table is joined with EmployeeKey in the same table which is modeled as a parent-child hierarchy. You learn parent-child hierarchies in Chapter 5.

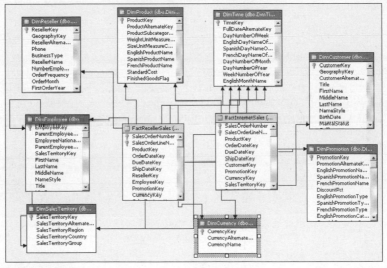

Figure 2-13

Create a Data Source

Cubes and dimensions of an Analysis Services database must retrieve their data values from tables in a relational data store. This data store, typically part of a data warehouse, must be defined as a data source. An OLE DB data provider or .NET data provider is used to retrieve the data from the data source. OLE DB and .NET data providers are industry standard technologies for retrieving data from relational databases. If your relational database provider does not provide a specific OLE DB data provider or a .NET data provider, you can use the generic Microsoft OLE DB provider to retrieve data. In this chapter you will be using the SQL Server database and hence you can use the OLE DB provider called Microsoft

OLE DB Provider for SQL Server or the Native OLE DB\SQL Native Client provider. If you need to use the .Net data provider then you need to select SqlClient provider.

To create a data source, follow these steps:

1. Select the Data Sources folder in the Solution Explorer.

2. Right-click the Data Sources folder and then click New Data Source, as shown in Figure 2-14.

Figure 2-14

This launches the data source wizard. This wizard is self-explanatory and you can easily create a data source by making the appropriate selection on each page of the wizard. The first page of the wizard is the welcome page that provides additional information of a data source. Click Next to continue.

3. You're now in the connection definition page of the data source wizard, as shown in Figure 2-15. In this page you provide the connection information to the relational data source that contains the "Adventure Works DW" database. Click the New button under Data Connection Properties to specify the connection details. The Connection Manager Dialog box launches.

4. On the page shown in Figure 2-16, you need to specify the connection properties to the SQL Server containing the Adventure Works DW database. The provider used to connect to any relational database by default points to Native OLE DB\SQL Native Client provider. Click on the drop down for the Provider and select Native OLEDB\SQL Native Client. or Microsoft OLE DB Provider for SQL Server. If you have installed SQL Server 2005 on the same machine, type localhost or the machine name under Server Name as shown in figure 2-16. If you have restored the sample Adventure Works DW database on a different SQL Server machine, type that machine name instead. You can either choose Windows authentication or SQL Server Authentication for connecting to the relational data source. Select Use Windows Authentication. If you choose the SQL Server authentication you need to specify SQL Server login name and password. Make sure you check the Save my password option. Due to security restrictions in Analysis Services 2005, if you do not select this option you will be prompted to key in the password each time you send the definitions of your database to the Analysis Services instance. From the drop-down list box under Select or enter database name, select AdventureWorksDW. You have now provided all the details for establishing a connection to the relational data on Adventure Works DW. Click OK.

Figure 2-15

Figure 2-16

5. The connection properties you provided in the connection dialog are now shown in the Select how to define the connection page of the Data Source wizard, as shown in Figure 2-17. Click the Next button.

Figure 2-17

6. In the Impersonation Information page you need to specify the impersonation details as to how Analysis Services will connect to the relational data source. There are four options for you to select as shown in Figure 2-18. You can provide a domain user name and password to impersonate or select the Analysis Service instance's service account for connection. If you choose the default option then the Analysis Services uses the impersonation information specified for the database. The option User the credentials of the current user is primarily used for data mining where you retrieve data from relational server for prediction. Select the Use the service account option and click Next.

7. On the final page, the Data Source wizard chooses the database you have selected as the name for the data source object you are creating (see Figure 2-19). You can choose the default name specified or specify a new name here. The connection string to be used for connecting to the relational data source is shown under Preview. Click Finish.

Super! You have now successfully created a data source.

Create a Data Source View (DSV)

The Adventure Works DW database contains 25 tables. The cube you build in this chapter uses 10 tables. Data Source Views give you a logical view of the tables that will be used within your OLAP database. A Data Source View can contain tables and views from one or more data sources. Although you could accomplish the same functionality by creating views in the relational server, Data Source Views provide additional functionality, flexibility, and manageability.

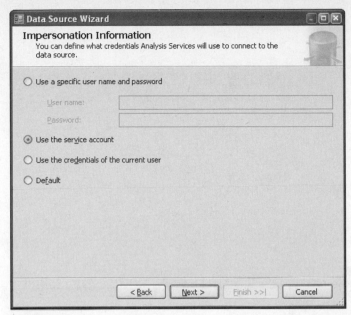

Figure 2-18

Figure 2-19

To create a Data Source View, follow these steps:

1. Select Data Source Views folder in the Solution Explorer.

2. Right-click Data Source Views and select New Data Source View, as shown in Figure 2-20.

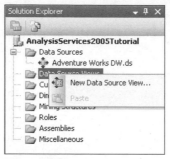

Figure 2-20

This launches the data source view wizard. Similar to the data source wizard, this wizard allows you to create a data source view just by choosing an appropriate selection on each page of the wizard. Click the Next button to go to the next page of the wizard.

3. The second page of the DSV wizard (see Figure 2-21) shows the list of data source objects from which you might want to create a view. The New Data Source button allows you to launch the data source wizard so that you can create new data source objects from the wizard. You have currently created a data source to the Adventure Works DW database. Select this data source and click the Next button.

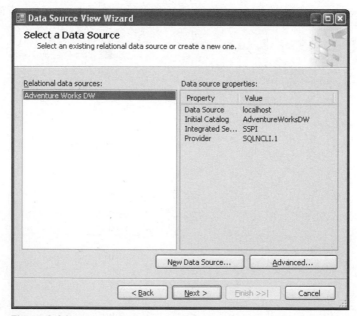

Figure 2-21

4. Upon clicking the Next button, the DSV wizard connects to the relational database Adventure Works DW using the connection string contained in the data source object. The DSV then retrieves all the tables, views, and their relationships from the relational database and shows them in the third page. You can now select the tables and views that would be needed for the Analysis Services database. For this tutorial navigate through the Available Objects list and select the FactInternetSales and FactResellerSales tables. Click the > button so that the tables move to the Included Objects list. Select the two tables in the Included Objects list by holding down the Shift key. As soon as you select these tables you will notice that the Add Related Tables button is enabled. This button helps you to add all the tables and views that have relationships with the selected tables in the Included Objects list. Now click the Add Related Tables button. You will notice that all the related dimension tables mentioned earlier as well as the FactInternetSalesReason table are added to the Included Objects list. In this tutorial you will not be using the FactInternetSalesReason table, so you should remove this table. Select the FactInternetSalesReason table in the Included Objects list and click the < button. You have now selected all the tables needed to build the cube in this tutorial. Your Included Objects list of tables should match what's shown in Figure 2-22.

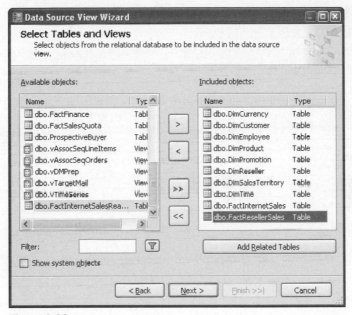

Figure 2-22

5. Click the Next button and you are at the final page of the DSV Wizard! Similar to the final page of the data source wizard, you can specify your own name for the DSV object or use the default name. Select the default name presented in the wizard and click Finish.

You have now successfully created the DSV that will be used in this chapter. The DSV object is shown on the Solution Explorer with a new designer page created in the main area of the BIDS as shown in Figure 2-23. This is called the data source view editor. The data source view editor contains three main areas: diagram organizer, table view, and the diagram view. The Diagram view shows a graphical representation of the tables and their relationships. Each table is shown with all the columns of the table along with the key attribute. Connecting lines show the relationships between tables. If you double-click the connecting line you will find the columns of each table that are used to form the join. You can make changes to the data source view by adding, deleting, or modifying tables and views in the DSV Editor. In addition, you can establish new relationships between tables. You learn further details about the DSV Editor in Chapter 4.

The number of tables you can see in the Diagram view depends on the resolution on your machine. In this view, you can zoom in to see a specific table enlarged or zoom out to see all the tables within the Diagram view. To use the zoom feature you can right-click anywhere within the Diagram view, select Zoom, and set the zoom percentage you want. Figure 2-24 shows a zoomed in Diagram view so that you can see the FactInternetSales table clearly.

The Diagram view in the DSV arranges the tables to best fit within the view. Sometimes the number of tables in the DSV can be quite large. In such circumstances navigating to the tables in the Diagram view can be difficult. For easier navigation you can use the Locator window (see Figure 2-24). The Locator window shows the full DSV diagram as a thumbnail. You can open it by performing a left mouse click on the 4-headed arrow in the lower-right corner of the diagram, as highlighted in Figure 2-23. The Locator window remains open while the mouse button is held down. This allows you to navigate through the visible area in the diagram view by moving the mouse.

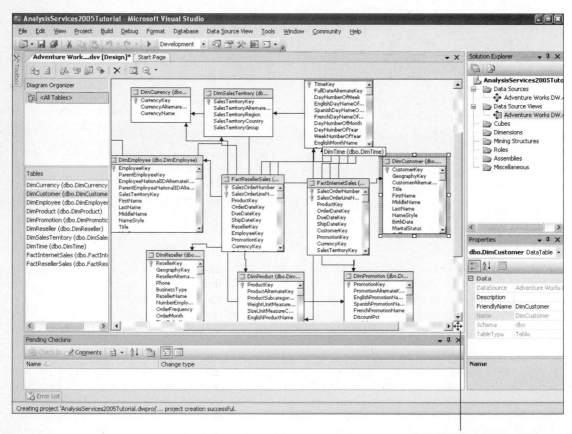

Four Headed Arrow

Figure 2-23

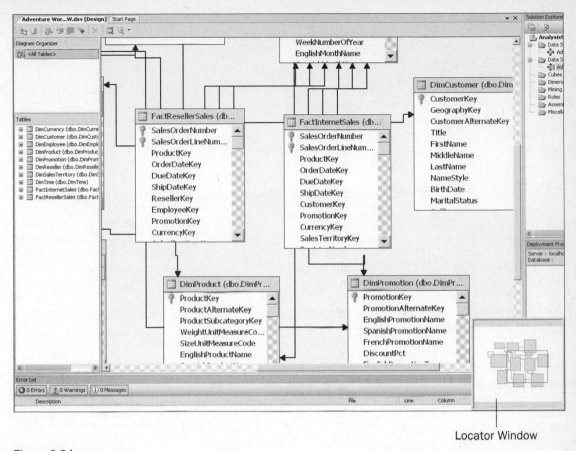

Locator Window

Figure 2-24

You have now learned the basic operations used within a data source view. Next, you move on to create the cube using cube wizard.

Create a Cube Using the Cube Wizard

In Analysis Services 2005 you can build cubes via two approaches — top-down or bottom-up. The traditional way of building cubes is bottom-up by building cubes from existing relational databases. In the bottom-up approach you need a data source view from which a cube can be built. Different cubes within a project can be built from a single DSV or from different DSVs. In the top-down approach you create the cube and then generate the relational schema based on the cube design.

A cube in Analysis Services 2005 consists of one or more measure groups from a fact table (typically you will have one measure group per fact table) and one or more dimensions (such as Product and Time) from the dimension tables. Measure groups consist of one or more measures (for example, sales, cost, count of objects sold). When you build a cube, you need to specify the fact and dimension tables you want to use. Each cube must contain at least one fact table, which determines the contents of the cube. The facts stored in the fact table are mapped as measures in a cube. Typically, measures from the same fact table are grouped together to form an object called measure group. If a cube is built from multiple fact tables, the cube typically contains multiple measure groups. Before building the cube the dimensions need to be created from the dimension tables. The cube wizard packages all the steps involved in creating a cube into a simple sequential process:

1. Launch the Cube Wizard by right-clicking the Cube folder in the Solution Explorer and selecting New Cube.

2. Click the Next button in the welcome page.

3. You are now asked to select the method to build the cube. Choose the default value and then click the Next button (see Figure 2-25). Note you are using the Cube Wizard.

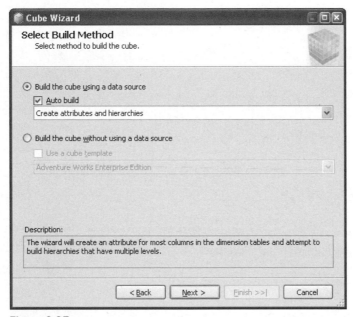

Figure 2-25

4. In the Select Data Source View page, select the Adventure Works DW DSV (see Figure 2-26) you created and click Next.

5. The wizard will detect the relationships between the tables in the DSV and detects the fact and dimension tables. The next page of the Cube Wizard, Detecting Fact and Dimension Tables (see Figure 2-27), performs the analysis. Click the Next button after the wizard has completed the analysis.

6. In the Identify Fact and Dimension Tables page (see Figure 2-28) the cube wizard presents you the fact and dimension tables from its analysis. If you feel the cube wizard's analysis does not match your design of fact and dimension tables you can make appropriate changes on this page so that the tables reflect the intended behavior for your design. In this example the cube wizard detects the DimReseller table as both fact and dimension table due to the relationships (outward relationship means fact table and inward relationship means dimension table) associated with

the DimReseller table. Deselect the check box so that DimReseller is used as a dimension in this design as shown in Figure 2-28. Click Next to go to the next page.

Figure 2-26

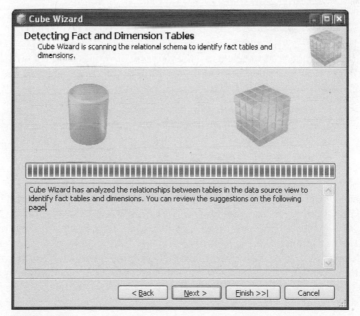

Figure 2-27

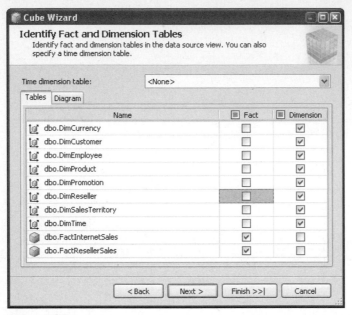

Figure 2-28

7.   In the Select Measures page (see Figure 2-29), the cube wizard shows you the columns of the fact table that have been analyzed by the wizard as potential measures. The cube wizard has automatically removed the columns that join to the dimension tables because these columns are typically not used as measures. The cube wizard creates a measure group that has the same name as the fact table and groups all the measures under this measure group name. If there are multiple fact tables, the cube wizard groups the measures under appropriate measure groups. By default the cube wizard selects all the measures from the fact table. You have the option to select or de-select measures you want to be built in the cube. Select all the measures (by default all measures are selected) and click Next.

8.   The cube wizard now scans all the dimension tables to identify hierarchies within the dimension tables. The wizard samples the relational data from each dimension table, analyzes the relationships between columns within each dimensional table, and detects hierarchies. Each dimension contains one or more hierarchies. As mentioned earlier, two kinds of hierarchies are created within a dimension in Analysis Services 2005: attribute hierarchies and user hierarchies. Each column in a dimension table can be created as a flat hierarchy called the attribute hierarchy. Flat hierarchies are hierarchies that are formed from a single column in the dimension table. All the members of an Attribute hierarchy are at the lowest level. The attribute hierarchy also contains an All level (explained in Chapter 5). User hierarchies, on the other hand, are typically created with more than one level and are called multi-level hierarchies. A typical example of a user hierarchy is a geography hierarchy that contains the levels Country, State, City, and Zip Code. Each level in a user hierarchy typically corresponds to a column in the dimensional table. The Detecting Hierarchies page (see Figure 2-30) shows you the tables analyzed. Click Next to proceed to the next page.

Figure 2-29

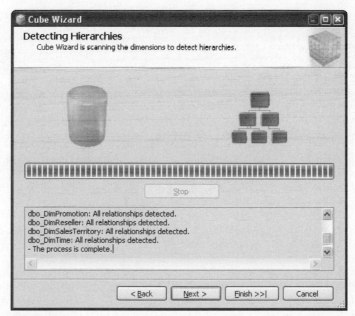

Figure 2-30

9. The Review New Dimensions page (see Figure 2-31) shows the dimensions that the wizard has detected. Here you can select or de-select the dimension you want the wizard to create based on the analysis. You can expand each dimension shown in this page to see the hierarchies detected by the wizard. The Attributes are shown under the Attributes folder and the Hierarchies are shown under the Hierarchies folder. After you have reviewed and selected the hierarchies and dimension, click Next.

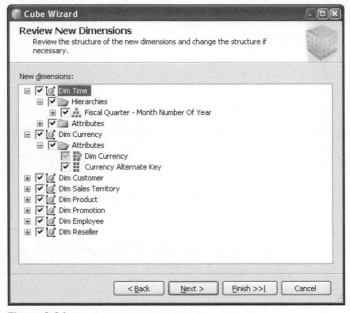

Figure 2-31

10. You are now in the last page of the wizard, as shown in Figure 2-32. Use the default name suggested by the wizard and click the Finish button.

11. After the completion of the wizard you will notice that the cube Adventure Works DW and dimensions Dim Time, Dim Currency, Dim Customer, Dim Sales Territory, Dim Product, Dim Promotion, Dim Employee and Dim Reseller are created in the Solution Explorer as shown in Figure 2-33.

    The cube Adventure Works DW in the Solution Explorer is automatically opened and that becomes your main window, called the Cube Editor, as shown in Figure 2-34.

The cube editor has several panes that allow you to perform various operations that could be performed on a cube object. Your default pane upon completion of the cube wizard is the Cube Structure pane. Other panes of the Cube Editor are Dimension Usage, Calculation, KPIs, Actions, Partitions, Perspectives, Translations, and Browser. In this chapter you will become familiar with basic operations in the Cube Structure and the Browser panes. You learn more about the Cube Editor in Chapters 6 and 9.

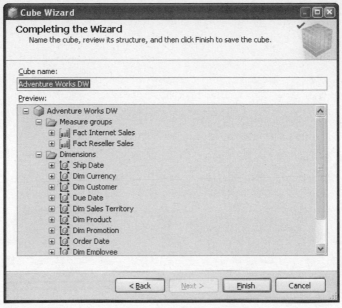

Figure 2-32

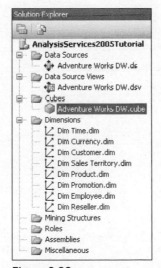

Figure 2-33

The Cube Editor pane has been divided into three windows: Measures, Dimensions, and the Data Source View. If you need to add or modify Measure groups or Measures you will do that within the Measures window. The Dimensions window is used to add or modify the dimensions relevant to the current cube.

The Data Source View shows all the fact and dimension tables used in the cube with appropriate colors (yellow for fact table and blue for dimension table). Actions such as zoom in, zoom out, navigation, finding tables, and different diagram layouts of the tables that are possible in the DSV Editor are available within the DSV of the Cube Editor.

If you right-click within the Measure, Dimension, or Data Source View windows you will be able to see the various actions that could be accomplished within the windows. The actions within the Measure, Dimension, or DSV windows of a Cube Editor can also be accomplished by clicking the appropriate icons (see Figure 2-34) in the Cube Editor.

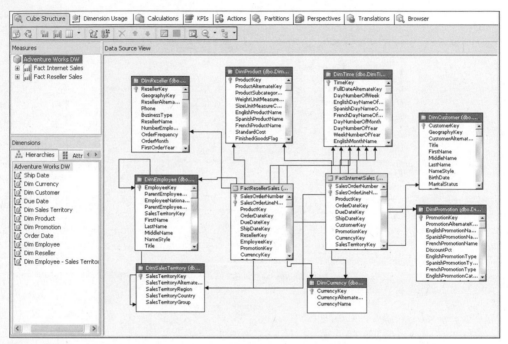

Figure 2-34

You have now successfully created a cube using the Business Intelligence Development Studio. All you have done, though, is create the structure of the cube. There has not been any interaction with the Analysis Services instance until this moment. This method of creating the cube structure without any interaction with the Analysis Services instance is referred to as project mode. Using BIDS you can also create these objects directly on the Analysis Services instance. The method of creating all the objects on the Server is called online mode, which is discussed in Chapter 9.

Next, you need to send the schema definitions of the newly created cube to the Analysis Services instance. This process is called *deployment*.

Deploying and Browsing a Cube

To deploy the database to the Analysis Server, right-click the project name and select Deploy, as shown in Figure 2-35. You can also deploy the project to the server from the menu items within BIDS by selecting the Debug⇨Start or just by pressing the function key F5 on your keyboard.

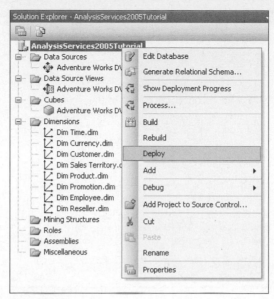

Figure 2-35

When you select Deploy, the BIDS first builds the project you have created and checks for preliminary errors such as invalid definitions within the project. After that, BIDS packages all the objects and definitions you have created in the project and sends them to the Analysis Services instance. By default all these definitions are sent to Analysis Services on the same machine (localhost). A database with the name of the project is created in Analysis Services and all the objects created in the project will be created within this database. Upon selecting the Deploy option, BIDS not only sends all the schema definitions of the objects you have created, but also sends a command to process the database.

If you want to deploy this to a different machine that is running Analysis Services 2005, you need to right-click the project and select Properties. This brings up the Properties page in which you can specify the Analysis Services name to deploy the project. This page is shown in Figure 2-36. Change the Server property to the appropriate machine and follow the steps to deploy the project.

After you deploy the project you will see a Deployment Progress window at the location of the Properties window. The Output window in BIDS shows the operations that occur after selecting Deploy — building the project, deploying the definitions to the server, and the process command that is sent to the server. BIDS retrieves the objects being processed by the Analysis Services and shows the details (the object being processed; the relational query sent to the relational database to process that object including the start and end time; and errors, if any) in the Deployment Progress window. Once the deployment has been completed, then appropriate status will be shown in the Deployment Progress window as well as the Output window. If there were errors reported from the server these will be presented to you in the Output window. You can use the Deployment Progress window to identify which object caused the error. BIDS waits for results from the server. If the deployment succeeded (successful deployment of schema and processing of all the objects), this information is shown as "Deploy: 1 succeeded, 0 failed, 0 skipped". You will also notice the message "Deployment Completed Successfully" in the Deployment Progress window. If there are any errors reported from Analysis Services, then deployment will fail and you will be prompted with a dialog box. The errors returned from the service will be shown in the Output window. In your current project, deployment will succeed as shown in Figure 2-37 and you will be able to browse the cube.

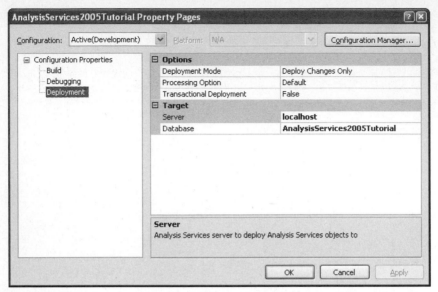

Figure 2-36

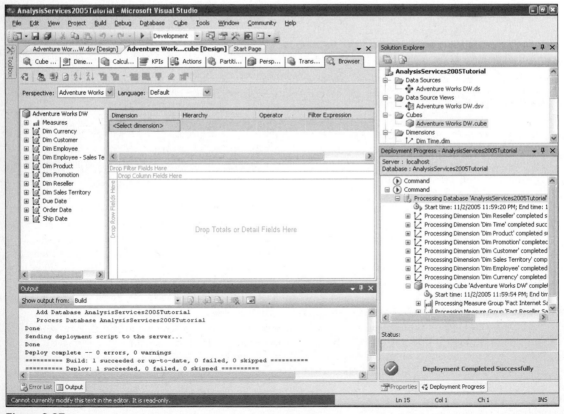

Figure 2-37

After a successful deploy BIDS automatically switches the Cube Editor pane from Cube Structure to Browser so that you can start browsing the cube you have created. The Browser pane has three main windows, as shown in Figure 2-38. The left window shows all the measures and dimensions that are available for your browser. This is called the Metadata window. You can expand the tree structures to see the measure groups, measures, and hierarchies. On the right side you have two windows split horizontally. The top pane is referred to as the Filter window because you can specify filter conditions while browsing the cube. The bottom pane hosts the Office Web Components (OWC) inside it, which is used for analyzing results. You can drag and drop measures and dimensions from the metadata pane to the OWC in the right bottom pane to analyze data.

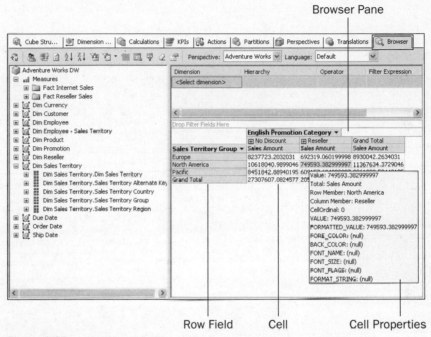

Figure 2-38

In Figure 2-38 you can see that the hierarchies "English Promotion Category" of dimension "Dim Promotion" and the hierarchy "Sales Territory Group" of dimension "Dim Sales Territory" are dropped on to the Column and Row fields of the OWC. Drag and drop the Measure Sales Amount in the Data area. You can similarly drag and drop multiple measures within the data area. You will now see the measure values that correspond to the intersection of the different values of the two hierarchies English Promotion Category and Sales Territory Group. As shown in Figure 2-38 you will notice "Grand Total" generated for each dimension along the Row and Column. This is provided by OWC and the values corresponding to the Grand Total are retrieved by OWC by sending appropriate MDX queries to the server. Each measure value corresponding to the intersection of the dimension values is referred to as a cell. If you hover over each cell you will see a window that shows all the properties of a particular cell. In Figure 2-87 you can also see the cell properties for the cell at the intersection of English Promotion Category = Reseller and Sales Territory Group = North America.

Using SQL Server Management Studio

SQL Server Management Studio (SSMS) is ground zero for administering the Analysis Servers resident on your network; not only that, you can also administer instances of SQL Server, Reporting Services, Integration Services and SQL Server Mobile from SSMS. In this book you learn administering and managing Analysis Servers, and this chapter specifically discusses the Analysis Services object as shown in the Object Explorer. Administering Analysis Services is discussed in detail in Chapter 11.

The first step in the process of adding objects to the Object Explorer calls for connecting to the services you wish to manage. In fact, as soon as you start Management Studio, you get a dialog to connect to one of the services as shown in Figure 2-39. Create a connection to the Analysis Services through your login.

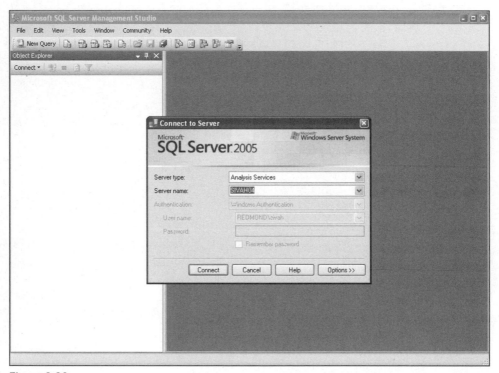

Figure 2-39

SSMS provides you a way to register your servers so that you do not have to specify the login credentials each time need to connect to a server. Click on View menu item and select Register Servers. You will now see a window called Registered Servers in SSMS as shown in Figure 2-40. In the Registered Servers pane, click the toolbar icon second from left; this enables you to register an Analysis Services instance instead of SQL Server. Now, right-click Microsoft Analysis Servers and select New⇨Server Registration. In the resulting New Server Registration dialog (see Figure 2-41) you need to specify the name of the Analysis Services instances you wish to connect to and optionally specify some of the connection parameters such as time out or enabling encryption. If it was a named instance, enter the name of the instance in the Server Name field, otherwise, type in localhost—this means you want to register the default instance of Analysis Services on your machine. This is the most common configuration. Once you have filled in the Server Name field, you can test the connection by clicking the Test button at the bottom of the dialog. If the connection does not succeed, you need to make sure Analysis Services is running and that your authentication scheme is correct. Once the connection is working, click Save.

Figure 2-40

Figure 2-41

Object Explorer Pane

When you connect to an Analysis Services instance you see the server in the Object Explorer pane (see Figure 2-42). This section reviews the various objects in Analysis Services with the help of the sample database, Adventure Works DW. Open the Databases object to see your Analysis Services database called AnalysisServices2005Tutorial and expand each object. Now you should be looking at a list of seven major objects (Data Sources, Data Source Views, Cubes, Dimensions, Mining Structures, Roles and Assemblies) as shown in Figure 2-42.

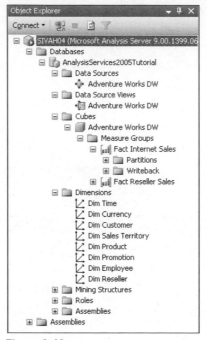

Figure 2-42

The following list describes each of the objects:

❑ **Databases:** The Databases object is where all your deployed Analysis Services projects are listed; note that these objects could have been created in On-line mode or Project mode.

❑ **Data Sources:** The Data Sources object will, at minimum, contain a single object pointing to a data source like SQL Server 2005 if you have cubes or dimensions or mining models. Behind the scenes, they are objects that store connection information to a relational data source which can be a .NET provider or an OLE DB provider. In either case you can establish a connection to a data source. In Figure 2-42, you can see the Adventure Works DW data source, which is called "Adventure Works DW." For any real-world scenario, it is likely you will have multiple data sources.

❑ **Data Source Views:** The data source views object will contain at least one object pointing to a sub-set of the data originally identified by the data source object. The reason this object type exists is because in the enterprise environment the data source might contain thousands of tables, though here you're interested in working with only a small subset of those tables. Using the DSV object, you can restrict the number of tables shown in a given view. This makes working on even the largest database a manageable task. On the other hand, you might want to create a DSV to contain not only all tables in one database, but a portion of tables from a second database. Indeed, you can have a DSV that uses more than one data source for an optimal work environment.

❑ **Cubes:** You have already looked at the details of cubes in BIDS; they are the lingua franca of Business Intelligence. Well, those cubes can be viewed in the Object Explorer pane. Further, three sections under the cubes object provide information about how the cube is physically stored and whether or not it will allow you to write back unique data to the cube for "what if" analysis:

  ❑ **Measure Groups:** Measure groups are comprised of one or more columns of a fact table which, in turn, is comprised of the data to be aggregated and analyzed. Measure groups help in grouping logical measures under a single entity.

  ❑ **Partitions:** Partitioning is a way of distributing data across disparate systems. You typically partition the fact data if you have a large fact table. In this way you can make the queries return faster; this works because scanning partitions in parallel is faster than scanning serially. There is a maintenance benefit as well; when you do incremental updates (process only data changed since the last update) it is more efficient for the system to update only those partitions that have changed. One variation of the partitioning technique is to partition on data categorized by year. In this way, a single fact table might have only up to five years of the most recent data and is therefore subject to queries, whereas the older, less often accessed data can lay fallow in a fact table partition. If you right-click the partitions object under the FactInternetSales measure group, you will see a number of administrative tasks associated with partitions that can be dealt with directly in SSMS.

  ❑ **Writeback:** Writeback provides a user the flexibility to perform a "what if" analysis of data or do perform a specific update to a measure such as budget where your budget for next year gets determined by using writeback. The writeback object is empty in AnalysisServices2005Tutorial because it has not been enabled. By default writeback is not turned on. To see what options are available, right-click the Writeback object.

❑ **Dimensions:** Dimensions are what cubes are made of and you can see what dimensions are available for use in a given project by looking at the contents of this object. Note that you can browse, process, and delete dimensions from here with a right-click of the mouse.

❑ **Mining Structures:** Data mining requires a certain amount of infrastructure to make the algorithms work. Mining structures are objects that contain one or more mining models. The mining models themselves contain properties like column content type, your data mining algorithm of choice, and predictable columns. You have to derive mining models based on a mining structure.

❑ **Mining Models:** This is where the Mining Model objects are stored. There is a one-to-one relationship between mining models and algorithms. If you want to use two algorithms based on the same mining model, you have to create a copy of your derived model and associate a different algorithm with it.

❑ **Roles:** Roles are objects that define a database-specific set of permissions; these categories can be for individual users or groups of users. Three types of permissions can be set for a role: Administrator level or Full control, Process Database level, and Read Database Metadata level. Roles are discussed with the help of a scenario in Chapter 19.

❑ **Assemblies:** You learned earlier in this chapter that assemblies are actually stored procedures (created with CLR or COM-based programming languages) used on the server side for custom operations. If you are familiar with Analysis Services 2000 and the UDF (User-Defined Function), note that assemblies can do anything the UDF can do and more. Also note that COM UDFs in Analysis Services 2000 form are also supported in Analysis Services 2005 for backwards compatibility of existing applications. The scope of these assemblies is OLAP database–specific; that is, an assembly can only operate on the database for which it is run.

❑ **Server Assemblies:** If you want to operate on multiple databases in Analysis Services, you have to create this sort of object, the server assembly. Server assemblies are virtually the same as assemblies, except their scope is increased; they work across databases in Analysis Services.

Querying Using the MDX Query Editor

Just to recap what MDX is, it is a query language that allows you to query multidimensional databases similar to SQL that is used to query relational databases. MDX is used to extract information from Analysis Services cubes or dimensions. Whereas SQL returns results along two axes — rows and columns — MDX returns data along multiple axes. You learn about MDX in depth in Chapters 3 and 7; for now, look at a simple MDX query to learn how to execute it and view the results.

The syntax of a typical MDX query is as follows:

```
SELECT [<axis_specification>
    [, <axis_specification>...]]
 FROM [<cube_specification>]
[WHERE [<slicer_specification>]]
```

The MDX SELECT statement contains a SELECT clause where you specify the data you need to retrieve across each axis and a FROM clause that is used to specify the cube from which you retrieve the data, with an optional WHERE clause that is used to slice a small section of data from which you need the results.

In Analysis Services 2000, an MDX Sample application was included with the shipping product; people used this application to send queries to cubes and retrieve results. In Analysis Services 2005, query editors are integrated right in the SSMS for sending queries to SQL Server and Analysis Services. These query editors have IntelliSense (dynamic function name completion) capabilities built in. When MDX queries are saved from the SSMS they are saved with the extension .mdx. You can open the MDX query editor in SSMS by selecting File⇨New⇨Analysis Services MDX Query as shown in Figure 2-43 or by clicking on the MDX query icon as shown in Figure 2-44.

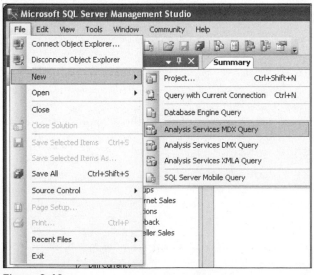

Figure 2-43

Figure 2-44

You will be prompted to connect to your Analysis Services instance. After you establish a connection to your Analysis Services instance, you can select the name of the database you wish to use from the available databases drop-down box shown in Figure 2-45. Select the AnalysisServicesTutorial2005 database that you created in this chapter. In this database you created one cube called Adventure Works DW, which is shown in the Cube drop-down box. The Query Editor is composed of two window panes, the Metadata pane on the left and the Query Construction pane on the right. In the Query Construction pane, you can make use of the IntelliSense feature by pressing Ctrl and Spacebar after typing in a few characters of an MDX keyword.

Now you can type the following query in the Query pane:

```
SELECT [Measures].members on COLUMNS
FROM [Adventure Works DW]
```

Database Selection Dropdown   Query construction pane

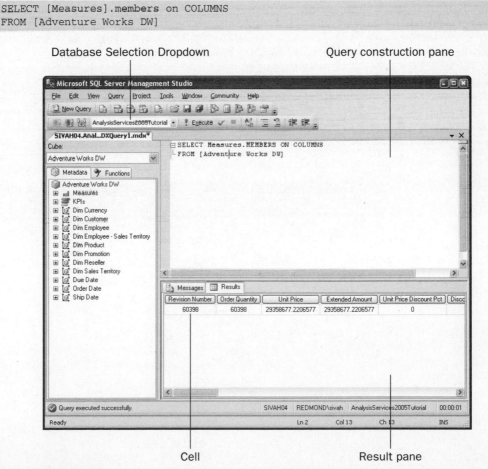

Cell   Result pane

Figure 2-45

You can now execute the query by pressing the Ctrl+E key combination or clicking the Execute button. On execution, the query construction pane splits in two and the results from the server are shown in the bottom half. All MDX queries cited in this book can be executed using this method. Congratulations, you just ran your first MDX query! You can see the results of the MDX query in the result pane where you can see the members on axes and the corresponding cell values as shown in Figure 2-45.

Summary

In this chapter you were introduced to Analysis Services 2005 and learned how it overcomes most of the limitations of its predecessor, Analysis Services 2000. In addition to trumping these limitations, Analysis Services 2005 provides a rich suite of tools for development and management of Analysis Services databases.

You were introduced to the Business Intelligence Development Studio, which is core to designing Analysis Services cubes and dimensions. You successfully created a cube using the cube wizard; in the course of building that cube you learned about data sources, data source views, dimensions, and relevant wizards used to create these objects. You successfully deployed the cube to Analysis Services and then browsed the cube within Business Intelligence Development Studio.

In the second half of this chapter you learned about the integrated management environment of SQL Server 2005, which is used to manage SQL Server and Analysis Services. You were familiarized with the various objects within an Analysis Services database by browsing the objects in the Object Explorer.

Finally, you learned that MDX does not require a Ph.D. in nuclear physics to use. The MDX Query Editor can be used easily to execute an MDX query, in this case, against the cube you built. Finally, you were able to view the results. In the next chapter you learn the basics of MDX, which will form the foundation for you to understand Analysis Services 2005 one level deeper.

3

Introduction to MDX

In Chapter 2 you ran a simple MDX query to retrieve data from Analysis Services 2005. Building on that, in this chapter you learn the fundamental concepts underlying MDX and how you can manipulate and query multidimensional objects within Analysis Services using MDX. This chapter forms the basis for much of the subsequent chapters in this book; in fact, in several places in this chapter and throughout the book it is shown how each interaction between client tools and the instance of Analysis Services results in the generation of MDX. You not only see the MDX that is generated, but also glean some insight as to what the MDX does.

SQL Server 2005 provides a sample Analysis Services project that contains the majority of the features supported by Analysis Services 2005. In this chapter you will use the sample Analysis Services project shipped with the product to learn MDX. The illustrations are limited to three dimensions for you to more easily understand the concepts. You can extend these concepts if you want to view data across additional dimensions. In this chapter you learn the basic concepts regarding cells, members, tuples, and sets. In addition, you learn how to create MDX expressions and MDX queries for data analysis from Analysis Services databases.

What Is MDX?

Just as SQL (Structured Query Language) is a query language used to retrieve data from relational databases, MDX (Multi-Dimensional eXpressions) is a query language used to retrieve data from multi-dimensional databases. More specifically, MDX is used for querying data from OLAP databases with Analysis Services and supports two distinct modes. When used as an expression, it can define and manipulate multidimensional objects and data to calculate values. As a query language, it is used to retrieve data from Analysis Services databases. MDX was originally designed by Microsoft and introduced along with Analysis Services 7.0 in 1998.

MDX is not a proprietary language; it is a standards-based query language used to retrieve data from OLAP databases. MDX is part of the OLEDB for OLAP specification sponsored by Microsoft. Many other OLAP providers support MDX, including Microstrategy's Intelligence Server, Hyperion's Essbase Server, and SAS's Enterprise BI Server. There are those who wish to extend the standard for additional functionality, and MDX extensions have indeed been developed by individual vendors. MDX extensions provide functionality not resident in the standard, but the constituent parts of any extension are expected to be consistent with the MDX standard. Analysis Services 2005 does provide several extensions to the standard MDX defined by the OLEDB for OLAP specification. In this book you learn about the form of MDX supported by Analysis Services 2005.

When one refers to MDX they might be referring either to the MDX query language or to MDX expressions. Even though the MDX query language has similar syntax as that of SQL, it is significantly different. Nonetheless, we will use SQL to teach you some MDX — we're not proud. Before you get into the details of MDX query language and MDX expressions, you need to learn some fundamental concepts.

Fundamental Concepts

The cube is the foundation of a multidimensional database. Each cube typically contains more than two dimensions. The Adventure Works cube in the sample database contains 21 dimensions. The Adventure Works sample project and relational database need to be selected explicitly during installation from Documents, Samples, and Sample Databases. Using BIDS open the sample Adventure Works project from Program Files\Microsoft SQL Server\90\Tools\Samples\AdventureWorks Analysis Services Project\Enterprise and deploy it to your Analysis Services instance. If you open the Adventure Works cube in BIDS you can see the measures and dimensions that make up the Adventure Works cube in the Cube Structure tab as shown in Figure 3-1.

The *Measures* object is basically a special dimension of the cube which is a collection of measures. Measures are quantitative entities which are used for analysis. Each measure is part of an entity called a measure group. *Measure Groups* are collections of related measures and each measure can only be part of a single measure group. Often you will want to have one measure group for each fact table in your data warehouse. Measure groups are primarily used for navigational purposes by design tools or client tools to have better readability or ease of use for end users. They are never used in MDX queries while querying measures. However, they can be used in certain MDX functions which, by the way, you will see in this chapter and in Chapter 7. By default Analysis Services generates a measure group for every fact table, so you don't have to worry about changing the measure group's design. If you want to, of course, you can.

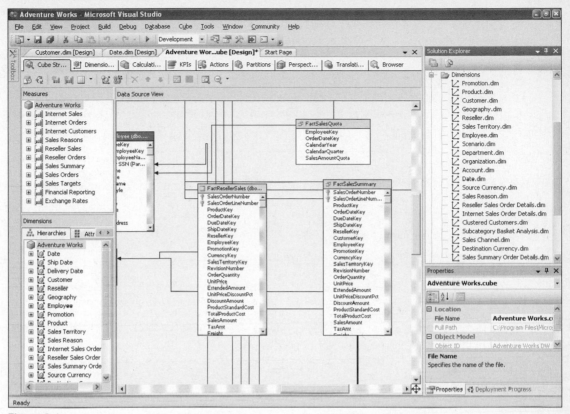

Figure 3-1

In Figure 3-1 you can see the twenty-one dimensions that are part of the Adventure Works cube. To understand the fundamental concepts of MDX through illustrations we will use three of the dimensions Product, Customer, and Date. Each dimension has one or more hierarchies and each hierarchy contains one or more levels. You learn about dimensions, hierarchies and levels in detail in Chapter 5. We will use the hierarchies Calendar, Product Line and Country from the dimensions Date, Product and Customer respectively to understand fundamental concepts in MDX. Figure 3-2 shows a section of the Adventure Works cube using the three hierarchies Calendar, Product Line and Country. The Calendar hierarchy of the Date dimension contains five levels: Calendar Year, Calendar Semester, Calendar Quarter, Month and Date. For illustration purposes only the top three levels of the Calendar hierarchy are used in Figure 3-2. The Product Line and Country are attribute hierarchies and have two levels, the All level and the Country level. Note that Figure 3-2 does not show the All level.

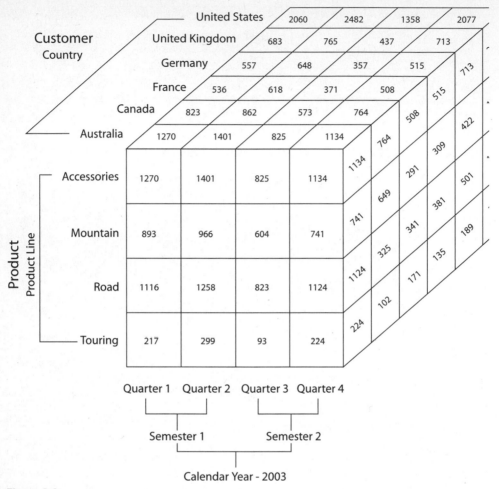

Figure 3-2

Members

Each hierarchy of a dimension contains one or more items that are referred to as *members*. Each member corresponds to one or more occurrences of that value in the underlying dimension table. Figure 3-3 shows the members of the Calendar hierarchy in the Date dimension. In the Calendar hierarchy the items 2004, H1 CY 2004, H2 CY 2004, Q1 CY 2004, Q2 CY 2004, Q3 CY 2004, and Q4 CY 2004 are the members. You can see that the items at each level together form the collection of the members of the hierarchy. You can also query the members of a specific level. For example Q1 CY 2004, Q2 CY 2004, Q3 CY 2004, and Q4 CY 2004 are members of the level Calendar Quarter.

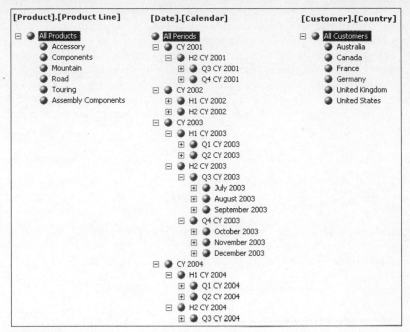

Figure 3-3

In MDX each member of a hierarchy is represented by a unique name. The unique name helps to identify specific members. The unique name for a member is dependent upon properties of a dimension within a cube such as MemberUniqueNameStyle and HierarchyUniqueNameStyle. The algorithm determining the unique name of a member is not discussed in this book. You can access members of a dimension by using the name path (using the name of the member) or the key path (using the key of the member). Using the default properties in BIDS to creating your cubes and dimensions you can access a member in a dimension with its dimension name, hierarchy name and level name. For example, member Q1 CY 2004 in the Calendar hierarchy is represented as

```
[Date].[Calendar].[Calendar Quarter].[Q1 CY 2004]
```

The brackets [and] are used to enclose the names of the dimension, hierarchy, levels, and members. It is not necessary that these names be enclosed within the square brackets every time, but whenever you have a name that is separated by a space, or has a number in it, or if the name is an MDX keyword, brackets must be used. In the preceding expression the dimension name Date is an MDX keyword and hence must be enclosed within brackets.

The following three representations are also valid for the member Q1 CY 2004.

```
[Date].[Calendar].[Q1 CY 2004]                              (1)
[Date].[Calendar].[CY 2004].[H1 CY 2004].[Q1 CY 2004]       (2)
[Date].[Calendar].[Calendar Quarter].&[2004]&[1]            (3)
```

In the first representation the member is represented in the format Dimension.Hierarchy.Member name. You can use this format so long as there are no two members of the same name. For example, if quarter 1 in each year is called Q1 then you cannot use the above format; you would need to qualify using the level name in the MDX expression. If you do use the above format it will always retrieve Q1 for the first year in the hierarchy. In the second format you can see the navigational path for the member clearly since you see all the members in the path. So far the formats for accessing members you have seen are all using the name of the members. The final representation uses the key path where you can see the key of members in a path is represented by &[membername]. When you use the key path the members are always preceded with the & symbol.

Another example is the member Australia of hierarchy Country in the Customer dimension, which would be specified as

```
[Customer].[Country].Australia
```

Notice that there are no square brackets in the expression for the member Australia. This is due to the fact that Australia is one word and no numbers are involved. In general, you can use the following format for accessing a member.

```
[DimensionName].[HierarchyName].[LevelName].[MemberName]
```

The above format is predominantly used in this chapter as well as the book. If you are developing client tools we recommend you make an effort to understand the unique name algorithm from product documentation based on the properties set for dimensions. In this way, you can use the best name format to access a member.

Cells

In Figure 3-2 you can see three faces of the cube. You can see the front face of the cube has been divided into 16 small squares, and each square holds a number. The number represented within each square is the measure "Internet Sales Amount" of the AdventureWorksDW cube. If you view the remaining visible faces of the cube you will realize that each square you analyzed in the front face of the cube is actually a small cube. The top-right corner square of the front face contains the value 1134; you will notice that the same number is represented on the other sides as well. This smaller cube is referred to as a *cell*.

The cell is an entity from which you can retrieve data that is pertinent to an intersection of the dimension members. The number of cells within a cube depends on the number of hierarchies within each dimension of a cube and the number of members in each hierarchy. As you can imagine, cells hold the data values of all measures in a cube. If the data value for a measure within a cell is not available, the corresponding measure value is a Null value.

If you are familiar with three-dimensional coordinate geometry you are aware of the three axes X, Y, and Z. Each point in three-dimensional coordinate geometry is represented by an X, Y, and Z coordinate value. Similarly, each cell within a cube is represented by dimension members. In the illustration shown in Figure 3-4, you can see the three dimensions: Product, Customer, and Date. Assume that each of these dimensions had exactly one hierarchy that is illustrated in the figure, namely, Product Line, Country, and Calendar Time. From the figure you can see that the Product Line has 4 members, the Calendar Time has 4 members (considering only the quarters), and Country has 6 members. Therefore the number of cells is equal to 4*4*6 = 96 cells.

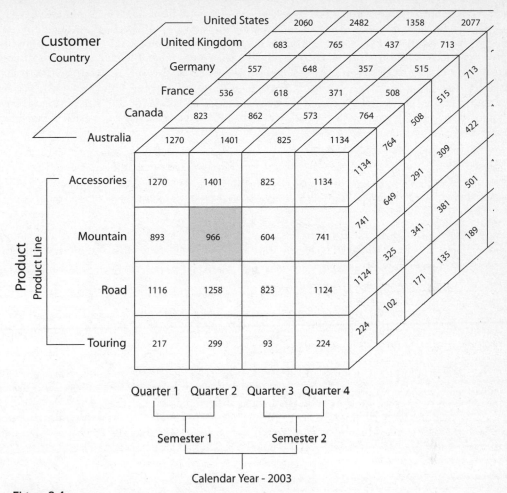

Figure 3-4

Now that you have learned what a cell is, you need to understand how to retrieve data from it. Assume you want to retrieve the data shown by the shaded area in the cube. The Sales amount represented in this cell is 966. This cell corresponds to the intersection of Product=Mountain, Date=Quarter2, and Customer=Australia. The value 966 corresponds to the total Sales of Mountain tires in Quarter2 bought by Customers residing in Australia. To retrieve data from the cube you need to send an MDX query to Analysis Services. What you need to do is retrieve the "Sales Amount" from the Cube based on the condition that uniquely identifies the cell that contains value 966. That MDX query is

```
SELECT Measures.[Internet Sales Amount] on COLUMNS
FROM [Adventure Works]
WHERE ( [Date].[Calendar].[Calendar Quarter].&[2004]&[1],
    [Product].[Product Line].[Mountain],
    [Customer].[Country].[Australia])
```

You can see from this query that you are selecting the Measures.[Internet Sales Amount] value from the Adventure Works cube based on a specific condition mentioned in the WHERE section of the MDX query. This condition specified in the WHERE clause uniquely identifies the cell. All you have done in the condition is to list the members (which you learned about in the previous section) that uniquely identify the cell, separated by commas. An MDX expression like this that uniquely identifies a cell is called a tuple.

Tuples

As you saw in the previous section, a *tuple* uniquely identifies a cell or a section of a cube. A tuple is represented by one member from each dimension, separated by a comma, and is enclosed within the parentheses characters, (and). A tuple does not necessarily have to explicitly contain members from all the dimensions in the cube. Some examples of tuples based on the Adventure Works cube are

1. ([Customer].[Country].[Australia])

2. ([Date].[Calendar].[2004].[H1 CY 2004].[Q1 CY 2004], [Customer].[Country].[Australia])

3. ([Date].[Calendar].[2004].[H1 CY 2004].[Q1 CY 2004], [Product].[Product Line].[Mountain], [Customer].[Country].[Australia])

In the preceding examples, Tuples 1 and 2 do not contain members from all the dimensions in the cube. Therefore they represent sections of the cube. A section of the cube represented by a tuple is called a slice since you are slicing the cube to form a section (slice) based on certain dimension members.

When you refer to tuple ([Customer].[Country].[Australia]) you actually refer to the sixteen cells that correspond to the country Australia for the example shown in Figure 3-4 (the cells in the front face of the cube). Therefore when you retrieve the data held by the cell pointed to by this tuple you are actually retrieving the Internet Sales Amount of all the customers in Australia. The Internet Sales Amount value for the tuple ([Customer].[Country].[Australia]) is an aggregate of the cells encompassed in the front face of the cube. The MDX query to retrieve data represented by this tuple is

```
SELECT Measures.[Internet Sales Amount] on COLUMNS
FROM [Adventure Works]
WHERE ([Customer].[Country].[Australia])
```

The result of this query is $9,061,000.58

The order of the members used to represent a Tuple does not matter. What this means is that the following tuples

1. ([Date].[Calendar].[2005].[H1 CY 2004].[Q1 CY 2004], [Product].[Product Line].[Mountain], [Customer].[Country].[Australia])

2. ([Product].[Product Line].[Mountain], [Customer].[Country].[Australia], ([Date].[Calendar].[2005].[H1 CY 2004].[Q1 CY 2004])

3. ([Customer].[Country].[Australia], [Date].[Calendar].[2005].[H1CY 2005].[Q1CY 2005], [Product].[Product Line].[Mountain])

are all equal and uniquely identify just one cell. Because a Tuple uniquely identifies a cell, it cannot contain more than one member from each dimension.

A tuple represented by a single member is called a simple tuple and does not have to be enclosed within the parentheses. ([Customer].[Country].[Australia]) is a simple tuple and can be referred to as [Customer].[Country].[Australia] or simply Customer.Country.Australia. When there is more than one member from each dimension, the tuple needs to be represented within the parentheses characters. A collection of tuples forms a new object called sets, which is frequently used in MDX queries and expressions.

Sets

A *set* is a collection of tuples that are defined using the exact same dimensions, both in type and number. A set is typically specified with the curly brace characters { and }. The following examples illustrate sets.

Example 1:

The Tuples (Customer.Country.Australia) and (Customer.Country.Canada) are resolved to the exact same dimension. A collection of these two Tuples is a valid Set and is specified as

```
{(Customer.Country.Australia), (Customer.Country.Canada)}
```

Example 2:

The tuples (Customer.Country.Australia, [Product].[Product Line].[Mountain]) and (Product.Country.Canada, [Date].[Calendar].[2004].[H1 CY 2004].[Q1 CY 2004]) cannot be combined to form a set. Even though they are formed by two dimensions, the dimensions used to resolve the tuple are different. Both tuples have the Customer dimension but the second dimensions are different.

Example 3:

Each of the following tuples has the three dimensions Date, Product, and Customer.

```
1.   ([Date].[Calendar].[2004].[H1 CY 2004].[Q1 CY 2004], [Product].[Product
Line].[Mountain], [Customer].[Country].[Australia]),
2.   ([Product].[Product Line].[Mountain], [Customer].[Country].[Australia],
([Date].[Calendar].[2002].[H1 CY 2002].[Q1 CY 2002])
3.   ([Customer].[Country].[Australia], Date.[Calendar].[2003].[H1 CY 2003].[Q1 CY
2003], [Product].[Product Line].[Mountain] )
```

The members in the date dimension of the three tuples above are different and therefore these tuples refer to different cells. As per the definition of a set, a collection of these tuples is a valid set and is shown here

```
{ ([Date].[Calendar Time].[2004].[H1 CY 2004].[Q1 CY 2004], [Product].[Product
Line].[Mountain], [Customer].[Country].[Australia]), ([Product].[Product
Line].[Mountain], [Customer].[Country].[Australia], ([Date].[Calendar].[2003].[H1
CY 2003].[Q1 CY 2003]),([Customer].[Country].[Australia],
[Date].[Calendar].[2002].[H1 CY 2002].[Q1 CY 2002], [Product].[Product
Line].[Mountain] )}
```

A set can contain zero, one, or more tuples. A set with zero tuples is referred to as an empty set. An empty set is represented as

```
{   }
```

A set can contain duplicate tuples. An example of such a set is

```
{Customer.Country.Australia, Customer.Country.Canada, Customer.Country.Austrailia}
```

This set contains two instances of the tuple Customer.Country.Australia. Because a member from a dimension by itself forms a tuple, it can be used in MDX queries. If there is a tuple that is specified by only one dimension, you do not need the parentheses to specify the cell. Similarly, when there is a single tuple specified in the query you do not need curly braces. When an MDX query is being executed, implicitly this tuple is converted to a set in the query rather than representing the object as a tuple.

Now that you have learned the key concepts that will help you to understand MDX better, the following section dives right into the MDX query syntax, the operators used in an MDX query or an MDX expression.

MDX Query

Chapter 2 introduced you to the MDX SELECT statement. The syntax for an MDX query is as follows

```
[WITH <formula_expression> [, <formula_expression> ...]]
SELECT [<axis_expression>, [<axis_expression>...]]
FROM [<cube_expression>]
[WHERE [slicer_expression]]
```

You might be wondering whether the SELECT, FROM, and WHERE format is similar to the Structured Query Language (SQL), serve a purpose similar to SQL. Even though the SELECT-FROM-WHERE looks identical to SQL in MDX, you can do more complex operations in MDX. You learn some of these operations in this chapter and throughout the book.

The keywords WITH, SELECT, FROM, and WHERE along with the expressions following them are together referred to as a *clause*. In the preceding MDX query template anything specified within the square brackets means it is optional; that is, that section of the query is not mandatory in every MDX query.

You can see that the WITH and WHERE clauses are optional because they are enclosed within [and] characters. Therefore, you might be thinking that the simplest possible MDX query should be the following

```
SELECT
FROM [Adventure Works]
```

Super! You are absolutely correct. This MDX query returns a single value; the tuple corresponding to this value uses the default members of the dimension to retrieve the value. You might recall that the fact data is stored in a special dimension called Measures. When you send the preceding query to the Analysis Services instance you get the default member from the Measures dimension, which is one of the measures in the cube. The result of this query is the aggregated result of all the cells in the cube of this measure for the default values of each dimension in the cube.

The WITH clause is typically used for custom calculations and operations, and you learn about this in the later part of this chapter. First, take a look at the SELECT, FROM, and WHERE clauses.

SELECT Statement and Axis Specification

The MDX SELECT statement is used to retrieve a subset of the multidimensional data from an OLAP Server. In SQL the SELECT statement is used to retrieve columnar data, that is, data is retrieved as columns. Columnar data is one-dimensional and therefore a single axis is sufficient for projecting this data. In SQL you retrieve data as ROWS and COLUMNS, which is viewed as two-dimensional data. If you consider the two-dimensional coordinate system, you have the X and Y axes. The X axis is used for the COLUMNS and the Y axis is used for ROWS. Multidimensional data, however, are specified in a way such that data can be retrieved on multiple axes. Indeed, MDX provides you with the capability of retrieving data on multiple axes.

The syntax of the SELECT statement is

```
SELECT [<axis_expression>, [<axis_expression>...]]
```

The axis_expression specified after the SELECT refers to the dimension data you are interested in retrieving. These dimensions are referred to as axis dimensions because the data from these dimensions are projected onto the corresponding axes. The syntax for axis_expression is

```
<axis_expression> := <set> ON Axis (axis number)
```

Axis dimensions are used to retrieve multidimensional result sets. A set, the ordered collection of tuples, is defined to form an axis dimension. MDX provides you with the capability of specifying up to 128 axes in the SELECT statement. The first five axes have aliases. They are COLUMNS, ROWS, PAGES, SECTIONS, and CHAPTERS. Subsequent axes are specified as Axis (axis number). Take the following example:

```
SELECT    Measures.[Internet Sales Amount] ON COLUMNS,
          [Customers].[Country].MEMBERS on ROWS,
          [Product].[Product Line].MEMBERS on PAGES
```

Three axes are specified in the SELECT statement. Data from dimensions Measures, Customers, and Product are mapped on to the three axes to form the axis dimensions.

Axis Dimension

The axis dimension is what you build when you define the SELECT statement. When you build a SELECT statement, it functions by assigning a set to both COLUMNS and ROWS or additional axes — if you have more than two axes in your query. Unlike the slicer dimension (described later in this chapter), the axis dimension retrieves and retains data for multiple members, not by single members.

> **No Shortcuts! In MDX you cannot create a workable query that omits lower axes. If you want to specify a PAGES axis, you must also specify COLUMNS and ROWS.**

FROM Clause and Cube Specification

The FROM clause in the MDX query determines the cube from which you retrieve and analyze data. It's similar to the FROM clause in a SQL query where you specify a table name. The FROM clause is a necessity for any MDX query. The syntax of the FROM clause is

```
FROM <cube_expression>
```

The cube_expression denotes the name of a cube or a sub section of the cube from which you want to retrieve data. In SQL's FROM clause you can specify more than one table, but in an MDX FROM clause you can define just one cube name. The cube specified in the FROM clause is called the *cube context* and the query is executed within this cube context. That is, every part of the axis_expression to be retrieved from the cube context is specified in the FROM clause:

```
SELECT [Measures].[Internet Sales Amount] ON COLUMNS
FROM [Adventure Works]
```

This query is a valid MDX query that retrieves the [Internet Sales Amount] measure on the X-axis. The measure is retrieved from the cube context [Adventure Works]. Even though the FROM clause restricts you to working with only one cube or section of a cube, you can retrieve data from other cubes using the MDX function LookupCube. When there are two ore more cubes having common dimension members then the LookupCube function helps you to retrieve measures outside the CURRENTCUBE's context with the help of the common dimension members.

WHERE Clause and Slicer Specification

In pretty much any relational database work that you do, you will want to issue queries that return only specific portions of the overall data available in a given table or set of joined tables, and/or joined databases. This is accomplished using SQL statements to map out what data you do and do not want returned as a result of running your query. Here is an example of an unrestricted SQL query on a table named Product that contains sales information for products:

```
SELECT *
FROM    Product
```

This query results in five columns being retrieved with several rows:

Product ID	Product Line	Color	Weight	Sales
1	Accessories	Silver	5.00	200.00
2	Mountain	Grey	40.35	1000.00
3	Road	Silver	50.23	2500.00
4	Touring	Red	45.11	2000.00

The * represents "all," meaning that query will dump the entire contents of the table. If you want to know the Color by each Product Line, you have to restrict the query so that it returns only the information you want. The following simple example demonstrates a query constructed to return just two columns from the table:

```
SELECT ProductLine, Color
FROM Product
```

This query returns the following:

Product Line	Color
Accessories	Silver
Mountain	Grey
Road	Black
Touring	Red

The concept of crafting queries to return only what you need maps directly to MDX from SQL. In fact, they share a conditional statement that adds a whole new level of power to restricting queries to return only desired data. It is called the *WHERE* clause. After taking a look at the SQL use of WHERE you will see how the concept applies to MDX. Here is a SQL query that uses WHERE to return two columns for those products with a silver color from the Product table:

```
SELECT ProductLine, Sales
FROM    Product
WHERE   Color = 'Silver'
```

This query returns the following:

Product Line	Sales
Accessories	200.00
Road	2500.00

The same concept applies to MDX. Indeed, MDX uses both SELECT and WHERE statements. The SELECT statement is used to identify the dimensions and members a query will return and the WHERE statement limits the result set by some criteria; the preceding example is restricted by Color = 'Silver'. Note that members are the elements that make up a dimension's hierarchy. The Product table, when modeled as a cube, will contain two measures, Sales and Weight, and a Product dimension with the hierarchies ProductID, ProductLine, and Color. In this example the Product table is used as a fact as well as dimension table. An MDX query against the cube that produces the same results as that of the SQL query is

```
SELECT Measures.[Sales] ON COLUMS,
[Product].[Product Line].MEMBERS on ROWS
FROM   ProductsCube
WHERE ([Product].[Color].[Silver])
```

The two columns selected in SQL are now on the axes COLUMNS and ROWS. The condition in the SQL WHERE clause, which is a string comparison, is transformed to an MDX WHERE clause, which refers to a slice on the cube that contains products that have silver color. Even though the SQL and MDX queries look similar, the operations in SQL Server and Analysis Services are quite different.

Slicer Dimension

The *slicer dimension* is what you build when you define the WHERE statement; it is a filter that removes unwanted dimensions and members. What makes things even more interesting is that the slicer dimension then includes any axis in the cube not overtly included in any of the queried axes. The default members of the hierarchies not included in the query axes are used in the slicer axis. Regardless of how it gets its data, the slicer dimension will only accept MDX expressions (described later in this chapter) that evaluate to a single tuple. When there are multiple tuples specified on the slicer axis then MDX will evaluate these tuples as a set and the results of the tuples are aggregated based on the measures included in the query and the aggregation function of that specific measure.

WITH Clause and Calculated Member

Often business needs involve calculations that must be formulated within the scope of a specific query. The WITH clause in the MDX query provides you with the ability to create such calculations within the context of the query. In addition, you can also retrieve results outside the context of the current cube identified using the LookupCube MDX function.

Typical calculations that are created using the WITH clause are named sets and calculated members. In addition to these, the WITH clause also provides you with functionality to define cell calculations, load a cube into an Analysis Server cache for improving query performance, alter the contents of cells by calling functions in external libraries, and additional advanced concepts such as solve order and pass order. You learn about the named sets, calculated members, and calculated measures in this chapter, and Chapter 7 covers the rest.

The syntax of a WITH clause is

```
[WITH <formula_expression> [, <formula_expression> ...]]
```

The WITH clause provides with you the capability of specifying several calculations within one statement. The formula_expression will vary depending upon the type of calculation, and each such calculation is separated by a comma.

Named Sets

As you learned earlier, a set is a collection of tuples. The set expression, even though simple, can often be quite lengthy and this might make the query appear to be complex and unreadable. MDX provides you with the capability of dynamically defining sets with a specific name so that the name can be used within the query. Think of it as an alias for the collection of tuples in the set you are interested in retrieving data from. This is called a *named set*. A named set is nothing but an alias for a regular MDX set expression that can be used anywhere within the query as an alternative to the actual set expression.

Consider the case where you have customers in various countries. Suppose you want to retrieve the Sales information for customers in Europe, and then you need to use the customer members in the various countries in Europe. Your MDX query would look like this:

```
SELECT Measures.[Internet Sales Amount] on COLUMNS,
{[Customer].[Country].[Country].&[France],
[Customer].[Country].[Country].&[Germany],
[Customer].[Country].[Country].&[United Kingdom]} ON ROWS
FROM [Adventure Works]
```

This query is not too lengthy, but you can imagine a query that would contain a lot of members and functions being applied to this specific set several times within the query. Instead of using the completed set every time in the query, you can create a named set and then use the alias in the query as follows:

```
WITH SET [EUROPE] AS '{[Customer].[Country].[Country].&[France],
[Customer].[Country].[Country].&[Germany],[Customer].[Country].[Country].&[United
Kingdom]}'

SELECT Measures.[Internet Sales Amount] on COLUMNS,
[EUROPE] ON ROWS
FROM [Adventure Works]
```

The formula_expression of the WITH clause for named sets is

```
Formula_expression :=  SET <set_alias_name> AS [']<set>[']
```

The alias name can be any alias name and is typically enclosed within angle brackets. Note the keywords SET and AS that are used in this expression to specify a named set. The actual set of tuples do not have to be enclosed within single quotes (''). The single quotes are still available for backwards comparability reason since Analysis Services 2000 expected the set to be included within single quotes.

Calculated Members

Calculated members are calculations specified by MDX expressions. These MDX expressions are resolved as a result of MDX expression evaluation rather than just the retrieval of the original fact data. A typical example of a calculated member is the calculation of year-to-date sales of products. Let's say the fact data only contains sales information of products for each month and you need to calculate the year-to-date sales. This can be specified by MDX expressions using the WITH clause so that you can retrieve the sales information not only for each month, but also the year-to-date sales up to that month.

The formula_expression of the WITH clause for calculated members is

```
Formula_expression := MEMBER <MemberName> AS [']<MDX_Expression>['],
                [ , SOVLE_ORDER = <integer>]
                [ , <CellProperty> = <PropertyExpression>]
```

MDX uses the keywords MEMBER and AS in the WITH clause for creating calculated members. The MemberName should be a fully qualified member name that includes the dimension, hierarchy, and level under which the specific calculated member needs to be created. The MDX_Expression should return a value that corresponds to the member. The SOLVE_ORDER, which is an optional parameter, should be a positive integer value if specified. The SOLVE_ORDER determines the order in which the members need to be evaluated when multiple calculated members are defined. The CellProperty is also an optional parameter and it is used to specify cell properties for the calculated member such as text formatting of the cell contents including background color.

All the measures in a cube are stored in a special dimension called Measures. Calculated members can also be created on the measures dimension. In fact, most of the calculated members that are used for business are usually on the measures dimension. Calculated members on the measures dimension are referred to as calculated measures. Following are examples of calculated member statements.

Example 1:

```
WITH MEMBER [MEASURES].[Profit] AS '([Measures].[Internet Sales Amount] -
          [Measures].[Total Product Cost])'
SELECT [MEASURES].[Profit] ON COLUMNS,
      [Customer].[Country].MEMBERS ON ROWS
FROM [Adventure Works]
```

In example 1 a calculated member Profit has been defined as the difference of the measures [Internet Sales Amount] and [Total Product Cost]. When the query is executed for every country, this calculated member will be evaluated based on the MDX expression.

Example 2:

```
WITH
SET [ProductOrder] AS 'Order([Product].[Product Line].members, [Internet Sales
Amount], BDESC)'
MEMBER [Measures].[ProductRank] AS 'Rank([Product].[Product Line].CURRENTMEMBER,
[ProductOrder])'
SELECT {[ProductRank],[Sales Amount]} on COLUMNS,
[PRoductOrder] on ROWS
FROM [Adventure Works]
```

Example 2 includes creation of a named set and a calculated member within the scope of the query. The query orders the Products based on the Internet Sales Amount and returns the sales amount of each product along with the rank. The named set [Product Order] is created so that the members within this set are ordered based on the Sales. This is done by using an MDX function called Order (you learn more about the Order in Appendix A). To retrieve the rank of each product, a calculated member [ProductRank] is created using the MDX function Rank.

The results of the preceding query on the sample Adventure Works Analysis Services database is

	Product Rank	Sales Amount
All Products	1	$109,809,274.20
Road	2	$48,262,055.15
Mountain	3	$42,456,731.56
Touring	4	$16,010,837.10
Accessory	5	$2,539,401.59
Components	6	$540,248.80

Example 3:

```
WITH MEMBER Measures.[Cumulative Sales] AS 'SUM(YTD(),[Internet Sales Amount])'
SELECT {Measures.[Internet Sales Amount], Measures.[Cumulative Sales]} ON 0,
[Date].[Calendar].[Calendar Semester].MEMBERS on 1
FROM [Adventure Works]
```

In example 3 a calculated member is created so that you can analyze the sales amount of each month along with the cumulative sales. For this two MDX functions are used: the SUM and the YTD. The YTD MDX function is called without any parameter so that the default Time member at that level is used in the calculation. The SUM function is used to aggregate the sales amount for that specific level. The result of the preceding query on the sample Analysis Services database is shown in the table below. You can see that the Cumulative Sales corresponding for the members H2 CY 2002, H2 CY 2003, and H2 CY 2004 show the sum of Internet Sales Amount for that member and the previous half year for the corresponding year.

	Internet Sales Amount	Cumulative Sales
H2 CY 2001	$3,266,373.66	$3,266,373.66
H1 CY 2002	$3,805,710.59	$3,805,710.59
H2 CY 2002	$2,724,632.94	$6,530,343.53
H1 CY 2003	$3,037,501.36	$3,037,501.36
H2 CY 2003	$6,753,558.94	$9,791,060.30
H1 CY 2004	$9,720,059.11	$9,720,059.11
H2 CY 2004	$50,840.63	$9,770,899.74

Example 4:

```
WITH MEMBER [Date].[Calendar].[%Change] AS
100* ((([Date].[Calendar].[Calendar Quarter].[Q2 CY 2002] -
   [Date].[Calendar].[Calendar Quarter].[Q1 CY 2002])    /
   [Date].[Calendar].[Calendar Quarter].[Q2 CY 2002])

SELECT {[Date].[Calendar].[Calendar Quarter].[Q1 CY 2002],
[Date].[Calendar].[Calendar Quarter].[Q2 CY 2002],
[Date].[Calendar].[%Change]} ON COLUMNS,
Measures.[Internet Sales Amount] ON ROWS
FROM [Adventure Works]
```

The above query shows an example of a calculated member defined in the Date dimension to return a quarter-over-quarter comparison of the sales amount. In this example, quarter 1 and quarter 2 of the year 2002 are being used. The result of this query is

	Q1 CY 2002	Q2 CY 2002	%Change
Sales Amount	$1,791,698.45	$2,014,012.13	11.038

MDX Expressions

MDX expressions are partial MDX statements that evaluate to a value. They are typically used in calculations or in defining values for objects such as default member and default measure, or used for defining security expressions to allow or deny access. MDX expressions typically take a member, a tuple, or a set as a parameter and return a value. If the result of the MDX expression evaluation is no value, a Null value is returned. Following are some examples of MDX expressions.

Example 1:

```
Customer.[Customer Geography].DEFAULTMEMBER
```

This example returns the default member specified for the hierarchy Customer Geography of the Customer dimension.

Example 2:

```
(Customer.[Customer Geography].CURRENTMEMBER, Measures.[Sales Amount]) –
(Customer.[Customer Geography].Australia, Measures.[Sales Amount)
```

This MDX expression is used to compare the sales between customers of different countries with sales of customers in Australia.

Such an expression is typically used in a calculation called the calculated measure. Complex MDX expressions can include various operators in the MDX language along with the combination of the functions available in MDX. One such example is shown in Example 3.

Example 3:

```
COUNT(INTERSECT( DESCENDANTS( IIF( HIERARCHIZE(EXISTS[Employee].[Employee].MEMBERS,
STRTOMEMBER("[Employee].[login].[login].&["+USERNAME+"]")),
POST).ITEM(0).ITEM(0).PARENT.DATAMEMBER is
HIERARCHIZE(EXISTS([Employee].[Employee].MEMBERS,
STRTOMEMBER("[Employee].[login].[login].&["+USERNAME+"]")), POST).ITEM(0).ITEM(0),
HIERARCHIZE(EXISTS([Employee].[Employee].MEMBERS,
STRTOMEMBER("[Employee].[login].[login].&["+username+"]")),
POST).ITEM(0).ITEM(0).PARENT,
HIERARCHIZE(EXISTS([Employee].[Employee].MEMBERS,
STRTOMEMBER("[Employee].[login].[login].&["+USERNAME+"]")), POST).ITEM(0).ITEM(0))
).ITEM(0) , Employee.Employee.CURRENTMEMBER))  > 0
```

The above example is a cell security MDX expression to allow employees to see Sales information made by them or by the employees reporting to them and not to other employees. This MDX expression uses several MDX functions (you learn some of these in the next section). You can see that this is not a simple MDX expression. The above MDX expression returns a value "True" or "False" based on the employee that is logged in, and Analysis Services provides appropriate cells to be accessed by the employee based on the evaluation. This example is analyzed in more detail in Chapter 18.

MDX has progressed extensively since its birth and you can pretty quickly end up with a complex MDX query or MDX expression like the one shown above in Example 3. There can be multiple people working on implementing a solution and hence it is better to have some kind of documentation for the queries or expressions. Similar to programming languages where you can embed comments, MDX supports commenting within queries and MDX expressions. At this time there are three different ways to comment your MDX. They are:

```
// (two forward slashes) comment goes here
-- (two hyphens) comment goes here
/* comment goes here */ (slash-asterisk pairs)
```

We highly recommend that you add comments to your MDX expressions and queries so that you can look back at a later point in time and interpret or understand what you were implementing with a specific MDX expression or query.

Operators

The MDX language, similar to other query languages such as SQL or programming languages, has several operators. An operator is a function that is used to perform a specific action and takes arguments. MDX has several types of operators. Similar to other languages, MDX contains the arithmetic operators, logical operators, and special MDX operators.

Arithmetic Operators

Regular arithmetic operators such as +, –, *, and / are part of the MDX arithmetic operators. Just as with programming languages, these operators can be applied between two numbers. The + and – operators can also be used as unary operators for numbers. Unary operator means the operator can be used with a single operand (single number) in MDX expressions such as + 100 or -100.

Set Operators

The +, -, and * operators, in addition to being arithmetic operators, are also used to perform operations on the MDX Sets. The + operator is used to union two Sets, the – operator is used to evaluate the difference of two Sets, and the * operator is used find the cross product of two sets. Cross product of two sets results in all possible combinations of the tuples in each set and helps in retrieving data in a matrix format. For example if you have the two sets {Male, Female} and {2003, 2004, 2005} then the cross product of the two sets represented as {Male, Female} * {2003, 2004, 2005} is {(Male,2003), (Male,2004), (Male,2005),(Female,2003),(Female,2004),(Female,2005)}. The following examples show some of the operations on sets using the set operators.

Example 1:

The result of the MDX expression

```
{[Customer].[Country].[Australia]} + {[Customer].[Country].[Canada]}
```

is the union of the two sets as shown here:

```
{[Customer].[Country].[Australia], [Customer].[Country].[Canada]}
```

Example 2:

The result of the MDX expression

```
{[Customer].[Country].[Australia],[Customer].[Country].[Canada]}*
{[Product].[Product Line].[Mountain],[Product].[Product Line].[Road]}
```

is the cross product of the sets as shown here:

```
{([Customer].[Country].[Australia],[Product].[Product Line].[Mountain])
([Customer].[Country].[Australia],[Product].[Product Line].[Mountain])
([Customer].[Country].[Canada],[Product].[Product Line].[Road])
([Customer].[Country].[Canada],[Product].[Product Line].[Road])}
```

Comparison Operators

MDX supports the comparison operators <, <=, >, >= , =, and <>. These operators take two MDX expressions as arguments and return TRUE or FALSE based on the result of comparing the values of the MDX expression.

Example:

The following MDX expression uses the (greater than) comparison operator, >

```
Count (Customer.[Country].members) > 3
```

In the above example Count is an MDX function that is used to count the number of members in Country hierarchy of Customer dimension. Because there are more than three members, the result of the preceding MDX expression is TRUE.

Logical Operators

The logical operators that are part of MDX are AND, OR, XOR, NOT, and IS, which are used for logical conjunction, logical disjunction, logical exclusion, logical negation, and comparison, respectively. These operators take two MDX expressions as arguments and return TRUE or FALSE based on the logical operation. These logical operators are typically used in MDX expressions for cell and dimension security, which you learn about in Chapter 18.

Special MDX Operators — Curly Braces, Commas, and Colons

The curly brace represented by the characters { and } is used to enclose a tuple or a set of tuples to form an MDX set. Whenever you have a single tuple, the curly brace is optional because Analysis Services implicitly converts the single tuple to a set. When there is more than one tuple to be represented as a set or when there is an empty set, you need to use the curly brace.

You have already seen the comma character used in several earlier examples. The comma character is used in forming a tuple that contains more than one member. By doing this you are eventually creating a slice of data on the cube. In addition, the comma character is used to build sets comprised of tuples where the tuples are separated by the comma character. In the set {(Male,2003), (Male,2004), (Male,2005),(Female,2003),(Female,2004),(Female,2005)} the comma character is not only used to form tuples but also to form the set of tuples.

The colon character is used to define a range of members within a set. The members within a set are ordered based on the key or the name of the member, whichever is specified while creating the set. The colon character is used between two non-consecutive members in a set to indicate inclusion of all the members between them, based on the ordering. For example, if you have the following set

```
{[Customer].[Country].[Australia], [Customer].[Country].[Canada],
[Customer].[Country].[France], [Customer].[Country].[Germany],
[Customer].[Country].[United Kingdom], [Customer].[Country].[United States]}
```

The following MDX expression

```
{[Customer].[Country].[Canada] : [Customer].[Country].[United Kingdom]}
```

results in the following set

```
{[Customer].[Country].[Canada], [Customer].[Country].[France],
[Customer].[Country].[Germany], [Customer].[Country].[United Kingdom]}
```

MDX Functions

MDX functions can be used in MDX expressions or in MDX queries as you carve up axis dimensions like a Thanksgiving turkey. MDX forms the bedrock of Analysis Services 2005; BIDS builds MDX expressions that typically include MDX functions to retrieve data from the Analysis Services database based upon your actions like browsing dimensions or cubes. MDX functions help address some of the common operations that are needed in your MDX expressions or queries. Including ordering tuples in a set, counting the number of members in a dimension, and string manipulation required to transform user input into corresponding MDX objects.

This section splits the MDX functions into various categories and provides some basic examples. The best way to learn MDX functions is to understand their use in business scenarios so that you can apply the right MDX function in analogous cases. In this book, you will often see MDX which the product generates; paying attention to and experimenting with such MDX is critical to your transition from basic understanding of Analysis Services 2005 to complete mastery—and though it is a profound challenge, mastery is attainable. You can do it. Again, when you slice a dimension in any cube-viewing software, like Office Web Components, it is MDX that is generated and executed to back-fill the newly exposed cells. Also, when you create a report based on a cube (UDM) using Excel (to be seen in Chapter 15) or using Reporting Services (Chapter 17) it is MDX that is created behind the scenes to capture the contents with which to populate the report. Almost all these MDX queries or expressions generated by BIDS or by client tools use various MDX functions; some of which you will learn about in detail as you work through this book.

In Chapter 10 you learn about the new stored procedures support in Analysis Services 2005 and how you can write your custom functions in .NET programming languages that can be called within your MDX expression or queries. For example, the following MDX query contains a custom function MyStoredProc that takes two arguments and returns an MDX object.

```
SELECT MyStoredProc (arg1, arg2) ON COLUMNS
FROM CorporateCube
```

What we expect will get you even more excited about Chapter 10 is that the .NET assemblies themselves can contain MDX expressions within them due to an object model that exposes MDX objects! It should be obvious if you are experienced with Analysis Services 2000 that the new version opens up whole new approaches to problem solving in the BI space. Because MDX functions are so central to successful use of Analysis Services 2005, it is best if you jump right in and learn some of the functions. Putting those functions together to accomplish more meaningful tasks will come later in the book. For now, please snap on your seatbelt; it's time to learn about MDX functions.

MDX Function Categories

MDX functions are used to programmatically operate on multidimensional databases; from traversing dimension hierarchies to calculating numeric functions over the data, there is plenty of surface area to explore. In this section the MDX functions have been categorized in a specific way for you to understand the MDX functions efficiently. You also see some details on select functions of interest, where interest level is defined by the probability you will use a given function. You can see all of the MDX functions in detail in Appendix A. We have categorized the MDX functions into several categories very similar to the product documentations on MDX functions. The category *set functions*, which makes it the largest category. MDX functions can be called in several ways:

1. Function (read *dot* function)

    Example: `<Dimension>.Name` returns the name of the object being referenced (could be a hierarchy or level/member expression). Perhaps this reminds you of the dot operator in VB.NET or C# programming — that's fine. It's roughly the same idea.

    ```
    WITH MEMBER measures.LocationName AS [Customer].[Country].CurrentMember.Name
    SELECT measures.LocationName ON COLUMNS,
    Customer.country.members on ROWS
    FROM [Adventure Works]
    ```

2. Function

    Example: `Username` is used to acquire the username of the logged-in user. It returns a string in the following format: domain-name\user-name. Most often this is used in dimension or cell security related MDX expressions. The following is an example of how username can be used in an MDX expression:

    ```
    WITH MEMBER Measures.User AS USERNAME
    SELECT Measures.User ON 0 FROM [Adventure Works]
    ```

3. Function ( )

    Example: The function CalculationCurrentPass ( ) requires parentheses, but takes no arguments. More on what CalculationCurrentPass ( ) can be seen in Appendix A.

4. Function (with arguments)

    Example: OpeningPeriod ([Level_Expression [, Member_Expression]]) is an MDX function that takes an argument that can specify both level_expression with member_expression or just the member_expression itself. This is most often used with Time dimensions, but will work with other dimension types. This function returns the first member at the level of the member_expression; for example, the following returns "Day 1":

```
OpeningPeriod (Day, [April])
```

Set Functions

Set functions, as the category title suggests, operate on sets. The take sets are arguments and often the result of the set functions is a set. Some of the widely used set functions are Crossjoin and Filter which we are quite sure you would be using in your MDX queries. Hence these two functions are discussed here with examples.

Crossjoin returns all possible combinations of sets as specified by the arguments to the crossjoin function. If there are N sets specified in the crossjoin function, this will result in a combination of all the possible members within that set on a single axis. You see this with the following example:

```
Crossjoin ( Set_Expression [ ,Set_Expression ...] )

SELECT Measures.[Internet Sales Amount] ON COLUMNS,
CrossJoin( {Product.[Product Line].[Product Line].MEMBERS},
{[Customer].[Country].MEMBERS}) on ROWS
FROM [Adventure Works]
```

This query produces the cross product of each member in the Product dimension with each member of the Customer dimension along the sales amount measure. Following are the first few rows of results from executing this query:

		Sales Amount
Accessory	All Customers	$604,053.30
Accessory	Australia	$127,128.61
Accessory	Canada	$82,736.07
Accessory	France	$55,001.21
Accessory	Germany	$54,382.29
Accessory	United Kingdom	$67,636.33
Accessory	United States	$217,168.79
Components	All Customers	(null)
...	...	...

Sometimes the result of the combination of the members of the set might result in values being null. For example, assume that there is one product that is sold only in Australia. The sales amount for this product in other countries and the sales amount for other products in Australia are going to be Null. Obviously you are not interested in the empty results. It does not help in any business decisions. Instead of retrieving all the results and then checking for null values, there is a way to restrict these on the server side of the Analysis Services instance. In addition to this, Analysis Services optimizes the query so that only the appropriate result is retrieved and sent. For this you use nonemptycrossjoin function or the nonempty function. The syntax for these two functions are

```
NonEmptyCrossjoin(
      Set_Expression [ ,Set_Expression ...][ ,Crossjoin_Set_Count ] )

NonEmpty(
      Set_Expression [ ,FilterSet_Expression])
```

Hence in order to remove the empty cells in the query using Crossjoin shown above you can use one of the following queries which use the nonemptycrossjoin and nonempty functions. While using the nonemptycrossjoin function you need to apply the filter condition on Internet Sales Amount and then retrieve the crossjoin of members from the first two sets. This is due to the fact that the default measure for the Adventure Works cube is not Internet Sales Amount and hence if the measure is not included as a parameter in the function nonemptycrossjoin function will be using the default measure. While using the nonempty function you first do the crossjoin function and then filter out the tuples that have null values for the Internet Sales amount as shown in the second query below. The nonempty MDX function is new in Analysis Services 2005.

```
SELECT Measures.[Internet Sales Amount] ON COLUMNS,
NonemptyCrossJoin( {Product.[Product Line].[Product Line].MEMBERS},
{[Customer].[Country].MEMBERS},Measures.[Internet Sales Amount],2 ) on ROWS
FROM [Adventure Works]

SELECT Measures.[Internet Sales Amount] ON COLUMNS,
Nonempty(CrossJoin( {Product.[Product Line].[Product Line].MEMBERS},
{[Customer].[Country].MEMBERS}),Measures.[Internet Sales Amount]) on ROWS
FROM [Adventure Works]
```

Most users and client tools interacting with an instance of Analysis Services use the nonemptycrossjoin function extensively. You see more details on this function in several chapters of this book.

Another MDX function that is quite useful is the Filter function. The Filter function helps restrict the query results based on one or more conditions. The Filter function takes two arguments: a set expression and a logical expression. The logical expression is applied on each item of the set and returns a set of items that satisfy the logical condition. The function argument for the Filter function is:

```
Filter( Set_Expression , { Logical_Expression | [ CAPTION | KEY | NAME ]
=String_Expression } )
```

The result of the example query shown for the Crossjoin function results in 43 cells. If you are only interested in the products for which the sales amount is greater than a specific value and are still interested in finding out the countries, you can use the Filter function as shown here:

```
SELECT Measures.[Internet Sales Amount] ON COLUMNS,
Filter(CrossJoin( {Product.[Product Line].[Product Line].MEMBERS},
{[Customer].[Country].MEMBERS}),[Internet Sales Amount] >2000000) on ROWS
FROM [Adventure Works]
```

This query filters out all the products for which the sales amount is less than 2,000,000 and returns only the products that have the sales amount greater than 2,000,000. The result of execution of this query is as follows:

		Sales Amount
Mountain	All Customers	$10,251,183.52
Mountain	Australia	$2,906,994.45
Mountain	United States	$3,547,956.78
Road	All Customers	$14,624,108.58
Road	Australia	$5,029,120.41
Road	United States	$4,322,438.41
Road	All Customers	$3,879,331.82

Member Functions

Member functions are used for operations on the members such as retrieving the current member, ancestor, parent, children, sibling, next member, and so on. All the member functions return a member. One of the most widely used member functions is called ParallelPeriod. The ParallelPeriod function helps you to retrieve a member in the Time dimension based on a given member and certain conditions. The function definition for ParallelPeriod is

```
ParallelPeriod( [ Level_Expression [ ,Numeric_Expression [ , Member_Expression ] ]
    ] )
```

Figure 3-5 shows an illustration of ParallelPeriod function. ParallelPeriod is a function that returns a member from a Time dimension (you will learn about time dimension in Chapter 5) relative to a given member for a specific time period. For example ParallelPeriod([Quarter], 1, [April]) is [January]. You might be wondering how this result came about. The following steps show the execution of the ParallelPeriod function and how Analysis Services arrives at the result:

1. The ParallelPeriod function can only be used in conjunction with time dimensions. For the illustration shown in Figure 3-5 assume you have a time dimension with a hierarchy Calendar which contains levels Year, Semester, Quarter and Month.

2. The Parallel Period function first finds the parent member of last argument, April, in the specified level Quarter which is the first argument. It identifies that level of April is Quarter2.

3. The sibling of [Quarter2] is then evaluated based on the numeric expression. A positive number indicates that the sibling of interest exists as a predecessor to the current member in the collection of members at that level. A negative number indicates that the sibling of interest is a successor of the current member. In this example, the sibling of interest is [Quarter1] because the numeric expression is 1.

4. Next, the member at the same position as that of member [April] is identified in [Quarter1], which is January.

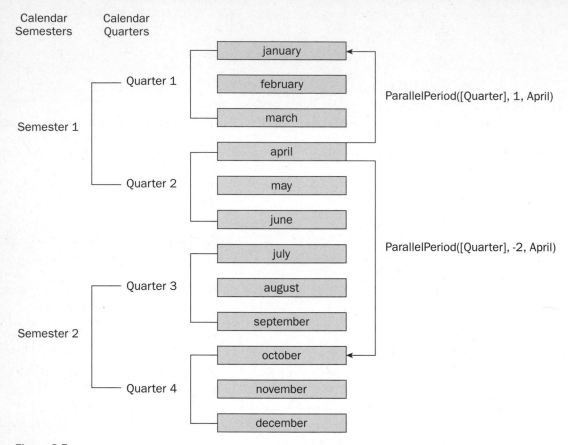

Figure 3-5

The ParallelPeriod function is used to compare measure values relative to various time periods. Typically a customer would be interested in comparing Sales between Quarters or over Years, and this function really comes in handy when you want to make relative comparisons. Most of the client tools interacting with Analysis Services use this function.

Numeric Functions

Numeric functions come in very handy when you are defining the parameters for an MDX query or creating any calculated measure. Note that there are plenty of statistical functions in this group, including standard deviation, sample variance, and correlation. The most common of the numeric functions is a simple one called Count along with its close cousin, DistinctCount. The Count function is used to count the number of items in the collection of a specific object like Dimension, Tuples, Set, or Level. The DistinctCount, on the other hand, takes a Set_Expression as an argument and returns a number that indicates the number of distinct items in the Set_Expression, not the total count of all items. Here are the function definitions for each:

```
Count ( Dimension | Tuples | Set| Level)
DistinctCount ( Set_Expression )
```

Please take a look at the following query:

```
WITH MEMBER Measures.CustomerCount AS DistinctCount(
Exists([Customer].[Customer].MEMBERS,[Product].[Product Line].Mountain,
"Internet Sales"))
SELECT Measures.CustomerCount ON COLUMNS
FROM [Adventure Works]
```

The DistinctCount function counts the number of distinct members in the who have purchased products of the product line Mountain. If a customer has purchased a product twice then the distinct count function will just count the customer once. The MDX function Exists is introduced in Analysis Services 2005 and is used to filter customers who have only purchased product line Mountain through the Internet. You will learn the Exists function in Chapter 7. The result of the Exists function is a set of customers who have purchased product line Mountain. The result of the above query is 9590.

Dimension Functions, Level Functions, and Hierarchy Functions

Functions in these groups are typically used for navigation and manipulation. Here is an example of just such a function, the "Level" function from the Level group:

```
SELECT [Date].[Calendar].[Calendar Quarter].[Q1 CY 2004].LEVEL ON COLUMNS
FROM [Adventure Works]
```

This query actually results in a list of all the quarters displayed in the results. The reason is because [Date].[Calendar].[Calendar Quarter].[Q1 CY 2004].LEVEL evaluates to [Date].[Calendar Year].[Calendar Semster].[Calender Quarter]. From this, you get the list of all quarters for the relevant calendar year.

String Manipulation Functions

To extract the names of sets, tuples, and members in the form of a string, you can use functions like MemberToStr (<Member_Expression>) and to do the inverse, take a string and create a member expression, you can use StrToMember (<String>). Consider the following case, in which there is a client application that displays sales information for all countries. When a user selects a specific country, you need to extract the sales information for the specific country from Analysis Services. Because the countries are represented as strings in the client application, you need to translate this string to a corresponding member, and then you can retrieve the data. String manipulation functions are useful while accepting parameters from users and transforming them to corresponding MDX objects. However there is a significant performance cost involved while using string manipulation functions. Hence we recommend you try to use these functions only if necessary.

```
SELECT STRTOMEMBER ('[Customer].[Country].[Australia]' ) ON COLUMNS
FROM [Adventure Works]
```

Other Functions

Four other function categories exist: Subcube and Array both have one function each. The final two categories are logical functions, which allow you to do Boolean evaluations on multidimensional objects, and tuple functions that you can use to access tuples. In addition to that, Analysis Services 2005 has introduced several new MDX functions. You have seen some of them in this chapter such as Nonempty and Exists. You will learn more about these in Chapter 7 and Appendix A.

Summary

Congratulations, you have made it through the first three chapters! Ostensibly you should now feel free to take on the rest of the chapters in no particular order, but you got this far, so why not go immediately to Chapter 4 and jump right in? Now you know the fundamental elements of MDX — cells, members, tuples, and sets. Further, you learned that MDX has two forms: queries and expressions.

You saw that MDX queries, which are used to retrieve data from Analysis Services databases, retain a superficial resemblance to SQL, but that the resemblance breaks down the more you drill down on the details. MDX expressions, on the other hand, are simple yet powerful constructs that are partial statements — by themselves they do not return results like queries. The expressions are what enable you to define and manipulate multidimensional objects and data through calculations, like specifying a default member's contents, for example.

To solidify your basic understanding of MDX, you learned the common query statements, WITH, SELECT, FROM, and WHERE, as well as the MDX operators like addition, subtraction, multiplication, division, and rollup, and the logical operators AND and OR. These details are crucial to effective use of the language. You got a good look at the eleven MDX function categories; saw the four forms MDX functions can take, and even saw some detailed examples of some commonly used functions like Filter, ParallelPeriod, MemberToStr, and StrToMember. You learn more advanced MDX concepts and functions in Chapters 7, 8, and 9. All the MDX functions supported in Analysis Services 2005 are provided in Appendix A with examples. Coming up next in Chapter 4 are the details of creating a data source, a data source view, and how to deal with multiple data source views in a single project.

4

Working with Data Sources and Data Source Views

You have completed the first three chapters of the book where you learned the concepts of data warehousing, worked hands on with Analysis Services tools and finally learned the basics of the MDX language to retrieve data from Analysis Services. The next three chapters of the book guide you to use the product to design your cubes and dimensions. The traditional approach of designing your cubes and dimensions is based upon an existing single-source data set. You will be working with multiple relational data sources in the real world when you develop business intelligence applications. In this chapter you learn what data sources are and how they feed into the creation of Data Source Views (DSVs). These DSVs provide you a consolidated view on just the tables and joins on tables of interest across the one or more data sources you defined. The data source and DSVs literally form the foundation for subsequent construction of both dimensions and cubes. Note that more than one data source per project is supported as are multiple DSVs per project; you learn how this infrastructure plays out in this chapter.

Data Source

In order to retrieve data from the source you need information about the source such as name of the source, type of method to retrieve the data, security permissions needed to retrieve the data etc. All this information is encapsulated into an object called *Data Source* in Analysis Services 2005. An Analysis Services database contains a collection object called Data Sources which stores all the data sources needed to build cubes and dimensions within that database. Analysis Services will be able to retrieve source data from data sources via the OLEDB interface or using the managed .Net provider interface.

In the simplest case you will have one data source that contains one fact table with some number of dimensions linked to it by joins; that data source is populated by data from an OLTP database and is called an *Operational Data Store* (ODS). Figure 4-1 shows a graphical representation of this data source usage. The ODS is a single entity storing data from various sources so that it can feed as a source of data for your data warehouse.

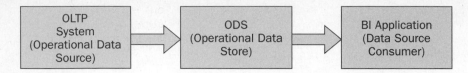

Data Source path commonly used in Analysis Services 2000; the data
is first transformed to a more usable format and stored in the ODS.

Figure 4-1

A variant on the data source usage, which is enabled by the UDM in Analysis Services 2005, is the ability
to take data directly from the OLTP system as input to the decision support software. This is shown in
Figure 4-2.

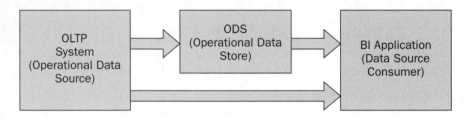

Data Sources used in Analysis Services 2005; the data is transformed
to a more usable format and stored in the ODS. However, with the
UDM technology, it is even easier to take data input from different sources.

Figure 4-2

In Analysis Services 2000, certain limitations were associated with the use of data sources. Analysis
Services 2000 only supported one fact table per cube. Therefore, only one data source could be used for
specifying the fact table of a cube. You could still specify multiple data sources within Analysis Services
2000, because dimensions referenced did not have to be in the same data source as the fact table. A
workaround addressing the single fact table constraint was to create a SQL view on the multiple fact
tables to create what appeared to Analysis Services 2000 as a single fact table. A more common and
straightforward solution adopted by many users was to have multiple cubes based on disparate data
sources and combine them into a single cube that was called a *virtual cube*.

Analysis Services 2005 natively supports the capability of specifying multiple fact tables within a single
cube. Each of these fact tables can be from a different data source. Analysis Services 2005 still provides
you with the capability of creating what are essentially virtual cubes; this is accomplished using linked
objects (discussed in Chapter 9). Since Analysis Services 2005 provides you with the capability of creating
cubes from various data sources you need to be extremely careful about how you model your cube —
that is, you must specify the right relationships (primary key and foreign key mappings) between tables
from various data sources. In this way you can make sure your cube is designed to provide you the
results you want.

Using the Analysis Services 2000 data source methods is like carving on a bar of soap with a butter knife:
you could create a statue, but it might not win any awards for beauty. Conversely, the kind of power and
flexibility in Analysis Services 2005 puts you in a position similar to that of carving a bar of soap with a

razor blade. Carving with a razor blade, you can make a gorgeous and intricate statue, but if you're not careful, you could cut the heck out of your fingers. So, be careful and craft some beautiful dimensional schemas! To do so, keep your schemas as simple as possible relative to the flexibility requirements imposed by the application specification you're working with.

Data Sources Supported by Analysis Services

Strictly speaking, Analysis Services 2005 supports all data sources that expose a connectivity interface through OLE DB or .Net Managed Provider. The data sources need to support certain basic methods based on the interface that conform to the standard since Analysis Services 2005 uses those methods to retrieve schema (tables, relationships, columns within tables and data types) information. If the data source is a relational database then by default it uses the standard SQL to query the database. Analysis Services uses a cartridge mechanism that allows you to specify extensions and customization in SQL that are used by a specific relational database. This allows Analysis Services to efficiently query data from the relational database.

The major data sources for Analysis Services databases are the relational databases Microsoft SQL Server, IBM's DB2, Teradata and Oracle. Figure 4-3 shows various data sources supported by Analysis Services 2005 on one of the machines that has SQL Server 2005 installed. For a specific data source you need to install the client components of the data provider so that the OLE DB provider and/or .Net provider for that specific data source is installed on your machine. These client components should not only be supported on your development machine where you use BIDS to design your database but also on the server machine where an Analysis Services instance will be running. For relational databases DB2 and Oracle it is recommended you use the Micorosoft's OLE DB data provider for Oracle or DB2 instead of the OLE DB providers provided those databases. Please make sure appropriate connectivity components from Oracle and IBM's DB2 are installed on your machine in addition to the OLE DB providers from Microsoft.

Figure 4-3

In Chapter 2 you used the data source wizard to create a data source which included impersonation information. In addition to providing impersonation information you can optionally specify additional connection properties such as query time out for connection, isolation level, and maximum number of connections as shown in Figure 4-4. The isolation level property has two modes: Read Committed and Snapshot. By default the Read Committed is used for all the data sources. The Snapshot isolation mode which is supported by the relational data source SQL Server 2005 and Oracle are used to ensure that the data read by Analysis Services 2005 is consistent across multiple queries sent over a single connection. What this means is that if the data on the relational data source keeps changing and if multiple queries are sent by Analysis Services 2005 to SQL Server 2005 to query data then all the queries will be seeing consistent data seen by the first query. Any new data that arrived between the results of first query and Nth query sent over a specific connection will not be included in the results of the Nth query. All these connection properties will be stored and applied whenever a connection is established to that specific data source. The data source wizard also allows you to create data sources based on an existing data source connection already created so that a single connection is shared by Analysis Services for multiple databases. The wizard also allows you to establish connections to objects within the current Analysis Services project such as establishing an OLE DB connection to the cube being created in the project. Such a connection is typically useful while creating mining models (to be seen in Chapter 13) from cubes.

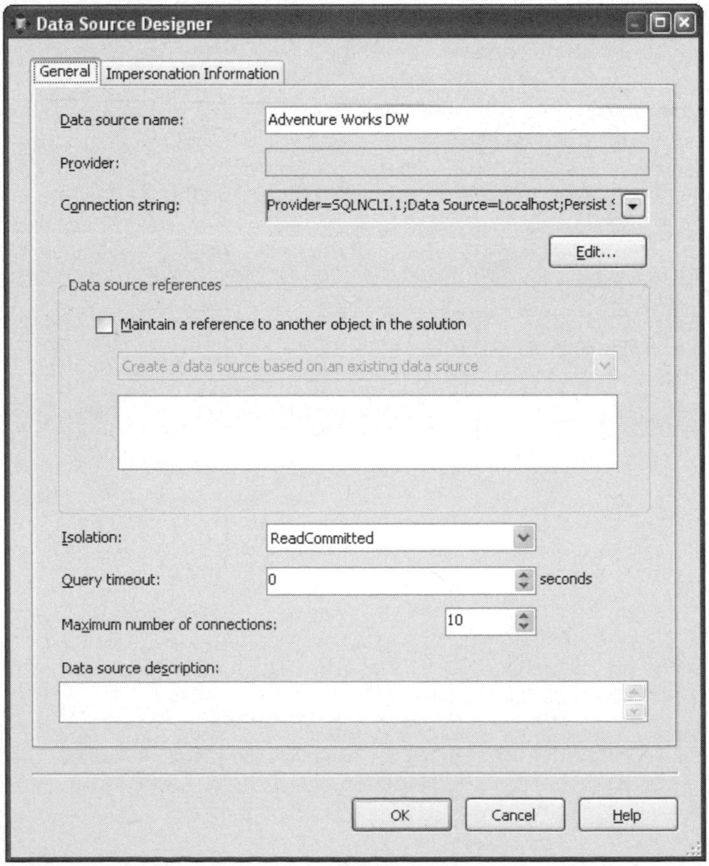

Figure 4-4

.NET versus OLE DB Data Providers

There are two types of data provider which most data sources support. OLE DB is a common set of interfaces implemented through COM components that help you to access data from data sources. Similar to OLE DB; a common interface is being exposed using managed code. Providers exposing the interface using .NET technology are called .NET providers. Analysis Services 2005 has the ability to use OLE DB or .NET providers to access data from data sources such as flat files to large scale databases such as SQL Server, Oracle, Teradata and DB2. Analysis Services retrieves data from the data sources using the chosen provider's (OLE DB or managed) interfaces for processing of Analysis Services objects. If any of the Analysis Services objects are defined as ROLAP then the provider is used to retrieve data during query time. Updating the data in the UDM is called writeback. Analysis Services also uses the provider interfaces to update the source data during writeback (you learn writeback in Chapter 12).

.NET Providers

Microsoft has created the .NET Framework and programming languages that use the framework to run in a Common Language Runtime (CLR) environment. The relationship between the Microsoft languages and the CLR are analogous to that of Java the language and the Java Runtime (the virtual machine). The .NET Framework itself is a huge class library that exposes tons of functionality and does so in the context of managed code. The term *managed* refers to the fact that memory is managed by the CLR and not the coder. You can write your own managed provider for your data source, or you can leverage .NET providers that use the .NET Framework. With the installation of SQL Server 2005 you will have .NET providers to access data from Microsoft SQL Server and Oracle which is shown way back in Figure 4-3. If your relational data source has a .NET provider, you can install it and use that provider. In the Connection Manager page of the data source wizard, you can choose the .NET provider to connect to your data source.

OLE DB Data Providers

OLE DB is an industry standard that provides a set of COM (Component Object Model) interfaces that allow clients to access data from various data stores. The OLE DB standard was created for client applications to have a uniform interface from which to access data. Such data can come from a wide variety of data sources using this interface, such as Microsoft Access, Microsoft Project, and various database management systems.

Microsoft provides a set of OLE DB data providers to access data from several widely used data sources. These OLE DB providers are delivered together in a package called MDAC (Microsoft Data Access Components). Even though the interfaces exposed by the providers are common, each provider is different in the sense they have specific optimizations relevant to the specific data source you perform on data retrieval. OLE DB exposes the COM interface and is written in unmanaged code (code that runs outside the .NET Framework CLR). The .NET Framework provides you with a way of having interoperability between managed and unmanaged code by which you can create a .NET wrapper that uses the unmanaged code but provides the functionality of a managed provider. There is such a wrapper on top of the OLE DB that is called the Unmanaged .NET Data Provider for the data sources that do not have a native implementation of the .NET data provider.

The Microsoft OLE DB provider for SQL Server has been the primary way of connecting to a Microsoft SQL Server to date. In the SQL Server 2005 release, this OLE DB provider has been repackaged and named SQL Native Client. SQL Native Client provides easy manageability of upgrades to the OLE DB provider. Analysis Services 2005 provides the capability of connecting to any data source that provides the OLE DB interface, including the Analysis Server OLE DB provider by which you can retrieve data from another Analysis Server.

The Trade-Offs

Analysis Services 2000 supported connection to data sources through OLE DB providers only. Analysis Services 2005 has a much tighter integration with the .NET Framework and supports connections via OLE DB providers and .NET data providers. If you deployed the .NET Framework across your entire organization, we recommend you use the .NET providers to access data from relational data sources. You might encounter a certain amount of performance degradation by using the .NET provider; however, the uniformity, maintainability, inherent connection pooling capabilities, and security provided by .NET data providers are worth the risk of taking the hit on performance. If you are really concerned about performance, we recommend you use OLE DB providers for your data access.

Data Source Views

Data Source Views (DSV) enable you to create a logical view of only the tables involved in your data warehouse design; in this way system tables and other tables not pertinent to your efforts are excluded from the virtual workspace. In other words, you don't have to look at what you're never going to use directly anyway. DSVs are a powerful tool; in fact, you have the power to create DSVs that contain tables from multiple data sources which you learn later in this chapter. You need to create a DSV in your Analysis Services data since cubes and dimensions are created from the DSV rather than directly from the data source object. The DSV wizard retrieves the schema information including relationships so that joins between tables are stored in the DSV. These relationships help cube and dimension wizards to identify fact and dimension tables as well as hierarchies. If the relationships do not exist in the data source we recommend you to create the right relationships within the DSV. Defining the relationships between the tables in the DSV helps you to get a better overview of your data warehouse in the DSV. When you take the time to create a DSV it ultimately pays for itself in terms of speeding up the design of your data warehouse.

Back in Chapter 2 you used the DSV wizard to create a view on the Sales fact table in Adventure Works DW. The DSV wizard is a great way to get a jump-start on DSV creation. Then, once the DSV is created you can perform several operations on it such as adding or removing tables, specifying primary keys for tables, and establishing relationships between tables. These operations are accomplished within the DSV designer. You learn more about the DSV and operations within the DSV in the following sections.

DSV Designer

The DSV Designer contains three panes, as shown in Figure 4-5. The center pane contains a graphical view of all the tables in the DSV; its primary keys and the relationships between tables are represented by lines with an arrow at the end. The top-left pane is called the *Diagram Organizer*, which is helpful in creating and saving concise views within large DSVs. When a DSV contains more than 20 tables it is difficult to visualize the complete DSV within the graphical view. When there are a large number of tables, typically only a subset of the tables is related. Hence you will likely perform operations only on a subset of these tables at any given time, and the Diagram Organizer is a handy way to create several diagrams that include just such subsets of relevant tables. Note that operations done on the tables within this diagram are reflected real-time in the entire DSV. By default you get one diagram that is called All Tables.

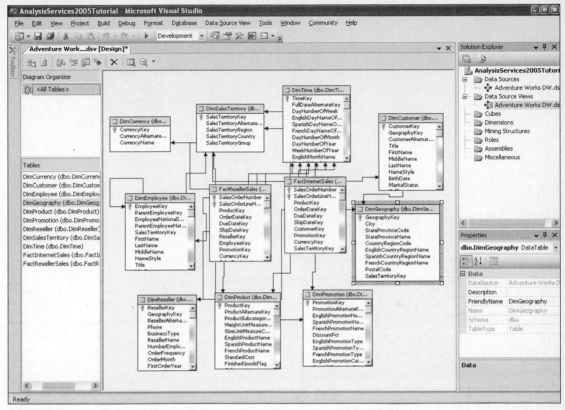

Figure 4-5

Figure 4-5 shows part of the default diagram All Tables that is created at the completion of the DSV wizard. The lower left pane is called Tables and is used to show the tree view of all the tables of the DSV along with their relationship with other tables. Figure 4-6 shows the Tables pane with detailed information of the DimCurrency table; you can see the primary key of the DimCurrency table and the CurrencyKey, which is distinguished by a key icon. In addition, there is a folder that indicates all the relationships between the DimCurrency table and other tables in the DSV. If you expand the Relationships folder (as shown in Figure 4-6) you will see that the DimCurrency table joins to the FactInternetSales and FactResellerSales through the CurrencyKey — where the join is specified within parentheses.

Adding/Removing Tables in a DSV

It is most common to initially create DSVs using the DSV wizard. Also common is the desire to modify what the wizard comes up with to maximize usefulness of the view; what you get initially is usually good, but subject to improvements. The DSV designer is what provides you with the capability to easily modify the existing tables in the DSV. To modify the existing tables, right-click the diagram view pane and select Add/Remove Tables, as shown in Figure 4-7.

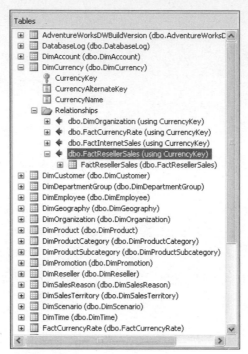

Figure 4-6

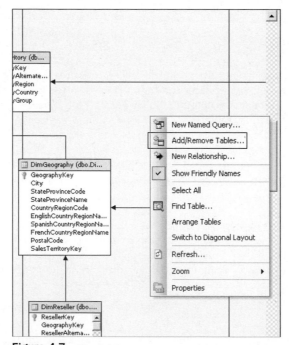

Figure 4-7

This invokes the Add/Remove Tables dialog shown in Figure 4-8. Using this dialog you can add additional tables to the DSV by moving tables from the Available objects to the Included objects or remove existing tables by moving them from Included objects to Available objects. If you want to remove a table from the DSV, you can do so either in the DSV Designer or in the table view by using the following steps:

1. Select the table to be deleted.

2. Right-click the table and click Delete.

3. Click OK in the confirmation dialog that appears.

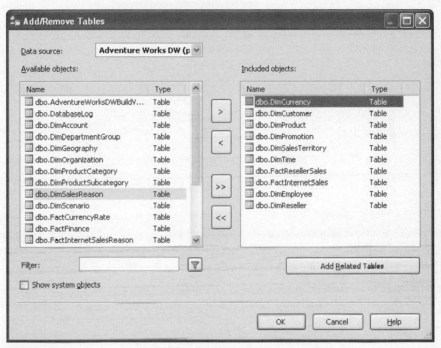

Figure 4-8

Specifying Primary Keys and Relationships in the DSV

It is likely that you will encounter underlying databases without the primary key to foreign key relationships that you will need in place for preparation of data for analysis; that is, building dimensions and cubes. The DSV wizard extracts primary keys and the relationships specified in the underlying relational database to form primary keys and the relationships represented in the DSV. As mentioned, perhaps some of the OLTP systems you use do not have the primary keys and relationships specified in the relevant tables — or when you design your data warehouse you might want to change these to suit your data warehouse design. The DSV designer provides you with the functionality to specify primary keys for the tables that do not have them already, and in this way you can effectively modify or add new relationships between the tables in the DSV.

To specify the primary key(s) for a table, you need to do the following in the DSV Designer:

1. Select the column in the table that you want to specify as a primary key. If there is more than one column that forms the primary key, you can do multiple selections by holding the Ctrl key. If the tables have auto-increment setup for the key column in the database then you will not be able to change the primary key(s) of the tables.

2. Right-click and select Set Logical Primary Key.

When there is a relationship between two tables F and D, you typically have columns A and B in tables F and D that are involved in the join. Typically column B is the primary key in table D, but not always. Column A is referred to as the foreign key. An example would be a Sales fact table that has a product id as a column that joins with the product id in the dimension table Products. In order to specify relationships between tables in the DSV, you need to use the following steps:

1. Select the column A in table F that is involved in the join to another table.

2. With column A selected, drag and drop it to column B in table D.

This forms a relationship between tables F and D and a line will be created between these two tables with an arrow pointing toward table D. If you double-click this line you will see details on the relationship — tables involved in the relationship and columns used for the join. Figure 4-8 shows the relationship between FactResellersSales and DimReseller tables. You can modify the relationship using this edit relationship dialog by either changing the columns involved in the join or by adding additional columns that are involved in the join.

You can also create a new relationship by right-clicking a table and selecting New Relationship. You will be asked to specify the relationship in the Create Relationship dialog which is similar to the Edit Relationship dialog shown in Figure 4-9 where you need to choose the columns in the source and destination tables are involved in the join.

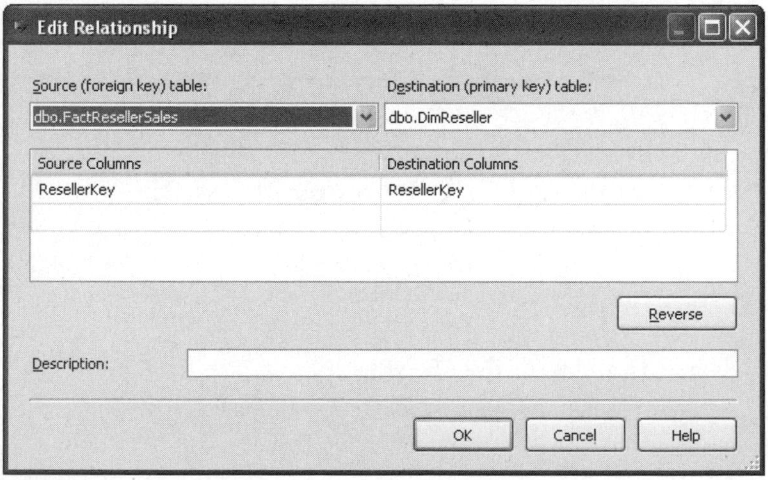

Figure 4-9

> All graphical operations such as drag and drop and specifying primary keys that are accomplished in the diagram view can also be accomplished in the table view.

Customizing Your Tables in the DSV

While modeling your data warehouse often you will want to select a few columns from tables, or restrict the fact table rows based on some specific criteria. Or you might want to merge columns from several tables into a single table. All these operations can be done by creating views in the relational database. Analysis Services 2005 provides the functionality of performing all these particular operations within the DSV using *Named Query*. You can invoke Named Query editor by right-clicking a table and then selecting Replace Table➪With New Named Query..., as shown in Figure 4-10. If you want to add a specific table twice in your DSV or add some columns of a new table, you can launch the query designer by right-clicking the DSV Designer and selecting "With New Named Query...".

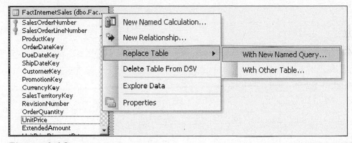

Figure 4-10

Named Query manifests itself as a query designer that helps you to build custom queries to create a view. The Create Named Query designer dialog is invoked when "With New Named Query..." is selected as shown in Figure 4-11. In this dialog you can add tables from the data source; select specific columns from the tables and apply restrictions or filters using the graphical interface. A SQL query is created based on your selections and is displayed in a pane. If you're a SQL wizard, you can forego filling out the dialog elements and paste a valid SQL query in the query pane. We recommend that you then execute the query to make sure the query is correct. The results from the underlying relational database will then be visible in a new pane beneath the query pane. Click OK once you have formed and validated your query. The table is now replaced with results from the query you have specified in the DSV with selected columns.

In certain instances you might want to create a new column in the table. An example of this would be to create a Full Name of an Employee from the first name, middle initial, and last name. One way to accomplish this task would be to replace the table with a named query and write the appropriate SQL to create this additional column. However, Analysis Services 2005 provides a simpler way to do the same operation. Right-click on the Employee table and select New Named Calculation. This action invokes the Edit Named Calculation dialog shown in Figure 4-12. To add a column called Full Name to the Employee table you just need to combine the first name, middle name, and last name. You can type the expression for this in the Expression pane as shown in Figure 4-12 and then click the OK button.

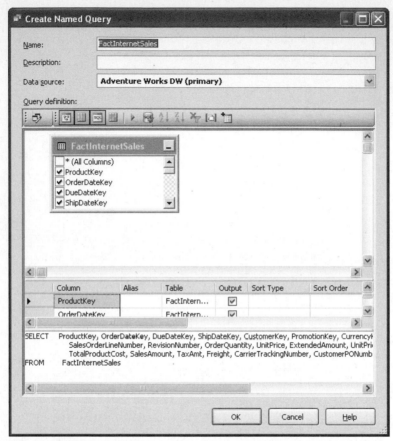

Figure 4-11

Figure 4-12

A new column is added to the Employee table as shown in Figure 4-13. The data type of this calculated column will be determined based on the data types of the actual columns involved in the calculation or data used within the expression. If the expression results in a number, the data type for this column will be an integer. In the preceding example the data type of this column is a string.

The DSV maintains the calculated column of a table as a computed column in the metadata; it does not write it out to the underlying tables. When you want to view the data of this table (which you see later in this chapter), the expression must be added to the SQL query so that you can see the data of this computed column.

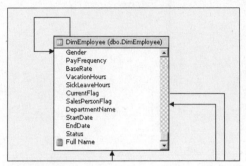

Figure 4-13

Data Source Views In Depth

Data warehouse designs consist of several fact tables and all the associated dimension tables. Small data warehouses are usually comprised of 10 to 20 tables, whereas the larger data warehouses can have more than a hundred tables. Even though you have a large number of tables in your data warehouse, you will likely work with a small subset of those tables; each of which has relationships between them. For example, assume you have sales, inventory, and human resources (HR) data to analyze and the HR data is not strongly related to the sales and inventory data but there is a desired linkage. Then you might create two cubes, one for Sales and Inventory information and another one for HR. It is quite possible the Sales, Inventory, and HR information could be stored in a single data source—in the ODS or OLTP system.

Employee information (HR) could be related to the sales and inventory information within the company so far as there is a link between a given sales event and the employee who made the sale. You might want to slice the sales data by a specific employee, but to do so you must access information that is a part of a separate cube only accessible to the HR department (for security reasons). You can get around this problem by making a single DSV containing all the tables that store sales, inventory, and HR information of a company. From that DSV, both cubes can be formulated and permissions set such that only members of the HR group can drill down on employee personal data.

Having a lot of tables in the DSV definitely makes the navigation and usability a bit complex. When you are working on the data of HR you will only want to see the tables related to this alone. For easy manageability you will need customizable views within your DSV that show only certain tables. Analysis Services 2005 provides you with the capability of having several views within the DSV that contain a subset of the tables in the DSV. These views are actually called diagrams. By default you get a diagram called <All Tables> when you complete the DSV wizard. You can create additional diagrams and select the tables that you want to include within this diagram. This feature was actually added to the product based on requests from the customers. Next, you learn how to create a new diagram and include only the tables you need within this diagram.

To create a new diagram, you need to do the following:

1. Right-click the Diagram Organizer pane and select New Diagram, as shown in Figure 4-14. Name this diagram view "Internet Sales."

Figure 4-14

2. You now have an empty diagram view. Right-click the diagram view and select Show Tables (see Figure 4-15). You are presented with the dialog where you can choose the table(s) you want to include in this diagram view.

Figure 4-15

3. Select all the tables that are part of the InternetSales fact table in this diagram view and click OK.

This gives you a diagram view of the InternetSales that contains the InternetSales fact table and the related dimension tables as shown in Figure 4-16. This InternetSales diagram has six of the eleven tables in the DSV and it makes it much easier to understand the relationship between these tables only.

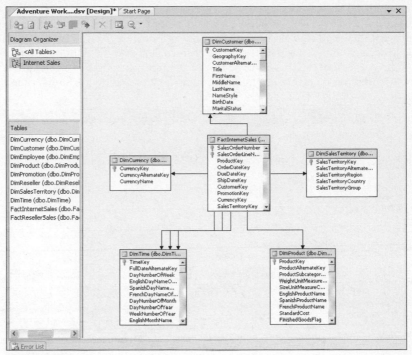

Figure 4-16

If you do not want a specific table in your diagram view you can right-click the table and select Hide. Instead of steps 2 and 3 you can add tables to the diagram view by dragging and dropping tables from the Table pane to the Diagram pane. Create another diagram for ResellerSales and add the FactResellerSales table and related tables.

Data Source View Properties

Each object created within the BIDS has certain properties. Within the DSV you can view the properties of the object's DSV, tables, columns, and relationships. Properties of these objects are shown in the Properties window within the BIDS, as shown in Figure 4-17.

Figure 4-17 shows the properties of a column in a table, calculated column, a table, and a relationship. For the regular columns in a table you have the properties AllowNull, Data Type, Description, Friendly Name, Length, and Name. The properties of a column are populated by retrieving the corresponding property from the data source. The data type of this column is retrieved from the data source. Based on the properties defined in the data source, the properties AllowNull, Data Type, Length, Name, and Friendly Name are populated. The length is applicable only for the data type string. For all data types other than string the Length has a value of –1. You cannot change certain properties. Those properties are not editable in the Properties window and are grayed out. You can change the Friendly Name and provide a description to each column. Often columns of a table in the relational database might not have user-friendly names. User-friendly means the name of the column should indicate clearly what the data held by the column is. The Friendly Name is a property that can be changed by you so that this friendly name is shown in the DSV for an easier understanding of the model. You can provide an optional Description to each column if needed. The DSV provides you with the option of switching between the original column names and the friendly names. You can right-click in the DSV diagram view and toggle between the friendly name and the original column name by selecting the Show Friendly Name option.

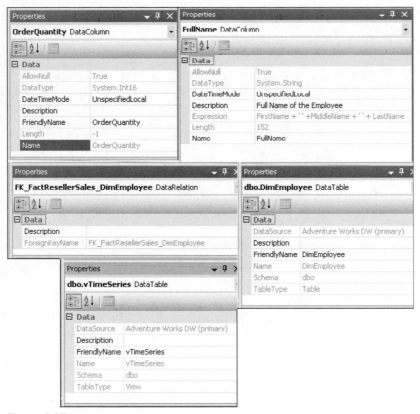

Figure 4-17

Named columns created in the DSV do not have a Friendly Name property because you will be defining the name to this column which will be easily understandable. Instead, named columns have the Expression property because each named column is just a SQL expression. You can only change this expression in the Named Column dialog and not in the Properties window.

Tables have the properties Data Source, Description, FriendlyName, Name, Schema, and Table Type. The Data Source indicates the name of the data source of the Table. The Table Type shows whether the object in the underlying data source is a table or a view. Similar to the columns, tables also have the option to specify a friendly name that can be used in the DSV.

Relationships between tables are provided with a name that includes the tables that participate in the relationship. Similar to named columns, named queries do not have a Friendly Name property. They have a property called Query Definition that shows the query used to specify the named query object.

Different Layouts in DSVs

The DSV designer provides you with two layouts to view the tables in the DSV. When you create a DSV the default layout selected is called the rectangular layout. In the default layout the lines representing the relationships between tables are composed of horizontal and vertical lines, and these emerge from any of the sides of the table. The second layout offered by the DSV designer is called the diagonal layout. In the diagonal layout the tables are arranged in the way such that the lines showing the relationships between tables are originating at the end points of the table so that these lines appear to be along the diagonal of the tables — hence the name "diagonal layout." You can switch between the rectangular layout and the diagonal layout in the DSV by right-clicking in the DSV designer and selecting the layout of your choice. Figures 4-18 and 4-19 show the rectangular and diagonal layout, respectively, of the Internet Sales diagram.

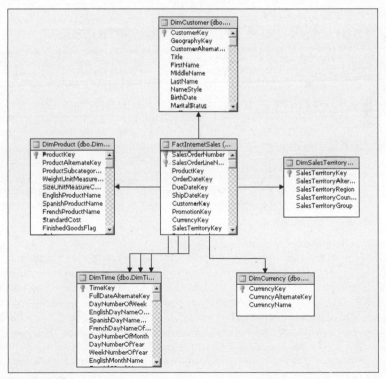

Figure 4-18

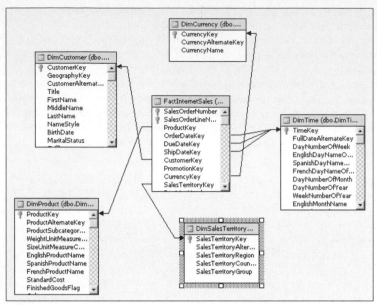

Figure 4-19

Validating Your DSV and Initial Data Analysis

The relationships specified in the DSV will be used in creating your dimensions and cubes. Therefore, validating your DSV is crucial to your data warehouse design. The DSV designer provides a first level of validation when you specify relationships. If the data types of column(s) involved in the relationship do not match, the DSV will not allow you to establish the relationship. This forces you to make sure you cast the data types of the column(s) involved in the relationships appropriately. You might need another level of validation by looking at the data within each table. You can do this by issuing queries to the tables in a relational data source. The DSV provides a way of looking at sample data for validation. A few validations you can do within the DSV by looking at sample data are as follows:

1. Looking at the fact table data helps you in making sure this table contains fact data, the primary key has been specified correctly, and appropriate relationships needed for dimensions are established.

2. Analyzing the dimension table's sample data ensures that you have all the relationships established between the fact and dimension and any relationships within the table are established correctly. For example, if you have an Employee table that contains an employee and his manager, you might want to establish a relationship so that your model can take advantage of this.

In addition, a sample of data from the tables in the DSV helps you in identifying the measures of the cube as well as the hierarchies of each dimension. Analyzing sample data in DSV also helps you to identify dimensions that can be created from the fact table data. The analysis of sample data within the DSV is even more important in creating your Data Mining models. You learn more about analyzing the data with respect to Data Mining in Chapter 13.

To see a sample of the data you need, right-click a table in the DSV and select Explore Data. You can now see rows from the underlying table presented within the Explore <tablename> Table window as shown in Figure 4-20. The data presented is only a subset of the underlying table. By default the first 5,000 rows are retrieved and shown within this window. You can change the number of rows retrieved by clicking the Sampling Options button. Clicking the Sampling Options button launches the Data Exploration options where you can change the sampling method, sample count, and number of states per chart which is used for displaying data in the chart format. Once you have changed the sample count value you can click the Resample Data button to retrieve data based on the new settings. The Explore Table window has four tabs: Table, Pivot Table, Chart, and Pivot Chart. The Table tab shows the raw sampled data from the data source as rows and columns with column headings. 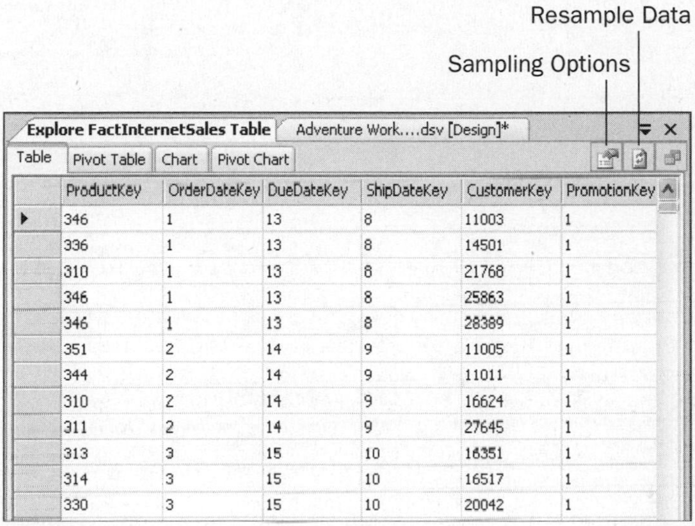

Figure 4-20

When you click the Pivot Table tab you get an additional window called PivotTable Field List that shows all the columns of the table, as shown in Figure 4-21. You can drag and drop these columns inside the pivot table in the row, column, details, or filter areas. The values in the row and column provide you with an intersection point for which the detailed data is shown. For example, you can drag and drop ProductKey, CustomerKey, and Sales Amount to the row, column, and detail data areas. The pivot table now shows you sales amount of each product by each customer. The pivot table actually allows you to view multidimensional data from a single table. You learn more about pivot tables in Chapter 15.

Analysis Services analyzes the sample data, identifies the most important columns within the table, and provides you distributions in the Chart tab. The Pivot Chart tab provides you functionality similar to the Pivot Table tab but in a chart view. The Chart and Pivot Chart tabs are typically used to do an initial analysis of the data so that appropriate columns can be used to create good Data Mining models. You learn more about these in Chapter 14.

Figure 4-21

Multiple Data Sources within a DSV

Data warehouses usually consist of several data sources. Some examples of data sources are SQL Server, Oracle, DB2, and Teradata. Traditionally, the OLTP database is transferred from the operational data store to the data warehouse — the staging area combines the data from the disparate data sources. This is not only time intensive in terms of design, maintainability, and storage, but also in terms of other considerations such as replication of data and ensuring data is in sync with the source. Analysis Services 2005 helps you avoid this and gives you better return on your investment.

The DSV designer provides you with the capability of adding tables from multiple data sources from which you can build your cubes and dimensions. You first need to define the data sources that include the tables that are part of your data warehouse design using the data source wizard. Once this has been accomplished, you create a DSV and include tables from one of the data sources. This data source is called the primary data source and needs to be a SQL Server. You can then add tables in the DSV designer by right-clicking in the diagram view and choosing Add/Remove Tables. The Add/Remove Tables dialog allows you to choose a data source as shown in Figure 4-22 so that you can add tables from that data source. You should be aware that there might be performance implications due to retrieving data from secondary data sources since all the queries are routed through the primary data source.

Once you have added the tables from multiple data sources within your DSV, you can start creating your cubes and dimensions from this DSV as if these came from a single data source. The limitation that the primary data source needs to be a SQL Server is due to the fact that Analysis Server uses a specific feature called OPEN ROWSET query of Microsoft SQL Server to retrieve data from other data sources.

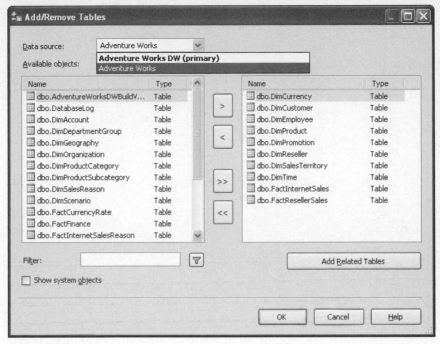

Figure 4-22

Summary

You now have the skills to deal with the challenges real-world data warehouses will throw at you in terms of multiple data sources. You learned about OLE DB and managed data providers that are supported by Analysis Services 2005 to retrieve data from data sources and trade offs of using one versus another. Indeed, you learned to tame the disparate data source beast by using multiple data sources. Then you learned to consolidate the tables and relationships of interest in Data Source Views (DSVs), and finally, to prune the tables and relationships in the DSVs so you only have to deal with what's relevant.

Note that when key changes are made in the DSV, that is where the changes stay — in the DSV. The changes are not written out to the underlying tables as you might expect. This is a good thing. To see why, take a look at the alternative to using the DSV capability. The alternative method is to create a view in SQL with real relationship transforms in the underlying tables. It's not that we strongly oppose this method, but if your data spans multiple databases, you have to create linked servers and that can become time consuming. Analysis Services 2005 provides an easy way to specify these cross-database relationships within a DSV without the overhead of creating linked servers. However when multiple data sources are included in a single DSV the primary data source should support the ability to send queries and retrieve results from other server. You can incur a performance degradation due to this method; however you do have the flexibility of not having to manage the data on multiple servers to create your data warehouse.

You're doing great! In fact, you're ready to tackle core business intelligence constructs like dimension design (Chapter 5) and cube design (Chapter 6). If you already know these topics from working with Analysis Services 2000, we recommend working through the chapters anyway; there have been some important changes.

5

Dimension Design

Prior to the advent of cable, when you brought home a new television, the first order of business was to manually tune in one of the few existing local channels. To accomplish this you manipulated the dials, rabbit-ear antennae positioning, and other controls to eventually obtain an optimal picture, audio, and vertical hold configuration. The process of designing a data warehouse using Analysis Services 2005 is similar to this. Analysis Services 2005 provides you with various wizards that help you build the initial framework, just like the rotary tuner on the television got you close to the desired channel. With the basic infrastructure in place, some fine-tuning can optimize the initial framework to your needs. In fact, you saw this approach in the previous chapter when you learned about creating data sources and DSVs. Likewise, here you learn creating dimensions using the Dimension Wizard and then using the Dimension Designer to fine-tune the dimension based on your business needs.

Cubes are made of dimensions and measures where the measures are aggregated along each dimension. Without an understanding of dimensions and how measures are aggregated along dimensions, you can't create and exploit the power of cubes, so let's jump right in learning about building and viewing dimensions. Once the dimensions are created they need to be added to the cube and the right relationship type between the fact data and dimension needs to be defined. Analysis Services 2005 supports six relationship types which you learn in this chapter and Chapter 8. In addition you learn the attributes and hierarchies that form an integral part of dimensions. You learn to model the Time dimension and Parent-Child dimensions in Analysis Services 2005 which are unique from regular dimensions and quite often found in many data warehouses. Finally, you find out how to process and browse the dimensions.

Working with the Dimension Wizard

Dimensions help you to define the structure of your cube so as to facilitate effective data analysis. Specifically, dimensions provide you with the capability of slicing data within a cube, and these dimensions can be built from one or more dimension tables. As you learned in Chapter 1, your data warehouse can be designed as a star or snowflake schema. In a star schema, dimensions are created from single tables that are joined to a fact table. In a snowflake schema, two or more joined dimension tables are used to create dimensions where one of the tables is joined to the fact table. You create both of these dimension types in this chapter.

You also learned in Chapters 1 and 3 that each dimension contains objects called hierarchies. In Analysis Services 2005 you have two types of hierarchies to contend with: the attribute hierarchy, which corresponds to a single column in a relational table, and multilevel hierarchies, which are derived from two or more attribute hierarchies where each attribute is a level in the multi-level hierarchy. A typical example of an attribute hierarchy would be zip code in a Dim Geography dimension, and a typical example for a multilevel hierarchy would be Country-State-City-Zip Code also in a Geography dimension. In everyday discussions of multilevel hierarchies, most people leave off the "multilevel" and just call them *"hierarchies."*

For the exercises in this chapter, you use the project you designed in Chapter 2. If you don't happen to have the project handy, you can download it from www.wrox.com. If you download or not, you will still need to add the Geography Dimension (dbo.DimGeography) to the DSV. To add this dimension to your DSV follow the steps below.

1. Double click on the DSV named "AdventureWorksDW.dsv" in Solution Explorer.

2. Click on the "Add/Remove Objects" icon (top left icon in the DSV Designer) as shown in Figure 5-1.

Figure 5-1

3. In the Available objects list, select dbo.DimGeography and click on the > (right arrow) button as shown in Figure 5-2. This will move the Geography dimension into Included objects lists in the Add/Remove tables dialog. Click OK to continue.

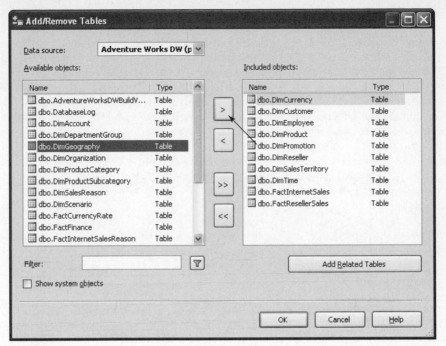

Figure 5-2

Now you are ready to explore use of the Dimension Wizard in Analysis Services 2005. The Dimension Wizard is capable of scanning the dimension table(s), detecting relationships between columns within the table, and suggesting hierarchies for the formation of the dimension. The following exercise shows you how to create a dimension using the Geography table in the Adventure Works DW data source. To do so, follow the steps below:

1. Launch the Dimension Wizard by right-clicking Dimensions in the Solution Explorer and selecting New Dimension... as shown in Figure 5-3. If the welcome screen of the Dimension Wizard opens up, click Next.

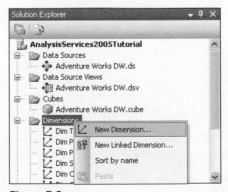

Figure 5-3

2. You will see the Select Build Method screen, as shown in Figure 5-4. You can create dimensions from a data source or from pre-existing templates provided by Analysis Services. In this chapter we're concerned with creating dimensions from a data source; dimensions created from templates are detailed in Chapter 8. By default the Dimension Wizard uses the "Auto build" cube option to create dimensions from data sources. When the Auto build option is enabled, the wizard retrieves a sample of data, detects relationships, and then suggests potential hierarchies for that dimension; but it is up to you to evaluate the Auto build. If you expect to create your own hierarchies and fine tune them then you can disable the Auto build option in this page. You can also choose to create attributes and hierarchies or just attributes by changing the selection in the drop-down list. For now, accept the default options and click Next.

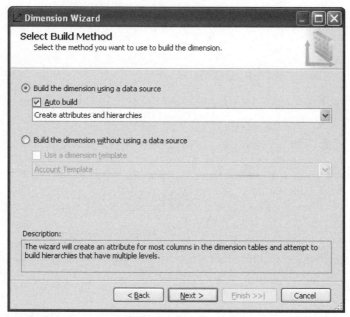

Figure 5-4

3. In the Select Data Source View page (shown in Figure 5-5) you need to select the DSV for creating the dimension. By default the first DSV in your project is selected. Because your current project has only one DSV the Adventure Works DW DSV is selected. Click the Next button to process to the next page of the Dimension Wizard.

4. On the dimension type selection page of the Dimension Wizard (see Figure 5-6) you see three options: Standard Dimension, Time Dimension, and Server Time Dimension. A Standard dimension can be modified to become any sophisticated dimensional variant and makes for a great generic starting point. A Time dimension, on the other hand, is a unique type of dimension typically created from a table that contains time information such as year, semester, quarter, month, week, and date. A Time dimension is unique because its members are fixed (a year always has 12 months in it) and typical business analyses are performed over time. Due to the uniqueness of the Time dimension and how it is used for business analysis, there are special MDX functions that can be used along with time dimension. Furthermore, aggregation of data on a time dimension does not have to be a garden variety aggregation like sum or count.

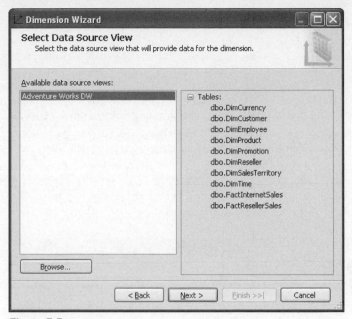

Figure 5-5

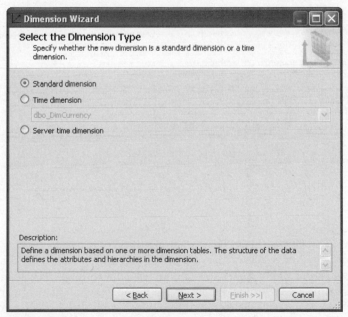

Figure 5-6

Most business decision makers want to analyze their data across a time dimension to understand the month with maximum sales for a quarter or other time frame. Analysis Services provides you a distinct way to aggregate measure data across a time dimension; this is done with semi-additive measures. You learn more about semi-additive measures in Chapter 9. In a Time dimension, several hierarchies are commonly used, such as fiscal year and calendar year, for example; both of which can be built automatically. And without any associated tables in the data source either! To do so you need to use the Server time dimension. You learn about Server time dimension in Chapter 8. Select the Standard Dimension option and click Next.

5. In the "Select the Main Dimension Table" screen, you need to select the main table from which the dimension is to be designed. If a dimension is to be created from a star schema, the dimension is created from the single pertinent table. A snowflake schema dimension actually contains several tables, one of which is the primary table of the dimension. This primary table is chosen as the main table in the "Main table" selection screen of the Dimension Wizard. Select the DimGeography table from the Main table drop-down list as shown in Figure 5-7 and click Next.

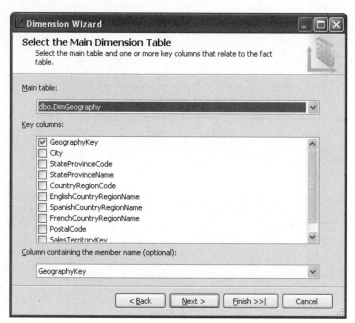

Figure 5-7

6. At this point, the Dimension Wizard analyzes the DSV to detect any outward-facing relationships from the DimGeography table. An outward-facing relationship is a relationship between the DimGeography table and another table, such that a column in the DimGeography table is a foreign key related to another table. Figure 5-8 shows that the wizard detected an outward relationship between the DimGeography table and the DimSalesTerritory table. If you want to model the selected main table as a star-schema table, deselect any of the tables shown on that screen. You can try this out in the Geography dimension you are creating now. Make sure the DimSalesTerritory table is deselected and click Next.

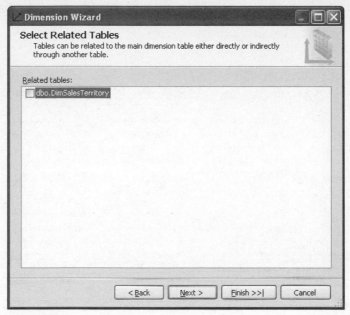

Figure 5-8

7. As shown in Figure 5-9, the Dimension Wizard selects the columns of all the table(s) that have been selected for the dimension you're creating. Each selected column on this screen results in an equivalent attribute being created in the new dimension. Even though you are building a dimension here, this dimension is going to be part of a cube (which is described by the Unified Dimensional Model). The UDM combines the best of the relational and OLAP worlds — one of the important uses of the relational model is the ability to query each column for reporting purposes. The columns in the relational table are transformed to attributes of a dimension that can then be used for querying from the UDM. Select all the attributes and click Next.

8. Analysis Services 2005 is aware of some common dimension types often used in business intelligence applications. These common dimension types have dimension attributes associated with them that typically form levels of a hierarchy within the dimension. In the Dimension Wizard you can choose the dimension type and specify the columns in the table that correspond to the dimension attributes. In the Specify Dimension Type drop-down menu shown in Figure 5-10, the default dimension type selected is Regular, though several other types are supported, some of which can be seen in the figure. The Regular dimension type does not have predefined dimension attributes. If you click a different dimension type such as Organization or Promotion you will see the dimension attributes that are commonly associated with it. You can select the dimension attributes and specify the column in the data source that corresponds to them. When you complete the wizard, these dimension attributes will be defined and you will be able to see them in the Dimension Designer. For designing the Geography dimension, select the Regular dimension type and click Next.

Figure 5-9

Figure 5-10

9. The next screen in the Dimension Wizard is to define Parent-Child relationship within a dimension. A commonly used example of a Parent-Child relationship is readily seen in any organizational chart; it is the relationship between managers and their direct reports. You learn more about Parent-Child relationships later in this chapter. There is no Parent-Child relationship in the DimGeography table. You don't need to make any change here, so click Next.

10. On the Detecting Hierarchies screen, the wizard gets a sample of the data from the data source and scans for relationships between the columns in the table. If one-to-many relationships are detected within this sample, the wizard suggests hierarchies. The attributes that form the different levels within the hierarchies will be detected and shown to you on the following screen. The wizard gives you the option of including or excluding the detected hierarchies; in this example the Dimension Wizard does not detect any such hierarchies (see feedback from the Dimension Wizard after it analyzed the DimGeography table as shown in Figure 5-11). Hence the following screen does not have any hierarchies. Click Next on this screen, and click Next again on the following screen of the wizard.

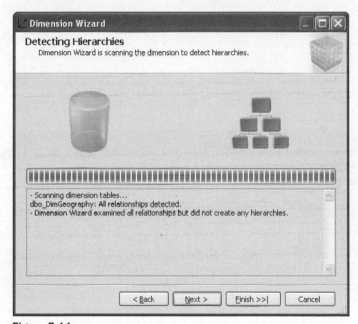

Figure 5-11

11. The final screen of the Dimension Wizard summarizes all the attributes and hierarchies that you selected (see Figure 5-12). If there were hierarchies included, you will see another folder called Hierarchies under the dimension in this screen. Click the Finish button.

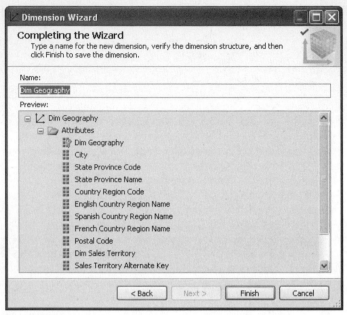

Figure 5-12

12. The wizard has created the dimension object Dim Geography and opens it up within the Dimension Designer. Congratulations!!! You have successfully created your first dimension using the Dimension Wizard. Next, you learn the various parts of the Dimension Designer and how to enhance the dimension as per your business needs.

Working with the Dimension Editor

The Dimension Designer, shown in Figure 5-13, is an important tool that helps you to refine the dimension hierarchies created by the Dimension Wizard. You can define the properties such as unary operators, custom roll-ups, and so forth which help you to define how data should be aggregated for cells referred to by members of hierarchies in the dimension. The Dimension Designer itself is composed of three main window panes called Attributes, Hierarchies and Levels, and the DSV. In addition to that you have the toolbar, which contains several icons that help you to enhance the dimension. The Attributes pane shows all the attributes, the Hierarchies and Levels pane shows all the hierarchies along with the levels, and the DSV pane shows the tables that are part of the dimension. If you hover over each one of the icons you will be able to see the functionality that is supported by the icon. Some of the icons are the same as the ones you saw in the DSV and are used for operations within the dimension DSV. The functionality of the remaining icons is discussed later in this chapter and in Chapter 8.

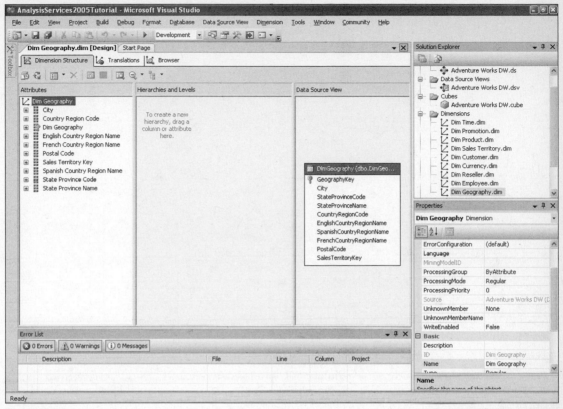

Figure 5-13

Attributes

Attributes are hierarchies that only have two levels; the All level and another level that has the name of the attribute that contains all the members. Each attribute directly corresponds to a column in the relational table. Therefore when the dimension is part of UDM that is used for relational reporting, attributes are selected from the UDM for the corresponding relational column. The Attributes pane in the Dimension Designer shows all the attribute hierarchies of the dimension. The default view of all the attributes within the Attributes pane window is called the Tree view as shown in Figure 5-14. The two additional views supported in the Dimension Designer are the List view and the Grid view. These views show the attributes and associated properties in different views. We have seen the Tree view to be the most flexible view in the Dimension Designer. In the Tree view you can see the attributes along with the member properties. Member properties are attributes within the same dimension that have a one-to-many relationship with the current attribute. For example, if you have the attributes Country, State, and City, you have one-to-many relationships between country and state, as well as between state and city. Member properties are also referred to as related attributes because these attributes have a one-to-many relationship between them.

Each dimension has to have at least one attribute that is defined as the key attribute. By definition, the key attribute has a one-to-many relationship with every attribute in the dimension. The Dimension Wizard automatically establishes relationships, such that all attributes of the dimension are related to key attributes. You can see the related attributes of the key attribute Dim Geography in the tree view of Figure 5-14. Just choose the view that best suits you to visualize and design your dimension easily. You can toggle between the different views by right-clicking in the Attributes pane and selecting the view type you desire, as shown in Figure 5-14.

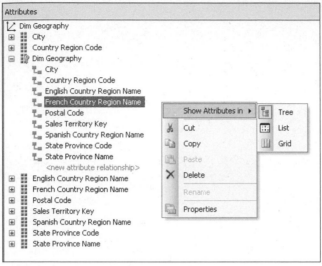

Figure 5-14

Figure 5-15 shows the List view and Grid view of the attributes shown in Figure 5-14. The List view provides you a concise view where the attributes pane is below the Hierarchies and Level pane. The List view is useful when you have a lot of multi-level hierarchies in the dimension. Since you get a wider area for the hierarchies and levels pane you get a visually optimized view where you can see the attributes and hierarchies. In the Grid view you can see all the attributes with a subset of properties for each attribute. Each property specified in the Grid view is an editable drop-down list box so you can change the properties in this view. All the properties shown in the Grid view are also a part of the Properties window.

If you are aware of a one-to-many relationship between attributes, we highly recommend that you specify this relationship in the Dimension Designer as a related attribute. Specifying the member property helps improve query performance as well as changing the aggregation design so as to include the attributes that are part of a hierarchy. You learn more about this in Chapter 12. Because the Dim Geography dimension contains one-to-many relationships, you need to specify the member properties to get query performance improvement. In order to specify that the attribute State Province Name is a member property of City, you need to do the following:

1. Expand the node showing the attribute City.

2. Drag and drop the attribute State Province Name from the attribute list to the area shown as new attribute relationship under the City node. Establishing the relationship between attributes serves dual purpose – member properties as well as related attributes. Establishing the relationship between attributes not only helps in processing performance (you learn in Chapter 12) but also affects calculations that are aggregated across these attributes. You can define the type of relationship between the attributes you established now using the property Cardinality in the Properties window. By default the Cardinality is set to many. If you know that the relationship between the attributes is one to one then you can change the cardinality to one. For example the cardinality between a customer's id and their social security number is one to one, however the cardinality between state and city is one to many.

List View

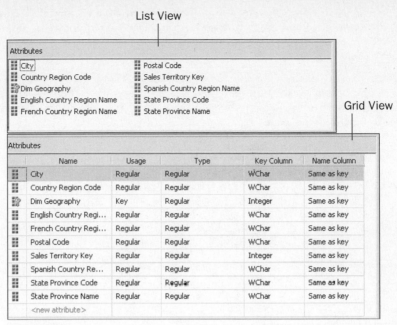

Grid View

Figure 5-15

Follow the same two steps for the English Country Region Name attributes. You have now specified member properties for city attribute. Similarly specify English Country Region name as member property for attribute State Province Name. Often in business analysis when you are analyzing a specific member of a dimension, you need to see the properties of the dimension member to understand it better. In such circumstances, instead of traversing the complete hierarchy you can retrieve the member by querying the member properties. This once again is a performance improvement from the end user's perspective. A wide variety of client tools support the ability to retrieve member properties of a specific member when needed by the data analyst. You can add additional attributes by dragging and dropping a column from the DSV to the Attribute pane or delete an existing attribute by right-clicking that attribute and selecting Delete.

Hierarchies and Levels

Hierarchies (also called multi-level hierarchies) are created from attributes of a dimension. Each multi-level hierarchy contains one or more levels, and each level is an attribute hierarchy. Based on the attributes of the Geography dimension you created, the logical hierarchy to create would be Country-State-City-Dim Geography. Do not expand any of the attributes, stay at the highest level for now. You can create this hierarchy using the following steps:

1. Drag and drop the attribute English Country Region Name from the Attributes pane to the Hierarchy and Level pane. This creates a multi-level hierarchy called Hierarchy with one level English Country Region Name. This level actually corresponds to Country. Hence rename the "English Country Region Name" to "Country" by right clicking on the attribute within the multi-level hierarchy and selecting "Rename."

2. Drag and drop State Province Name from the Attributes pane to the Hierarchy pane such that the State Province Name attribute is below the Country in the multi-level hierarchy designer.

Rename "State Province Name" to "State-Province" by right clicking on the attribute and select-ing "Rename." Drag and drop attributes City and Dim Geography attributes to the multi-level hierarchy in that order so that you now have a four level hierarchy Country-State-City-Dim Geography.

3.   The default name of the hierarchy you have created is Hierarchy. Rename the hierarchy to Geography by right-clicking the name and selecting Rename (see Figure 5-16). You can also rename the levels of the Geography hierarchy by selecting each attribute and changing its name value in the Properties pane.

Figure 5-16

4.   You have created a multi-level hierarchy called Geography that has four levels, as shown in Figure 5-17. You can click the arrows to expand the attribute in each level to see all the member properties. You can create additional hierarchies in the Hierarchy and Level window pane.

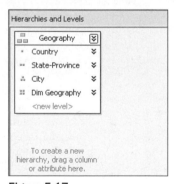

Figure 5-17

Browsing the Dimension

After successfully creating the Dim Geography dimension, you definitely would like to see the results of what you have created and find out how you can see the members of the dimension. So far the dimen-sion has been designed, but not deployed to the server. Indeed, there has been no interaction with the instance of Analysis Services instance yet. In order to see the members of the dimension, Analysis Services needs to receive the details of the dimension (the attributes, member properties and the multi-level hierarchies you have created). You learned in Chapter 3 that the Analysis Services 2005 tools communicate to the instance of Analysis Services via XML/A (XML for Analysis).

XML/A is a Simple Object Access Protocol (SOAP)-based XML Application Programming Interface (API), which is an industry standard, designed for OLAP and Data Mining. The XML/A specification defines the two functions, Execute and Discover, which are used to send actions to and retrieve data from the host instance. The Execute and Discover functions take several parameters that help in various actions the instance of Analysis Services will perform. One of the parameters of the Execute function is the command sent to an instance of Analysis Services — note that in addition to supporting XML/A, Analysis Services supports extensions to the standard. Following is a sample Execute request sent to an instance of Analysis Services using XML/A. The Execute request is a modified version of the one in XML/A specification available at `http://www.xmla.org`.

```
<Execute xmlns="urn:schemas-microsoft-com:xml-analysis"
SOAP-ENV:encodingStyle="http://schemas.xmlsoap.org/soap/encoding/">
<Command>
<Statement> select [Measures].members on Columns from Adventure Works</Statement>
<Command>
<Properties>
<PropertyList>
<DataSourceInfo> Provider=SQL Server 2005;Data Source=local; </DataSourceInfo>
<Catalog>AnalysisServices2005Tutorial</Catalog>
<Format>Multidimensional</Format>
<AxisFormat>ClusterFormat</AxisFormat>
</PropertyList>
</Properties>
</Execute>
</SOAP-ENV:Body>
</SOAP-ENV:Envelope>
```

In the above XML/A, a request is sent to execute an MDX query that is specified within the command Statement on the catalog AnalysisServices2005Tutorial. The XML request shown above results in the query being executed on the server side and the results sent to the client side via XML/A.

Several commands are used to communicate to Analysis Server 2005. Some of the common commands are Create, Alter, Process, and Statement. These commands are used to change the structure of objects described. Each object in Analysis Services 2005 has a well-defined set of properties. The complete definition of the objects is referred to as Data Definition Language in this book. You will learn some of the DML and DDLs used in Analysis Services 2005 in various chapters of the book through examples. For in depth understanding of DMLs and DDLs we recommend you to read the Analysis Services 2005 documentation.

You might recall that you deployed the Analysis Services 2005 tutorial project in Chapter 2. What actually happens when you deploy a project is that the BIDS packages all the design change information in the project as a single XML/A request and sends it as a whole. In this case, you want to see the contents of the dimension you have created. Therefore you need to deploy the project to an instance of Analysis Services. Deploy the project to your Analysis Services instance by right clicking on the solution AnalysisServices2005Tutorial and selecting Deploy or using the F5 function key. When you deploy the entire project using BIDS to Analysis Services, several XML/A requests are sent by BIDS. They are:

1. Request for a list of the databases from Analysis Services to determine if the current project already exists on the instance. The project name you specified while creating the object will be used as the database name. Based on the deployment settings in your project, BIDS either sends the entire definition of all the objects or only the changes you have made since the last deploy. The BIDS will either use a Create or Alter statement based upon the fact the database already exists on the Analysis Services instance. We have not included the Create/Alter XML/A request below since it is quite large. You can use the SQL Profiler to analyze the XML/A request (you learn to use SQL Profiler in Chapter 12).

2. BIDS then sends an XML/A request to process the objects on the instance of Analysis Services. Following is the request that is sent to the server to process the dimension Dim Geography:

```
<Batch Transaction="false"
xmlns="http://schemas.microsoft.com/analysisservices/2003/engine">
  <Process>
    <Type>ProcessDefault</Type>
    <Object>
       <DatabaseID>AnalysisServicesTutorial2005</DatabaseID>
       <DimensionID>Dim Geography</DimensionID>
    </Object>
  </Process>
</Batch>
```

3. BIDS requests schema information through several Discover requests to retrieve information such as the hierarchies and levels. BIDS finally requests Dim Geography dimension data through another XML/A request and automatically changes the tab on the Dimension Designer from Dimension Structure to Browser so that you can view the data. The MDX query that is sent to the server by BIDs to retrieve dimension data is:

```
SELECT HEAD( [Dim Geography].[Geography].LEVELS(0).MEMBERS, 1000 ) on 0
FROM [$Dim Geography]
```

Since you are familiar with MDX by now you might have deciphered most of the query. This query uses the HEAD function to request the first 1,000 members from Level 0 of the hierarchy Geography in dimension [Dim Geography]. In the FROM clause you see [$ Dim Geography]. Though you have not created any cube in your data warehouse project yet, you know that the FROM clause should contain a cube name, so how does this MDX query work? When a dimension is created the server internally stores the values of the dimension as a cube. This means that **every dimension is internally represented as a cube** with a single dimension that holds all the attribute values. The dimension you have created is part of the Analysis Services database AnalysisServicesTutorial2005 and is called a database dimension. Because each database dimension is a one-dimensional cube, they can be queried using MDX using the special character $ before the dimension name. This is exactly what you see in the query, [$Dim Geography].

The Dimension Designer has switched to the Browser pane as shown in Figure 5-18. The hierarchy first shown in the hierarchy browser is the most recently created multi-level hierarchy Geography. You can choose to browse any of the multilevel hierarchies or attribute hierarchies by selecting one from the drop-down list labeled Hierarchy. This list contains the multilevel hierarchies followed by the attribute hierarchies. Each attribute hierarchy and multilevel hierarchy within a dimension has a level called the All level. In Figure 5-18 you can see the All level for the hierarchy Geography. The All level is the topmost level of most hierarchies (the All level can be removed in certain hierarchies) and you can change the name of the All level by changing the property of the hierarchy. It makes sense to call the level "All" because it encompasses all of the sub-levels in the hierarchy. If a hierarchy does not contain the All level then the members of the top most level would be displayed as the first level in the dimension browser.

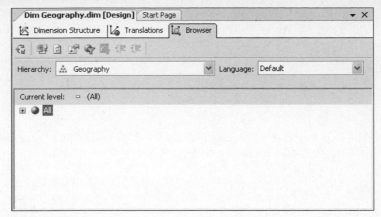

Figure 5-18

Assume you want to change the All level of the Geography hierarchy to "All Countries." The following steps show you how to do this:

1. Go to the Dimension Structure view of the Dimension Designer.

2. Click on the Geography hierarchy in the Hierarchies and Levels pane.

3. The properties window now shows all the properties of this hierarchy. The first property is AllMemberName and it displays no value. Add a value by typing **All Countries** in the text entry box to the right of AllMemberName.

4. Deploy the project once again.

5. After the deploy is successful the Dimension Designer automatically switches to the Browser tab. In the Browser tab BIDS requests you to reconnect to retrieve the latest data from the Analysis Services instance. Click on the Reconnect link shown in the Browser.

You can now see that the All level of the Geography hierarchy has changed to All Countries, as shown in Figure 5-19. You can also see in the figure that the All Countries level has been expanded to show all members in the next level.

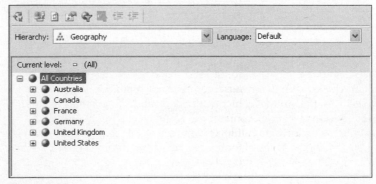

Figure 5-19

When you expand the All Countries level, the following MDX query is sent to the Analysis Services instance to retrieve the members in the next level:

```
WITH MEMBER [Measures].[-DimBrowseKey 0-] AS
      '[Dim Geography].[Geography].currentmember.properties("key0", TYPED)'
SELECT { [Measures].[-DimBrowseKey 0-] } ON 0,
HEAD( [Dim Geography].[Geography].[All Countries].CHILDREN, 1000) ON 1
FROM [$Dim Geography]
```

The goal of the MDX query is to retrieve all the members that are children of the All Countries level. Similar to the MDX query that was sent to retrieve members in level 0, this query only retrieves the first 1,000 children of All Countries level. This is accomplished by use of the HEAD function as seen in the MDX query. This query includes a calculated measure called Measures.[-DimBrowseKey 0-], which is selected in the MDX query. The calculated measure expression in this query retrieves the key of the current member by using the MDX function *Properties*. The MDX function Properties returns a string value based on the parameters passed to it. The Properties function returns the value of the member property that is specified as the first argument to the expression. In this query the value requested is the Key of the current member.

Other parameters that can be passed to the Properties function are NAME, ID, and CAPTION, or the name of a member property or related attribute. The properties NAME, ID, KEY, and CAPTION are called as intrinsic member properties since all attributes and hierarchies will have these properties. The second argument passed to the Properties function is optional and the only value that can be passed is TYPED. If the Properties function is called without the second parameter, the function returns the string representation of the property. If the second argument TYPED is passed to the Properties function, the function returns the data type of the property (data type that was defined in the data source) requested. For example, if the first argument is Key and if the Key of this attribute is of type integer, the Properties function returns integer values. Typically the second parameter TYPED is useful if you want to filter the results based on a member property. For example, if the key of the Geography hierarchy is an integer and if you want to see only the children of member United States, you can use the FILTER function along with the calculated measure that has been created using the parameter TYPED.

The result of the preceding MDX query is shown in the following table. The dimension browser retrieves this information and shows the names of the members in the hierarchical format shown in Figure 5-19.

	-DimBrowseKey 0-
Australia	Australia
Canada	Canada
France	France
Germany	Germany
United Kingdom	United Kingdom
United States	United States

You defined the member property for the State and City earlier. Now you want to see these member properties in the dimension browser. To do that you can either click the Member Properties icon in the Dimension Designer toolbar (highlighted in Figure 5-20) or choose Member Properties from the Menu Dimension. A dialog appears that has all the attributes of the dimension. Select the attributes Country, State-Province, and City and click OK. The member properties you have selected are now shown in the dimension browser as shown in Figure 5-20.

Figure 5-20

Expand the members of United States to see the member properties of the States and Cities under United States. The member properties of a member are also retrieved with the help of an MDX query. For example, when you want to see all the cities in Alabama, the following MDX query is sent to the server:

```
WITH MEMBER [Measures].[-DimBrowseLevelKey 0-] AS '[Dim
Geography].[Geography].currentmember.properties("key0", TYPED)'
MEMBER [Measures].[-DimBrowseProp City-] AS '[Dim
Geography].[Geography].currentmember.properties("City", TYPED)'
MEMBER [Measures].[-DimBrowseProp Country-] AS '[Dim
Geography].[Geography].currentmember.properties("Country", TYPED)'
MEMBER [Measures].[-DimBrowseProp State-Province-] AS '[Dim
Geography].[Geography].currentmember.properties("State-Province", TYPED)'
SELECT { [Measures].[-DimBrowseLevelKey 0-], [Measures].[-DimBrowseProp City-],
[Measures].[-DimBrowseProp Country-], [Measures].[-DimBrowseProp State-Province-] }
ON 0,
Head( [Dim Geography].[Geography].[City].&[Huntsville].Children, 1000) ON 1
FROM [$Dim Geography]
CELL PROPERTIES VALUE
```

Similar to the MDX query you analyzed earlier to retrieve all the members of the All level, this query retrieves all the Alabama City members. The member properties City, State-Province, and Country are retrieved with the same query as calculated members using the WITH MEMBER clause as seen in the above query.

Sorting Members of a Level

Members of a level are members of the attribute that are defined for that level. For example, members of the level Country in the Geography hierarchy are actually members of the attribute English Country Region Name. The member name that is shown in the dimension browser is the text associated with the Name of the Country. It is not uncommon for the dimension tables to have one column for the descriptive name and one column for the key of that column. You can use the descriptive name column to display the name of the attribute and the key column to sort the members in that attribute. The attributes' properties help you sort members of a level.

Each attribute in a dimension has two properties, KeyColumns and NameColumn. The KeyColumns property is used to specify the column(s) that is used for sorting the members and the NameColumn is used for the descriptive name of the member. By default the Dimension Wizard and the Dimension Designer set the KeyColumns attribute when an attribute is added to the dimension. The NameColumn attribute is empty. If the NameColumn is empty, Analysis Services uses the KeyColumns by default for the descriptive names for client requests.

Figure 5-21 shows these properties for the attribute Country. The data type of the attribute is also shown in the KeyColumns property. Country is of data type Wchar, which means all the members are strings. Therefore, when you view the members in the dimension browser the members are sorted by the names. The Dim Geography dimension table has the column Country Region Code. You can define the sort order of the countries based on the Country Region Code instead of their names by changing the KeyColumns and NameColumn properties appropriately. The following exercise demonstrates exactly how you can change the order of the countries based on the order of Country Region Code (AU, CA, DE, FR, GB, and US) instead of the country names:

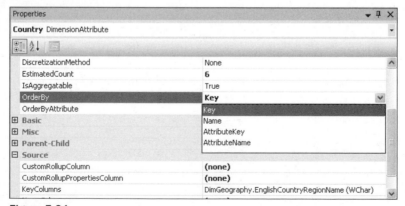

Figure 5-21

1. Click on English Country Region Name in the Attributes pane, then in the properties pane, click the NameColumn property value drop-down and select New. This opens an Object Binding dialog showing all the columns in the Dim Geography table. Select the column English Country Region Name and click OK.

2. Click the KeyColumns property value (the three dots button). This action launches the DataItem Collector dialog. Delete the column EnglishCountryRegionName from the collection and then click the Add button. A new item New Binding (WChar) appears in the list box Members. Under the Misc section in the dialog select the Source property and click on the ... button. The Object Binding dialog is now launched. Change the binding type from Generate Column to Column Binding and select CountryRegionCode from the Source column list. The DataItem Collector dialog should look like Figure 5-22. Click the OK button.

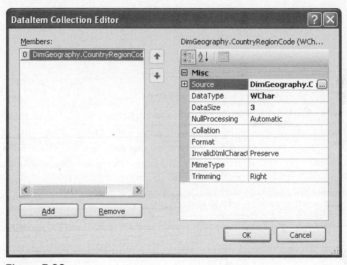

Figure 5-22

3. Click the Advanced Properties for the attribute EnglishCountryRegionName. Change the value of property OrderBy from Name to Key. This instructs the server to order this attribute using the Key attribute (CountryRegionCode), which you specified in step 2.

4. Deploy the project to the Analysis Services instance. Deploying the project to Analysis Services instance results in sending the new changes defined in steps 1 through 3 followed by processing the dimension. Once you are in the Browser tab click on the Reconnect option to retrieve the latest dimension data.

In the dimension browser select the Geography hierarchy. The order of the countries has now changed based on the order of Country Region Code (AU, CA, DE, FR, GB, and US) instead of the country names you viewed in Figure 5-19. The new order of countries is shown in Figure 5-23.

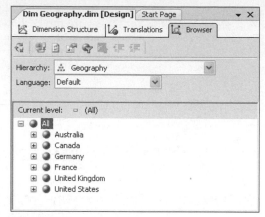

Figure 5-23

Optimizing Attributes

During the design of a dimension you might want to include certain attributes in the dimension, but not want to make the attribute hierarchies available to end users for querying. Two properties of the attributes help you to manipulate visibility of attributes to end users. One property, AttributeHierarchyEnabled, allows you to disable the attribute. By setting this property to False you are disabling the attribute in the dimension; you cannot include this attribute in any level of a multilevel hierarchy. This attribute can only be defined as a member property (related attribute) to another attribute. Members of this attribute cannot be retrieved by an MDX query, but you can retrieve the value as a member property of another attribute. If you disable an attribute you might see improvements in processing performance depending on the number of members in the attribute. You need to be sure that there will be no future need to slice and dice on this attribute.

Another property called AttributeHierarchyVisible is useful for setting an attribute hierarchy to invisible for browsing; but even with this set, the attribute can be used as a level within a hierarchy or can be used for querying. If you set this property to False, you will not see this attribute in the dimension browser. The properties AttributeHierarchyEnabled and AttributeHierarchyVisible are part of the Advanced property section in the properties window, as shown in Figure 5-24.

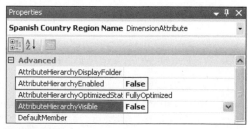

Figure 5-24

If you want to create a dimension that contains only multilevel hierarchies and no attributes, you can mark the AttributeHierarchyVisible property to False for all the attributes. When you go to the dimension browser you will only see the hierarchies. Even though you have disabled the attribute for browsing, you will still be able to query the attribute using MDX.

Defining Translations in Dimensions

If your data warehouse is to be used globally, you want to show the hierarchies, levels, and members in different languages so that customers in those countries can read the cube in their own language. Analysis Services 2005 provides you with a feature called Translation (not a super-imaginative name) that helps you create and view dimension members in various languages. The benefit of this feature is that you do not have to build a new cube in every language. For implementation you need to only have a column in the relational data source that will have the translated names for all the members of a a specific attribute in the dimension.

In the Dim Geography table you have two attributes: Spanish Country Region Name and French Country Region Name. These columns have the translated names of the country names which are members of the attributes English Country Region Name. The following steps describe how to create a new translation:

1. Switch to the Translations tab in the Dimension Designer.

2. Click the New Translation icon shown in Figure 5-25 or choose New Translation from the Dimension menu item to create a new translation and choose a language. The Selection language dialog now pops up.

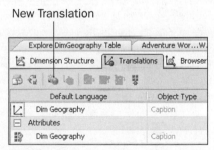

Figure 5-25

3. Select the language French (France) and click OK.

4. A new column with the title French (France) is added as shown in Figure 5-26. Click the row English Country Region Name on the column French (France). You now see the Attribute Data Translation dialog. Select the French Country Region Name column and click OK.

5. Repeat steps 1 through 4 for the language Spanish (Spain).

You have now created two translations in French and Spanish languages. In addition to specifying the columns for member names, you can also change the metadata information of each level. For example, if you want to change the level Country in the Geography hierarchy in French and Spanish languages, you can do that by entering the names in the row that show the Country level. Type **Pays** and **Pais** as shown in Figure 5-26 for French and Spanish translations respectively. You have defined translations for the Country attribute in two languages making use of the columns in the relational data source. To see how this metadata information is shown in the dimension browser, first deploy the project to your Analysis Services instance.

Default Language	Object Type	French (France)	Spanish (Spain)
Dim Geography.dim [Design] / Adventure Wor...W.dsv [Design] / Start Page			
Dimension Structure / Translations / Browser			
Dim Geography	Caption		
Attributes			
Dim Geography	Caption		
City	Caption		
State Province Code	Caption		
State-Province	Caption		
Country Region Code	Caption		
French Country Region ...	Caption		
Postal Code	Caption		
English Country Region ...	Caption		
Hierarchies			
Geography	Caption		
All Countries	AllMemberName		
Country	Caption	Pays	Pais

Figure 5-26

To see the effect of the translations you have created, select language French (France) from within the Dimension Browser as shown in Figure 5-27. Select the Geography hierarchy and expand the All level. Now you can see all the members in French. If you click any of the countries, the metadata shown for the level is "Pays" (French for country) as shown in Figure 5-27. There is a negligible amount of overhead associated with viewing dimension hierarchies, levels, and members in different languages from your UDM.

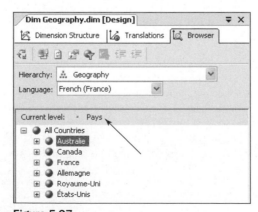

Figure 5-27

Creating a Snowflake Dimension

A snowflake dimension is a dimension that is created using a set of dimension tables. A snowflake dimension normally suggests that the tables in the data source have been normalized. Normalization is the process by which tables of a relational database are designed to remove redundancy and are optimized for frequent updates. Most database design books, including *The Data Warehouse Toolkit* by Ralph Kimball (Wiley, 1996) and *An Introduction to Database Systems* by C. J. Date (Addison Wesley, 2003), talk about the normalization process in detail.

The columns from different tables of a snowflake dimension often result in levels of a hierarchy in the dimension. The best way to understand a snowflake dimension is to create one yourself. To create one we're going to need two additional tables added from the source to our DSV. Here is how to add the two tables:

1. Open the AdventureWorksDW DSV and click on the Add/Remove Tables icon (top left icon in the DSV).

2. Control-Click on "dbo.DimProductCategory" and "dbo.DimProductSubcategory" and click the right arrow > to move the two tables from the source to the DSV. Click OK to continue.

Now that you have the necessary tables, the following steps describe how to create a snowflake dimension called DimProducts from AdventureWorksDW.

1. Launch the Dimension Wizard, accept the defaults, and proceed through the pages of the Wizard to the "Select Main Dimension Table" screen. Select the dbo.DimProduct Table from the drop-down list box for Main Table, then click Next.

2. The Select Related Tables screen shows the tables DimProductCategory and DimProductSubCategory. These tables together with the DimProduct table form the snowflake dimension "DimProduct" which we're creating. Select DimProductCategory and the DimProductSubCategory tables on this page and proceed to the next screen by clicking Next.

3. Accept the defaults and proceed through the pages until you get to the "Review New Hierarchies" screen. The Dimension Wizard detects a hierarchy with three levels, as shown in Figure 5-28. This hierarchy is created from columns in the three dimension tables that you selected earlier in the wizard.

4. Accept the defaults and complete the wizard. You've now successfully created a snowflake dimension with one hierarchy and several attributes in Analysis Services 2005. The DSV of this dimension shows the three dimension tables.

You can perform most of the same operations in a snowflake dimension as you can in a star schema dimension, including adding attributes, creating hierarchies, and defining member properties. Notice that the levels of the hierarchy are actually referring to attributes that have been created from the three dimension tables in the DSV pane. The wizard also defines the member properties for the levels in the multi-level hierarchy. The member properties of a specific level defined by the Dimension Wizard are all the columns that are part of the dimension table. The member properties for the level Dim Product Category are English Product Category Name, French Product Category Name, Spanish Product Category Name. and Product Category Alt Key which are all the remaining columns in the Dim Product Category table from which the attribute Dim Product Category has been defined. You have successfully created a snowflake dimension. You can now deploy the project and browse the dimension similar to that of a star schema dimension.

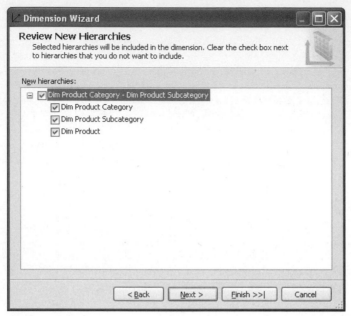

Figure 5-28

Creating a Time Dimension

Almost every data warehouse designed will have a Time dimension. The Time dimension can be comprised of the levels Year, Semester, Quarter, Month, Week, Date, Hour, Minute, and Seconds. Most data warehouses contain the levels Year, Quarter, Month, and Date. The Time dimension helps in analyzing business data across similar time periods; for example, determining how the current revenues or profit of a company compare to those of the previous year or previous quarter.

Even though it appears that the Time dimension has regular time periods, irregularities often exist. The number of days in a month varies across months, and the number of days in a year changes each leap year. In addition to that, a company can have its own fiscal year, which might not be identical to the calendar year. Even though there are minor differences in the levels, the Time dimension is often viewed as having regular time intervals. Several MDX functions help in solving typical business questions related to analyzing data across time periods. ParallelPeriod is one such function, which you learned about in Chapter 3. Time dimensions are treated specially by Analysis Services and certain measures are aggregated across the Time dimension uniquely and are called semi-additive measures. You learn more about semi-additive measures in Chapter 9.

The following steps show you how to create a Time dimension on the Dim Time table of the AdventureWorksDW database:

1. Launch the Dimension Wizard and accept the defaults in the initial screens of the Dimension Wizard. On the Dimension Type page of the Wizard, select Time dimension and choose the dbo_DimTime table as shown in Figure 5-29. Click Next to continue.

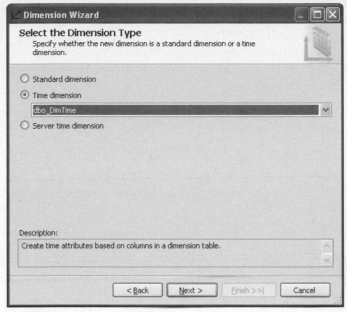

Figure 5-29

2. On the Define Time Periods screen you need to define the columns in the relational table that correspond to the levels within a Time dimension. This page allows you to define the most common time hierarchies used in the business world: fiscal year, calendar year, reporting year, and manufacturing year. Define the properties Year, Half Year, Quarter, Month, and Date as shown in Figure 5-30 and click Next.

Figure 5-30

3. The Review New Hierarchies screen shows the hierarchies that will be created by the Dimension Wizard based on the time property names you defined in the previous screen. Figure 5-31 shows that one hierarchy will be created. If you had defined other time properties, additional hierarchies might be shown in this screen. You have the option of selecting the hierarchies that you want the wizard to generate. You also have the option of including or excluding the default levels shown by the wizard. Accept the defaults and click Next.

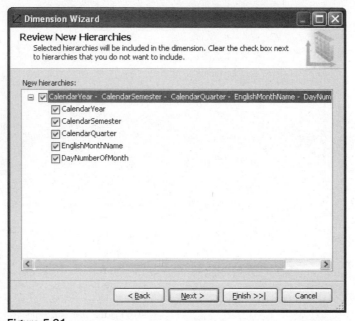

Figure 5-31

4. Complete the Time Dimension Wizard. The Time dimension with one hierarchy and several attributes will be created as shown in Figure 5-32. Go ahead and deploy and process the project.

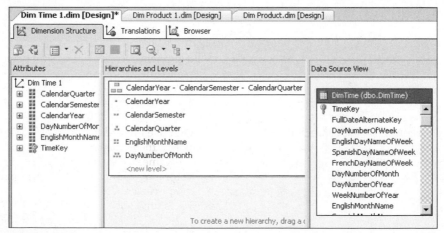

Figure 5-32

Figure 5-33 shows the hierarchy that you created. Notice that the order of months within a quarter is not the default calendar order. For example, the order of months of CY Q1 of year 2002 is February, January, and March. To change the order, change the KeyColumns, NameColumn, and SortOrder appropriately and re-deploy the project.

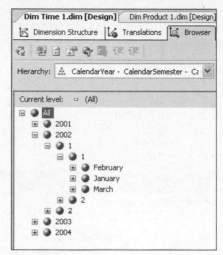

Figure 5-33

You have now successfully created a Time dimension. If you review the basic properties of each attribute in the Time dimension, you will notice that the property Type has values such as Quarters, HalfYears, Years, Days, and Months. You can define the right property type for the chosen attribute. Defining the right property type is important since a client application could use this property to apply the MDX functions for the Time dimension.

Creating a Parent-Child Hierarchy

In the real world you come across relationships such as that between managers and their direct reports. This relationship is similar to the relationship between a parent and child in that a parent can have several children. In the data warehousing world such relationships are modeled as a Parent-Child dimension and in Analysis Services 2005 the relationships are modeled as a hierarchy called the Parent-Child hierarchy. The key difference between this relationship and any other hierarchy with several levels is how this relationship is represented in the data source. Well, that and certain other properties which are unique to the Parent-Child design. Both of these are discussed in this section.

When you created the Geography dimension, you might have noticed that there were separate columns for Country, State, and City in the relational table. Similarly, the manager and direct report can be modeled by two columns, ManagerName and EmployeeName, where the EmployeeName column is used for the direct report. If there are five direct reports for a manager, there will be five rows in the relational table. The interesting part of the Manager-DirectReport relationship is that the manager is also an employee and is a direct report to another manager. This is unlike the Columns City, State, and Country in the Dim Geography table. It is probably rare at your company, but employees can sometimes have new managers due to managerial reorganization. The fact that an employee's manager can change at any time of the year is very interesting when you want to look at facts such as sales generated under a specific manager, which is the sum of sales generated by the manager's direct reports. A dimension modeling such a behavior is called a slowly changing dimension since the manager of an employee changes over time. You can learn slowly changing dimensions and different variations in detail in the book *The Microsoft Data Warehouse Toolkit: With SQL Server 2005 and the Microsoft Business Intelligence Toolset* by Joy Mundy et al. (Wiley, 2006).

The Employee table in AdventureWorksDW has a Parent-Child relationship because it has a join from ParentEmployeeKey to the EmployeeKey. You can use the Dimension Wizard to create a dimension on the DimEmployee table. Accept the defaults on each screen of the Dimension Wizard. On the Define Parent-Child Relationship screen shown in Figure 5-34, you will notice that the Dimension Wizard has identified a Parent-Child relationship as well as the Parent attribute based on a sample of the data. The wizard was able to identify the Parent-Child relationship due to join within the same table in the DSV.

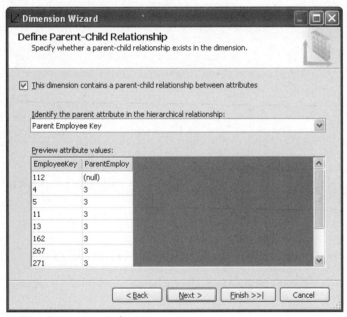

Figure 5-34

On the Review New Hierarchies screen, shown in Figure 5-35, the Dimension Wizard shows the multi-level hierarchies detected from the data sample.

By default the Dimension Wizard defines the properties for the attribute modeling the Parent-Child hierarchy at the completion of the Dimension Wizard, as shown in Figure 5-36.

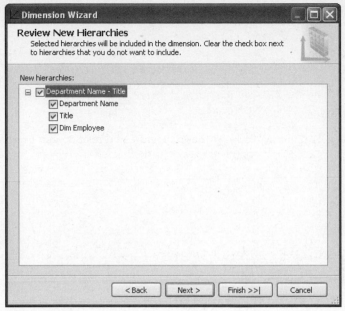

Figure 5-35

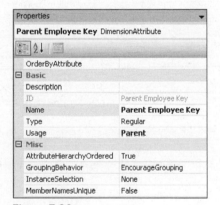

Figure 5-36

The Parent-Child hierarchy is actually a special attribute hierarchy because it can contain multiple levels, unlike the other attributes. The Parent-Child hierarchy that you created is the attribute ParentEmployeeKey. The Usage property for this attribute is set to Parent, which indicates that this attribute is a Parent-Child hierarchy. If you deploy the project and browse the Parent-Child hierarchy, you will notice that you see the ids of parent and employee as a multilevel hierarchy. Typically, you would want to see the names of the employees rather than their ids. You learned earlier that you can use the named column to specify the name that is shown in the browser and use the key column for ordering. Because the Parent-Child hierarchy retrieves all the information from the Key attribute, which is the DimEmployee attribute in this example, you need to modify the named column of the DimEmployee attribute rather than the named column of the Parent-Child hierarchy attribute. Change the named column of the Key attribute to LastName. When you deploy the project and browse the Parent-Child hierarchy, you will see the members of the hierarchy, as shown in Figure 5-37.

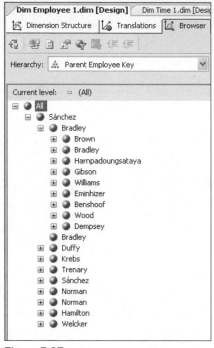

Figure 5-37

Summary

At the beginning of each episode of the television serial "The Twilight Zone" the viewer was exhorted to not adjust their television set. With all due respect to Rod Serling, just the opposite is true with Analysis Services 2005. Yes, you will get great results from using the Dimension Wizard and other wizards in BIDS, but for optimal results, you will want to fine-tune what those wizards produce. A great example is using the Properties window to assign descriptive names to an attribute which might otherwise harbor some obscure name coming from a source database. More profoundly, you can use the Dimension Designer to create translations for the attributes and hierarchies of a dimension into another language.

In addition to learning about dimensions, you learned the necessity of deploying your dimension to the instance of Analysis Services where the dimension is processed by retrieving the data from the data source. Processing is essential to enable the user to browse a dimension. The communication between BIDS and an instance of Analysis Services is accomplished through a SOAP-based XML API called XML/A (XML for Analysis), which is an industry standard. Even more interesting is that dimensions stored in Analysis Services are represented internally as cubes — one-dimensional cubes; and what a coincidence, because cubes are the topic of Chapter 6.

6

Cube Design

In Chapter 5 you learned to create dimensions using the Dimension Wizard and to refine and enhance dimensions using the Dimension Designer. Dimensions eventually need to be part of your UDM for you to analyze data across various dimension members. In previous chapters, you read about the Unified Dimensional Model (UDM). Now, prepare yourself for significantly more detail because all the fact and dimension tables you see when you're looking at a DSV in the Cube Designer comprise the UDM. Yes, the UDM is more than a multiple data-source cube on steroids, but to make it as clear as possible, think of the UDM as a cube for now. In this chapter you learn how to create cubes using the Cube Wizard and enhance the cube using the Cube Designer. You learn to add calculations to your cube that facilitate in effective data analysis followed by analyzing the cube data itself in the Cube Designer.

The Unified Dimensional Model

To generate profits for a business, key strategic decisions need to be made based on likely factors such as having the right business model, targeting the right consumer group, pricing the product correctly, and marketing through optimal channels. To make the right decisions and achieve targeted growth you need to analyze data. The data can be past sales, expected sales, or even information from competitors. The phrase "Knowledge is power" is very fitting here because in the world of business, analyzing and comparing current sales against the expected sales helps executives make decisions directly aligned with the goals of the company. Such sales information is typically stored in a distributed fashion and must be collected from various sources. Executives making the business decisions typically do not have the capability to access the raw sales data as formed from various locations and subsequently optimized for use. The decision-makers typically rely on the aggregated data, which is easy to understand and which facilitates the decision-making process. Presenting aggregated data to the decision-makers quickly is a key challenge for business intelligence providers. Analysis Services 2005 enables you to design a model that bridges the gap between the raw data and the information content that can be used for forming business decisions. This model, designed through Analysis Services 2005, is called the Unified Dimensional Model (UDM).

The UDM is central to your Analysis Services database architecture. UDM is your friend because it helps you narrow the gap between end users and the data. Analysis Services provides you with several features that help you design a unified model that will serve the needs of end users. UDM, as the name suggests, provides you with a way to encapsulate access to multiple heterogeneous data sources into a single model. The UDM buffers you from the difficulties of managing the integration of various data sources so you can build your model easily. The UDM provides you with the best of OLAP and relational worlds, exposing rich data and metadata for exploration and analysis.

Figure 6-1 (originally shown in Chapter 2, but reprinted here for your convenience) shows you the architecture of the Unified Dimensional Model that has been created using Analysis Services 2005. As shown in the figure, the UDM helps you to integrate data from various data sources such as Oracle, SQL Server, DB2, Teradata, and flat files all into a single model that merges the underlying schemas into a single schema. The end users do not necessarily have to view the entire schema of the UDM. Instead, they can view sections of the UDM relevant to their needs through the functionality provided by Analysis Services 2005 called *perspectives*.

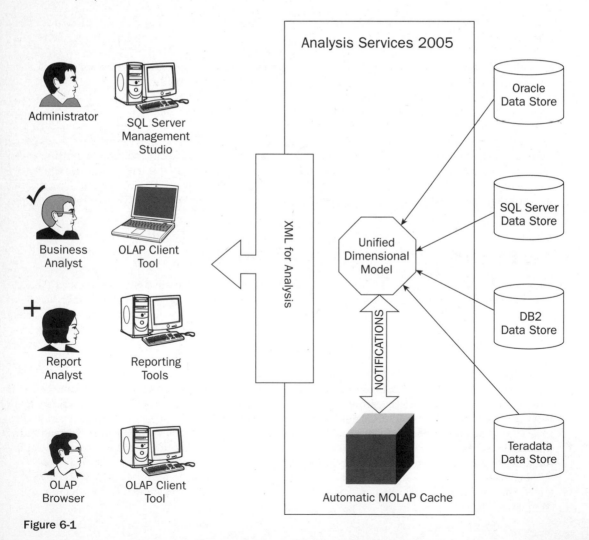

Figure 6-1

In the OLAP world, data analyzed by end users is often historical data that might be a few days, months or even years old. However, the responses to the OLAP queries are typically returned within a few seconds. In the relational world the end users have instant access to the raw data but the responses to queries can take much longer, on the order of minutes. As mentioned earlier, the UDM merges the best of both the OLAP and relational worlds and provides the end users with real-time data with the query performance of the OLAP world. The UDM is able to provide the query performance of the OLAP world with the help of a feature in Analysis Services 2005 that creates a cache of the relational data source that also aggregates the data on an instance of Analysis Services. During the time the cache is being built, the UDM retrieves the data directly from the data sources. As soon as the cache is available, the results are retrieved from the cache in response to relevant queries. Whenever there is a change in the underlying data source, the UDM receives a notification and appropriate updates are made to the cache based on the settings defined for cache updates.

The UDM also provides rich, high-end analytic support through which complex business calculations can be exploited. Such complex calculations can be extremely difficult to formulate in the relational world at the data-source level. Even if such calculations are defined on the relational data source; query responses to OLAP style queries from relational data source might be really slow as compared to the responses from Analysis Services. UDM natively interfaces to end-user clients through the XML for Analysis standard which allows client tools to use XMCA to retrieve data from Analysis service. Client tools such as Office Web Components (OWC) and Excel pivot tables allow the end users to create ad-hoc queries for data analysis. In addition to that, UDM supports rich analytic features such as Key Performance Indicators (KPIs), Actions and Translations that help surface the status of your business at any given time so that appropriate actions can be taken.

The UDM provides an efficient interface for detail-level reporting through the dimension attributes that are common in the relational world. In addition to that the UDM is easily understandable by a relational user. The ability to transform the UDM catered towards end user's views and the ability to perform ad-hoc queries on aggregated data to detail-level data make the UDM a powerful construct indeed. The UDM also allows you to design the model in the end user's language, which is needed in a global market.

Creating a Cube using Cube Wizard

Cubes are the principal objects of an OLAP database that help in data analysis. Cubes are multidimensional structures that are primarily composed of dimensions and facts. The data from a fact table that is stored within the cube for analysis are called *measures*. In Analysis Services 2005 you can store data from multiple fact tables within the same cube. In Chapter 2 you became familiar with the Cube Wizard and in this chapter you see more details of the Cube Wizard followed by refinements to your cube in the Cube Designer.

Similar to the Dimension Wizard you used in Chapter 5, the Cube Wizard facilitates creation of cube objects from the DSV. For this exercise, you continue with the AnalysisServices2005Tutorial project you created in Chapter 5, which contained the dimensions Geography, Employees, and Time. To start with a clean slate, please delete the existing cube Adventure Works DW if it is still there from Chapter 2. To delete, just right click on the cube in Solution Explorer and select Delete. To completely understand the functionality of the Cube wizard follow the steps below to build a new cube.

1. Right-click the Cubes folder and select New Cube, as shown in Figure 6-2. Click Next on the introduction page to proceed.

Figure 6-2

2. In the Select Build Method page you have the option to build the cube from an existing data source or without a data source. In this tutorial you build the cube from the Adventure Works DW data source. In Figure 6-3 please notice the checkbox option, Use Auto Build. If you select this option the Cube Wizard will detect and create dimensions as part of the creation of the cube. Further, you have the option to enable Cube Wizard detection of attributes and hierarchies within dimensions and to create them as part of the cube building process. Or you can have the detection only for the creation of dimension attributes. Select the option for creating attributes and hierarchies. You can refine the attributes and hierarchies after creation using the dimension editor. If you do not use the Auto build option you can add existing dimensions to the cube in the Cube Wizard or Cube Editor. You can also launch the Dimension Wizard and create dimensions using the Cube Wizard. Accept the defaults as shown in Figure 6-3 and click Next.

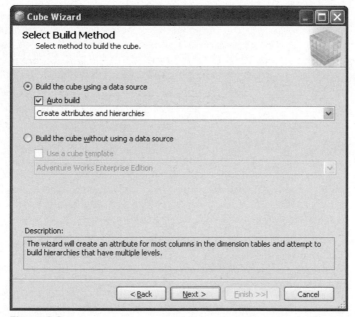

Figure 6-3

3. The next page of the Cube Wizard is the DSV selection page. If you have multiple DSVs you need to select the DSV upon which you are creating the cube. In the current project you only have the AdventureWorksDW DSV. The Cube Wizard allows you to select the DSV from which you want to create the cube. Select the AdventureWorksDW data source and Click Next.

The Cube Wizard now scans the DSV to detect the fact and dimension tables in the DSV and presents these in the Detecting Fact and Dimension Tables page as shown in Figure 6-4. Any table that has an outgoing relationship is identified as a fact table, whereas a table that has an incoming relationship is detected as dimension table.

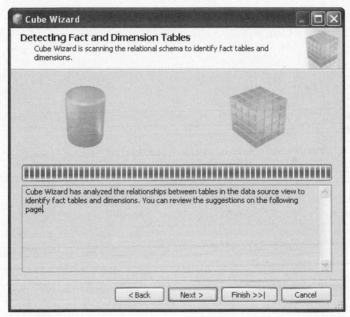

Figure 6-4

Click Next after the fact and dimension detection has been completed.

On the Identify Fact and Dimension Tables page you see the tables that have been identified as fact and dimension tables by the Cube Wizard as shown in Figure 6-5. You have the option to select or deselect a table as a fact or dimension table. The wizard has identified the FactInternetSales, FactResellerSales, and DimReseller tables as fact tables and identified the DimReseller table and the remaining tables as dimension tables. The DimReseller table was detected as both a fact and dimension table because there are incoming as well as outgoing relationships from it. The default view of this page shows the tables with checkboxes indicating selection status.

You can also see a graphical view of the fact and dimension tables. If you click the Diagram tab you will see the tables as shown in Figure 6-6. In the diagram view, fact tables are shown in color yellow, the dimension tables are shown in color cyan, and the tables that have been identified as both dimension and fact tables are shown in green. In this tutorial DimReseller table is considered as only a dimension table and not a fact table.

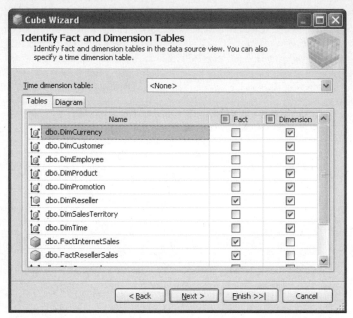

Figure 6-5

4.   Switch to the Tables view and deselect the DimReseller table from being a fact table and click Next.

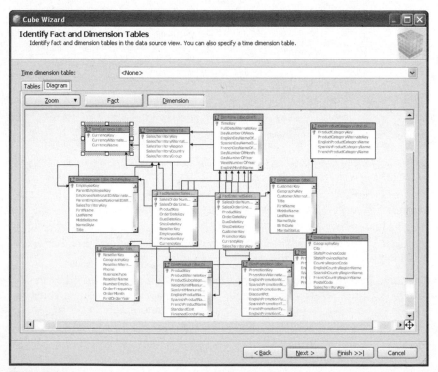

Figure 6-6

5. Figure 6-7 shows the Review Shared Dimensions page. This page is shown in the Cube Wizard only when you have tables selected as dimension tables in the Cube Wizard as well as shared dimensions already created from these tables in the database. Select all the dimensions from the Available Dimensions area and move them to the Cube Dimensions area as shown in Figure 6-7 and click Next.

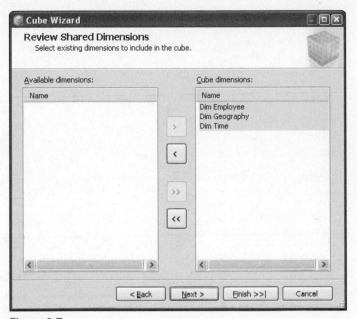

Figure 6-7

6. In the Select Measures page, the Cube Wizard shows all the columns from the fact tables that it detects as potential measures of the cube as shown in Figure 6-8. The Cube Wizard does not select the primary and foreign keys in a table as measures. There is a one-to-one mapping between a column in the fact table and a measure in the cube. The Cube Wizard groups measures from a fact table under an object called a *Measure Group*. Therefore, by default, there will be one measure group for each fact table included in the cube. In the DSV you are using there are two fact tables, and therefore two measure groups named Fact Internet Sales and Fact Reseller Sales are created. You can select or deselect the measures you want to be part of the cube in this page. Use the default selection and Click Next.

7. In the Detecting Hierarchies page the Cube Wizard scans all the dimension tables for which dimensions have not been created to detect hierarchies. The Next button will be enabled after the Cube Wizard has analyzed the relations within the tables. Click the Next button as soon as it is enabled.

8. The Cube Wizard now shows all the dimensions that will be created by the Cube Wizard as shown in Figure 6-9. You can expand the dimensions to see the hierarchies and attributes that have been detected by the Cube Wizard for creation. Review the dimensions and hierarchies within the dimension on this page. You can deselect attributes, hierarchies and dimensions that are not needed for your cube on this page. Select the defaults on this page and click Next.

Figure 6-8

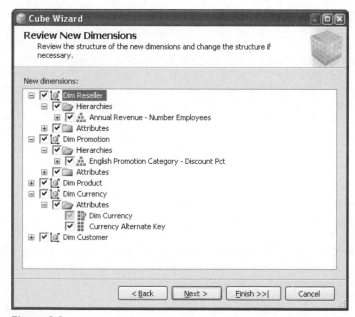

Figure 6-9

9. In the final page of the Cube Wizard (shown in Figure 6-10) you can specify the name of the cube to be created and review the measure groups, measures, dimensions, attributes and hierarchies. Use the default name Adventure Works DW suggested by the Cube Wizard and click Finish.

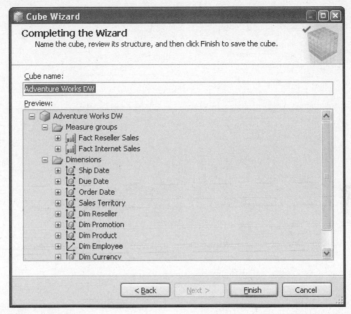

Figure 6-10

The Cube Wizard creates the dimension objects and the cube after you hit the finish button. The created cube Adventure Works DW is opened within the Cube Designer as shown in Figure 6-11. The Cube Designer contains several tabs that help perform specific operations that will refine the initial cube created by the Cube Wizard. The default tab is the Cube Structure as shown in Figure 6-11. The Cube Structure view you can see three panes that show the Measures, Dimensions, and the DSV. The DSV contains all the tables that are part of the cube. Operations such as adding or deleting tables in the DSV and zooming in or out with the DSV Designer are possible within the cube DSV. The Dimensions pane shows the dimensions that are part of the current cube and the Measures pane shows the measure groups and measures that are part of the current cube. You can add or delete measures and dimensions in the Cube Structure view. The dimensions within the cube shown in Dimensions pane are called cube dimensions. You can have multiple instances of the shared dimensions of the database within a cube. For example, the Fact tables FactInternetSales and FactResellerSales have relationship with the Dim Time dimension through Order Date, Ship Date and Due Date. Hence you can see three cube dimensions Ship Date, Due Date and Order Date in the Dimensions pane which refer to the Dim Time database dimension. A dimension such as Dim Time which plays the role of three cube dimensions is called as role playing dimension. You will learn role playing dimensions in Chapter 8. Within the Dimensions pane you have two views with which to see the Hierarchies and Attributes of each dimension.

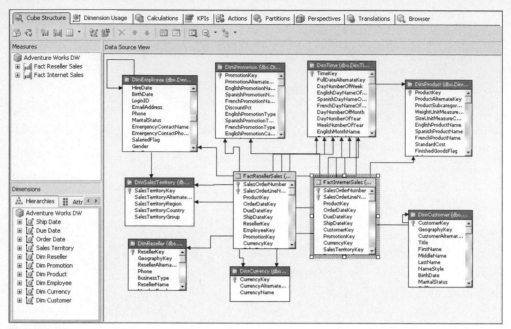

Figure 6-11

What you have done so far is created the Adventure Works DW database containing the Adventure Works cube. You have to deploy the project to the Analysis Services instance so that you can analyze the data within the cube. You can deploy the project to the server in one of the following ways:

1. Select Debug⇨Start Debugging from the menu.

2. Right click on the database AnalysisServices2005Tutorial in solution explorer and select Deploy.

3. Right-click the Adventure Works DW cube and choose Process — from which you will first be prompted to deploy the project and then followed by Process dialog to process the cube.

4. Use the shortcut key F5 to deploy and process.

When you deploy the project to the server, the BIDS sends an XML/A request containing object definitions to the default instance of the Analysis Server selected in the project. By default the Analysis Services project is deployed to the default instance of Analysis Services on your machine. The object definitions are of the cubes and dimensions you created. If you have installed your Analysis Services 2005 as a named instance, you need to change the deployment server name. The BIDS sends another request to process the objects within the database. If you are in the Cube Designer the BIDS assumes that you want to analyze the data after deployment and processing and therefore switches the Cube Designer from Cube Structure to Browser, which is discussed in the next section.

Browsing Cubes

If you deployed a cube to Analysis Services instance the BIDS switches to the Browser tab. Alternately you can open a cube in the Cube Designer and click on the Browser tab. In the Browser view you will see three panes: a Metadata pane, a Filter pane, and a Data pane along with a tool bar as shown in Figure 6-12.

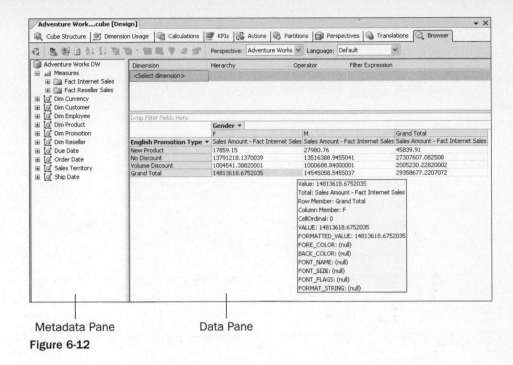

Metadata Pane   Data Pane

Figure 6-12

The Metadata pane, at the left-side pane of the Cube Browser, shows the measure groups (includes measures) and dimensions (includes attributes and hierarchies) of the cube. The Data pane, at the bottom right, is the Office Web Components (OWC) control used for analyzing multidimensional data. You can drag and drop hierarchies on the rows and/or columns and measures in the data area to analyze the data. Indeed, you can have multiple hierarchies on a rows or columns. The OWC has a filter control that can be used to filter the data being analyzed. You can slice the data you want to analyze based on specific members of a hierarchy. The top-right pane is also a filter control to slice multidimensional data for analysis, but has additional options to slice data other than the ones provided by OWC. While the filter control in OWC allows you to select or deselect members of a hierarchy the Filter pane allows you to perform comparison operations like equal, not equal, contains, in, not in, begins with, range operations, and any MDX expression. With the help of the filter controls in Filter pane and OWC, you will be able to analyze your multidimensional data.

Suppose you want to analyze the Internet sales of products based on the promotions offered to customers and the marital status of those customers. First you would need to drag and drop [Dim Promotion] .[English Promotion Type] from the metadata browser to the OWC rows. You will learn the MDX statements that are generated by OWC. SQL Server Profiler in SQL Server 2005 has the ability trace statements sent to Analysis Services instances. The MDX statements sent to the Analysis Services instance can be obtained by using SQL Server Profiler. For more information on how to obtain traces please refer to section on using SQL Server Profiler in Chapter 13.

The first statement sent from OWC to Analysis Service instance is:

```
DROP VISUAL TOTALS for [Adventure Works DW]
```

When you drag and drop members of a hierarchy on a row (or column), or a measure in the fields area, OWC creates a row (or column) called Grand Total, which will automatically provide totals of the measure value for that hierarchy. By default the OWC in Cube Browser shows you the totals of visible members of the hierarchy in the OWC. This is called Visual Totals because the total is calculated only for the members that are visible in the Browser. You have the option of disabling Visual Totals in the OWC. To do so, right-click OWC, select Command and Options, click the Report tab, and select the All Items option (including hidden items) for Calculate Totals. When OWC has the option of having a Grand Total to have the sum of visible members it uses Visual Totals. The above statement DROP VISUAL TOTAL for [Adventure Works DW] removes references to visual totals for cells and clears the memory cache for visual totals thereby ensuring values for current members selected is accurate. The full syntax for Drop Visual Totals statement is shown below where you can optionally specify the MDX set upon which the visual totals need to be dropped. If the MDX set expression is not specified the visual totals is dropped for the entire cube.

```
DROP VISUAL TOTALS FOR <cube name> [ON '<MDX set expression>']
```

The second statement sent to Analysis Server by OWC is:

```
CREATE SESSION
  SET [Adventure Works DW].[ {7868741D-072F-458A-8A8D-EA3FED4A3FA7}Pivot13Axis1Set0]
AS
    '
        {
                { [Dim Promotion].[English Promotion Type].[All] },
                AddCalculatedMembers([Dim Promotion].[English Promotion
Type].[English Promotion Type].MEMBERS)
        }
    '
```

This statement creates a set called {7868741D-072F-458A-8A8D-EA3FED4A3FA7}Pivot13Axis1Set0, which contains the members of the hierarchy [Dim Promotion].[English Promotion Type]. Since OWC creates the queries in an automated manner it includes the session id and dynamically creates a name (Pivot13Axis1Set0) that is attached along with the session id. The Analysis Server allows you to create sets and other MDX objects within a specific scope. You can create objects within the scope of the database or within the scope of your connection. In the previous statement OWC creates the set within the scope of the current session and the set will only be available for this specific session. Finally, OWC sends the following query to retrieve and show the members of the hierarchy [Dim Promotion].[English Promotion Type].

```
SELECT
  NON EMPTY [{7868741D-072F-458A-8A8D-EA3FED4A3FA7}Pivot13Axis1Set0]
  DIMENSION PROPERTIES MEMBER_NAME, PARENT_UNIQUE_NAME ON COLUMNS
  FROM [Adventure Works DW]
CELL PROPERTIES VALUE, FORMATTED_VALUE, FORE_COLOR, BACK_COLOR
```

Next, drag and drop [Dim Customer].[Marital Status] from the metadata browser to the OWC columns. OWC now sends a series of MDX statements followed by an MDX query to retrieve the members on rows and columns. The following code shows the statements sent by OWC. First OWC drops visual totals followed by creating two sets for the members of the hierarchies selected on rows and columns of the OWC. OWC then queries the members from the created sets and finally drops the earlier set Pivot13Axis1Set0 since OWC has created new sets for members on rows and columns of the OWC.

```
Drop visual totals for [Adventure Works DW]
CREATE SESSION
 SET [Adventure Works DW].[{7868741D-072F-458A-8A8D-EA3FED4A3FA7}Pivot14Axis0Set0]
AS
     '
        {
                { [Dim Customer].[Gender].[All] },
                AddCalculatedMembers([Dim Customer].[Gender].[Gender].MEMBERS)
        }
     '
 SET [Adventure Works DW].[{7868741D-072F-458A-8A8D-EA3FED4A3FA7}Pivot14Axis1Set0]
AS
     '
        {
                { [Dim Promotion].[English Promotion Type].[All] },
                AddCalculatedMembers([Dim Promotion].[English Promotion
Type].[English Promotion Type].MEMBERS)
        }
     '

SELECT
 NON EMPTY [{7868741D-072F-458A-8A8D-EA3FED4A3FA7}Pivot14Axis0Set0]
 DIMENSION PROPERTIES MEMBER_NAME, PARENT_UNIQUE_NAME ON COLUMNS,
 NON EMPTY [{7868741D-072F-458A-8A8D-EA3FED4A3FA7}Pivot14Axis1Set0]
 DIMENSION PROPERTIES MEMBER_NAME, PARENT_UNIQUE_NAME ON ROWS
 FROM [Adventure Works DW]
CELL PROPERTIES VALUE, FORMATTED_VALUE, FORE_COLOR, BACK_COLOR

DROP SET [Adventure Works DW].[{7868741D-072F-458A-8A8D-
EA3FED4A3FA7}Pivot13Axis1Set0]
```

Finally, drag and drop the measure [Sales Amount – Fact Internet Sales] to Detail Fields. OWC once again generates statements to drop existing sets and create new sets for members on rows and columns. These sets are used in the query to retrieve the measure along with the properties of the cells. The cell properties returned by the instance of Analysis Services are used by OWC to display values. From the query you can see the properties of formatted values, foreground color, and background colors are being retrieved by OWC. OWC uses the formatted value to display the cell values. The statements and query sent to Analysis Services by OWC are shown below.

```
Drop visual totals for [Adventure Works DW]

CREATE SESSION
 SET [Adventure Works DW].[{7868741D-072F-458A-8A8D-EA3FED4A3FA7}Pivot15Axis0Set0]
AS
     '
        {
                { [Dim Customer].[Gender].[All] },
                AddCalculatedMembers([Dim Customer].[Gender].[Gender].MEMBERS)
        }
     '
 SET [Adventure Works DW].[{7868741D-072F-458A-8A8D-EA3FED4A3FA7}Pivot15Axis1Set0]
AS
     '
```

```
            {
                { [Dim Promotion].[English Promotion Type].[All] },
                AddCalculatedMembers([Dim Promotion].[English Promotion
Type].[English Promotion Type].MEMBERS)
            }
        ,


SELECT
  NON EMPTY [{7868741D-072F-458A-8A8D-EA3FED4A3FA7}Pivot15Axis0Set0]
  DIMENSION PROPERTIES MEMBER_NAME, PARENT_UNIQUE_NAME ON COLUMNS,
  NON EMPTY [{7868741D-072F-458A-8A8D-EA3FED4A3FA7}Pivot15Axis1Set0]
  DIMENSION PROPERTIES MEMBER_NAME, PARENT_UNIQUE_NAME ON ROWS,
  {
        [Measures].[Sales Amount - Fact Internet Sales]
  }
  ON PAGES
  FROM [Adventure Works DW]
  CELL PROPERTIES VALUE, FORMATTED_VALUE, FORE_COLOR, BACK_COLOR

DROP SET [Adventure Works DW].[{7868741D-072F-458A-8A8D-
EA3FED4A3FA7}Pivot14Axis0Set0]

DROP SET [Adventure Works DW].[{7868741D-072F-458A-8A8D-
EA3FED4A3FA7}Pivot14Axis1Set0]
```

If you hover over a particular cell you can see the cell values without formatting, along with the row and column member values that correspond to that cell as shown in Figure 6-12.

Cube Dimensions

The Cube Wizard helps you create your cube object from the DSV by creating appropriate dimension objects. The wizard detects the relationships between dimension tables and fact table(s) in the DSV, creates appropriate dimensions if needed, and establishes appropriate relationships between the dimensions and measure groups within the cube. As mentioned in the previous section a cube contains an instance of the database dimension referred to as cube dimension. There can be multiple instances of a database dimension within a cube There exists a relationship between the cube dimension and the measure groups within the cube. In this section you will learn about various types of relationships between the cube dimensions and the measure groups within, as well as refine the Adventure Works DW cube created by Cube Wizard by addition of a new dimension.

The Cube Wizard establishes relationships between the measure groups and cube dimensions based on the analysis of relationships in the DSV. You might have to refine these relationships based on your business needs. You can change these relationships in the Dimension Usage tab of the cube editor. If you switch to the Dimension Usage tab you will see the dimensions, measure groups of the cube, and the relationships between them, as shown in Figure 6-13.

The cube dimensions and measure groups are represented in a matrix format as rows and columns, respectively, where the relationship between them corresponds to the intersection cell. The intersection cell shows the dimension type along with the attribute that is used in the relationship to join.

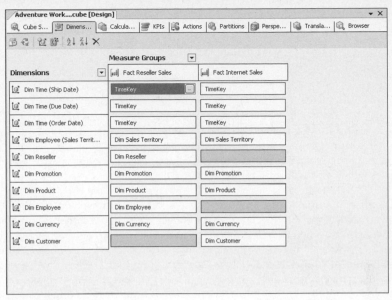

Figure 6-13

Dimension Types

Six different relationships can exist between a dimension and a measure group: No Relationship, Regular, Fact, Referenced, Many-to-Many, and Data Mining. In Figure 6-13 you see two of the six relationship types; No Relationship and Regular. Cells corresponding to a specific dimension and measure group can have an attribute specified that indicates that the dimension type is Regular. Further, such attributes can be used in the join condition between the dimension and the measure group. Often this attribute is the key attribute of the dimension and is called the *granularity attribute*. The granularity attribute can be an attribute that is above the key attribute of the dimension. When you browse a dimension along with measures of a measure group where the dimension and measure group have a regular relationship then Analysis Services aggregates the data appropriately. The relationship between Dim Customer and Fact Internet Sales measure group is a regular relationship. The granularity attribute is shown in the cell intersecting the dimension and measure group as shown in Figure 6-13.

Cells that are shaded gray indicate there is no relationship between the dimension and measure group. Whenever there is no relationship between a dimension and measure group, the measure group property IgnoreUnrelatedDimension controls the results of queries involving any hierarchy of that dimension and any measure from the measure group. The measure values will either be null (IgnoreUnrelatedDimension= False) or the same value for each member of the dimension (IgnoreUnrelatedDimension=True). For example, there is no relationship between dimension [Dim Employee] and the [Fact Internet Sales] measure group. If you browse the Gender hierarchy of [Dim Employee] and measure [Internet Sales Amount] you see that the measure values for each member of Gender hierarchy are the same value as the Grand Total as shown in Figure 6-14. This is because the IgnoreUnrelatedDimension value is set to True by the Cube Wizard as a default. You learn more about properties of measure groups and measures later in this chapter.

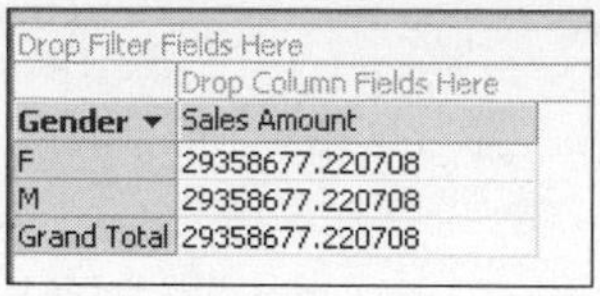

Figure 6-14

When a table is used as both a fact and dimension table, it constitutes a unique relationship between the dimension and measure group called the *fact* relationship. The relationship is similar to that of the regular dimension, but specifying it as a Fact dimension helps improve query performance for a certain class of MDX queries which you will learn more about in Chapter 9.

Typically there is a one-to-many relationship between a fact and a dimension member for regular relationships. When you have a one-to-one relationship between a fact and a dimension member, you typically have a fact relationship. When there is a many-to-many relationship between a fact and a dimension member, the dimension member has a one-to-many relationship with various facts and a single fact is associated with multiple dimension members. The definition for a many-to-many relationship can be well understood via an example. Assume you have a fact table (for sales of books data) that is related to a dimension table containing author information. There is another fact table that contains authors' salary information, which is related to the Authors dimension table as well as the geographical information of the publisher who is paying the authors. In this example you have a one-to-many relationship between authors and books. The salary fact data is related to the publisher's geographical information and the authors. If you want to analyze the book sales based on the geographical information of the publisher, the Geography dimension of publishers acts as a many-to-many relationship with the fact Book Sales. You learn the usage of fact and many-to-many relationships in Chapter 9.

Data Mining dimensions are another item type in the list of relationships; these are used to establish linkage between a cube and a dimension created from a Data Mining model. You learn more about this in Chapters 9 and 14.

When a dimension is related to the fact data through another dimension, you define this dimension as having a reference relationship with the measure group. You might recall that you added the Dim Geography dimension in the Review Shared Dimension page of the Cube Wizard. However the Cube Wizard was not smart enough to figure out there is a relationship between the Fact tables and the Dim Geography dimension table through other dimension tables. Hence the Cube Wizard did not add the Dim Geography dimension as a cube dimension. Since the relationship between the Dim Geography dimension and the measure groups in the Adventure Works DW are through another dimension you can say that there is an indirect relationship between Dim Geography dimension and the measure groups. This indirect relationship between the measure groups and dimensions is called a *reference relationship*.

Follow the steps below to add the Dim Geography dimension to the cube and establish the reference relationship:

1. To add the Dim Geography database dimension to the cube, right-click in the Dimension pane of the Cube Structure tab and select Add Cube Dimension, as shown in Figure 6-15.

2. A dialog showing all the shared dimensions within the project launches, as shown in Figure 6-16. Select the Geography dimension and click OK.

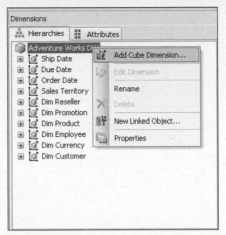

Figure 6-15

Figure 6-16

3. The cube editor identifies a default relationship through an attribute between existing measure groups and the Geography dimension and defines a relationship. If you go to the Dimension Usage page you will see the relationship established by the editor as shown in Figure 6-17. This cube editor has established a regular relationship with the attribute Dim Sales Territory with both the measure groups. The BIDS detects there are columns named Sales Territory key in the dimension table Dim Geography as well as both the fact tables. Since the column names are matching it establishes a regular relationship. However if you look at the fact and dimension tables and the relationships in the DSV you will notice this is an incorrect relationship. There exists an indirect relationship between Dim Geography dimension and Fact Internet Sales measure group through the Dim Customer dimension. There is an indirect relationship between Dim Geography dimension and the Fact Reseller measure group through the Dim Reseller dimension. You need to define a reference relationship.

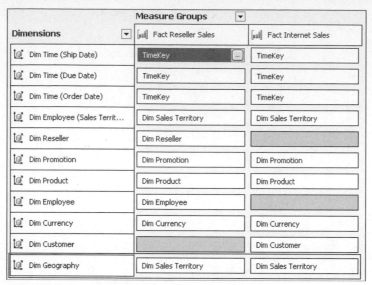

Figure 6-17

4. To define the relationship between [Dim Geography] and [Fact Internet Sales] measure group, select the corresponding cell in the matrix and you will see an ellipses in that cell. Click the ellipsis ("..."). This opens the Define Relationship dialog shown in Figure 6-18. Select Referenced from the Select Relationship Type drop-down list box. The [Dim Geography] dimension forms an indirect or reference relationship with the [Fact Internet Sales] measure group through the [Dim Customer] dimension. You define the intermediate dimension through the Intermediate Dimension option. Once you have defined the intermediate dimension, you need to select the attributes that are involved in the join of the relationship. Reference Dimension Attribute is the attribute in the reference dimension that is used in the join between the intermediate dimension ([Dim Geography]) and the reference dimension ([Dim Customer]). The Intermediate Dimension Attribute is an attribute of the intermediate dimension that is involved in the join between the reference dimension and the intermediate dimension. Define the Intermediate dimension as Dim Customer, Reference dimension attribute as Dim Geography, and Intermediate dimension attribute as Geography Key as shown in Figure 6-18 and click OK.

In Figure 6-18 you see a check box with text Materialize. This check box is enabled by default. By enabling this check box you are ensuring Analysis Services will build appropriate indexes so that get improved query performance while querying fact data along with reference dimension hierarchies.

5. Similar to step 4, establish a referenced relationship between the [Dim Geography] dimension and the [Fact Reseller Sales] measure group through the [Dim Reseller] dimension. Once you have completed specifying the relationship between [Dim Geography] and the two measure groups of the cube, your Dimension Usage tab will resemble Figure 6-19.

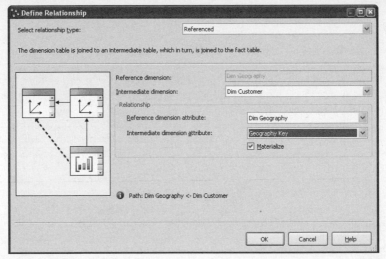

Figure 6-18

Dimensions	Measure Groups	
	Fact Reseller Sales	Fact Internet Sales
Dim Time (Ship Date)	TimeKey	TimeKey
Dim Time (Due Date)	TimeKey	TimeKey
Dim Time (Order Date)	TimeKey	TimeKey
Dim Employee (Sales Territ...	Dim Sales Territory	Dim Sales Territory
Dim Reseller	Dim Reseller	
Dim Promotion	Dim Promotion	Dim Promotion
Dim Product	Dim Product	Dim Product
Dim Employee	Dim Employee	
Dim Currency	Dim Currency	Dim Currency
Dim Customer		Dim Customer
Dim Geography	Dim Reseller	Dim Customer

Figure 6-19

The reference relationship between a dimension and a measure group is indicated by an arrow pointing to the intermediate dimension as shown in Figure 6-19. This graphical view of the reference relationship helps you identify the type of relationship between a dimension and measure group when you are looking at the Dimension Usage tab of the cube editor. Similar graphical representations are available for fact, many-to-many, and Data Mining dimensions, and you learn about these relationships in later Chapters 9 and 14.

Browsing Reference Dimensions

Having added the [Dim Geography] dimension as the reference dimension to the cube, assume you want to analyze the Reseller Sales based on different business types in various countries. To do so you need to go to the Cube Browser and drag and drop the English Country Region Name hierarchy from the [Dim Geography] dimension to the rows, the Business Type hierarchy of Dim Reseller dimension to the columns, and the measure Sales Amount of the Fact Reseller Sales measure group to the details area. You can now analyze the Sales data based on the business type in each country, as shown in Figure 6-20. Based on this sales knowledge, the costs associated with the products, and your business goals, you can strategically promote the business type yielding the maximum profit for your company. Reference dimensions help you to analyze fact data even though they are not directly related to the facts.

Drop Filter Fields Here				
	Business Type ▼			
	Specialty Bike Shop	Value Added Reseller	Warehouse	Grand Total
English Country Region Name ▼	Sales Amount	Sales Amount	Sales Amount	Sales Amount
Australia	327171.5382	799552.060499997	467611.778	1594335.3767
Canada	1216909.29569999	4855218.34759999	8305797.95319992	14377925.5965001
France	418643.6974	948247.751599999	3240646.48599999	4607537.93499999
Germany	164090.0319	625523.4215	1194374.5839	1983988.03729999
United Kingdom	330178.3808	1793112.8225	2155717.6233	4279008.82659999
United States	4299173.23570002	25945862.9237999	23362765.0507001	53607801.2102
Grand Total	6756166.17970001	34967517.3274999	38726913.4751	80450596.9823001

Figure 6-20

OWC sends the following statements and queries to retrieve data for analyzing the reseller sales fact of various business types across in various countries of the resellers. OWC creates sets for the members on the columns and rows of OWC and then queries the facts added to the detail data along with the sets.

```
Drop visual totals for [Adventure Works DW]

CREATE SESSION
  SET [Adventure Works DW].[{76D2D6C7-D50B-4C12-8DBF-DA53595646F5}Pivot24Axis0Set0]
AS

    '      {
              { [Dim Reseller].[Business Type].[All] },
              AddCalculatedMembers([Dim Reseller].[Business Type].[Business
Type].MEMBERS)
         }
  '
  SET [Adventure Works DW].[{76D2D6C7-D50B-4C12-8DBF-DA53595646F5}Pivot24Axis1Set0]
AS
  '
         {
              { [Dim Geography].[English Country Region Name].[All] },
              AddCalculatedMembers([Dim Geography].[English Country Region
Name].[English Country Region Name].MEMBERS)
         }
  '

SELECT
  NON EMPTY [{76D2D6C7-D50B-4C12-8DBF-DA53595646F5}Pivot24Axis0Set0]
```

```
   DIMENSION PROPERTIES MEMBER_NAME, PARENT_UNIQUE_NAME ON COLUMNS,
   NON EMPTY [{76D2D6C7-D50B-4C12-8DBF-DA53595646F5}Pivot24Axis1Set0]
   DIMENSION PROPERTIES MEMBER_NAME, PARENT_UNIQUE_NAME ON ROWS,
   {
          [Measures].[Sales Amount]
   }
   ON PAGES
   FROM [Adventure Works DW]
   CELL PROPERTIES VALUE, FORMATTED_VALUE, FORE_COLOR, BACK_COLOR


   DROP SET [Adventure Works DW].[{76D2D6C7-D50B-4C12-8DBF-
   DA53595646F5}Pivot23Axis0Set0]

   DROP SET [Adventure Works DW].[{76D2D6C7-D50B-4C12-8DBF-
   DA53595646F5}Pivot23Axis1Set0]
```

OWC provides you with the option of slicing the data you are analyzing. Therefore OWC creates the MDX statements to create sets within the specified session. It then queries the multidimensional data on three different axes and displays them on the Rows, Columns, and Fields area. Because the query used by the OWC control retrieves data on three-dimensional axes, you cannot execute the same query in SQL Server Management Studio (SSMS). SSMS will only be able to display two-dimensional results. Therefore if you need to see the exact same results in SSMS, you need an MDX query that will retrieve results in a two-dimensional format. The MDX query generated by OWC can be re-written using the CrossJoin function or the cross join operator * so that the results can be retrieved on two axes. The simplified MDX query that will return the same results as the OWC is:

```
   SELECT
   {
          [Measures].[Sales Amount]
   }
   ON COLUMNS,
   NON EMPTY {[Dim Reseller].[Business Type].members  *
   [Dim Geography].[English Country Region Name].members}
   DIMENSION PROPERTIES MEMBER_NAME ON ROWS
   FROM [Adventure Works DW]
   CELL PROPERTIES VALUE, FORMATTED_VALUE, FORE_COLOR, BACK_COLOR
```

So far you have learned about Cube dimensions, how to add them to a cube, define relationships and then query data along with the dimensions. Cube dimensions and their attributes and hierarchies contain several properties. Some properties such as AttributeHierarchyEnabled, AttributeHierarchyVisible, and the AttributeHiearchyOptimizedState reflect the state of the cube dimension hierarchies or attributes in the shared dimension by default. You can override these properties so that appropriate settings are applied for the cube dimensions within the cube. The properties AggregationUsage for attributes and AllMember AggregationUsage for cube dimensions control the behavior of aggregations designed on the cube. You learn more about these properties in Chapters 9 and 13.

Measures and Measure Groups

You learned about editing cubes dimensions and establishing the right relationships between dimensions and measure groups in a cube. Similarly, you can add or delete objects called measures and measure groups in a cube. Measures are the focus point for data analysis and therefore they are the core objects of a cube. Measures are columns from the fact table that contain meaningful information for data analysis. Usually measures are of type numeric and can be aggregated or summarized along hierarchies of a dimension. You can specify the type of aggregation that needs to be applied for each measure. You can apply several types of aggregate functions to each measure. The most widely used aggregate functions are Sum, Count, and Distinct Count. A collection of measures forms an object called a measure group, and a collection of measure groups forms the dimension called *Measures* in the cube. Measures is a keyword in Analysis Services that refers to a special dimension that only contains the fact data.

If you click the Cube Structure tab in the cube editor you will see the Measures pane on the top-left corner. Click the cube named Adventure Works DW within the Measures pane to see the associated properties in the Properties window located on the bottom-right corner of the BIDS. Figure 6-21 shows the Measures and Properties panes. The Measures pane shows the cube name and the measure groups within the cube. You can see the two measure groups Fact Reseller Sales and Fact Internet Sales that correspond to the two fact tables. Fact table columns that become measures of the cube are contained within the corresponding measure group. There is typically a one-to-one relationship between a fact table and measure group in the cube.

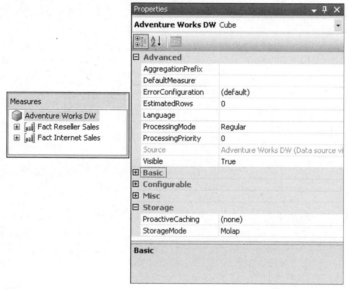

Figure 6-21

In your source data, if you had partitioned your fact data into multiple fact tables across a specific dimension, that needs to be handled differently while designing the cube. For example, if you have Fact Internet Sales data stored in separate fact tables for each quarter (fact data has been partitioned into multiple fact tables across the Time dimension), then with respect to the cube all these are considered a single fact table because they have the same schema. You have partitioned your relational fact data into multiple fact tables due to design or scalability considerations, but when you want to analyze the data you will be looking forward to aggregating the data appropriately across various dimensions, especially the Time dimension. You can either merge the data from all the fact tables within the DSV with a named query or you can utilize the partitioning feature in Analysis Services so that Analysis Services aggregates the data correctly during browsing. You learn more about partitions in Chapters 12 and 13.

You can see several properties of the cube in Figure 6-21. The most important property is DefaultMeasure. As the name indicates, this property is used to define the measure used by default whenever queries are sent to the cube. The reason why the default measure is important is that whenever your MDX query does not contain the explicit measures specified, the default measure is returned. In addition to that, the default measure is used whenever restrictions are applied in the query with the WHERE clause, and based on the default measure your results can be different. If you select the DefaultMeasure property you can see a drop-down list box that shows all the measures of the cube. You can choose the measure you want to define as the default measure of the cube. If the default measure is not specified, the first measure of the first measure group of the cube (as seen in the Measures pane) will be the default measure of the cube.

The next most important property is the StorageMode property. This defines whether your fact data will be stored on Analysis Services or your relational data source or both. The Storage mode has three different options: Multidimensional OLAP (MOLAP), Relational OLAP (ROLAP), and Hybrid OLAP (HOLAP). The default value is MOLAP, which means that when the cube is processed Analysis Services reads the relational data and stores it in a proprietary format for fast retrieval. You learn more about the defining storage modes in Chapter 9. In Analysis Services 2005, you have the option to instruct the server to automatically update cube and dimension objects if there was a change in the relational data. The ProactiveCaching property helps in controlling the frequency of the update of the cube data based on changes in the relational data. You learn more about the ProactiveCaching with the help a complete scenario in Chapter 18. The ErrorConfiguration property helps in handling the various errors that can occur while processing the fact data and defining what actions should be taken under such error circumstances such to ignore the error, converting to a specific value or stopping processing when errors are encountered. One of the main features of an OLAP database is the ability to create aggregations that facilitate fast query response times. The AggregationPrefix property is used to prefix the name of the aggregations that are created for the cube. The remaining properties are self-explanatory and you can find detailed information for each property in Analysis Services 2005 product documentation.

If you click one of the measure groups, you will see the properties associated with that measure group. Most of the properties at the cube level are also applicable to the measure group. If you specify a value for a property at the cube level as well as the measure group level for a common property, the value specified at the measure group level will be honored by the server. Expand the measure group Fact Internet Sales and select the measure Sales Amount – Fact Internet Sales. The Properties pane now shows the properties of a measure, as shown in Figure 6-22. Now let us learn the important properties for the measures in detail.

The AggregateFunction property defines how the measure value is to be aggregated from one level to another level of a hierarchy in a dimension. For example, the Product dimension contains a hierarchy called Products that contains two levels, Model Name and Product Name. Each model contains one or more products. If you want the sales of a specific product to be aggregated to the model, you need to specify the aggregate function to be Sum. Whenever you browse the cube along the Products hierarchy, you will see that the sales of each product are aggregated to the corresponding model. However, sometimes you might not want the measure value to be aggregated while browsing a hierarchy. Therefore, Analysis Services 2005 provides you with several aggregate functions.

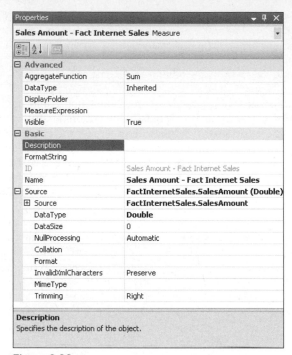

Figure 6-22

Other than the Sum aggregate function the most commonly used aggregate functions are Count and Distinct Count. The Count aggregate function, as the name indicates, is used whenever you want to count each occurrence of the measure value rather than add the measure values. For example, if you want to find the number of transactions in a day or number of customers in a day, you would use a Count aggregate function on a fact table column that indicates the customers who came to the store on a specific day. The Distinct Count aggregate function, on the other hand, can be used to identify the unique number of occurrences of a specific measure. For example, a customer can buy a specific product every month. If you want to find the unique number of customers who purchase a specific product, you use the Distinct Count aggregate function. You will see examples of Count and Distinct Count aggregate functions in this section. The None aggregate function is used when you do not want to aggregate the values of a specific measure across a dimension. An example of where the None aggregate function would be used is for the price of a specific product or discount provided on a unit product.

When you build and browse a cube you will see all the measures occurring under the dimension called [Measures] in the Metadata pane of the Cube Browser. If you want to organize the related measures in a logical structure that is more meaningful for the customers, you use the property called DisplayFolder. You can specify a measure to be part of one or more display folders by editing the DisplayFolder property. If you enter a name in the DisplayFolder property, that specific measure will become part of the newly entered display folder. You can make a specific measure part of multiple display folders by specifying the display folders separated by a semicolon. When display folders are specified then while browsing the cube you will see the display folders under the appropriate measure group name in the metadata pane of the Browser. Therefore you cannot have measures from different measure groups under a single display folder.

In some business applications you only allow access to the aggregated results of a measure. For such applications you need a way to aggregate the results of a measure but do not want to show the base measure. You can aggregate the results of a measure by specifying a measure called the calculated measure (you learn more about calculations a little later in this chapter) and hide the base measure. The measure property Visible allows you to hide the base measure from viewing for such applications.

The FormatString property allows you to show the measure value in a format of your choice. If you select the FormatString property you will see the various format options available. The MeasureExpression property is used for specifying expression that evaluate the value for the measure. For example if you have Sales information you might want to ensure the Sales information is presented in the local currency based on the currency conversion rates. In such a case you will define appropriate expression for measure expression property for the measure Sales. You learn about the MeasureExpression property in Chapter 9.

The easiest way to see the effect of some of the properties mentioned is to try them yourself in your own project. Specify two display folders named DisplayFolder1 and DisplayFolder2 for the measure Sales Amount. Because the measure Sales Amount – Fact Internet Sales is a currency data type, you can select the currency format. Select the #,#.0 format from the FormatString property drop-down list. The properties window for the measure Sales Amount – Fact Internet Sales should resemble the Figure 6-23.

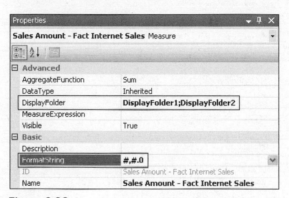

Figure 6-23

You learned examples of where the aggregate functions Count and Distinct Count can be useful. In your Adventure Works DW project if you want to count the number of customers and distinct customers who have bought specific products, you need to use these aggregate functions. Customer Key identifies the customer who has bought a specific product in the fact table. Therefore in order to see the counts of customers you need to create two new measures using the fact table column Customer Key. To create the two new measures follow the steps below.

1. Drag and drop the Customer Key column from the Fact Internet Sales table in the DSV of the cube editor to the Measures pane. A measure called Customer Key is now created. In the Properties pane change the name for this measure from Customer Key to Distinct Customers by right clicking on the measure selecting Rename. Change the aggregate function for this measure to be Distinct Count.

2. Drag and drop the Customer Key column once again from the DSV to the Measures pane. A measure called Customer Key is created. Rename the Customer Key to Total Customers and change the aggregate function from Sum to Count.

3. The Unit Price – Fact Internet Sales of a product is the same value. Therefore this value should not be aggregated. In order to see the same value for a specific product you need to choose the aggregate function FirstNonEmpty.

4. Create a hierarchy called Products in the Dim Product dimension with two levels Model Name and English Product Name. Rename the level English Product Name as Product Name.

5. Deploy the project to the Analysis Services instance.

Once the deployment is completed you will be in the Browser tab. When you expand the Measures folder you will see two folders called DisplayFolder1 and DisplayFolder2 that contain the measure Sales Amount as shown in Figure 6-24. You might recall that we mentioned you cannot have measures from multiple measure groups grouped under the same display folder. Display folders specified for a measure are always expected to be within the scope of the measure group. However due to minor issue in BIDS Browser you can see that the second display folder DisplayFolder2 specified for a measure is not under the measure group as shown in Figure 6-24. You can in fact specify multiple display folders for a measure and thereby have measures from various measure groups grouped under the same display folder. However display folders are expected to be used by client tools and based on the client tool you are using you might not be able to do this. This tip is helpful only while using BIDS and the issue is expected to be fixed in future releases of the product.

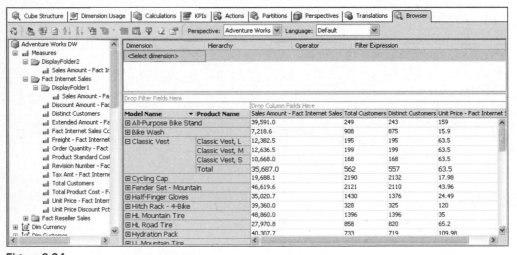

Figure 6-24

Drag and drop the measures Sales Amount – Fact Internet Sales, Total Customers, Unit Price – Internet Sales Amount and Distinct Customers to the data area of the OWC. Then drag and drop the hierarchy Products from the Dim Product dimension to the rows and expand the member Classic Vest. You can now see that the values for the measures are aggregated for the hierarchy Products that contains two levels, Model Name and Product Name, based on the aggregate function chosen. Choosing the aggregate functions Count and Distinct Count will not only count the values for the members of a hierarchy, but will also aggregate the counts to the next level. You can see that the Unit Price – Internet Sales Amount is aggregated from the members in the Product Name level to Model Name level based on FirstNonEmpty aggregate function. You see the Total value for the measure Unit Price – Fact Internet Sales for Classic Vest model as 63.5. The Unit Price value shown for the Model-100 model name is the Unit Price Mountain-100 Silver 42, one of the members of the Model-100. In the example shown in Figure 6-24, all the products under the model name Classic Vest have the same unit price. If you expand the Model Name member Mountain-100 you will see different values for the Products under the model Mountain-100. If these were different values, you could see the effect of this aggregate function. Notice that the values of Sales Amount are formatted based on the format string you specified earlier.

You have now successfully enhanced the cube created by the Cube Wizard by adding cube dimensions and measures to the cube. In the process you have also learned about the properties of cube dimensions, measures, and measure groups. Most often businesses need complex logic to analyze the relational data. Analysis Services 2005 provides you with the ability to embed the complex calculations required for solving business problems in several ways. The most basic operation that every business will need is creating simple arithmetic operations on the base measures or dimension members. Objects created via such operations are called calculated members.

Calculated Members

The term *calculated member* refers to the creation of any MDX object through a calculation. The calculated member can be part of the Measures dimension where a simple MDX expression such as addition or subtraction of two or more base measures results in a new measure. Such calculated members on the Measures dimension are referred to as *calculated measures*. You can also create calculated members on other dimensions by specifying an MDX expression. These members are simply referred to as calculated members. To create a calculated member, click the Calculations tab of the cube editor. This takes you to the Calculations view, as shown in Figure 6-25. The Calculations view contains three window panes: Script Organizer, Calculation Tools, and Script.

The Script Organizer window pane shows the name of the calculation objects of the cube. Various types of calculations can be created in the Calculations view and one of them is the calculated member or calculated measure. You can apply a name to a subset of dimension members that is referred to as named sets. In addition to calculated members and named sets, you can define a script containing complex MDX expressions to perform complex business logic calculations. If you right-click within the Script Organizer you can see the selections to create a calculated member, named set, or a script command. These operations can also be performed by clicking the icons in the toolbar as indicated in Figure 6-25. You create calculated measures in this chapter, and the creation of named sets and script commands is detailed in Chapter 9.

The Calculation Tools window is identical to the Metadata browser window you have become familiar with in the Browser view. The Calculation Tools window contains three tabs: Metadata, Functions, and Templates. The Metadata view shows the measures and dimensions of the current cube. The Functions view shows all the MDX functions along with a template of the arguments needed for each function. In the Templates view you can see the templates for some of the common calculations used for certain applications such as budgeting and financial.

The Script window pane shows the details of the calculations. The default view of the Script window is called the Form view. The Script window can be toggled to a different view called the Script view. If you are in the Form view, the Script Organizer window will be visible and you can see the calculations of each object in the Script command window. If the Script window is switched to the Script view (using the appropriate icon) then all the calculations are shown as a single script and the Script Organizer pane becomes invisible. You can toggle between the two views by clicking the icons shown in Figure 6-25 or by selecting the option through the menu item Cube⇨Show Calculations In, which contains options for Script or Form views.

New Named Set

New | New | Form View | Calculation Properties
Calculated | Script
Member | Command | Script View | Change User

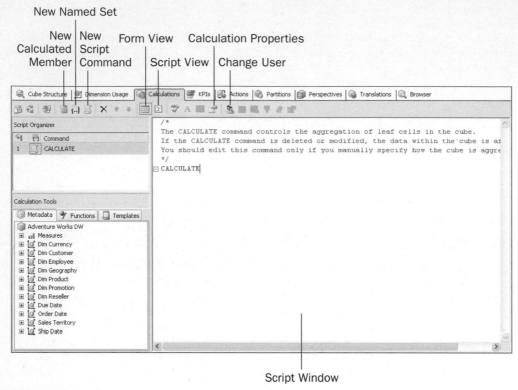

Script Window

Figure 6-25

*All commands and selections available in Analysis Services 2005 are accessible via keyboard controls.
You can switch between the three panes of the Script tab of the Cube Designer using the F6 function key
and making the appropriate selection via menu items.*

Calculated Measures

Calculated measures are the most common type of calculated members created in a cube. In your project
you have the measures Sales and Product Cost in the two measure groups, Internet Sales and Reseller
Sales. An important question to ask about any business concerns profits gained. Profit gained is the difference between total sales and cost of goods sold. In the Adventure Works DW cube you have created
you have Sales through Internet as well as Reseller. Therefore you need to add these to sales amounts to
calculate the total sales of products. Similarly, you need to calculate the total product cost by adding the
costs of products sold through Internet and Reseller. Two calculated measures must be formed to perform these operations. Once you have created these two calculations, you can calculate the profit. Follow
the steps below to create the calculated measure for profit.

1. Right-click in the Script command window and select New Calculated Member, as shown in
    Figure 6-26.

    An object called Calculated Member is created in the Script command window. The Script win-
    dow now shows several text boxes for you to specify the name of the calculation, the MDX
    expression for the calculated member, and certain properties for the calculated member.

Figure 6-26

2. Specify the name of the calculated member as [Total Sales Amount] in the Script window. In the Expression text box you need to type the MDX expression that will calculate the Total Sales Amount. As mentioned earlier, the Total Sales Amount is the sum of sales from the sales amounts in Fact Internet Sales and Fact Reseller Sales measures groups. Drag and drop these measures from the Metadata window and add the MDX operator "+" between these measures as shown in Figure 6-27.

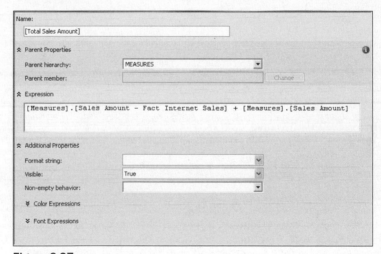

Figure 6-27

3. For cost of goods sold, create a new calculated measure called [Total Product Costs] using a method similar to the one described in step 2 but with appropriate Product Cost measures from the two measure groups.

4. Create a calculated measure called Profit. The MDX expression to evaluate Profit is the difference of the calculated measures you have created in steps 2 and 3. Enter the MDX expression [Measures].[Total Sales Amount] – [Measures].[Total Product Costs] in the Expression text box as shown in Figure 6-28.

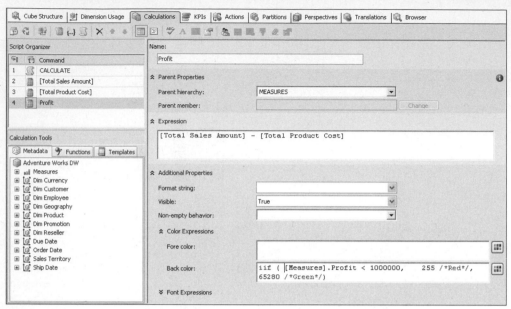

Figure 6-28

5. You have the option of specifying certain additional properties for the calculated measures you have created based on an MDX expression. By default all the calculated measures created are visible. You can specify color, font, and format strings for the calculated measures based on certain conditions. For example, if you want to highlight the profit in red if the amount is less than one million dollars and in green if it is greater than or equal to one million, you can do so by specifying the appropriate background color for the calculated member. Enter the following MDX expression for the background color:

```
iif (
[Measures].Profit < 1000000,     255 /*Red*/,
        65280 /*Green*/)
```

The MDX expression uses the IIF function. This function takes three arguments. The first argument is an expression that should evaluate to true or false. The return value of the iif function is either the second or the third argument passed to the function. If the result of the expression is true, the IIF function returns the second argument; if the expression is false, it returns the third argument. The first argument passed to the IIF function is to see if the profit is less than one million. If second and third arguments passed to the function are the values for the colors red and green. The values for the colors can be selected by clicking the color icon next to the background color text box.

6. To see the effect of the calculations you have created, go to the Cube Browser tab and deploy the project. As soon as the deployment is complete you will be asked to reconnect to the server in the Cube Browser. Reconnect to the server. If you expand the Measures folder you will see the calculated measures you have created. Drag and drop the measure Profit to the OWC detail area, hierarchy English Country Region name of the Dim Geography dimension on rows and hierarchy Style of the Dim Product dimension on columns. You will see the background color for the cells are either red or green based on the Profit value as shown in Figure 6-29.

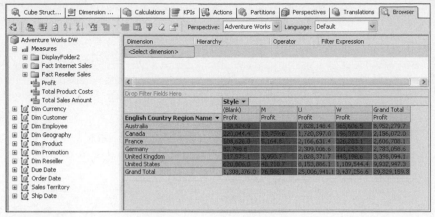

Figure 6-29

Querying Calculated Measures

You can query the calculated measures similar to other measures in the cube by referencing them with the name. For example, if you want to query the calculated member Profit based on Model Name, you execute the following query.

```
SELECT [Measures].[Profit] on COLUMNS,
[Dim Product].[Model Name].MEMBERS on ROWS
FROM [Adventure Works DW]
```

If you want to retrieve all the measures in the cube instead of specifying each measure, you use [Measures].MEMBERS. However, calculated members are not returned when you select [Measures].Members. You need to execute the following MDX query to retrieve the base measures along with the calculated members:

```
SELECT [Measures].ALLMEMBERS on COLUMNS,
[Dim Product].[Model Name].MEMBERS on ROWS
FROM [Adventure Works DW]
```

You have enhanced the Adventure Works DW cube by creating calculated measures and learned to set certain properties for the calculated measures via MDX expressions. The NonEmptyBehavior property for calculated measures is discussed in Chapters 7 and 13 along with creation of named sets and script commands.

Creating Perspectives

Analysis Services 2005 provides you with the option of creating a cube that combines many fact tables. Each cube dimension can contain several attributes and hierarchies. Even though the cube might contain all the relevant data for business analysis combined into a single object, the users of the cube might only be interested in sections of the cube. For example you can have a cube that contains sales and budgeting information of a company. The Sales department is only interested in viewing sales-relevant data, whereas the users involved in budgeting or forecasting next year's revenue are only interested in budget-relevant sections of the cube. Typically, users do not like to see too much extra information. In order to accommodate this, Analysis Services 2005 provides you with the option of creating a view of a cube that only contains a subset of objects within the cube, called a *perspective*.

In the Adventure Works DW cube you have created you have two fact tables, FactInternetSales and FactResellerSales. To understand the behavior of perspectives, create a perspective for Internet Sales and a perspective for Reseller Sales. The cube itself is the default perspective. The following steps show you how to create new perspectives:

1. Click the Perspective tab in the Cube Designer. You will see a column on the left showing the measures, dimensions, and calculated members as shown in Figure 6-30.

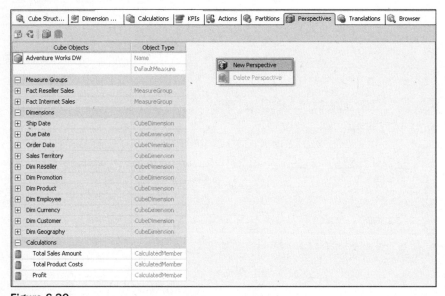

Figure 6-30

2. Right-click in the window pane and select New Perspective as shown in Figure 6-30. You can also create a new perspective by clicking the icon in the toolbar. A new column with the name Perspective is created. You have a checkbox next to each object in the cube and these are selected by default. Rename the perspective Internet Sales. Deselect the Fact Reseller Sales measure group and the dimensions Dim Employee and Dim Reseller.

3. Create another perspective called Reseller Sales. Deselect the Fact Internet Sales measure group and Dim Customer.

Your Perspective window will now look similar to Figure 6-31. Now deploy the project. The BIDS sends the definitions for the new perspectives to the server. Perspectives are not new cubes on the server, but only a view of the main cube object. Keep in mind that these are represented as different cubes with the cube names represented as the perspective name when a client queries for the cube in a database.

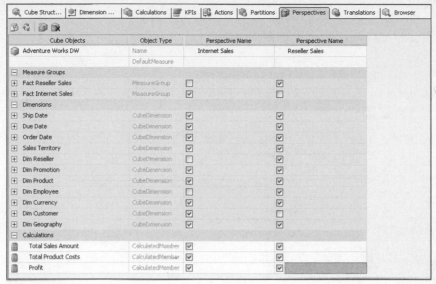

Figure 6-31

In Chapter 5 you learned to specify translations to attributes in a dimension. Similarly, you can create translations for the cube. You see the effect of perspectives along with translations after learning how to create translations for a cube.

Creating Translations

Translations facilitate display of data and metadata in a regional language. Unlike translations for dimensions (a column is specified in the relational table that contains the translation for members of an attribute hierarchy), in the cube translations are specified for the cube metadata objects.

To create a new translation for the Adventure Works DW cube, do the following:

1. Click the Translations tab in the cube editor. Similar to the Perspective view, the left column shows the names of all the metadata objects in the default language. There is another column that indicates the object type, which indicates Caption because defining translations for a cube is only providing translated names for the metadata object names.

2. Right-click in the Translation window pane and select New Translation. You can also create a new translation using the icon in the toolbar. The Select Language dialog box appears. Select French (France) as the language. You now have a new column where you can provide the translations of each object (measure, display folders, dimension name, attribute names). If you know French or you want to key in the translations in a language of your choice, you can do so. If you want to experiment with French you can specify the French translations, as shown in Figure 6-32. You can define translations for each metadata object in the cube such as measure names, measure group names, dimension names, perspective names, as well as calculated member names.

3. Deploy the project to Analysis Server.

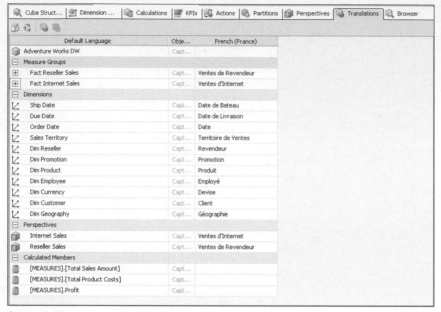

Figure 6-32

Browsing Perspectives and Translations

You have successfully created perspectives and translations for the Adventure Works DW object. To see the effect you need to be in the Browser tab of the Cube Designer. In the Browser, if you click the Perspective drop-down list box you will see three perspectives: Adventure Works DW, Internet Sales, and Reseller Sales. Select the Internet Sales perspective. If you expand the measures in the Metadata window you will notice that all the measures relevant to the reseller are now not visible. Drag and drop the Sales Amount – Fact Internet Sales, English Product Name hierarchy in the Dim Product dimension, and the English Education Name hierarchy of the Dim Customer dimension to the OWC browser. You will see the sales amount data along with product names and education of customers as shown in Figure 6-33.

To see the translated names in French you need to select the language French (France) in the Cube Browser. As soon as you select the French (France) language you will notice that all the metadata and data members for the hierarchies in the OWC automatically change to values in French, as shown in Figure 6-34. Thus you have created translated values in French for a French client who wants to analyze the same values, but who would be able to understand and interpret the results better in French than English. Each language has a corresponding id called the locale id. When you select a specific language in the Browser BIDS connects to the server with the corresponding locale id for the language. Analysis Services automatically provides you with the metadata and data corresponding to the locale id whenever queries are sent to the server on the same connection.

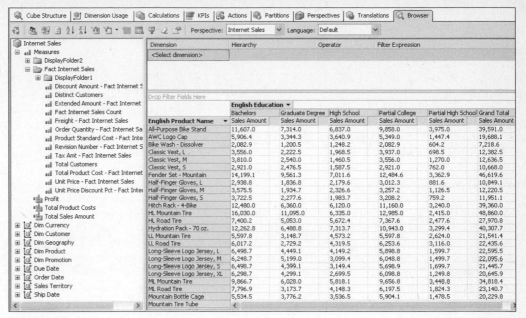

Figure 6-33

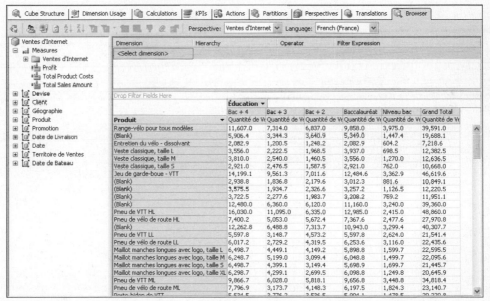

Figure 6-34

Instead of creating new cubes for various users and clients understanding different languages and the overhead of maintaining the cubes in each language, Analysis Services 2005 provides you with the functionality through the perspectives and translations features.

Summary

You traversed the Cube Wizard for a second time in this book, but also at a much lower level of granularity and hopefully with a lot more understanding of what was going on. You learned how to create calculated members and set properties concerning the display of those members; for example, different color foregrounds and backgrounds. And finally, you learned how to create and browse perspectives and translations. In the real world of business, you will have additional enhancement requirements to meet after running the Cube Wizard. These requirements may include creating calculated members on dimensions, creating cube scripts containing complex MDX expressions to meet your business needs, and adding Key Performance Indicators (KPIs), which will graphically represent the state of your business in real time. The Cube Designer contains additional tabs for KPIs and Actions. These features help enhance your cubes for business analysis. In addition to that, the Cube Designer helps in partitioning fact data, and defining aggregations which in turn, help you achieve improved performance while querying your UDM. These are covered in Chapter 9, with additional coverage in other chapters as well.

Part II
Advanced Topics

Advanced Topics in MDX

This chapter follows up on and extends what you learned back in Chapter 3: the basic concepts of the MDX language and how to write MDX queries. You also learned about the MDX operators and functions that are supported by the MDX language; including calculated member and named sets creation. If you are thinking, "that was so four chapters ago, I already forgot everything!" you might want to go back and review the material before continuing here. In Analysis Services 2005 majority of the calculations are defined as a script called MDX scripts. MDX scripts constitute complex calculations on multidimensional data which consist of MDX statements. CALCULATE, SCOPE, IF-THEN-ELSE and CASE are some of the MDX statements that are used within MDX scripts that help you define complex calculations that affect cube data. MDX scripts are structured in a way that the flow of the statements are simple and readable. The scripting language itself is based on a procedural programming model and although it may sound complex, it is actually simpler to use than certain predecessor technologies. This is due to simplifications in syntax. You can actually step through statements in MDX scripts and see results formulated in real-time; a real boon to the debugging process which you learn in chapter 9.

Of particular importance for successful MDX Script usage is an understanding and mastery of the various ways calculation order can be specified. In this chapter, you learn more about that functionality — specifically, about how calculations are implemented and evaluated in Analysis Services 2005 using MDX scripts. There is a new flow model that replaces explicit manipulation of solve order and calculation pass precedence which were used for ordering calculation is Analysis Services 2000. Additionally, this chapter provides you with examples of common MDX queries that users could write to solve real business problems. These examples are created for use with the sample Adventure Works DW project that ships with the product. For details on the process of debugging calculations, see Chapter 9, which covers this and other advanced topics related to cubes. Some of the MDX queries you will need to write to solve business problems necessitate the use of cube space restriction, empty cell removal, and parameterized queries — all concepts covered in this chapter.

Calculation Fundamentals

At the core of the Analysis Services engine is the ability to model various complex business problems using calculations. In Analysis Services 2000, calculations were based on dimensions such that each dimension typically contained one or more multilevel hierarchies. The calculation model of Analysis Services 2005 differs from the previous version because it combines the traditional OLAP and relational worlds. That combination occurs by leveraging the Unified Dimensional Model through attribute hierarchies (which are entities within a dimension). The attributes and the relationships between the attributes form the basis of the calculation model. The hierarchies (attribute or multilevel) are a way of navigating the dimensional space. Attribute hierarchies typically have two levels, the optional "All" level and another level that contains all the members of the attributes. Hence cells in the cube space can be accessed directly through the attribute hierarchies or multilevel hierarchies, and you will get the same results. Most of the calculation definitions for a cube are defined within an entity called MDX Script, which is part of every cube object. Some calculations are specified as properties of dimension attributes. Even while defining security for various hierarchies within a dimension, you specify the security restrictions through the attribute hierarchies of the dimension. Hence, attributes form the fundamental building blocks for all calculations in Analysis Services 2005.

MDX Scripts

MDX Scripts contains a set of MDX Statements separated by semicolon. MDX Scripts typically contain the calculations that need to be applied to a cube including creation of calculated members, named sets and calculations for the cells in Analysis Services 2005 cubes. The cube is populated based on the calculations defined in the cube. Users of the cube can have different security permissions defined for dimensions and cubes within a database (you learn about securing data in chapters 9 and 19). Therefore when a user connects to a cube Analysis Services 2005 evaluates the security permissions for the user. After the security permissions are evaluate the user gets assigned a cube context. The calculations being applied to a user's cube context is based up on the security permissions. The data populated within the cube for the user is based on the security permissions for that user. If a cube context for a specific set of permissions already exists then the user is automatically assigned to that specific cube context.

You use MDX Scripts to write your complex business calculations in an easy-to-read manner. All the calculations are a sequence of statements that are self contained, similar to a procedural language. Analysis Services 2005 allows multiple people to collaborate and develop the UDM for a company. Even if more than one user is defining the calculations for the UDM, the calculation can be included in a single MDX script with appropriate comments, which can reduce potential errors. No more quarrels with your co-worker about who made the mistake and why the cube is not working. Analysis Services 2005 tools help you debug MDX scripts interactively, more like debugging a program to identify any semantic errors in calculations defined in the script. Syntactic errors are automatically flagged by Analysis Services when the cube is deployed to Analysis Services. The real value of the MDX script is to define calculations that assign values to cells in the cube space based upon complex business conditions. Analysis Services 2005, with the help of the SCOPE statement, helps you narrow down the cube space to which the calculation needs to be applied. For complex conditions that cannot be covered using the SCOPE statement, use the CASE operator. An example of an assignment is to allocate your sales quota based for next year based on the sales of the current year. You see more about this later in this chapter.

When you have a large script with several calculations, there might be instances where you will want the calculations to be applied in a different order than that dictated by the MDX script. Some calculations are specified as properties of dimension attributes, such as custom rollup column and unary operator column (this is shown in Chapter 8). Calculations applied to a cell not only depend on the calculations in MDX scripts but also how the calculations custom rollups and unary operators change the cell value. Analysis Services 2005 applies the calculations to cube cells based on a set of precedence rules.

CALCULATE Statement

When you create a cube using the Cube Wizard within the Business Intelligence Development Studio, a default MDX script is created for you. You can see the script definitions in the Calculations tabs of the Cube Designer as shown in Chapter 6 and again in Chapter 9. The CALCULATE statement is added to the script by the Cube Wizard. This statement indicates that the Analysis Services instance is to aggregate the data from the lowest level of attributes and hierarchies to higher levels. Aggregation of data to various levels of a hierarchy is illustrated in Figures 7-1 through 7-3. Assume you have a cube that has three dimensions: Geography, Products, and Time, with hierarchies Customer Geography, ProductLine, and Date, respectively. For illustration purposes assume Customer Geography and ProductLine are single-level hierarchies and Date is a multilevel hierarchy with levels Quarter, Semester, and Year.

When a user accesses the cube, the fact data first gets loaded into the cube as shown in Figure 7-1; which represents data for a specific year. Depending on the storage type (ROLAP, MOLAP, or HOLAP) the fact data would be retrieved from the relational data source or from local Analysis Services storage. This is referred to as PASS 0 within Analysis Services. Consider PASS as an analogy of doing a first visit of all the cells within the cube. Once the fact data has been loaded into the cube, Analysis Services applies calculations for the cells based on the calculations specified in the MDX scripts or dimensions attributes. Assume this cube has the default MDX script with a CALCULATE command. After loading the fact data, Analysis Services executes the MDX script. When the CALCULATE statement is encountered, the fact data aggregated for appropriate levels of the dimension hierarchies is made accessible to end users. Because the Product Line and Customer Geography hierarchies have only one level, there is no need to aggregate the data. The Date hierarchy has the levels Semester and Year for which the data needs to be aggregated from the Quarter level. When the CALCULATE statement is encountered a new PASS; PASS 1, is created where aggregated data can be seen for various levels. Analysis Services aggregates the data for the Semester level from the Quarter level as shown in Figure 7-2 and then to the Year level as shown in Figure 7-3. You will be able to query the aggregated data.

If the CALCULATE statement is not specified in the MDX script, you will not be able to query the aggregated data for Semester and Year. If you query the data for the levels Semester and Year you will get null values. A concern about missing a CALCULATE statement in the MDX script is that you can retrieve the fact level data only when you include all hierarchies of all dimensions in your query. For example, if you have the following query:

```
SELECT [Measures].[Internet Sales Amount] on COLUMNS,
Product.[Product Line].Members on ROWS
FROM [Adventure Works]
```

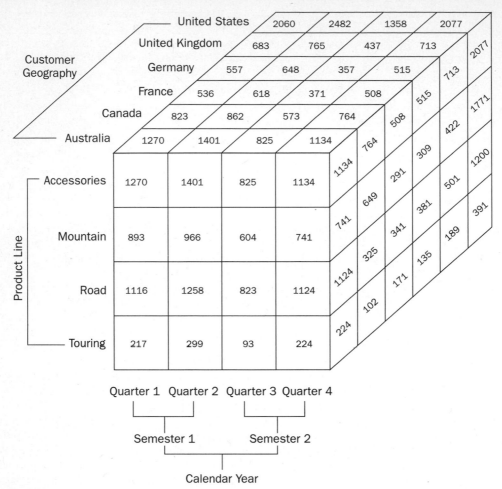

Figure 7-1

You will only see null values. In order to retrieve the fact data, you would need to send the following query to Analysis Services:

```
SELECT [Measures].[Internet Sales] on COLUMNS,
Product.ProductLine.Members *
Customer.[Customer Geography].members *
Time.Quarter.Members *
Time.Semester.Members *
Time.Year.Members *
Time.Date.Members
on ROWS
FROM [Adventure Works]
```

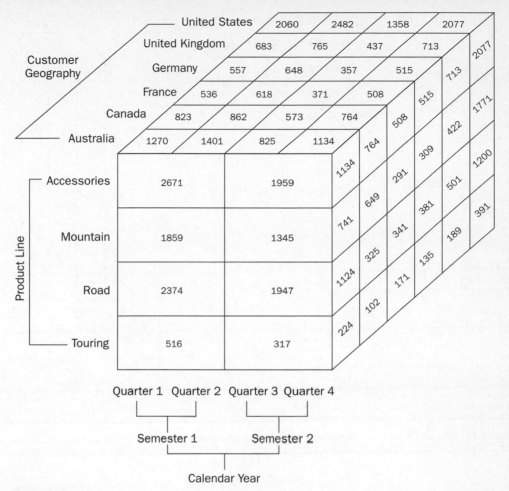

Figure 7-2

If a cube does not have an MDX script defined then a default MDX script with CALCULATE statement is used as default by Analysis Services. We do not expect users to have MDX scripts without the CALCU-LATE statement other than by mistake. If you do not have any calculations defined in MDX scripts and your queries return null values for various hierarchies we recommend you check if the CALCULATE statement is included in the MDX script.

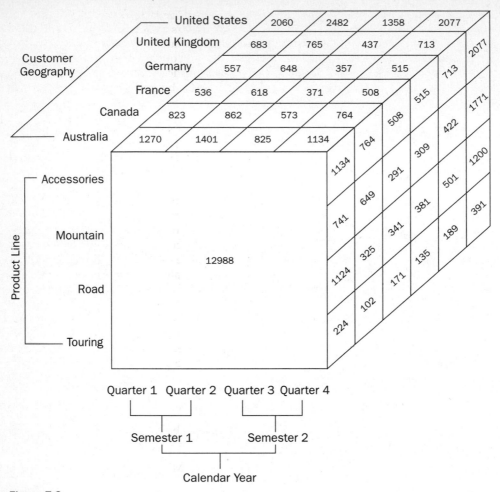

Figure 7-3

Named Sets

In Chapter 3 you learned about Named Sets. You learned that you can create these named sets within your MDX queries and access them. Following is the example of named sets created within an MDX query in Chapter 3:

```
WITH SET [EUROPE] AS {[Customer].[Country].[Country].&[France],
[Customer].[Country].[Country].&[Germany],[Customer].[Country].[Country].&[United
Kingdom]}
SELECT Measures.[Sales Amount] on COLUMNS,
[EUROPE] ON ROWS
FROM [Adventure Works]
```

When the named sets are created within an MDX query they can only be accessed within the scope of the query. Other queries within the same session or other users in different sessions cannot access these named sets in their queries. Some of the named sets might be useful for several users, and it would be better to create them so that they can be shared across several queries or even several users. Analysis Services provides ways of defining named sets within a specific session where you can send multiple queries, or in a cube's MDX script where they can be accessed by multiple users using the CREATE statement. In both cases you create sets as shown here:

```
CREATE SET [Adventure Works].[EUROPE]
AS '{[Customer].[Country-Region].[Country-Region].&[France],
[Customer].[Country-Region].[Country-Region].&[Germany],[Customer].[Country-
Region].[Country-Region].&[United Kingdom]}';
```

Instead of the WITH clause that you used in the MDX query for set creation, the CREATE statement allows you to create a set within the scope of a session or the entire cube. When you define sets using the CREATE command, you need to specify the cube name as a prefix as shown in the CREATE statement as seen above with the [Adventure Works] cube. You do not specify the name of the dimension when you specify the set. This is because a set can contain tuples that are formed by multiple hierarchies that are from one or more dimensions. Hence irrespective of whether all the tuples in a set are from a single hierarchy or multiple hierarchies, it is not considered to be part of any single dimension.

Once the set has been created using the CREATE command, it can be accessed in any query. If the named set was created within a session, it would be valid only within that specific session and could not be used by users in other sessions. If the named sets are to be used by several users, we recommend you create them in the cube scope by defining them in the MDX script. Named sets can be in one of the three scopes when an MDX query is being executed:

❑ They can be within the query scope where they are defined with the WITH clause in MDX.

❑ They can be within the session scope where they can be created within a specific session using the CREATE statement you learned now.

❑ They can be scoped as global and defined within an MDX script using the CREATE statement.

Analysis Services checks for resolving members or sets in an MDX query within query, session, and global scopes, respectively. Once you have created the named sets (either in session or global scope) executing the following query will result in the same values that you obtained when you had the named set created using the WITH clause:

```
SELECT Measures.[Sales Amount] on COLUMNS,
[EUROPE] ON ROWS
```

Named sets are really convenient and useful for querying because the MDX queries using them are easy to read and allow multiple users to access them. However, you should be aware that there is a memory cost associated with holding them in Analysis Services. If you need to create a large number of named sets that are quite large in terms of number of tuples, then exercise caution. We recommend you drop any named sets whenever they are not used. Just as there is a CREATE statement, there is a statement to delete named sets or calculated members as well. The DROP statement does the job of deleting sets and calculated members. The syntax for the DROP statement is simple:

```
DROP SET <setname>
```

Calculated Members

Similar to named sets, you learned that calculated members can be created using the WITH clause within a query. Following is the query used in Chapter 3 for creating a calculated member:

```
WITH MEMBER [MEASURES].[Profit] AS '([Measures].[Sales Amount] -
            [Measures].[Total Product Cost])'
SELECT [MEASURES.[Profit] ON COLUMNS,
       [Customer].[Country].MEMBERS ON ROWS
FROM [Adventure Works]
```

As with named sets, calculated members can also be created using the CREATE statement as follows:

```
CREATE MEMBER [Adventure Works].[Measures].[Profit]
AS '([Measures].[Sales Amount] - [Measures].[Total Product Cost])';
```

For creating a member you use the CREATE MEMBER followed by the member name. While creating named sets you did not specify which dimension the named set belonged to. However, while creating calculated members you do specify the cube and dimension name. Notice that all measures within a cube are always within a special dimension called Measures. Hence in the preceding CREATE statement, the cube name and the dimension Measures is specified. The calculated members that are most often created by users are calculated measures, that is, calculated members on the Measures dimension. For convenience Analysis Services 2005 assumes that a calculated member will be in the Measures dimension if it is not prefixed with Measures. Hence the following statement is a valid syntax:

```
CREATE MEMBER [Profit]
AS '([Measures].[Sales Amount] - [Measures].[Total Product Cost])';
```

Once the calculated members have been created, you can use them as shown in the following query. The query scope, session scope, and global scope seen for named sets also apply to calculated members.

```
SELECT [MEASURES.[Profit] ON COLUMNS,
       [Customer].[Country].MEMBERS ON ROWS
FROM [Adventure Works]
```

Similar to named sets, calculated members can also be dropped using the DROP MEMBER statement. The syntax for DROP MEMBER is

```
DROP MEMBER <member name>
```

Typically, client tools interacting with Analysis Services that create MDX queries dynamically based on user actions on the front end create and drop calculated members within sessions. One example is the OWC Pivot table control, which is used with the Cube Browser. You will see some of the MDX queries that are sent to the Analysis Services instance by client tools in Chapter 15, with detailed explanations of what these MDX queries mean.

Analysis Services 2005 provides a new way to define calculated members at the global scope within MDX scripts. This helps you create a member first without any definition and later define the expression. The MDX statements below help demonstrate this new definition for calculated members. The statements below will evaluate to the same results as that of the CREATE MEMBER statement. If the dimension name is not specified it is assumed the calculated member is part of the Measures dimension.

They are semantically the same but it is a matter of convenience if say, you want to create a calculated measure and are not sure about the actual expression. You can define the calculated member, use it in statements and finally create the actual expression in the MDX script.

```
CREATE MEMBER [Profit];

[Measures].[Profit] = [Measures].[Sales Amount] - [Measures].[Total Product Cost];
```

Named sets and calculated members are the basic objects created within MDX scripts most likely to be exploited by users of the cube. You can specify properties such as format string, font, color, and background color for the calculated members as discussed in Chapter 6. Next, you see some of the additional statements that are used within MDX scripts and how they help you define your business calculations.

Cube Space and Autoexists

The cube space (cells) in an Analysis Services cube can be calculated as the product of the member count in each attribute from each dimension. As you can imagine, this space is quite large even for a small cube that contains less than ten dimensions, with each dimension containing around ten attributes. The entire cube space is quite large and often the cells that have the data are quite sparse as compared to the entire space. When we refer to the data in the cube space we do not just refer to the data in the fact table. You can apply calculations through MDX expressions to various cells in your cube space. Most of these calculations are defined within MDX scripts.

Before you learn to specify cell calculations you need to have a better understanding of the cube space that comprises all the cells. Some cells in the cube space retrieve data through calculations or are aggregated up across dimensions based on your business definitions within the cube. For example, consider the budget of your company for next year or the sales quota for next year, which are typically calculated based on profit or sales of the current year. This data is not available in the fact table but is likely based on a calculation of the data in the fact table. Similarly, you can have cell values for which data is aggregated from fact data due to cube modeling scheme.

Assume you have a sales cube with a Time dimension containing a Time hierarchy with levels Year, Quarter, Month, and Date. In this case, the fact table contains data for each day. Analysis Services would aggregate the data for cells corresponding to month, quarter, and year. We refer to the cube space that is accessible to the users, and which can be manipulated through calculations, as the real cube space. Certain cells in the cube space can be accessed through MDX queries but are actually not of the real cube space. For example, assume a Customer dimension that has attributes Name, Gender, and Marital Status. There is customer named Aaron Flores who is Male in the Adventure Works DW sample database. The cell corresponding to Customer.Customer.[Aaron Flores] and Customer.Gender.Female does not exist in the cube space:

```
select [Customer].[Customer].[Aaron Flores] on 0,
[Customer].[Gender].&[F] on 1
from [Adventure Works]
```

You can request the cell corresponding to this coordinate with the preceding MDX query and you will get a null value. You might want to see multiple attributes of a dimension on a specific axis. If you do a cross-join of multiple attributes you will get the entire cross product of all the member of the attributes involved in the cross-join. However, if you do a cross-join of attributes within the same dimension, Analysis Services eliminates the cells corresponding to attributes members that do not exists with one another in the cube space. This specific behavior is called AUTO EXISTS, which can be interpreted as an EXISTS function automatically being applied to attributes within the same dimension. The EXISTS MDX function, which you learn about later in this chapter, takes two sets and returns members of one set that exist with one or more tuples of one or more other sets. Analysis Services 2005 automatically applies EXISTS for attributes within the same dimension when they are included on the same axis. For example, if you query Internet Sales Amount along with customers across states and countries, your MDX query will be:

```
SELECT [Measures].[Internet Sales Amount] on COLUMNS,
[Customer].[Country].[Country].MEMBERS *
[Customer].[State-Province].[State-Province].MEMBERS
ON ROWS
FROM [Adventure Works]
```

The results of the above MDX query will only have the states that are within a specific country instead of a regular cross-join of the members of both hierarchies. Alberta, which is a state in Canada, does not exist in Australia and hence you do not have a tuple containing Australia and Alberta in your result.

SCOPE Statement

If you want to perform certain operations within the scope of the entire cube, you will typically have the calculations defined within the MDX scripts. CREATE and DROP SUBCUBE statements (you learn later in this chapter) are statements that can be used to restrict the cube space within the session scope at query time. You cannot use the CREATE SUBCUBE statement within MDX scripts. However, Analysis Services provides another statement called SCOPE. The SCOPE statement restricts the cube space so that all MDX statements and expressions specified within the SCOPE statement are evaluated exactly once against the restricted cube space. Named Sets in the MDX script are not affected by the SCOPE statement. The syntax of the SCOPE statement is:

```
SCOPE <SubeCubeExpression>
  <MDX Statement>
  <MDX Statement> ...
END SCOPE
```

You can have one or more MDX statements within the SCOPE statement and you can have nested SCOPE statements. Nested SCOPE statements can often be simplified as a single SCOPE statement as long as all the MDX statements are within the innermost SCOPE statement. MDX statements expressed within SCOPE statements are really cell calculations, which you learn about in the next section. An example of SCOPE statement is:

```
SCOPE
  (
     [Date].[Fiscal Year].&[2002],
     [Date].[Fiscal].[Month].Members,
     [Measure].[Sales Quota Amount]
  ) ;

        This = [Date].[Fiscal].CurrentMember.Parent / 3 ;

End Scope ;
```

In the above example the SCOPE statement restricts the cube space for Year 2002 all the members of the Month under the Fiscal hierarchy of Date dimension and the measure Sales Quota Amount. The default members of the hierarchies not specified in the subcube expression become part of the subcube. The MDX expression specified within the SCOPE statement use "this" as the keyword. "This" refers to the current subcube. In the preceding example the MDX expression evaluated will take the Sales Quota Amount measure and iterate through all the members in Fiscal hierarchy of the Date dimension and replace existing measure values to one-third the value of the parent of the current member. This MDX expression is referred to as an assignment since the cells referenced within the subcube (using "This") are assigned values based on the MDX expression. In this specific example, the Fiscal hierarchy level month has Sales Quota Amount allocated based on the Quarter level. A nested SCOPE statement can re-scope a hierarchy that was already scoped by an earlier SCOPE statement. For example if you have a SCOPE statement to create a subcube for Fiscal Year 2002 and a nested scope to create a subcube for Fiscal Year 2003 then the Fiscal Year hierarchy is re-scoped to subcube of 2003.

Cell Calculations and Assignments

Now you have learned about the cube space and were introduced to calculations affecting cell values. In this section you learn about cell calculations in depth. MDX provides several ways to specify calculations, such as calculated members, calculated measures, custom rollups (to be discussed in Chapter 8), and unary operators (also discussed in Chapter 8). Using these features to affect a group of cell values or even a single cell value is not easy. Analysis Services allows you to create or apply calculations to cell values, which can help you in scenarios such as budgeting. Analysis Services 2000 introduced the statement CREATE CELL CALCULATION, which, similar to calculated members and named sets, can be specified at a query, session, or cube scope. The syntax for CREATE CELL CALCULATION statement is:

```
CREATE CELL CALCULATION  <CubeName>.<formula name>
FOR <SetExpression> AS <MDX Expression>, <cell property list> CONDITION = <Logical
Expression>
```

In the above syntax, the <formula name> is an identifier for the cell calculation statement. The Set expression resolves to a set of tuples for which the cell values will be changed based on the MDX expression. The cell property list is an optional set of properties for the cell such as DISABLED, DESCRIPTION, CALCULATION_PASS_NUMBER, and CALCULATION_PASS_DEPTH, which can be applied to the cells being evaluated separated by commas. These properties help in application of specific properties to certain cells so that the calculations are evaluated in the right order. Further, correct use of cell properties can help client tools identify these cells uniquely so that they can be represented appropriately to the end users.

An example of the CREATE CELL CALCULATION statement for the Adventure Works DW sample database can be applied to the task of making the Sales Quota Amount for the Fiscal Year 2005 set twice the value of the Actual Sales in the Fiscal Year 2004 set:

```
CREATE CELL CALCULATION [Adventure Works].[SalesQuota2005]
FOR '([Date].[Fiscal Year].&[2005],
    [Date].[Fiscal].[Month].Members,[Measures].[Sales Amount Quota]
    )'

AS '(ParallelPeriod( [Date].[Fiscal].[Fiscal Year],
1,[Date].[Fiscal].CurrentMember),[Measures].[Sales Amount])*2 '
```

Here the set expression returns tuples for which the cell values need to be updated — in this case the months of Fiscal Year 2005. The MDX expression evaluates to the Sales Amount values of fiscal year 2004, which is then multiplied by 2. You can verify the results of the the cell calculation via the following MDX query:

```
SELECT {[Measures].[Sales Amount Quota],[Measures].[Sales Amount]} on 0,
Descendants({[Date].[Fiscal].[Fiscal Year].&[2004],
[Date].[Fiscal].[Fiscal Year].&[2005]},3,SELF) on 1
from [Adventure Works]
```

You can see that the Sales Amount Quota for the months July and August 2004 (which are months in fiscal year 2005) are exactly twice the Sales Amount for the months July and August of 2003 (the corresponding months for the fiscal year 2004). The particular variant of Descendants function (there are others) used in the preceding MDX query is used to retrieve the months of the fiscal years 2004 and 2005. The second parameter indicates the level in the hierarchy from which members need to be retrieved and the last parameter indicates whether to retrieve members only from the current level or from other levels before or after the current level. For further details on the descendants function, please refer to Appendix A.

For the session scope and global scope you can follow the example mentioned above. For global scope you need to define the cell calculation statements within MDX scripts. If you want to use this within the query scope, you need to use the CREATE CELL CALCULATION statement with the WITH clause, like this:

```
WITH CELL CALCULATION [Adventure Works].[SalesQuota2005]
FOR '([Date].[Fiscal Year].&[2005],
    [Date].[Fiscal].[Month].Members,[Measures].[Sales Amount Quota]
    )'

AS '(ParallelPeriod( [Date].[Fiscal].[Fiscal Year],
1,[Date].[Fiscal].CurrentMember),[Measures].[Sales Amount])*2 '

SELECT {[Measures].[Sales Amount Quota],[Measures].[Sales Amount]} on 0,
Descendants({[Date].[Fiscal].[Fiscal Year].&[2004],
[Date].[Fiscal].[Fiscal Year].&[2005]},3,SELF) on 1
from [Adventure Works]
```

The above example can be re-written with a condition clause as shown in the next code snippet, which will result in exactly the same behavior. In the following MDX statement the condition checks for the Current Member of the Fiscal Year hierarchy and only applies the calculation to the cells if the condition is satisfied. Even though both these cell calculation statements result in the same behavior, we recommend you use the first flavor because the condition gets evaluated for each and every cell. Analysis Services restricts the cube space in the above example due to the selection of Fiscal Year 2005, which would give better performance if the number of cells to be updated is large.

```
CREATE CELL CALCULATION [Adventure Works].[SalesQuota2005]
FOR '([Date].[Fiscal].[Month].Members,[Measures].[Sales Amount Quota]
    )'
AS '(ParallelPeriod( [Date].[Fiscal].[Fiscal Year],
1,[Date].[Fiscal].CurrentMember),[Measures].[Sales Amount])*2 ',
CONDITION = '[Date].[Fiscal Year].CurrentMember is [Date].[Fiscal Year].&[2005]'
```

Cell calculations not only help you evaluate specific cell values, but also avoid the addition of members in the cube space. The properties CALCULATION_PASS_NUMBER and CALCULATION_PASS_DEPTH provide the functionality to specify complex recursive calculations such as goal-seeking equations. The CALCULATION_PASS_NUMBER specifies the PASS number at which the calculation is to be performed.

Analysis Services 2005 supports the CREATE CELL CALCULATION syntax for backward compatibility reasons. Assignment statements are the recommended way for global cell calculations in Analysis Services 2005. This new syntax allows you to model complex business logic through the SCOPE statement, the CASE operator, and new MDX functions such as Root and Leaves. You must be familiar with the SCOPE statement along with assignments using the "This" keyword from the previous section. Each assignment statement in MDX Scripts results in a new PASS value. The cell calculation example with SCOPE is as follows:

```
SCOPE([Date].[Fiscal Year].&[2005],
     [Date].[Fiscal].[Month].Members,
     [Measures].[Sales Amount Quota]);
This = (ParallelPeriod( [Date].[Fiscal].[Fiscal Year],
1,[Date].[Fiscal].CurrentMember),[Measures].[Sales Amount])*2;
END SCOPE;
```

The preceding cell calculation is simple in the sense that it does not require special conditions. It is referred to as a simple assignment because the cell value for the current coordinate indicated by "This" is assigned a value, which is evaluated from the MDX expression on the right-hand side. If you have a complex expression with several conditions to apply the cell calculation, the simple assignment will not be sufficient. You can use the IF statement to check for conditions before applying the cell calculation. For example, if you want the Sales Amount Quota to be two times the previous year's Sales Amount just for the first quarter, your calculation using the IF statement will be:

```
SCOPE
([Date].[Fiscal Year].&[2004],
     [Date].[Fiscal].[Month].Members,
     [Measures].[Sales Amount Quota]);
This =
(ParallelPeriod( [Date].[Fiscal].[Fiscal Year],
1,[Date].[Fiscal].CurrentMember),[Measures].[Sales Amount])* 1.3;

IF ([Date].[Fiscal].Currentmember.Parent is [Date].[Fiscal].[Fiscal
Quarter].&[2004]&[1])
THEN This = (ParallelPeriod( [Date].[Fiscal].[Fiscal Year],
1,[Date].[Fiscal].CurrentMember),[Measures].[Sales Amount])* 2.0
END IF;

END SCOPE;
```

The syntax of the IF statement is:

```
IF <conditional_expression> THEN <assignment_expression> END IF;
```

As you can you see from the statement it is pretty straightforward. In fact it is quite easy to debug statements in MDX scripts with the help of the MDX debugger within the Cube Designer (you will learn debugging MDX scripts in Chapter 9). The assignment_expression is a valid MDX assignment statement. Examples of assignment_expression include MDX expressions assigned to a subcube or calculation properties applied to a subcube. END IF indicates the end of the IF statement. In the preceding example, you first assign values to all the cells corresponding to the subcube to be 1.3 times the value of the Sales amount in the previous year. Later you have the conditional IF statement to update the cell values corresponding to the first quarter to be two times the Sales Amount.

You can get into more complex expressions which may require multiple IF statements which can lead to updating cells multiple times. The cube space is large, and applying cell calculations on a large cube space can lead to performance degradation. Hence, Analysis Services provides the CASE expression to perform assignments.

The syntax for the CASE expression is:

```
Statement =
CASE <value_expression>
WHEN <value_expression> THEN <statement>
ELSE  <statement>
END;
```

Here an MDX statement is assigned one of the values being returned by the CASE expression. Assume for the Fiscal Year 2004, you need to specify the Sales Amount Quota based on some condition, such as the Sales Quota for the first quarter must be 1.3 times the previous year's sales amount, for the second quarter the quota is 2 times the previous year's sales amount, and for the third and fourth quarters the quota is 1.75 times the previous year's sales amount. You can specify this condition easily using the CASE statement as follows:

```
SCOPE
([Date].[Fiscal Year].&[2004],
    [Date].[Fiscal].[Month].Members,
    [Measures].[Sales Amount Quota]);
This =
CASE WHEN ([Date].[Fiscal].Currentmember.Parent is [Date].[Fiscal].[Fiscal
Quarter].&[2004]&[1])

THEN

(ParallelPeriod( [Date].[Fiscal].[Fiscal Year],
1,[Date].[Fiscal].CurrentMember),[Measures].[Sales Amount])* 1.3

WHEN ([Date].[Fiscal].Currentmember.Parent is [Date].[Fiscal].[Fiscal
Quarter].&[2004]&[2])

THEN
(ParallelPeriod( [Date].[Fiscal].[Fiscal Year],
1,[Date].[Fiscal].CurrentMember),[Measures].[Sales Amount])* 2.0

ELSE

(ParallelPeriod( [Date].[Fiscal].[Fiscal Year],
1,[Date].[Fiscal].CurrentMember),[Measures].[Sales Amount])* 1.75

END;

END SCOPE;
```

The preceding CASE expression applies the correct calculations based on the Quarter the month belongs to. The CASE expression is similar to the switch case statement in C/C++. Based on the conditional expression provided after the WHEN, the statement is assigned to the expression on the left hand side ("This" in the above code sample). You can have multiple WHEN-THEN's within the CASE expression as shown in the preceding example.

In the all previous examples you have seen SCOPE-END SCOPE being used. Use SCOPE when you have multiple calculations that need to be applied within the SCOPE. However, if it is a single MDX expression, you can write the cell calculation by direct assignment to the subcube as shown below.

```
([Date].[Fiscal Year].&[2005], [Date].[Fiscal].[Month].Members,
      [Measures].[Sales Amount Quota]) =
              (ParallelPeriod( [Date].[Fiscal].[Fiscal Year],1,
[Date].[Fiscal].CurrentMember) ,[Measures].[Sales Amount])*2;
```

You have so far learned about the cell calculations using assignments in Analysis Services 2005, which is recommended over the CREATE CELL CALCULATION syntax. You learned about the IF statement and the CASE expression to apply cell calculations based on business conditions. There are two MDX functions in Analysis Services 2005 that help you write cell calculations with ease. These functions are Root and Leaves, which are great if you want to apply cell calculation to the leaf-level members or the root of a hierarchy. These functions appropriately position the coordinate so that the cell calculations can be applied to that coordinate. Following are some examples that use the Root and Leaves MDX functions:

```
CREATE MEMBER CurrentCube.[Measures].[Ratio to All Products]

 As [Measures].[Sales Amount]
    /
    (
     Root( [Product] ),
     [Measures].[Sales Amount]
    ),

Format_String = "Percent",
Non_Empty_Behavior = [Sales Amount] ;

SCOPE(Leaves([Date]),[Measures].[Sales Amount Quota]);
    this = this*1.2;
END SCOPE;
```

In the first example, you can see a calculated measure that calculates contribution of Sales of a product as a portion of total product sales. This is accomplished through use of the Root(Product), which will provide the sales information for all the products. Root(Product) is often used to calculate ratios of a measure for a single member against all the members in the dimension. In the second example, the Sales Amount Quota is being applied to Leaf members of the Date dimension so that the Sales Amount Quota can be increased by 20%. Leaves MDX function would help in budgeting and financial calculations where you want the calculations applied only to the leaf-level members and then rolled up to the members at other levels. The Root and Leaves MDX functions are new in Analysis Services 2005. Both take a dimension as the argument and return the leaf-level members of the dimension that exists with the granularity attribute of the dimension.

Recursion

Recursive calculations can be quite common in MDX. Recursive calculation occurs when a calculated member references itself for calculations. For example if you want to calculate the cumulative sales over time then you can apply an MDX expression which calculates the Sales of current time member and the cumulative sales for previous time member. This leads to recursion since the cumulative sales of previous time member needs to be evaluated with the same MDX expression for the previous time member. In Analysis Services 2000 you can end up with a calculation that can lead to infinite recursion. You need to have special conditional checks to avoid infinite recursion errors. In Analysis Services 2005 infinite recursions due to single expression are avoided since a new PASS value. Consider the following MDX statements in your MDX script.

```
SCOPE ([Date].[Fiscal Year].&[2004])
[Sales Amount Quota] = [Sales Amount Quota] * 1.2;
END SCOPE
```

In the above statement the evaluation of [Sales Amount Quota] leads to infinite recursion. In such a situation where single expression leads to infinite recursion, Analysis Services 2005 detects it and assigns a value from the previous PASS value.

Freeze Statement

Freeze Statement is used in circumstances where you might want to change the cell value that was used in an MDX expression to determine results for another cell value without changing the cell value from an earlier calculation. The syntax for Freeze Statement is:

```
Freeze <subcube>
```

This Freeze statement is only used within MDX Scripts. It is easier to understand the Freeze statement with an example. Assume the following MDX statements below where A, B, and C are MDX expressions.

```
A=B;
B=C;
```

Due to recursion the final value for A will be equal to the value of C. However, if you want to ensure that the value of A is pinned to the value assigned by MDX expression B, you would introduce a Freeze statement between the two assignments as shown here.

```
A=B;
Freeze(A);
B=C;
```

You can use the Freeze statement when you perform budget allocations. An example of Freeze statement is used in the sample Adventure Works DW database. Budget is first allocated the current year's quarters based on the previous year's quarter values and Freeze statement is applied to the quarters so that their values are not changed. Then the months are allocated weights based on the previous years followed by the budget for the months which allocated as a ratio of the quarter value. If the Freeze statement is not applied to the budget value for quarters their values would be overwritten when the ratios for the months are calculated.

Restricting Cube Space/Slicing Cube Data

A typical cube contains several dimensions and each dimension has several hundred or thousands of members. For example, if you have a sales cube that contains products, the products dimension would have at least hundreds of products if not thousands. During analysis of your data you would typically want to slice the data or drill down into specific sections of the cube to glean insights hidden in the data. Client tools help you to do slice, dice, and drill down in cubes. These client tools dynamically generate the MDX to restrict the cube space. Such tools dynamically generate MDX queries. In this section, "restricting cube space" is used loosely in the sense that we refer to restricting the cube space in the context of MDX scripts or restricting the data being returned to the client where users typically slice or dice the data. Several ways exist to restrict the cube space and analyze data and this section discusses some of the ways of restricting cube space using MDX to appropriately retrieve the section of the data.

Using the SCOPE STATEMENT

You already learned some techniques to restrict searchable cube space; use of which would depend on the context of your problem and what you are trying to accomplish by restricting the cube space. To refresh your memory, the SCOPE statement within MDX Scripts is used to restrict the cube space to form a subcube, which is a part of the cube projected along the dimensions mentioned within the SCOPE statement. The SCOPE statement is often used for cell calculations where the assignment statement typically is used with the "This" function. An example to recap what you learned in the previous section is:

```
SCOPE([Date].[Fiscal Year].&[2005],
     [Date].[Fiscal].[Month].Members,
     [Measures].[Sales Amount Quota]);

This = (ParallelPeriod( [Date].[Fiscal].[Fiscal Year],
1,[Date].[Fiscal].CurrentMember),[Measures].[Sales Amount])*2;
END SCOPE;
```

Using CREATE and DROP SUBCUBE

By default you retrieve all cells from the entire cube space. You might want to restrict your analysis to specific slices or sections of the cube though. For example, if you are analyzing the sales information for the year 2005, you might want to reduce your search space to just the year 2005. There are several ways to restrict your cube space in Analysis Services 2005. If you are querying the cube you can restrict the cube space with the CREATE SUBCUBE statement, which then restricts the cube space for subsequent queries. Assume you are analyzing the Internet Sales information in the Adventure Works DW database for various quarters. You use the following MDX query:

```
select [Measures].[Internet Sales Amount] on 0,
[Date].[Fiscal].[Fiscal Quarter].members on 1
from [Adventure Works]
```

If you want to restrict your cube space and only analyze the Internet sales data for the year 2004, one way to do so is to use the CREATE SUBCUBE statement. The syntax of the statement is

```
CREATE SUBCUBE <SubCubeName> AS <SELECT Statement>
```

where the SELECT clause is an MDX SELECT clause that returns the results for the restricted cube space based on specific criteria.

The following MDX statements help you restrict the cube space to year 2006 by using the CREATE SUBCUBE statement and then querying the Internet sales for all the quarters in that year.

```
CREATE SUBCUBE [Adventure Works] as SELECT ([DATE}{FISCAL]. [FISCAL YEAR] & [2004],
OK)
on 0 from [Adventure Works]

select [Measures].[Internet Sales Amount] on 0,
[Date].[Fiscal].[Fiscal Quarter].members on 1
from [Adventure Works]

DROP SUBCUBE [Adventure Works]
```

In the above CREATE SUBCUBE statement, the * in the SELECT statement indicates selection of the default members in the remaining hierarchies of the dimensions. If the All member of a hierarchy is included, all the members of that specific hierarchy are included in the subcube. Subsequent queries to the Adventure Works cube will evaluate to the restricted cube space corresponding to the year 2004. The query selecting Fiscal Quarters provides the results shown in the following table. If you did not create the subcube, you will see quarters for all the Fiscal Years in the cube.

	Internet Sales Amount
Q1 FY 2004	$2,744,340.48
Q2 FY 2004	$4,009,218.46
Q3 FY 2004	$4,283,629.96
Q4 FY 2004	$5,436,429.15

Once you have completed your analysis on the restricted cube space you can revert back to the original cube space by dropping the subcube using the DROP SUBCUBE statement followed by the name of the subcube you just created. The CREATE SUBCUBE statement is typically used within the scope of a query session where you want to perform analysis on restricted cube space. At query time you can reduce the cube space using the CREATE SUBCUBE statement and use the CREATE CELL CALCULATION statement for applying cell calculation. You can later query within the context of the subcube created.

Using EXISTS

As mentioned earlier, the cube space in Analysis Services 2005 is quite large and typically sparse given the nature of the attribute model. Remember AUTOEXISTS? That's where querying the cross-join of attributes within the same dimension results in reducing the cross-join set so that only members that exist with one another are returned. Well, EXISTS is a function that explicitly allows you to do the same operation of returning a set of members that exists with one or more tuples of one or more sets. The EXISTS function can take two or three arguments. The syntax of the EXISTS function is:

```
EXISTS( Set, <FilterSet>, [MeasureGroupName])
```

The first two arguments are Sets that get evaluated to identify the members that exist with each other. The third optional parameter is the Measure group name so EXISTS can be applied across the measure group. EXISTS identifies all the members in the first set that exist with the members in the FilterSet and returns those members as results. The following is an example of EXISTS where you analyze the sales of all customers who have four cars. In this example we use restricting cube space loosely to restrict the members in the Customer hierarchy. You can achieve similar results using a FILTER or NONEMPTY-CROSSJOIN function, which you explore later in this chapter.

```
WITH SET [HomeOwnerCustomer] AS
EXISTS([Customer].[Customer].[Customer].members,[Customer].[Number of Cars
Owned].&[4] )
SELECT [Measures].[Internet Sales Amount] on 0,
HomeOwnerCustomer on 1
from [Adventure Works]
```

Out of 18,000 customers in the customer dimension, the query returns 1,262 customers.

An example of using EXISTS with the measure group name follows:

```
WITH SET [HomeOwnerCustomer] AS
EXISTS([Customer].[Customer].[Customer].members, [Product].[Product Model
Categories].[Category].&[1],
"Internet Sales")
SELECT [Measures].[Internet Sales Amount] on 0,
HomeOwnerCustomer on 1
from [Adventure Works]
```

The above example identifies the customers who have bought products of category 1, which is Bikes. The measure group name [Internet Sales] is specified so that EXISTS uses the measure group to determine the set of customers who have bought bikes.

Using EXISTING

By now, you are quite familiar with the WHERE clause in the MDX SELECT statement. The WHERE clause only changes the default members of the dimensions for the current subcube and does not restrict the cube space. It does not change the default for the outer query and gets a lower precedence as compared to the calculations specified within the query scope. For example, look at the following MDX query:

```
WITH MEMBER measures.x AS COUNT([Customer].[Customer Geography].[State-
Province].MEMBERS)
SELECT measures.x ON 0
FROM [Adventure Works]
WHERE ([Customer].[Customer Geography].[Country].&[United States])
```

The query returns a value of 71. You know that there are 50 states within the United States and the count of customers should be <= 50. You get the value 71 because calculations are done at a scope larger than the one defined by the WHERE clause. In order to restrict the cube space so that calculations are done within the scope of the conditions specified in the WHERE clause, you can use several methods. One way to accomplish this is using the keyword EXISTING, by which you force the calculations to be done on a subcube under consideration by the query rather than the entire cube. Following is an MDX query using EXISTING:

```
WITH MEMBER measures.x AS COUNT(
EXISTING [Customer].[Customer Geography].[State-Province].MEMBERS)
SELECT measures.x ON 0
FROM [Adventure Works]
WHERE ([Customer].[Customer Geography].[Country].&[United States])
```

The EXISTING keyword forces sets to be evaluated in the current context. One can argue that the current context is defined due to the WHERE clause, which does not actually restrict the cube space. As mentioned earlier we are using the term "restricting cube space" loosely just to show examples of how you can restrict the data in a cube to retrieve the results you are looking for.

Using SUB-SELECT

Analysis Services 2005 introduces a new clause called SUB-SELECT, by which you can query a subcube instead of the entire cube. The syntax of the SUB-SELECT clause along with SELECT is:

```
[WITH <formula_expression> [, <formula_expression> ...]]
SELECT [<axis_expression>, <axis_expression>...]]

FROM [<cube_expression> | (<sub_select_statement>)]
[WHERE <expression>]
[[CELL] PROPERTIES <cellprop> [, <cellprop> ...]]

<sub_select_statement> =
SELECT [<axis_expression> [, <axis_expression> ...]]
FROM [<cube_expression> | (< sub_select_statement >)]
[WHERE <expression>]
```

The cube_expression in the MDX SELECT statement can now be replaced by another SELECT statement called the sub_select_statement, which queries a part of the cube. You can have nested SUB-SELECT statements up to any level. The SELECT clause in the SUB-SELECT statement restricts the cube space on the specified dimension members in the SUBSELECT clause. Outer queries will therefore be able to see only the dimension members that are specified in the inner SELECT clauses. Look at the following MDX query that uses SUBSELECT syntax:

```
SELECT NON EMPTY { [Measures].[Internet Sales Amount] } ON COLUMNS,
NON EMPTY { ([Customer].[Customer Geography].[Country].ALLMEMBERS ) }
DIMENSION PROPERTIES MEMBER_CAPTION, MEMBER_UNIQUE_NAME ON ROWS
FROM (
    SELECT ( { [Date].[Fiscal].[Fiscal Year].&[2004],
              [Date].[Fiscal].[Fiscal Year].&[2005]
            }
          )
    ON COLUMNS
    FROM (
        SELECT ( { [Product].[Product Categories].[Subcategory].&[26],
                  [Product].[Product Categories].[Subcategory].&[27] } )
        ON COLUMNS
        FROM [Adventure Works]
        )
    )
WHERE ( [Product].[Product Categories].CurrentMember,
        [Date].[Fiscal].CurrentMember
      )
CELL PROPERTIES VALUE, BACK_COLOR, FORE_COLOR, FORMATTED_VALUE
```

The query contains SUB-SELECT clause twice. The innermost query returns a subcube that only contains Products of SubCategory ids 26 and 27. Assume that this subcube is named subcube A. The second

SUB-SELECT uses subcube A and returns another subcube with the restriction of Fiscal Years 2004 and 2006 . Finally, the outermost SELECT statement retrieves the Internet Sales for Customers in various countries. Here SUB-SELECT queries restrict the cube space to certain members on Product and Date dimensions, thereby the outermost SELECT statement queries data from a subcube rather than the entire cube space. If you execute the preceding query in SSMS, you will see the results shown in the following table. You can rewrite most queries using SUB-SELECT with the WHERE clause in Analysis Services 2005, which accepts Sets as valid MDX expressions. There are instances where subsets and where clause can return different results. More information is provided in the book *MDX Solutions 2nd edition* by George Spofford, et, al. (Wiley Publishing, Inc., 2006). Analysis Services 2005 only uses SUBSELECT syntax for queries built through the designer that creates reports. You learn more about creating reports on Analysis Services UDM in Chapter 17.

	Internet Sales Amount
Australia	$16,335.00
Canada	$12,168.00
France	$6,021.00
Germany	$6,060.00
United Kingdom	$7,932.00
United States	$30,435.00

Removing Empty Cells

The number of cells in a cube is the uniquely identifiable space within the cube. It is the product of the number of members in each attribute of each dimension. This is referred to as the cube space. As you can imagine, the entire cube space can be quite large. Of the entire cube space, the cells which constitute the product of attribute hierarchies of each dimension can potentially have fact data. However, in a typical cube most of these cells will not have fact data. For example, take a simple cube that contains dimensions product, time, and store. Assume the fact table contains IDs for dimensions, product time, and the sales amount. The product dimension table typically contains columns pertaining to the dimension, such as product name, product category, product weight, product color, and discount. The store dimension table would contain information about the store such as city, state, country, and number of employees. The time dimension might contain day, month, and year. As the owner of existing stores you might be interested in looking at the sales of various products in stores across various time periods every week, month, or quarter to make a decision on what product lines to enhance to grow your business. The store manager may be interested in identifying the sales of the products along with discounts so that he can stock products that sell the most while having discounts to maximize the profit of the store. Hence, the types of questions that might be requested from your UDM might be different based on the user.

Because the cube space is typically quite large, a vast majority of the cells might be nulls, meaning no data is available. If your queries include attributes from the same dimension such as sales of products that have 10% discount, Analysis Services automatically returns the sale of products that have exactly 10% discount. As you learned earlier in this chapter, Analysis Services uses AUTO EXISTS and eliminates all members in the products hierarchy that do not exist with the 10% discount member in the discount hierarchy. Hence the results you get will not contain null values. However, if you query for data across dimensions, you can end up with several cells that are nulls. Often you are not interested in the cells with null values and you do not want to retrieve them in the result set to begin with. Analysis Services provides several functions and keywords that help you in eliminating null values in your result set.

Assume you want to analyze the Internet Sales amount across various countries for various products. Every product might not be sold in every country and so you can end up with certain country-product combinations that do not have any sales. To eliminate the null values you can use the keyword NON EMPTY on the axis or the MDX functions NONEMPTYCROSSJOIN, NONEMPTY, and FILTER. These are some basic ways to remove empty cells from the result set and you can certainly write many more ways of removing empty cells.

The operator NON EMPTY is used on an axis to remove the members that result in empty cell values. When NON EMPTY is applied then cells with null values are eliminated in the context of member on other axes. You can see this in the following query:

```
SELECT  [Measures].[Internet Sales Amount]  on 0,
NON EMPTY [Customer].[Customer Geography].[Country].members *
[Product].[Product Model Categories].members on 1
FROM [Adventure Works]
```

You can use the FILTER function as shown in the following query with the condition to eliminate null values for Internet Sales Amount:

```
SELECT  [Measures].[Internet Sales Amount]  on 0,
FILTER ( [Customer].[Customer Geography].[Country].members *
[Product].[Product Model Categories].members, [Measures].[Internet Sales Amount])
on 1
FROM [Adventure Works]
```

The following two queries use the NONEMPTYCROSSJOIN and NONEMPTY functions, which have similar arguments of taking a set and a filter set and eliminating cells that contain nulls. If you use the NONEMPTY-CROSSJOIN function, you can specify the sets that need to be crossjoined, and in the final result you can specify the sets that need to be included in the result set. In this example, two sets are specified:

```
SELECT  [Measures].[Internet Sales Amount]  on 0,
NONEMPTYCROSSJOIN([Customer].[Customer Geography].[Country].members,
[Product].[Product Model Categories].members, [Measures].[Internet Sales Amount],2
) on 1
FROM [Adventure Works]
```

If you use the NONEMPTY function, the set passed as an argument needs to be a crossjoin of the sets involved as shown in the following query:

```
SELECT   [Measures].[Internet Sales Amount]  on 0,
NONEMPTY([Customer].[Customer Geography].[Country].members*
[Product].[Product Model Categories].members, [Measures].[Internet Sales Amount])
on 1
FROM [Adventure Works]
```

When NONEMPTY function is used then the members in the set are filtered based on the argument passed (Measures.[Internet Sales Amount]) in the above example.

To sum up, there are several ways of removing the nulls in your result set so that you can analyze the results that are meaningful. You can choose one of the preceding examples to restrict the null cell values. However, you should be aware that the NONEMPTYCROSSJOIN function is being deprecated because there are certain limitations while using this function with calculated members.

Filtering Members on Axes

Filtering members on axes is a pretty common requirement. The filtering process can be extremely simple or an advanced MDX expression. The Filter function is one of the most common uses of filtering sets and projecting onto axes. You saw some examples of the FILTER function in Chapter 3. To refresh, assume you want to look at the gross profit of all the products whose Sales have been greater than $50,000. You will have a simple FILTER condition in the MDX query as shown in the following example:

```
SELECT {[Measures].[Gross Profit]} on 0,
FILTER( [Product].[Product Categories].[SubCategory].members,[Sales Amount] >
50000) on 1
from [Adventure Works]
```

You have already learned that you can eliminate empty cells in a variety of ways. Assume you have a large crossjoin on one of the axes and you want to apply complex filter conditions. In such a case the filter condition needs to evaluate over all the cells being represented by the crossjoin, and it might be quite a performance hit. It is more efficient to eliminate cells that have null values and then apply the filter condition on the resulting set. Analysis Services provides a new clause called the HAVING clause, which allows you to do this. The syntax for the HAVING clause is:

```
SELECT <axis_specification> ON 0,
NON EMPTY <axis_specification> HAVING <filter condition> ON 1
FROM <cube identifier>
```

The following MDX query uses the HAVING clause to analyze the gross profit of all the products that have sales amounts of $5,000 for a product in any city within a month:

```
SELECT {[Measures].[Gross Profit]} on 0,
NON EMPTY [Product].[Product Categories].[Product] * [Customer].[Customer
Geography].[City]
* [Date].[Fiscal].[Month].members
HAVING [Sales Amount] > 5000 on 1
from [Adventure Works]
```

Ranking and Sorting

Ranking and Sorting are pretty common features in most business analysis. MDX provides several MDX functions such as TOPCOUNT, BOTTOMCOUNT, TOPPERCENT, BOTTOMPERCENT, and RANK that help you stack rank information for better business decisions. You saw an example of RANK in Chapter 3. This section uses the Adventure Works DW sample database to show a few examples of some common business questions in the retail industry that business analysts might be looking at.

Example 1

If you want to get an overview of the various products sold across various countries and through internet sales, the following MDX query will provide you the results. You can set a Sales Quota for subsequent years to improve revenue on specific countries or specific products to have an overall impact for the company.

```
SELECT [Customer].[Customer Geography].[Country] on 0,
[Product].[Category].members on 1
from [Adventure Works]
WHERE (Measures.[Internet Sales Amount])
```

Example 2

In the case of companies which manufacture and sell products, it is desirable to take a look at how various products are performing on a periodic basis. If you are looking for the top N product categories or subcategories based on the sales in all the countries, the following queries will provide you the answer. Based on the results you can invest more in marketing campaigns and other initiatives to further boost the sales and revenue for the company.

```
SELECT Measures.[Internet Sales Amount] on COLUMNS,
TOPCOUNT([Product].[Product Categories].[Category].Members,
3, Measures.[Internet Sales Amount]) ON ROWS
from [Adventure Works]

SELECT Measures.[Internet Sales Amount] on COLUMNS,
TOPCOUNT([Product].[Product Categories].[SubCategory].Members,
10, Measures.[Internet Sales Amount]) ON ROWS
from [Adventure Works]
```

Example 3

If you want to drill down further on the top 10 product categories within the United States, you can use the following query. Based on this information you can improve sales on products that are doing well or try to boost sales on the remaining products after some market research on why they are not doing well.

```
SELECT Measures.[Internet Sales Amount] on COLUMNS,
TOPCOUNT([Product].[Product Categories].[SubCategory].Members,
10, Measures.[Internet Sales Amount]) ON ROWS
from [Adventure Works]
WHERE ([Customer].[Customer Geography].[Country].&[United States])
```

Example 4

If you want to see growth figures for the top 5 products in the last 4 quarters, you can use the following MDX query. This query provides you with the trend information that allows you to see if the top 5 products have been consistently increasing in sales. If you see that some products do not show a positive trend, you do need to drill down further for details and take appropriate action.

```
 WITH SET [Top5Products] as 'TopCount( [Product].[Product
Categories].[SubCategory].Members,
     5,Measures.[Internet Sales Amount]   )'
SET [CurrentQuarter] as 'Tail(Filter([Date].[Fiscal].[Fiscal Quarter].Members,
        Not IsEmpty([Date].[Fiscal].CurrentMember)),1)'
SET [Previous4Quarters] as ' [CurrentQuarter].item(0).item(0).Lag(4) :
[CurrentQuarter].item(0).item(0).Lag(1) '
MEMBER Measures.Growth AS
([Date].[Fiscal].currentmember ,[Measures].[Internet Sales Amount])
-
([Date].[Fiscal].currentmember.prevmember, [Measures].[Internet Sales Amount])/
([Date].[Fiscal].currentmember, [Measures].[Internet Sales Amount])* 100

select [Top5Products]  on COLUMNS,
 [Previous4Quarters] on ROWS
from [Adventure Works]
WHERE  [Growth]
```

Example 5

In order to maximize your business you might discontinue products that are not providing your best sales. Typically companies might cut their work force by 10% to increase the company's bottom line. Assume you want to analyze the products to see the bottom 10% of the products in terms of Internet sales. You can send the following MDX queries from SSMS. You can see that there are 159 products that contribute toward internet sales and out of these, 95 products contribute to the bottom 10% of the overall sales. Now you can further drill down at each product and identify the cost of selling them over the internet and see if it really makes sense to keep selling these products.

```
//Total number of products contributing towards internet sales - 159 products
select {[Measures].[Internet Sales Amount]} on COLUMNS,
 Non Empty[Product].[Product Categories].[Product Name].Members on ROWS
from [Adventure Works]

//Bottom 10% (Sales) of the products sold through the internet - 95 products
select {[Measures].[Internet Sales Amount]} on COLUMNS,
 Non Empty BottomPercent([Product].[Product Categories].[Product Name].Members, 10,
 [Measures].[Internet Sales Amount]) on ROWS
from [Adventure Works]
```

Parameterize Your Queries

Parameterized queries in MDX, as the name suggests, help in passing parameters to a query where the values for the parameters are substituted before query execution. Why are parameterized queries important? You might have heard about attacks on web sites where users hack the sites by entering their own SQL, and as a result see data they should not see or change the data in the relational databases. This is because of those applications that are used to get input from users and concatenate the input string to form SQL queries. Often such applications run the queries under administrative privileges. Knowing this, hackers can enter inputs that are SQL constructs and that are executed along with the full SQL query. This is called *SQL injection* because hackers inject their own SQL queries within the overall query.

Similar threats exist for MDX as well. One of the main reasons why such attacks are possible is because user input is not validated.

Analysis Services overcomes the MDX injection by allowing parameters to be passed along with queries. Analysis Services validates these parameters, replaces the parameters in the query with the values, and then executes the query. The parameters to a query are represented within the query prefixed with the @ symbol. The following is a parameterized query. In this query the Number of children of a customer is the parameter.

```
SELECT NON EMPTY { [Measures].[Internet Sales Amount] } ON COLUMNS, NON EMPTY {
([Customer].[Customer Geography].[Country].ALLMEMBERS ) } DIMENSION PROPERTIES
MEMBER_CAPTION, MEMBER_UNIQUE_NAME ON ROWS FROM ( SELECT (
STRTOSET(@CustomerTotalChildren, CONSTRAINED) ) ON COLUMNS FROM ( SELECT ( {
[Date].[Fiscal].[Fiscal Year].&[2004], [Date].[Fiscal].[Fiscal Year].&[2005] } ) ON
COLUMNS FROM ( SELECT ( { [Product].[Product Categories].[Subcategory].&[26],
[Product].[Product Categories].[Subcategory].&[27] } ) ON COLUMNS FROM [Adventure
Works]))) WHERE ( [Product].[Product Categories].CurrentMember,
[Date].[Fiscal].CurrentMember, IIF( STRTOSET(@CustomerTotalChildren,
CONSTRAINED).Count = 1, STRTOSET(@CustomerTotalChildren, CONSTRAINED),
[Customer].[Total Children].currentmember ) ) CELL PROPERTIES VALUE, BACK_COLOR,
FORE_COLOR, FORMATTED_VALUE, FORMAT_STRING, FONT_NAME, FONT_SIZE, FONT_FLAGS
```

Your client application would send the preceding query along with the list of parameters and values. When you execute the query you will get the results similar to executing regular queries. The following is an XMLA script that shows how the parameters are sent to Analysis Services. You have a name and value pair specified for each parameter in the query under the Parameters section of the XMLA script for query execution.

```
<Envelope xmlns="http://schemas.xmlsoap.org/soap/envelope/">
  <Body>
    <Execute xmlns="urn:schemas-microsoft-com:xml-analysis">
      <Command>
        <Statement>
select [Measures].members on 0,
       Filter(Customer.[Customer Geography].Country.members,
              Customer.[Customer Geography].CurrentMember.Name =
              @CountryName) on 1
from [Adventure Works]
</Statement>
      </Command>
      <Properties />
      <Parameters>
        <Parameter>
          <Name>CountryName</Name>
          <Value>'United Kingdom'</Value>
        </Parameter>
      </Parameters>
    </Execute>
  </Body>
</Envelope>
```

You will see an example of parameterized queries using the client object model ADOMD.Net in Chapter 9.

New MDX Functions

Analysis Services 2005 introduces several new MDX functions to facilitate data extraction from the UDM. The following table covers some of the functions and gives a brief description about their behavior for quick reference. Detailed information about these functions is provided in Appendix A. We recommend you learn more about the MDX functions used in MDX scripts with scenarios in *MDX Solutions 2nd Edition* by George Spofford et al. (Wiley, 2006).

MDX Function	Description
MeasureGroupMeasures(<Measure Group Name>)	This function retrieves all the measures within a specific measure group. Because the UDM can contain several measure groups, this function helps by making the query more specific.
EXISTS (<set>,<filterset> EXISTS(<set>,<filterset>,<measuregroup name>	This function is used to determine if tuples in the set exist with the tuples in the filter set. If yes, those tuples are returned. When the measure group argument is used, the measure group is used to determine the EXISTS operation.
KPI Functions – KPICURRENTTIMEMEMBER(«String Expression») KPIGOAL(«String Expression» KPISTATUS(«String Expression» KPITREND(«String Expression») KPIVALUE(«String Expression») KPIWEIGHT(«String Expression»)	KPI functions help in retrieving the values for the KPI, which help in displaying the status of KPI through KPI graphic icons. Some of these functions return normalized values between -1 and 1. All the KPI functions except KPICurrentTimeMember take the KPI name as an argument and return values that can be matched with the corresponding graphic. These functions are helpful for client-side programming where you retrieve the value and show the corresponding icon that visually represents the status. Analysis Services internally treats these as just calculations. KPICurrentTimeMember retrieves the time member corresponding to the KPI, which can be different from the default member on the Time dimension.

Table continued on following page

MDX Function	Description
UnOrder(<set>)	MDX usually returns an order set in the results. Often this ordering takes additional overhead on the server. The UnOrder function instructs Analysis Services to return results without ordering. This often helps in improving performance on large results sets, which are typically crossjoins of several hierarchies.
Error(<Error message>) Error	This helps in throwing user-defined errors in cases where certain operations are not possible.
Root (Dimension) Leaves(Dimension)	Root and Leaves functions are used in Scripts for appropriately positioning the coordinate on a dimension for allocations or assignments.

Summary

You have learned the calculation fundamentals in Analysis Services 2005 and the use of MDX scripts to apply global scope calculations. MDX scripting includes creating calculated members, named sets, and assignments. Kind of makes you want to specialize in MDX, doesn't it? This is great stuff! This chapter does not provide an in-depth view of the Analysis Services 2005 calculations and various overwrite semantics of calculations due to the relationship between attributes simply because it is too vast to cover here. This chapter is meant to serve as an introduction to the Analysis Services 2005 calculation model with some examples of solving common problems. Several sections in this chapter cover the sort of MDX used to solve some of the common business questions and some MDX enhancements in Analysis Services 2005. MDX is like an ocean. Even when you think you have mastered it you might end up finding there are things you have not learned. Typically you will learn a lot of MDX as and when you implement customer solutions. If you want to dive fully into MDX, understand the concepts discussed in the chapter in detail including the calculation precedence rules; we highly recommend you read *MDX Solutions 2nd Edition* by George Spofford et al. (Wiley, 2006).

Having learned some of the fundamental concepts of calculations in Analysis Services 2005, you are ready for a deeper understanding of the dimensions and cubes discussed in the next two chapters. Don't think you are done learning MDX in this book. You will be learning additional MDX in subsequent chapters through illustrations and examples wherever applicable. Your journey through the Analysis Services landscape will become even more interesting and exciting as you work your way through the book.

Advanced Dimension Design

In this look at advanced dimension design, you learn to aggregate data up to the parent member through custom rollup operations and learn about the effects of dimension and hierarchy properties. Also, you learn about business intelligence wizards which help you enhance dimensions. Finally, you are introduced to dimension writeback, which is a way to make changes to dimension members for "what" if analysis. Consider first the details you already learned about dimension design back in Chapter 5; you learned how dimensions, which are made up of hierarchies, consist of tiers called levels. The two types of hierarchies were described, both attribute and multi-level hierarchies, and the Time dimension and Parent-Child dimensions were discussed in some detail.

Here you learn about the ways you can leverage and extend dimensions to get even more value out of them. Normally, you would expect the data to be aggregated to its parent. For example, if you have a hierarchy such as Time, then Sales per month will be rolled up to calculate first the Sales of a quarter, and Sales Quarters will be rolled up to calculate the Sales of a year. Even though this is the most common way a user would expect the data to be aggregated, there are dimensions in which the data does not get rolled up by a simple sum. Another take-away from Chapter 5 was that parent-child hierarchies are special, and Analysis Services 2005 provides properties that help enhance dimensions that contain parent-child hierarchies.

If you don't get the in-depth details of this chapter just from reading the narrative descriptions, don't worry; the concepts are demonstrated through examples as well. This area is a classic example of "It seems profoundly difficult until you get it, but once you get it, it is so simple as to seem obvious." If you already know the concepts mentioned above or otherwise understood them after reading this paragraph, read the chapter anyway, it goes far beyond the basics.

> If you came to this chapter looking for information on calculated members or Data Mining dimensions, both being perfectly reasonable to expect here, well, they are not covered here. For information on Calculated Members, please see Chapter 3 and for Data Mining dimensions, please see Chapter 14.

Custom Rollups

The name "custom rollup" is very much self describing. Custom refers to the "user defined" nature of a rollup, such that a measure value for a member is not a simple sum of values of its children as you move up a hierarchy. Rollup describes how those calculations typically start at the leaf or lower-level node and move (roll) up toward the root. There are several ways in which you can apply a custom rollup to a hierarchy: by using the attribute property CustomRollup column, using unary operators (used for parent-child hierarchies), and by using MDX scripts to specify custom rollup for members in a level. Note that unary operators can be used on non-parent-child hierarchies too.

A business scenario will help you better understand the need for and concept of the custom rollup. Perhaps you are familiar with the word *depreciation*.Technically, the definition of depreciation is "mapping an asset's expense over time to benefits gained through use of those assets." It simply means that the value of an asset decreases over time. When working on the financial side of business intelligence it is only a matter of time before you encounter the concept of depreciation, so if you don't already know it, study this carefully. As you may already know, the value of a car decreases over the years. In fact, after the moment you drive off the lot, the new car's value starts to decrease. This is a common example of depreciation.

There are two types of depreciation you should be familiar with and understand. They are called straight-line and accelerated. Typically, businesses keep two (sometimes more) sets of accounting books, which, by the way, is completely legal. One set of books is for the IRS and one set is for investors. The books for the IRS often use accelerated depreciation because this provides optimal tax benefits (less taxable income is initially reported) and the books for investors use straight-line depreciation because this yields higher net earnings per share for that quarter or year and a more favorable ROE (Return on Equity), which is the net income divided by the shareholder's equity.

Accelerated depreciation on a delivery van, illustrated in Figure 8-1, can be thought of as "front loaded" depreciation; the percentages associated with each year indicate the percentage of total value depreciated or "written off" for that year. The fact that 40% is depreciated the first year and 10% the last year speaks to the notion that the depreciation is front loaded. There is no cash involved in recognizing depreciation, yet there is a reduction in asset value and an expense is logged; hence it is called a non-cash expense. The company can write off more of the van's value earlier on their taxes. That means less taxable income for the company in the earlier years and that is a good thing.

Straight-line depreciation on the same delivery van, illustrated in Figure 8-2, again happens over time until the van is essentially worthless with no salvage value (in this case after five hard-driving years). Notice that the rate at which the van falls apart is the same, regardless of how depreciation is logged on the financial records. In this case, the non-cash expense is logged in equal amounts over the life of the asset at 20% per year. The effect this method has is that an investor sees an asset retaining value for a longer period. That is a good thing because value ultimately relates to stock price.

Having learned about depreciation you can understand the need for custom rollup of member values in a hierarchy to their parent—it all depends on the type of depreciation being logged and therefore will be custom, by definition. In order to calculate the net profit of your company, you would typically add up the sales revenue, any increase in asset values, and subtract the expenditures (Cost of Goods Sold) and depreciation values appropriately. You might be wondering if these are just measure values, what is so complex about them. Why not just write a calculated measure appropriately? That would be a reasonable question to ask. And if it is just measures you're dealing with, you don't have a problem.

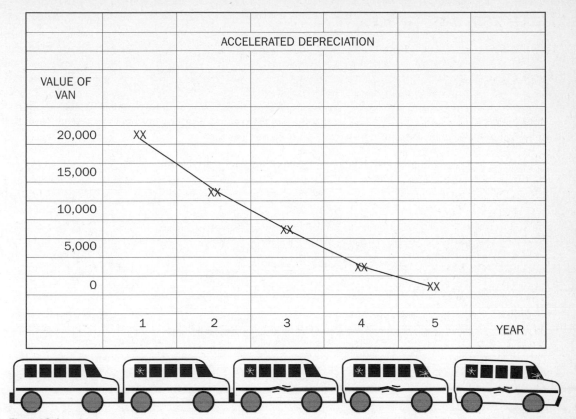

Figure 8-1

By definition, depreciation indicates that values change over time. So, your calculations that reflect the value of physical assets (like delivery vans) should be adjusted for appropriate percentage changes based on the Time dimension you are querying. Similarly, there might be other dimensions or measure groups that calculations might depend on. For example, say you have a Budget measure group and a Sales measure group in your cube. Your budget for next year might depend on the sales of the previous year and you need to use appropriate MDX expression to arrive at the budget amount. You can create such custom calculations using MDX scripts with appropriate SCOPE statements, but it will be quite a lengthy script, especially if the calculations are different for each member in a dimension. Also, verifying that your calculations are giving the correct values will be time-consuming. Analysis Services 2005 allows you to specify the calculations through MDX expressions as a property to the hierarchy.

Here is an example. If there is an Account dimension that indicates the types of accounts of your company, such as asset, liability, income, and expenditure, and you have a measure called Amount, the rollup of the values to the parent member is not a simple sum. In such a case, you need to specify a custom rollup. If the hierarchy is a parent-child hierarchy, Analysis Services 2005 allows you to perform a custom rollup using a feature called the unary operator if it is a simple operation (addition, subtraction, do not rollup the values), which is discussed in the next section. However, if the value of a member has not derived from its children or you have a user hierarchy where you have to rollup the values to the parent using a complex operation or custom formula, you specify the custom rollup using a property called CustomRollupColumn for an attribute hierarchy.

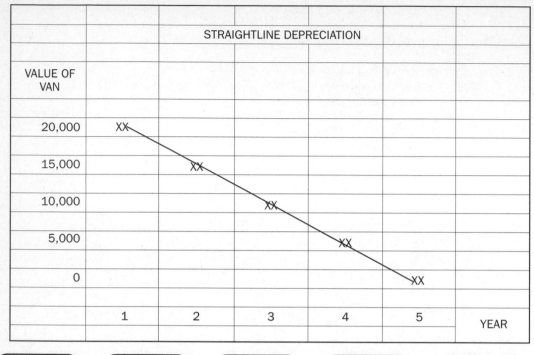

Figure 8-2

The CustomRollupColumn property of an attribute should be set as a column in the relational table that will contain the custom rollup calculation — which is an MDX expression. For example, in the Account dimension in Adventure Works DW sample, the value for Account Average Unit is calculated from the Accounts Net Sales and Units, which are members in the Account dimension under different parents. In order to specify the custom formula for a member, the column in the relational table should contain an MDX expression that evaluates the value for the member. You need to specify an MDX expression for each member a custom formula needs to be applied to. In Analysis Services 2000 you had properties to specify custom formulas to members and Custom Rollup Formulas to levels within dimensions. You can consider the CustomRollupColumn property for a hierarchy in Analysis Services 2005 as merging the two properties in Analysis Services 2000. It would have probably been better to name this property CustomFormula instead of CustomRollup. Follow the steps below to understand the behavior of a custom rollup by using the sample Adventure Works DW relational database.

1. Create a new Analysis Services project called AnalysisServicesTutorial using BIDS.

2. Create a data source to the AdventureWorksDW relational database on your SQL Server instance.

3. Create a Data Source View that contains all the tables except AdventureWorksDWBuildVersion, DatabaseLog, and ProspectiveBuyer within the Adventure Works DW data source, as shown in Figure 8-3.

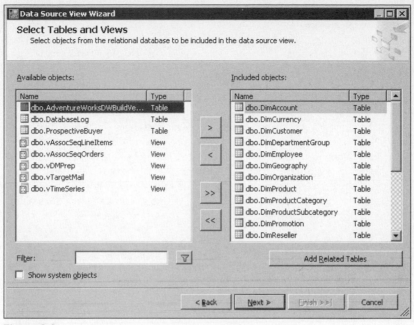

Figure 8-3

4. Create the dimensions using the Dimension Wizard and select the defaults so that you end up with the dimensions shown in Figure 8-4. Include the table DimProductCategory and DimProductSubcategory along with DimProduct while creating the DimProduct dimension so that you have a snowflake dimension. All the remaining dimensions are created using the appropriate dimension table from the DSV. The Dimension Wizard will automatically detect parent-child hierarchies for dimensions DimEmployee, DimAccount, DimDepartmentGroup, and DimOrganization. The wizard will create appropriate parent-child hierarchies with that information. Go ahead and create the Time dimension Dim Time by defining appropriate time periods.

Figure 8-4

5. Create a new cube using the Cube Wizard. In the "Identify Fact and Dimension Tables" dialog mark all tables beginning with the word Fact as fact tables only, all tables beginning with Dim as dimension tables, and specify the time dimension table as shown in Figure 8-5. Add all the dimensions created in step 4 as cube dimensions and complete the Cube Wizard with the defaults. You will now have Adventure Works DW cube created. The Cube Wizard detects the relationship between the fact and dimension tables based on relationships in the DSV and creates appropriate dimension usage. If you do need to change the relationships you can do so on the Dimension Usage tab within the cube editor. If you look at the relationships in the Dimension Usage tab you will notice that there are multiple instances of certain dimensions. For example, you will see four instances of the DimTime dimension Dim Time, Dime Time (Due Date), Dim Time (Order Date), and Dim Time (Ship Date). Instead of creating four database dimensions and using them within the cube, Analysis Services 2005 creates cube dimensions from a single dimension. Typically when you have multiple relationships between a fact table and dimension table then the optimal way to model them is with a single database dimension. Such dimensions are called *role playing* dimensions.

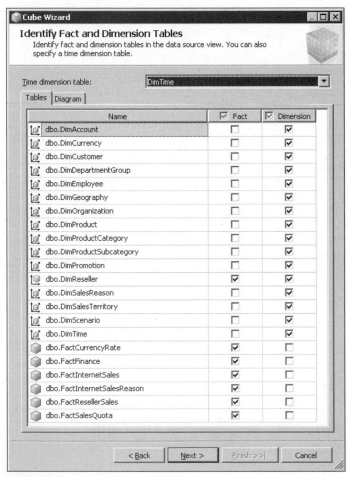

Figure 8-5

6. Double-click the Dim Account dimension in Solution Explorer. Notice the attribute hierarchies of Dim Account dimension within the Dimension Designer. If you switch to the Dimension Browser and browse the parent-child hierarchy, you will see the account numbers. In order to view the Account names while browsing the parent-child hierarchy you need to specify the NameColumn property for the key attribute, which you learned about in Chapter 5. Select the key attribute Dim Account and specify the relational column AccountDescription as the NameColumn property for the key attribute and then deploy the changes to the Analysis Services instance. If you go to the Dimension Browser you will see the name of the accounts.

In the properties for an attribute you will see a property called CustomRollupColumn, as shown in Figure 8-6. This property needs to be set to the relational column that has the MDX expression for custom rollup formula. The MDX expression specified in this property gets evaluated on the cells when the value's corresponding members of the hierarchy are being retrieved in the query.

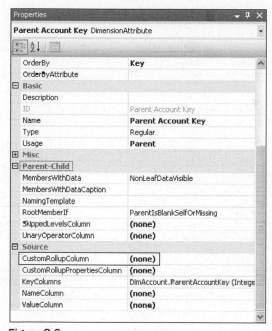

Figure 8-6

7. The sample AdventureWorksDW relational database provides a column with custom rollups for the Account dimension. Right-click the DimAccount table in the DSV of the dimension DimAccount and select Explore Data. You will see the data in the relational table as shown in Figure 8-7. The relational column CustomMembers contains the MDX expression for custom rollup. In the AdventureWorksDW relational sample there is an MDX expression defined for an Account, which has AccountKey = 98 as shown in Figure 8-7. There are no children for the Account with AccountKey = 98 (Account Name is "Average Unit Price") and there are no corresponding fact rows in the fact table FactFinance. Therefore, if you browse the current Adventure Works DW cube in Cube Browser, you will see a null value for the Average Unit Price account. The MDX expression in the relational table for Average Unit Price account is:

```
[Account].[Accounts].[Account Level 04].&[50]/[Account].[Accounts].[Account Level
02].&[97]
```

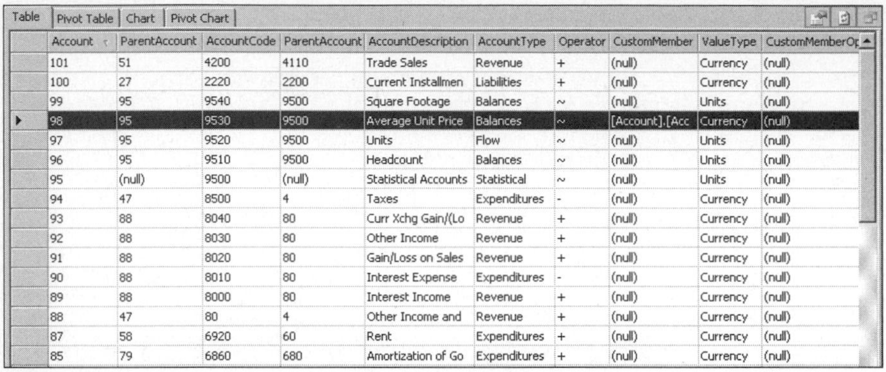

Table | Pivot Table | Chart | Pivot Chart

Account	ParentAccount	AccountCode	ParentAccount	AccountDescription	AccountType	Operator	CustomMember	ValueType	CustomMemberOp
101	51	4200	4110	Trade Sales	Revenue	+	(null)	Currency	(null)
100	27	2220	2200	Current Installmen	Liabilities	+	(null)	Currency	(null)
99	95	9540	9500	Square Footage	Balances	~	(null)	Units	(null)
98	95	9530	9500	Average Unit Price	Balances	~	[Account].[Acc	Currency	(null)
97	95	9520	9500	Units	Flow	~	(null)	Units	(null)
96	95	9510	9500	Headcount	Balances	~	(null)	Units	(null)
95	(null)	9500	(null)	Statistical Accounts	Statistical	~	(null)	Units	(null)
94	47	8500	4	Taxes	Expenditures	-	(null)	Currency	(null)
93	88	8040	80	Curr Xchg Gain/(Lo	Revenue	+	(null)	Currency	(null)
92	88	8030	80	Other Income	Revenue	+	(null)	Currency	(null)
91	88	8020	80	Gain/Loss on Sales	Revenue	+	(null)	Currency	(null)
90	88	8010	80	Interest Expense	Expenditures	-	(null)	Currency	(null)
89	88	8000	80	Interest Income	Revenue	+	(null)	Currency	(null)
88	47	80	4	Other Income and	Revenue	+	(null)	Currency	(null)
87	58	6920	60	Rent	Expenditures	+	(null)	Currency	(null)
85	79	6860	680	Amortization of Go	Expenditures	+	(null)	Currency	(null)

Figure 8-7

When evaluated this MDX expression will provide the amount for Account Average Unit Price from Accounts Net Sales and Units. Accounts Net Sales and Units are not children of the Average Unit Price account and hence the custom formula mentioned earlier calculates the value for Average Unit Price Account. In the preceding expression you see that the dimension and hierarchy names specified are Account and Accounts, respectively. Notice the members specified in the MDX expression for custom rollup include the level names Account Level 04 and Account Level 02. By default, the level names for parent-child hierarchies have the names "Level xx". Hence you also need to make sure you specify appropriate property to have the level names as shown in the MDX expression. Hence you need to change the name of the dimension and the parent-child hierarchy in your database.

8. Right click on the dimension name Dim Account and click Rename. Enter the name Account. When asked if the object name needs to be changed, click Yes. Open the Account dimension in Dimension Designer. Right-click the parent-child hierarchy Parent Account Key and rename it Accounts. You now need to specify the level names for the parent-child hierarchy. Enter the value "Account Level *;" next to the Accounts parent-child hierarchy property Naming template and set the property IsAggregatable to False. You learn more about these properties later in this chapter. Don't think you have completed all the renaming yet. You have currently renamed the dimension and hierarchy. When an MDX expression within a cube is calculated, the dimension name addressed with the cube is the cube dimension and not the database dimension that you just renamed. Hence you also need to rename the cube dimension name for dimension Account. Open the cube Adventure Works Cube. Click the Cube Structure tab; right-click the Account dimension in the Dimensions pane and select Rename. Enter the name Account. You have successfully made changes to your cube to define the custom rollup formula for the Accounts hierarchy.

9. Select the property CustomRollupColumn for the Accounts hierarchy in the Account dimension. Click the drop-down list box and select New. In the Object binding dialog select the CustomMembers column in the Dim Account table as the column for the CustomRollupColumn property as shown in Figure 8-8. You have successfully specified a custom formula for members of the Accounts hierarchy. In addition to specifying a custom formula using CustomRollupColumn, you can also specify the CustomRollupPropertiesColumn property to apply custom properties on the cell value. The CustomRollupPropertiesColumn property also takes a column in the relational

table as input and that column should contain the MDX expression. Typically you would specify the cell properties such as background color and foreground color using an MDX expression. The sample relational database does not contain values for CustomRollupPropertiesColumn and hence we leave the exercise of exploring the properties to you.

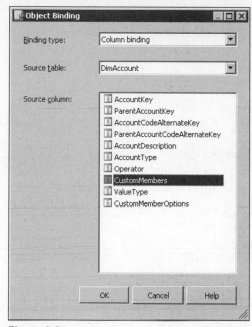

Figure 8-8

Deploy the project to the Analysis Services instance. To make sure the custom rollup column MDX expression is correctly evaluated for the Average Unit Price account, go to the Cube Browser and browse the Accounts dimension and the measure Amount from the Fact Finance measure group. You will see the value for Average Unit Price is now calculated using the MDX expression as shown in Figure 8-9. Using a calculator you can easily verify that the value for Average Unit Price is equal to the value of Net Sales divided by the Units.

Drop Filter Fields Here

Account Level 01 ▾	Account Level 02	Account Level 03	Account Level 04	Amount
				1107010918.52
⊞ Balance Sheet				
⊟ Net Income	⊟ Operating Profit	⊟ Gross Margin	⊞ Net Sales	140448069.35
			⊞ Total Cost of Sales	41007898.98
			Total	181455968.33
		⊞ Operating Expenses		50055025.2
		Total		231510993.53
	⊞ Other Income and Expense			502384.64
	⊞ Taxes			7243791.01
	Total			239257169.18
⊟ Statistical Accounts	⊞ Headcount			7002
	⊞ Units			201323
	⊞ Average Unit Price			697.625553712193
	⊞ Square Footage			12164000
	Total			12373022.6255537

(Drop Column Fields Here)

Figure 8-9

You have now successfully learned to apply a custom formula to members of a hierarchy. In this example, a parent-child hierarchy was used for you to understand the CustomRollupColumn property; however, the custom rollup is not limited to parent-child hierarchies but can be used on any hierarchy. As mentioned, Analysis Services 2000 provided a way to specify a custom formula for a level within a hierarchy. You can specify such a formula in your MDX script or specify the custom formula for the members in a relational column and use the CustomRollupColumn property for that hierarchy. If an attribute hierarchy is part of multiple user hierarchies and you need to apply different custom rollup behavior based on the hierarchy, you need to apply these custom formulas in the MDX script. Analysis Services 20005 provides another way to aggregate data for members in parent-child hierarchies using a property called *UnaryOperatorColumn*. The next section provides further details.

Enhancements to Parent-Child Hierarchies

The parent-child hierarchy structure is particularly common in business so it is very important for you to master the techniques related to it. In this section, the concepts discussed in the previous section are extended. Several important properties are supported by Analysis Services 2005 for parent-child hierarchies. One of the important properties for a parent-child hierarchy is called the *UnaryOperatorColumn*.

Unary Operators

Unary operators are used for custom rollup of members to their parent where the rollup operation is a unary operation. A unary operator, as the name suggests, is an operator that takes a single argument — the member — and rolls up the value of the member to its parent. As with the custom rollup column, you need to have the unary operators specified as a column in the relational table, and this column must be set as a property for the parent-child hierarchy. Unary operators can be applied also to non parent-child hierarchies, but that scenario will not be covered here. The following table shows the various unary operators supported by Analysis Services and a description of their behavior.

Unary Operator	Description
+	The value of the member is added to the aggregate value of the preceding sibling members. This is the default operator used if no unary operator column is specified.
-	The value of the member is subtracted from the aggregate value of the preceding sibling members.
*	The value of the member is multiplied by the aggregate value of the preceding sibling members.
/	The value of the member is divided by the aggregate value of the preceding sibling members.
~	The value of the member is ignored.
N	The value is multiplied by N and added to the aggregate values. N can be any numeric value (typically N is between 0 and 1).
	An empty unary operator is equivalent to "+".

A business scenario commonly used to demonstrate the usefulness of rollups using unary operators is the case where Net Income equals Sales minus Cost of Goods Sold. As for the calculation of tax at different rates depending on tax bracket, that will come a little later because calculating those values will require custom rollups, and for now the topic of discussion is the unary operator. In this example, Sales figures will be added, hence the "+" operator is used, and for Cost of Goods Sold, which is subtracted, the "-" operator is used. Were depreciation included in the following example, given that it is a non-cash expense, you might choose to ignore it in the hierarchy by using the tilde (~) unary operator. Follow the steps below to set up unary operators for the parent-child hierarchies in the Account and Organization dimensions.

1. Open the Account dimension and click the Accounts hierarchy. In the Properties window you will see the properties associated with parent-child hierarchies under a section called Parent-Child, as shown in Figure 8-10. Click the drop-down list box next to UnaryOperatorColumn and select New.

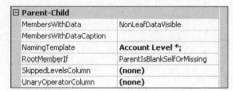

Parent-Child	
MembersWithData	NonLeafDataVisible
MembersWithDataCaption	
NamingTemplate	**Account Level *;**
RootMemberIf	ParentIsBlankSelfOrMissing
SkippedLevelsColumn	(none)
UnaryOperatorColumn	**(none)**

Figure 8-10

2. In the Object Binding dialog select Operator as the column, as shown in Figure 8-11.

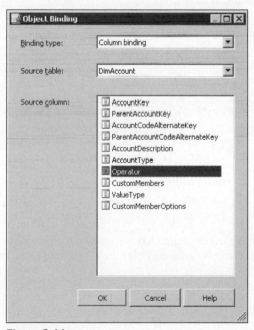

Figure 8-11

If you explore the data for DimAccount table, you can see the unary operators associated for each account as shown earlier in Figure 8-7. Note that there are "~" operators indicating "ignore this" for certain items. Deploy the changes to your Analysis Services instance. Because the Operator column is an attribute hierarchy in the Account dimension, it automatically becomes a member property of the key attribute. All member properties of the key attribute are automatically inherited by the parent attribute, the parent-child hierarchy. Therefore you can view the unary operators associated with each account in the Dimension Browser by enabling the member property Operator as shown in Figure 8-12.

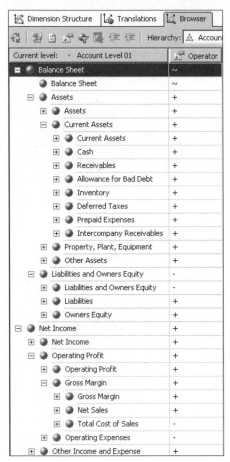

Figure 8-12

3. The next step is to ensure that you have set the unary operators correctly and the rollup to parent occurs as desired. For verification, edit the Adventure Works DW cube and click the Browser tab. Drag and drop the Amount measure and the parent-child hierarchy Accounts from the Metadata pane to the data and row area within the Cube Browser, and then expand the levels Net Income→Operating Profit→Gross Margin. Before specifying the unary operator, Analysis Services aggregates the values for Net Sales and Total Cost of Sales as a sum to calculate the value for Gross Margin. Because a unary operator has been specified, you should see the value for Gross Margin is the difference of Net Sales and Total Cost of Sales, as shown in Figure 8-13.

Account Level 01 ▾	Account Level 02	Account Level 03	Account Level 04	Account Level 05	Amount
					Drop Column Fields Here
⊞ Balance Sheet					2.38418579101563E-07
⊟ Net Income	⊟ Operating Profit	⊟ Gross Margin	⊞ Net Sales		127234148.59
			⊞ Total Cost of Sales		41007898.98
			Total		86226249.6099999
		⊞ Operating Expenses			50055025.2
		Total			36171224.41
	⊞ Other Income and Expense				50937.4600000001
	⊞ Taxes				7243791.01
	Total				28978370.86

(Drop Filter Fields Here)

Figure 8-13

Analysis Services 2005 introduces a new unary operator, which is referred to as N in the unary operator table. N is a numerical value that is used as a weighting factor so that the value of the member is multiplied by the value N and then aggregated to the parent. For example a company might calculate overhead costs for utilities like electricity at the level of an entire factory. Electricity consumption is not evenly distributed across the organizations within the factory, though; the manufacturing floor might be sucking up power at a rate completely disproportionate to the administrative section. This disparity is something that should be accounted for when doing internal costing analysis. One way managerial accountants address the problem is to calculate the overhead at the departmental level and at the factory level. The amount of electricity consumed can be weighted by some predetermined amount such that cost assignments are rolled up to the correct parents. For example, the manufacturing department could be assigned a ratio of 1 to 9 for factory level overhead versus department level overhead. That is, 10% of the electricity used by manufacturing facilities is assigned to factory overhead, while the other 90% is assigned as a department-specific cost.

In some organizations, even though a group is reporting to a parent (higher level group), the measure value of the sub-group might be rolled up as a fraction of the total measure value to the parent. This is because parent groups only own a part of the organization. If you know the percentage of ownership for various organizations as a measure, you can specify CustomRollupColumn with an appropriate MDX expression. However, with Analysis Services 2005's unary operator N, you can simply specify the rollup using numerical values.

The AdventureWorksDW relational database provides an example of the unary operator N for the Organization dimension, where the percentage of ownership is specified in a column in the Dim Organization table. Follow the steps below to enhance the Dim Organization dimension created by the Dimension Wizard so that the dimension is modeled to match the actual business results:

1. Open the Dim Organization Dimension. Specify the NameColumn property for the key attribute as OrganizationName.

2. Rename the Parent Organization Key parent-child hierarchy to Organizations. Click the UnaryOperatorColumn and select New. In the Object Binding dialog, select the PercentageOfOwnership column.

At this point, you have specified the weighted average for the Organizations parent-child hierarchy. You might immediately want to see the results by deploying the changes. However, if you do deploy as such, you might see weird results because of the way calculations are applied in the cube. This is because when Analysis Services retrieves data for measures across a specific hierarchy, it takes the default members of other hierarchies while doing this evaluation. For most hierarchies the All member is the default. In the Account dimension the IsAggregatable property is set to false because aggregating the data for the top-level members in the Account dimension does not make business sense. In such circumstances, Analysis Services uses the default member of the hierarchy. If a default member is not specified, Analysis Services retrieves the first member of the hierarchy. The first member of the Accounts hierarchy is Balance Sheet and the unary operator for Balance Sheet, ~ (tilde), will result in very weird or non-intuitive results. In order for you to see meaningful results, you need to make sure you choose the right default.

3. For the Accounts hierarchy, click the DefaultMember property. In the Set Default Member dialog, choose a member to be the default option, select Net Income, and click the OK button. The Net Income member has a unary operator of +, which will result in meaningful data being seen while browsing the Amount measure for other dimensions. Now, deploy the changes to the Analysis Services instance. This percentage of ownership will be applied for the measures being queried.

4. If you browse the Organization dimension along with the measure Amount you will notice appropriate rollups based on the weighted unary operator. Figure 8-14 shows the amount for various organizations, and you can see that the amount from the Canadian organization is aggregated as 0.75 to the North American organization.

Drop Filter Fields Here				
				Drop Column Fields
Level 02 ▾	Level 03	Level 04	Level 05	Amount
⊟ AdventureWorks Cycle	⊟ North America Operations	⊞ Canadian Division		9366434.10000001
		⊞ USA Operations		18193403
		Total		25218228.575
	⊞ European Operations			566471.697499999
	⊞ Pacific Operations			64215.0749999985
	Total			25832861.57875
Grand Total				25832861.57875

Figure 8-14

When multiple calculations are specified for a cell, Analysis Services 2005 uses a specific order in which calculations are evaluated. Due to the order of calculations, cell values might not always be intuitive and you can sometimes see results other than expected. This is mostly due to the way in which calculations are being applied. We highly recommend you know your cube design well and the calculation precedence (order of calculations) and to subsequently verify the results. Several calculations can be applied to a measure: semi-additive calculation, unary operator, and custom rollup. You learn more about semi-additive measures briefly in this chapter and in detail in Chapter 9. When Analysis Services is evaluating the measure value for a member, it initially calculates the regular aggregate of the measure value. This aggregate can be Sum, Count, or any of the semi-additive functions (to be discussed later). If a unary operator is specified, the unary operator rollup is applied for the member across that specific dimension and the value of the measure is overwritten. Finally, if a custom rollup is specified for the member, the value resulting from the custom rollup MDX expression is evaluated as the final result. The evaluation of a cell value is done across each dimension and if dimensions have custom rollups and unary operators then all the unary operators are applied followed by custom rollups based on the order of the dimensions within the cube.

Specifying Names to Levels of a Parent-Child Hierarchy

When you create multi-level hierarchies, various attribute hierarchies form the levels of the hierarchy. For example, in a Geography hierarchy you will have Country, State, City, and Zip Code as levels and when you browse the dimension you can see the names of the levels as the names of the attribute hierarchies. Parent-child hierarchies are unique and different from the user hierarchies. While creating regular hierarchies, you can see the various levels in the dimension editor, but for parent-child hierarchies you cannot visually see the number of levels unless you process and browse the hierarchy. The levels within a parent-child hierarchy are embedded within the relationship. Analysis Services allows you to define a name for each level of the parent-child hierarchy. Typically, parent-child hierarchies can contain multiple levels and the total number of levels corresponds to the depth of the parent-child hierarchies. By default, Analysis Services 2005 provides names for the levels — Level 01, Level 02, and so on. Level N is based on the depth of the parent-child hierarchy.

If you want custom names to be specified for each level, Analysis Services 2005 provides a property for just that. For example, if you have an org-structure parent-child hierarchy, you can name the levels CEO, Presidents, Vice Presidents, General Managers, Product Unit Managers, Managers, Leads, and Individual Contributors. If you want to specify common prefix, use the parent-child property called NamingTemplate. If you click the selection for NamingTemplate, you will launch the Level Naming Template dialog, as shown in Figure 8-15. In this dialog you can specify the name for each level in the parent-child hierarchy. If you want a constant prefix name followed by the level number, such as Employee Level 1, Employee Level 2, and so on, you just need to specify Employee Level * as shown in Figure 8-15 and Analysis Services will automatically append the level number at the end of each level. Edit the Dim Employee dimension and specify the level names as Employee Level * for the Parent Employee Key hierarchy as shown in Figure 8-15. Change the name of the parent-child hierarchy to Employees, add a new calculated column called Full Name in the DimEmployee table within the DSV, which is the sum of FirstName and LastName, and make the Full Name relational column as the NameColumn for the key attribute of employees. Deploy the changes to the Analysis Services instance.

When you browse the Employees hierarchy you will see the new level names as shown in Figure 8-16. When you click on a member, you will see the level name shown next to the Current Level.

In Figure 8-16 you can see that the member David Bradley also reports to David Bradley. This is because each parent member is also included as its child, so that the value for that parent member is an aggregate of all its children and its own value. By way of example, if you have a Sales organization of employees and each manager manages a few sales employees in a region in addition to being in charge of certain sales, the total sales by the manager is a sum of all the direct reports plus the manager's own sales. That is why you sometimes see a member reporting to him- or herself while browsing a parent-child hierarchy. If you know that the non-leaf members (as with managers in an employee organization) do not have fact data associated with them and are just an aggregate of the children, Analysis Services 2005 provides a property by which you can disable a member being a child of itself. This property is called MemberWithData and setting the value to NonLeafDataHidden, as shown in Figure 8-17, allows you to disable a member being shown as reporting to itself.

You have now learned several enhancements to parent-child hierarchies. The properties for parent-child hierarchies provided by Analysis Services help you model requirements for different business scenarios. In the next section you will look at other properties of attributes and dimensions that help you enhance dimensions.

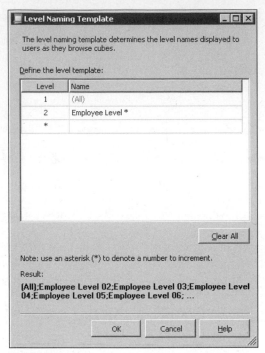

Figure 8-15

Figure 8-16

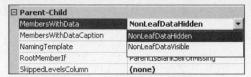

Figure 8-17

Using Properties to Customize Dimensions

Analysis Services provides several properties for use with hierarchies and dimensions. If every property were explained with illustrations and examples, this chapter would be quite large, so in this section you learn about the properties that are likely to be used in fulfillment of most common business requirements.

Ordering Dimension Members

In Chapter 5 you learned to order dimension members of a hierarchy based on key or named columns specified for the attribute. Based on that, Analysis Services sorted the members in the hierarchy and you were able to see the order while browsing the dimension. In certain business scenarios, you might have a need to sort the members based on a specific value or based on some other condition. Analysis Services 2005 provides properties to sort members of a hierarchy in a variety of ways other than the key or named columns.

Analysis Services 2005 provides you an option to sort members of a hierarchy based upon another attribute that is related or included as member property for the primary attribute you want to sort. For example, if you have an Employees hierarchy and if you have the age of the employees defined as a related attribute, you can set the appropriate properties to achieve a sorting of employees based on age. You need to set the property OrderByAttribute to age and then set the property OrderBy to either AttributeKey or AttributeName depending on your requirements, and then deploy the changes to the Analysis Services instance. These properties are shown in Figure 8-18. You can see the changes take effect by viewing the members in the Dimension Browser.

Figure 8-18

The All Member, Default Member and Unknown Member

Each hierarchy within a dimension has a member that is called the *default member*. When a query is sent to Analysis Services, Analysis Services uses the default member for all the hierarchies that are not included in the query in order to evaluate the results for the query. If a default member is not specified, Analysis Services uses the first member in the hierarchy based on the default ordering for the hierarchy. If the property IsAggregatable is set to True, that means that the values of members of the hierarchy can be aggregated to form a single member. This single member by default is called the "All" member and is usually the default member for the hierarchy. You can change the name of the All member for the attribute hierarchies within the dimension by changing the dimension property AttributeAllMemberName, as shown in Figure 8-19. In order to select the Properties window for the dimension, you can click the dimension name in the Attributes pane in the dimension editor or anywhere in the Hierarchies and Levels pane. If you deploy the change for AttributeAllMemberName as shown in Figure 8-19, you will see that the All member for various hierarchies now shows up as AllMember. For multi-level hierarchies the property to set the default member is AllMemberName.

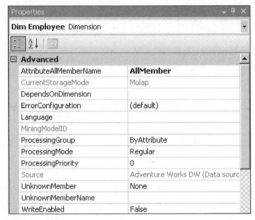

Figure 8-19

You can change the default member for each hierarchy. To change the default member, you need to set the property DefaultMember with the correct member in the hierarchy. Click the ellipses next to the DefaultMember property for the Employees hierarchy and you will see the Set Default Member dialog shown in Figure 8-20. You have three options for specifying the default member: using the system default member, selecting the member by browsing the hierarchy, or specifying an MDX expression to arrive at the default member. For the last option you can paste the MDX expression that evaluates the default member for the hierarchy or use the dialog to build the MDX expression that will evaluate the default member. Once the default member has been set for a specific hierarchy, Analysis Services uses that default member in query evaluation. You can send the following MDX query to ensure the default member you have set in the property is being used by Analysis Services:

```
SELECT [Dim Employee].[Employees].defaultmember on 0
from [Adventure Works DW]
```

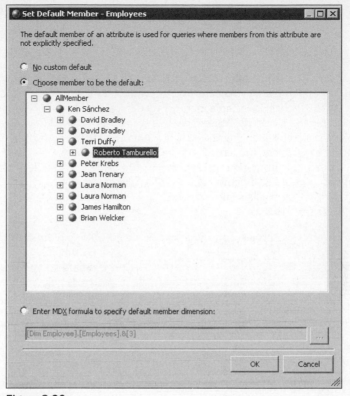

Figure 8-20

UnknownMember is a property for each dimension in your database. If there are referential integrity issues in your relational database, then during partition processing Analysis Services will raise appropriate errors. If you have set specific processing options to ignore errors, but include the fact data corresponding to errors in the cube, then Analysis Services allocates the fact data to a member called the Unknown member in the dimensions for which it is unable to find members due to referential integrity issues. You have the option of allowing the Unknown member to be visible or hidden, using the dimension property UnknownMember. When the UnknownMember is set to be visible, the member name is set to UnknownMember and will be included in the results of the MDX queries that contain the hierarchy. Similar to the All member name, Analysis Services gives you the option of changing the name of the Unknown member to a more meaningful name corresponding to that specific dimension.

Error Configurations for Processing

One of the challenges in designing a data warehouse is creating a perfect schema without any referential integrity issues. However, this is often not possible and a significant amount of the time spent in designing a data warehouse is typically spent in data cleansing. Analysis Services, by default, will stop processing dimensions whenever it encounters specific referential integrity issues. Some data warehouse designers might want to ignore the referential integrity issues by ignoring the records causing errors and include corresponding fact data to Unknown member of dimensions so that they can see the results of their cube design. Analysis Services gives you fine-grain control for various referential integrity issues that can happen during processing. The dimension property ErrorConfiguration allows you the fine-grain control for dimension processing. If you click the ErrorConfiguration property and select Custom, you will see all the properties that allow you fine-grain control as shown in Figure 8-21.

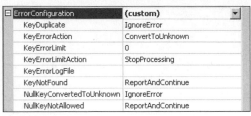

ErrorConfiguration	(custom)
KeyDuplicate	IgnoreError
KeyErrorAction	ConvertToUnknown
KeyErrorLimit	0
KeyErrorLimitAction	StopProcessing
KeyErrorLogFile	
KeyNotFound	ReportAndContinue
NullKeyConvertedToUnknown	IgnoreError
NullKeyNotAllowed	ReportAndContinue

Figure 8-21

The possible errors Analysis Services can encounter while processing a dimension are related to key attributes of the dimension. Typically, when you have a snowflake dimension you can encounter dimension key errors while processing whenever Analysis Services is unable to find corresponding keys in the dimension tables involved in the snowflake schema. The main errors that Analysis Services encounters are duplicate key errors (multiple occurrences of the key attribute in the dimension table), key not found error (unable to find a key in the dimension table in the snowflake schema), and null keys being encountered when you do not expect null keys to be present in the dimension tables. You can set properties to stop processing after a specific number of errors have been reached, continue processing by reporting the errors, or ignoring all errors. We believe the error configuration properties are self-explanatory. We leave it to you as an exercise to set various error configurations while building your data warehouses.

Storage Mode

Analysis Services supports two storage modes for dimensions. Your dimensions can be configured to be MOLAP or ROLAP dimensions. If a dimension is configured as MOLAP, at the time of processing Analysis Services reads all the dimension data from the relational data sources and stores the data in a compressed format. Due to the proprietary patented format, Analysis Services is able to retrieve dimension data efficiently, resulting in fast query response times. When the storage mode is set to ROLAP, Analysis Services does retrieve the data from the relational data source. At the time of processing it updates appropriate metadata information. For each query involving retrieval of data from the ROLAP dimension, Analysis Services sends corresponding SQL queries directly to the relational data source to retrieve the members in the dimension, performs necessary calculations on the Analysis Services engine, and then results of the query are provided to the client. Typically, ROLAP storage mode is chosen whenever there are a large number of members in a dimension (on the order of hundreds of millions of members). You need to evaluate the trade-off between query performance versus storage or business requirement for your business and set the correct storage mode for your dimensions. Disks have become quite cheap these days and we recommend setting the storage mode for dimensions as MOLAP. However, in certain business scenarios where you have the dimension data constantly changing and you need real-time data, you might want to set the storage mode to ROLAP. Even in cases where your customers need real-time data, you might be able to set the property called Proactive Caching that helps in providing real-time data to your customers. For more details on real-time data, see Chapter 18. Figure 8-22 shows the dimension property for storage mode.

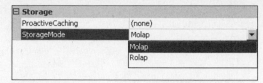

Figure 8-22

Grouping Members to Form a Single Member

Some of the hierarchies might have continuous data, and typically you might not be interested in view-ing each and every member. An example of such a hierarchy is the salary of customers. Typically one would be interested in customers within a specific salary range rather than querying for customers with a specific salary. In such circumstances, Analysis Services allows you to model your hierarchy so that the members of the hierarchy are ranges rather than individual values. Analysis Services provides two prop-erties to control this behavior so that you can group a set of members to a single group.

Follow these steps to understand the behavior:

1. Open the Dim Customer dimension in the Dimension Designer.

2. The Yearly Income attribute hierarchy of Dim Customers has the salaries for all the customers. In order to group the values into a few members, you need to set the properties DiscretizationBucketCount and DiscretizationMethod. Set the DiscretizationBucketCount to 10 and the DiscretizationMethod to Automatic, as shown in Figure 8-23. The DiscretizationBucketCount instructs Analysis Services to generate N members in the hierarchy where N is the number of members. The DiscretizationMethod specifies the way in which you want the customer salaries to be grouped. The Automatic setting instructs Analysis Services to find the most efficient way of grouping the values after analyzing all the values. Deploy the changes to your Analysis Services instance.

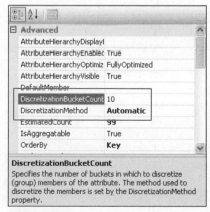

Figure 8-23

You will see the various buckets generated by Analysis Services in the Dimension Browser, as shown in Figure 8-24.

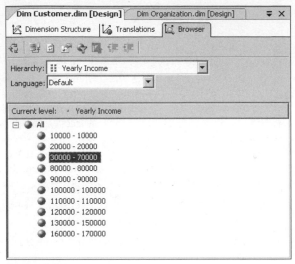

Figure 8-24

You have learned most of the commonly used properties that will help you in enhancing your dimensions and hierarchies for your business. In the next section you add intelligence to your dimensions by means of the wizards provided by Analysis Services 2005. These business intelligence wizards help in creating calculations that are widely used in business with the help of a few selections.

Dimension Intelligence using the Business Intelligence Wizard

Analysis Services 2005 provides you with a Business Intelligence wizard that allows you to enhance your dimensions with appropriate calculations added to your cube. Three specific enhancements are discussed in this section: Account intelligence, Time intelligence, and Dimension intelligence. Analysis Services 2005 supports the Account dimension natively in the engine. In this way, Analysis Services is able to aggregate data for members in the Account dimension based on the account names. The Time intelligence enhancement creates calculations for common business questions, such as year-over-year or quarter-over-quarter revenue. Such calculations are typically created as session calculated measures by various client tools in Analysis Services 2000. Analysis Services 2005 enables support of these calculations natively, so that all client tools and custom tools can take advantage of these calculations. The Dimension intelligence enhancement allows you to map your dimension to commonly used dimension types, so that client tools can discover and present them to customers in a unique way that is easily interpreted.

Account Intelligence

In Chapter 6 you learned about measures and aggregation functions that are specified for measures such as Sum, Count and Distinct Count. Analysis Services 2005 supports calculations specifically for the Account dimension so that an appropriate aggregation function is applied based on account names. In fact, there is a special type of aggregation function called ByAccount. Based on the type of account Analysis Services can apply the right aggregation function. The account intelligence wizard allows you to qualify dimension as an Account dimension and then map type of accounts to well known account types. Based on these mappings the wizard informs you of the type of aggregation function that will be applied for the accounts. If your Account uses a specify account type and aggregation function then you will be able to specify that at the database level. Follow the steps below to map the dimension with name Account as a dimension of type Account and specify necessary attributes so that appropriate aggregation functions are applied to account types.

1. Double click on the dimension with name Account to open it in Dimension Designer.

2. Launch the Dimension Intelligence Wizard from the menu item Dimension→Add Business Intelligence or by clicking on the first icon in the Dimension Designer. If you see the welcome screen click the Next button.

3. In the Choose Enhancement page select Define account intelligence as shown in Figure 8-25 and click Next.

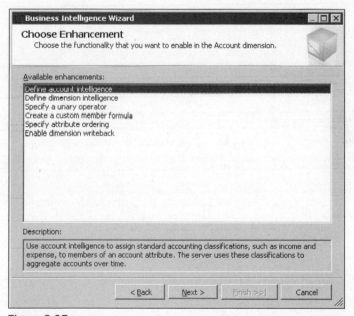

Figure 8-25

4. In the Configure Dimension Attributes page, Figure 8-26, you need to define the mapping between the attributes in the current dimension named Account to the standard attributes of the Account dimension. Map the Chart of Accounts to the parent-child hierarchy Accounts, Account Name to the key attribute Dim Account that contains the name of the Accounts, Account Number to the Account Code Alternate Key (Account Code Alternate Key uniquely identifies a member in the account) and the Account Type to the attribute Account Type and press Next.

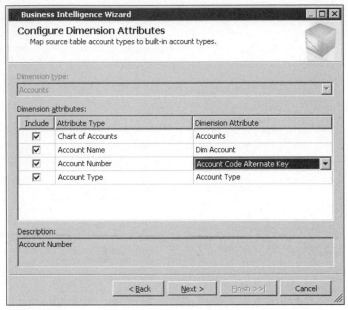

Figure 8-26

The Account Type identifies the type of an account member and is used by Analysis Services to use the appropriate aggregation function for measures that have the AggregationFunction property set to ByAccount.

5. In the Define Account Intelligence page the account types from the source table are mapped to the built-in account types in Analysis Services 2005. If the name of account types in the source table do not directly map to the built-in account types you would need to map them correctly in this page. In this example all the account types are mapped correctly and hence press Next.

6. The final page of the Business Intelligence Wizard shows the various account types along with the aggregation functions associated with accounts. Please review the aggregation functions and click Finish (see Figure 8-27 and Figure 8-28).

You have now successfully enhanced your Account dimension. If you look at the properties for the Account dimension you will see the Account dimension property Type is set to Accounts. The aggregation functions for various account types are pre-defined in Analysis Services. However Analysis Services allows you the flexibility to add additional account types as well as to make changes to the AggregationFunction for the account types to suit your business needs. To make modifications right click on the project name AnalysisServicesTutorial in solution explorer and select Edit Database. You will see a new designer to make changes at the database level as shown in Figure 8-29.

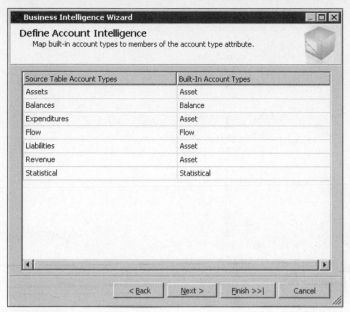

Figure 8-27

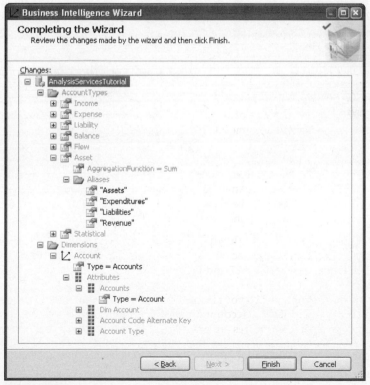

Figure 8-28

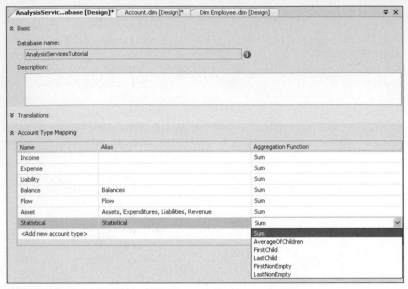

Figure 8-29

As mentioned earlier the enhancement made to the Account dimension will only be applicable for measures that aggregation function defined as ByAccount. Open the Adventure Works DW cube. In the Cube Structure pane select the measure Amount in the Fact Finance measure group and set the Aggregation Function for this measure to ByAccount as shown in Figure 8-30. Deploy your changes to the Analysis Services instance.

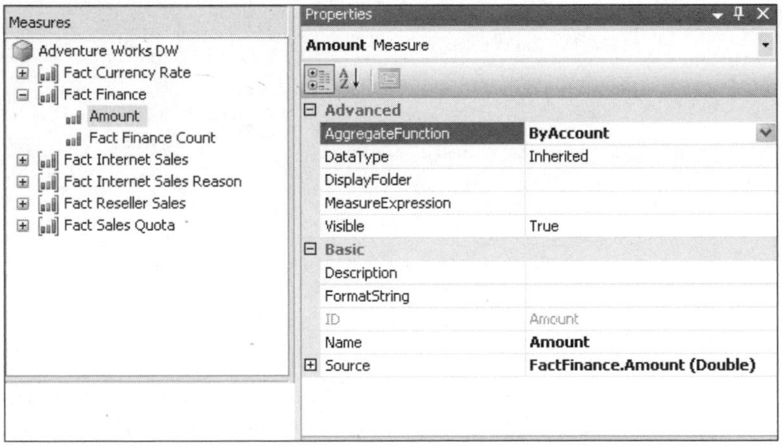

Figure 8-30

In the Cube Browser you can now browse the measure Amount along with the Account dimension members, and you can notice that the right aggregation functions are used to aggregate the measure values based on the account type. However you will notice that the member Statistical Accounts is not visible in the OWC browser. This is due to the fact that accounts of type Statistical should have the value rolled up based on the aggregation function Sum; however all the children of member Statistical Accounts have unary operator column set to ~ which means those values are not rolled up to the parent. In order to view the Statistical Accounts member and its children you need to define a value for member. Switch to the Calculations tab in the Cube Designer. Right click on the Script Organizer pane and select New Script Command. In the script command window enter the following statement to set the Amount for the Account member Statistical Account to be NA. Save the changes and deploy them to your Analysis Services instance.

```
( [Account].[Accounts].&[95], [Measures].[Amount] ) = "NA"
```

If you reconnect to Analysis Services instance in the Cube Browser you will the Statistical Account member and its children as shown in Figure 8-31. You can see the Amount for Statistical Accounts is set to NA even though the aggregation function is Sum. This is because of the fact that Analysis Services applies Unary operation evaluation on a cell after the regular rollup across the dimension (in this specific case ByAccount aggregation).

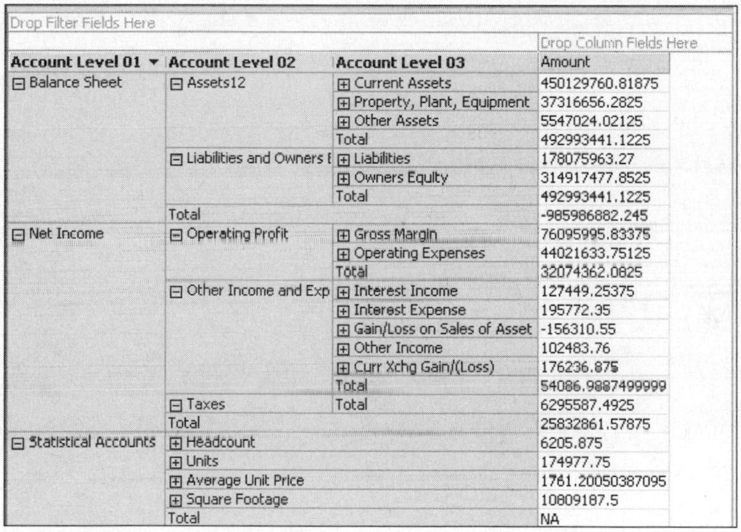

Account Level 01 ▾	Account Level 02	Account Level 03	Amount
⊟ Balance Sheet	⊟ Assets12	⊞ Current Assets	450129760.81875
		⊞ Property, Plant, Equipment	37316656.2825
		⊞ Other Assets	5547024.02125
		Total	492993441.1225
	⊟ Liabilities and Owners I	⊞ Liabilities	178075963.27
		⊞ Owners Equity	314917477.8525
		Total	492993441.1225
	Total		-985986882.245
⊟ Net Income	⊟ Operating Profit	⊞ Gross Margin	76095995.83375
		⊞ Operating Expenses	44021633.75125
		Total	32074362.0825
	⊟ Other Income and Exp	⊞ Interest Income	127449.25375
		⊞ Interest Expense	195772.35
		⊞ Gain/Loss on Sales of Asset	-156310.55
		⊞ Other Income	102483.76
		⊞ Curr Xchg Gain/(Loss)	176236.875
		Total	54086.9887499999
	⊟ Taxes	Total	6295587.4925
	Total		25832861.57875
⊟ Statistical Accounts	⊞ Headcount		6205.875
	⊞ Units		174977.75
	⊞ Average Unit Price		1761.20050387095
	⊞ Square Footage		10809187.5
	Total		NA

Figure 8-31

Since the aggregation functions specific to an Account Type are done natively with Analysis Services rather than calculations in scripts you should expect better performance while querying appropriate cells.

Time Intelligence

There are certain calculations that are frequently used in business such as calculating Year to Date and Year over Year Growth for measures such as Sales. These calculations are related to the Time dimension and can be created within the scope of the query or session as necessary. Several client tools have utilized query or session scope calculations to create such calculations while using Analysis Services 2000. Analysis Services 2005 provides a wizard to enhance your cube to add such calculations. The Time Intelligence enhancement is part of the cube enhancement since calculations such as Year to Date and Year over Year Growth are all calculated in context with measures. Since this enhancement add appropriate calculations to the cube as well as attributes in the Time dimension, it is included in this chapter. Follow the steps below to define Time Intelligence enhancement.

1. Open the cube Adventure Works DW in Cube Designer.

2. Launch the Business Intelligence Wizard from the menu Cube→Add Business Intelligence or by clicking on the Add Business Intelligence icon (first icon in the Cube Structure tab). If you see the Welcome screen press next.

3. In the Choose Enhancement page select Define time intelligence as shown in Figure 8-32.

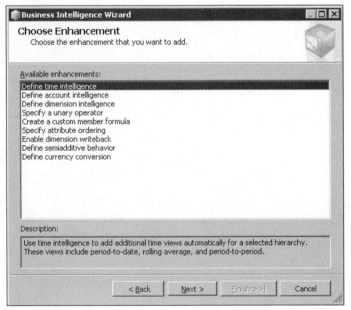

Figure 8-32

4. In the Choose Target Hierarchy and Calculation page you need to select the calculations as well as hierarchy in Time dimension that is expected to use the calculations. In the drop down list box for Use the following hierarchy to analyze time calculations you will see the four Time dimensions Dim Time, Order Date, Delivery Date, and Ship Date. All these cube dimensions are role playing dimensions of the database dimension Dim Time. Select the multi-level hierarchy in the cube dimension Order Date as shown in Figure 8-33. Select the calculations Year to Date, Year Over Year Growth, and Year Over Year Growth % and press Next.

5. In the Define Scope of Calculations you need to select the measures for which you need the time calculations to be applied. Select the measure Sales Amount as shown in Figure 8-34.

Figure 8-33

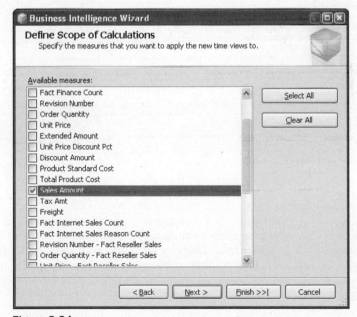

Figure 8-34

6. The final page of the wizard shows the changes to the database Time dimension Dim Time as well as the calculations as shown in Figure 8-35. You can see that the wizard adds a column in the Dim Time table within the DSV and adds that as an attribute in the Dim Time database dimension in addition to the calculations that will be added to the cube's script.

Figure 8-35

Switch to the Calculations tab of the cube and explore the calculations created by Business Intelligence Wizard. Also look at the Named Calculation added to the Dim Time table in the DSV. These will help you to understand the calculations you need to create if you didn't have the Time Intelligence enhancement. The Business Intelligence Wizard makes it easy for data warehouse designers to add the enhancements related to Time without defining and verifying the calculations which can take a considerable amount of time.

You have successfully enhanced your cube and Time dimension to analyze growth on Internet Sales (Sales Amount measure). To use the calculations for analysis deploy the enhancements to your Analysis Services instance and switch to the Cube browser. Drag and drop the measure Sales Amount to the data area, CalendarYear - CalendarSemester - CalendarQuarter - EnglishMonthName on Rows and CalendarYear - CalendarSemester - CalendarQuarter - EnglishMonthName Order Date Calculations on Columns. You will be able to see the Year to Date, Year over Year Growth, and Year over Year Growth % as shown in Figure 8-36.

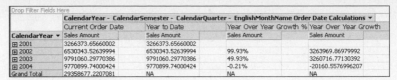

CalendarYear ▾	CalendarYear - CalendarSemester - CalendarQuarter - EnglishMonthName Order Date Calculations ▾			
	Current Order Date	Year to Date	Year Over Year Growth %	Year Over Year Growth
	Sales Amount	Sales Amount	Sales Amount	Sales Amount
⊞ 2001	3266373.65660002	3266373.65660002		
⊞ 2002	6530343.52639994	6530343.52639994	99.93%	3263969.86979992
⊞ 2003	9791060.29770386	9791060.29770386	49.93%	3260716.77130392
⊞ 2004	9770899.74000424	9770899.74000424	-0.21%	-20160.5576996207
Grand Total	29358677.2207081	NA	NA	NA

Figure 8-36

Dimension Intelligence

Analysis Services 2005 provides you a way to define your dimensions to map to standard dimension types such as Customer, Organization, Currency. These mappings can help client tools which might have customized views of presenting such dimensions to end users. To map your dimensions to standard dimension types follow the steps below:

1. Open the Dim Organization dimension in Dimension Designer.

2. Launch the Business Intelligence Wizard by clicking on the icon Add Business Intelligence or from the menu Dimension→Add Business Intelligence. If you see the welcome screen press Next.

3. In the Choose Enhancement page select Define dimension intelligence (as shown in Figure 8-37) and press Next.

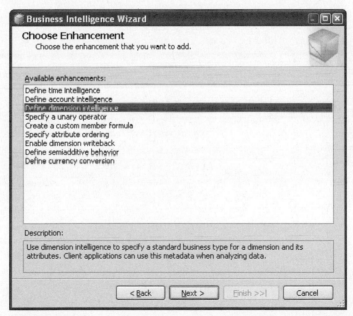

Figure 8-37

4. In the Define Dimension Intelligence page enable the default Attribute Types Company and Ownership Percentage and map them to corresponding attributes in the Dim Organization dimension Organizations and Percentage of Ownership (see Figure 8-38) and press Next.

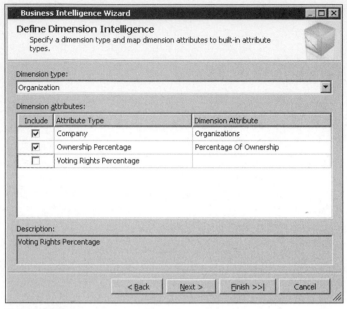

Figure 8-38

5. The final page of the wizard shows the definitions specified in the previous page. It shows that Dim Organization is of standard dimension type Organization. This dimension contains several companies which are represented by the attribute Organizations and the PercentOwnership is determined by the attribute Percentage Of Ownership (see Figure 8-39).

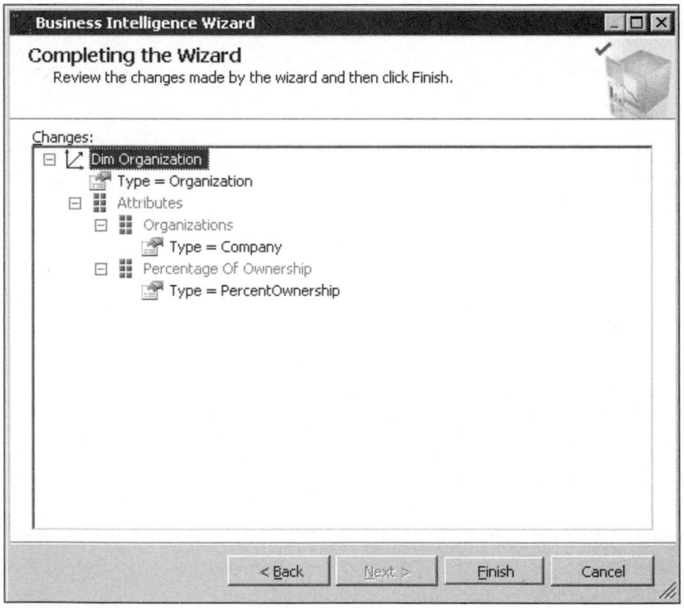

Figure 8-39

You have successfully defined dimension intelligence for the Dim Organization dimension. You can see that the property Type for the dimension and the attributes selected in the dimension intelligence enhance has been set appropriately. Apply the Dimension Intelligence Enhancement to the remaining dimensions. You will be able to view the effect of these only through client tools that utilize the property type.

Server Time Dimension

In certain data warehouses you might not have a special table for Time. However the fact table might contain date as a column. Analysis Services 2005 provides you the functionality of creating a Time dimension based on time range with appropriate hierarchies. You can configure the range based on the beginning and end dates found in your fact tables. This range-based Time dimension is created on Analysis Services and is called Server Time dimension. Once a Server Time dimension is created you can add this to the cube and specify appropriate granularity. Follow the steps below to create a Server Time dimension.

1. Right click on the Dimensions folder in Solution Explorer and select New Dimension to launch the Dimension Wizard.

2. Select the default value in the Select Build Method as shown in Figure 8-40 and click Next.

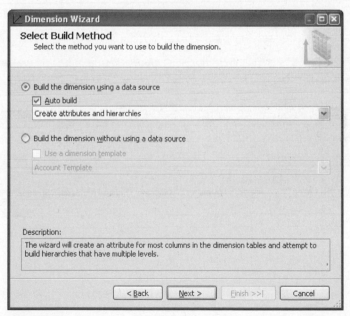

Figure 8-40

3. In the Select Data Source View page select the default as shown in Figure 8-41 and press Next.

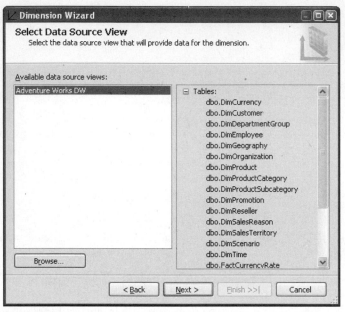

Figure 8-41

4. In the Select the Dimension Type page select the option Server time dimension as shown in Figure 8-42 and click Next.

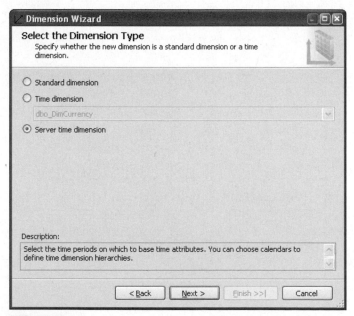

Figure 8-42

5. In the Define Time Periods page select the date ranges as shown in Figure 8-43 and the Time periods Year, Quarter, Month, Week, and Date and press Next.

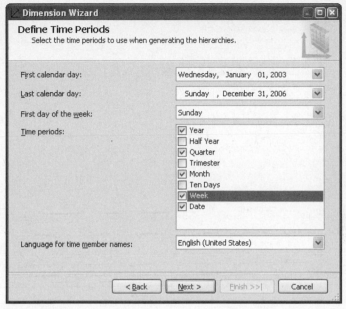

Figure 8-43

6. In the Select Calendars page select Fiscal calendar as shown in Figure 8-44 and click Next.

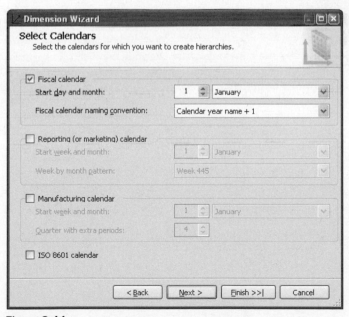

Figure 8-44

7. In the Review New Hierarchies page the wizard shows the various hierarchies to be created within the dimension as shown in Figure 8-45. Please review them and click Next.

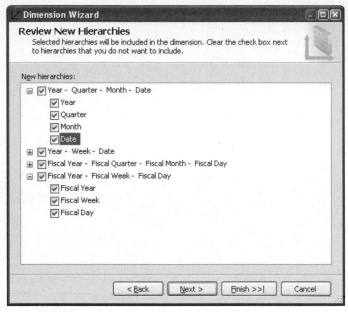

Figure 8-45

8. In the final page of the Wizard enter the name of the dimension as ServerTimeDimension as shown in Figure 8-46 and click Next.

The ServerTimeDimension is now created and you can see all the hierarchies and attributes in the Dimension Designer as shown in Figure 8-47. Since this dimension is created from Analysis Services instead of the DSV you will see a pane called Time Periods that lists all the periods that are available for selection. You can add additional Time Periods as attributes in the dimension. Date is the key attribute of this dimension and it cannot be deleted.

Deploy the changes to Analysis Services instances. You can now browse the hierarchies in ServerTimeDimension as shown in Figure 8-48. The formats used for members in various levels cannot be changed. You can add this ServerTimeDimension to your cubes and define the relationship. If you want to establish a relationship at the key level with the ServerTimeDimension you do need to have a column of type Date in the fact table(s). If a time table was not present in your data warehouse then you do need to create that table and then create a dimension from that time. However Analysis Services simplifies the creation Time dimension with the help of Server Time dimension.

Figure 8-46

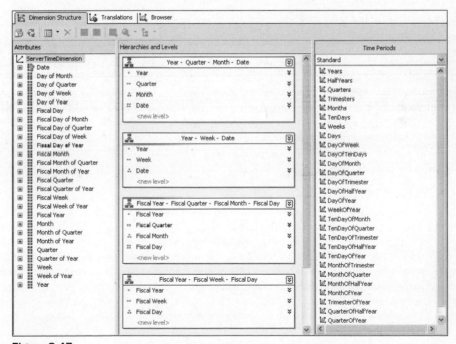

Figure 8-47

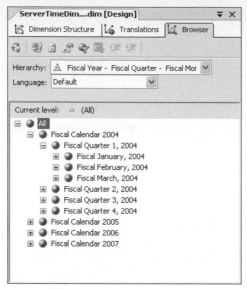

Figure 8-48

Dimension Writeback

Dimension writeback is another enhancement to dimensions and is available through the Dimension Intelligence Wizard. This is an important feature that allows you to create or modify members in your dimension without having to go to your relational data source. Once you enable your dimension for writeback, Analysis Services provides you the functionality to add or modify members through the Dimension Browser pane. Some business scenarios where dimension writeback can be used are:

❑ When employees of an organization move from one location to another and their reporting structure in the organization and attributes of employee such as address and phone number change.

❑ When an employee's status changes due to marriage or childbirth and these changes need to be updated in the dimension.

❑ When you have an Account dimension and new types of accounts are being introduced and you need to add members to the dimension.

When you writeback data to the dimension, Analysis Services propagates the change in the data to the relational data source and does an incremental process of the dimension, so that affected members are processed. During this time the dimension and cube will be available for querying for other users. The following steps show how to enable writeback on the Employee dimension and will help you understand the dimension writeback behavior by performing writeback operations on certain employees:

1. Open the Employee dimension in the dimension editor.

2. Click the icon to launch the Business Intelligence Wizard or select Dimension→Add Business Intelligence from the menus. Select Enable Dimension Writeback in the Business Intelligence Wizard as shown in Figure 8-49 and click Next.

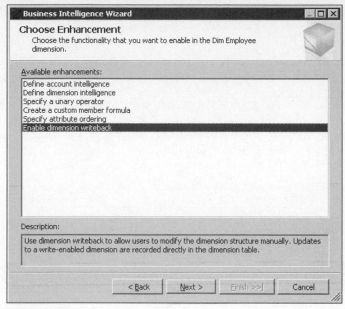

Figure 8-49

3.   On the Enable Dimension Writeback page make sure the checkbox is enabled, as shown in Figure 8-50, and click Finish.

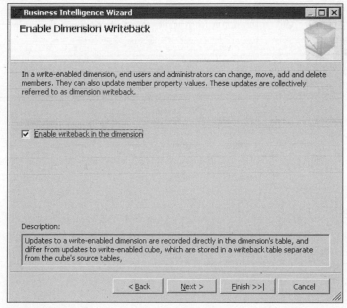

Figure 8-50

4. The wizard changes the dimension property WriteEnabled to True. Instead of using the wizard, you can just change the WriteEnabled property to be True for all the dimensions for which you might have to update the data. Deploy the changes to the server.

5. After deployment succeeds, BIDS automatically switches the view from the Dimension Structure pane to the Dimension Browser pane. Click the Member Properties icon and select all the member properties related to the Employees dimension. Assume the employee John Wood got married and you need to update his marital status to married. Click the Writeback toolbar button or from the top menus select Dimension→Writeback to enter writeback mode. Double-click the member property Marital Status for John Wood. The Marital Status field for John is now editable, as shown in Figure 8-51.

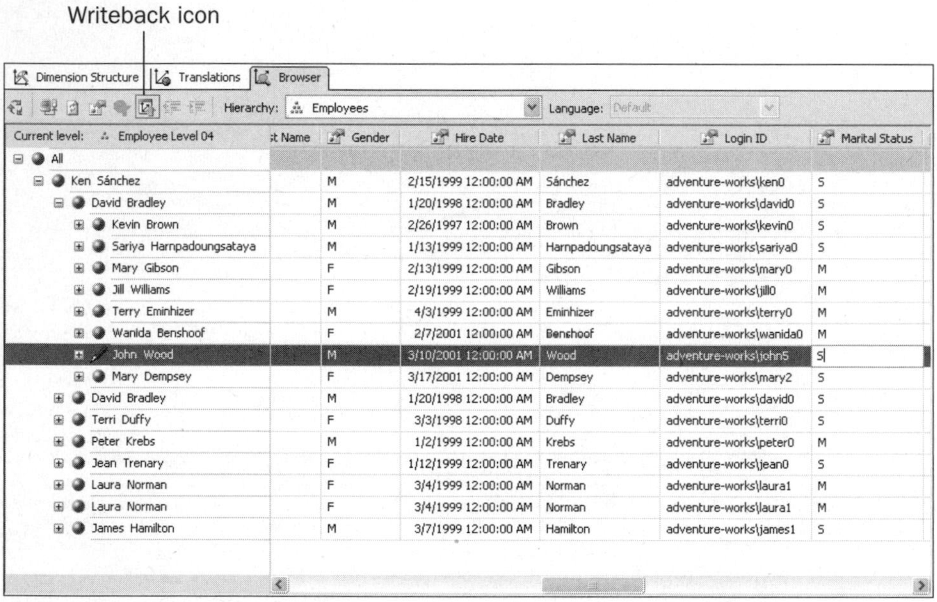

Figure 8-51

6. Change the Marital Status field to M and then move the cursor to a different line. At this time BIDS sends the following dimension writeback request to the Analysis Services instance. You can see that an Update statement for the cube dimension $ Dim Employee is sent to the Analysis Services instance. Note the key attribute is critical for Analysis Server to make the appropriate update:

```xml
<Update xsi:type="Update" xmlns:xsd="http://www.w3.org/2001/XMLSchema"
xmlns:xsi="http://www.w3.org/2001/XMLSchema-instance"
xmlns="http://schemas.microsoft.com/analysisservices/2003/engine">
  <Object>
    <Database>AnalysisServicesTutorial</Database>
    <Cube>$Dim Employee</Cube>
    <Dimension>Dim Employee</Dimension>
  </Object>
  <Attributes>
    <Attribute>
```

```
          <AttributeName>Marital Status</AttributeName>
          <Keys>
            <Key xsi:type="xsd:string">M</Key>
          </Keys>
        </Attribute>
      </Attributes>
      <Where>
        <Attribute>
          <AttributeName>Dim Employee</AttributeName>
          <Keys>
            <Key xsi:type="xsd:int">275</Key>
          </Keys>
        </Attribute>
      </Where>
  </Update>
```

7. If the operation was successful you will be able to make other operations. If there are errors you should get feedback from the Analysis Services with the appropriate error messages.

You have successfully completed enabling a dimension for writeback in the Employee dimension. You can perform additional operations such as creating new members, moving a member along with descendants, and deleting members through dimension writeback. These are operations that update the members or properties of members on dimensions and you will learn these operations with examples in detail in Chapter 11. You should be aware that you cannot change the values of the existing key attributes in the dimension because the key attribute is used by the Analysis Services instance to perform the writeback operation.

Summary

You have experienced more chapter flashbacks than usual here, but that merely suggests certain loose ends are getting tied together and certain mental connections are being reinforced. In this chapter you learned about custom rollups using the common business concept of depreciation, which addresses the nature of value change over time. Any type of change over time is a recurrent theme in business intelligence, and this chapter discussed use of the Time Intelligence enhancement, which can be used on cubes with a Time dimension to provide views by time period. Similarly, the Account Intelligence enhancement was explored; it maps known business entities like Income, Expense, Asset, and Liability to the dimensions in your cube so that appropriate rollup can be done for accounts natively in Analysis Services.

The Account Intelligence enhancement also allows you to add additional accounts and change aggregation functions for specific accounts based on your business requirements. The Server Time dimension helps you to define range-based time dimension quickly when there is no time table in your data source. The Dimension Wizard also provides you the ability to create the standard dimension types such as Customers, Organizations, Time, Currency, etc., along with appropriate attributes and hierarchies and generate appropriate schemas in your data source which is not discussed in this chapter. You would need to populate these tables with appropriate data before processing the dimensions. We leave it you to explore this option from the Dimension Wizard by selecting the build method "build the dimension without a data source." Finally, dimension writeback was discussed and you learned how data can be written to a relational table, and an incremental process is kicked off so that related members in the dimension are processed along with the corresponding cube. Speaking of cubes, that is what the next chapter is about. Now that you have learned about dimension enhancement, it is time to move on to advanced cube design!

9

Advanced Cube Design

You landed the job! You got the coveted "Cube Enhancement Analyst" position, which coincidentally requires you to read this chapter before starting. But are you even qualified to read this chapter? The answer is yes if you meet the following criteria: you learned about creating and browsing a cube in Chapter 5, and in Chapter 8 you learned about enhancing dimensions by using special dimension properties and by adding business intelligence — oh, and some understanding of MDX, which you learned in Chapters 3, wouldn't hurt either. Please review those topics if you are not confident in your understanding of them. Indeed, this chapter builds on what you have learned already, focusing on enhancements to your cube in support of specific business requirements. The focus here is on working with measures in your cube by modifying properties to change how measures appear in cubes and how values are aggregated. There is also focus on using enhanced dimension relationships which are new to Analysis Services. You also work with Actions, an enhanced feature, and Key Performance Indicators (KPIs), a new feature, to add functionality that helps end users view and interpret data efficiently. To implement many of the techniques described in this chapter, you use advanced MDX. In some cases, you can use the Business Intelligence wizard to simplify the addition of complex MDX. Once you have the design techniques mastered, attention is turned to techniques for managing scalability through partitioning, assigning storage modes, and building aggregations.

If this book were the movie "The Matrix," now is the time when Morpheus would hold out a red pill in one hand and a blue pill in the other, and say, "You put the book down and take the blue pill — the story ends, you wake up in your bed and believe whatever you want to believe. You take the red pill — and I show you how to build powerful cubes." To be honest, this chapter might not be as dramatic as all that, but it will bring together many of those gnarly concepts you have learned so you can fine-tune the process of turning data into information (the essential theme of this book.) At the risk of belaboring the point, this chapter really is central, not just in the sense it is near the middle of the book, but in the sense it will help you understand some of the more important features in Analysis Services 2005. In this chapter, you use the Adventure Works DW sample project included with Microsoft SQL Server 2005 to understand how to apply advanced design techniques to cubes. So, gear up and get ready for a deep dive into the core of Analysis Services 2005.

Measure Groups and Measures

In Chapter 6, you learned about measure groups and measures within a cube. To recap, a cube can contain one or more measure groups and each measure group can contain one or more measures. You also learned about the various aggregation functions for each measure, and reviewed some MDX examples of how measure values are rolled up while browsing the cube. In this section, you'll learn how to use an MDX function to simplify querying measure groups and how to group measures within a measure group to help users navigate them more easily. You'll also learn how to use properties to control how measure values are aggregated when unrelated to dimensions in the same query or when performing currency conversions. Lastly, you'll learn how to reuse measure groups in multiple cubes.

With Analysis Services 2005 it is quite possible to end up with a cube containing several measure groups. If you open the Adventure Works cube in the Enterprise version of the Adventure Works DW sample project (located at C:\Program Files\Microsoft SQL Server\90\Tools\Samples\AdventureWorks Analysis Services Project\Enterprise) you see 11 measure groups for the Adventure Works cube as shown in Figure 9-1.

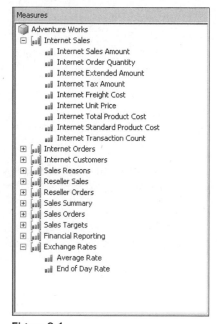

Figure 9-1

If you expand each measure group, you can see that most measure groups contain multiple measures. For example, the Internet Sales measure group has 9 measures and the Reseller Sales measure group has 11. Often, business analysis questions are targeted at measures within a single measure group rather than all the measures within a cube. One way to write an MDX query targeting a specific measure group is to include each measure one by one. For instance, if you want all visible regular measures (that is, no calculated measures and no measures with the Visible property set to False) within the Internet Sales measure group, your MDX query could look like this:

```
select
{[Measures].[Internet Sales Amount],
 [Measures].[Internet Order Quantity],
 [Measures].[Internet Extended Amount],
 [Measures].[Internet Tax Amount],
 [Measures].[Internet Freight Cost],
[Measures].[Internet Total Product Cost],
 [Measures].[Internet Standard Product Cost]
} on columns
from [Adventure Works]
```

It is time-consuming to form an MDX query that includes each measure of the measure group within the query because you need to drag and drop each measure individually or type the name of each measure into the query. Fortunately, an MDX function called MeasureGroupMeasures is provided to retrieve all the measures within a measure group. The following query shows how to use this function to return the same results as the preceding query:

```
SELECT MeasureGroupMeasures("Internet Sales") ON 0
FROM [Adventure Works]
```

Lots of measures in a single measure group can also be overwhelming for end users. Another feature can be used to create logical groupings of measures within each measure group so users can locate measures more easily while browsing a cube. Simply assign the same value to the DisplayFolder property of each measure (in the same measure group) that you want to group together.

Not only do you need to consider measure groups and how measures appear in a cube, but also consider how they interact with dimensions. For example, when you have multiple measure groups within a single cube, you will find that certain dimensions do not have relationships with certain measure groups. Recall from Chapter 6 that relationships between dimensions and measure groups are defined on the Dimension Usage tab of the cube designer. If you look at Dimension Usage in the Adventure Works cube of the Adventure Works DW sample project, you see there is no relationship between the Internet Sales measure group and the Reseller dimension. A query that includes a measure from the Internet Sales measure group and members from the Reseller dimension, as shown below, returns the same value for each Reseller member — the value for the All member:

```
SELECT {[Measures].[Internet Extended Amount]} ON 0,
[Reseller].[Reseller Type].members ON 1
FROM [Adventure Works]
```

If users find this result confusing, you can override this default behavior by changing the value of the IgnoreUnrelatedDimensisons property for the measure group, as shown in Figure 9-2.

If the IgnoreUnrelatedDimensions property is set to False, a query that includes a measure with a dimension having no relationship to it will return null values. If, for example, you change the IgnoreUnrelatedDimensions property of the Internet Sales measure group to False and then deploy the project, the previous MDX query returns null cell values for each member of the Reseller dimension except the All Reseller member.

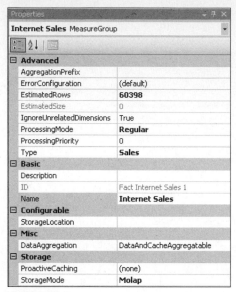

Figure 9-2

IgnoreUnrelatedDimensions is a new property that provides the functionality of the ValidMeasure MDX function, often used when working with virtual cubes in Analysis Services 2000. A virtual cube, you may recall, simulates the consolidation of multiple fact tables within a single cube. The ValidMeasure function returns a cell value corresponding to the All member for a dimension that does not have a relationship with the current measure. In other words, the dimension is not represented by a foreign key column in the fact table containing the current measure.

To continue the previous example, with the IgnoreUnrelatedDimensions property for the Internet Sales measure group set to False, you can execute the following MDX query to see that the cell values for all the members in Reseller Type hierarchy have the same value for measure x, while the real measure Internet Extended Amount has null values:

```
WITH MEMBER measures.x AS Validmeasure(([Measures].[Internet Extended Amount],
[Reseller].[Reseller Type]))
SELECT { measures.x,[Measures].[Internet Extended Amount]} ON 0,
[Reseller].[Reseller Type].members ON 1
FROM [Adventure Works]
```

Another important measure property to know about is MeasureExpression. On the Cube Structure tab of the cube designer, click the Internet Sales Amount measure in the Internet Sales measure group to see its properties, as shown in Figure 9-3. A valid value for MeasureExpression is an MDX expression that typically includes product (multiplication operator) or ratio (division operator) of two measures (or constant). This type of expression is used for currency conversions or when aggregating values with many-to-many dimensions, which are both discussed later in this chapter. When you specify a measure expression, Analysis Services 2005 evaluates the expression for each dimension member first and then aggregates the values across the dimension.

Measures used in the MDX expression can be from the same measure group or from different measure groups. In Figure 9-3, for example, the MeasureExpression divides Internet Sales Amount, from the Internet Sales measure group, by Average Rate, from the Exchange Rates measure group. The Exchange Rates measure group contains Average Rate and End of Day Rate to be used for currency conversions.

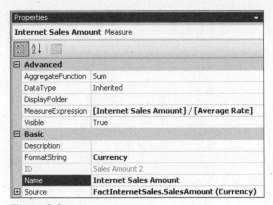

Figure 9-3

If you look at the Dimension Usage tab of the Cube Designer, you can see both measure groups, Internet Sales and Exchange Rates, have a direct relationship with the Time dimension. You can also see that dimension Destination Currency is directly related to the Exchange Rate measure group, but has a many-to-many relationship with the Internet Sales measure group. These relationships are required when you store transaction data, such as sales amounts, in the fact table using the local currency, but need the ability to summarize that data in reports using a different currency. For instance, you have sales recorded in the fact table in Mexican pesos, but you need to report sales in Euros.

Since exchange rates vary over time, you might choose to average the exchange rate at the day or month level (depending on your business situation) to calculate the total sales in a specific currency. In the Adventure Works cube, the Average Rate measure is stored in the fact table at the day level. Because it's defined as a semi-additive measure, which you learn more about later in this chapter its value is determined by calculating the average of the children of the current member of the time dimension. That is, if the current member is a month member, then the average rate is calculated by averaging the Average Rate measure for all days in that month.

You can best see the effect of Average Rate on Internet Sales Amount by browsing the cube. Place Destination Currency on rows, and add the measures Average Rate and Internet Sales Amount as shown in Figure 9-4.

In Figure 9-4 you can see the U.S. dollar is the base currency because it has an Average Rate of 1. Please note that the Internet Sales Amount for the other currencies is not derived from the division of Internet Sales Amount shown in U.S. dollars by the destination currency's Average Rate. The MeasureExpression defined for Internet Sales Amount causes Analysis Services to calculate a value for each individual transaction, dividing Internet Sales Amount in US dollars by the Average Rate for that day, and then aggregating the calculated values to show the Internet Sales amount in the desired currency. (You'll learn later in this chapter how the individual transactions were converted to US dollars before the MeasureExpression is applied.) Incidentally, because the FormatString property for Internet Sales Amount is set to Currency, all values for this measure are shown as dollars in the browser. Ideally, you should use an MDX expression for this property to format the value based on the user's selected destination currency.

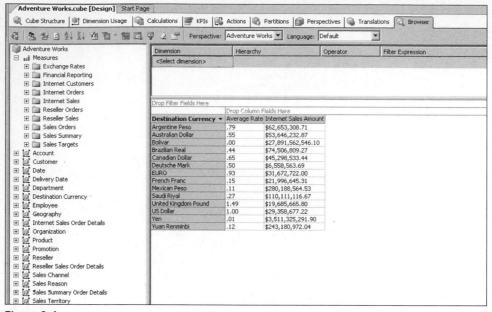

Figure 9-4

Once you have a measure group and its measures designed just right, you can add that measure group into another cube. If you are familiar with Analysis Services 2000, you will recognize this capability as the functional equivalent of adding a cube to a virtual cube without the associated activities related to creating and maintaining the individual cubes. With Analysis Services 2005, you can use the Linked Object wizard to add a measure group from another cube in the same database, a cube on the same server, or a cube in any other Analysis Services instance. You can launch the wizard from either the Cube Structure tab, as shown in Figure 9-5, or from the Dimension Usage tab.

Using the wizard, you define a data source for the Analysis Services database containing the measure group you want to include in your current cube, and then select the desired measure group from the list of available objects. The linked measure group wizard is self-explanatory and hence we leave it to you to add a linked measure group.

Take a look at the Mined Customers cube in the Adventure Works DW sample project to see how all measure groups in a cube can be linked measure groups, as shown in Figure 9-6. Linked measure groups are identified by a linking chain icon.

After adding a linked measure group, you still need to define the right relationships between the dimensions in the cube and the linked measure group. By using a linked measure group, you have access to data in the source cube without the maintenance overhead of separate measure groups for the same data.

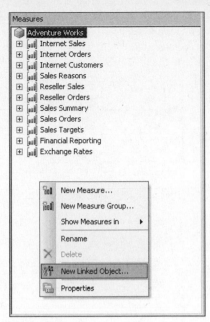

Figure 9-5

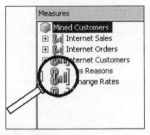

Figure 9-6

You can have a cube where all the real measures are hidden. All the measures exposed to the end users are calculated measures. Some Analysis Services customers design their cubes this way to model specific business requirements.

Adding and Enhancing Dimensions

Dimensions are an integral part of a cube. In this section, you learn about specific properties that affect a dimension's behavior within a cube as well as special types of relationships that can be defined between a dimension and a measure group. These features allow you to address special business requirements and thereby enhance overall analytical capabilities.

When you create a dimension within an Analysis Services 2005 database, you are actually creating a *database dimension*, which can be shared across multiple cubes within the same database or used multiple times within a single cube. Each instance of a database dimension within a cube is called a *cube dimension*. Right-click within the Dimensions pane of the Cube Structure as shown in Figure 9-7 to add a new cube dimension.

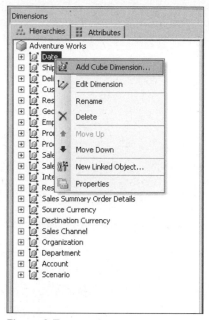

Figure 9-7

For each cube dimension, you can selectively exclude certain hierarchies or attributes by modifying properties. In the Dimensions pane on the Cube Structure tab, select the hierarchy or the attribute to be hidden and then change the applicable property in the Properties window to False. If you want to hide a hierarchy, use the Visible property. To hide an attribute, use the AttributeHierarchyVisible property.

Another important property of a cube dimension is AllMemberAggregationUsage. This property is associated with the cube dimension object itself. Changing the value of this property affects how Analysis Services builds aggregations to improve query performance. You learn about other cube dimension properties for hierarchies and attributes in Chapter 13.

Most changes to database dimensions, such as the addition or deletion of attributes or hierarchies as well as changes to most properties, are automatically reflected in the corresponding cube dimensions. However, certain changes, such as renaming a database dimension, will not result in a similar change to the cube dimension. In such circumstances you could either delete the existing cube dimension and then re-add the database dimension within the cube, or simply rename the cube dimension.

As soon as you add a cube dimension, Analysis Services 2005 attempts to detect relationships based on the DSV and to create appropriate relationships between the newly added dimension and the existing measure groups in the cube. You should switch to the Dimension Usage tab of the Cube Designer to verify relationships between dimensions and measure groups were detected correctly.

The most common type of relationship between a dimension and a measure group is a regular relationship, but there are several other types that could be defined: regular, referenced, fact, many-to-many, data mining, and no relationship. You reviewed regular and referenced relationships in depth in Chapter 6. In this chapter, you learned how to use the IgnoreUnrelatedDimensions property to determine whether you see values or nulls when there is no relationship between a measure group and a dimension. The following sections discuss the remaining three relationship types.

Fact Dimension

A fact relationship is a relationship that exists between a dimension and a measure group that are both based on the same relational table. In the Adventure Works DW sample project, the Internet Sales Order Details dimension and the Internet Sales measure group retrieve data from the FactInternetSales relational table. Fact dimensions are typically created to support detail-level reporting or scenarios in which the database does not have a well-structured star or snowflake schema but contains all information in a single table. Figure 9-8 shows the fact relationship defined between the measure group Internet Sales and the dimension Internet Sales Order Details.

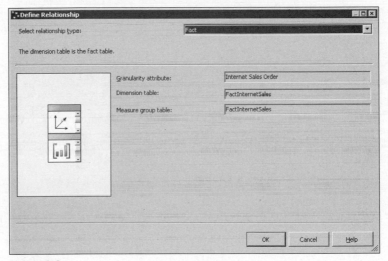

Figure 9-8

To define a fact relationship, switch to the Dimension Usage tab, and then click the cell that intersects the measure group and the dimension. When you select the Fact relationship type, the Define Relationship dialog automatically assigns the key attribute of the dimension as the granularity attribute. You can define a fact relationship only when the dimension and measure group are based on the same table; a validation in the Define Relationship dialog enforces this requirement. Otherwise, a fact relationship is very similar to a regular relationship. For example, browsing the dimension with this measure group, whether in a cube browser or with your own custom MDX, will look similar to browsing data in a regular relationship. If that's the case why do we need a fact relationship type? Two reasons:

1. Specific optimizations are done by Analysis Services during drill-through (discussed later in this chapter) when a fact relationship is defined between a measure group and a ROLAP dimension.

2. Certain client tools can present data from this relationship in a way that makes it easier for users to interpret the data during analysis.

Many-to-Many Dimension

Analysis Services 2005 supports another new relationship type called many-to-many. You were introduced to many-to-many dimensions during the discussion of measure expressions. You can recognize a many-to-many relationship when a single fact row is associated with multiple members in the dimension table. Figure 9-9 shows an example of a many-to-many relationship that exists in the Adventure Works DW sample database.

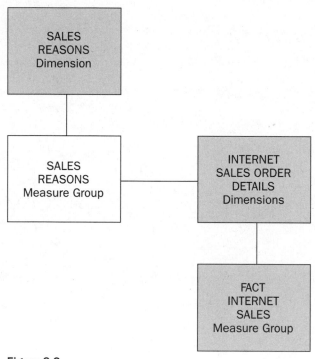

Figure 9-9

As you learned in the previous section, the Internet Sales measure group is related to the Internet Sales Order Details dimension through a fact relationship. Figure 9-9 adds new relationships — the Sales Reasons measure group is related to the Sales Reasons dimension through a fact relationship and to the Internet Sales Order Details dimension through a regular relationship. In other words, each line item in a sales order (in the Internet Sales measure group as a single fact row) can have one or more sales reasons (in the Sales Reasons dimension). An *intermediate dimension*, Internet Sales Order Details, joins the two measure groups, one of which is an *intermediate fact table*. This intermediate fact table, Sales Reasons (the measure group) joins the intermediate dimension to the many-to-many dimension, Sales Reasons (the dimension). When Analysis Services 2005 aggregates the values for each many-to-many dimension member, it aggregates the values in the measure group based on the set of distinct regular dimension members related to the current many-to-many dimension member. As a result, data is aggregated to each level exactly once. For example, consider a sales order that has two different sales reasons A and B. If you request Internet Sales measure values for that sales order by Sales Reasons — specifically members A, B, and All — you will see that the measure values are aggregated to the All member exactly once because there is only one distinct sales order related to the All member. Similarly, there is only one distinct sales order related to A and to B, so all three members will display the same values in this example.

Many-to-many relationships are common in data warehouses, and now, you have the ability to model and analyze the data from many-to-many dimensions. You can use a many-to-many relationship to perform currency conversion as you saw previously in this chapter when learning about measure expressions. You can also perform weighted average calculations using the many-to-many relationship in combination with a measure expression. Many-to-many relationships can be modeled for any schema that contains at least one common dimension between the regular measure group and the intermediate measure group. If there are multiple common dimensions between the measure groups, Analysis Services 2005 aggregates values for each distinct combination of members in those dimensions related to the current many-to-many dimension member.

On the Dimension Usage tab, click the cell that intersects the measure group and the dimension for which you want to define a many-to-many relationship. In the Adventure Works sample cube, take a look at the many-to-many relationship between the Sales Reason dimension and the Internet Sales measure group. You can see the relationship requires the intermediate measure group Sales Reasons, as shown in Figure 9-10.

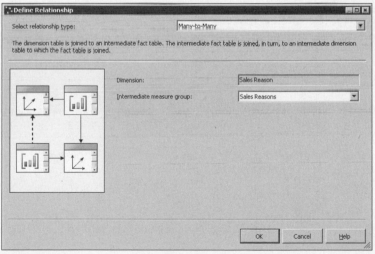

Figure 9-10

With this relationship defined, you can browse the many-to-many dimension Sales Reason along with the Internet Sales measure group, as shown in Figure 9-11.

Drop Filter Fields Here			
		Drop Column Fields Here	
Sales Reason Type	Sales Reason	Internet Sales Amount	Internet Order Quantity
Marketing	Television Advertisement	$27,475.82	730
	Total	$27,475.82	730
Other	Manufacturer	$5,998,122.10	1,818
	Other	$248,483.34	3,653
	Price	$10,975,842.56	47,733
	Quality	$5,549,896.77	1,551
	Review	$1,694,881.98	1,640
	Total	$18,678,948.02	51,314
Promotion	On Promotion	$6,361,828.95	7,390
	Total	$6,361,828.95	7,390
Grand Total		$29,358,677.22	60,398

Figure 9-11

The sum of the Internet Order Quantity values for the various Sales Reasons grouped with Sales Reason Type Other is 56,395 which is greater than the Total shown for Other, which is 51,314. Because a many-to-many relationship is defined between the Internet Sales measure group, which includes Internet Order Quantity, and the Sales Reason dimension, the aggregated measure values correctly use the distinct members to avoid double-counting

Data Mining Dimension

The technical definition of data mining is the process of automatic or semi-automatic discovery of hidden patterns in a data set that are not intuitive. Several data mining algorithms are available to discover different kinds of patterns. Some data mining algorithms predict future values based on the patterns detected. For example, you can first use data mining to classify customers of a retail store as Platinum, Gold, Silver, and Bronze members based on selected attributes, such as income, number of children, and so on. You can use data mining to automatically classify new store customers based on the patterns discovered for existing customers. Additionally, the retail store could decide to boost sales by providing coupons to targeted customers based on the buying patterns of existing customers. Analysis Services 2005 supports several data mining algorithms which you learn in detail in Chapter 14.

In Analysis Services 2005, the UDM is tightly integrated with the data mining features. You can, for example, create a data mining model not only from a relational data source, but also from an existing cube. When a data mining model is created from a cube, you can also create a data mining dimension from the mining model. You can then add this new dimension to the source cube to form a new cube with which you can perform analysis of cube data right alongside the data mining results.

Figure 9-12 shows the relationship definition for a data mining relationship. The target dimension, Clustered Customers, is a dimension that was derived from a data mining model. The source dimension, Customers, is the dimension from which the data mining model was originally created.

If you open the Mined Customers cube in the Adventure Works DW sample project and switch to the Dimension Usage tab, you can see the data mining relationship defined between the Cluster Customers dimension and Internet Sales measure group. Open the Cube Browser to view the breakdown of Internet sales based on the Clustered Customers dimension as shown in Figure 9-13. This dimension represents the data mining model's classification of all members in the Customers dimension into 10 different clusters. To see the characteristics of each cluster, you need to review the mining model. By combining data mining results with cube data, you can make specific business decisions. For example, using the sales information shown in Figure 9-13 in combination with the characteristics of clusters defined by the data mining model, you could decide to boost sales by developing promotions or other incentives for a specific set of customers.

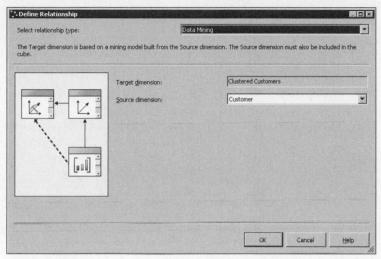

Figure 9-12

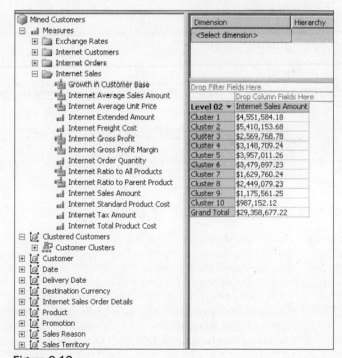

Figure 9-13

Role-Playing Dimensions

A role-playing dimension is a database dimension that acts as multiple dimensions within a cube. Instead of requiring to create two database dimensions that serve different purposes, but depend on the same data source table(s), a single database dimension can be used to create separate cube dimensions. For example, if you have a geography dimension as a database dimension, you can add it to a cube as Customer Geography and Employee Geography cube dimensions. Similarly, you can have one Time dimension called Date, and then you can add Ship Date and Received Date as cube dimensions. In these examples, Geography and Date dimensions are role-playing dimensions because they can each serve different roles within the same cube.

Figure 9-14 shows how the Date dimension is used as a role-playing dimension in the Adventure Works cube of the Adventure Works DW sample project. The Date dimension plays the role of three date dimensions: Date, Ship Date, and Delivery Date. When a dimension plays multiple roles in a single measure group, the fact table for the measure group contains one foreign key column for each role, each of which must have a relationship to a single dimension table defined in the DSV.

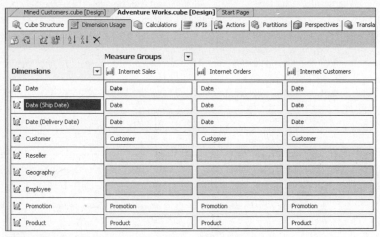

Figure 9-14

Adding Calculations to Your Cube

In Chapter 6, you learned how to use the Calculations tab in the cube designer for creating calculated members and named sets. In Chapter 7, you learned about the calculation model in Analysis Services 2005 and how cell calculations are created within MDX Scripts. In this section, you learn how to review and test cell calculations.

You use the Calculations tab in the cube designer to define all calculations which then become part of the MDX script of your cube. In this section, you continue using the Adventure Works DW sample project included with Microsoft SQL Server 2005 product to explore the functionality available in the Calculations tab.

The following steps show how to review the definitions of some of the calculations defined in the Adventure Works sample cube and how to verify the results as the calculations are applied to the specific cells:

1. Open the Adventure Works DW sample project located at C:\Program Files\Microsoft SQL Server\90\Tools\Samples\AdventureWorks Analysis Services Project\Enterprise and, if you haven't done so already, deploy the project to the Analysis Services instance on your machine. If you have a default Analysis Services instance, you can deploy the project without changing the project properties. However, if you have installed named instances of Analysis Services and SQL Server you must change the project's deploy properties to target the right instance of Analysis Services and you must also change the relational data source in the project to point to your SQL Server instance.

2. Open the Adventure Works cube and click the Calculations tab. You will see all the calculated members, named sets, and calculations specified within the MDX script as shown in Figure 9-15. The first command selected in the Script Organizer, which is also the first command in the MDX script, is the Calculate statement. The Calculate statement is automatically added to each cube created by the cube wizard. The Calculate statement can be anywhere within the MDX script, but it must be included so be careful not to delete it. You can also add comments to the MDX script to make it easier to understand the purpose of the calculations by inserting your comments between the /* and */ characters as shown in Figure 9-15. All comments within the MDX script are detected by the cube designer and converted to a green font color for easier reading.

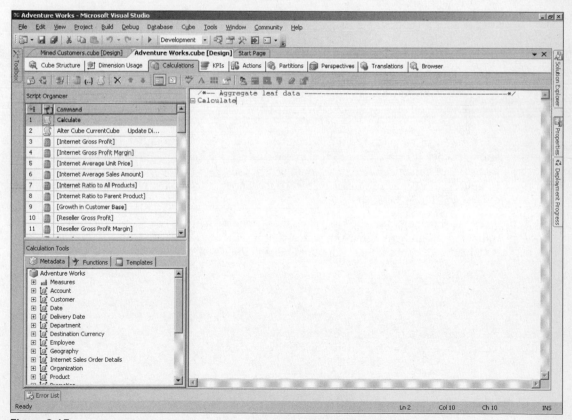

Figure 9-15

3. The Calculations tab has two views: the Form View and the Script View. Figure 9-15 shows the Form View in which you can select a command listed in the Script Organizer pane to see its definition independently. Figure 9-16 shows the Script View, which displays when you click the Script View icon in the Calculations toolbar. In Script View, you can see all the commands together in the script pane.

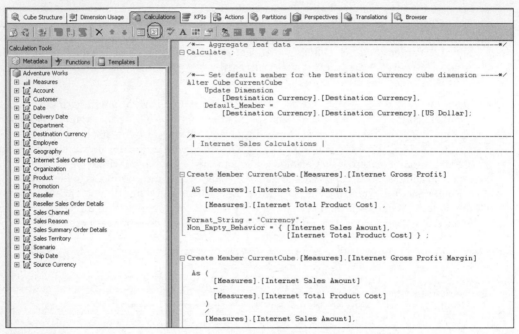

Figure 9-16

4. Click the Form View icon on the Calculations toolbar, scroll through the Script Organizer pane, and then click the first Scope statement. As you can see in Figure 9-17, when you select an item in the Script Organizer, the corresponding script displays on the right side. As you learned in Chapter 7, this Scope command restricts the cube space to Sales Amount Quota for Fiscal Quarters in Fiscal Year 2005.

5. Click the statement that appears below the Scope statement in the Script Organizer to see the following assignment statement, which allocates the Sales Amount Quota for the Fiscal Year 2005 based 135% of the Sales Amount Quota in the Fiscal Year 2004:

```
This = ParallelPeriod
       (
           [Date].[Fiscal].[Fiscal Year], 1,
           [Date].[Fiscal].CurrentMember
       ) * 1.35
```

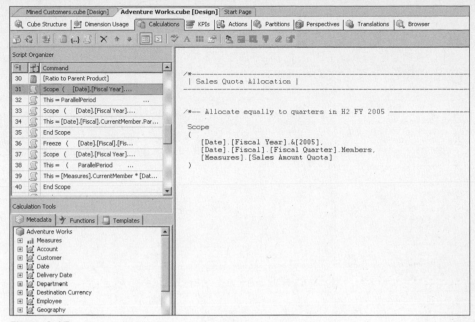

Figure 9-17

6. As you add statements and commands to the MDX script, you should test the script to ensure the affected cells or members get the correct values. One way to test an MDX expression is to use it in a query and evaluate the results. This approach can become time-consuming, especially when you have complex expressions like those shown in Chapter 7. A better alternative is to use the debugging capabilities of the Analysis Services 2005 Cube Designer in which you can quickly validate results. Because a cube's MDX Script is just a sequence of MDX statements, you can evaluate each statement separately by using the Cube Designer's debugging feature. Debugging your MDX script is similar to debugging application code. You can set breakpoints to evaluate a sequence of MDX statements that precede the statement specified as a breakpoint. To try the debugging capabilities, click the Script View icon in the Calculations toolbar, scroll through the list of MDX statements to locate the first Scope statement in the MDX script, and then set a breakpoint as shown in Figure 9-18. Set the break point by clicking in the margin to the left of the Scope statement. The breakpoint appears as a solid red circle as shown in Figure 9-18. Once you have set the break point, you see the statement being highlighted in red.

7. To start debugging mode, press the function key F10. After deploying the database, the Cube Designer switches to debugging mode which divides the script pane into two sections, as shown in Figure 9-19. Standard Visual Studio environment debugging windows, such as Autos, Locals, and Breakpoints, among others, might also automatically open when debugging starts. Close these windows to allocate more screen space to the script pane. The top half of the script pane now contains the MDX script with the breakpoint statement highlighted in yellow. The bottom half now includes an Office Web Components Pivot Table control loaded as well as several sub panes labeled MDX1, MDX2, MDX3, and MDX4. The Pivot Table is useful for browsing the dimensions and measures as you execute the statements. The MDX panes 1 through 4 can be used to execute regular MDX queries during the debugging session.

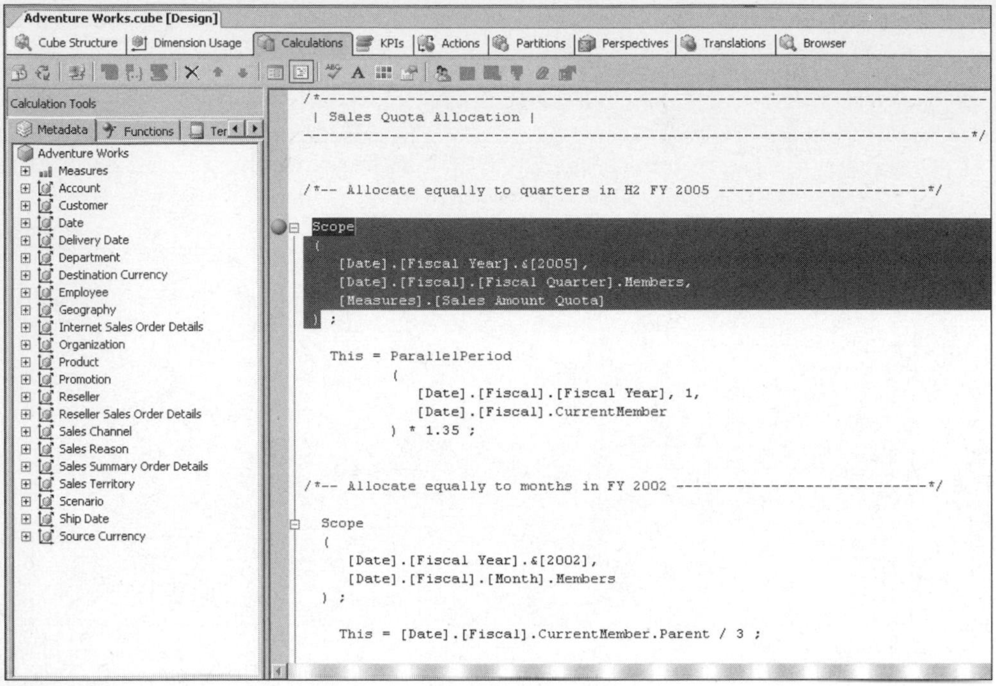

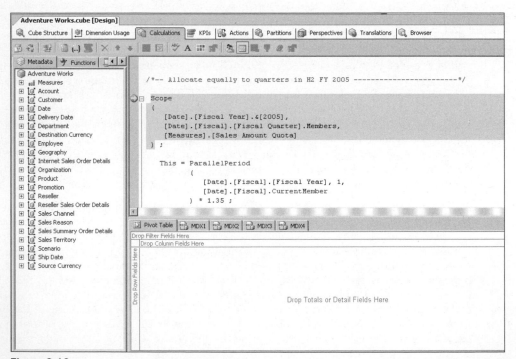

Figure 9-18

Figure 9-19

8. The debugger stopped execution of the MDX script at the statement with the breakpoint. You can monitor the effect of the subsequent statements by placing the Fiscal hierarchy of the Date dimension and the Sales Amount Quota measure in the Pivot Table, as shown in Figure 9-20. Expand the Fiscal Years 2004 and 2005 to see the Fiscal Semesters. All the measure values are currently highlighted in yellow for each quarter because the option to highlight affected cells is enabled by default. You can use the fifth icon from the right in the Calculations toolbar "Highlight changed cells" to toggle this behavior.

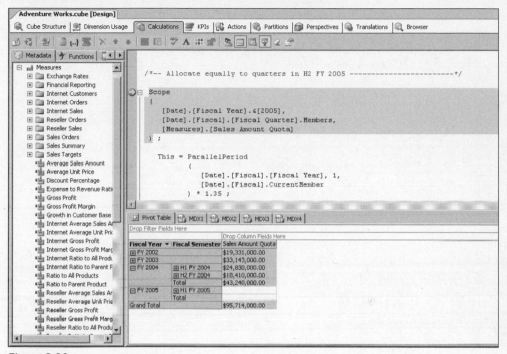

Figure 9-20

9. The next statement, which is the assignment MDX expression to specify the Sales Amount Quota for the Fiscal year 2005, is now ready for execution. Press F10 to step through the Scope statement. The assignment statement is now highlighted with a yellow background, shown in Figure 9-21, but has not yet been executed.

10. Execute the assignment statement by pressing the F10 key, which executes one statement at a time. As soon as the assignment statement is executed, the Sales Amount Quota value for the year 2005 changed from empty to 18,539,550.00. The cells corresponding to Fiscal Year 2005 and the Grand Total are both affected by the assignment statement and are the only cells highlighted, as shown in Figure 9-22.

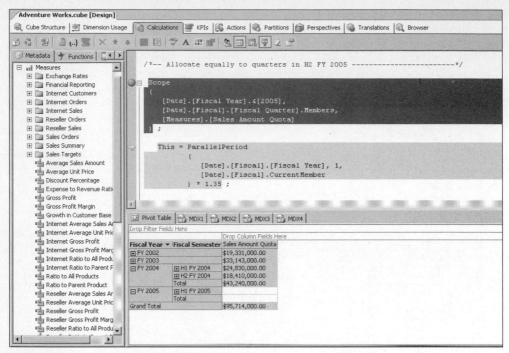

Figure 9-21

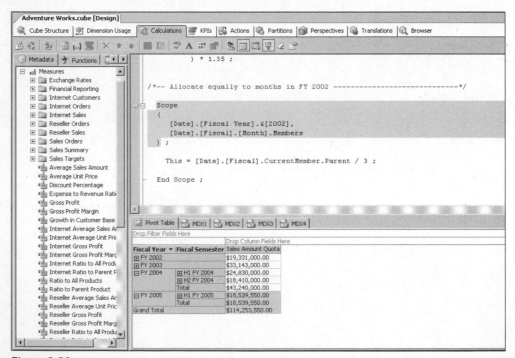

Figure 9-22

You have now successfully tested the MDX script calculations you learned about in Chapter 7. You can also use the MDX1 through MDX4 panes for additional debugging. For example, before stepping into the statement that assigns values to the quarters of year 2005 you can send the following MDX query to query the current values for 2005 quarters:

```
SELECT [Measures].[Sales Amount Quota] ON 0,
[Date].[Fiscal].[Fiscal Quarter].members ON 1
FROM [Adventure Works]
```

Just click one of the MDX tabs as shown in Figure 9-23, type the MDX query, and click the Execute MDX button. The Execute MDX button is the button containing the green arrow. The MDX query executes in the current context of debugging and retrieves the cells specified by the query, and displaying the results in the results pane.

Execute MDX

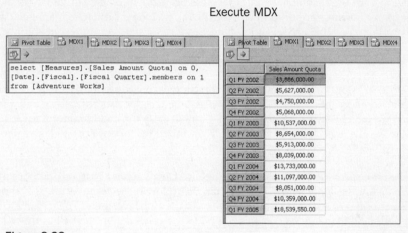

Figure 9-23

If you currently have one of the MDX panes open during execution of the MDX script, the results of the executed statements are immediately reflected in the results. Figure 9-24 shows the results of the MDX query before and after the execution of the MDX script to assign a sales quota for the year 2005.

	Sales Amount Quota			Sales Amount Quota
Q1 FY 2002	$3,886,000.00		Q1 FY 2002	$3,886,000.00
Q2 FY 2002	$5,627,000.00		Q2 FY 2002	$5,627,000.00
Q3 FY 2002	$4,750,000.00		Q3 FY 2002	$4,750,000.00
Q4 FY 2002	$5,068,000.00		Q4 FY 2002	$5,068,000.00
Q1 FY 2003	$10,537,000.00		Q1 FY 2003	$10,537,000.00
Q2 FY 2003	$8,654,000.00		Q2 FY 2003	$8,654,000.00
Q3 FY 2003	$5,913,000.00		Q3 FY 2003	$5,913,000.00
Q4 FY 2003	$8,039,000.00		Q4 FY 2003	$8,039,000.00
Q1 FY 2004	$13,733,000.00		Q1 FY 2004	$13,733,000.00
Q2 FY 2004	$11,097,000.00		Q2 FY 2004	$11,097,000.00
Q3 FY 2004	$8,051,000.00		Q3 FY 2004	$8,051,000.00
Q4 FY 2004	$10,359,000.00		Q4 FY 2004	$10,359,000.00
Q1 FY 2005	(null)		Q1 FY 2005	$18,539,550.00

Figure 9-24

The debugger also allows you to simulate a different user during execution. Click the Change User icon (sixth icon from the right on the Calculations toolbar) to change to a different user or a role when you need to verify the results of an MDX script with appropriate security for your end users. Obviously, you don't want users to view data that they aren't supposed to see.

Now that you have learned how to use and debug calculations in Analysis Services 2005, you're ready to learn about two other important types of cube enhancements, KPIs and Actions.

Key Performance Indicators (KPIs)

Key Performance Indicators, most often called KPIs, may also be referred to as Key Success Indicators (KSIs). Regardless of what you call them, they can help your organization define and measure quantitative progress toward organizational goals. Business users often manage organizational performance using KPIs. Many business application vendors now provide performance management tools (namely dashboard applications) that collect KPI data from source systems and present KPI results graphically to end business users. Microsoft Office Business Scorecard Manager 2005 is an example of a KPI application that can leverage the KPI capabilities of Analysis Services 2005.

Analysis Services 2005 provides a framework for categorizing the KPI MDX expressions for use with the business data stored in cubes. Each KPI uses a predefined set of data roles — actual, goal, trend, status, and weight — to which MDX expressions are assigned. Only the metadata for the KPIs is stored by an Analysis Services instance, while a new set of MDX functions for applications is available to easily retrieve KPI values from cubes using this metadata.

The Cube Designer provided in Business Intelligence Development Studio (BIDS) also lets cube developers easily create and test KPIs which you learn in the following section. Figure 9-25 shows the KPIs in the Adventure Works cube using the KPI browser in the Cube Designer. You can get to the KPI browser by clicking on the KPI tab in the Cube Designer and then clicking on the KPI browser icon (second icon in the tool bar in the KPI tab).

Display Structure	Value	Goal	Status	Trend
Customer Perspective				
Expand Customer Base				
Growth in Customer Base	NA	NA	⬆	→
Financial Perspective				
Grow Revenue				
Channel Revenue	$80,450,596.98	$114,253,550.00	▭	↑
Financial Variance	1.26	0	↕	↓
Internet Revenue	$29,358,677.22	29358677.22	▭	↑
Return on Assets	0.92	Not Budgeted	▭	↑
Revenue	$109,809,274.20	109809274.2	▭	↑
Maintain Overall Margins				
Net Income	12609503	5583900	⬆	↑
Operating Profit	16728234.5	5583900	▮	↑
Financial Gross Margin	44390103	11848650	▮	↑
Operating Expenses	27661868.5	6264750	▮	↓
Product Gross Profit Margin	11.43%	0.12	▭	↑
Internal Perspective				
Increase Operational Efficiency				
Expense to Revenue Ratio	25.19%	0.25	◗	↓

Figure 9-25

KPI Creation

Consider the following scenario: The Adventure Works sales management team wants to monitor the sales revenue for the new fiscal year. Sales revenue for prior fiscal years is available in the Adventure Works cube. The management team has identified the goal of 15% growth for sales revenue year over year. If current sales revenue is over 95% of the goal, sales revenue performance is satisfactory. If, however, the sales revenue is within 85% to 95% of the goal, management must be alerted. If the sales revenue drops under 85% of the goal, management must take immediate action to change the trend. These alerts and calls to action are commonly associated with the use of KPIs. The management team is interested in the trends associated with sales revenue; if the sales revenue is 20% higher than expected, the sales revenue status is great news and should be surfaced as well — it's not all doom and gloom.

Use the following steps to design the KPIs for the sales management team:

1. Open the Adventure Works DW sample project located at C:\Program Files\Microsoft SQL Server\90\Tools\Samples\AdventureWorks Analysis Services Project\Enterprise.

2. Double-click the Adventure Works cube in Solution Explorer to open the Cube Designer.

3. Click the KPIs tab to open the KPI editor.

4. Click the New KPI icon in the KPI toolbar to open a template for a new KPI. As you can see in Figure 9-26, there are several properties to fill in.

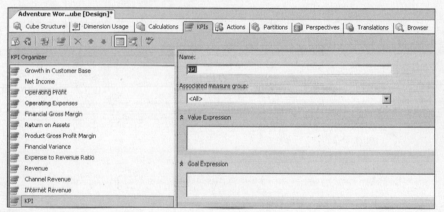

Figure 9-26

5. Type Sales Revenue KPI in the Name text box and then choose Sales Summary in the drop-down box for Associated Measure Group. The revenue measure is Sales Amount which is included in the Sales Summary measure group.

6. Type the following MDX expression in the Value Expression text box.

```
[Measures].[Sales Amount]
```

When managers browse the KPI, the value of Sales Amount value will be retrieved from the cube.

7. Now you need to translate the sales revenue goal to increase 15% over last year's revenue into an MDX expression. Put another way, this year's sales revenue goal is 1.15 times last year's

sales revenue. Use the ParallelPeriod function to get the previous year's time members for each current year time member. Type the resulting MDX expression, shown below, in the Goal Expression text box.

```
1.15 *
        (
            [Measures].[Sales Amount],
            ParallelPeriod
            (
                [Date].[Fiscal].[Fiscal Year],  1,
                [Date].[Fiscal].CurrentMember
            )
        )
```

8. In the Status section of the KPI template, you can choose a graphical indicator for the status of the KPI to display in the KPI browser. You can see several of the available indicators in Figure 9-27. For your own KPI applications, you must programmatically associate the KPI status with your own graphical indicator. For now, select the Traffic Light indicator. The MDX expression that you define for status must return a value between -1 and 1. The KPI browser displays a red traffic light when the status is -1 and a green traffic light when the status is 1. When the status is 0, a yellow traffic light displays.

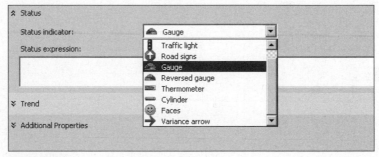

Figure 9-27

9. Type the following expression in the Status Expression text box.

```
Case
  When KpiValue("Sales Revenue KPI")/KpiGoal("Sales Revenue KPI" )>=.95
    Then 1
  When KpiValue("Sales Revenue KPI")/KpiGoal("Sales Revenue KPI")<.95
    And
      KpiValue("Sales Revenue KPI")/KpiGoal("Sales Revenue KPI")>=.85
    Then 0
    Else -1
End
```

The above expression uses the Case MDX statement available for use with Analysis Services 2005. In addition, you now have a set of MDX functions to use with KPI metric values. In the previous MDX expression, the KpiValue function retrieves the value of Sales Revenue KPI, and the KpiGoal function retrieves the goal value of Sales Revenue KPI. More precisely, the KpiValue function is a member function that returns a calculated measure from the Measures dimension. By using KPI functions, you can avoid a lot of typing if your value or goal expression is complex. This Status expression will return one of three discrete values — 1 if revenue exceeds 95% of goal, 0 if revenue is between 85%–95% of goal, and –1 if revenue is below 85% of goal.

10. Choose the default indicator (Standard Arrow) for Trend indicator. Type the following MDX expression in the Trend Expression text box. This expression compares current KPI values with last year's values from the same time period to calculate the trend of the KPI.

```
Case
    When (
            KpiValue( "Sales Revenue KPI" ) -
            (
              KpiValue ( "Sales Revenue KPI" ),
              ParallelPeriod
              (
                [Date].[Fiscal].[Fiscal Year],
                1,
                [Date].[Fiscal].CurrentMember
              )
            )) /
            (
              KpiValue ( "Sales Revenue KPI" ),
              ParallelPeriod
              (
                [Date].[Fiscal].[Fiscal Year],
                1,
                [Date].[Fiscal].CurrentMember
              )
            )
          <=-.02
    Then -1
    When ( KpiValue( "Sales Revenue KPI" ) -
          (
            KpiValue ( "Sales Revenue KPI" ),
            ParallelPeriod
            (
              [Date].[Fiscal].[Fiscal Year],
              1,
              [Date].[Fiscal].CurrentMember
            )
          )) /
          (
            KpiValue ( "Sales Revenue KPI" ),
            ParallelPeriod
            (
              [Date].[Fiscal].[Fiscal Year],
              1,
              [Date].[Fiscal].CurrentMember
            )
          )  >.02
    Then 1
    Else 0
End
```

11. Expand the Additional properties section at the bottom of the KPI template to type a name in the Display Folder combo box for a new folder, or to pick an existing display folder. The KPI browser will show all KPIs in a folder separate from other measures and dimensions, but you can further group related KPIs into folders and subfolders. A subfolder is created when the folder names are separated by a backslash, "\". In the Display Folder combo box, type SampleKPI\RevenueFolder as shown in Figure 9-28.

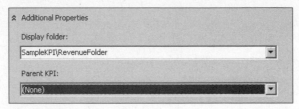

Figure 9-28

You can also choose to set Parent KPI so that the KPI browser displays KPIs hierarchically. Using the Parent KPI setting is for display purposes only and doesn't actually create a physical relationship between parent and child KPIs. You could, however, design a Parent KPIs that uses values from child KPIs via KPI functions; there is even a Weight expression to adjust the value of a Parent KPI. The display folder setting is ignored if you select a Parent KPI because the KPI will display inside its parent's folder. To complete your KPI, leave the Parent KPI as (None).

Congratulations, you just created your first KPI! Deploy the project to an instance of Analysis Services 2005 so you can view the KPI values. To deploy, select the Build menu item and then select Deploy Adventure Works DW. Like MDX scripts, KPI definitions are only metadata, so changing and saving the KPI definitions will only update the metadata store. A cube reprocess is not required, allowing you to use a KPI right after deploying it to the Analysis Services instance.

To view the KPI, follow these steps:

1. In the cube designer, click the Browser View icon in the KPI toolbar, as shown in Figure 9-29.

Figure 9-29

Your new KPI is at the bottom of the view window and should look like Figure 9-30

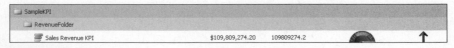

Figure 9-30

2. The KPI browser supports the standard slicer window at the top of the browser. You can select specific members to narrow down the analysis to areas of interest. For example, suppose you are interested in the sales revenue KPI for August 2003. In the slicer window, select the Date dimension, Fiscal hierarchy, and August 2003 (found in semester H1 FY 2004 and quarter Q1 FY 2004) as shown in Figure 9-31.

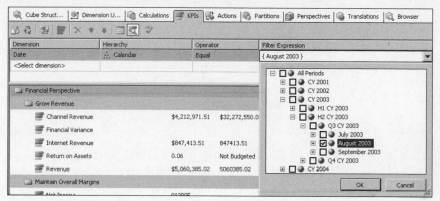

Figure 9-31

You will notice the KPI values have changed as shown in Figure 9-32, as have the Goals — August beats the goal!

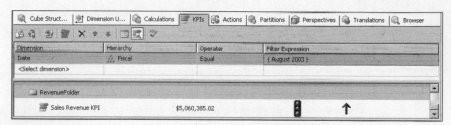

Figure 9-32

KPIs In Depth

Every Analysis Services cube can have an associated collection of KPIs, and each KPI has five properties as its set of metadata. These properties are MDX expressions that return numeric values from a cube as described in the following table.

KPI Specific Properties	Description
Value	An MDX expression that returns the actual value of the KPI. It is mandatory for a KPI.
Goal	An MDX expression that returns the goal of the KPI.

Table continued on following page

KPI Specific Properties	Description
Status	An MDX expression that returns the status of the KPI. To best represent the value graphically, this expression should return a value between –1 and 1. Client applications use the status value to display a graphic indicator of the KPI trend.
Trend	An MDX expression that returns the trend of the KPI over time. As with Status, the Trend expression should return a value between –1 and 1. Client applications use the trend value to display a graphic indicator of the KPI trend direction.
Weight	An MDX expression that returns the weight of the KPI. If a KPI has a parent KPI, you can define weights to control the contribution of this KPI to its parent.

Analysis Services 2005 creates hidden calculated members on measure dimensions for each KPI metric (value, goal, status, trend, and weight). However, if a KPI expression directly references a measure, Analysis Services optimization uses the measure directly instead of creating a new calculated measure. You can query the calculated measure used for KPIs in an MDX expression, even though it's hidden.

To see how this works, open SSMS, and connect to Analysis Services. Click the Analysis Services MDX Query icon in the toolbar to open a new MDX query window. Make sure you're connected to the Adventure Works DW database in the Available Databases list box, type the following query in the MDX query window, and then click the Execute button.

```
SELECT {Measures.[Sales Revenue KPI Goal] } ON 0,
[Date].[Fiscal].[Fiscal Quarter].members on 1
FROM [Adventure Works]
```

Figure 9-33 shows the results of executing the query.

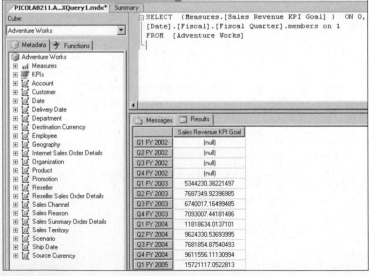

Figure 9-33

Using ADOMD.NET to Query KPIs

The Analysis Services instance hosting the database cubes also maintains the KPI definition metadata. As you learned in the previous section, you can access KPI values directly by using KPI functions. Client applications can also access this KPI metadata information and retrieve values programmatically through an Analysis Services client-side component ADOMD.NET.

ADOMD.NET provides native support for KPIs. It includes a KPI class that contains a method called Kpi.Properties("KPI_XXX"), which is used to retrieve properties of each KPI. This method returns a string of unique measures for the developer to use in the construction of MDX queries that retrieve the KPI values. The following code example demonstrates how to access a KPI using ADOMD.NET and how to construct a parameterized MDX query. Because KPI metrics are just calculated measures, you execute a KPI query with ADOMD.NET the same way you execute regular MDX queries.

```
using System;
using System.Collections.Generic;
using System.Text;
using Microsoft.AnalysisServices.AdomdClient;

namespace QueryKPIs
{
    class Program
    {
        static void Main(string[] args)
        {
            string connectionString = "Provider = MSOLAP.3;Data
Source=localhost;Initial Catalog=Adventure Works DW";
            AdomdConnection acCon = new AdomdConnection(connectionString);
            try
            {
                acCon.Open();
                CubeDef cubeObject = acCon.Cubes["Adventure Works"];
                foreach (Microsoft.AnalysisServices.AdomdClient.Kpi cubeApi in
cubeObject.Kpis)
                {
                    string commandText = @"SELECT { strtomember(@Value),
strtomember(@Goal), strtomember(@Status), strtomember(@Trend) }
    ON COLUMNS FROM [" + cubeObject.Name + "]";
                    AdomdCommand command = new AdomdCommand(commandText, acCon);
                    foreach (Microsoft.AnalysisServices.AdomdClient.Kpi kpi in
cubeObject.Kpis)
                    {
                        command.Parameters.Clear();
                        command.Parameters.Add(new AdomdParameter("Value",
kpi.Properties["KPI_VALUE"].Value));
                        command.Parameters.Add(new AdomdParameter("Goal",
kpi.Properties["KPI_GOAL"].Value));
                        command.Parameters.Add(new AdomdParameter("Status",
kpi.Properties["KPI_STATUS"].Value));
                        command.Parameters.Add(new AdomdParameter("Trend",
kpi.Properties["KPI_TREND"].Value));
                        CellSet cellset = command.ExecuteCellSet();

                        Console.WriteLine("KPI Name:" + kpi.Name);
```

```
                            Console.WriteLine("Value:" +
            cellset.Cells[0].FormattedValue);
                            Console.WriteLine("Goal:" +
            cellset.Cells[1].FormattedValue);
                            Console.WriteLine("Status:" +
            cellset.Cells[2].FormattedValue);
                            Console.WriteLine("Trend:" +
            cellset.Cells[3].FormattedValue);
                        }

                    }
                }
                finally
                {
                    acCon.Close();
                }
            }
        }
    }
```

Note that this example uses a parameterized MDX query and the StrToMember function to avoid MDX injection. The developer of a client-side application needs to be cautious with user input; a simple string concatenation would allow a malicious user to input and run harmful code. You can create a new C# program called QueryKPI, copy the above code, add the Microsoft.AnalysisServices.AdomdClient DLL as a reference and run the program. We recommend you explore the .NET Adomd client object model by writing client programs that leverage the object model.

Drill-Through

Drill down is the process of navigating from a summary level to more detailed levels across a cube dimension. Drill-through is a completely different animal. Drill-through retrieves fact data corresponding to a cell or some specified range of cells. Often the lowest level of detail in a cube is still comprised of aggregated values, but users occasionally have a need to see the associated row-level data from the fact table. In Analysis Services 2005, even if you use the MOLAP storage mode (discussed later in this chapter), you can still use drill-through. You can modify a server configuration advanced property, OLAP\Query\DefaultDrillthroughMaxRows, control the default size of the returned dataset.

By default, drill-through returns the granularity attribute of each dimension and all measures. If you want your drill-through action to behave like drill-through in Analysis Services 2000, you can create a ROLAP dimension from the fact table that contains the measures to return. And just how do you define drill-through? You could create an application that performs drill-through programmatically using the SQL query supported by Analysis Services 2005. A new option in Analysis Services 2005 is to create a drill-through action. The following sections describe the available action types, including how to create a drill-through action.

For some insight on how drill-through actually works in Analysis Services 2005, it is informative to contrast it to the implementation of drill-through in Analysis Services 2000. Analysis Services 2000 fetched all requested measures directly from the relational data source which is potentially a slow process. Analysis Services 2005 fetches the requested measures from the MOLAP database directly and therefore runs much faster. Indeed, the system is self-contained and requires no connection to SQL Server. Drill through can be defined as an Action (to be seen in next section) and can drill through on cells that have drill through action defined. You will learn to define Drill through and understand it's behavior in the next section.

Actions

Actions are predefined metadata components stored on the server that send commands to client applications to perform certain operations based on a selection by the user in the cube browser. For example, the user could select dimension members, levels, a set, specific cube cells, and so on. An action command usually includes a command string, such as a URL, and the suggested command behavior, such as opening a Web browser for the URL. MDX expressions are often built into commands to include the context of the user selection in the action. If a user initiates an action by selecting a product, for example, an MDX expression could be used to generate a URL for a catalog page describing the selected product.

Action Types

Analysis Services 2005 supports seven action types. These action types empower client applications with more analytical capabilities than traditional OLAP analysis drill up, drill down, and pivot activities. For example, if a sales manager is analyzing sales for cities in Washington State, the ability to click on a city member to view an MSN city map would be helpful. Similarly, if your implementation includes Reporting Services, you could link a report that analyzes sales reasons by product category to the product category members by adding an action to the cube. When the sales manager clicks a product category, the action passes the selected product category as a parameter to the report which then displays in a Web browser. If a sales number for a specific region appears to be surprisingly high or low, the sales manager could use a Drill-through action to retrieve all detailed transactions contributing to the value. The seven action types supported in Analysis Services 2005 are listed in the following table along with the information on what can be done by a client when such an action type is returned by Analysis Services 2005.

Action Type	Description
CommandLine	Returns a command that can be run under command prompt.
HTML	Returns an HTML script that can be rendered using HTML browser.
URL	Returns a URL that can be launched using a browser. Report Action (to be see later) uses this Action type.
Statement	Returns a statement that can be run as an OLE DB command.
Rowset	Returns a rowset to a client application.
Proprietary	Performs an operation by using an interface other than those listed in this table. The client application retrieving this action type should know how to use this proprietary action type.
Dataset	Returns a dataset to a client application.

Action Target Types

Each action is tied to a target type. Target types refer to a specific object or objects, inside the cube. If a user clicks an object that has been defined as a target for an action, the action will be enabled in the client application for that specific object. For example, if you define a URL action to be associated with attribute members of the geography.city attribute, that action will be available when the user selects any member of the city attribute. When you define an action, you must specify the type of objects that will be targets of the action. Analysis Services 2005 supports the following Action Target Types.

Target Type	Description
Attribute Members	Only valid selection is a single attribute hierarchy. The target of the action will be all members of attribute wherever they appear (that is, it will apply to multilevel hierarchies as well).
Cells	All Cells is the only selection available. If you choose Well Cells as a target type, type an expression in Condition to restrict the cells with which the action is associated.
Cube	CURRENTCUBE is the only selection available. The action is associated with the current cube.
Dimension members	You need to select a single dimension. The action will be associated with all members of the dimension.
Hierarchy	You need to select a single hierarchy. The action will be associated with the hierarchy object only. Attribute hierarchies appear in the list only if their AttributeHierarchyEnabled and AttributeHierarchyVisible properties are set to True.
Hierarchy members	You need to select a single hierarchy. The action will be associated with all members of the selected hierarchy. Attribute hierarchies appear in the list only if their AttributeHierarchyEnabled and AttributeHierarchyVisible properties are set to True.
Level	You need to select a single level. The action will be associated with the level object only.
Level members	You need to select a single level. The action will be associated with all members of the selected level.

URL Action

In this section you will learn to create a few actions. The URL Action is probably one of the actions which we expect customers to use widely. Follow the steps below to create a URL action.

1. Using BIDS, open the Adventure Works DW sample project (located at C:\Program Files\ Microsoft SQL Server\90\Tools\Samples\AdventureWorks Analysis Services Project\ Enterprise), and double-click the Adventure Works cube in Solution Explorer to open the cube designer. Click the Action tab to open the actions editor, as shown in Figure 9-34.

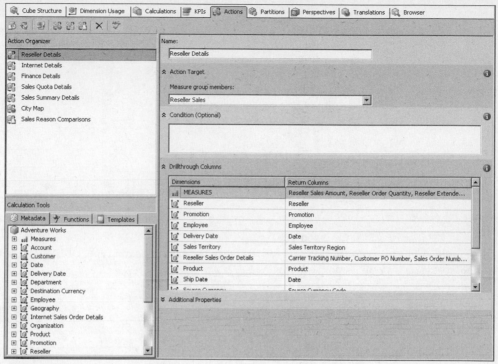

Figure 9-34

2. Click the New Action button in the Actions toolbar. Type a name for the new action: My City Map. Open the Target type list box (by clicking on the down arrow) to see the available action target types, and then choose Attribute Members, as shown in Figure 9-35.

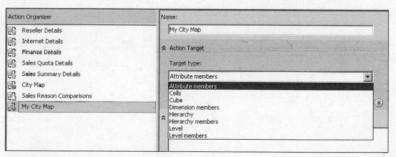

Figure 9-35

3. In the Target object drill down box, pick Geography.City as the attribute target (shown in Figure 9-36).

4. Leave the Action Condition text box blank. If you want to enable the action only under certain conditions, you can enter an MDX expression that returns a Boolean value. Because you always want the My City Map action to be enabled, you don't need an Action Condition expression here.

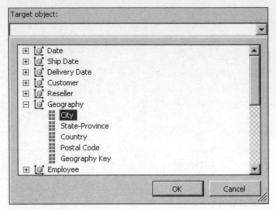

Figure 9-36

5. In the Action Content section of the editor, keep the default action type, URL. In the Action Expression text box, type the following MDX expression:

```
// URL for linking to MSN Maps
"http://maps.msn.com/home.aspx?plce1=" +

// Retreive the name of the current city
[Geography].[City].CurrentMember.Name + "," +

// Append state-province name
[Geography].[State-Province].CurrentMember.Name + "," +

// Append country name
[Geography].[Country].CurrentMember.Name +

// Append region parameter
"&regn1=" +

// Determine correct region parameter value
Case
    When [Geography].[Country].CurrentMember Is
        [Geography].[Country].&[Australia]
    Then "3"
    When [Geography].[Country].CurrentMember Is
        [Geography].[Country].&[Canada]
        Or
        [Geography].[Country].CurrentMember Is
        [Geography].[Country].&[United States]
    Then "0"
    Else "1"
End
```

This MDX expression returns a string URL used by the client application to open MSN Map for the user-selected City. The user's selection is passed into the MDX expression as:

```
[Geography].[City].CurrentMember
```

If the user selects a different city and launches the action, the MDX expression is re-evaluated and returns a different URL.

6. Scroll down to the section Additional Properties, and expand the section to review the available properties. There are three options for the property Invocation shown in the table below along with their meaning. Since you want the action to be triggered by the user, leave the default Invocation value Interactive. You can also leave the application and description fields blank, because they are informational properties.

The following table describes the possible values for the Invocation property:

Method	Description
Interactive	The action is triggered by user interaction.
Batch	The action runs as a batch operation.
On Open	The action runs when a user opens the cube.

7. In the Caption text box, type the following MDX expression:

```
[Geography].[City].CurrentMember.Member_Caption + " City Map ..."
```

The specified caption is displayed to end users to indicate an action is available. The user clicks the caption to initiate the action. The "Caption Is MDX" property controls how the server evaluates the contents of the caption. If you leave this property value as false, the server treats the caption as a static string.

8. Change the Caption Is MDX value to True. The server evaluates the MDX expression in the Caption text box to construct the caption, which in this case will result in different city names included in the caption as different cities are selected in the browser.

Now that you've created a My City Map action, deploy the project to save the action to the server. Just as with KPI definition, an action definition is metadata stored on the server with the cube. Adding or changing the action won't impact the cube data and doesn't require a reprocess. When the project deploys, you can verify the newly created action right away.

Browse URL Action in the Cube Browser

Many standard OLAP client applications such as pivot tables in Office Web Components and the BIDS Cube Browser support actions out of the box. In this section, you learn to invoke the action My City Map from Cube Browser.

1. In the cube designer, click the Browser tab to open the cube browser for the Adventure Works cube.

2. In the metadata pane on the left, open the Geography dimension. Then, open the Geography hierarchy and drag the City level from metadata window to Rows in the data window on the right side, as shown in Figure 9-37.

3. Right-click on any city in the data window. Notice actions listed on the pop-up menu. Corresponding city camp action captioned as <CityName> City Map... is one of the actions listed. Figure 9-38 show the action for the city Newcastle.

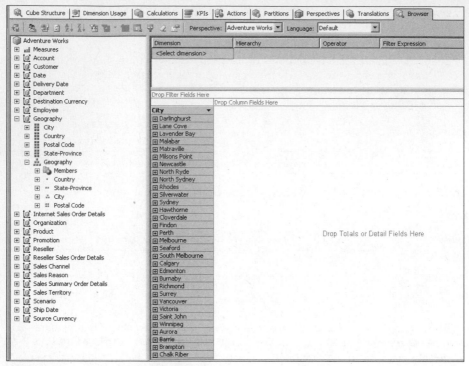

Figure 9-37

Figure 9-38

4. Click Newcastle City Map.... BIDS will invoke a Web browser and construct a URL from the predefined MDX expression. The result of the action is shown in Figure 9-39.

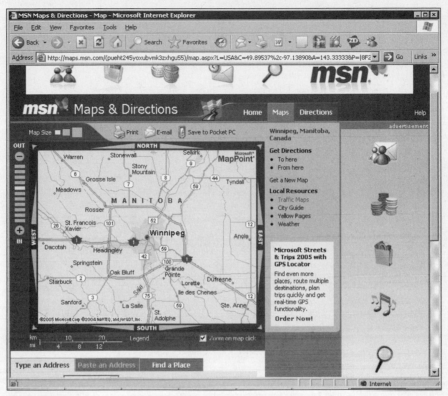

Figure 9-39

Report Actions

Report actions are similar to URL actions, except a Report action has additional properties to build the report server access to a URL for you. These properties are described in the following table:

Property	Description
ReportServer	The name of Report server
Path	The path exposed by report server
ReportParameters	Extra parameters for report
ReportFormatParameters	Extra parameters for report format

When a Report action is invoked, Analysis Services generates a URL string similar to the string here:

```
http://ReportServer/Path&ReportParameter1Name= ReportParameter1Value&
ReportParameter2Name= ReportParameter2Value.......&
ReportFormatParameter1Name=ReportFormatParameter1Value&
ReportFormatParameter2Name=ReportFormatParameter2Value ...
```

To review a Report action, follow these steps:

1. With the Adventure Works DW sample project still open in BIDS, click the Actions tab of the Cube Designer and then click Sales Reason Comparisons Report in the Action Organizer. Let's take a look at the properties of this report action (see Figure 9-40). The optional parameter values are MDX expressions that provide the action with the context of the user selection.

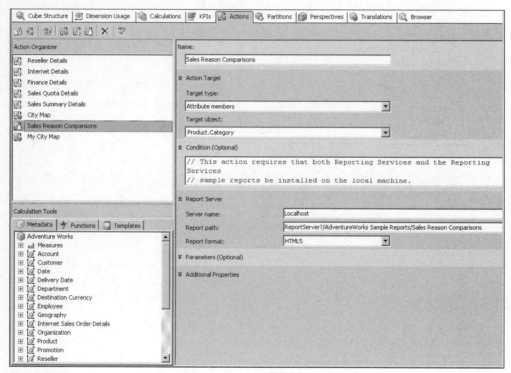

Figure 9-40

2. As with a URL action, you can invoke a Report action from the Cube Browser. Click the Clear Results button in the toolbar to start a new query. Sales Reasons Comparisons action's target is members of the Product.Category hierarchy. Drag, and drop Product.Category hierarchy from metadata pane to OWC's rows or columns. Right-click on the member Bikes to see the action's caption on the pop-up menu as shown in Figure 9-41.

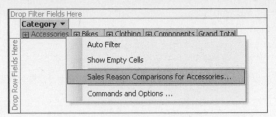

Figure 9-41

3. Click Sales Reason Comparions for Bikes. A browser window will open. If Reporting Services 2005 is installed, you will see a message, The item '/AdventureWorks Sample Reports/Sales Reason Comparisons' cannot be found; in other words, rsItemNotFound. This is because the report is fictitious. Were it a valid report, the report would display the sales reasons for the Bike category.

Drill-Through Action

OLAP is all about aggregating data and serving aggregating data to end users quickly. Users want to analyze data hierarchically by drilling up and drilling down which requires aggregated data from millions of daily transaction rows. Sometimes it is very useful for users to be able to retrieve the transaction rows that have been aggregated into a particular cell. Access to such details often helps business users understand any abnormal business activities (such as extremely large or small numbers) and investigate root causes. Drill-through provides this access to details by enabling users to fetch the fact table rows that contribute to an aggregation value of a cube cell.

Drill-through in Analysis Services 2000 is a special MDX command which is also supported in Analysis Services 2005. However in Analysis Services 2005 you can also create a special action type called Drillthrough. A Drillthrough action's target is always one or more cube cells associated with a specific measure group. In other words, cells with measures in the target measure group will display the available drill-through actions on the pop-up menu. Drillthrough actions return the related fact table rows in a tabular rowset. As the action developer, you specify which columns the action returns. The columns in the return rowset when a drill through action is executed are not limited to the actual fact table columns. Any dimension attributes linked to the selected measure group target can be included. Many-to-many dimensions and referenced dimensions are also supported, so attributes from these special dimensions are available for drill-through return columns as well.

In Analysis Services 2000, you explicitly had to set the Enable drillthrough flag in the Drillthrough options dialog for each cube. This flag to allow drill through is deprecated in Analysis Services 2005. Cube designers in Analysis Services 2005 can allow or deny drill through by defining a security role on each cube. Only an Analysis Services 2005 administrator can perform drill through against any cube without explicit permissions. If a user does not have drill through rights on a specific cube, then the drill-through will not execute and an error message displays

In addition, the cubes and partitions properties DrillthroughFilter, DrillthroughFrom, and DrillthroughJoin in Analysis Services 2000 are no longer valid in Analysis Services 2005. The same functionality can now be achieved using Data Source View.

Follow the steps below to understand an existing drillthrough action in the Adventure Works DW sample database and enhance it.

1. With the Adventure Works DW sample project still open in BIDS, click the Actions tab.

2. Click Finance Details in the Action Organizer, as shown in Figure 9-42.

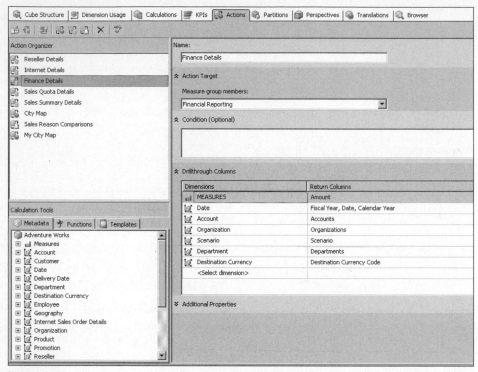

Figure 9-42

You can see the action target is the Financial Reporting measure group. The Drillthrough columns to be returned by the action are Amount, Fiscal Year, Date, and Calendar Year from the Date dimension, Accounts from the Account dimension, and so on.

3. Suppose the business user also wants Account Type and Account Number to be included as additional Drillthrough columns. Click the Accounts dimension attribute in the column labeled Return Columns to open the drop-down box. All available attributes for the Account dimension are listed here. Choose Account Type and Account Number as shown in Figure 9-43. Click OK.

4. In the Additional Properties section, the Maximum Rows setting is very useful for the designer to limit the maximum number of rows that can be returned for a drill-through action. This is important because a cell, especially a top-level cell, could be aggregated from millions of fact table rows. Setting the maximum rows value is always a good practice to protect your server from accidental or malicious operations, which will consume huge server resources. If the property is not set, the default max drill-through row count from server property Olap\Query\DefaultDrill-throughMaxRows is used. The default value of the setting is 10000. In the Maximum Rows text box, type in 5000 as shown in Figure 9-44. Deploy the project to save the action to the server.

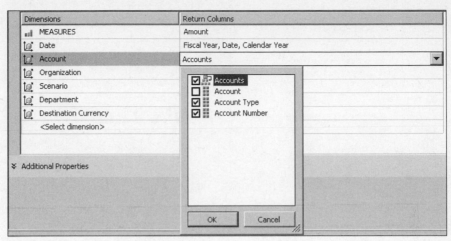

Figure 9-43

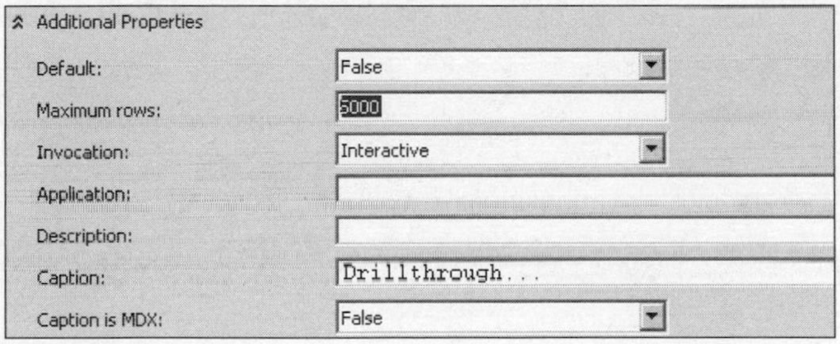

Figure 9-44

You can now view the drill-through results in the cube browser.

5. Click the Browser tab to open the Cube Browser. Since the action for Finance details is on the measure group Financial Reporting, you need to drag and drop Measures.Amount in the Financial Reporting folder to the OWC's Detail Fields ara. Right-click on the cell and you will see Drillthrough... as a menu item on the pop-up menu, as shown in Figure 9-45, indicating you can invoke the Drillthrough action for the cell. Before you actually invoke the action, you should limit your drill-through to a much narrower data region to prevent the action from returning all fact tables rows if no maximum row count limit is specified.

6. Drag and drop the Account dimensions on rows, drag and drop the Date.Fiscal hierarchy (in the Fiscal folder) on columns. Then set the slicers at the top of the cube browser for customers in the city Redmond (in USA and Washington) and the Research and Development department, as shown in Figure 9-46.

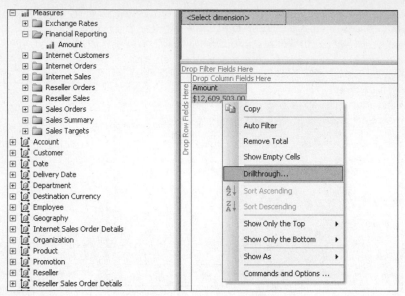

Figure 9-45

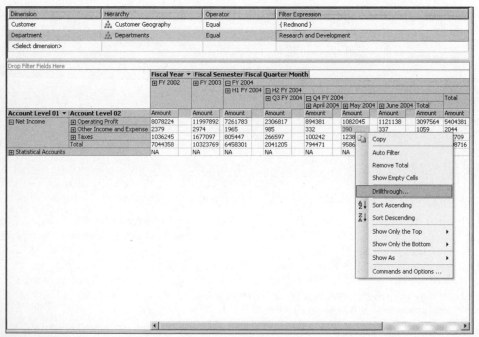

Figure 9-46

7. Suppose you are interested in Other Income and Expense from May 2004. Expand Net Income on rows, and on columns expand FY 2004, H2 FY 2004, and Q4 CY2004. Right-click on the cell intersection of May 2004 and Other Income and Expense, and then choose Drillthrough, as shown in Figure 9-46. A new window opens to display the fact table rows that aggregate to the cell value, as shown in Figure 9-47. Note that the newly added account type and account number is returned.

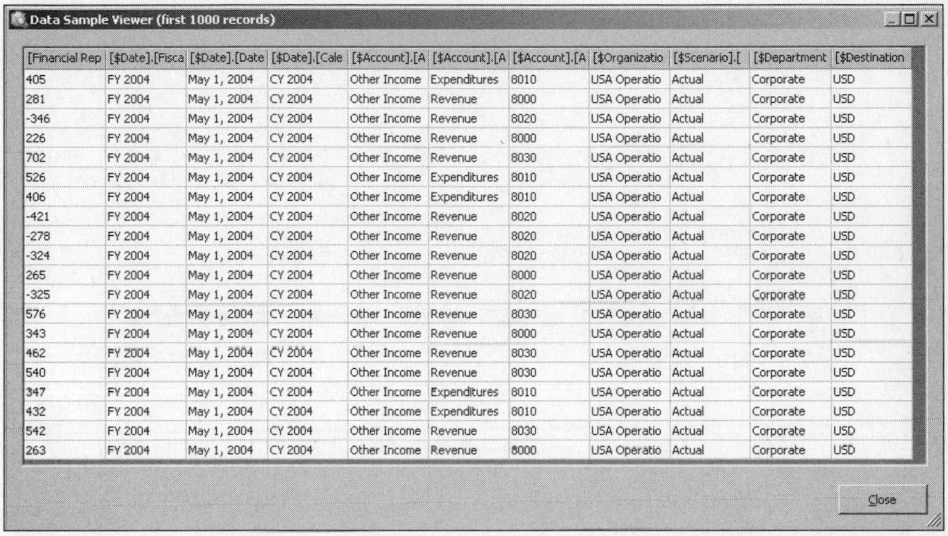

[Financial Rep	[$Date].[Fisca	[$Date].[Date	[$Date].[Cale	[$Account].[A	[$Account].[A	[$Account].[A	[$Organizatio	[$Scenario].[	[$Department	[$Destination
405	FY 2004	May 1, 2004	CY 2004	Other Income	Expenditures	8010	USA Operatio	Actual	Corporate	USD
281	FY 2004	May 1, 2004	CY 2004	Other Income	Revenue	8000	USA Operatio	Actual	Corporate	USD
-346	FY 2004	May 1, 2004	CY 2004	Other Income	Revenue	8020	USA Operatio	Actual	Corporate	USD
226	FY 2004	May 1, 2004	CY 2004	Other Income	Revenue	8000	USA Operatio	Actual	Corporate	USD
702	FY 2004	May 1, 2004	CY 2004	Other Income	Revenue	8030	USA Operatio	Actual	Corporate	USD
526	FY 2004	May 1, 2004	CY 2004	Other Income	Expenditures	8010	USA Operatio	Actual	Corporate	USD
406	FY 2004	May 1, 2004	CY 2004	Other Income	Expenditures	8010	USA Operatio	Actual	Corporate	USD
-421	FY 2004	May 1, 2004	CY 2004	Other Income	Revenue	8020	USA Operatio	Actual	Corporate	USD
-278	FY 2004	May 1, 2004	CY 2004	Other Income	Revenue	8020	USA Operatio	Actual	Corporate	USD
-324	FY 2004	May 1, 2004	CY 2004	Other Income	Revenue	8020	USA Operatio	Actual	Corporate	USD
265	FY 2004	May 1, 2004	CY 2004	Other Income	Revenue	8000	USA Operatio	Actual	Corporate	USD
-325	FY 2004	May 1, 2004	CY 2004	Other Income	Revenue	8020	USA Operatio	Actual	Corporate	USD
576	FY 2004	May 1, 2004	CY 2004	Other Income	Revenue	8030	USA Operatio	Actual	Corporate	USD
343	FY 2004	May 1, 2004	CY 2004	Other Income	Revenue	8000	USA Operatio	Actual	Corporate	USD
462	FY 2004	May 1, 2004	CY 2004	Other Income	Revenue	8030	USA Operatio	Actual	Corporate	USD
540	FY 2004	May 1, 2004	CY 2004	Other Income	Revenue	8030	USA Operatio	Actual	Corporate	USD
347	FY 2004	May 1, 2004	CY 2004	Other Income	Expenditures	8010	USA Operatio	Actual	Corporate	USD
432	FY 2004	May 1, 2004	CY 2004	Other Income	Expenditures	8010	USA Operatio	Actual	Corporate	USD
542	FY 2004	May 1, 2004	CY 2004	Other Income	Revenue	8030	USA Operatio	Actual	Corporate	USD
263	FY 2004	May 1, 2004	CY 2004	Other Income	Revenue	8000	USA Operatio	Actual	Corporate	USD

Figure 9-47

Under the hood, client applications, including the Cube Browser, use a schema rowset to get the proper drill-through query for a specific action. Then the client application sends the drill-through query to the server, which returns a rowset with the detailed fact table rows. Following is the query sent by the Cube Browser to get the previous drill-through results. You can find the maximum rows setting and the return column settings in various sections of the query. The SELECT clause of the query is the specific cell that was selected when activating drill-through.

```
DRILLTHROUGH MAXROWS 10000 Select
([Date].[Fiscal].[Month].&[2004]&[5],[Measures].[Amount],[Account].[Accounts].&[88]
)  on 0
 From [Adventure Works]
 RETURN [Financial Reporting].[Amount],
       [$Date].[Fiscal Year],
       [$Date].[Date],
       [$Date].[Calendar Year],
       [$Account].[Accounts],
       [$Account].[Account Type],
       [$Account].[Account Number],
       [$Organization].[Organizations],
       [$Scenario].[Scenario],
       [$Department].[Departments],
       [$Destination Currency].[Destination Currency]
```

Adding Intelligence to the Cube

Similar to adding intelligence to Dimensions that you learned in Chapter 8 you can add intelligence to the Cube. Figure 9-48 shows the various enhancements that can be done to a Cube using the Business Intelligence Wizard. You have learned most of these enhancements in earlier chapters. In this chapter you will learn the enhancements to define and understand semi-additive behavior as well as defining currency conversion whenever fact data needs to be converted to appropriate local currency.

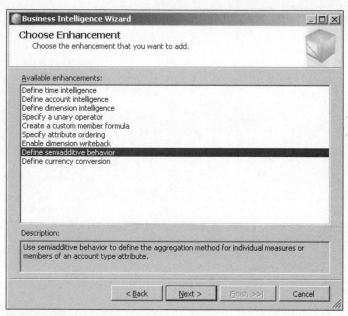

Figure 9-48

Semi-Additive Measures

Semi-additive measures are measures whose data is not aggregated as sum or count to over the various levels on a hierarchy. The semi-additive aggregate functions for measures are ByAccount, AverageOfChildren, FirstChild, LastChild, FirstNonEmpty, LastNonEmpty and None. For example, assume you have a Time hierarchy and the measure Sales value to be rolled up average of the sales of it's children. Assume the levels in the Time hierarchy are Year, Half Year, Quarters, Months and Date. If you have a member Quarter 1 of the year 2004 whose children are months July, August and September then the value for Quarter 1 will be average of of the sales values for the three months.

Using the Business Intelligence Wizard you can change the behavior of the Aggregation Function of various measures in the cube. Launch the Business Intelligence Wizard, select "Define semi-additive behavior in the Choose Enhancement page and click Next. In the Define Semi-additive Behavior page (shown in Figure 9-49) you have three options. The default option is the detection of a dimension of type account which contains semi-additive members. You learned in Chapter 8 to define semi-additive behavior for various Account types. If this selection is made then the Business Intelligence Wizard sets the aggregate function to ByAccount for all the measures of the measure group that has relationship defined with the dimension of type account. In the sample Adventure Works DW database there is only one measure Amount that has the ByAccount aggregation function. The first option turns off all the semi-additive behavior for all the measures that have the AggregateFunction property set to a semi-additive behavior. When this option is selected any measure that has a semi-additive aggregation function will be set to the Sum aggregation function. The last option "Define semiaddtive behavior for individual measures" allows you to change the Aggregation Function for each measure. Once you make the selections in this Define Semiaddtive Behavior page press Next. The final page of the Business Intelligence Wizard shows the new Aggregate Function for the measures that will be affected. You can review the changes to be applied to the measures and click Finish. BIDS then changes the AggregateFunction property for the measures.

Figure 9-49

You can verify the AggregateFunction property of the measures that are expected to be changed by the selections in the semi-additive behavior enhancement through the Business Intelligence Wizard. You learned the semi-additive behavior of the ByAccount AggregateFunction in Chapter 8. In order to see the results of LastNonEmpty and AverageOfChildrence semi-additive aggregate functions deploy the sample Adventure Works DW database and browse the measures in the Exchange Rate in the Cube Browser along with the Date.Fiscal hierarchy and DestinationCurrency.DestinationCurrency hierarchy as shown in Figure 9-50. You can see the value for the members in the Date.Fiscal hierarchy are calculated based on the aggregate functions LastNonEmpty (for End of Day Rate measure) and AverageOfChildren(for AverageRate measure) applied to their children.

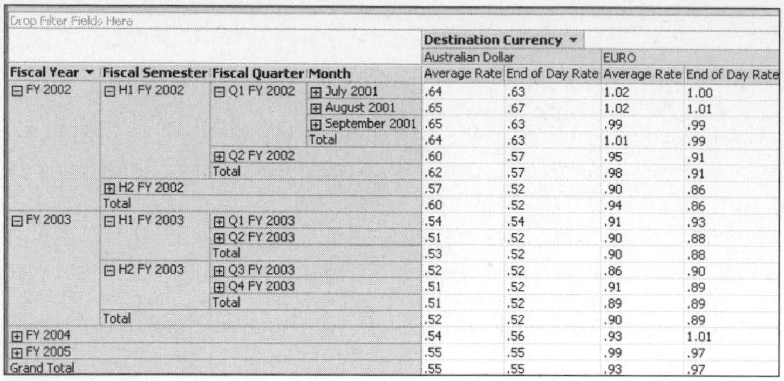

Fiscal Year	Fiscal Semester	Fiscal Quarter	Month	Australian Dollar		EURO	
				Average Rate	End of Day Rate	Average Rate	End of Day Rate
FY 2002	H1 FY 2002	Q1 FY 2002	July 2001	.64	.63	1.02	1.00
			August 2001	.65	.67	1.02	1.01
			September 2001	.65	.63	.99	.99
			Total	.64	.63	1.01	.99
		Q2 FY 2002		.60	.57	.95	.91
		Total		.62	.57	.98	.91
	H2 FY 2002			.57	.52	.90	.86
	Total			.60	.52	.94	.86
FY 2003	H1 FY 2003	Q1 FY 2003		.54	.54	.91	.93
		Q2 FY 2003		.51	.52	.90	.88
		Total		.53	.52	.90	.88
	H2 FY 2003	Q3 FY 2003		.52	.52	.86	.90
		Q4 FY 2003		.51	.52	.91	.89
		Total		.51	.52	.89	.89
	Total			.52	.52	.90	.89
FY 2004				.54	.56	.93	1.01
FY 2005				.55	.55	.99	.97
Grand Total				.55	.55	.93	.97

Drop Filter Fields Here

Destination Currency ▾

Figure 9-50

Currency Conversion

If your organization does business in more than one country, then you might need to deal with converting currencies between countries. Analysts and managers may want to analyze transactions in the currency used for the transaction (also known as the local currency), while corporate management may want to convert all transactions to a single currency to get a complete view of all transactions globally. This scenario can be thought of as a many-to-one currency conversion. Or you might load data in the data warehouse in one currency, but need to report financial results in different currencies. This scenario describes a one-to-many currency conversion. Yet another possibility is a combination of these two scenarios in which transactions data is in the local currency and needs to be reported in more than one different currency — a many-to-many currency conversion. Fortunately, Analysis Services 2005 provides a wizard to make it easy for you to add currency conversions to a cube for any of the three scenarios described above.

Before you can use the wizard, however, you need to build a currency dimension and an exchange rate measure group in your cube. These database objects are already in the Adventure Works cube that you've been using throughout this chapter, which gives you an opportunity to take a look at the proper structure before you have to build your own.

To review database objects used for currency conversion, follow these steps:

1. Using BIDS, open the Adventure Works cube in the Enterprise version of the Adventure Works DW sample project (located at C:\Program Files\Microsoft SQL Server\90\Tools\Samples\ AdventureWorks Analysis Services Project\Enterprise). Double-click the Adventure Works cube in Solution Explorer to open the cube designer.

2. Click the Exchange Rates measure group in the Measures page, then take a look at the Type property for the measure group, shown in Figure 9-51. You must set the Type property value to Exchange Rates so that Analysis Services can correctly specify this measure group in the currency conversion calculations added to the MDX script when you use the wizard. The Exchange Rates measure group is based on a fact table that contains daily average and end of day exchange rates by day and by currency.

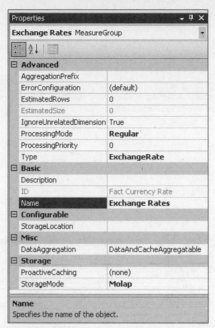

Figure 9-51

3. Open the Exchange Rates measure group; click on the Average Rate measure, and look at its AggregateFunction property. As you learned earlier in this chapter, Average Rate is a semi-additive measure that cannot be summed to get value for the month, quarter, or year level. Instead the aggregate function AverageOfChildren is used.

4. Now double-click the Source Currency dimension in Solution Explorer. In the Properties window, you can see the Type property for this dimension is set to Currency. Click the Source Currency attribute in the Attributes pane. You can see its Type property is CurrencySource. Lastly, click the Source Currency Code attribute and verify its Type property is CurrencyIsoCode. You can make sure you get the property settings right by selecting Currency as the Dimension Type when using the Dimension Wizard to create the dimension. The wizard will prompt you for the column in your table containing the currency's ISO code and for the key attribute. Alternately you can change the properties after the dimension is created.

5. Now you're ready to start the Business Intelligence Wizard. The wizard will create a second currency dimension, one used for reporting the converted currencies, for you as well as updating the MDX script with calculations that ensure the currency conversion is correctly applied to affected measures. Right-click the Adventure Works cube in Solution Explorer, click Add Business Intelligence, click Next, click Define Currency Conversion, and then click Next.

6. In the Set Currency Conversions Options dialog the wizard looks for measure groups of type ExchangeRate and pre-selects that measure group. If such a measure group does not exist then it selects the first measure group. Click Exchange Rates in the "Select the measure group that contains exchange rates" list. In the "Specify the pivot currency" list box, click USD, and then click OK. Lastly, click the N USD Per 1 ARS radio button, as shown in Figure 9-52. The FactCurrencyRate table, on which the Exchange Rate measure group is based, has rates to convert one unit of local currency (such as one Australian dollar) into a standard currency

(US dollars in this case), which is called a pivot currency. If the table contained rates to convert 1 unit of the pivot currency into the local currency, you would select the N ARS Per 1 USD radio button. The drop down list contains a pre-defined list of currencies to help you make the right selection. Click Next to continue.

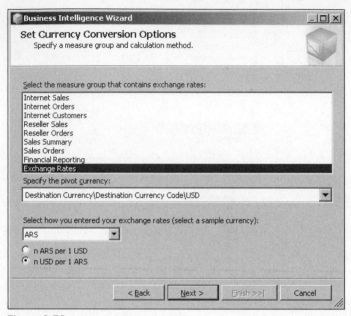

Figure 9-52

7. In the Select Members page select the check boxes next to Internet Sales Amount and Reseller Sales Amount, as shown in Figure 9-53. This page of the wizard identifies the members that will be converted. Another approach to currency conversion involves converting specific members in an attribute hierarchy of an Account dimension, such as certain expense accounts, or certain account types, such as all revenue accounts. You can select the measure from the measure group selected in the previous page of the dialog which is to be used for currency conversion. The Average Rate measure is selected by default. These options are useful when your cube is dedicated to financial data for balance sheets and profit and loss statements.

8. Click Next to view the next page of the wizard, as shown in Figure 9-54. Here you describe your conversion scenario for the wizard. Your selection here determines what information you must supply on subsequent pages of the wizard. The selections are self explanatory. Select the Many-to-many selection and click Next.

9. In the Define Local Currency Reference page (Figure 9-55), you define the location of the column that contains the currency key. After you specify whether it's in a fact table (which it is in the Adventure Works DW sample data) or in a dimension table, you select the attribute with which a currency is associated. If a currency attribute is in the fact table, it is likely to be a dimension key that is related to a dimension table. Otherwise, the attribute is a column in a dimension table that typically corresponds to geography, such as business divisions that are located in separate countries.

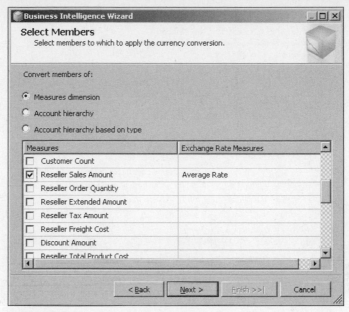

Figure 9-53

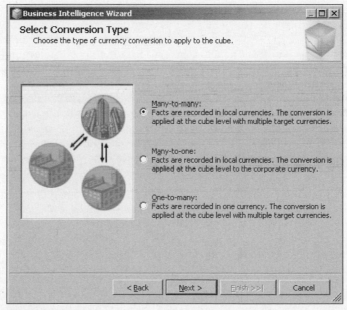

Figure 9-54

In this example, the Destination Currency is automatically selected because the currency conversion definition is already in the Adventure Works cube. If you were to start completely from scratch, you would choose the Source Currency dimension's key attribute on this page.

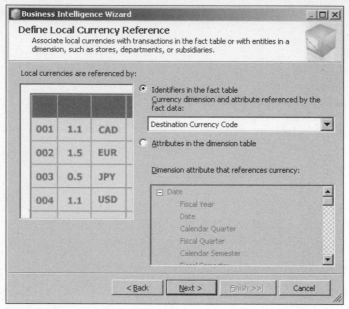

Figure 9-55

10. Click Next again, and then click the box to the left of Reporting Currencies to select all of the available items as shown in Figure 9-56. On this page, you identify the currencies to include in the reporting currency (called Destination Currency in the Adventure Works cube). The Business Intelligence Wizard builds a new dimension according to your selections here. If you forget to select a currency that exists in the exchange rate fact table, cube processing will fail—be careful!

11. Click Next, and then click Cancel on the final page of the wizard. Because the Destination Currency and currency conversion calculations are already in the cube, the wizard doesn't need to do anything. But if you are adding this capability to your own cube, there's still more to explore to better understand what the wizard would do if you started the process with only a Source Currency dimension and an Exchange Rates fact table.

12. Double-click the Adventure Works data source view in Solution Explorer. In the Tables pane, right-click DimDestinationCurrency, and then click Edit Named Query. A query similar to the following query would be created by the Business Intelligence Wizard when creating a reporting currency. The WHERE clause of this query would detail currencies selected on the Specify Reporting Currencies page of the wizard (see Figure 9-56) if you picked some, but not all, available currencies. Notice that the main foundation for the named query is the DimCurrency table which is also used for the Source Currency dimension in the Adventure Works DW database.

```
SELECT     CurrencyKey, CurrencyAlternateKey, CurrencyName
FROM       DimCurrency
WHERE     (CurrencyKey IN
                    (SELECT DISTINCT CurrencyKey
                     FROM           FactCurrencyRate))
```

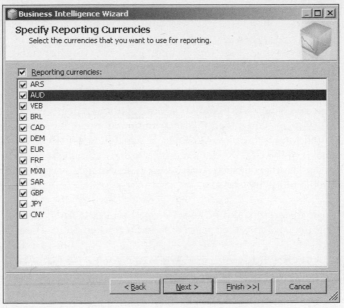

Figure 9-56

13. Switch to the Cube Designer, click the Dimension Usage tab, and locate the relationships between the Exchange Rate measure group and other dimensions. Only the Date and Destination Currency dimensions have a regular relationship with Exchange Rate. Recall that you learned about many-to-many relationships earlier in this chapter. In the current example, Internet Sales has sales amounts in many local currencies which need to be converted — by way of Exchange Rates — to multiple destination currencies. Accordingly, Internet Sales has a regular relationship with Source Currency (representing the local currency) and a many-to-many relationship with Destination Currency with Exchange Rate as the intermediate measure group.

A simple Analysis Services project based on the AdventureWorksDW relational database, along with instructions to use the currency conversion wizard and verify the results, are available at the download site for this book.

Working with Partitions

When building business intelligence solutions at the enterprise level it is common to work with terabytes of source (also known as fact or detail) data. You can bet a company like Wal-Mart has many terabytes of detailed data feeding into its business intelligence solutions. Even if you are working with just a few hundred gigabytes, you will find the use of partitions to be critical to your success.

By adding partitions to your overall cube design strategy, you can manage how and where cube data is physically stored, how a cube is processed as well as the time required for processing, and how efficiently Analysis Services 2005 can retrieve data in response to user queries. One key benefit of partitioning is the distribution of data over and across one or more hard disk drives. And in the case of remote partitions, the data can be spread over various machines. Partitions can even be processed in parallel on the remote machines. In this section, you first learn how to set up a local partition. Then, in the section that follows, you learn how to set up a remote partition configuration — which, by the way, is not the simplest procedure.

In order to work with partitions, you first need administrator privileges on both the local and remote instances of Analysis Services you intend to use. Administrator privileges are granted to member groups or users assigned to the Analysis Services 2005 server role. Being a member of the server role is analogous to being a member of the OLAP Administrator's group in Analysis Services 2000. To join the Server role first open SSMS and connect to each Analysis Services instance you plan to use. For each instance, you need to perform the following steps:

1. Right-click the instance name and select Properties. In the Analysis Services Properties dialog, shown in Figure 9-57, click the Security tab in the top-left pane. Then, click the Add button.

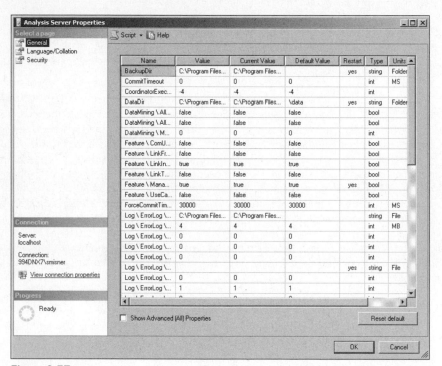

Figure 9-57

2. Next you need to enter your fully articulated user name in the Enter the Object Names to Select box. In Figure 9-58, you can see how redmond\stephenq was entered. To validate your entry, just click the Check Names button. Finally, click OK to close all dialogs. You now have server-wide administrator rights. Be sure to repeat these steps on the local and the remote servers.

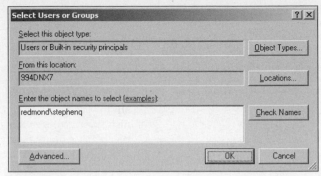

Figure 9-58

Building a Local Partition

An important thing to know about partitions is that one partition per measure group in a cube is created behind the scenes to accommodate the storage of data and metadata of your cube — so without any action on your part, beyond the creation of the measure groups, you already have partitions on your computer. When you explicitly create a local partition, you add it to the existing partition for a measure group. So, why should you take extra steps to add partitions? Well, by using partitions, you can spread data across multiple hard disk drives on a single computer. Because very large partitions slow down cube-related activities, dividing one large partition into multiple smaller partitions can improve processing and query times.

In the following exercise, your goal is to replace the single Internet Sales partition for 2004 into two partitions of equal size. This will require you to change the parameters on the existing partition to make room for the new partition; otherwise, Internet sales for 2004 would be double-counted because both partitions would contain the same data. Double-counting, by the way, is something you must be very alert for because it will result in incorrect results.

To create a local partition, follow these steps:

1. Using BIDS, open the Adventure Works DW sample project located at C:\Program Files\ Microsoft SQL Server\90\Tools\Samples\AdventureWorks Analysis Services Project\ Enterprise. Double-click the Adventure Works cube name in Solution Explorer to open the cube designer.

2. Click the Partitions tab. Your screen should look similar to Figure 9-59.

3. If necessary, expand the Internet Sales section by clicking the arrows to the left of Internet Sales. Click the Source box for Internet_Sales_2004, and then click the button with two dots appearing in the box to open the Partition Source dialog.

4. Because you need to use a very similar filter query when you create the second Internet Sales 2004 partition, highlight the query and copy it to the clipboard or Notepad. You will modify the query to change the partition such that it contains only data with OrderDateKeys between 915 and 1098 (inclusive) as shown in Figure 9-60, and click OK.

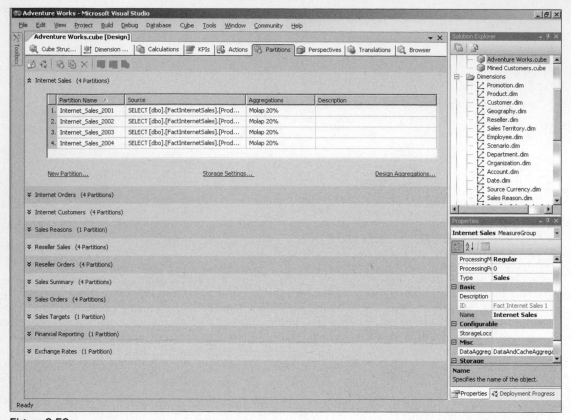

Figure 9-59

5. Next, click the Partition Name "Internet_Sales_2004" and change it to "Internet_Sales_2004a."

6. Click the New Partition link to launch the Partition Wizard.

7. In the Partition Wizard, under Available Tables select the check box next to dbo.FactInternetSales and then click Next. You should see the wizard page as shown in Figure 9-61.

8. Click the Specify a Query to Restrict Rows check box. Delete the default query that shows up in the query window and paste in the query you previously saved. Edit the WHERE clause to limit partition data to rows with OrderDateKey >= '1099' AND OrderDateKey <= '1280'.

9. Click Finish (you're storing your partition to the default location). In the Name box, type Internet_Sales_2004b, click the Design Aggregations Later radio button, and then click Finish.

Naturally, you would want to design aggregations for your new partition, and deploy and process it. In this case, you have learned how to use the partition wizard for creating a new partition without duplicating data in the process. Again, data duplication must be guarded against because it leads directly to wrong results. The next section takes on the formidable and powerful remote partition.

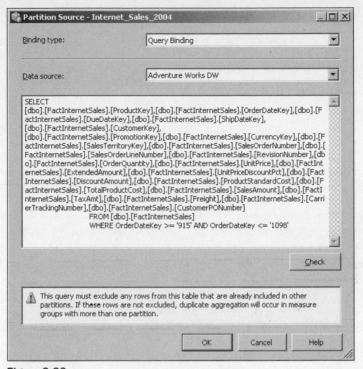

Figure 9-60

Figure 9-61

Building a Remote Partition

The basic architecture of the remote partition keeps data definitions (metadata) in the cube on the master (or parent) machine and off-loads the measure or detail data to the remote partitions on subordinate machines. In terms of administration tasks related to remote partitions, the host machine containing the cube metadata acts as the point of control for all related remote partitions.

To implement a remote partition in the most meaningful way, you need two computers. Earlier in this chapter, you followed steps to make sure the permissions were set to work with the local and remote computers with appropriate credentials. In addition, you must have the firewall settings on the master computer (the host box) and subordinate box configured to accept outside connections for Analysis Services. The computer storing the remote partition on it is called the Subordinate (Target) computer. In the tutorial that follows, we are using two instances on one machine (localhost and localhost\I2) to demonstrate remote partitions; in this case, firewall settings are not necessary. If you are going for a two machine configuration, of course, you will need to set the firewalls appropriately. Before working with the subordinate computer, you set the stage for successful inter-server interactions by starting your work on the Master computer.

1. In BIDS, open the Adventure Works DW sample project located at C:\Program Files\Microsoft SQL Server\90\Tools\Samples\AdventureWorks Analysis Services Project\Enterprise.

2. Right-click the project name, Adventure Works DW, in Solution Explorer and click Properties to access the Property Pages, as shown in Figure 9-62. Select the third item down below Configuration Properties in the pane on the left (Deployment). Make your settings consistent with those shown in the figure; be sure the correct name is listed for the Master Server which, if you're not using a named instance, should be localhost. Click OK.

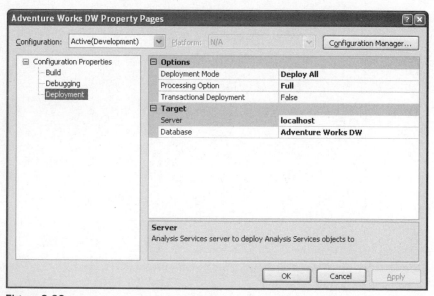

Figure 9-62

3. In Solution Explorer, right-click the Adventure Works DW database icon and select Deploy to deploy and process the project.

4. Now it's time to work on the target, or subordinate, machine (or instance). Open BIDS, and then create a new Analysis Services project called Target.

5. Right-click the Data Sources folder in Solution Explorer and select New Data Source. In the Data Source Wizard dialog, click the New button to open the Connection Manager dialog.

6. First, change the Provider to Native OLE DB\Microsoft OLE DB Provider for Analysis Services 9.0. In the Connection Manager dialog, there is a Server Or File Name text box, into which you type the name of your master Analysis Services instance. If you are using an unnamed instance (the default instance) on the Master machine, type the machine name (or "localhost"). Set the authentication properties in Log on to the Server consistent with your own configuration. Finally, click the down arrow for Initial Catalog and select Adventure Works DW (the dialog should look like Figure 9-63) and click OK.

Figure 9-63

7. In the Data Source Wizard, click Next. Set the Impersonation Information at this time to verify correct security settings. If you are unsure what to use, try Default. Click Next.

8. You need to provide a new name on this page; we suggest "ASDB_AdvWorksDW" and then click Finish to dismiss the dialog.

9. Just to be clear, you're still on the subordinate machine or instance. Right-click the project name in Solution Explorer and choose Edit Database. Now, change the MasterDataSourceID from empty to "ASDB_AdvWorksDW" as shown in Figure 9-64.

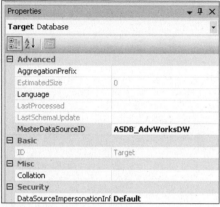

Figure 9-64

10. Right-click the database name in Solution Explorer and choose Properties. Click Configuration Properties and then click Deployment. Finally, click Server and set the name to the subordinate instance of Analysis Services as shown in Figure 9-65. Click OK to close the dialog.

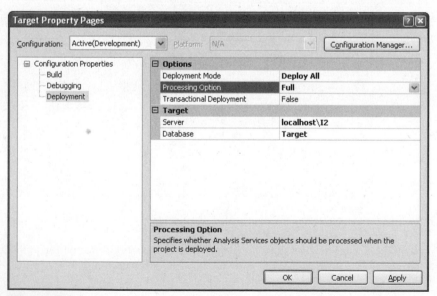

Figure 9-65

11. Deploy the project to move the metadata to the Analysis Services instance (localhost\I2).

12. For both localhost and localhost\I2 do the following in SSMS:

   a. Connect to the service.

   b. Right-click the instance name, and select Properties.

   c. Change the Value (first column) of both Feature\LinkToOtherInstanceEnabled and Feature\LinkFromOtherInstanceEnabled to True.

   d. Click OK to close the Analysis Servier Properties dialog. To make these changes stick, you need to restart the instance of Analysis Services; just right-click the instance name in Object Explorer and click Restart and click Yes when asked for verification.

13. In BIDS, create a second data source in the Adventure Works DW project to connect to the subordinate (target) instance of Analysis Services, and specifically at the target project (named Target here). Use the Native OLE DB\ Microsoft OLE DB Provider for Analysis Services 9.0 (see Figure 9-66).

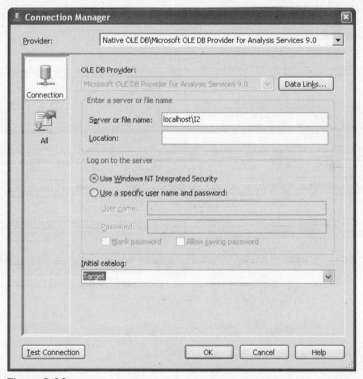

Figure 9-66

14. Click OK to close the Connection Manager dialog. Select the created data source for the Target database; then click Next. On the Impersonation Information page, select Default and click Next. Accept the default name provided by the Data Source Wizard and click Finish.

15. It is nearly time to create the remote partition; but first you need to make room for one by deleting an existing partition. Let's sacrifice one of the Fact Internet Sales partitions by opening the

Adventure Works cube and clicking the Partitions tab; then click the double down arrows next to Fact Internet Sales to open the section for the Internet Sales measure group. To delete the Internet_Sales_2001 partition, right-click on the partition and click delete as shown in Figure 9-67.

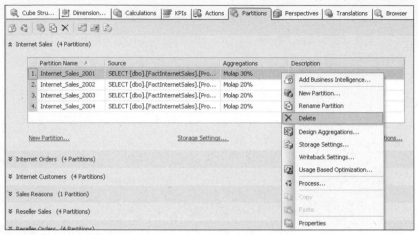

Figure 9-67

16. To build the remote partition, click the New Partition link. On the first page, click the checkbox next to dbo.FactInternetSales under Available Tables, and then click Next.

17. On the Restrict Rows page of the wizard; enable "Specify a query to restrict rows."

The partition wizard creates a relational select query up to the WHERE clause. At the end of the WHERE clause, type in "OrderDateKey<=184" as shown in Figure 9-68 and click Next.

18. In the Processing and Storage Locations page, select the option "Remote Analysis Services Data Source," select the data source Target as shown in Figure 9-69 and click Next.

19. Select the "Design aggregations later" radio button, name the partition "Internet_Sales_2001" as shown in Figure 9-70 and click Finish.

20. Open the Internet Sales Order Details dimension and change the storage mode from ROLAP to MOLAP in the Properties window.

Important Security Information for Remote Partitions: We have chosen the Impersonation mode to be "Default" for the Data Sources within the master and subordinate databases (instances). By choosing default, at the time of processing, Analysis Services instances use the service's start-up account while connecting to Analysis Services 9.0 databases. If your server start-up account for both instances is a Windows domain (user) account, then you would have appropriate permissions to access the databases (so long as that start-up account has admin permissions). However, if both instances were installed with server start-up accounts as "Local System" then you might encounter an access permissions error when the master database is trying to connect to the subordinate. This is due to the fact that connections to named instances of Analysis Services are routed via SQL Browser and by default, the server start-up account for SQL Browser is "Network Service." If your installation has the SQL Browser server start-up account as "Network Service" and the Analysis Services instances server start-up account is "Local System," please change the server start-up account of SQL Browser and the two Analysis Services instances to a windows domain account using SQL Server Configuration Manager. The

Configuration Manager can be launched from Start → All programs → Microsoft SQL Server 2005 → Configuration Tools → SQL Server Configuration Manager. For more information on changing a server start-up account, please refer to Chapter 12.

Figure 9-68

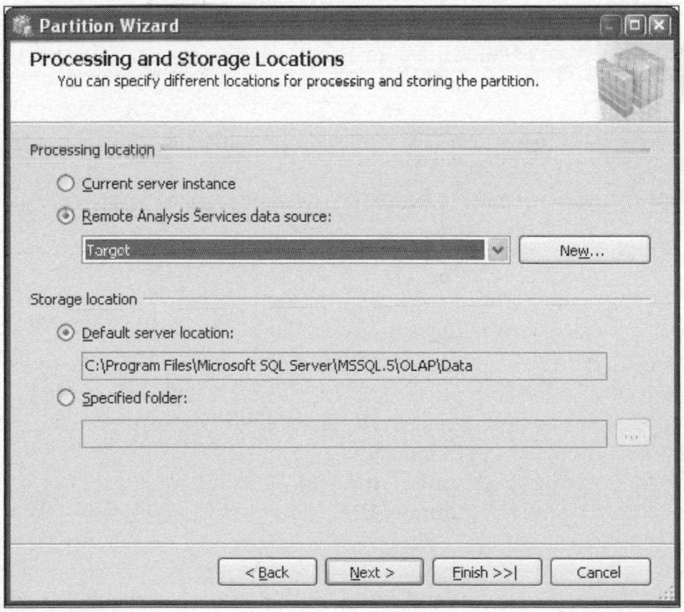

Figure 9-69

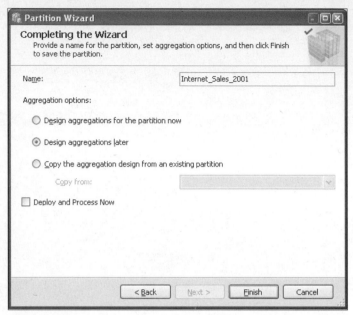

Figure 9-70

21. Finally, to populate the partition on the remote machine, right-click the Adventure Works cube name in the Solution Explorer, and choose Process. When asked whether to deploy the project first, select Yes. After processing is complete you will be able to query data from the remote partitions.

If you were successful, you can see the remote partitions quite clearly after processing as shown in Figure 9-71. And if it doesn't work for you the first time, don't worry, there are a lot of steps and therefore lots of opportunities to get things messed up. Most likely though, are security errors; be sure to verify you have all the correct Firewall settings and Impersonation settings. Impersonation settings are changed in a secondary tab in the Data Source wizard.

Storage Modes & Storage Settings

Where you store partition data is just one part of the storage picture; the mode in which you store it is the other. The storage modes used with Analysis Services solutions include MOLAP (Multi-dimensional OLAP), ROLAP (Relational OLAP), and HOLAP (Hybrid OLAP). These storage types were discussed in some detail way back in Chapter 1, so this section contains only a brief review. The main difference between these storage modes concerns where the data and (or) aggregated fact data is stored. MOLAP is the traditional storage mode for OLAP Servers and involves keeping both data and aggregations on the server. This results in fast query response times, but it is not as scalable as other solutions. ROLAP is the storage mode in which the data is left in the relational database. Aggregated or summary data is also stored in the relational database. The key advantage here is that the ROLAP will scale as well as your relational hardware/software will supportIt can sometimes result in slower queries, though. The HOLAP storage mode combines the best features of MOLAP and ROLAP. The data in the relational database is not touched while the aggregated or summary data is stored on the OLAP Server in a proprietary format; queries that can be resolved in the OLAP Server are, and those that cannot be are redirected to the relational backend.

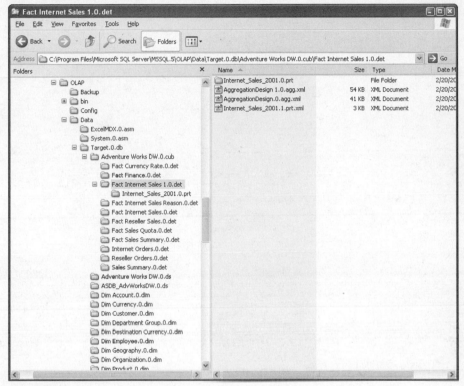

Figure 9-71

MOLAP is generally the preferred mode due to the performance gains and efficiency in its use of storage space. If you need to analyze real-time data, ROLAP is probably more appropriate. ROLAP is also a better option when you have a very large data warehouse and you do not want to duplicate the data. Each partition can have its own storage mode, which you specify on the Partitions tab of the cube designer in BIDS. Just click the Storage Settings link as shown in Figure 9-72.

When you click Storage Settings, the first page in the wizard is for Proactive Caching configuration (see Figure 9-73). Proactive Caching is a mechanism that control over the latency associated with moving data to MOLAP and reprocessing data too. You learn more about Proactive Caching options suited for various real world scenarios in Chapter 18.

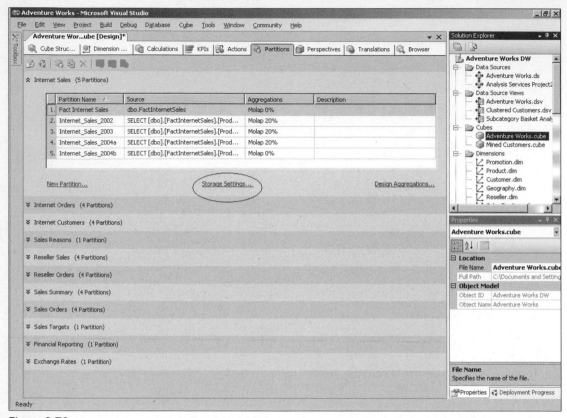

Figure 9-72

Building Aggregations

Aggregations are what make OLAP fast to use. They are pre-calculated summaries of the data. In Analysis Services, the storage and processing schemes are linked through the setting of caching options. Caching is a way to increase query response time by keeping the data used most often on a local disk.

To start the Aggregations Design wizard, click Design Aggregations in the Partitions tab of the cube designer. You use this wizard to create aggregations for each partition to improve overall query performance. You learn about aggregations in detail in Chapter 13. When you run the wizard, the performance benefits gained are graphically compared to the storage space required to store the aggregations, as shown in Figure 9-74 where you can see that the Performance Gain is set to 30%. A good starting target should be around 25% to 30%, but you will learn about the Usage Based Optimization Wizard in Chapter 13 for fine-tuning performance gains even further.

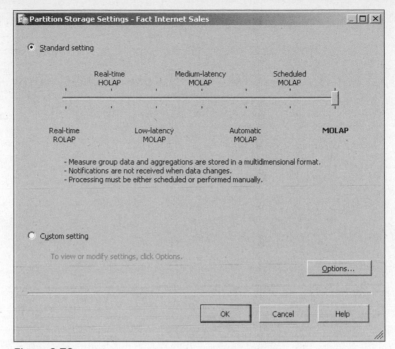

Figure 9-73

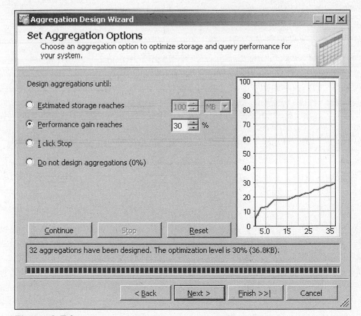

Figure 9-74

You can validate that the aggregations were defined by the wizard by looking at the partitions tab with the relevant measure group open and showing the partitions, as shown in Figure 9-75.

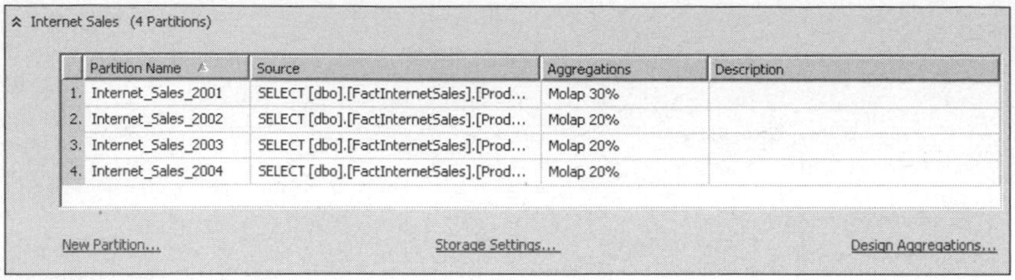

Figure 9-75

To validate the aggregations defined by the wizard are useful you need to trace the query execution using SQL Server Profiler which you learn in Chapter 13.

Defining Security

Now that you know how to create and enhance a cube to meet your business needs, you also need to know how to provide the right level of access to end users. Many people consider security to be a management task to be assigned to the administrators. However, your solution might be require Analysis Services to perform fine-grain security checks, which can adversely impact calculations. Hence, the cube developer should be actively involved in defining and testing security to verify users see the right data and experience good query performance.

Analysis Services 2005 provides you with fine-grain security to control access to metadata and data. You can also grant permissions to certain users who need the ability to process a database, but who do not need full control of the database. You can choose to secure data at the cube level, the dimension level, or even the cell level. Because security is an important topic for you to understand, especially with regard to dimension and cell security, Chapter 19 provides a complete example of a security definition. In this section, you learn the basic steps involved in granting write access permissions to a cube and its dimensions. The following steps will help you better understand how access permissions can be applied to your cube and dimensions:

1. Right-click the Roles folder in the Solution Explorer of the sample Adventure Works DW project and choose New Role. BIDS will create a new role called Role.role and opens the Roles designer as shown in Figure 9-76.

2. In the General tab, you can give members you assign to this role full control of the database, or you can limit their activities to processing the database or simply reading the database definitions. Selecting Full Control automatically grants full access including write permissions to change the objects within the current database. The Process Database option grants access to the users so that they can read the metadata about database objects and to process the objects. Users who have Process Database control will not be able to make changes to dimensions and cubes or even data within these. Read Definition allows the users to read metadata of the objects within the database, however it does not give you access to the data. Select the option that is best-suited for your users and provide some description for the current role in the role description box.

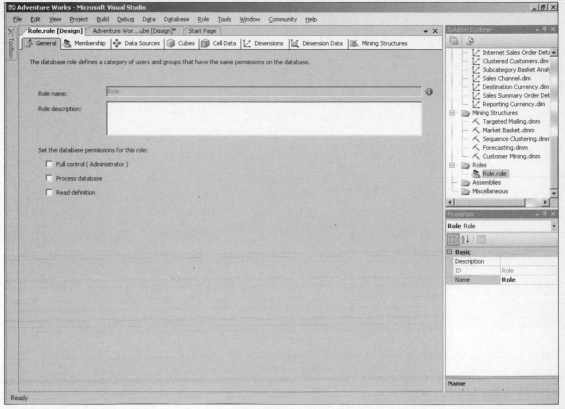

Figure 9-76

3. Click the Membership tab. In the Membership tab, you can add the list of users for whom you want the specific access you have selected. Analysis Services accepts all domain users or machine users in this dialog. Analysis Services verifies that the user entered is a valid user and then stores the id of the user within the database. Add a local machine user or a domain user in your company to the membership list and then click the Data Sources tab.

4. Figure 9-77 shows the Data Sources tab which you use to restrict users from accessing the cube's data sources. By default, access to data sources is None. Typically, access to data sources might be needed in data mining scenarios in which you might query the relational source data for prediction. Enabling the Read Definition option allows the users to retrieve information such as database name, tables, views, and so on of the data source.

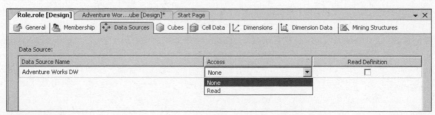

Figure 9-77

5. The Cubes tab is shown in Figure 9-78. Here you have the option to grant access to specific cubes. By default, users have no access to any cube in a database to ensure that developers or administrators do not accidentally provide cube access to users who are not supposed to have access. You have the option of providing read access only or read/write access to each cube in the database. You can also see there is the option of Local Cube/Drillthrough Access. These options allow you to specifically grant users the ability to create local cubes or drill-through to more detailed data. In addition, you can limit access to Drillthrough only or to Drillthrough and Local Cube. Local cubes are typically created from Excel so that small versions of cubes can be shared with other users. Local cubes (also called offline cubes) are covered in Chapter 15. The Process option allows you to grant users the ability to process selected cubes. Select Read/Write access to the Adventure Works cube, and then click the Dimensions tab.

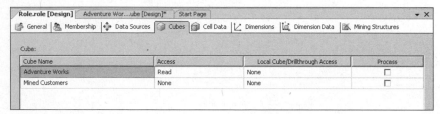

Figure 9-78

6. In the Dimensions tab, you have the option to control which database dimensions or cube dimensions a user can access if they've already been granted access to the cube. Figure 9-79 shows how you can define security for the database dimensions or the cube dimensions of the Adventure Works cube. If you select the databases dimensions option, you will see all the dimensions listed with three columns in which you specify the type of access, Read Definition access, and Process capabilities. The Process column is used to provide process permission to specific dimensions. By default, Read access is applied to all the dimensions, but you can change the access type to Read/Write for any dimension. If you allow the Read/Write option, the users have the ability to alter the dimension structure or data. The Read Definition access allows users to query for certain properties of the dimension such as count of hierarchies, members, and levels in the dimension.

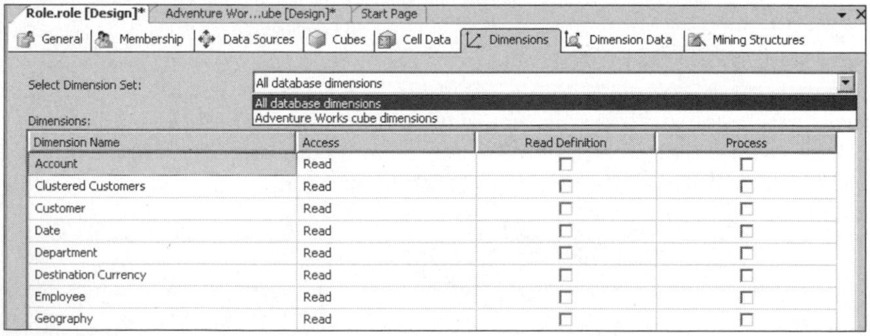

Figure 9-79

If you select the cube dimensions option, you will see two columns called Inherit and Access for each of the dimensions, as shown in Figure 9-80. By default, the Inherit column is selected, meaning that all the permissions specified for the database dimension are inherited by the cube dimension. You do have the option of overriding the database dimension access permissions. For example, you might provide Read access to all the database dimensions, Inherit for all the cube dimensions, and then Read/Write permissions on a specific dimension so that you allow certain users to writeback data to the dimension or alter dimension structure. In order to override the database dimension permission access, you need to deselect the Inherit option and then select the Read/Write option from the Access column.

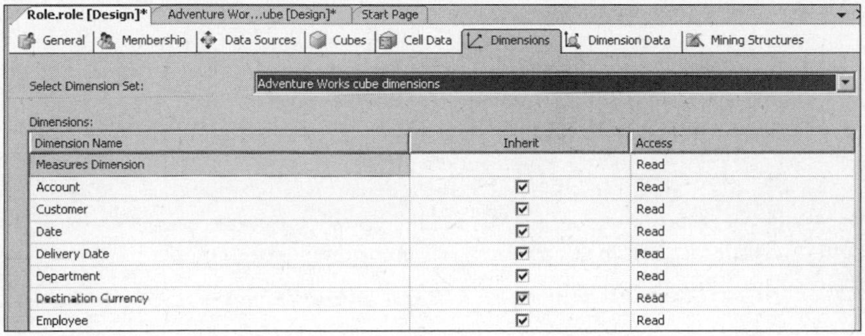

Dimension Name	Inherit	Access
Measures Dimension		Read
Account	☑	Read
Customer	☑	Read
Date	☑	Read
Delivery Date	☑	Read
Department	☑	Read
Destination Currency	☑	Read
Employee	☑	Read

Figure 9-80

As you can see, the role of designer lets you easily specify the right access permissions to the dimensions and cubes within an Analysis Services database. If you have provided access only to the Adventure Works cube, but not to the Mined Customers cube, then when you connect to Analysis Services through SQL Server Management Studio as one of the users listed in the role's membership, you will not see the Mined Customers cube. On the other hand, if you assign a user to two roles, with one role granting access to the Adventure Works cube and the other role granting access to the Mined Customers cube, the user will see both cubes because role permissions are additive. In BIDS, you can test the effect of security, including membership in multiple roles, by browsing the cube under a specific role or a user. If you try to browse a cube for which the current user or role has not been granted permissions, you will get an error message that says you do not have access to the cube.

In this section, you have learned how to define access permissions (read or write permissions) for cubes and dimensions. This ensures correct access restriction to a specific cube or a dimension as a whole to certain users querying the database. Some business scenarios call for restricted access to just a part of the dimension or cube. For example, if I am a sales manager in a chain of retail stores, I might only be given access to view sales information specific to my store. Defining the right security for dimension and cell data is best learned through a scenario; expect to find out more about restricting data access to users in Chapter 19. As for mining models, the Mining Structures tab allows you to define security for mining models, which we will not be covering in this book.

Summary

Ok, Neo, crawl up out of the rabbit hole; you have reached the conclusion of this chapter. And what a profound trip that was! This chapter has provided you with amazing new tools for your BI repertoire. In fact, consider yourself admitted to the knowledgeable inner-circle of BI professionals because you know that you can add measure groups from any accessible cube to your own cube without the use of views in SQL Server. This is functionally equivalent to the virtual cube scenario in Analysis Services 2000 without the extra steps associated with creation and maintenance of all those sub-cubes. This one change encapsulates a lot of power, and you are going to have fun discovering that power. Similarly, with remote partitions there is that compelling scalability factor that kicks in; it's great! The Cube Wizard also provides you the ability to create Cubes without a data source through templates similar to the Dimension Wizard which was not discussed in this chapter. The Cube Wizard has two templates to choose from. Once the Cube has been created you would need to populate the tables with appropriate data before processing the cube. We leave it to you to explore this option from the Cube Wizard by selecting the build method "build a cube without a data source."

Much of this chapter was dedicated to cube enhancements, which fall directly to the bottom line of providing business information; using actions and KPIs both will enhance any digital dashboard you might create. In fact, when you start building custom front ends for consumption of your business intelligence applications, like digital dashboards which reflect current business operations, there are cases where you will have to write your own application for filtering based on real-time data. Indeed, some complex and custom operations cannot even be defined in a cube. For such operations, Analysis Services provides support for the writing of custom code in ActiveX components or in managed code. There is more on the programmatic approach in the next chapter.

10

Extending MDX using External Functions

The MDX language supports an extensive set of functions for business analysis. In addition to that Analysis Services exposes certain VBA (Visual Basic for Applications) and Excel functions as built-in external functions which can be accessed through MDX. These functions supported in Analysis Services should meet most of your design and query requirements. However there is always a need for custom operations. Analysis Services provides an extensible architecture by which you can add your custom function to Analysis Services and access them through MDX. These external functions are also referred to as user-defined functions (UDF).

The UDF offers seamless integration with existing Microsoft Business Intelligence technology with all the power to be found in the programming language of your choice. This suggests you can accomplish anything your coding skills will support and that it will be leveraged by the existing benefits of Analysis Services. As an example, it would not be unusual to use recent stock data for calculations within MDX queries or expressions. By building a UDF to collect and pass along relevant data, your MDX query can reflect such up-to-date information.

Two types of external functions are described and demonstrated in this chapter: COM-based UDFs and .NET-based UDFs (commonly referred to as . NET assemblies). There are some crucial nuggets of data any Business Intelligence informavore will want to consume. You should already be aware that COM UDFs are created using C or C++ or even VB6, the output of which are COM DLLs. This functionality was available in Analysis Services 2000 — so there is nothing new there and is supported in Analysis Services 2005 for backwards compatibility of existing applications. On the other hand, the relatively new technology called .NET assemblies is supported with Analysis Services 2005. Your custom function written in .NET language, like VB.Net, C#, or even managed C++ for that matter needs to be compiled as a DLL (Dynamic Link Library).

Analysis Services provides native support for .NET assemblies and therefore debugging these procedures is quite straightforward within an instance of Analysis Services. Typically a person other than the administrator of the instance creates the UDFs. In such a case the administrator might not trust the coding abilities of the person—not an usual state of affairs. The good news is .NET assemblies provide several levels of code security hence, constraints are made on what the code can do. You see that concept demonstrated in the .NET assembly example in this chapter.

Microsoft has shipped a client object model called ADOMD.Net (ActiveX Data Objects for Multi-dimensional Databases), which is a programming interface for querying multidimensional data from Analysis Services. The client object model has classes for the objects on the server, which help in easy traversal of the objects at the client side. In addition to that the object model supports querying data and traversing through the result set. Analysis Services 2005 provides you with an equivalent ADOMD Server object model that can be used within your UDFs for custom operations on the server. One example is when the result set is really large and you are working on a low-bandwidth network. Where you would want to restrict the data on the server side rather than on the client. You can also include custom calculations for your business being applied to the objects directly on the server side with your custom C# code.

All told, Analysis Services 2005 allows you to write your custom code as a COM (Component Object Model) UDF or as an assembly with one of the .NET languages. Further, you can add them to the database so long as the dot net assembly has the appropriate credentials—for extra security only an Analysis Services administrator is allowed to add all assemblies. In this chapter you see examples of COM UDF creation in Visual Basic 6.0 and .NET assemblies using C#.

COM User Defined Functions

COM is Microsoft's architecture for building software from binary components that expose the function-ality with a well-defined interface. Analysis Services understands the COM interface and has the ability to interface with any COM DLLs so that functions within the DLL can be accessed through MDX. In order to create a function that will perform a customized operation for your business, you need to create a DLL using any of the languages that allow you to create a COM DLL, such as Microsoft Visual Basic or Microsoft Visual C++. In this chapter you learn how to create a COM UDF using Visual Basic 6.0.

Built-in COM UDFs

The MDX language provides certain functions (for example, SettoStr, TupletoStr, StrtoTuple, StrtoSet, and StrtoMember) that are helpful in translating MDX objects to external data structures such as string or arrays or from external structures to MDX objects. The MDX language does not support certain com-mon utility functions like performing operations on strings, such as trimming or getting the first sub-string match, or date operation functions. Such functions are natively supported in SQL, and they might be quite commonly used during MDX queries. Because Visual Basic for Applications (VBA) and Excel contain a rich set of such functions, they are readily available as a COM DLL. Analysis Services 2005 takes advantage of this and exposes certain functions in Excel and VBA out of the box. Analysis Services 2000 also supported certain VBA functions out of the box. However, on 64-bit platforms, VBA functions were not supported because VBA dll is 32 bit. Hence in Analysis Services 2005 the supported VBA func-tions are implemented using native and managed code instead of delegating the call to the VBA dll. Important functions that can impact performance are implemented natively, while the remaining sup-ported VBA functions are implemented as a built-in .NET assembly. If you want to use the COM VBA functions and do not want to use the VBA functions that have been implemented in .NET language then Analysis Services 2005 provides a configuration setting to switch back to the native VBA. By changing the server property VBANet to 0, you force Analysis Services to load the default VBA dll. However, you would have to delete the entire data folder of Analysis Services and then restart the server.

Calling a user-defined function in MDX is similar to calling a function in most programming languages. You make the call with the function name followed by an opening parenthesis, with each argument in the correct order separated by commas, and finally a closing parenthesis. For example, if you want to get today's date, you can use the VBA function Now(). The following MDX query will retrieve today's date:

```
WITH MEMBER Measures.[Today's Date] AS 'Now()'
SELECT Measures.[Today's Date] on 0
From [Adventure Works DW]
```

In the above example the value returned by the VBA function Now() is stored as a calculated measure and then retrieved using the MDX query. The functions provided by VBA and Excel will likely help you meet your business application requirements. However, each business need is unique and your business might require special computing that cannot be solved using the MDX, VBA, or Excel functions. You might have to base all your calculations on an external data source that is dynamically changing. In such circumstances you can write a custom COM DLL and add this to Analysis Services 2005.

Creating Your COM UDFs

Creating a COM user-defined function is quite simple. All you have to do is to create an ActiveX DLL using one of the COM languages such as Microsoft Visual Basic or Microsoft Visual C++. Analysis Services 2000 provided support for extending MDX by means of COM UDFs. The arguments that you can pass to COM UDF functions are numbers, strings, and arrays. You cannot use any of the MDX objects within your functions nor can you pass the MDX objects as parameters to your COM UDFs. Your COM UDF can return either strings or numbers that can be stored as calculated members or parameters to other functions in your MDX query. When you create your COM UDF function you would typically declare the types of arguments in the function declaration, such as COMUDFFunction (integer argument1, double argument 2, string argument3). The value passed from Analysis Services for that argument will be coerced into that specific type in the function signature when the function is called.

The Adventure Works DW cube you created in the previous chapters contains the calculated measure profit. Assume you want to see a cumulative sum of the profits based on the ship date along with the net profit for each year. In order to perform a cumulative sum, you can write a function that takes three arguments of the dimension, the measure value, and the location up to which the cumulative sum has to be performed. The dimension members along with their values need to be passed to your UDF. Analysis Services 2005 provides a function called SetToArray, which translates an MDX Set into an Array object. Using this function you can pass the measure values and the dimension members as arrays to the function.

Following is Visual Basic code to perform a cumulative sum. The function takes two arrays and a string. The first argument is an array of numbers, the second contains the dimension members, and the third argument is the member name up to which the cumulative total needs to be applied. The function returns the cumulative sum as the return value.

```
Public Function PartialSum(ByRef ArgVals() As Variant, ByRef ArgNames() As Variant,
ByVal StopAt As String) As Double

Dim Start As Integer
Dim Finish As Integer
```

```
Dim i As Integer
Dim s As String
Dim SubTotal As Double

Start = 0 ' for safety
Finish = UBound(ArgVals)
PartialSum = 0
'initialize working sum to zero
SubTotal = 0
For i = Start To Finish
    'add value for this tuple
    SubTotal = SubTotal + ArgVals(i)
    s = ArgNames(i)
    'leave if we have encountered the stopping point
    If s = StopAt Then
        PartialSum = SubTotal
        Return
    End If
Next i

End Function
```

You can create a new Visual Basic 6.0 project of ActiveX DLL type and enter the preceding code. Once you have entered the code you can create the DDL with the option File⇨Make DLL. When you are creating the DLL, make sure you select the option to create debug symbols so that you can debug your COM UDF if needed. The preceding Visual Basic code and project are available under Chapter 10 directory in the COMPartialSum folder on the web site that accompanies this book. Once you have created your COM DLL, you need to add this to your database.

Adding a COM UDF to an Analysis Services Database

You can add a COM UDF to your Analysis Services database using SQL Server Management Studio, through scripting or programmatically using the object model AMO that is used for managing your Analysis Server. We recommend that you add assemblies using the SQL Server Management Studio because it is easy to do.

You can add a COM UDF to Analysis Services at the scope of the Analysis Services instance or at the scope of an existing database. If your UDF is added at the server scope, it can be shared across multiple databases similar to the Excel and VBA DLLs that default to server-level scope. The following steps show you how to add the COM UDF you created.

1. Deploy the AnalysisServices2005Tutorial project provided under the Chapter10 directory available on the accompanying web site for this book to your Analysis Services instance. (If you already have the AnalysisServices2005Tutorial project deployed on your server you can skip this step.)

2. Connect to the Analysis Services instance using SQL Server Management Studio.

3. Expand the object AnalysisServices2005Tutorial database.

4. Right-click the node assemblies and select New Assembly.

5. You will now see the register assembly dialog shown in Figure 10-1. Change the type of assembly from .NET to COM. Under the file name, browse through the directory where the COM assembly is located and select the assembly file PartialSum.dll. The PartialSum.dll is also available under the Chapter 10 directory on the accompanying web site for this book.

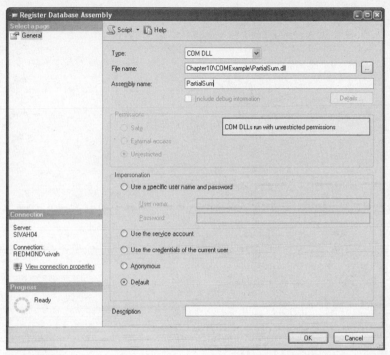

Figure 10-1

All COM assemblies added to Analysis Services have unrestricted permissions, which mean they can access files or network services in addition to any computation. You can have a finer grain of permissions and you can allow for .NET assemblies, which you learn more about in the next section. Analysis Services runs under a specific account credential. However, the assembly being added to Analysis Services might need a specific set of credentials because it needs to access specific external resources. Analysis Services allows you to specify the credential under which the COM UDF needs to be executed. The various options in the dialog are self-explanatory, but you will learn each option in detail when you are adding .NET assemblies to the Analysis Services instance. Select the default option and click OK. You can now use the assembly in your MDX Query.

Analysis Services 2000 provided syntax to add assemblies called "USE LIBRRARY <library name>". The majority of computations were done on the client side in Analysis Services 2000 and hence this syntax helped in loading libraries on the client side. Analysis Services 2005 performs all the operations on the server side. Therefore this syntax has been deprecated. You do not have to specify this syntax in Analysis Services 2005 since the DLL gets loaded when a query uses a function in the DLL. For backward-compatibility reasons the USE LIBRARY syntax is accepted by Analysis Services 2005, but it is just a NO OP (no operations are executed when the statement is encountered).

Accessing COM UDFs in MDX Queries

In order to retrieve the cumulative profit along with profit for various years, you need to use the MDX function SettoArray to translate a set of members in Analysis Services to an array that can be passed to a UDF. The following query calculates the cumulative profit across various years of ship date:

```
WITH
Member [Measures].[Year] AS '[Ship Date].[CalendarYear - CalendarSemester -
CalendarQuarter - EnglishMonthName].Currentmember.UniqueName'
member [Measures].[Cum Profit] AS '
PartialSum(
SettoArray([Ship Date].[CalendarYear - CalendarSemester - CalendarQuarter -
EnglishMonthName].[CalendarYear],[Measures].[Profit]),
SetToArray( [Ship Date].[CalendarYear - CalendarSemester - CalendarQuarter -
EnglishMonthName].[CalendarYear],[Measures].[Year] ),
[Ship Date].[CalendarYear - CalendarSemester - CalendarQuarter -
EnglishMonthName].CurrentMember.Uniquename)'

SELECT { [Measures].[Profit], [Measures].[Cum Profit]} on columns,
[Ship Date].[CalendarYear - CalendarSemester - CalendarQuarter -
EnglishMonthName].[CalendarYear] ON ROWS
from [Adventure Works DW]
```

You will see the results shown in the table below when you execute this query against the Adventure Works DW database.

	Profit	Cum Profit
2001	1,576,032.17	1576032.1682
2002	2,705,927.15	4281959.3152
2003	−168,557.73	4113401.5814
2004	−13,288.53	4100112.0547

Analysis Services calls the UDF for each member of the ship date to calculate the cumulative sum up to that year, thereby resulting in calculating the cumulative profit for each year. In this query the UDF is called four times because there are four members returned in the result.

Disambiguating Between Functions

You can add multiple COM UDFs that contain the same function names to a database or Analysis Services instance. If you have more than one function with the same name within Analysis Services, any query using the function name will result in an error. This is due to the inability to resolve to the correct function name. In such a circumstance you can explicitly specify the fully qualified name of the function by pre-pending it with the classID of the library. The classID of a function looks like this: AssemblyName.ClassName. If you have created your UDF using a Visual Basic project that contains a package name called COMExample and a class name COMExampleClass, you need to access the function as COMExample!_COMExampleClass.Function.

.NET User Defined Functions (Stored Procedures)

If you have been programming on the Microsoft platform, you must be familiar with the .NET framework and the .NET languages. .NET (Dot Net) is Microsoft's framework and strategy to connect people, business, systems, and devices. Several programming languages help in building applications using the framework, which helps in seamless integration with other applications. Analysis Services 2005 couples tightly with UDFs based on .NET languages. In addition to the tight integration, the .NET framework provides leverage through use of its security model. The model is provided by the framework and can be used to support fine-grain security on .NET assemblies added to Analysis Services. We refer to UDFs built using .NET languages as .NET assemblies as well as stored procedures in this book.

Creating Stored Procedures

You can create a .NET assembly using any of the .NET languages, such as C# or VB.Net. Similar to COM UDFs you can create your stored procedures to perform complex business computations catered towards your business applications. A few examples of stored procedures would be to perform custom business computations that will involve business logic based on certain conditions, accessing external resources such as stock price of the company from a web service to perform calculations, and accessing external resources such as data from a SQL Server to apply permissions on Analysis Services. Chapter 19 shows an example of applying permissions on Analysis Services by means of a stored procedure that retrieves data from an external service.

Analysis Services 2005 provides you with much more than fine-grain code access security for administrators when they add .NET assemblies to Analysis Services 2005. Analysis Services 2005 exposes all the MDX objects via a Server object model called ADOMD Server, where you can access all the Analysis Services such as cubes, dimensions, sets, and tuples within the object model. The server-side object model exposed to the programmer is similar to the client-side ADOMD.Net object model, but certain minor differences exist between these two object models. These differences result from the kinds of applications they support. In addition to supporting a complete object model for programming server-side stored procedures, Analysis Services 2005 also allows you to perform management operations via stored procedures using the Analysis Services Management Object, which you learn about in some detail in Chapter 12. In this section you see examples of stored procedures using the object models AMO and ADOMD server. Stored procedures using the AMO are referred to as AMO stored procedures and those using ADOMD server object model as ADOMD stored procedures

Before you look at AMO and ADOMD stored procedures you will look at the COM example in the previous section being written as a .NET stored procedure using C#. Open Visual Studio 2005 and create a C# class library application called PartialSumSproc. Enter the code shown below and compile the class library.

```
using System;
using System.Collections.Generic;
using System.Text;

namespace PartialSumSproc
{
    public class PratialSumSproc
    {
        public static double PartialSum(double [] Val, string [] Member,
```

```
            string stopMember)
    {
        double PartialSum = 0;
        int l = 0; //Lower bound value of the array
        int u = Val.Length; //upper bound value of the array.

        for(int i=l;i<u;i++)
        {
            //add tuple into the return set
            PartialSum = PartialSum + Val[i];

            //if the unique name of both tuple is same then break and return

            if (string.Compare(Member[i], stopMember) == 0)
                break;
        }

        //return the set back to server
        return PartialSum;
    }
  }
}
```

The .NET assembly needs to be added to the database and you can use the function PartialSum in your queries. If you already have your COM UDF added to your database then you need to access the function PartialSum in the .NET assembly along with the assembly name as PartialSumSproc.PartialSum.

AMO Stored Procedures

Analysis Management Objects (AMO) is the object model used to perform management operations on an Analysis Services object. You will learn more about AMO in Chapter 12. One of the common operations in any database is backup. Assume you are the DBA for Analysis Services in your company and you want to leave on vacation. Obviously you want to enjoy your vacation and not worry about work. But if there is a mission-critical need and you are in the middle of, say, the Tasmanian ocean and are called for help, you would want to have the flexibility and control required to remotely perform operations on your Analysis Services instance. Analysis Services 2005 allows you to query the server over an HTTP connection. With Analysis Services 2005 you can send XMLA requests to the server. These requests can be for management operations, but you'll want to know the disposition of those requests, that is, pass or fail status. An easier way to do a management operation is to create an AMO-stored procedure, which can be launched via an MDX query for which you can code a return value as a status indicator.

The following code is an AMO-stored procedure in C# that contains a function that does a backup of a database. This function takes the name of the database to backup and the name of the file under which the backup has to be taken as parameters. The stored procedure connects to the Analysis Server instance via a stored procedure. You can then access the databases on the server, and iterate through the entire database till you find the database passed as the parameter. Once you have identified the database, you just need to issue a backup command. The backup of the database is taken on the default backup database directory of Analysis Services instance.

```
#region Using directives

using System;
using System.Collections.Generic;
using System.Text;
using AMO = Microsoft.AnalysisServices;

#endregion

namespace AmoSprocExample
{
    public class AmoSprocExample
    {
        public AmoSprocExample() {}

        public static bool Backup(string sDatabaseName, string backupFileName)
        {
            try
            {
                AMO.Server asServer = new Microsoft.AnalysisServices.Server();
                 // Connect through AMO with connection string that has server name
                 // Here . indicates connecting to itself.
                asServer.Connect(".");
                 //Iterate through the databases on the server till you
                 //find the specified database and then perform backup
                for (int i = 0; i < asServer.Databases.Count; i++)
                {
                    AMO.Database asDB =
asServer.Databases.FindByName(sDatabaseName);
                    if( asDB != null)
                    {
                        asDB.Backup(backupFileName + ".abf");
                        return true;
                    }
                }

            }
            catch (AMO.AmoException e)
            {
                System.Console.WriteLine(e.Message);
            }
            return false;
        }
    }
}
```

To create this stored procedure, first create a new C# project for a class library using Visual Studio. Then add the .NET assembly Analysis Management Objects (Microsoft.AnalysisServices.dll) to the references as shown in Figure 10-2. Add the preceding code to your project and compile the project. Congratulations, you just created a dot net assembly. You can write similar functions within the same stored procedure that can perform various management operations on your server.

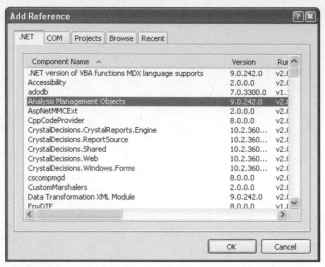

Figure 10-2

ADOMD Server Stored Procedure

A key attribute of Analysis Services 2005 stored procedures is the server object model called ADOMD Server, which is exposed by Analysis Services. You can now leverage the server ADOMD object model and create a stored procedure that will perform some of your custom business operations that were previously done on the client side. You can restrict the amount of data being retrieved from the server as well as perform many of the operations on the server, thereby getting improved performance.

Following is a C# code that uses the Server ADOMD object model. This stored procedure contains a function called custom filter that filters a set of tuples based on a sampling percentage. This is a stored procedure that is useful when you want a sample of customers for whom you want to do a marketing study. For example, you identify that there are one million customers who are extremely important for your business. Assume they are highly valued customers based on the purchases they make. Now you want to do a marketing study of a sample of such customers or send surveys to a subset of these customers to expand your line of business. How would you go about getting the sample of customers? You can retrieve all the customers, pick the top N percentage of customers, and perform a sampling operation on the server side using a stored procedure. The following stored procedure shows how this is done. The stored procedure contains a function called CustomFilter that takes an MDX Set and a sampling percentage as inputs and returns an MDX Set as an output. The CustomFilter function is simple in the sense that it takes the every Nth member based on the sampling percentage from the Set and adds them to a new Set. You can definitely write your own custom filter function based on your requirements.

```
#region Using directives

using System;
using System.Collections.Generic;
using System.Text;
using AdomdServer = Microsoft.AnalysisServices.AdomdServer;

#endregion
```

```
namespace AdoMdServerExample
{
    public class AdoMdServerExample
    {
        public AdoMdServerExample()
        {
        }
        Public static AdomdServer.Set CustomFilter(AdomdServer.Set mdxSet,
                                        int samplingPercentage)
        {
            AdomdServer.SetBuilder sampleSet = new
                    Microsoft.AnalysisServices.AdomdServer.SetBuilder();

            int iTupleCount = mdxSet.Tuples.Count;
            int iTupleSample = iTupleCount * samplingPercentage/100;

            for (int i = 0; i < iTupleCount; i++)
            {
                if (i % (samplingPercentage) == 0)
                {
                    sampleSet.Add(mdxSet.Tuples[i]);
                }
            }
            return sampleSet.ToSet();

        }
        public int TupleCount(AdomdServer.Set mdxSet)
        {

            return mdxSet.Tuples.Count;

        }

    }
}
```

This code is just an example of how to create a stored procedure that uses the ADOMD Server object model. Using the server object model you can execute MDX expressions and, based on the result, you can perform custom operations. Analysis Services 2005 uses the ADOMD server object model for some of the viewers used in Data mining (you will learn about data mining and its viewers in Chapter 14). There are built-in system stored procedures that make use of the ADOMD Server object model to restrict the amount of data being sent to the server to achieve the best performance and user experience in the viewers. To create an ADOMD stored procedure you need to include the assembly msmgdsrv.dll inside your C# class library references. You can find msmgdsrv.dll under the Analysis Services bin directory.

Static vs Non-Static Functions

Analysis Services 2005 supports using static as well as non-static functions. If a function is defined as non-static (static keyword is not defined in function definition) then each time the function is called Analysis Services needs to create an instance of the class and then needs to load the function. This could be quite expensive if the function is called several times within a query. Unless and until you absolutely need non-static functions we recommend you to define static functions. When static functions of a class are called then Analysis Services directly invokes the function after loading the assembly. The assembly load operation occurs only once and hence you do not incur performance degradation as compared to non-static functions when the function is called several times within a query.

Adding Stored Procedures

Once you have created the stored procedures you can add them to Server scope assemblies or database scope assemblies. Similar to adding the COM assembly, you need to use the SQL Server Management Studio to add the stored procedures. The following steps show how to add a stored procedure:

1. Connect to your database using SQL Server Management Studio.

2. Navigate to your database, right-click the Assemblies folder, and select New Assembly.

3. You will now be in the register assembly dialog that you used earlier for adding COM assemblies. Leave the type of the assembly as .NET assembly and specify the assembly file as shown in Figure 10-3.

4. Select the option to include debug information so that you can debug the assembly within the Analysis Server in case you run into problems. If you click the Details button you will see all the functions that are part of the assembly as shown in Figure 10-4. This is because .NET assemblies are compiled to an intermediate language and, using reflection, Analysis Services Tools is able to retrieve the functions available in the assembly. During runtime this code is compiled into machine language and then executed by the .NET framework.

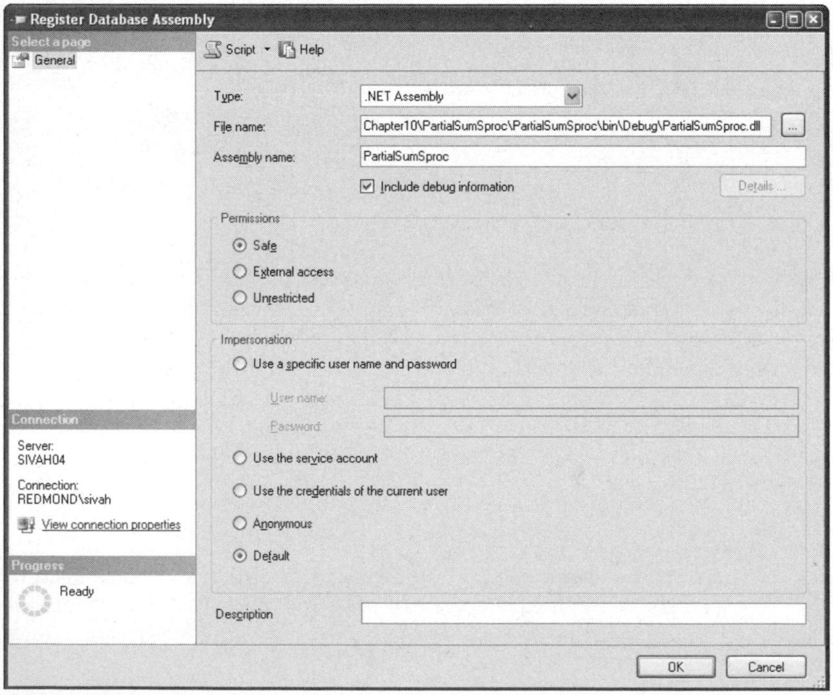

Figure 10-3

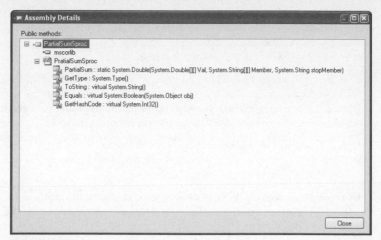

Figure 10-4

5. Select a permission set option for the assemblies you are adding. Analysis Services leverages permission sets from the .NET framework to provide fine-grain security on the assemblies being added to Analysis Services. You can select three different permission set options:

    a. **Safe:** The Safe permission set forces the assembly to only perform computation operations. Whenever a stored procedure marked with the Safe permission set tries to access external resources, the .NET framework restricts the permission and throws an error.

    b. **External Access:** The External Access permission set is intended to allow managed code to access external resources from the server, without compromising the reliability of the server. You can use this if you as the DBA trust the programmer's ability to write good code and if there is a need to access external resources such as data from an outside file.

    c. **Unrestricted:** If an assembly has been marked with the Unrestricted permission set, it can perform any operations on the server or on any external resources. The Unrestricted permission set should be used with caution and only for operations that need it. If you are the DBA and you have full confidence in the programmer and treat him equivalent to a DBA of the Analysis Server, you can give the Unrestricted permission set.

    Note: Only database administrators can add assemblies to Analysis Server.

6. The PartialSumSproc and AdomdSproc stored procedures only perform computation, hence the Safe permission set is sufficient.

7. Next, you need to specify the impersonation of the assembly. Don't let the verbiage throw you; it just means you need to indicate what credentials Analysis Services will execute this assembly under. Analysis Services 2005 provides five options for impersonation modes:

    a. **Use a Specific user name and password:** This option should be used whenever you have an assembly that has to be executed only under certain account credentials because that specific account has access to an external source that is used within the stored procedure. This is typically used whenever you want to read some data from a web service or from a relational data source or any other external resource.

b. **Use the service account:** Whenever you have operations that need to be performed under the credentials of the Analysis Services instance, you need to specify this operation. An example of a stored procedure that would need this is an AMO stored procedure that does management operations on the server.

c. **Use the credentials of the current user:** This option is recommended when you want the stored procedure to be executed under the credentials of the user accessing it. This is a safe option to select but if your stored procedure accesses external resources and the user does not have permissions the stored procedure would be executed.

d. **Run the assembly under an anonymous account.** This is the least-privileged account and will not have any access to any data. Typically, stored procedures that are computation-intensive can be specified with this option.

e. **Default.** When the default option is chosen it is actually translated to one of the four options you just learned based on the selected permission set. If the permission set is Safe, selecting the default option for impersonation will set the impersonation mode to Impersonate Service Account. If the permission set is Unrestricted or External Access, selecting the default impersonation mode results in the impersonation mode being set as Impersonate current user.

8. Select the default option and click OK.

9. Following steps 2 through 6, add the AMO stored procedure AMOSproc but select the permission as Unrestricted. You will learn why Unrestricted permission is used for AMOSproc in the next section.

You have successfully created stored procedures and added them to the AnalysisServices2005Tutorial database. Next you see examples of using them in queries.

Querying Stored Procedures

Similar to COM UDFs, you can call the stored procedures using the assembly name, interface name and function name. However, for .NET assemblies you need to specify the assembly name followed by the fully qualified class name and then the function name. You can just specify the assembly name followed by function name if there is no ambiguity in the function name.

You can use the PartialSumSproc assembly's PartialSum function to calculate the cumulative profit as shown in Figure 10-5.

Now that you have added the ADOMD stored procedure, you'll want to see how to use it. Assume you want to see all the cities that contributed to a profit of $1000 or more; you would use the following MDX Query.

```
SELECT measures.profit ON 0,
FILTER([Dim Geography].[City].[City].MEMBERS, measures.profit > 1000) ON 1
FROM [Adventure Works DW]
```

The query results in 287 cities that have a profit greater than $1000. If you want to do a marketing campaign in only 10 percent of those cities, you can use the CustomFilter function in addition to the MDX Filter function as follows:

```
SELECT measures.profit ON 0,
AdoMdServerExample.CustomFilter(
FILTER([Dim Geography].[City].[City].MEMBERS, measures.profit > 1000),
10)
ON 1
FROM [Adventure Works DW]
```

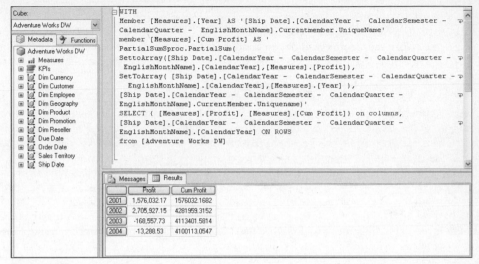

Figure 10-5

As you can see, your stored procedure takes the results of an MDX function because the Filter function returns an MDX set. That set is the parameter taken by your stored procedure. Vice versa, your stored procedure also has the capability of taking in MDX objects as parameters and returning MDX objects. Stored procedures are powerful features in Analysis Services 2005.

You have seen how stored procedures can be used within MDX queries. Another way of invoking stored procedures being executed in Analysis Services 2005 is via the CALL statement. You have added the AMO Stored procedure assembly to your database. If you are not concerned about the return result of the stored procedure and just have to execute it, you can use the CALL statement. To take a backup of the AnalysisServices2005Tutorial database you can send the following MDX statement:

```
CALL AmoSprocExample.Backup("AnalysisServices2005Tutorial","AS2K5")
```

Executing the query results in the backup of the database AnalysisServices2005Tutorial under the name AS2K5.abf in the Analysis Services backup directory.

You have added the AMO stored procedure with Unrestricted permission set access. Now see what happens if you change the permission set to External Access. You can change the permission set of an assembly by selecting the properties of the assembly and then changing the appropriate permission set.

Executing the preceding CALL statement to perform a backup now results in the following error message:

```
Execution of the managed stored procedure Backup failed with the following error:
Exception has been thrown by the target of an invocation.That assembly does not
allow partially trusted callers.
```

As mentioned earlier, when you specify the external access permission set, the .NET framework only allows assemblies to have external access. In this case your assembly AMOExample uses an assembly Microsoft.AnalysisServices that is not fully trusted by the .NET framework and does not have the full privilege of performing any operation in the specified permission set. Therefore, the .NET framework raises the error and does not execute the assembly. If you are a DBA and you restrict access to assemblies that you do not fully trust, your Analysis Server will be well secured and reliable.

Debugging Stored Procedures

Whenever you write code there are bound to be instances or conditions under which your stored procedure might not operate in accord with expectations. You can obviously test your stored procedure external to Analysis Services in conditions where you do not use the object models of Analysis Services. If you are using the ADOMD Server object model, debugging the stored procedure external to Analysis Services is difficult especially in the conditions where differences between client and server models exist. For example, the server ADOMD has an object called MDXExpression that helps you to evaluate MDX expressions within your stored procedure. This is not available in the client object model, so you will need a different method for debugging your stored procedure. The new method is not that complicated and is similar to debugging any program, but you need to debug within Analysis Services. Assume you want to debug your ADOMD stored procedure example in this chapter because you are not getting expected results. The following steps show how to debug it:

1. Execute the MDX query using the stored procedure.

2. Launch Visual Studio and attach it to your Analysis Server instance. You can attach the debugger to Analysis Services by selecting Tools⇨Attach to Process. In the Attach to process window search for the process msmdsrv.exe, select the process. Select Managed and Native options for Attach to as shown in Figure 10-6 and click Attach.

3. Now you need to make sure you load all the symbol information of your stored procedure. For this, select Debug⇨Window⇨Modules in Visual Studio. You will now see the modules window that shows all the DLLs loaded by Analysis Services executable msmdsrv.exe. Search for the DLL AdoMdServerExample.DLL, right-click and select Load Symbols. In the find symbol dialog, point to the folder that contains the symbol information for the AdoMdServerExample.DLL (that is, the file AdoMDServerExample.pdb).

4. In Visual Studio select File⇨Open and select the source file for AdoMDServerExample, which is AdoMDServerExample.cs.

5. Select break points at certain lines within the CustomFilter function.

6. Execute the MDX query once again. You will now hit the break point within Visual Studio as shown in Figure 10-7.

7. You can see all the local variables and you will be able to perform all the debugging operations that are feasible within Visual Studio. If your function calls other functions within the same stored procedures or other stored procedures, you will be able to debug those similar to debugging any of your programs.

8. Once you have identified your problem and made changes to the code and a new version of the binary, add the new version of the binary to Analysis Services by deleting the older version and adding the new version using the Register assembly dialog.

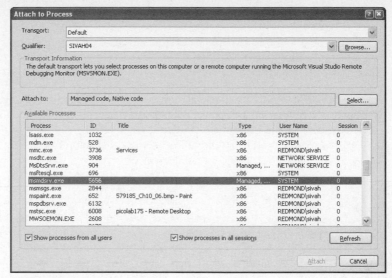

Figure 10-6

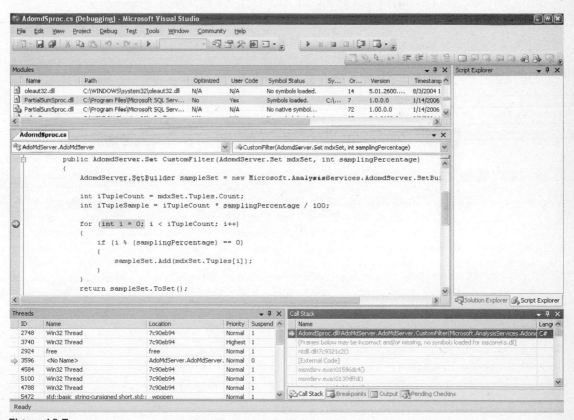

Figure 10-7

COM UDFs vs .NET Assemblies

Analysis Services supports COM UDF primarily due to backward compatibility because there might be several existing applications using it in production. If you are migrating your Analysis Services 2000 databases containing COM UDFs to Analysis Services 2005 using the migration wizard and need existing applications to utilize UDFs, we recommend using the COM UDFs. If you are very passionate about COM UDFs, you can develop your UDFs as COM libraries. However, COM is being deprecated in Analysis Services 2005, which means that the support for COM UDFs might not be available in future versions. COM UDFs are best suited for applications that do not need significant fine-grain security considerations. Hence we recommend you use COM UDFs only if it is absolutely essential due to backward compatability or for very special circumstances in which you are unable to develop your UDFs in .NET languages.

Even if you have COM UDFs in your Analysis Services implementation, you might be able to port these to .NET using VB.Net. We highly recommend that you use .NET languages for UDFs. Analysis Services 2005 has been architected to leverage maximum benefits of the .NET framework and provides the developers the best aspects of .NET languages, such as the memory management and garbage collection technology provided by .NET languages coupled with fine-grain security settings for the assemblies provided by Analysis Services 2005. If you are already familiar with .NET languages, that is great. If not, seriously consider ramping up and learning at least one .NET language. That ramp-up time will be time well spent. We don't recommend that you attempt to learn a new programming paradigm under some tight development schedule. If you have fine-grain security considerations associated with your business application, then use .NET assemblies. Note that if you will want to perform custom operations on your multidimensional data on your Analysis Services instance using the ADOMD Server Object model, you will have to use the dot Net languages to check stored procedures.

Summary

Did the impending sense of programming power make you dizzy while reading? You no doubt experienced a thrill akin to a roller coaster ride while reading this chapter. Think about it. There is a way to do basically whatever you want programmatically as long as you are capable of coding it up in concert with all the power of SQL Server Analysis Services 2005. Consider what you learned in the three sections of this chapter; in the first section you learned how to create a COM UDF and how to use them in MDX queries. In the second section on .NET UDFs you learned how to create stored procedures using the object models AMO and ADOMD Server. In the third section, you learned under what circumstances COM UDF is preferred over a .NET UDF. Most importantly you can use the MDX objects on the server using the ADOMD Server Object model which is only available for .NET UDFs. With the help of the UDFs you can now perform any custom operations that you need to in your multi-dimensional database. You have so far learned to design and refine your databases. In the next chapter you will learn the intricacies of updating underlying UDM data on dimensions as well as cells.

Part III

Administration, Performance Tuning Integration

11

Updating Your UDM Data

In previous chapters you saw how metadata constituting OLAP databases (the UDM) can be manipulated using the Analysis Services 2005 development environment. You learned that the metadata changes are propagated to Analysis Services instance through Create or Alter statements. Similarly, dimension and fact data within your UDM might have to be updated. For example, change of marital status for an employee, where marital status is an attribute within the employee dimension. Or perhaps an update for next fiscal year's budget based on the current year's revenue where budget is a measure within your UDM. Analysis Services 2005 provides you the ability to update dimension as well as cube data. Data updates within your UDM are referred to as a writeback because you are writing data back into an existing UDM. Updating members within your dimension is referred to as dimension writeback and updating the measure values within your cube is called cell writeback. By the way, don't let the three letter acronym throw you off; a UDM is another way of referring to a cube.

Dimension writeback enables a user to add, update, or delete dimension members; such as when a new employee joins the company, the user can update the employee dimension by adding a new member. Likewise, when an employee changes departments or leaves the company altogether, the user can update or delete relevant dimension members. When you update dimension members, Analysis Services automatically updates the corresponding tables in the data source, processes the dimension, and then cascades changes to affected cubes. In Analysis Services 2005, the operations Delete, Add, Move, and Update on dimension members are supported through BIDS, and through XML/A statements. Cell writeback supports user writeback values referred to by tuples in a cube. In a typical user scenario, a company's budget for next year is allocated based on market conditions and other factors. Analysis Services supports in-session writeback (what-if), which enables the user to change cell values directly in memory, and check resulting effects such as aggregate results and calculated values. The user can then choose to commit or discard (abort transaction) the changes. If the changes are committed, other users will be able to see those changes. You learn to writeback to dimension and cube data in this chapter through examples with the help of the sample Adventure Works DW relational data.

Updating Dimension Data in UDM

There are several circumstances where dimension data requires an update. If an organization is selling products, then adding new products to the catalog may end up on the "to do" list and hence the changes need to be reflected in the product dimension. You might come up with new promotions for a holiday season line to increase your sales and hence need to update data in your promotions dimension. One of the most common scenarios is changing data for employees. As new employees join the organization their information needs to be added to the appropriate dimension. Or existing employees' information might have to be updated due to a change in properties of the employees. Analysis Services 2005 allows you to change the dimension data through the BIDS as well as SSMS. In order to update the dimension data, the dimension first needs to be write-enabled, which means the users with write permissions on the dimension can update data. You learned the basics of dimension writeback in Chapter 8, and in this chapter you learn dimension writeback through a user scenerio.

In this section you learn how to add, delete, and update dimension members using the dimension write-back technique. Before you start implementing the scenario, you should understand that certain pre-requisites must be addressed to write data to a dimension. These prerequisites are as follows:

1. The dimension property WriteEnable needs to be set to True. This can be done in BIDS.

2. The dimension to be write-enabled must be derived from a single table, which means all dimension attributes' key and name columns have to come from a single table; that is, a snowflake dimension cannot be write-enabled.

3. If a dimension has been created from a named query, that dimension cannot be write-enabled. When dimension data is being updated, the data is updated in the backend relational database and Analysis Services needs to know the table to which the update needs to be done. In sum, Analysis Services does not support write-enabling dimensions that have been created from named queries or views in a relational database.

4. Analysis Services should have write permissions for the tables while impersonating the account specified in the data source and the dimension table cannot have auto increment key column while adding new rows.

Now that you know the limitations of the dimension writeback in Analysis Services, you can try dimension writeback on a database to understand the behavior better. Follow these steps to perform dimension writeback operations:

1. Create a UDM from a subset of the relational AdventureWorks DW data. Execute the following SQL script against the relational database to create the subset of data needed for this scenario. The following SQL script (CreateWriteBackExampleTables.sql in the Chapter 11 folder that can be downloaded from this book's accompanying web site) creates three tables, WB_Employee, WB_Period, and WB_Fact, and retrieves a subset of the data from the DimEmployee, DimTime, and FactSalesQuota tables of the Adventure works relational sample database. You are now ready to create an UDM on top of these three tables. Note that you should ignore any "cannot drop the table" messages if you get them.

```
USE [AdventureWorksDW]
GO
DROP TABLE [WB_Employee]
GO
DROP TABLE [WB_Period]
GO
DROP TABLE [WB_Fact]
```

```
GO

CREATE TABLE [dbo].[WB_Employee](
 [EmployeeKey] [int] NOT NULL,
 [ParentEmployeeKey] [int] NULL,
 [FullName] [nvarchar](101) COLLATE SQL_Latin1_General_CP1_CI_AS NOT NULL,
 [DepartmentName] [nvarchar](50) COLLATE SQL_Latin1_General_CP1_CI_AS NULL
) ON [PRIMARY]
GO


SELECT DISTINCT [CalendarQuarter]+[CalendarYear]*10 as QuarterKey,
    CAST([CalendarYear] AS VARCHAR(10) )+' Q'+
    CAST(CalendarQuarter AS VARCHAR(10)) AS QuarterName
  ,[CalendarYear]
INTO WB_Period
FROM [AdventureWorksDW].[dbo].[DimTime]

GO

INSERT INTO [WB_Employee]
SELECT [EmployeeKey]
   ,[ParentEmployeeKey]
   ,[LastName]+','+ [FirstName] AS FullName
   ,[DepartmentName]
FROM [AdventureWorksDW].[dbo].[DimEmployee]
GO

SELECT [EmployeeKey]
   ,[CalendarYear]*10 +[CalendarQuarter] AS Quarterkey
   ,[SalesAmountQuota] AS BudgetExpenseAmount
INTO WB_Fact
FROM [AdventureWorksDW].[dbo].[FactSalesQuota]
GO


INSERT INTO WB_Fact
SELECT 275, quarterkey, budgetexpenseamount
FROM dbo.WB_Fact
GO
```

2. Create a new Analysis Services project using BIDS and name it WriteBackExample.

3. Create a data source to the Adventure Works DW sample database. Make sure you set the Impersonation mode for the data source to default in the data source wizard.

4. Create a DSV and include the tables WB_Fact, WB_Period, and WB_Employee from the Adventure Works DW data source. Make sure the primary keys for all the tables are marked appropriately and establish the relationships between the tables in the DSV as shown in Figure 11-1. Note that to get the parent-child relationship, just drag and drop ParentEmployeeKey on to EmployeeKey.

5. Launch the Cube Wizard, select the defaults on various pages to create the cube. The wizard will create two dimensions: WB_Employee and WB_Period. Rename the dimensions to Employee and Period in Solution Explorer and then again in the Dimensions pane of the Cube Designer.

6. Open the Employee dimension. Rename the key and the parent attributes as Employee and Manager, respectively, for better readability. Set the NameColumn for the key attribute (Employee) in the Employee dimension to point to the Full Name column so that you can see the employee names while browsing the employee dimension's parent-child hierarchy.

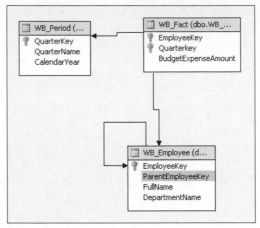

Figure 11-1

7. Delete the FullName attribute from the dimension because it is used only as the named column for the key attribute in this example. Do this by right clicking on "FullName" in the Attributes pane and selecting Delete.

8. To write-enable the WB Employee dimension, click the Employee dimension in the attribute pane of the Dimension Designer and change the dimension property WriteEnabled to True, as shown in Figure 11-2.

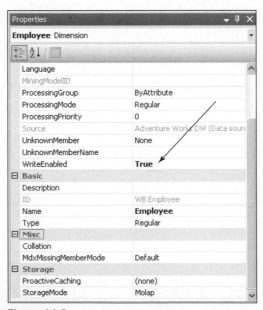

Figure 11-2

9. Deploy the Analysis Services project to your Analysis Services instance.

Adding a Member to a Dimension

In this scenario, a new employee named "Smith, James" who just joined the Adventure Works company needs to be added as a member to the Employee dimension. James will report to "Bradley, David" in the Marketing department. You can add a member to the Employee dimension through the key attribute or the parent attribute of the employee dimension because the employee dimension contains a parent-child hierarchy. You need to enter the values for all the properties for the dimension member to be added. Because you need to add a member under "Bradley, David," it is most convenient to use the Parent attribute of the Employee dimension, which is the parent-child hierarchy. Follow the steps below to add "Smith, James" to the Employee dimension:

1. Open the Employee dimension and switch to the Browser tab.

2. In the Hierarchy drop-down box, choose Manager hierarchy.

3. Click the member properties icon in the dimension Browser as shown in Figure 11-3. Select the Show All checkbox to select all the member properties and click OK.

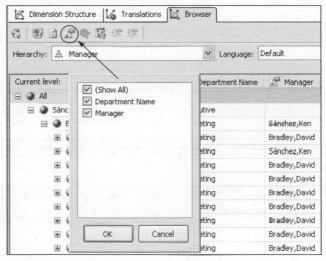

Figure 11-3

4. Click the Writeback icon (shown in Figure 11-4) to add a new member to the dimension. You will now see a new column called Key added to the Browser view, as shown in Figure 11-4. This column shows the Id of the manager. The id of the manager is the value in the key attribute hierarchy (Employee) in the dimension. If you browse the Employee attribute you will see these values for the members of the attribute.

5. In the dimension browser you can see two David Bradleys (Figure 11-4), which indicates David Bradley is a manager as well as an employee. In the tree view showing the employees, right-click the first "Bradley, David" and choose Create Child from the pop-up menu as shown in Figure 11-5. Notice that you can also create James Smith as a sibling member by selecting one of the employees reporting to David Bradley.

Writeback icon

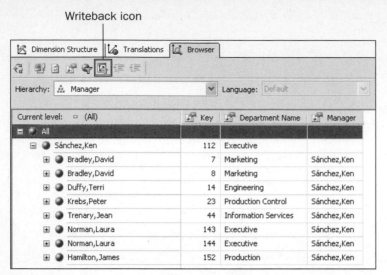

Figure 11-4

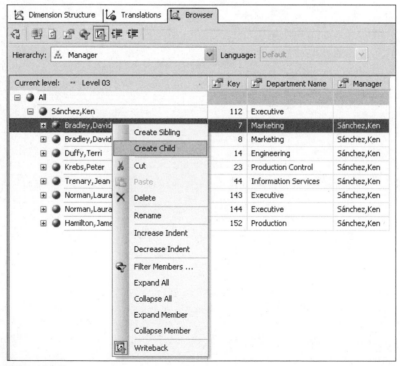

Figure 11-5

6. You will now see a new row being created under "Bradley, David" with the ParentEmployee already pre-populated with "Bradley, David". The cursor is located in the column where all the members are shown so that you can enter the name of the new employee. Enter the name "Smith, James". Enter the value 300 for the member key and Marketing as the Department Name as shown in Figure 11-6.

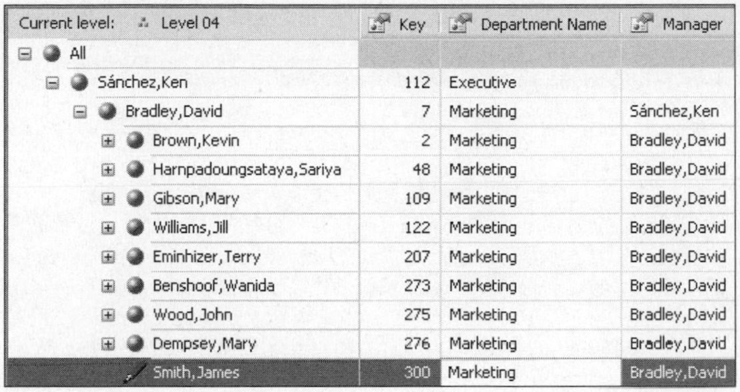

Current level: ⏶ Level 04	🔳 Key	🔳 Department Name	🔳 Manager
⊟ ⬤ All			
⊟ ⬤ Sánchez,Ken	112	Executive	
⊟ ⬤ Bradley,David	7	Marketing	Sánchez,Ken
⊞ ⬤ Brown,Kevin	2	Marketing	Bradley,David
⊞ ⬤ Harnpadoungsataya,Sariya	48	Marketing	Bradley,David
⊞ ⬤ Gibson,Mary	109	Marketing	Bradley,David
⊞ ⬤ Williams,Jill	122	Marketing	Bradley,David
⊞ ⬤ Eminhizer,Terry	207	Marketing	Bradley,David
⊞ ⬤ Benshoof,Wanida	273	Marketing	Bradley,David
⊞ ⬤ Wood,John	275	Marketing	Bradley,David
⊞ ⬤ Dempsey,Mary	276	Marketing	Bradley,David
✎ Smith,James	300	Marketing	Bradley,David

Figure 11-6

This parent-child hierarchy has a member property called Manager which is a column in the dimension browser. That column is read only because when you input a new member under a certain manager, the existing parent is populated into the Manager column automatically. Note that if you want to undo changes to a new member that was created, hit the "ESC" key. Otherwise, after you have entered all necessary values, move the cursor to a different member to add the new member to the dimension. BIDS sends the values for the new member "Smith, James" to the Analysis Services instance. The DDL sent by BIDS to Analysis Services for the dimension writeback is shown below. The Insert command is new in Analysis Services 2005 and does the writeback of the new member's values in the dimension.

```xml
<Insert xsi:type="Insert" xmlns:xsd="http://www.w3.org/2001/XMLSchema"
xmlns:xsi="http://www.w3.org/2001/XMLSchema-instance"
xmlns="http://schemas.microsoft.com/analysisservices/2003/engine">
 <Object>
  <Database>WriteBackExample</Database>
  <Cube>$WB Employee</Cube>
  <Dimension>WB Employee</Dimension>
 </Object>
 <Attributes>
  <Attribute>
   <AttributeName>Employee</AttributeName>
   <Name>Smith, James</Name>
   <Keys>
    <Key xsi:type="xsd:int">300</Key>
   </Keys>
  </Attribute>
  <Attribute>
   <AttributeName>Manager</AttributeName>
```

```
      <Keys>
       <Key xsi:type="xsd:int">7</Key>
      </Keys>
    </Attribute>
    <Attribute>
     <AttributeName>Department Name</AttributeName>
     <Keys>
       <Key xsi:type="xsd:string">Marketing</Key>
     </Keys>
    </Attribute>
   </Attributes>
 </Insert>
```

The DDL has two sections, Object and Attribute. The Object section is where the object is defined and where the cube and dimension names are specified. You already learned that each database dimension is considered a cube of single dimension within that Analysis Services database. Hence the new member is being created in the database dimension rather than the cube dimension. Therefore, you see the name $WB Employee being used to refer to the WB Employee database dimension. The newly added dimension member and its properties are specified as part of the Attributes section. Whenever dimension data is being updated, the corresponding data gets updated in the relational database and then Analysis Services does an incremental update of that dimension. Analysis Services, after receiving the command to add the new members, creates a corresponding SQL statement to update the data in the relational table WB_Employee. If there are some constraints set on this table, such as FullName cannot be null, the corresponding SQL update will fail and this will get propagated back to the dimension browser and shown to the user. If the relational update statement succeeds, the Analysis Services instance automatically does an incremental update of the dimension so that the newly added dimension gets added to the database dimension, and thereby can be accessed in all the cubes that use the dimension. Once the incremental update is successful, Analysis Services sends a response back to the dimension browser and you can proceed with additional operations.

If you query the relational table WB_Employee, you will see that a new row has been added to the relational table with the values you had entered as shown in the following table:

Key	Parentkey	FullName	Department
300	7	Smith, James	Marketing

You have now successfully added a new member to the employee dimension using the dimension writeback functionality supported through the BIDS. Next, you learn about modifying member properties of existing members.

Modifying Data of Members in a Dimension

Assume that James Smith worked for a year in the Marketing department and wanted to move to a different department for his career growth. He interviewed with the Engineering group and secured a new position. This data needs to be reflected in the Employee dimension. Assume James' new manager is Gail Erickson. Updating James' information in the employee dimension so that he has moved to a different organization needs to be done as a two-step process. You need to update the reporting structure for

James so that Erickson becomes his manager and then you need to update his new department information. Now let's go ahead and update James' information.

As mentioned in the previous section, the dimension browser does not allow you to edit the parent attribute (Manager column in this example) when you add a new member. Similarly, you cannot update or edit the Manager column directly. Therefore the BIDS provides the functionality of dragging and dropping James' information under Erickson so that his manager's name gets updated. Select the record for James in the dimension browser view with writeback enabled and then drag and drop James under "Erickson, Gail". The drag-and-drop operation can also be accomplished by cut-and-paste options available in the dimension browser. To do so, select James' record, right-click, and select Cut to remove the link from James' current manager. Then select "Erickson Gail," right-click, and select Paste so that James is moved under "Erickson, Gail".

You will see that James has now moved under "Erickson, Gail" and his manager information has been automatically updated as shown in Figure 11-7. However, other attributes of James do not get updated automatically. There are several reasons why this is true; Analysis Services does not know what attributes of a child are to be inherited from the parent. For example, you might have an attribute join date instead of department. James' join date and Erickson's join date need not be the same and hence join date for James should not be updated automatically. In this example, you see that the Department Name is one of the attributes that can be updated. It would have been nice if the Department Name updated had been done automatically. It is not, because you can have a business scenario where your manager might be a person from a different department but the work you are doing might still be the same. For example, you might have two departments coming under a general manager. A person from one of the departments might get promoted and might have to report directly to the general manager due to new responsibilities, even though he or she is working for his/her original department. Hence BIDS does not automatically update the member properties of a member when the member is moved from one parent to another. Appropriate values need to be updated by the end user.

Current level: ⁞⁞ Level 06	🔲 Key	🔲 Department Name	🔲 Manager
⊟ 🌑 All			
⊟ 🌑 Sánchez,Ken	112	Executive	
⊟ 🌑 Bradley,David	7	Marketing	Sánchez,Ken
⊞ 🌑 Brown,Kevin	2	Marketing	Bradley,David
⊞ 🌑 Harnpadoungsataya,Sariya	48	Marketing	Bradley,David
⊞ 🌑 Gibson,Mary	109	Marketing	Bradley,David
⊞ 🌑 Williams,Jill	122	Marketing	Bradley,David
⊞ 🌑 Eminhizer,Terry	207	Marketing	Bradley,David
⊞ 🌑 Benshoof,Wanida	273	Marketing	Bradley,David
⊞ 🌑 Wood,John	275	Marketing	Bradley,David
⊞ 🌑 Dempsey,Mary	276	Marketing	Bradley,David
⊞ 🌑 Bradley,David	8	Marketing	Sánchez,Ken
⊟ 🌑 Duffy,Terri	14	Engineering	Sánchez,Ken
⊟ 🌑 Tamburello,Roberto	3	Engineering	Duffy,Terri
⊞ 🌑 Walters,Rob	4	Tool Design	Tamburello,Roberto
⊞ 🌑 Walters,Rob	5	Tool Design	Tamburello,Roberto
⊟ 🌑 Erickson,Gail	11	Engineering	Tamburello,Roberto
🌑 Smith,James	300	Marketing	Erickson,Gail

Figure 11-7

BIDS sends the following update DDL to the Analysis Services instance server:

```
<Update xsi:type="Update" xmlns:xsd="http://www.w3.org/2001/XMLSchema"
xmlns:xsi="http://www.w3.org/2001/XMLSchema-instance"
xmlns="http://schemas.microsoft.com/analysisservices/2003/engine">
 <Object>
  <Database>WriteBackExample</Database>
  <Cube>$WB Employee</Cube>
  <Dimension>WB Employee</Dimension>
 </Object>
 <Attributes>
  <Attribute>
   <AttributeName>Manager</AttributeName>
   <Keys>
    <Key xsi:type="xsd:int">11</Key>
   </Keys>
  </Attribute>
 </Attributes>
 <Where>
  <Attribute>
   <AttributeName>Employee</AttributeName>
   <Keys>
    <Key xsi:type="xsd:int">300</Key>
   </Keys>
  </Attribute>
 </Where>
 <MoveWithDescendants>true</MoveWithDescendants>
</Update>
```

Similar to adding a new member, Analysis Services updates James' information in the relational data-base through appropriate relational update queries as shown in the following SQL query followed by an incremental process of the dimension. The update queries sent to the relational database can be seen if you monitor the trace (with progress events enabled) coming back from Analysis Services. You will learn to trace events on Analysis Services instances using SQL Profiler in Chapter 13. Analysis Services creates parameterized relational queries (the ? symbol indicates a parameter) to avoid SQL injection (a type of security vulnerability). The queries generated will depend on the relational backend and Analysis Services use of an appropriate cartridge (information that tells Analysis Services how to form the rela-tional queries for this database provider) for that specific relational database.

```
UPDATE [dbo].[WB_Employee]
     SET [dbo].[WB_Employee].[ParentEmployeeKey]=  ?
     WHERE
     (
     (
        [dbo].[WB_Employee].[EmployeeKey]  =  ?
     )
     )
```

In order to correctly update James' department to Engineering, you need to right click James' record and select Rename. James' record is now enabled for updates. Then click the Department Name column and change the department value from Marketing to Engineering. To complete the writeback, move the cursor to a different member. The record in the dimension table will be changed as shown in the following table:

Key ParentKey	key	FullName	Department
300	11	Smith, James	Engineering

In the DDL that was sent to the Analysis Services instance when you moved Smith, you can see a tag MoveWithDescendants set to true as shown in the following code. This tag informs Analysis Services to move all the descendants of the current member to the new parent. This is an example of a business scenario where an entire organization or division moves under a new manager.

```
<MoveWithDescendants>true</MoveWithDescendants>
```

Another common scenario is when a manager moves to a different department and all his or her direct reports automatically report to the second line manager until a new manager is identified. In such a circumstance, the MoveWithDescendants tag should be set appropriately to achieve the behavior. The dimension browser does not allow this functionality; however, you can create your own DDL and send it directly to the Analysis Services instance to achieve this behavior.

The BIDS dimension browser also facilitates moving members from one parent to another parent. All you have to do is to select multiple members by holding the Ctrl key down, and move the members to the new parent by using drag-and-drop or cut-and-paste operations. This would be helpful in circumstances where you have a re-org in your organizations.

Deleting Dimension Data

One scenario that eventually happens in all companies is an employee leaves the company. The human resources department often deletes the employee record from the main database so that payroll and benefits are terminated for the ex-employee. Analysis Services provides you support to delete members in a dimension from the dimension browser. Assume John Wood leaves the company and you need to delete the member corresponding to him in Employee dimension. To delete the member from the dimension, select the record for "Wood, John" and hit the delete button. The Delete Members dialog is launched, as shown in Figure 11-8. This dialog prompts to either delete all the descendants reporting to John Wood or make them report to John Wood's manager. If an entire group of employees under John Wood are leaving the company to start a new business or getting laid off, you would choose the Delete their descendants option. A more common scenerio is the second choice, which is Promote their descendants. Click OK after making the selection.

Figure 11-8

The BIDS dimension browser sends the drop statement to the Analysis Services instance as shown in the following code. Analysis Services sends a relational command to delete the member from the relational table and then does an incremental process of the dimension.

```
<Drop xsi:type="Drop" xmlns:xsd="http://www.w3.org/2001/XMLSchema"
xmlns:xsi="http://www.w3.org/2001/XMLSchema-instance"
xmlns="http://schemas.microsoft.com/analysisservices/2003/engine">
 <Object>
  <Database>WriteBackExample</Database>
  <Cube>$WB Employee</Cube>
  <Dimension>WB Employee</Dimension>
 </Object>
 <Where>
  <Attribute>
   <AttributeName>Employee</AttributeName>
   <Keys>
    <Key xsi:type="xsd:int">275</Key>
   </Keys>
  </Attribute>
 </Where>
</Drop>
```

If the dimension member had fact data in a fact table associated with him or her, the fact data will not be available for querying. Even though the data is processed inside the cube while querying, Analysis Services will not be able to identify the associated member and hence not return results for this member. You can send the following query to the Analysis Services instance before and after deletion of the member John Wood to see the difference between the returned result sets.

```
select measures.members on columns,
{[WB Employee].[Manager].&[7],
[WB Employee].[Manager].&[7].children } on rows
from [Adventure Works DW]
```

Be aware that Analysis Services automatically deletes dimension entries from a dimension table, but does not automatically delete the corresponding fact table entry from the fact table. The fact table entries for the deleted "Wood, John" (key 275) is still in the fact table. Before you remove the dimension member, you need to make sure that the dimension member doesn't have any data in the fact table. The fact data does exist within the UDM; it is just being restricted by Analysis Services. It is being restricted because the corresponding dimension member was deleted. Such fact data is referred to as orphan fact data. Because the dimension data corresponding to John Wood has been deleted and the fact data is still available, if you do a full process of the database you will see processing errors because Analysis Services by default checks for referential integrity. You can change the error configuration settings on the cube to handle the rows (delete or associate it with Unknown member of the dimension) associated with John Wood or you can delete the entries corresponding to John Wood using the following SQL statement and then reprocess the entire database:

```
delete from WB_Fact
where employeekey = 275
```

Analysis Services 2005 provides you BIDS and SSMS for you to directly add, edit, and remove dimension members. You can manually create dimension members for small dimensions within dimension browser. It is very helpful to users during the development phase of your UDM so that you can make appropriate modifications to your dimension data. In order to update the dimension data in your UDM, Analysis Services updates the data in the underlying relational table and then does an incremental process to update the data in the UDM. You should be aware that using BIDS for updating dimension data can reduce performance, because Analysis Services sends relational queries for each member update separately to update the dimension data in the relational database followed by the incremental process. If your scenario is to do a bulk operations such as moving an entire organization from one geographical location to another and you need to update all the dimension members, you are better off updating the relational database through bulk update and then processing the dimension.

We consider the dimension writeback supported by the dimension browser in BIDS or SSMS to be helpful under specific circumstances. This would be helpful during modeling and adding new members to see the dimension structure. Most often the relational database that stores the dimension data might not be accessible to the person who is involved in maintenance of your cubes and dimensions. The Analysis Services administrator might have granted permissions to a specific account that can access the relational backend that is part of the server role of Analysis Services or specified as part of the database data source impersonation, as seen in Chapter 2. Under such circumstances, as an administrator of the Analysis Services database you can update the dimension data through the dimension writeback supported by Analysis Services tools. We recommend the use of dimension data update through the dimension browser whenever you have limited data to update or the frequency of updates is quite low, once a month, for example. Everyone accessing the UDM cannot perform updates on dimensions. Users who are part of a role that has explicit write permissions and process permissions specified for dimensions can only do dimension writeback.

Now that you have learned how to update dimension data using the dimension browser, you should also be aware of the prerequisites which you learned earlier and the limitations in the Analysis Services tools. The developer designing the dimension needs to take into account the limitations. Two limitations we are aware of that you can potentially encounter while using dimension browser for writeback are:

1. If attributes within the dimension have different name and key columns defined, you cannot writeback to the dimension. The only exception is for the attributes that have Usage set to Key and Parent.

2. Dimension attributes need to have Discretization Method specified to None. This is because if an attribute has been discretized into a specific bucket, you cannot write the discretized value back to the relational data. It would have been better if Analysis Services would have disabled writeback on those specific attributes rather than not allowing writeback on the entire dimension.

These limitations are only due to the design of the dimension writeback through the dimension browser. If you write your own tool to update dimension data, you can send appropriate DDLs to Insert, Update, or Delete members to overcome the limitations.

Now that you have successfully learned to update dimension data, the following section discusses the need to update cell values in your cube. This is a common scenario for a lot of business organizations and we hope you will find the next section extremely useful.

Updating Your Cube Data

The ability to create "hypothetical" what-if scenarios is central to business intelligence because it enables the executive to explore contingencies associated with the financial landscape. In this way, the executive can seek out the profit maximizing potential of the firm while minimizing risk and generally mitigating threats. Because these concepts are so much better explained by way of example, here are two specific examples to help you understand what is meant by what-if scenarios.

In the first example, a company president is considering her options in terms of resource allocation for the coming fiscal year. Her BI team has astutely developed UDM that calculate key business drivers for the company. Because the user can writeback new values into those seed measures, new configurations of company resource allocation can be tried and the results assessed. The key business metrics will be re-calculated due to new values entered into the system. The sorts of questions that can be "asked" of the system through the use of these simulations depend on how many measures are designed to act as seed values. Typical questions include, "What if we increase our advertising budget for the next fiscal year?" "What if we charge more (or less) for our product?" and "What if we take on more debt to expand production facilities and therefore enhance manufacturing capacity?" Keep in mind that not just any question could be asked of the system. Only those questions that have the required measures available for use as seed values and underlying calculations or KPIs in support of cascading correct changes will provide meaningful results.

The second example considers the needs of a bank. The vice-president is considering strategies for the coming year regarding appropriate risk distribution for commercial loan application acceptance. The bank has good metrics from which to base calculations on successful loan repayments versus defaults and those metrics have been entered into the relevant cubes. If banks are anything like most bureaucratic organizations, they likely have regulations that mandate certain minimum distributions of loans to different risk categories. For example, in the interest of economic development and creating new active bank customers in the future, a certain percentage of high-risk loans should be accepted. The vice-president is most likely looking to give loans so as to maximize income from loans for the bank; with a fund of $500 million from which to make loans, the president can consider the manipulation of multiple seed values like interest rates and risk acceptance percentages. In the end, some optimal state will emerge, such as allocating $100 million to low risk, $250 million for moderate risk, and $150 million to high risk businesses.

In financial applications (corporate plan, budget, and forecast systems), most of the time the UDM is applied as a data gathering and analysis business model to gather data input from all departments, and perform many what-if analyses for future business decisions. Once the analysts make a final decision, the data values need to be updated in the cube for appropriate actions to be taken. For example, the budget for a department might get allocated based on the current year's revenue and that department would have to plan the next fiscal year's financial plans based on the allocated budget. If the executives have made a forecast of achieving specific revenue for the next year, other business decisions need to be propagated to the people in the corporate food chain appropriately. For example, if the sales target for the organization was to have 500 million dollars (10% growth over the current year), the business goals or commitments for the individual sales employees need to be appropriately set to reach the organization goal. In this section you learn how to effectively use Analysis Services to provide what-if scenarios to top executives and to update the cube data so that it can be appropriately propagated to the entire organization. Updating the data in an Analysis Services cube is referred to as cell writeback because you are updating the cell values in the cube space.

You will use the cube created in the previous section to learn about updating data within the cube. Consider the scenario where you need to allocate the budget amount for the group lead by Amy Alberts. Amy has three employees reporting to her and the budget needs to be distributed to her reports based on certain business factors. You will consider examples of various ways in which allocation of data can be accomplished with the cube's data. Analysis Services 2005 does not provide a front-end interface to update cube data unlike updating dimension data through the dimension browser. However, you can build your own application once you know what MDX statements to send to Analysis Services. Hence the examples you see in this section are primarily MDX statements, which you need to execute through SQL Server Management Studio to help you understand how to update the cube data. The following steps show how to make modifications to the cube so that you can use the database for understanding data allocation and update of cube data:

1. Execute the SQL queries (CreateWriteBackExampleTables.sql in the Chapter 11 folder that can be downloaded from the accompanying web site) initially executed to ensure you have all the dimension members. Open the dimension WB Period in the Analysis Services cube used in the previous section.

2. Rename the key attribute as Quarter, and have the name column for the key attribute set to QuarterName. Remove the attribute hierarchy QuarterName and create a user hierarchy Period that has two levels, Calendar, Year and Quarter, as shown in Figure 11-9. Open the Adventure Works DW cube in the WriteBackExample database and delete the measure WB_Fact Count that was created by intellicube. You will learn later in this section why you need to delete the measure with aggregation function Count.

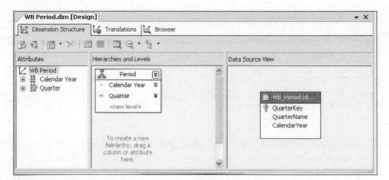

Figure 11-9

3. Deploy the changes to your Analysis Services instance.

4. Send the following MDX query to the cube:

```
select {[WB Employee].[Manager].&[290],
[WB Employee].[Manager].&[290].children} on 1 ,
[WB Period].[Period].&[2004].children on 0
from [Adventure Works DW]
```

5. The results of this MDX query are shown in the following table. The cell values show the Budget Expense amount for various quarters for employees reporting to Amy Alberts. Notice that the value for 2004 Q3 is not available.

	2004 Q1	2004 Q2	2004 Q3
Alberts,Amy	2072000	2865000	(null)
Alberts,Amy	116000	1000	(null)
Pak,Jae	883000	1329000	(null)
Varkey Chudukatil,Ranjit	707000	908000	(null)
Valdez,Rachel	366000	627000	(null)

6. You are aware that a cube contains one or more measure groups. When a cube is enabled to update data, that means that one or more measure groups are enabled for updating data in the cube. Typically, a fact table would correspond to a measure group in the cube. Each measure group contains one or more partitions. The data from the relational data source is read and stored within partitions by Analysis Services. In order to update the data within the cube you need to have a new partition called the writeback partition for each measure group you need to enable for updating data. Any data (measure values) that gets updated in the cube space will be entered into this writeback partition. The writeback partition is a partition that points to a relational data source. This data can reside within the same relational data source used by the cube or in a different relational database. Similar to restrictions in writing back to dimensions, Analysis Services has restrictions in writing back to a measure group. You can write enable a cube for updating data only when all the measures in the measure group have an aggregation function as Sum. Even if one of the measures has an aggregation function as count, distinct count, or any of the semi-additive aggregation functions, the measure group cannot be write-enable for writeback. Hence whenever you want to enable a cube for cell writeback you need to have measures that have aggregation function other than Sum to be in a separate measure group.

7. In order to enable updating data within the cube, connect to the database you have deployed; you can either use BIDS or SQL Server Management Studio. Within the BIDS, click the partitions tab of the Adventure Works DW cube. Select the partition WB Fact, right-click, and then select Writeback Settings as shown in Figure 11-10.

8. You will now be presented with the Enable Writeback dialog shown in Figure 11-11. When data is being written back to the cells of a cube, Analysis Services stores appropriate information in a relational database table. You learn about this information later in this chapter. For now assume it is stored in a table. Because Analysis Services needs to store some information in a relational table, you need to specify a data source that points to a database where Analysis Services has write permissions. In the enable writeback dialog you need to specify the data source and the name of the table to store the cell writeback data. By default, Analysis Services chooses the existing data source that is used by the partition with the writeback table name as WritebackTable_ <PartitionName>. If you do not want the writeback table within the same database as that of your relational backend, you can specify a new data source in the enable writeback dialog by clicking New. Once you have specified the writeback table, click the OK button. You can write-enable a measure group even through SQL Server Management Studio. To do so, connect to the Analysis Services database using SQL Server Management Studio, navigate to the measure group, right-click the measure group, and select Writeback Options⇨Enable Writeback. You will see the same enable writeback dialog similar to Figure 11-11 to specify the data source and the writeback table.

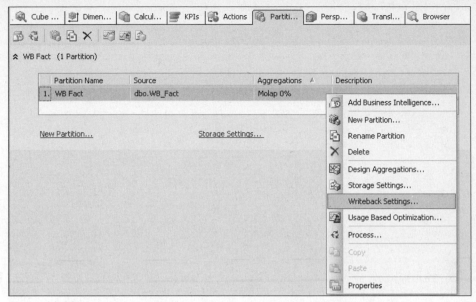

Figure 11-10

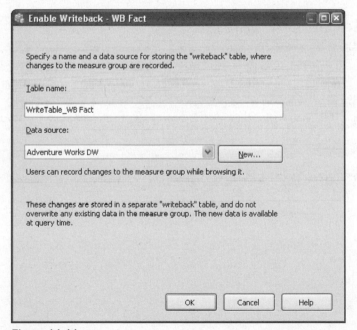

Figure 11-11

9. Once you click OK in the enable writeback dialog, the Partition editor automatically creates a ROLAP partition for Writeback_WB Fact. You can see a new partition called Writeback_WB Fact added to the measure group WB Fact in the partition list. When you deploy the entire project to the Analysis Services instance, the writeback partition metadata gets updated for the WriteBackExample database. The BIDS then sends a process command to process the database. At the time of processing the writeback partition, Analysis Services checks if the writeback table exists in the specified data source. If not, Analysis Services instance creates the writeback table by sending the following CREATE SQL statement. You do have the option of forcibly creating the writeback table at the time of each process of the measure group in the DDL, but by default Analysis Services creates the table only if it does not exist in the database.

```
CREATE TABLE [dbo].[WriteTable_WB Fact](
 [BudgetExpenseAmount_0] [float] NULL,
 EmployeeKey_1] [int] NULL,
 [QuarterKey_2] [int] NULL,
 [MS_AUDIT_TIME_3] [datetime] NULL,
 [MS_AUDIT_USER_4] [nvarchar](255) COLLATE SQL_Latin1_General_CP1_CI_AS NULL
) ON [PRIMARY]
```

10. Once the writeback table has been created, the cube has been enabled for writeback. You can now update the budget values for 2004 Q3. You have the option to writeback to a single cell or multiple cells depending on where you write the data. You will learn the various options in the next few sections.

Update a Single Cell Value

One of the scenarios is to update a single cell value in the cube. For example, you need to allocate a budget of $1000 for Jae Pak. Follow these instructions to update the cell value corresponding to Jae Pak:

1. Open SSMS and create two new MDX query windows.

2. Select the database WriteBackExample and the Adventure Works DW cube.

3. In step 5 of the previous section you saw the budget value for 2004 Q3 for employee Jae Pak was null. Send the following update statement to update the budget value for employee Jae Pak:

```
UPDATE CUBE [Adventure Works DW]
SET ( [WB Employee].[Manager].&[291]
, [WB Period].[Period].&[20043]) = 1000
//Updating the budget for employee Jae Pak for Quarter 3 of year 2004
```

4. The update statement is used to update the cell values in the cube. The syntax of the update statement is shown below.

```
UPDATE CUBE <CubeName>
SET <Tuple Expression> = Numeric or String value
[ALLOCATION TYPE clause]
```

5. The UPDATE CUBE syntax is pretty straightforward where you specify the coordinates in the cube to update the new value. The allocation type clause is an optional clause by which you can specify the nature of the allocation. You see examples of various allocation types later in this chapter through examples.

6. In the update statement the coordinate pointed by the tuple ([WB Employee].[Manger].&[291], [WB Period].[Period].&[20043]) refers to the budget value for Jae Pak. The statement updates the cell value to 1000.

7. If you send the following query to the cube you will see that the budget value for Jae Pak is now 1000:

```
SELECT {
[WB Employee].[Manager].&[291] } ON 1 ,
[WB Period].[Period].&[20043] ON 0
FROM
[Adventure Works DW]
```

8. Send the same query in the second MDX query editor window. You will see the original value null rather than the new value 1000. The update statement and the value only take effect for the first MDX window, which holds one connection (or session). Other connections (or sessions) are not affected by the updated value. This is because Analysis Services updates the new cell value only if you request it to make these changes permanently in the cube. In order to do that you need to send the commit statement to the server as shown below.

```
COMMIT
```

9. COMMIT is a short form for COMMIT TRANSACTION statement. By default, when you start executing new queries within SQL Server Management Studio, an implicit statement called BEGIN TRANSACTION is executed. Due to the changes, cell values will get updated only after you call the COMMIT TRANSACTION or just the COMMIT statement. When the COMMIT statement is executed, Analysis Services gets the new value to be written, subtracts the original cell value for that tuple, and then writes back the difference in the ROLAP partition that has been set up for writeback. Because the original cell value was null and the new value is 1000, you should see 1000 in the ROLAP partition.

10. Send the following query to the relational table in the Adventure Works DW database. You will see that there is a new entry in the relational table that has a value of 1000.

```
select * from [WriteTable_WB Fact]
```

11. If you go to the second MDX query window and query the cell value for Jae Pak, you will see the new value 1000.

12. Analysis Services allows you to send multiple updates within a transaction so that you have the ability to roll back or commit the entire transaction that does an update to cube. You can include one or more update queries within the statements Begin Transaction and Commit Transaction query, to start a transaction for cell update.

13. After the update statement, send the first MDX query in the same query window:

```
SELECT {[WB Employee].[Manager].&[290],
[WB Employee].[Manager].&[290].children
} on 1 ,
[WB Period].[Period].&[2004].children on 0
FROM [Adventure Works DW]
```

14. You will see the results shown in the following table. Notice that Alberts, Amy, parent member of Pak, Jae, got the 1000 aggregated. Analysis Services takes care of calculations and aggregations of the data written back to the cells automatically.

	2004 Q1	2004 Q2	2004 Q3
Alberts,Amy	2072000	2865000	1000
Alberts,Amy	116000	1000	(null)
Pak,Jae	883000	1329000	1000
Valdez,Rachel	366000	627000	(null)
Varkey Chudukatil,Ranjit	707000	908000	(null)

15. Switch to the first MDX window, and send the following query to update the same cell to 800. If you are executing the following statements in SQL Server Management Studio, execute them as separate statements by selecting the statement and then pressing execute or Ctrl+E to execute; that is, Begin Transaction should first be highlighted and executed, followed by the update statement and then the Commit Transaction statement.

```
BEGIN TRANSACTION


UPDATE CUBE [Adventure Works DW]
SET ( [WB Employee].[Manager].&[291]
, [WB Period].[Period].&[20043]) = 800


COMMIT TRANSACTION
```

16. If you send a query to retrieve the data for Jae Pak for Quarter 3 of 2004 in both MDX query windows, you will see the exact same value of 800.

Analysis Services uses the ROLAP partition to implement the cell writeback; when you send the update cell query the cell data value is held in memory for that specific session and transaction. When a user sends the commit statement, the change in cell value is written to the writeback table by Analysis Services. Because the writeback partition is ROLAP, other connections or users will pick up the data change immediately without reprocessing the cube.

Now open a SQL query window and connect to Adventure Works DW relational database and send the SQL query to retrieve all the rows in the Writeback table. You will see the results shown in the following table.

Budget Expense Amount_0	EmployeeKey_1	QuarterKey_2	MS_AUDIT_TIME_3	MS_AUDIT_USER_4
1000	291	20043	42:31.0	Sivah04\sivah
−200	291	20043	45:40.0	Sivah04\sivah

In the table you will see two rows being entered for the measure value. Recall that the first value of 1000 was the first update statement you executed. When you executed the second update statement, you updated the cell value to 800. The difference of -200 is therefore entered for the same tuple within the writeback table. When a new query comes in, the aggregated data of 1000-200 + the cell value within the cube is seen by the user. Note Analysis Services logs the time and the user who did the update to the cell. Consider this as a tracking mechanism for you to trace the writeback operations. If you notice serious discrepancies in your data, due to the logging of user and time when the update was done, users cannot deny what they did and this might come in handy if you are audited.

Update NON-Leaf Cell Value using Allocation

The previous example demonstrates how to update for Jae Pak who is a leaf member in the dimension who does not have any reports under him. A leaf-level cell in Analysis Services means all dimension members of that cell are on the granularity level; for example, member "Pak, Jae" doesn't have children and you choose to write to Q4. If you have another dimension, you would have to include a member from that dimension for the granularity attribute. However, in many cases, a user might want to input a number at a higher level granularity and allocate down to the leaf-level members via different rules. For instance, a user can input an entire year's budget and allocate to each quarter by last year's sales. In this section, you would allocate the budget for each employee reporting to Amy Alberts using the value allocated to Amy Alberts. Analysis Services provides several ways to allocate/update values for non-leaf level cells. Because the actual data being allocated cannot be held directly in a non-leaf cell within Analysis Services, the data needs to be propagated to the non-leaf-level cells. The most obvious and easiest way to allocate in this way is to allocate the value equally to all the leaf-level cells.

Equal Allocation

Consider the scenario where Amy Alberts is allocated $1,000 and this needs to be propagated to her and all her direct reports, because she also needs to budget for the work she does. As seen with the UPDATE statement syntax you have an optional allocation clause. In order to allocate this value equally to her direct reports, you need to specify the keyword USE_EQUAL_ALLOCATION. Before you execute the update statement below send an update statement to set the budget value for Jae Pak to 0. Following MDX query will update the budget value for Amy Alberts by equally allocating the value to her direct reports:

```
UPDATE CUBE [Adventure Works DW]
SET (
[WB Employee].[Manager].&[290]
, [WB Period].[Period].&[20043]) = 1000
USE_EQUAL_ALLOCATION
```

After this update statement, if you send the following query you will see that each of the employees reporting to Amy Alberts will get a value of 250 as shown in the following table.

```
SELECT {[WB Employee].[Manager].&[290],
[WB Employee].[Manager].&[290].children
} on 1 ,
[WB Period].[Period].&[2004].children on 0
FROM [Adventure Works DW]
```

	2004 Q1	2004 Q2	2004 Q3
Alberts,Amy	2072000	2865000	1000
Alberts,Amy	116000	1000	250
Pak,Jae	883000	1329000	250
Varkey Chudukatil,Ranjit	707000	908000	250
Valdez,Rachel	366000	627000	250

If you did not specify the allocation clause to be USE_EQUAL_ALLOCATION, Analysis Services assumes that the data allocated needs to be equally distributed to all the children. Therefore, the following UPDATE statement will also result in the same results as shown in the previous table:

```
UPDATE CUBE [Adventure Works DW]
SET (
[WB Employee].[Manager].&[290]
, [WB Period].[Period].&[20043]) = 1000
```

Now that you have learned how to update data to a non-leaf member, you will learn the remaining allocation options provided by Analysis Servivces.

Weighted Allocation

In a more complex scenario, allocation of budgets depends on the size of the organization or the revenue generated by the person (or group) in the previous year. A common form of allocation in the real-world is to allocate values based on rates calculated by using last period's budget rate plus some percentage increase to determine this period's value, or just use last year's sales to allocate this year's budget. Analysis Services provides a way to write back data to leaf levels using various proportions, and hence such an allocation is called weighted allocation.

Consider a case such that Amy Alberts gets $1,000 as a budget and she wants to allocate it to her direct reports and herself based on the ratio calculated from the previous quarter. Now, how do you go about forming an update statement that will accomplish this scenario? Let's first break it down and build the MDX.

First, you know the update statement to allocate to Amy Alberts is:

```
UPDATE CUBE [Adventure Works DW]
SET (
[WB Employee].[Manager].&[290]
, [WB Period].[Period].&[20043]) = 1000
```

Next, you need to add the allocation clause. For weighted or ratio allocation you need to use the keyword USE_WEIGHTED_ALLOCATION BY, which gets added at the end of the preceding statement. Following the USE_WEIGHTED_ALLOCATION BY you need to specify a ratio or weight that will derive the rate based on the previous quarter. The following MDX expression calculates the ratio of budget for the previous quarter for the employees reporting to Amy Alberts.

```
([WB Period].[Period].[20042], [WB Employee].[Manager].currentmember)/
([WB Employee].[Manager].&[290],[WB Period].[Period].[20042])
```

The first part of the MDX expression takes the current member in the context of the query, which will be one of the direct reports of Amy Alberts and their budget value in the second quarter of 2004. The second part of the MDX query provides the budget value for Amy Alberts for the second quarter of 2004. Because the value for Amy Alberts is an aggregated data of all her reports, you get a ratio of each employee's budget as compared to the overall budget allocated to Amy Alberts in the second quarter of 2004.

Combining all the sections of the MDX you have seen, you will have the following MDX query to allocate the budget to Amy Albert's team based on a ratio of the previous quarter:

```
update cube [Adventure Works DW]
set (
[WB Employee].[Manager].&[290]
, [WB Period].[Period].&[20043]) = 1000 use_weighted_allocation by
([WB Period].[Period].&[20042], [WB Employee].[Manager].currentmember)/
([WB Employee].[Manager].&[290],[WB Period].[Period].&[20042])
```

If you execute the MDX query to retrieve the budget amount for all the children of Amy Albets for various quarters of 2004 after executing the update statement, you should see the results shown in the following table. In the RTM version of the product the allocation does not get distributed. We believe this is a bug that might be resolved in service packs. We will provide an update through the download site on this example.

	2004 Q1	2004 Q2	2004 Q3
Alberts,Amy	2072000	2865000	1000
Alberts,Amy	116000	1000	0.34904014
Pak,Jae	883000	1329000	463.8743455
Valdez,Rachel	366000	627000	218.8481675
Varkey Chudukatil,Ranjit	707000	908000	316.9284468

Incremental Allocation

The third scenario is where a cell already has a value and you need to allocate values to leaf-level cells so that they are incremented by the new value allocated — based on equal allocation or weighted allocation. Consider an organization that receives funding from multiple sources and these funds need to be allocated to subdivisions one by one. Further, you do not want to overwrite the previous data. Before you learn about incremental allocation, please delete the Writeback table in the relational data source and reprocess the WriteBackExample database.

Lets say Amy Alberts obtained funding in the amount of $1,000 for Jae Pak in support of the project he is working on. Amy allocates this budget directly to Jae for quarter 3 of 2004. Send the following update statement to allocate the budget to Jae.

```
UPDATE CUBE [Adventure Works DW]
SET (
[WB Employee].[Manager].&[290]
, [WB Period].[Period].&[20043]) = 1000
```

Now assume Amy gets funding in the amount of $1,000 for the entire group and she wants to allocate this equally to all her direct reports. She obviously does not want to overwrite the existing budget value allocated for Jae already. Analysis Services provides a way to allocate this new budget amount to the leaf-level cells either through equal or through weighted allocation. The allocation clause keyword that needs to be used is USE_EQUAL_INCREMENT or USE_WEIGHTED_INCREMENT along with the weight as seen in the Weighted allocation example.

Consider the scenario where Amy wants to allocate the amount equally. The MDX query to do this allocation is:

```
update cube [Adventure Works DW]
set (
[WB Employee].[Manager].&[290]
, [WB Period].[Period].&[20043]) = 2000 use_equal_increment
```

Send the following MDX query to see if the allocation with increment worked correctly:

```
select {[WB Employee].[Manager].&[290],
[WB Employee].[Manager].&[290].children
} on 1 ,
[WB Period].[Period].&[2004].children on 0
from
[Adventure Works DW]
```

You will see the results shown in the following table whereby Jae Pak's budget for 2004 Q3 is now $1,250 and the budget for remaining employees is $250 each. Note the total budget allocated for Amy and her direct reports is $2,000, which is sum of the budget of all employees reporting to her.

	2004 Q1	2004 Q2	2004 Q3
Alberts,Amy	2072000	2865000	2000
Alberts,Amy	116000	1000	250
Pak,Jae	883000	1329000	1250
Valdez,Rachel	366000	627000	250
Varkey Chudukatil,Ranjit	707000	908000	250

Similarly you can use the USE_WEIGHTED_INCREMENT option to writeback to the cell corresponding to Amy Alberts and see that the budget gets distributed based on weights and also gets added to existing budget amounts.

You learned how to update a cube's cell data using the cell writeback feature of Analysis Services 2005. You also learned that the changes are propagated back to the cube only when you issue a commit statement. Therefore, you can perform many what-if scenarios by doing allocations followed by queries; this will surface the influence of the allocations on the financial status of the company. Typically we expect calculations to be defined in MDX scripts that make use of the measure values such as budget, which will reflect the overall profit or key performance indicators of the company. If the updates you have done do not yield the expected results, you can roll back the complete transaction thereby preventing the entire update operation to be propagated to the writeback table.

You learned how to writeback values to your cube and do what-if analysis or scenarios by sending MDX queries to see the effects of the writeback. Similar to dimension writeback where you had certain limitations, there are some things you should be aware of while updating cell values using the UPDATE statement. Assume you have a large cube with several dimensions (greater than twenty dimensions). Due to multidimensionality, a specific cell is now referred to by multiple dimensions. If you do an allocation using the UPDATE statement that includes only a few dimension's granularity attributes, Analysis Services will try to equally distribute the value allocated to a cell in the cube to all the leaf-level cells (across all the hierarchies in each dimension). Hence if you do an update on a cell that is referred to by the topmost-level on certain dimensions, the update to leaf levels can be quite expensive because Analysis Services needs to equally distribute the value across all members of all dimensions. Such an update will result in a lot of rows being entered into the writeback table. Hence whenever possible please make sure you do the writeback to the appropriate level intended. We are just warning you about data expansion.

To understand the data expansion problem better, consider the following example of updating Amy Alberts's budget for the year 2003 which is referred to by the tuple ([WB Employee].[Manager].&[290], [WB Period].[Period].&[2003]). This will update all the leaf-level members, which is the product of all the members reporting to Amy Alberts and all the quarters in 2003. This update results in changes to 16 cells at the leaf level. Imagine dimensions that have hundreds or even thousands of members. As with a Product dimension, a simple mistake of updating at the topmost level will cascade out with millions of leaf-level cells being updated — and you will see millions of rows in the writeback table. To mitigate this problem you need to identify meaningful leaf-level cells and then writeback to just those specific cells.

Keep in mind that you can still do what-if analysis on a cube, even if the cube is not enabled for writeback. The changed measure cannot be committed back to the server if the cube doesn't have a writeback partition. However, you can still do a "begin transaction," update cell values, and send MDX queries to view the results of the measure (cell value) change, and then simply "rollback transaction" when finished.

Summary

In this chapter you worked with simple examples that demonstrated dimension writeback and cell writeback; specifically, how updates of cell values in cubes are executed. Many possible forms of data manipulation can be used to address the scenarios discussed in this chapter, from the most basic mathematical manipulations to weighted allocations. The changes to cells in a cube will affect the leaf level cells in the cube. Once the leaf level cells are updated, then dependent cells are updated through a cascading effect. Hence measures, calculations, and KPIs dependent on these updates are all impacted and their new values can be queried through MDX for data analysis.

You have so far learned to design dimensions and cubes, extend MDX using stored procedures, and finally to update data in dimensions in cubes. These abilities are all targeted towards data warehouse designers and developers. As with any server product, administrators are required to provide high availability of the servers and maintain a secure environment. In the next chapter you learn to perform administrative tasks on the Analysis Services instances through SSMS as well as use custom code through the management objects model Analysis Management Objects (AMO).

12

Administering
Analysis Services

Administration is an important task on any server product. As an administrator of Analysis Services you need to make sure Analysis Services is secure, reliable and provides efficient access to the end users. You can administer Analysis Server in two ways; through the SQL Server 2005 Tool set (SSMS or BIDS) or programmatically using an object model called AMO (Analysis Management Objects). You can accomplish tasks like processing objects, providing access to Analysis Services objects in databases and synchronization of databases between Analysis Services instances using SSMS. You can use BIDS to connect to a specific OLAP database to perform design changes and accomplish follow-on tasks such as processing and providing access to users. SSMS and BIDS both use AMO behind the scenes to accomplish all management tasks. The AMO object model itself is installed and registered into the GAC (Global Assembly Cache) when the product is installed. The AMO .NET assembly, by the way, is Microsoft.AnalysisSevices.dll. In the first section of this chapter you learn about key administrative tasks and how to accomplish those tasks using SSMS and BIDS, and in the second section you learn more about the programmatic approach, using AMO, to accomplish the same tasks and others.

Administration using
SQL Server 2005 Tools

Let's just jump in and get our feet wet, shall we? In chapter 2 you used SSMS to view the objects found in an Analysis Services 2005 database. We'll start here on a similar footing; first, open SSMS, connect to Analysis Services, and open the Databases folder. You will see a tree view of those databases you have saved on the server to date, as shown in Figure 12-1. One of those databases should be titled AnalysisServices2005Tutorial—you should take a moment to review the tree nodes and what they contain because you will be learning the administrative tasks associated with those objects.

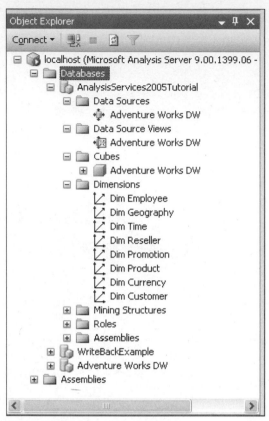

Figure 12-1

Managing the Server

SSMS, the integrated management environment for SQL Server 2005 products, provides you the flexibility of managing several Analysis Servers. In this chapter we use the word "server" to denote an instance of Analysis Services, and "servers" to denote one or more. If you have a set of Production Servers that are being used for customers and a set of Test Servers that are being used for development and testing purposes, you typically want to manage them differently. The most logical thing is to group these servers. Using the Register Servers windows of SQL Server Management Studio you can group a set of Analysis Servers to form a Server group as shown in Figure 12-2. You can register several Analysis Servers or organize a few Analysis Servers into a group and manage them using the Server Group and Server Registration dialogs that can be launched by right clicking on Analysis Services folder in the Register Servers window.

Some of the common tasks of starting, stopping, restarting or configuring Analysis Services instances can be accomplished from the Registered Servers window. You can right-click the specific Analysis Services instance and choose the appropriate operation. In addition to that you can connect to the server in the object explorer or launch the MDX query editor from this window.

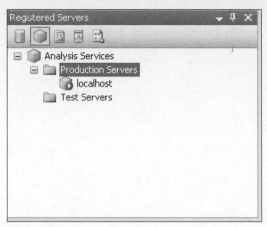

Figure 12-2

Once you are connected to an Analysis Services instance in the Object Explorer window you can accomplish various administrative tasks on the server, such as creating new databases, providing permissions, creating new databases, processing objects, and moving databases from test servers to production servers. First and foremost for the Analysis Server admin is to provide access permissions to the users who will be administering the server. The following steps show how you can add a user as an administrator of an Analysis Services instance by making them part of the object called Server Role:

1. In the Object Explorer window right-click on the Analysis Services instance and select Properties.

2. You will now see the Analysis Services properties dialog.

3. Click Security in the page as shown in Figure 12-3. Click the Add button to add a user to Analysis Services administrators group. You can only add domain users or groups as part of the administrator group for Analysis Services. If your user is a local user you can specify machinename\username to add the user to this server administrator group.

Another important management task is to set appropriate properties for Analysis Services for enabling features or configuring certain properties so that Analysis Services performs optimally. You can change the properties using the Analysis Services properties dialog shown in Figure 12-4. Analysis Services needs to be restarted for certain properties to take effect. This is indicated by a "yes" in the Restart column in the Analysis Server Properties dialog. Some of the most important properties involve control of parallelism for processing and querying; changing the read buffer size for reading data from disk for faster query response time. Equally important are maximum amount of memory to be used by the Analysis Services processes, controlling the maximum number of connections to the server, and the ability to turn server features on and off. You learn some of these properties in this chapter and others in Chapter 13.

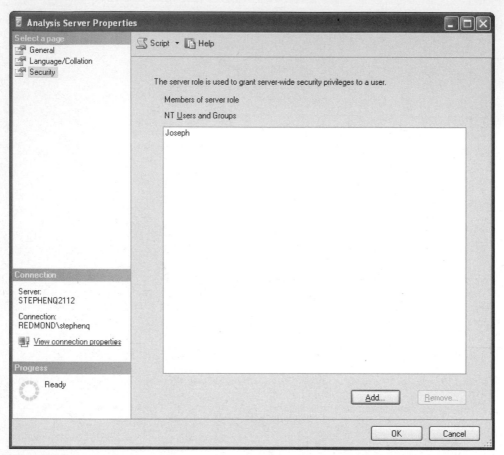

Figure 12-3

Managing Analysis Services Objects

Several management tasks can be performed on Analysis Services objects. Some of the most important tasks are processing of cubes and dimensions, providing access permissions to various objects within a database, managing the partitions of a cube based on usage, and adding assemblies to databases. Even though the SQL Server Management Studio provides a great interface to manage Analysis Services 2005 and abstracts all the internal details, it is beneficial to understand the underlying operations that take place when you perform the management operations. Knowledge of the server internals gives you the edge of understanding the operations better and effectively managing the server when unforeseen problems occur.

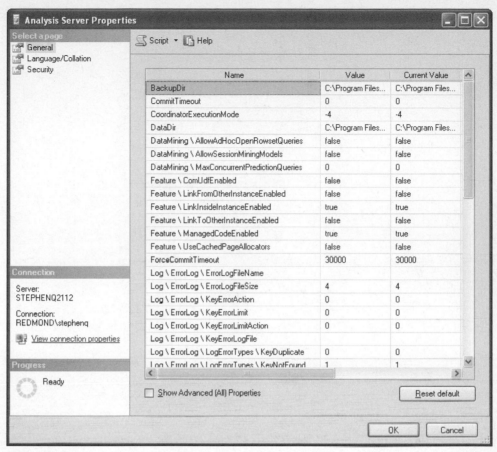

Figure 12-4

All communications to Analysis Services is through XML for Analysis (XML/A). The management tasks executed through SSMS use the management object model AMO (Analysis Management Objects), which in turn sends XML/A Execute commands to the Analysis Services instance. You will see some of the commands sent to the server while performing the management tasks in this chapter.

Processing Analysis Services Database Objects

One of the important jobs of an Analysis Services DBA (database administrator) is to process the objects resident in databases. Analysis Services 2005 provides fine-grain control to the Analysis Services DBA to process the objects within an Analysis Services database using the Process dialog. You can launch the Process dialog by right-clicking the object folders such as Cubes, Dimensions, and Mining Structures — this works just as well on individual objects or groups of objects too. Based on the location from which the Process dialog is launched, the options for processing the object or group of objects will vary. In addition to this you can select an object and launch the process dialog. To process the database AnalysisServicesTutorial2005, do the following:

1. Right-click the database AnalysisServicesTutorial2005 and click Process as shown in Figure 12-5.

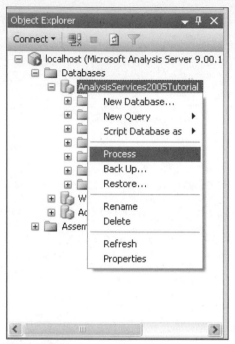

Figure 12-5

2. You will see the Process dialog as shown in Figure 12-6. This dialog shows the name of the object to be processed along with the type of object. There are several processing options for each object. The default option for the database object is Process Full. As the name implies, the Process Full option allows you to process the object completely even if the object had been processed earlier. It will clear any data that was processed earlier. Click OK in this dialog.

When you click OK the process dialog uses AMO to send the Process command to the Analysis Services instance. You can see the process command that is to be sent to the server by clicking the Script⇨Script Action to new Query window. You will see the following script command:

```
<Batch xmlns="http://schemas.microsoft.com/analysisservices/2003/engine">
  <Parallel>
    <Process xmlns:xsd="http://www.w3.org/2001/XMLSchema"
xmlns:xsi="http://www.w3.org/2001/XMLSchema-instance">
      <Object>
        <DatabaseID>AnalysisServices2005Tutorial</DatabaseID>
      </Object>
      <Type>ProcessFull</Type>
      <WriteBackTableCreation>UseExisting</WriteBackTableCreation>
    </Process>
  </Parallel>
</Batch>
```

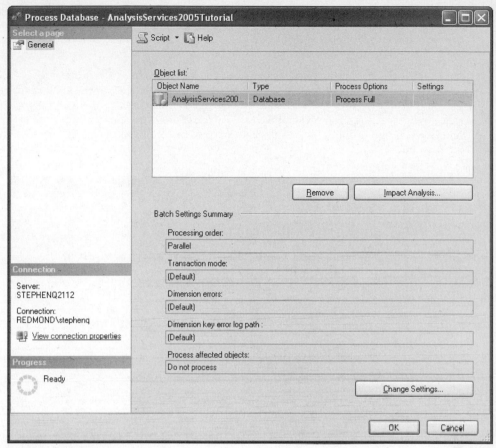

Figure 12-6

The above script contains several commands that are interpreted by Analysis Services. Since the medium of communication to Analysis Services is XML/A request, the script is embedded within SOAP Envelope tags. This script can be executed from XMLA editor within SQL Server Management Studio. SSMS adds the appropriate SOAP envelope tags to send the script to Analysis Services. The commands in the script are Batch, Parallel, and Process. The Process command is part of a set of commands that manipulate the data in Analysis Services. These commands that change the data in Analysis Services databases are called the DML (data manipulation language). The Batch command allows multiple commands to be executed within a single statement. The Parallel command allows you to instruct the server to execute all the commands within the command in parallel. The Process command is used to process an Analysis Services object and needs several properties such as DatabaseID and Processing Type.

3. When you click OK in the Process dialog, a Process command with appropriate options is sent to the Analysis Services instance. This command requests the server to process the database. For processing the objects within a database the server needs to read data from the data source, which is done by issuing queries to the data source. You will now see the Process progress

dialog that shows fine-grain details of each processing operation on the server. As you can see from Figure 12-7, each object within the database that is being processed is reported along with the timing information and whether the process succeeded or failed. You can see the query sent to the data source to retrieve the data.

4. Once all the objects have been processed you will see the status of the processing. If all the objects were successfully processed you will see Process Succeeded in the status as shown in Figure 12-7. If there were errors during processing, the status bar will show an appropriate message. The processing of objects that results in an error are shown in red in the tree view of the processing progress dialog. You can drill down into the details of the processing to understand the reason for failure.

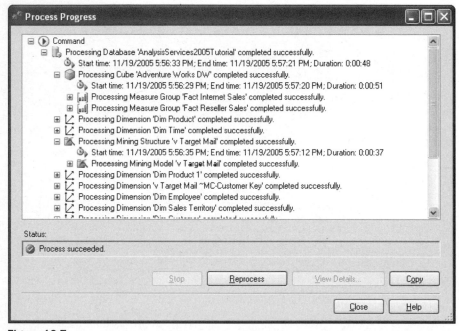

Figure 12-7

There are several operations that take place in the preceding processing command. All the objects within the database are processed in parallel based on the settings of the Analysis Services instance. If there are dependencies, the dependent objects are processed first. For example, the dimensions that are part of a cube need to be processed before the cube can be processed. Analysis Services processes all the objects of the database under a single transaction. What this means is that if one of the objects failed during processing, the remaining objects will not be processed. For example, if all the dimensions of a cube were successfully processed and if there were errors while processing the cube, the processing of the dimension objects will be rolled back. Once all the objects have been successfully processed, the server commits the transaction, which means that the objects are marked as processed and are available for querying.

Assume an Analysis Services object has been processed and is being queried by users. At the time users are querying the object, you can initiate processing on the same object. Because a version of the object is currently being queried, Analysis Service stores the uncommitted processed object under a temporary file. At the time of commit, the server first ensures that the user is not using the objects, removes the previous version of the processed objects, and then marks the temporary files as primary. You see this in detail in the following section.

Processing a Cube

An Analysis Services database can contain several cubes and dimensions within it. You have the flexibility to control the processing of individual cubes and dimensions by launching the process dialog from appropriate cube or dimension objects. There are several processing options for processing a cube, as shown in Figure 12-8. All of the same processing options available for partitions and measure groups are available for the cube because a cube is a collection of measure groups, which in turn is a collection of partitions.

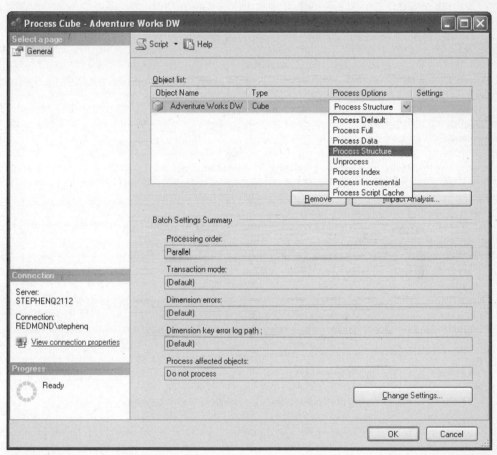

Figure 12-8

When a cube is created you will typically do a full process (*Process Full* in process dialog) of it so that you can browse the cube. Usually the cube structure might not change after the initial design. You will be getting additional fact data that you would want to add to an existing cube. For example, you might have a Sales cube that you have created and you might be getting sales fact data from each store every month. Processing the entire cube every time will take a considerable amount of time and end users might have to wait for a long period to see the most up to date data. Analysis Services 2005 provides you with an option to process only the new fact data instead of the entire cube. This is called incremental processing. In order to add the new fact data to the cube you can add a new partition to the cube and process that partition. Alternately you can use the *Process Incremental* option in process dialog and specify the query that provides the new fact data that needs to be processed. Process incremental is a common management task for data warehouses. If you specify the *Process Default* option in process dialog, the server checks for all the objects that have not been processed and only processes those objects. If the cube data had been processed and if aggregations and indexes are not processed then those are processed.

When you choose the *Process Full* option for processing a cube, the server performs three internal operations. If the storage mode for the cube is MOLAP, the server first reads the data from the relational data and stores the data in a compact format. If there were aggregations defined for the cube, the server will build those aggregations during this processing. Finally, the server creates indexes for the data that helps speed access to data during querying. Even if there were no aggregations specified for the cube, the server still creates the indexes. The *Process Data* option actually is the first step of the Process Full option where the server reads data from relational data sources and stores it in proprietary format. The second and third steps of processing aggregations and indexes can be separately accomplished by the *Process Index* option. You might be wondering why you have the Process Data and Process Index option when the Process Full and Process Default option actually accomplish the same task. These options provide the administrator a fine grain of control. These are especially important when you have limited time to access the relational data source and want to optimize the processing. Under such instances, you first process data. Once you have all the data on the Analysis Service you can then create your aggregations and indexes, which do not need access to the relational data source.

If you choose the *Process Structure* option, the server processes all the cube's dimensions and the cube definitions so that the cube's structure is processed without any processing of the data. The server will not process the partitions or measure groups of the cube, therefore you cannot see any of the fact data; however, you can browse the cube because the cube definitions are processed. You can retrieve metadata information about the cube (measure names, measure groups, dimensions, KPIs, actions, and so on) after processing the cube's structure. However, you will not be able to query the cube data. For a cube that has been processed with Process Structure, you can see the cube in SQL Server Management Studio MDX query editor when you select the drop-down list for the cube. If your cube linked measure groups has been processed with Process Structure option, you will be able to query the measures in linked measure groups. Often when you design your UDM you will want to make sure your design is correct and your customers are able to see the right measures and dimensions. Process Structure is helpful in validating your design. As soon as the data for the cube is available the cube can be processed with the Process Default option so that end users can query the data from the cube.

You can clear the data in the cube using the *Unprocess* option. The *Process Script Cache* option can be used when you want Analysis Services to cache the calculations specified in the MDX script. Analysis Services evaluates calculations specified using the CACHE statement in the MDX scripts. You have learned the various processing options for the Cube. The processing options provided in the process dialog are different than the process types that are specified in the process command sent to Analysis Services. The following table shows how the various processing options map to the process types sent to Analysis Services.

Process Options in Process Dialog	Process Type in Process Command
Process Full	ProcessFull
Process Default	ProcessDefault
Process Data	ProcessData
Process Structure	ProcessStructure
Unprocess	ProcessClear
Process Index	ProcessIndexes
Process Incremental	ProcessAdd
Process Script Cache	ProcessScriptCache

The processed data of a cube are stored in a hierarchical directory structure that is equivalent to the structure you see in the object explorer. Figure 12-9 shows the directory structure of the processed data of the Adventure Works DW sample database in Analysis Services 2005. The directory also shows the files within a partition. The metadata information about the cubes and dimensions are stored as XML files, while the data is stored in a proprietary format of Microsoft. Every time an object is processed, a new version number is appended to the object. For example, the files shown in Figure 12-9 are under a specific partition directory. The file info.<versionnumber>.xml is used to store the metadata information about the partition. Similar metadata files are stored within the directories of each object, cube, dimension, and measure groups. We recommend you to browse through each object folder to see the metadata information. The fact data is stored in the file with extension data. The key to an OLAP database is the fast access to data. You learned about a cell, which was represented by a Tuple. A Tuple is the intersection of various dimension members. For fast data access, Analysis Services builds indexes to access data across multiple dimensions. The index files in Analysis Services have the extension "map". In Figure 12-9 you can see the .map files that have the format <version>.<Dimension>.<Hierarchy>.fact.map. There is an associated header file for each map file. Analysis Services stores the data as blocks called segments for fast access. The associated header file contains offsets to the various segments for fast access during queries.

The processing dialog provides you the flexibility of processing objects in parallel or within the same transaction. If errors are encountered during processing, you can set options to handle these errors. You can configure the parallelism and error options by selecting the Change Settings button in the process dialog. You will see the Change Settings dialog as shown in Figure 12-10 which enables you to configure certain processing operations and error settings during processing. Setting the parallelism option is as simple as selecting the appropriate option in the processing order. By default all the objects are processed in parallel and within the same transaction. If you do want failure of one object to impact other objects, you should process the objects under different transactions by choosing the sequential option.

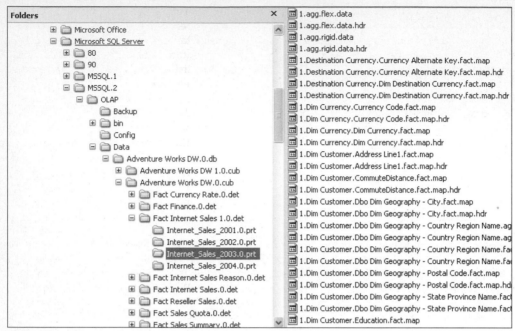

Figure 12-9

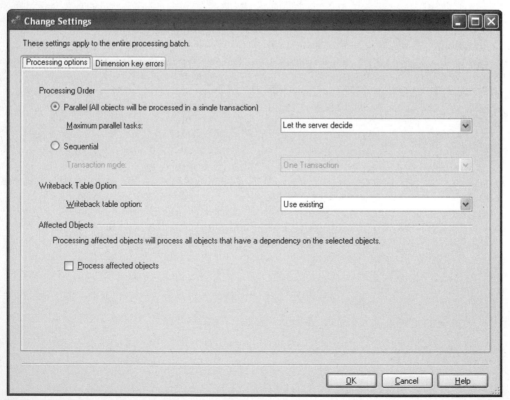

Figure 12-10

You might encounter errors while processing your Analysis Services objects due to incorrect design or referential integrity problems in the relational data source. For example, if you have a fact record that contains a dimension id that is not available in the dimension table, you will see a "Key not found" error while processing the cube. By default, when an error is encountered during processing the processing operation fails. You can change the settings in the processing dialog to take appropriate action other than failing the processing operation. The Change Settings dialog helps in changing the error configuration settings for all the objects selected for processing. Whenever you encounter Key errors you can either convert the values to unknown or discard the erroneous records. You can run into key errors while processing the facts or the dimensions. If you encounter a key error while processing a cube, that means Analysis Services was unable to find a corresponding key in the dimension. You can assign the fact value to the member called Unknown member for that specific dimension. You can encounter key errors while processing a snowflake dimension when an attribute defined as a foreign key does not exist in the foreign table or when there are duplicate entries. The two most common types of key errors that you might encounter during dimension processing are key not found and duplicate key errors.

Processing a Dimension

You can process dimensions independent of the cube. After the initial processing of a dimension, you might process the dimensions on a periodic basis if additional records are added in the dimension table or there were changes to columns of an existing row. An example of additions to a dimension is new products being added to the products dimension. You would want this information to be reflected in the dimensions so that you can see the sales information for the new products. Another example of changes in dimension is when an employee moves from one city to another city; the attributes of the employee will need to change. Therefore the process dialog provides you with various options for processing the dimension, as shown in Figure 12-11.

While processing a dimension Analysis Services reads data from the dimensions table(s). When a dimension is processed, each attribute of the dimension is processed separately. Based on the parallelism specified on Analysis Services, these attributes can be processed in parallel. Each dimension contains an attribute called the All attribute. This is not exposed to the user but used internally by Analysis Services. You can see the files associated with this attribute as <version>.(All).<extension> in Figure 12-12. When each attribute is processed, several files are created. Similar to fact data, the dimension data is stored in a proprietary format. Each attribute of a dimension has a key column and a named column. These directly map into two different files with extensions kstore and sstore, which refer to key store and string store, respectively. In addition, there are additional files that get created for each attribute of the dimension, which help in fast access to name, key, and levels of attributes and hierarchies. The files with extension map are created when indexes are processed for each attribute and help in fast retrieval of related attributes of the dimension for a dimension member.

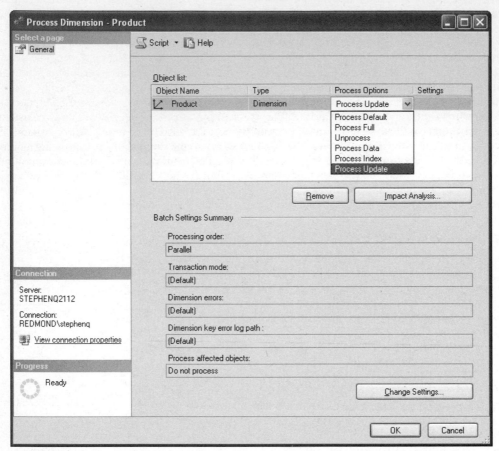

Figure 12-11

Name ▲	Size	Type	Date Modified
1.(All).ahstore	1 KB	AHSTORE File	11/19/2005 7:37 PM
1.(All).asstore	1 KB	ASSTORE File	11/19/2005 7:37 PM
1.(All).astore	1 KB	ASTORE File	11/19/2005 7:37 PM
1.(All).khstore	1 KB	KHSTORE File	11/19/2005 7:37 PM
1.(All).kstore	1 KB	KSTORE File	11/19/2005 7:37 PM
1.Account Description.(All).lstore	1 KB	LSTORE File	11/19/2005 7:37 PM
1.Account Description.(All).ostore	1 KB	OSTORE File	11/19/2005 7:37 PM
1.Account Description.(All).sstore	9 KB	SSTORE File	11/19/2005 7:37 PM
1.Account Description.Account Description.dstore	9 KB	DSTORE File	11/19/2005 7:37 PM
1.Account Description.Account Description.lstore	1 KB	LSTORE File	11/19/2005 7:37 PM
1.Account Description.Account Description.ostore	1 KB	OSTORE File	11/19/2005 7:37 PM
1.Account Description.Account Description.sstore	1 KB	SSTORE File	11/19/2005 7:37 PM
1.Account Description.ahstore	3 KB	AHSTORE File	11/19/2005 7:37 PM
1.Account Description.asstore	6 KB	ASSTORE File	11/19/2005 7:37 PM
1.Account Description.astore	2 KB	ASTORE File	11/19/2005 7:37 PM
1.Account Description.fact.data	1 KB	DATA File	11/19/2005 7:37 PM
1.Account Description.fact.data.hdr	1 KB	HDR File	11/19/2005 7:37 PM
1.Account Description.khstore	3 KB	KHSTORE File	11/19/2005 7:37 PM
1.Account Description.kstore	1 KB	KSTORE File	11/19/2005 7:37 PM
1.Account Description.ustore	1 KB	USTORE File	11/19/2005 7:37 PM
1.Account Type.(All).lstore	1 KB	LSTORE File	11/19/2005 7:37 PM
1.Account Type.(All).ostore	1 KB	OSTORE File	11/19/2005 7:37 PM
1.Account Type.(All).sstore	9 KB	SSTORE File	11/19/2005 7:37 PM

Figure 12-12

Time taken to process a dimension depends on the number of attributes and hierarchies in the dimension as well as the number of members in each hierarchy. When a processing command is sent to the server, the server reads the data from the relational data source and updates the dimension. SQL Server Analysis Services 2000 had a limitation of 64000 members for each parent and a maximum of 256 levels within a single dimension. Analysis Services 2005 does not have such a limitation. When a dimension is processed, the attributes of the dimension are processed separately. Some attributes can be processed in parallel, while some cannot. The order of processing of various attributes is dependent on the member property definition and resources available on the machine. For example, say you have a Customer dimension that contains the attributes Customer Name, SSN, City, State, and Country. Assume SSN is the Key attribute for this dimension and by default all attributes within the dimension are member properties of the key attribute. In addition, assume additional member property relationships have been established. They are Country⇨State, State⇨City, City⇨Customer Name, State⇨Customer Name, and Country⇨Customer Name. Due to the preceding relationship, the order of processing of the attributes in the Customer dimension is Country, State, City, Customer Name, and SSN. This is because Analysis Services needs to have information about Country in order to establish the member property relationship while processing the State, Customer Name, or SSN.

When the *Process Default* option is chosen for processing, the dimension's data or indexes are processed if they had not been processed. If the *Process Full* option is chosen, the entire dimension is re-processed. When *Process Full* option is used dimension data and indexes that have been processed initially will be dropped and data is retrieved from the data source. Based on dimension size (number of dimension members as well as number of attributes and hierarchies in the dimension) the processing operation can take a long time.

Similar to incremental processing of the cubes you can incrementally process dimensions using the *Process Update* option. The *Process Update* option in the process dialog maps to *ProcessUpdate* process type in the process command which is applied only for dimensions. Some of the dimensions such as Employees or Customers or Products can potentially contain a large number of members. Mostly additional members can be added to these dimension or some attributes of these dimension members might have changed. Often a full processing of the entire dimensions is not only necessary, but cannot be afforded due to business needs. Under these circumstances incremental processing of the dimension or an update of the attributes of the dimension should be sufficient. When you choose the *Process Update* option for the dimension, the server scans all the dimensions in the dimension table. If there were changes to the dimension caption or description, they are updated. If new members are added to the dimension table, these members are added to the existing dimension during incremental processing. When the *Process Update* option is chosen, attributes of each dimension member will be updated. The key of each dimension member is assumed to be the same, but expect some attributes to be updated. The most important attribute that is updated is the member property for each member. When you have a parent-child hierarchy in a dimension; and if the parent attribute has been changed, that information is updated during the Process Update processing option.

The *Process Data* option for dimensions is used to process the dimension data. The indexes will not be processed when the Process Data option is used. The *Process Index* option is used to create indexes for attributes in the dimensions. If the ProcessMode dimension property is set to LazyAggregations, Analysis Services builds indexes for new attributes of the dimension as a lazy operation in the background thread. If you want to rebuild these indexes immediately you can do so by choosing the *Process Index* option. The *Unprocess* option is to clear the data within the dimension.

Managing Partitions

In a fit of unrestrained metaphor use back in Chapter 4, we noted that carving bars of soap using razor blades could result in intricate little statues, but could also result in fingers covered with band aids. Well, use of partitions carries a similar warning. Partitions enable you to distribute fact data within Analysis Services and aggregate data so that the resources on a machine can be efficiently utilized. When there are create multiple partitions on the same server, you will reap the benefits of partitions since Analysis Services reads/writes data in parallel across multiple partitions. Fact data on the data source can be stored as several fact tables Sales_Fact_2002, Sales_Fact_2003 etc or as a single large fact table called Sales Fact. You can create multiple partitions within a measure group; one for each fact table in the data source or by splitting data from single large fact table through several queries. Partitions also allow you to split the data across two or more machines running Analysis Services which are called Remote partitions. As an administrator you might be thinking what the size of each partition should be to achieve the best results. Based on the performance analyzed on Analysis Services 2000 customers, Microsoft recommends each partition be 5 GB or 20 million records. You learn more about optimizing partitions in Chapter 13.

A sales cube's partition usually contains data spread across time, that is, a new partition might be created for every month or a quarter. As an administrator you would create a new partition from SQL Server Management Studio and process it so that is available for users. To create a new partition, perform the following steps in BIDS.

1. Open the AnalysisServices2005Tutorial project you have used in previous chapters.

2. Change the FactInternetSales table to a named query so that there is a where condition DueDateKey<700. In case you don't recall how this is done, we've included the steps here:

    a. Open Adventure Works DW.dsv under the Data Source Views folder.

    b. Right click on the FactInternetSales table in diagram view, select Replace Table->With New Named Query... menu items.

    c. In the Create Named Query dialog, In the DueDateKey Filter text entry box, enter <700. Your change will automatically be reflected in the query window. Click OK to continue.

3. In the DSV, right-click the Add/Remove tables and add the FactInternetSales table to Included objects.

4. In the diagram view, replace the FactInternetSales table with a named query. In the named query, set Filter to DueDateKey >=700. Rename the named query as FactInternetSalesNew. Deploy the project.

5. Connect to the AnalysisServices2005Tutorial database using SSMS. Navigate to the measure group FactInternetSales.

6. Right-click the Partitions folder and select New Partition. You will now be in the Partition Wizard. Click Next on the welcome screen.

7. Choose the named query FactInternetSalsNew to create a new partition as shown in Figure 12-13 and click Next.

8. If you want to split the data from the fact table into multiple partitions, you can do so by specifying the query on the page shown in Figure 12-14. Click the Next button.

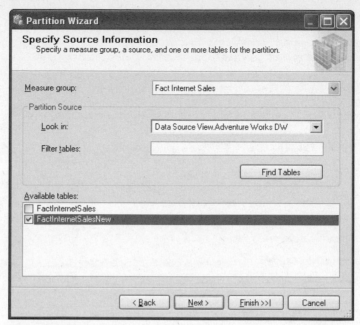

Figure 12-13

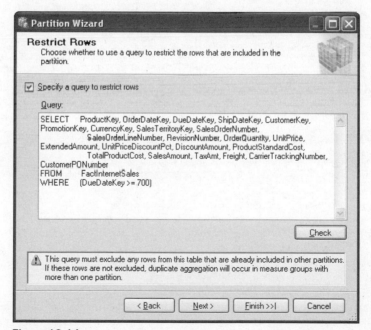

Figure 12-14

One way Analysis Services provides scalability is by use of remote partitions, where the partitions reside in two or more Analysis Services instances. On the Processing and Storage Location page as shown in Figure 12-15, you can specify where to store the partition. You can specify the remote Analysis Services instance on this page, but the data source to the remote Analysis Service instance should have been defined in this database. You can change the storage location where you want the partition to reside on any of the Analysis Service instances.

9. Choose the default options as shown in Figure 12-15 and click Next.

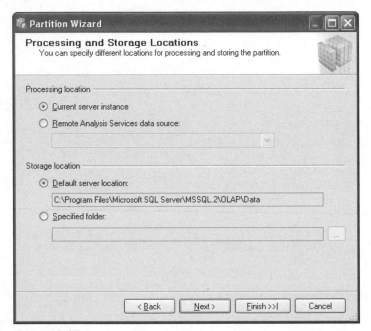

Figure 12-15

10. You will be in the final page of the Partition Wizard. Select Design aggregations later, Process Now and then click Finish. The partition will be processed and you can browse the cube data.

The number of partitions for a specific cube can typically increases over time. Users might not be browsing historical data with the same granularity as that of the recent data. For example, you might be more interested in comparing Sales data for the current month to that of the previous month rather than data from five years ago. However, you might want to compare year-over-year data for several years. By merging the partition data you can see some benefits during query performance. You learn the considerations you should take into account to merge partitions in Chapter 13.

There are two main requirements to merge partitions: the partitions should be of the same storage type, and they need to be on the same Analysis Services instance. Therefore if you have remote partitions, they can be merged together only if they are on the same Analysis Services instance. To merge partitions, do the following:

1. Launch the Merge partition dialog by right-clicking the Partitions folder within a measure group. You will see the Merge partition dialog as shown in Figure 12-16.

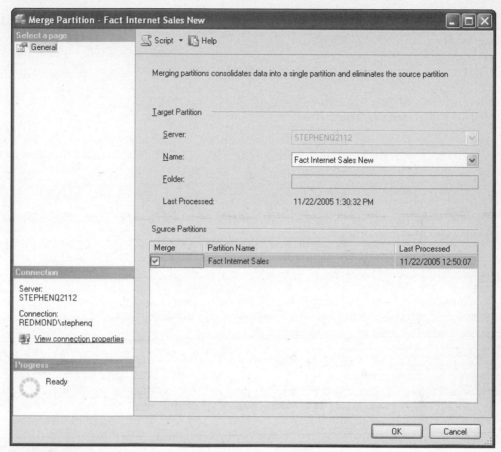

Figure 12-16

2. Select the Target partition that will contain the merged data and the list of partitions to merge data from in the Merge partition dialog as shown in Figure 12-16 and click OK.

All the data from the source partitions will merge into the target partition, and the source partitions are deleted due to this operation. SSMS sends the following command to Analysis Services to merge the partitions:

```
<MergePartitions xmlns="http://schemas.microsoft.com/analysisservices/2003/engine">
  <Sources>
    <Source>
      <DatabaseID>AnalysisServices2005Tutorial</DatabaseID>
      <CubeID>Adventure Works DW</CubeID>
      <MeasureGroupID>Fact Internet Sales</MeasureGroupID>
      <PartitionID>Fact Internet Sales New</PartitionID>
```

```
        </Source>
      </Sources>
      <Target>
        <DatabaseID>AnalysisServices2005Tutorial</DatabaseID>
        <CubeID>Adventure Works DW</CubeID>
        <MeasureGroupID>Fact Internet Sales</MeasureGroupID>
        <PartitionID>Fact Internet Sales</PartitionID>
      </Target>
    </MergePartitions>
```

Managing Assemblies

You learned about .NET and COM assemblies in Chapter 10. Assemblies, also referred to as stored procedures, can only be added by Analysis Services administrators. You need to make sure your instance of Analysis Services is safe and secure irrespective of the operations done by the stored procedures. Security is always a concern, and you do not want any assemblies to bring down the server. Because hackers try to hack servers, most software products now are built to be secure by default. The administrator needs to enable certain components and options to make them available to users. By default, Analysis Services does not allow execution of stored procedures. The administrator first needs to enable the server properties Feature\ManagedCodeEnabled and Feature\ComUdfEnabled to true (value of 1 in the Analysis Services config file) for enabling managed assemblies and COM DLLs respectively. This is accomplished by using the server properties dialog to enable registration and execution of assemblies.

The key to managing assemblies is to understand the nature of the assembly and setting appropriate properties while adding assemblies to your Analysis Services. Figure 12-17 shows the dialog to add assemblies to the Server or to a specific database.

You saw in Chapter 10 that Analysis Services supports two types of assemblies: COM and .NET CLR assemblies. Once you specify the type and name of the assemblies, you need to specify the security information for these assemblies. There are two parameters by which you can control the security of these stored procedures, Impersonation and Permissions. Permission allows you to define the scope of access for the assembly, such as accessing the file system, accessing the network, and accessing unmanaged code. There are three different values for permission sets:

❑ **Safe.** The most secure of the three permissions. When the safe permission set is specified for an assembly, it means that the assembly is only intended for computation and the assembly cannot access any protected resource. It guarantees protection against information leaks, elevation attacks by malicious code, and guarantees reliability.

❑ **External Access.** This set value provides access to external resources to the assembly without compromising reliability, but does not offer any specific security guarantees. You can use this if you as the DBA trust the programmer's ability to write good code and if there is a need to access external resources such as data from an outside file.

❑ **Unrestricted.** This set value is primarily intended for people who have a very good understanding of programming on servers and need access to all resources. This permission set does not guarantee any code security or reliability. Unrestricted access should only be allowed to assemblies that have been written by users who absolutely need access to external resources and have a very good understanding of all security issues, such as denial of service attacks and information leakage, and are able to handle all these within the stored procedures. We recommend you use this option only when it is absolutely essential and you have full confidence in the programming abilities of the developer who has developed the assembly.

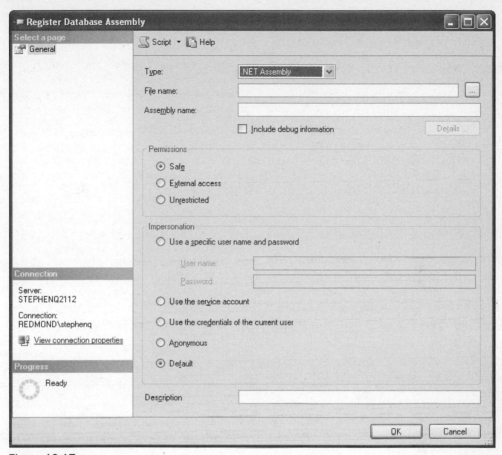

Figure 12-17

Impersonation allows you to specify the account under which the stored procedure needs to be executed. There are five different values for Impersonation information:

❑ **Default:** The default value allows you to execute the stored procedure under a secure mode with the minimum privileges. If the assembly is of type COM, the default value is Impersonate CurrentUser. For a .NET CLR assembly, the default value depends on the permission set defined. If the permission set is Safe, the Impersonation mode will be Impersonate Service Account but if the permission set is External Access or Unrestricted, the Impersonation mode will be Impersonate Current User.

❑ **Anonymous:** If you want the stored procedure to be executed as anonymous user, you need to select Impersonate Anonymous. You will have limited access when the stored procedure is executed as Impersonate Anonymous.

    ❑ **Use the credentials of the current user:** This Impersonation mode is typically used when you want the stored procedure to be executed with the user's credentials. This is a safe option to select. If the stored procedure accesses external resources and the current user executing the stored procedure does not have permissions then execution of the stored procedure will not cause any ill effects. A use of this impersonation mode is to define dynamic data security where the current user's credential is need to access external resources.

❑ **Use the service account:** If you choose the Impersonate Service Account, whenever the stored procedure is executed it will be executed under the credentials of service startup account for Analysis Services. An example of a stored procedure that would need this impersonation mode is an AMO stored procedure that does management operations on the server.

❑ **Use a specific username and password:** If your business needs a stored procedure to always be executed in the context of a specific user, you need to choose this option. You need to specify a Windows account name and password for this impersonation mode. A typical example where you might use this options is when you access an external source such as a data source or web service to retrieve data with this account and utilize that value within the stored procedure for computation.

To summarize, COM assemblies only support the credentials of the current user impersonation, whereas .NET CLR assemblies support all the impersonation modes. As an administrator of Analysis Services you need to choose the right impersonation and permission that suits your business needs.

When you register an assembly with a specific Analysis Services database or for the server using the Register Assembly dialog, Analysis Services 2005 Register Database Assembly dialog uses AMO to set up the correct properties. This, in turn, sends a Create command to the Analysis Services instance as shown below.

```
<Create AllowOverwrite="true"
xmlns="http://schemas.microsoft.com/analysisservices/2003/engine">
  <ParentObject>
    <DatabaseID>Adventure Works DW</DatabaseID>
  </ParentObject>
  <ObjectDefinition>
    <Assembly xmlns:xsd="http://www.w3.org/2001/XMLSchema"
xmlns:xsi="http://www.w3.org/2001/XMLSchema-instance" xsi:type="ClrAssembly">
      <ID>AmoSproc</ID>
      <Name>AmoSproc</Name>
      <Description />
      <ImpersonationInfo>
        <ImpersonationMode>Default</ImpersonationMode>
      </ImpersonationInfo>
      <Files>
        <File>
          <Name>AmoSproc.dll</Name>
          <Type>Main</Type>
          <Data>
            <Block>------------Content about the stored procedure------</Block>
            <Block>------------Content about the stored procedure------</Block>
            <Block>------------Content about the stored procedure------</Block>
            <Block>------------Content about the stored procedure------</Block>
          </Data>
        </File>
      </Files>
      <PermissionSet>ExternalAccess</PermissionSet>
    </Assembly>
  </ObjectDefinition>
</Create>
```

The information within the tag BLOCK is a huge amount of text, which for illustration purposes has been restricted to a single line. This text within the BLOCK tag is the assembly to be registered that will be stored within Analysis Services instance. When queries use functions within the assembly, Analysis Services loads the assembly within the same process and executes the CLR assembly with appropriate parameter passing. The results from the assembly are appropriately passed back to Analysis Services for further evaluation of a query.

Back-up and Restore

Backup is an operation that is part of every individual's life. If you have an important document you take a photocopy as a backup. Similarly, backup is an extremely critical operation for any data warehouse. There are several reasons why you should periodically back up your Analysis Services database. One reason is for disaster recovery, another is for auditing purposes. Irrespective of purpose, it is always a good idea to back up your database on a periodic basis. You can back up databases on your Analysis Services instance through SSMS. Follow the steps below to backup the AnalysisServiecs2005Tutorial database.

1. Connect to Analysis Services instance using SSMS.

2. Navigate to the database AnalysisServices2005Tutorial in the Object Explorer window.

3. Right-click the database and select Back Up...

You will see the backup dialog shown in Figure 12-18. By default the dialog chooses the database name as the backup name. By default the backup file will be created in the Backup folder your Analysis Services installation folder. If you want the backup location on a different drive or directory, you first need to change the Analysis Services server property AllowedBrowsingFolder by adding the appropriate directory. You can then choose the folder by clicking Browse in the Backup Database dialog and specifying a file name for backup.

You have the option to encrypt the database by specifying a password. You'll need that password to restore the database. If you have remote partitions in the database, you have the option of specifying the backup location for each remote partition. Backup of these partitions is done on respective Analysis Services instances on that machine.

4. Disable the option to encrypt the backup file.

5. Select the option to overwrite any existing backup files with the same name.

6. Choose the default backup file name and click OK.

Following command is sent to Analysis Services instance by SSMS to backup the database AnalysisServices2005Tutorial.

```
<Backup xmlns="http://schemas.microsoft.com/analysisservices/2003/engine">
  <Object>
    <DatabaseID>Analysis Services 2005 Tutorial</DatabaseID>
  </Object>
  <File>Analysis Services 2005 Tutorial.abf</File>
  <AllowOverwrite>true</AllowOverwrite>
</Backup>
```

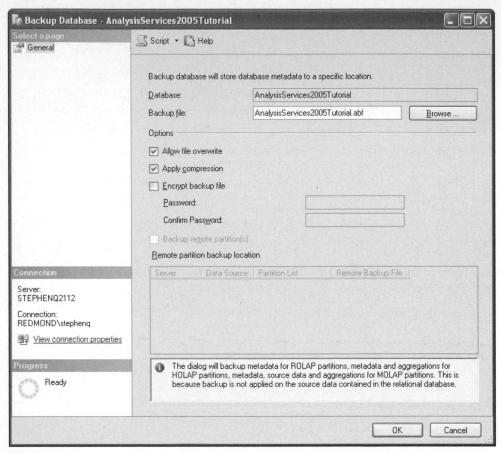

Figure 12-18

An Analysis Services 2005 backup file with the extension .abf will be created in the Backup folder. Analysis Services 2000 had a 2GB limitation on the file size for backup of a database. Analysis Services 2005 does not have any such limitation. Analysis Services 2005 allows you to back up multiple databases at the same time. Through the SQL Server Management Studio you can launch the backup dialog from each database you want to backup and run backups in parallel. Alternatively, you can create a DDL that will execute backup of multiple databases within the same command.

Whenever you want to restore an Analysis Services database for which you have a backup, you can do so by using the restore dialog. To a restore a database on an Analysis Services instance launch the restore dialog by right-clicking the Database folder from Object Explorer of SSMS and select Restore.... You will see the restore dialog shown in Figure 12-19.

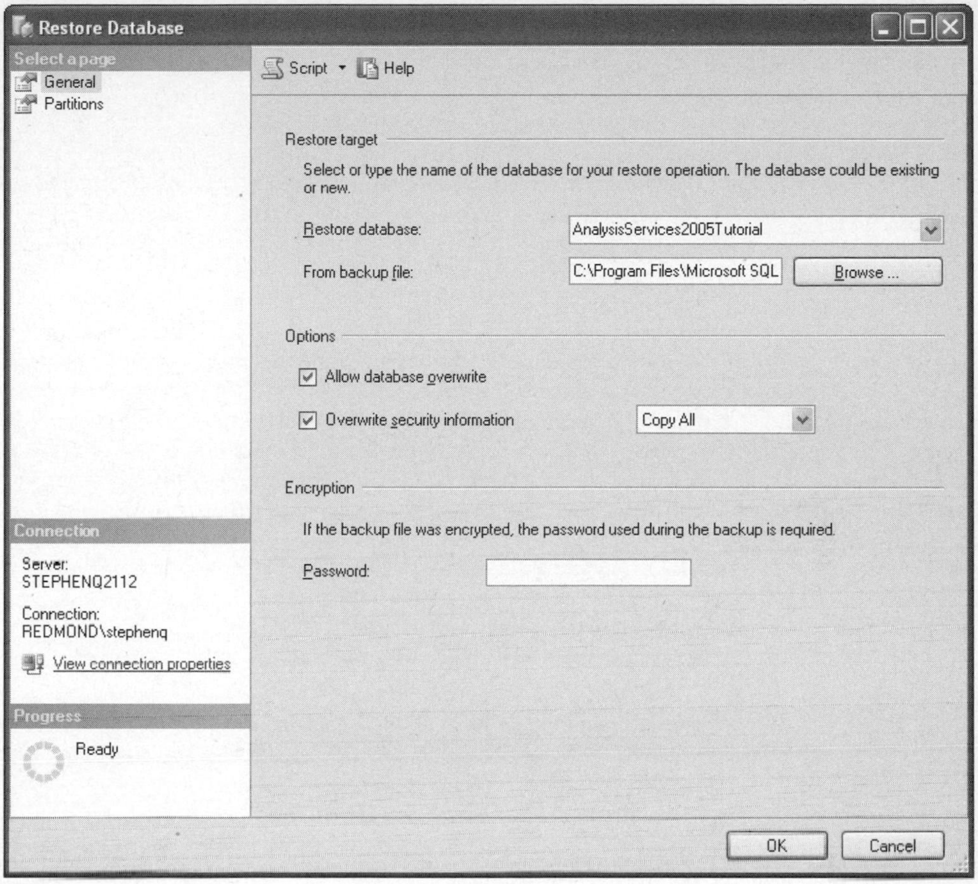

Figure 12-19

Specify the database you want to restore and the backup file for that database. If the database already exists and you want to overwrite the existing database object, you can do so by clicking the option Allow Database Overwrite. You can restore the entire database including security information or you can skip the security defined on the backup file during restore. If you had provided a password during backup of this database, you need to specify the same password for restore operation. Once the database has been restored you can query the database. You can take a backup of a database from your test servers and restore it on production server. In such a circumstance you might choose to skip the security information if the security defined on production servers is different from those on your test servers. In such a circumstance you would need to ensure you secure the database by defining the right security on production servers. In a circumstance where the backup was taken on your production server and you are restoring the database on an upgraded production machine we do expect users to restore the database with the security information.

Synchronization

Synchronization sounds like a sophisticated, highly technical area of endeavor, but actually, it couldn't be simpler; consider synchronization as just replication for Analysis Services 2005 databases. The name actually is suitable because it allows you to "synchronize" the Analysis Services database resident on an Analysis Services instance to another Analysis Services instance. Typically engineers test the designed Analysis Services database on a test environment before they move them to their production servers. Engineers often have to backup their database on test servers and restore them on production servers. However through the synchronization feature in Analysis Services 2005 engineers can move well tested database(s) from test servers to production servers with ease.

If you have an Analysis Services instance actively supporting a population of users, you want to be able to update the database they're querying against without taking the system down to do so. Using the Synchronize Database Wizard you can accomplish the database update seamlessly. The wizard will copy both data and metadata from your development and test machine (staging server) to the production server and automatically switch users to the newly copied data and metadata based on conditions defined on production server. To try this out, you need to have two instance of Analysis Services installed on another machine, or have a second instance of Analysis Services installed on your current machine. We recommend you to install another instance called I2 on the same machine. Follow the steps below to synchronize a database from default instance to the newly instance named instance.

1. Launch SSMS and connect to your default instance (localhost) and named instance (localhost\I2) of Analysis Services as shown in Figure 12-20.

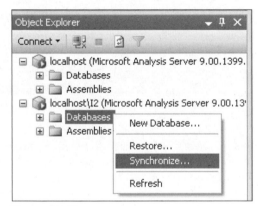

Figure 12-20

2. We assume that you have deployed the AnalysisServices2005Tutorial to your default instance. Right click on the Databases folder of the named instance and select Synhcronize... as shown in Figure 12-20.

3. If you see the welcome screen click Next.

4. In the Select Database to Synchronize page of the Synchronize wizard type the default instance localhost as the Source server and select the Source database AnalysisServices2005Tutorial as shown in Figure 12-21 and click Next.

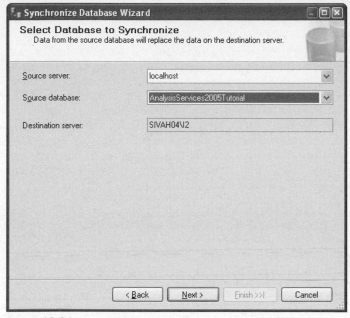

Figure 12-21

In the Specify Locations for Local Partitions page you can change locations of the partitions during synchronizations if the destination server allows it. In Figure 12-22 you can see that all the partitions of AnalysisServices2005Tutorial will be restored in the default location.

Figure 12-22

1. Click Next in the Specify Locations for Local Partitions page. In the Specify Query Criteria page you can choose to synchronize the database with or without the security permissions specified on the source server with the various options as shown in Figure 12-23. You can choose to copy all the roles, skip the membership information in the role(s) or skip all the security permissions. Analysis Services 2005 has been designed to provide these options since customers might choose to synchronize databases from test servers to production servers. While synchronizing databases from test to production servers you can choose to keep all roles if the security permissions in test environment are identical to the ones in production environment. If the security permissions have been defined in such a way that they can be utilized in the production environment but the users in production environment are different then you can use Skip membership information. If you choose the Skip membership option you would need to define the membership after synchronization. Select the Skip membership option as shown in Figure 12-23 and click Next.

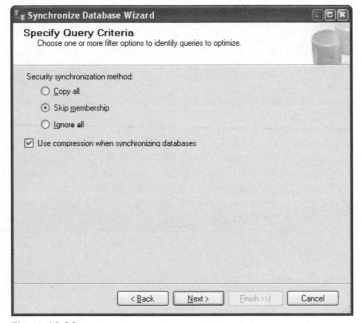

Figure 12-23

2. In the Select Synchronization Method page you can choose to start the synchronization process immediately or script the command to a file and later send the command to the destination server using SSMS or through custom programs. Choose the Synchronize now method as shown in Figure 12-24 and click Finish.

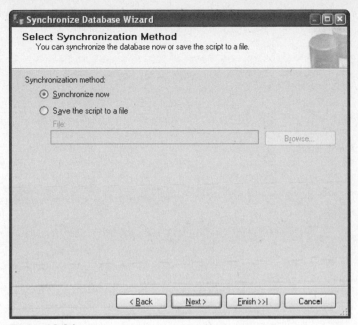

Figure 12-24

As soon as you hit the finish following Synchronization a command is sent to the server to synchronize the database.

```
<Synchronize xmlns:xsi="http://www.w3.org/2001/XMLSchema-instance"
xmlns:xsd="http://www.w3.org/2001/XMLSchema"
xmlns="http://schemas.microsoft.com/analysisservices/2003/engine">
  <Source>
    <ConnectionString>Provider=MSOLAP.3;Data
Source=localhost;ConnectTo=9.0;Integrated Security=SSPI;Initial
Catalog=AnalysisServices2005Tutorial</ConnectionString>
    <Object>
      <DatabaseID>AnalysisServices2005Tutorial</DatabaseID>
    </Object>
  </Source>
  <Locations>
  <SynchronizeSecurity>SkipMembership</SynchronizeSecurity>
  <ApplyCompression>true</ApplyCompression>
</Synchronize>
```

You should be aware that the destination server contacts the source server for synchronization using the credentials of the service startup account and not the user who initiated the synchronize operation from SSMS. You do need to make sure the service startup account of the destination server has credentials to access the database(s) on the source server. The source server creates a backup of the objects that have changed in the source server, compresses them, and then sends them to the destination server. On the destination server these objects are first restored under a temporary file. If there are active queries being executed against the database on the destination server, the server waits for those queries to complete and then updates the objects. On the source server, the objects are locked during synchronization. Until the time the objects are sent to the destination server you cannot perform operations, such as processing, or other actions that will modify the objects.

1. You will see the Synchronization Progress page as shown in Figure 12-25. You will see progress percentage of the synchronization shown in this page which gets updated periodically. After the synchronization is completed you will see the message in the page as shown in Figure 12-25. Click Close.

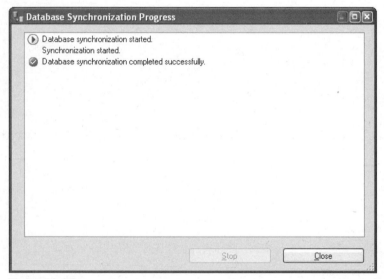

Figure 12-25

You can use the synchronization wizard periodically to synchronize the database from source server to destination server. We typically expect the source server is your test environment and the destination server to be the production environment. Synchronization is a pull model operation where the destination server pulls data from the source server. If a version of the database exists on the destination server then the source server only sends the data. Typically on the destination server you might have established new membership or security permissions. If you choose appropriate options to skip membership or Ignore roles during synchronization then security permissions on the destination servers will not be changed.

> There is an important security requirement you must implement to complete a successful synchronization. The destination server's service startup account must have access to the database(s) on the source server that are expected to be synchronized.

Managing Security

As an administrator, managing security is the most critical operation for the Analysis Services database. The phrase "managing security" can mean several things: managing the roles of Analysis Services databases, using the Analysis Services security features dimension and cell security, enabling and disabling features in Analysis Services, and setting up Analysis Services with appropriate firewall protection. The latter of which will ensure your Analysis Services instance can appropriately communicate via Internet and Intranet.

Server and Database Roles

Roles are of vital importance to secure databases on your Analysis Services instance. You will deal with two kinds of roles when using the product: the server role and database roles. The server role is required for use by a login that performs administrative functions through the user interface (SSMS) or programmatically using AMO. The database roles are defined on an as-needed basis where you can provide read/write permissions to users to all objects in the database or as fine grain as certain cells in a cube. You learned about the server role and how to specify membership earlier in this chapter. In Chapter 9 you learned to define read/write access to dimensions and cubes in a database. To provide access permissions to users you can use the Roles Dialog that can be launched by right clicking on the Roles folder within a specific database. Figure 12-26 shows the Roles Dialog in SSMS.

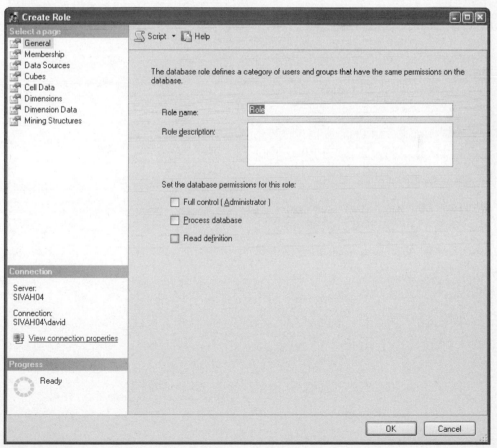

Figure 12-26

The Roles dialog is used to define access to database objects. The pages in the Roles dialog are identical to the Role designer you learned in Chapter 9. Please see to Chapter 9 for details. Chapter 19 provides extensive coverage of database role management through a scenario by which restrict access is restricted to specific dimension members (dimension security) or cells in a cube (cell security) to the users of the database. Just to recap briefly, you can add several roles to a specific database, add members to the role, and provide read, write, or read/write access to the role. In addition you can specify the cell security and dimension security for this role using MDX expressions to limit access to specific cell data or dimension members. When a user is part of multiple roles, Analysis Services provides you access to data in a least restrictive manner. If a user has been restricted access to members of a dimension in one role and has been provided access to the same members in another role then the user will be able to access the members.

Enabling or Disabling Features

Managing database roles is one aspect of securing data in Analysis Services. You can add users to the server role so that you can have several administrators for your Analysis Services instance. The administrator can define appropriate levels of access to databases and objects within a database. However, there is another level of protection that Analysis Services 2005 provides by which you can disable feature(s) that are not used by your users. One of the most common ways to protect your server from security attacks is to reduce your attack surface by running your server or application with minimum functionality. For example, you can turn off unused services of an operating system that listens for requests from users by default. As and when the features are needed, they can be enabled by the administrator. Similarly, Analysis Services allows you to enable or disable certain features to prevent security attacks, thereby making your Analysis Services more secure. Following is the list of features that can be enabled or disabled using the server properties of your Analysis Services instance:

❑ Feature\ManagedCodeEnabled

❑ Feature\LinkInsideInstanceEnabled

❑ Feature\LinkToOtherInstanceEnabled

❑ Feature\LinkFromOtherInstanceEnabled

❑ Feature\COMUDFEnabled

❑ Datamining\AllowAdhocOpenRowSetQueries

❑ Security\RequireClientAuthentication

The features LinkInsideInstanceEnabled, LinkToOtherInstanceEnabled, and LinkFromOtherInstanceEnabled help in enabling or disabling linked objects (measure groups and dimensions) within the same instance and between instances of Analysis Services. The features ManagedCodeEnabled and COMUDFEnabled help you to allow/disallow loading assemblies to Analysis Services. You can allow or deny ad-hoc open row set data mining queries using the property Datamining\AllowAdhocOpenRowSetQueries. The server property Security\RequireClientAuthentication helps you to allow or deny anonymous connections to Analysis Services.

SQL Server 2005 provides you a configuration utility called Surface Area Configuration to reduce the attack surface. You can launch the Surface Area Configuration dialog from Program Files⟹ Microsoft SQL Server 2005⟹Configuration Tools⟹ SQL Server Surface Area Configuration. The dialog provides you two options. The first option is to configure SQL Server 2005 services where you can start or stop services or enable local and remote connections to SQL Server 2005 services. The second option is to configure the features. If you select Surface Area Configuration for Features you will see the dialog shown in Figure 12-27. You can enable or disable the features for allowing Data Mining queries, Anonymous Connections, Linked Objects and COM User Defined functions from this dialog.

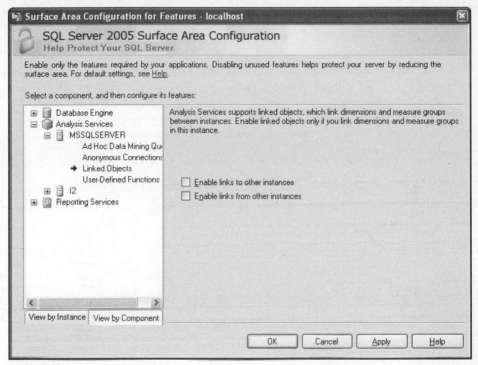

Figure 12-27

Online Mode

As an administrator you need to ensure databases and their objects are kept up to date. Otherwise, your end users will query out of date information. After creating an OLAP database in SSMS you can use the role dialog to create roles and provide permissions to specific users to be database administrators. To reduce confusion, deployed Analysis Services projects should be named the same as the database created by the server administrator. Once the database is created then the server or the database administrator can perform administrative operations using SSMS such as adding new roles, assemblies or processing objects periodically. There might be certain design changes which you will have to make to the database based on additional requirements from the end users. In such a circumstance you would not be able to make the changes in the original project and deploy that project to the Analysis Services instance since the new objects added to the database will likely be deleted. Analysis Services 2005 provides you two ways to make additional changes. You can connect to the Analysis Services database on the server directly through BIDS and then make the changes in a mode called "online mode". The second option is to import the database on your Analysis Services instance using the Import Analysis

Services 9.0 project (one of the Business Intelligence Project templates that can be used from BIDS), make changes to the database in project mode and then re-deploy the project to the Analysis Services instance. We recommend the former since you can not only make changes directly on the server which updates the objects immediately but also perform processing tasks on the objects through the online mode. Instead of designing your Analysis Services database in project mode and then deploying it to the Analysis Services instance you can design the entire database by connecting to the database in online mode. Follow the steps below to connect to an Analysis Services database in online mode using BIDS.

1. Launch BIDS from Program Files⇨Microsoft SQL Server 2005⇨SQL Server Business Intelligence Development Studio.

2. To open an Analysis Services database in online mode select File⇨Open⇨Analysis Services Database… as shown in Figure 12-28.

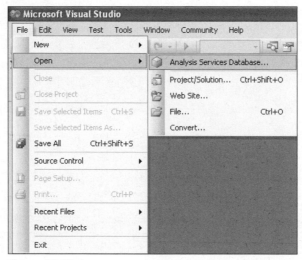

Figure 12-28

3. In the Connect to Database dialog you have the option to open an existing database or create a new database on the Analysis Services instance. You would need to be a server administrator to create a database on the Analysis Services instance. Type the Analysis Services instance name and select a database to open in online mode as shown in Figure 12-29 and click Ok.

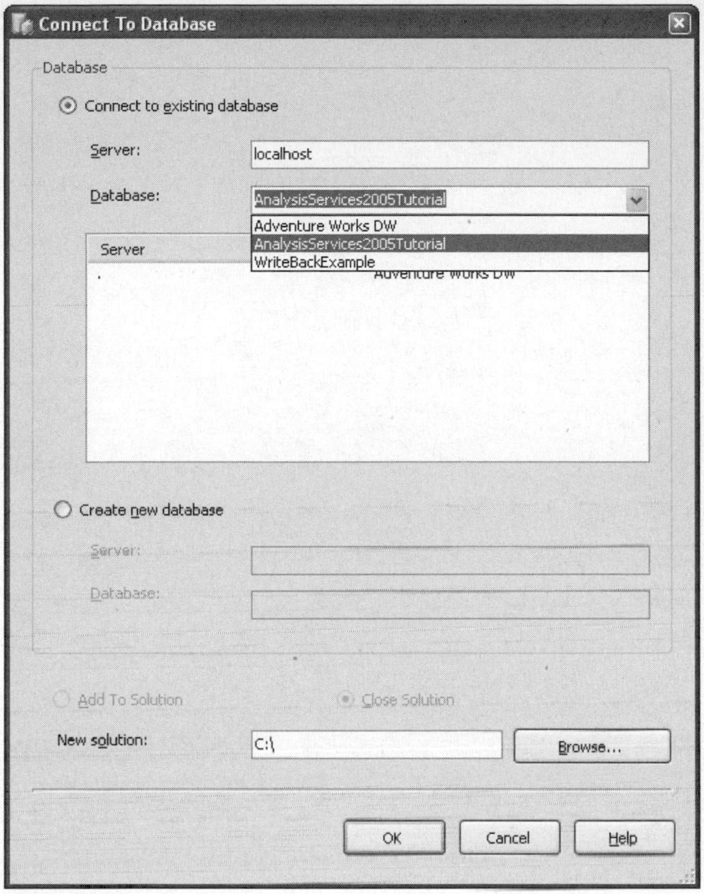

Figure 12-29

BIDS connects to the Analysis Services instance and retrieves all the database objects within BIDS. You will see all the objects of the database in the solution explorer similar to the project mode as shown in Figure 12-30. Notice that with the database connected in online mode the Analysis Services instance name is indicated next to the database name in the Solution Explorer. All the operations that you were able to perform on the objects within a database in the project mode can be performed in the online mode. You do not have the deployment option for the database. Instead you would need to save all your changes directly on the server. We recommend you to explore making changes or adding new objects in the online mode and then saving the changes directly on the Analysis Services instance.

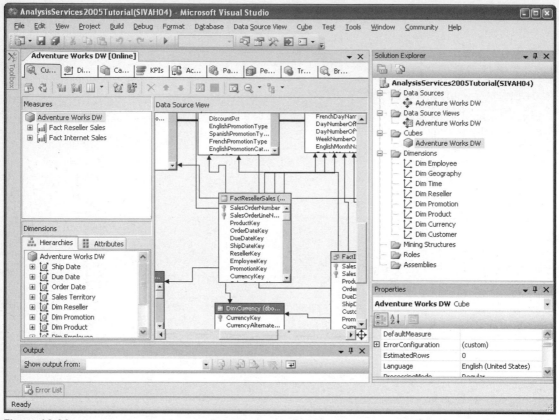

Figure 12-30

Administration via Programming

In Analysis Services 2005 you have the option of automating administrative processes using XML/A commands or using AMO, which in turn communicates with the server using XML/A. AMO provides a well-defined object model that extracts execute and discover XML/A commands that need to be sent to the server and is extremely helpful. Almost all the user interface you saw in SQL Server Management Studio uses the AMO object model while communicating to the server. You learn to manage Analysis Services using AMO in this section. You learn about using XML/A commands and Integration Services to automate some of the management tasks in Chapter 16. You don't have to type in the long code snippets that follow; they are available for download on the book's web site.

Analysis Management Objects (AMO)

In the introduction to this chapter, we mentioned that AMO is an object model that can be used for programmatic administration of an Analysis Services instance. AMO is the replacement for DSO (Decision Support Objects), which shipped in Analysis Services 2000. It is installed and registered into the GAC

(Global Assembly Cache) when Analysis Services is installed. The GAC itself is part of the .NET infrastructure where all commonly used .NET assemblies are registered. Now then, the best way to actually learn AMO is to jump in and use it! In this section you learn a few sample AMO applications that will perform some of the administrative operations you saw earlier in this chapter using SSMS. With the help of AMO you can automate almost all your administrative tasks.

Processing Analysis Services Databases

As you learned earlier in this chapter, processing is one of the most important operations for an administrator. Usually administrators want to automate this process using scripts or programs. You will learn to build an AMO-based console application that takes four command-line parameters: server name, target type (cube or dimension), processing type (full, incremental, update, or unprocess), and finally, the object's name (to be processed.) Before building this console app, please read the source code shown below in advance and don't worry if you don't get it right away; you will soon learn the purpose of all but the most self-explanatory lines of code. The following code is a sample to kick start you to learn AMO with some of the processing options for processing dimension or cube objects within a database.

```
#region Using directives
using System;
using System.Collections.Generic;
using System.Text;
using AMO = Microsoft.AnalysisServices;
#endregion
namespace ProcessASObjects
{
class ProcessASObjects
{
  Microsoft.AnalysisServices.Server myServer = null;
  bool isConnected = false;
  static void Main(string[] args)
  {
    if (args.Length != 6)
    {
          Console.WriteLine("ProcessASObjects <serverName> <1 for Cube/2 for
Dimension> <ProcessType = 1 for Full /2 for Inc /3 for Update /4 for UnProcess>
<databaseName> <objectName>");
          return;
    }
   ProcessASObjects pASObj = new ProcessASObjects(args[0]);
   if (pASObj.isServerConnected())
      pASObj.ProcessObject(Int32.Parse(args [1]), Int32.Parse(args [2]),
        args[3], args[4]);
  }
  public ProcessASObjects(string serverName)
  {
    myServer = new AMO.Server();
    try
    {
      myServer.Connect(serverName);
      isConnected = true;
    }
    catch (Exception e)
    {
```

```
          isConnected = false;
          Console.WriteLine("Error while connecting to the server:" + e.Message);
      }
  }
  bool isServerConnected()
  {
    return isConnected;
  }
  bool ProcessObject(int objectType,int processType, string dbName,
      string objectName)
  {
      AMO.ProcessType objectProcessType = AMO.ProcessType.ProcessDefault;
      switch (processType)
      {
          case 1: objectProcessType = AMO.ProcessType.ProcessFull; //ProcessFull
                  break;
          case 2: objectProcessType = AMO.ProcessType.ProcessAdd;
                  //ProcessIncremental of new members
                  break;
          case 3: objectProcessType = AMO.ProcessType.ProcessUpdate;
                  //Process to update existing members and their properties
                  break;
          case 4: objectProcessType = AMO.ProcessType.ProcessClear;
                  //Clear the object
                  break;
      }
      switch (objectType)
      {
          case 1: // Cube Processing
                  return ProcessCube(dbName, objectName, objectProcessType);
          case 2: //Dimension Processing
                  return ProcessDimension(dbName, objectName, objectProcessType);
      }
      return true;
  }
  bool ProcessDimension(string dbName, string DimName,
                        Microsoft.AnalysisServices.ProcessType pType)
  {
    try
    {
      foreach (AMO.Database db in myServer.Databases)
      {
        if (db.Name.Equals(dbName)) //Check if database name matches
        {
          foreach (AMO.Dimension dim in db.Dimensions)
          {
            if (dim.Name.Equals(DimName))
            //Check if dimension is found within the database
            {
              dim.Process(pType);
              // Process the dimension with the appropriate
              // processing type specified by the user.
              Console.WriteLine("Object {0} Successfully processed",DimName);
              Console.WriteLine("Last processed time is {0}",dim.LastProcessed);
```

```
          }
        } // end foreach
      } // end if
    } // end foreach
  } // end try
  catch (Exception e)
  {
    Console.WriteLine("Error while processing {0}", DimName + e);
    return false;
  } // end catch
  Console.WriteLine("Successfully processed the object");
  return true;
} // end ProcessDimension
bool ProcessCube(string dbName, string CubeName,
                 Microsoft.AnalysisServices.ProcessType pType)
{
  try
  {
    foreach (AMO.Database db in myServer.Databases)
    {
      if (db.Name.Equals(dbName)) //Check if database name matches
      {
        foreach (AMO.Cube cube in db.Cubes)
        {
          if (cube.Name.Equals(CubeName))
          //Check if dimension is found within the database
          {
            cube.Process(pType);
            // Process the dimension with the appropriate processing
            // type specified by the user.
            Console.WriteLine("Successfully processed the object");
            Console.WriteLine(cube.LastProcessed);
          }
        } //end for each
      } // end if
    } // end foreach
  } //end try
  catch (Exception e)
  {
    Console.WriteLine("Error while processing {0}", CubeName + e.Message);
    return false;
  } // end catch
  return true;
} // end ProcessCube
~ProcessASObjects()
{
  //Disconnnect the server when this process is being killed.
  try
  {

    if(myServer.Connected)
      myServer.Disconnect();
  }
  catch (Exception e)
```

```
    {
        Console.WriteLine("Exception occurred while disconnecting from
server"+e.Message);
    }
  } // end ~ProcessASObjects
 } // end class ProcessASObjects
} // end namespace ProcessASObjects
```

To create an AMO-based console application for Analysis Server administration, open Visual Studio 2005 and select New Project under the File menu. In the New Project dialog, select project type Visual C# and use the Console Application template. Name your project AnalysisServicesProcess and be sure the Create Directory for Solution checkbox is checked; finally, click OK to continue. The next step involves adding the AMO assembly to your project; this is accomplished by right-clicking References in the Solution Explorer and selecting Add Reference. In the Add Reference dialog, scroll down to find Analysis Management Objects (Microsoft.AnalysisServices.DLL) and double-click it. This causes the Microsoft.AnalysisServices to be added to your list References.

To accomplish the tasks required in this program, you will need the following directives; please add any you don't already have listed.

```
using System;
using System.Collections.Generic;
using System.Text;
using AMO = Microsoft.AnalysisServices;
```

Next, consistent with .NET coding conventions, create a namespace called ProcessASObjects with a class definition inside of that, also called ProcessASObjects. For more information on namespaces or classes, please see Microsoft's C# online documentation.

```
namespace ProcessASObjects
{
  class ProcessASObjects
  {
        // the rest of the code in this application will go here...
  }
} // end namespace ProcessASObjects
```

First, create and initialize variables of type Server and bool for use in the Main section:

```
Microsoft.AnalysisServices.Server myServer = null;
bool isConnected = false;
```

Next, you create the Main section and infrastructure for processing the command-line parameters; this requires the instantiation of the ProcessASObjects object using new. Then, call the object's method, ProcessObject, with the respective arguments supplied. Of course you can name these functions any way you like, but to keep things simple, you should use the names shown for now.

```
if (args.Length != 5)
{
        Console.WriteLine("ProcessASObjects <serverName> <1 for Cube/2 for Dimension>
        <ProcessType = 1 for Full /2 for Inc /3 for Update /4 for UnProcess> <databaseName>
        <objectName>");
```

```
        return;
    }
    ProcessASObjects pASObj = new ProcessASObjects(args[0]);
      if (pASObj.isServerConnected())
          pASObj.ProcessObject(Int32.Parse(args [1]), Int32.Parse(args [2]),
          args[3], args[4]);
    }
```

Next is the ProcessASObjects definition; you can see clearly that a new AMO server connection is created with appropriate error handling in the event of failure.

```
    public ProcessASObjects(string serverName)
    {
       myServer = new AMO.Server();
       try
       {
          myServer.Connect(serverName);
          isConnected = true;
       }
       catch (Exception e)
       {
          isConnected = false;
          Console.WriteLine("Error while connecting to the server:" + e.Message);
       }
```

If the server connection was successful, the following returns true back to Main in the last If clause in the Main section:

```
    bool isServerConnected()
    {
       return isConnected;
    }
```

What follows is the code necessary to decipher the type of processing to be carried out on the target cube or dimension based on user's command line input and to determine if it is, in fact, a cube or dimension to be processed:

```
    bool ProcessObject(int objectType,int processType, string dbName,
        string objectName)
      {
        AMO.ProcessType objectProcessType = AMO.ProcessType.ProcessDefault;
        switch (processType)
        {
          case 1: objectProcessType = AMO.ProcessType.ProcessFull; //ProcessFull
                  break;
          case 2: objectProcessType = AMO.ProcessType.ProcessAdd;
                  //ProcessIncremental of new members
                  break;
          case 3: objectProcessType = AMO.ProcessType.ProcessUpdate;
                  //Process to update existing members and their properties
                  break;
          case 4: objectProcessType = AMO.ProcessType.ProcessClear;
                  //Clear the object
```

```
                    break;
        }
        switch (objectType)
        {
            case 1: // Cube Processing
                    return ProcessCube(dbName, objectName, objectProcessType);
            case 2: //Dimension Processing
                    return ProcessDimension(dbName, objectName, objectProcessType);
        }
        return true;
    }
```

The two methods ProcessDimension and ProcessCube are the key methods that perform the processing operation. Both methods return a boolean value. These methods return true only in the event the processing operations was successful without any errors. If there are errors then the errors are typically thrown as exceptions and the method returns false. In both methods, you make sure the database name matches an existing database; likewise for dimensions and cubes in their respective methods. Then you use the Process method on the object along with processing type provided by the user which is indicated by the variable pType.

```
bool ProcessDimension(string dbName, string DimName,
                    Microsoft.AnalysisServices.ProcessType pType)
{
    try
    {
        foreach (AMO.Database db in myServer.Databases)
        {
            if (db.Name.Equals(dbName)) //Check if database name matches
            {
                foreach (AMO.Dimension dim in db.Dimensions)
                {
                    if (dim.Name.Equals(DimName))
                    //Check if dimension is found within the database
                    {
                        dim.Process(pType);
                        // Process the dimension with the appropriate
                        // processing type specified by the user.
                        Console.WriteLine("Object {0} Successfully processed",DimName);
                        Console.WriteLine("Last processed time is {0}",dim.LastProcessed);
                    }
                } // end foreach
            } // end if
        } // end foreach
    } // end try
    catch (Exception e)
    {
        Console.WriteLine("Error while processing {0}", DimName + e);
        return false;
    } // end catch
    Console.WriteLine("Successfully processed the object");
    return true;
} // end ProcessDimension
bool ProcessCube(string dbName, string CubeName,
```

```
                    Microsoft.AnalysisServices.ProcessType pType)
   {
     try
     {
       foreach (AMO.Database db in myServer.Databases)
       {
           if (db.Name.Equals(dbName)) //Check if database name matches
           {
             foreach (AMO.Cube cube in db.Cubes)
             {
               if (cube.Name.Equals(CubeName))
               //Check if dimension is found within the database
               {
                   cube.Process(pType);
                   // Process the dimension with the appropriate processing
                   // type specified by the user.
                   Console.WriteLine("Successfully processed the object");
                   Console.WriteLine(cube.LastProcessed);
               }
             } //end for each
           } // end if
       } // end foreach
     } //end try
     catch (Exception e)
     {
       Console.WriteLine("Error while processing {0}", CubeName + e.Message);
       return false;
     } // end catch
     return true;
   } // end ProcessCube
```

To wrap things up, you need only disconnect from the server which is done in the code below.

```
~ProcessASObjects()
{
  //Disconnnect the server when this process is being killed.
  try
  {

    if(myServer.Connected)
        myServer.Disconnect();
  }
  catch (Exception e)
  {
    Console.WriteLine("Exception occurred while disconnecting from
server"+e.Message);
  }
}
```

Once you have mastered the AMO and basic programming concepts shown in this section, you will find it easy to extend the code to take on other administrative tasks like tracing server events, designing aggregations, and writing custom AMO programs for your management tasks.

Back-up and Restore

To convince you that it really is not difficult to extend the concepts demonstrated in the preceding processing program to complete other console apps for administrative purposes, please read through these source code samples covering back-up and restore capabilities.

```csharp
using System;
using System.Collections.Generic;
using System.Text;
using AMO = Microsoft.AnalysisServices;

    /// <summary>
    /// This console program is backup an Analysis Services
    /// -------------------------------------------------------------------
    /// </summary>


namespace ASBackup
{
    class Program
    {
        static void Main(string[] args)
        {
            try
            {
                if (args.Length != 2)
                {
                    Console.WriteLine("Usage: ASBackup <servername>
<databasename>");
                    return;
                }
                AMO.Server myServer = new AMO.Server();
                myServer.Connect(args[0]);
                foreach (AMO.Database db in myServer.Databases)
                {
                    if (db.Name.Equals(args[1]))
                    {
                        db.Backup(args[1]+".abf",true); //Backup the database with
the provided file name
                    }//end if
                } //end forach

            } //end try
            catch (Exception e)
            {
                Console.WriteLine("Exception occurred:" + e.Message);
            }

        } // end Main
    } // end class
} // end namespace
using System;
using System.Collections.Generic;
using System.Text;
```

```
using AMO = Microsoft.AnalysisServices;

    /// <summary>
    /// This console program is restore an Analysis Services backup file
    /// ---------------------------------------------------------------------
    /// </summary>


namespace ASRestore
{
    class Program
    {
        static void Main(string[] args)
        {
            try
            {
                if (args.Length != 2)
                {
                    Console.WriteLine("Usage: ASRestore <backupfilename>");
                    return;
                }
                AMO.Server myServer = new AMO.Server();
                //Connect to the Server
                myServer.Connect(args[0]);
                myServer.Restore(args[1]);
            } //end try
            catch (Exception e)
            {
                Console.WriteLine("Exception occurred:" + e.Message);
            }
        } // end Main
    } // end class
} // end namespace
```

As you can see from the above code segments, it really is quite simple — create an AMO server object, connect to the Analysis Services instance. Depending on the operation (backup or restore) call the appropriate method to perform the operation using AMO. The more you experiment with AMO programming, the more interesting and useful solutions you will generate; so come up with some solutions yourself and code them up!

Adding Assemblies to Analysis Services

You can create your own application in AMO to register assemblies in an Analysis Services database. You just need to get the full path of the assembly, set the right permission and impersonation mode, and then register the assembly. The following is a sample code of a console application that registers the assembly to a specific database in an Analysis Services instance:

```
using System;
using System.IO;
using AMO = Microsoft.AnalysisServices;
```

```
namespace RegisterAssembly
{
    /// <summary>
    /// This console program is used to add .NET assemblies to Analysis Services
databases with appropriate permission set and impersonation mode.
    /// -------------------------------------------------------------------
    /// </summary>
    class RegisterAssembly
    {
        [STAThread]
        static void Main(string[] args)
        {
            int impersonationMode = 0;
            int permissionSet = 0;
            //This console application takes five command line parameters
            // Server name
            // Assembly name with full path that is to be registered
            // Database to which the assembly needs to be added
            // Permission
            // Impersonation Mode
            if (args.Length != 5)
            {
                Console.WriteLine("Usage ...");
                Console.WriteLine("RegisterAssembly {server} {assemPath} {database}
{PermissionSet(1-ExternalAccess,2-Safe, 3-Unrestricted) {ImpersonationMode (1-
Anonymous,2-CurrentUser, 3-ServiceAccount, 4-Default)} ");
                Console.WriteLine("Adds an assembly to database ");
                return;
            }

            try
            {

                //Connect to the Analysis Services instance
                AMO.Server server = new AMO.Server();
                server.Connect(args[0]);

                //get the assembly name
                FileInfo f = new FileInfo(args[1]);
                string assName = f.Name.Replace(f.Extension, "");
                assName = assName.Replace("AMO", "");
                AMO.ClrAssembly cAss = new AMO.ClrAssembly(assName, assName);
                cAss.LoadFiles(f.FullName, true);

                impersonationMode = Int16.Parse(args[4]);
                permissionSet = Int16.Parse(args[3]);
                if (impersonationMode == 0 || permissionSet == 0)
                {
                    Console.WriteLine("Usage ...");
                    Console.WriteLine("RegisterAssembly {server} {assemPath}
{database} {PermissionSet(1-ExternalAccess,2-Safe, 3-Unrestricted)
{ImpersonationMode (1-Anonymous, 2-CurrentUser, 3-ServiceAccount, 4-Default)} ");
```

```
                Console.WriteLine("Adds an assembly to database ");
                return;
            }

            cAss.ImpersonationInfo = new
Microsoft.AnalysisServices.ImpersonationInfo();
            //Set the correct impersonation Mode requested
            switch (impersonationMode)
            {
                case 1: cAss.ImpersonationInfo.ImpersonationMode =
AMO.ImpersonationMode.ImpersonateAnonymous;
                    break;
                case 2: cAss.ImpersonationInfo.ImpersonationMode =
AMO.ImpersonationMode.ImpersonateCurrentUser;
                    break;
                case 3: cAss.ImpersonationInfo.ImpersonationMode =
AMO.ImpersonationMode.ImpersonateServiceAccount;
                    break;
                case 4: cAss.ImpersonationInfo.ImpersonationMode =
AMO.ImpersonationMode.Default;
                    break;
            }
            //set the correct permissionSet requested
            switch (permissionSet)
            {

                case 1: cAss.PermissionSet =
Microsoft.AnalysisServices.PermissionSet.ExternalAccess;
                    break;
                case 2: cAss.PermissionSet =
Microsoft.AnalysisServices.PermissionSet.Safe;
                    break;
                case 3: cAss.PermissionSet =
Microsoft.AnalysisServices.PermissionSet.Unrestricted;
                    break;
            }

            //add assembly to database
            AMO.Database db = server.Databases.GetByName(args[2]);
            db.Assemblies.Add(cAss);

            cAss.Update(); //Sends the DDL to the Server
            server.Disconnect();
            Console.WriteLine("Registered Assembly");
        }
        catch (Exception e)
        {
            Console.WriteLine("Register Assembly failed, " + e.Source + " " +
e.Message);
        }
    }
    }
}
```

The AMO code samples provided in this section are primarily to help you start using AMO for the various management tasks. The samples provided in this chapter have been tested for appropriate operations. However these are still code samples and if you need to write your own AMO programs for management operations we expect you to write robust code for your production environment with appropriate error handling. AMO contains several classes that help you perform more than just management operations. You can design an entire database programmatically and deploy the entire database to an Analysis Services instance.

Synchronization is one of the administrative task operations to move database from test environments to production environments. However, AMO does not have methods to perform the synchronize operation. AMO allows you to send XMLA scripts to the Analysis Services instances. You can take the script that can be generated from the Synchronization Wizard and send the script using AMO to perform management operations for synchronization. We leave it to you to explore the AMO object model and write the code for synchronization. The AMO sample program for synchronization can be downloaded from the web site accompanying the book.

HTTP Connectivity to Analysis Services

We expect customers would want to expose the data from Analysis Services to the end users through web application. Analysis Services 2000 supported data access from the Web through a component called DATA PUMP. Analysis Services 2005 uses a similar architecture to support data access for Web applications. The PUMP component needs to be loaded within Internet Information Server (IIS) as an ISAPI dll. In order to provide web access to data from Analysis Services you need to configure your IIS appropriately. You need to set up virtual directories, copy appropriate DLLs provided by Analysis Services 2005 and setup appropriate permission on IIS so that users can access data from Analysis Services. The PUMP does not necessarily have to be setup on the same machine as Analysis Services. Using Analysis Services 2005 you can configure several data PUMPs to be directing queries to various Analysis Services instances. Each PUMP has a configuration file where the server name and certain other properties are configured. In order to access Analysis Services data over the web a user would connect to IIS using HTTP. IIS in turn directs the request to Analysis Services instance over TCP/IP with appropriate credentials set up on IIS. The architecture of the connection to Analysis Services over HTTP is shown in Figure 12-31.

You can configure security on IIS to either use anonymous connection to Analysis services, perform username and password authentication on IIS or perform windows authentication. The steps for setting up HTTP connectivity using data PUMP includes configuring your IIS by creating virtual directories and configuring the PUMP and security for the users. Microsoft has published a white paper called "Configuring HTTP Access to SQL Server 2005 Analysis Services on Microsoft Windows XP," Published: July 27, 2005. We recommend you to go to http://www.microsoft.com, search for the paper with the above provided title.

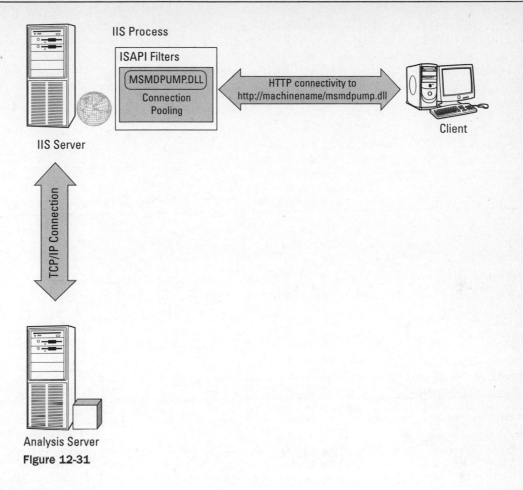

IIS Process

ISAPI Filters

MSMDPUMP.DLL

Connection
Pooling

HTTP connectivity to
http://machinename/msmdpump.dll

Client

IIS Server

TCP/IP Connection

Analysis Server
Figure 12-31

Legacy DSO Applications

If you have experience with DSO (object model used for managing Analysis Services 2000), we expect you will find AMO straightforward. The good news is that if you have imported your Analysis Services 2000 database to Analysis Services 2005, you can still make those client apps written for Analysis Services 2000 work. This is accomplished using the version of DSO shipped with Analysis Services 2000 Service Pack 4 along with some additions. We refer to the DSO installed with SQL Server 2005 as DSO8.5. If you have an existing DSO application you will be able to use that application to manage the upgraded or migrated database as long as there has been no changes to the migrated database using SQL Server 2005 tools. The overall architecture showing how an existing DSO application can communicate with Analysis Services 2005 is shown in Figure 12-32.

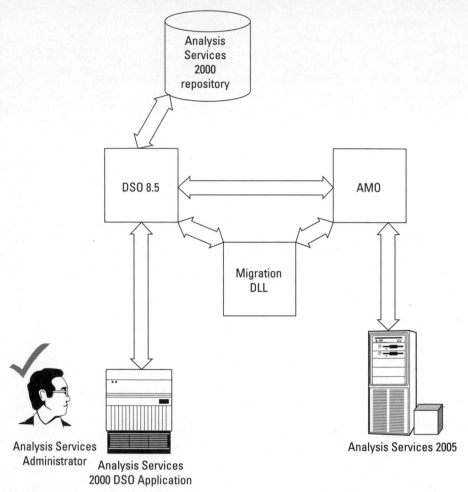

Figure 12-32

When an existing DSO-based application attempts to connect to Analysis Services 2005; DSO8.5 is used to make the connection. DSO 8.5 first tries to connect to Analysis Services 8.0 (Analysis Services 2000), followed by Analysis Services 7.0. When connections to both Analysis Services 8.0 and 7.0 fail DSO 8.5 connects to Analysis Services 2005 through AMO. Repository connection string information and the locks directory are garnered and stored as properties in the Analysis Services configuration file when Analysis Services 2000 is upgraded to Analysis Services 2005. AMO returns the repository connection string and lock directory properties to DSO 8.5. Changes to the Analysis Services database initiated by the DSO application such as modifications to dimensions, cubes or mining models, are only reflected in the repository. When the client application issues a process command; then DSO8.5 retrieves the meta-data for the database, uses the migration DLL to migrate to Analysis Services 2005 objects and then, using AMO, sends the entire database to be updated to Analysis Services 2005. Any information that is updated on the database in the meantime using SQL Server 2005 tools would be lost. After the migration or upgrade from Analysis Services 2000 to Analysis Services 2005 if you make any changes to the imported database, which uses features specific to Analysis Services 2005 we recommend you not continue on with your legacy DSO application. We encourage you to re-write your management application using AMO unless it is cost prohibitive to do so.

Analysis Services and Fail-over Clustering

Analysis Services 2005 provides fail-over clustering out of the box. By that we mean SQL Server 2005 setup supports Analysis Services to be installed on a windows clustered environment. You first need to have Microsoft Cluster Services (MSCS) setup to form a cluster of two or more nodes. We recommend you look at Windows product documentation to setup and configure MSCS. You need to have a shared disk with sufficient disk space that can hold the Analysis Services data files. After setting up a cluster; you can then use Microsoft SQL Server 2005 setup to install Analysis Services with fail-over capability. In the SQL Server 2005 setup you need to provide a virtual server name with an IP (internet protocol) address and the shared data folder for the Analysis Services data. The virtual server name will be the name of the Analysis Services server. SQL Server 2005 setup installs Analysis Services 2005 binaries on all the nodes of the cluster and the data folder is setup on the shared disk with appropriate permissions.

Figure 12-33 shows the overall architecture of the Analysis Services 2005 fail-over cluster setup. Users of Analysis Services will only be aware of the virtual server name. At a give time only one of the physical machines will service users requests and has access to the shared disk containing Analysis Services data. When one of the nodes in the cluster fails due to network or power problems then MSCS makes the second node as the primary and provides control to the shared disk. MSCS identifies failure in the primary node through the heart beat which is a typically a connection through a second network card between the machines involved in the cluster. The second node gains control to the Analysis Services data all future user requests are directed to the second node. Existing users originally connected to the first node would have to re-establish their connections. In order to make sure you are isolated from disk problems it is recommended that the shared disk is a RAID (Redundant Array of Independent (or Inexpensive) Disks to provide fault tolerance. Due to fail-over clustering support you have higher availability of Analysis Services to your users whenever there are hardware problems.

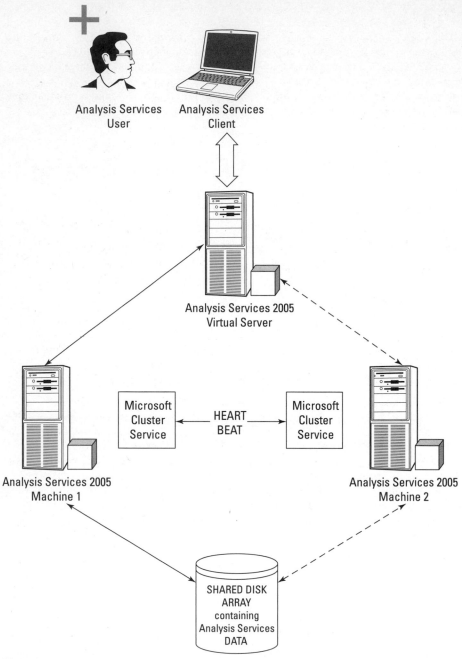

Figure 12-33

Summary

If you're a database administrator experienced with Analysis Services 2000 admin, this chapter may have been largely routine with a few interesting twists—like .NET or what it means to process a dimension versus a cube. If you have never created programs to dynamically administer a server, perhaps you found this to be one of the most exciting chapters yet! It is great how you can apply the power and flexibility of programming with direct access to server side functionality. What this ultimately provides is an unfettered ability to manage the server the way you want; not just the way the Analysis Services 2005 User Interface Designers thought you would want to. This is not to say the User Interface isn't good; it is, but let's face it—you know best what you want to accomplish.

In this chapter you learned that for each administrative task there is a way to execute it through the user interface using SSMS or BIDS; or through the coding and running of applications using the AMO .NET assembly called Microsoft.AnalysisServices.dll. One illustration of these parallel implementation modes was shown with the synchronization capability, which can be implemented in the user interface using the Synchronize Database Wizard in SSMS, or can be coded with the synchronize ( ) method as part of an AMO-based application. With all the excitement surrounding AMO it is easy to forget its predecessor, DSO. You found out that legacy client applications could be used to interface with Analysis Server 2000 databases after migration to Analysis Server 2005. To accomplish this, you need only use DSO8.5 to talk to the server.

You also learned how useful backup and restore can be for auditing purposes—specifically by providing snapshots in time of cubes to auditors and analysts. And how security is configured for administrative versus user access to the server; this by using server and database roles, respectively. Finally, in this chapter you were exposed to properties. In the next chapter on Performance Optimization, you will find several interesting ways to tweak properties to achieve maximal processing and query throughput.

13

Performance Optimization

As any good English dictionary will tell you, performance has several possible meanings. In computer science, performance most often refers to the functioning efficiency of software and can relate to both speed and scalability. There are established standards and benchmarks to measure and compare the performance of products and services. Why care about performance? Well, consider your job performance; assuming you are an employee, your job review and, therefore, salary raise and bonus, will hinge on how well you do your job. In order to get the best work out of you, your manager needs to know what your interests are, what motivates you, and then assign appropriate tasks to get the maximum performance from you. Your manager will be rewarding you for your performance. Usually in the currency you like most, cash.

It follows that if you are a data warehouse designer using Analysis Services you need to know how to get the best performance from the system so as to satisfy the customers. Just like your boss can push certain buttons to motivate you, Analysis Services provides various parameters that can be set to achieve maximum performance. As for server products such as Analysis Services, one can attribute performance results to how well server properties are tuned in the context of speed and scalability requirements.

The graph shown in Figure 13-1 is a typical server scalability graph. The query throughput lines show the server throughput (queries served per minute) as more users are using the system concurrently for two different hardware configurations. For Hardware 1, up to about 50 users, the server throughput increases linearly. That means the server has sufficient resources to support 50 concurrent users. Then after about 50 users, the throughput starts to flatten out. In the 50-to-100 user range, the server doesn't have enough resources (CPU or memory or disk) to serve requests of all concurrent users. In this circumstance, some user requests would be queued in the system request queue to keep the system from slowing down all the user requests. At about 100 users, the system is running at maximum capacity. The curve flattens off at high loads because internally, the server only executes a few queries concurrently, and queues the rest. This is so that with many outstanding queries, new users can still get reasonable response time while connecting to the server and executing non-query commands.

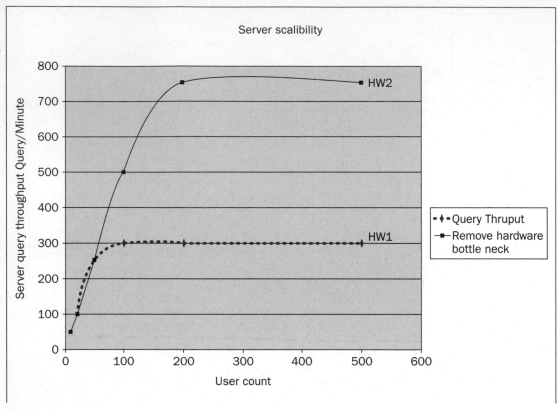

Figure 13-1

From the perspective of a user, when a server is under an extreme load with many outstanding queries, some of the execution time is spent waiting in the queue, and some time is spent actually working on the query. You might compare it to waiting in line for a food in a crowded baseball stadium. When the load is high, the wait time can easily exceed the time to actually do the business. Hardware 2 has better resources (CPUs, memory, network) as compared to Hardware 1. Hence if you run the server on Hardware 2 you obviously get a better throughput since the saturation to maximum users occurs at about 200 users.

If you have a well architected server then Figure 13-2 shows the average query response under load. The average response time starts to increase, and eventually the average response time will increase linearly. If your system only needs to support 10 to 50 members, you don't have to do anything. But if your system needs to support 100+ users, you need to identify the system bottlenecks. Typically servers will expose performance monitoring counters to expose internal values. You can use the task manager and performance counters to identify bottlenecks; whether the system is CPU-bound (such that the Server CPU is pegged at 100%) or memory-bound (memory usage is constantly maxed out) or disk-bound (reads or writes to disk). By removing the system hardware bottleneck and adding more CPU or memory to the server, you should be able to get performance improvements and support more concurrent users as shown in Figure 13-2 for Hardware 2.

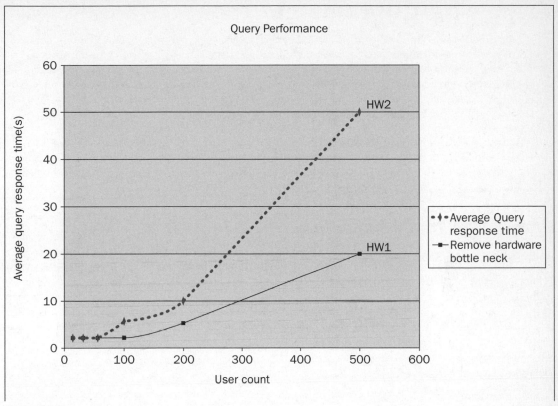

Figure 13-2

Note that while we expect to see the general shape of the curves described above, the limits will be different for your hardware, your cube design, the queries your users execute, and the frequency with which queries are executed. With respect to Analysis Services, in a typical query scenario, CPU, memory, and disk read speed can all be potential bottlenecks for your system. In a cube or dimension processing scenario, CPU, memory, disk writing speed, and network speed between the relational source and Analysis Services can all be candidate areas for system optimization work.

For Analysis Services performance we refer to four main areas — database design and processing, querying, and configuring Analysis Services (setting properties). The first involves design optimization to facilitate the optimized processing of dimensions and cubes. The second relates to optimization to speed up MDX queries. The third involves fine tuning Analysis Services or appropriate hardware acquisition based on requirements. Does performance imply both scalability and optimization of Analysis Services? Depending on whom you ask, one or both are true. The bottom line is that you need best query performance with regard to your OLAP cubes. That is true regardless of size, and however you can get it that doesn't involve the violation of federal or state laws is fine. In the next section you will learn some of the design techniques that can help in improving your Analysis Services performance.

Optimizing UDM Design

The data modeling completed during UDM creation has a significant impact on both query performance and processing performance, so it is not something to be rushed through. Even before starting to build your UDM, you must understand the business requirements of the system under assembly as much as possible. You need to have clarity regarding the goal of the system, and that, in turn, feeds directly into creating the analysis requirements, and what potential queries the system needs to support. That understanding will also provide insight into what attributes the user won't be interested in analyzing.

Every dimension, and attribute in a dimension, will demand processing time for your UDM. In addition, because adding unnecessary dimensions and attributes will increase the cube space, it can slow the query performance too. You should use the business requirements to drive your design, just be sure to avoid unnecessary dimensions and keep your system compact and performant.

Fine Tuning Your Dimensions

In Analysis Services 2005, dimensions can contain several hierarchies. Often when you create your dimension using the wizard, all the columns in the relational table(s) are added as attribute hierarchies in support of relational and OLAP querying. You can easily end up with a dimension that can have hundreds of attributes. In most business scenarios, the attributes within a dimension are not used in many queries. Only a subset of the attributes might be heavily used. In this section you learn various design techniques that will help you design the right dimension suited to your business needs and get the optimal performance acceptable for your business.

Choose the Right Key Attribute

Each dimension needs to have a key attribute. The relational dimensional tables will typically have a column defined as a key column, and that is automatically inferred as the key attribute by the dimension wizard. In certain relational databases, the relationships between the fact and dimension tables and the primary and foreign keys might not be defined. In such cases you would need to define the relationships between the tables in your DSV. Choosing the key attribute can actually impact processing and query performance. If you know that you have two columns in the dimension table that each uniquely identifies a row in the table and if they are of different data types, such as integer and string, try to choose the column that is an integer. Key attributes that are of integer data types occupy less storage and are faster to retrieve than those of type string, because the number of bytes used to store string types are typically larger than that for integer data types. In addition, if you have a choice of choosing a single column as a key attribute as compared to choosing multiple columns in the table, choose the single column as the key column. If you are already aware of these techniques and have designed your database accordingly, it's great. Some might think that all they need is just more disks — we consider that disk space is quite cheap to buy and they are much faster than before — and some might think a few bytes might not make a big difference. However, imagine your dimension has millions of members — no matter how much disk space you have, accessing each member during queries takes time.

The fastest processing time of fact-table partitions occurs when the fact table has integer foreign keys for the dimension, and the dimension contains the integer key as an attribute (perhaps hidden). This allows the SQL query sent by Analysis Services during processing to be efficient in terms of query performance. We are aware of several international major customers with large data warehouses using composite keys with long strings. Each of these companies had a data warehouse before they started using Analysis

Services and they consider a change prohibitively expensive. Their design works and their business benefits from using Analysis Services. But their time window for processing fact-table partitions would be much smaller if they had used integer keys.

Avoid Unnecessary Attributes

Because Analysis Services supports attributes hierarchies, you can create many attributes which allow the users to analyze their data along those attributes. However, if you create too many attributes that are never used in customer queries, it will waste system data storage slowing both processing and query performance. We recommend you look at each dimension in detail and eliminate attributes that will never be queried by users. Although your dimension table(s) might contain several columns it is usually not necessary to convert every single column in the dimension table(s) to attributes hierarchies in the dimension. You can see an example in the sample Adventure Works DW project's customer dimension. Figure 13-3 shows the Customer dimension, where you can see the list of columns in the DSV and compare it against the list of attribute hierarchies included within the dimension.

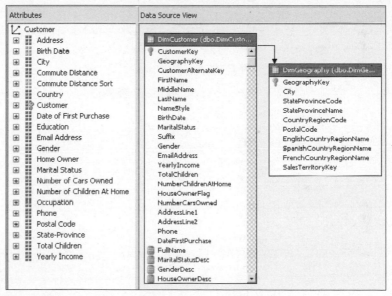

Figure 13-3

You can see that the Dim_Customer relational table contains several columns. However the Customer dimension includes only a subset of those columns that are essential for data analysis as attribute hierarchies. For example the column Title in the Customer's table is not used in data analysis and hence it is not included as an attribute in the Customer dimension.

Turn Off Optimization for Rarely Used Attributes

Although some attributes in a dimension are used for data analysis, they might be needed only on rare occasions. For example, you might be querying an employee's zip code or phone number infrequently for analysis. By default, Analysis Services creates indexes for each attribute; assuming the attribute hierarchy will be used often in queries. By turning off attributes' optimization via their AttributeHierarchy OptimizedState, you will save processing time and resources by not creating indexes for such attributes. A query involving any NotOptimized attribute will be slower; however, because it is rarely used, it won't hurt most of your users' query performance. Most often you will have certain attributes that are used as member properties. We recommend you set the AttributeHierarchyOptimizedState for member property attributes as well as attributes that might be used infrequently during querying to be NotOptimized because those attributes are not involved in queries. The improvement for data storage and processing time would justify this choice.

The AttributeHierarchyOptimizedState is a property for each attribute. If you click an attribute you will see this property under the advanced section in the properties window. Figure 13-4 shows the Attribute HierarchyOptimizedState property. To turn off the property for an attribute in the dimension, change the value from FullyOptimized to NotOptimized.

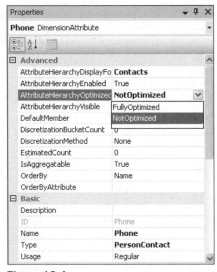

Figure 13-4

Turn Off AttributeHierarchy for Member Properties

Some attributes are not relevant to data analysis per se, which means user queries will never pivot on those attributes. Still, it is useful to display and use those attributes as member properties. Consider the "birth date" attribute; although customer queries may never break down fact data by birth date, customer birth date might be displayed next to customer names in reports, perhaps as a sorting criteria for listing customers. You can turn off the AttributeHierarchyEnabled property for "birth date" to tell the Analysis Services not to build an attribute hierarchy for this attribute, but keep it as a member property. This reduces the time and space needed for dimension processing. Figure 13-5 shows the AttributeHierarchyEnabled property for a dimension attribute. If this property is set to false for an attribute; you will not be able to browse the hierarchy. Rather, you can query the attribute members as member properties.

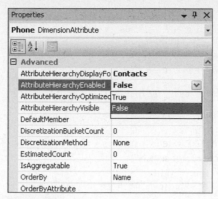

Figure 13-5

Define Hierarchy Relationships between Attributes

If attributes within a dimension are related by a one-to-many relationship, we recommend you establish that relationship in Dimension Designer. For example, in a geography dimension you will typically have Country, State, and City attributes know that there is a one-to-many relationship between these attributes. Define these relationships in the Dimension Designer for improved processing and query performance. If you create user hierarchies within a dimension, and if the user hierarchies have multiple levels and there is a natural relationship between these attributes, we highly recommend you define these relationships. Often when user hierarchies are created, they will be used in queries and defining the natural relationships helps significantly in query performance. The attribute relationship will help the server build efficient indices, which will benefit query performance along the user hierarchies significantly. To really understand this issue, you first need to learn about natural and unnatural hierarchies.

All attributes within a dimension are related to the key attribute because the key attribute is unique, and by definition a key has a one-to-many relationship with all the attributes. As for the natural hierarchy, consider the multilevel hierarchy Full Name⇨Postal Code⇨City⇨State-Province⇨Country shown in Figure 13-6. A hierarchy is called a natural hierarchy if there is a one-to-many relationship between every pair of attributes that are from successive levels of a user hierarchy. In the example shown in Figure 13-6, you can see that the relationship between attributes of various levels has been established in the Dimension Designer, namely, Customer attribute (called FullName in the multilevel hierarchy) has a relationship with Postal Code, Postal Code has an attribute relationship with City, City has an attribute relationship with State Province and State Province has an attribute relationship with Country. Essentially, a chain of relationships from the bottom-level attribute to the top-level attribute is created. Such a hierarchy is called a natural hierarchy.

In a natural hierarchy, the attribute at a given level maintains a many-to-one relationship with an attribute directly above it. The many-to-one relationship is defined by the attribute relationship, as shown in Figure 13-6, and the server builds indexes for fast navigations. A natural hierarchy for which indexes are created during processing time is referred to as a materialized hierarchy. For the customer hierarchy example shown in Figure 13-6, indices for state-province to country, city to state-province, and so on are built and stored in the server. Analysis Services will utilize those indices to accelerate query performance; it can easily find all states in the USA because the query can be directly resolved from the "State-Province to Country" index. Also, if the data cache or aggregated data that is stored in Analysis Services has data for State-Province, Analysis Services can use the same index to quickly get an aggregate value for Country.

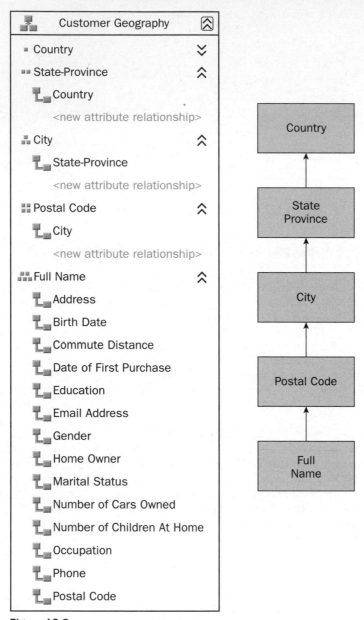

Figure 13-6

Defined relationships not only help during query performance but also during processing. Analysis Services processes the key attribute of the dimension after processing all the remaining attributes. If no relationships are defined, then at the time of processing the dimension the server needs to retrieve data for all the attributes while processing the key attribute. This increases the processing time of the key attribute and the dimensions. If you have defined the natural relationships between attributes, Analysis Services has an optimized code path that reduces the key attribute processing, thereby reducing the overall dimension processing time. You will see significant differences in processing times for large dimensions that have hundreds of attributes. For some large dimensions (> 10 million members and > 100 attributes) you might reach the physical processing limits of a 32-bit environment and might have to move to 64-bit servers. Establishing relationships (as discussed) combined with other dimension optimizations (also discussed) can facilitate processing for large dimensions on a 32-bit platform.

In the case of an unnatural hierarchy, only the key attribute has an attribute relationship to all other attributes, so the relationship graph resembles Figure 13-7. The system will only build indexes along attribute relationships, and build one-to-many indexes for Country to Customer, State-Province to Customer, City to Customer, and Zip Code to Customer. When you create a user hierarchy such as Customer⇨ZipCode⇨City⇨StateProvince⇨Country, no additional indices get created.

Unnatural hierarchies need to be materialized (identifying navigation paths for members from one level to the next level and data corresponding to members in a level need to be aggregated from the members at the lowest level) during query time and will result in slow query performance. For example, to resolve a simple USA.Children query, the server must use the Country⇨Customer relationship to find all customers in the USA; then use the Customer⇨State Province relationship to find all states for those customers in the USA. If there are millions of customers in the USA, the query will traverse the millions of records, thereby resulting in slow performance. In addition, if the server has cached values or pre-calculated aggregations for "State-Province," the cache cannot be used to resolve a country query because there are no direct relationships between country and state province.

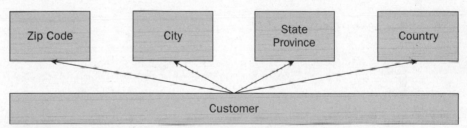

Figure 13-7

You should specify one-to-many relationships whenever possible. Not only will it help significantly for query performance, but it also will save storage space. For the Country to Customer index in the unnatural hierarchy example, every customer member in the USA will have an entry in the index. However, by moving the relationship to State-Province to Country, you will only need 50 entries for that index. To establish the attribute relationship as shown in Figure 13-8, you simply need to drag and drop the attribute to the "new attribute relationship" for the corresponding attribute.

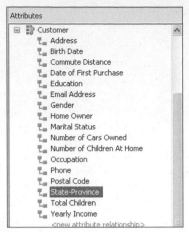

Figure 13-8

Fine Tuning Your Cube

You have so far seen some of the design techniques that will help you achieve improved dimension processing and query performance. Similarly, certain design optimizations within the cube can also help you in achieving better performance during processing or querying. This section discusses cube optimization design techniques.

Fact Table ⇨ Measure Groups or Partitions

When you run cube wizard on a DSV containing multiple fact tables, the wizard creates a separate measure group for each fact table identified. However, such a UDM may or may not be the right design for your business analysis. For example, if you have two fact tables, salesfact2005 and salesfact2006, which have the sales information of your business for the years 2005 and 2006 (containing identical columns), the cube wizard will be creating two measure groups. However, for your purposes these should actually be modeled within the same measure group as two partitions so that appropriate data can be rolled up. If you are creating the cube using the Cube Wizard, select one of the fact tables in the cube wizard table selection page, and then the other fact table can be added as a partition to the measure group. If you select both tables by mistake and the Cube Wizard has already created two measure groups for the two fact tables, you can delete one of them from the Cube Designer and add that table as a partition in the partitions tab. A way to think about this is a Measure Group contains the union of all partitions.

You can have fact data spread across multiple tables. For business reasons it might make sense to have all the fact data within the same measure group. Consider a measure group as an entity within your UDM that represents a set of measures which are grouped logically for business reasons; or in Analysis Services terms, share the same dimensionality and granularity. Hence even if you have fact data spread across multiple tables and for business reasons, you actually need to combine the data; make sure you have them added within a single measure group. You can join the fact tables containing measures into a single view within the DSV and create a measure group from that, or you can add measures from either of the fact tables within a single measure group using the Cube Designer.

Optimizing Reference Dimensions

If your UDM contains reference dimensions, you need to be aware of making optimizations for the reference dimensions. If you are querying a reference dimension that is not optimized then you might not get the best query performance. Figure 13-9 shows the relationship definition for a reference dimension. You have a small checkbox called Materialize. You learned in Chapter 5 about reference dimensions and materializing them. To recap, materializing the reference dimensions ensures that indexes are created for the dimension. Once you materialize the reference dimensions, Analysis Services views those reference dimensions as regular dimensions. This helps to improve the query performance. Also, materializing a reference dimension is the only way to create a chain of two or more dimensions as reference dimensions that include intermediate reference dimensions.

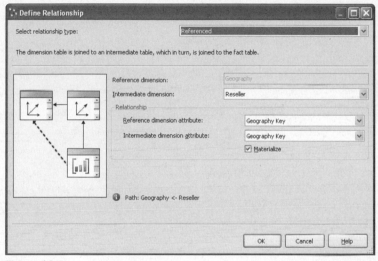

Figure 13-9

Partitions

Partitions store cube fact data in one of the storage modes — MOLAP, ROLAP, or HOLAP. By dividing the data in fact table(s) into multiple partitions you can take advantage of parallelism which can reduce the processing time for the cube and get improved query performance. Assume you have fact data for various months since the year 2002, which is part of a specific measure group. The following table shows a partition scheme that uses time to partition the fact data. Partitions 1–3 include data for past years, and they do not change. Partition 4 includes data for past months in the year 2005, which also do not change. Only Partition 5, that contains current month data, changes daily.

Partition 1	Partition 2	Partition 3	Partition 4	Partition 5
2002	2003	2004	2005	CurrentMonth

Assume the fact data is in a single fact table called Yearly Sales, and you have a measure group within your UDM that has been created from this fact table. By default the Cube Wizard creates a single partition that points to the relational table Yearly Sales. By dividing the data into multiple partitions, all the partitions can be processed in parallel, which will utilize the processor and memory resources of your machine more efficiently. Unlike Analysis Services 2000, which processed each partition serially, Analysis Services 2005 processes objects in parallel by default. If the Server machine has more than one CPU and sufficient memory, parallel processing will reduce total process time as compared to a machine with single CPU. During query time, if cubes contain several partitions, Analysis Services can scan those partitions in parallel, and queries can return results quickly because the server has multiple jobs running in parallel, each one scanning a partition. In addition to that, when you divide the data into multiple partitions based on specific dimension member, Analysis Services 2005 by default retrieves data only from relevant partitions needed for the query if the cube is of storage type MOLAP. For example, if a query requests data for partition 2002, Analysis Services will only query the data from partition containing 2002 data. In order to create multiple partitions, you can create multiple tables in the relational database and then create the partitions. Alternatively, you can create named queries within your DSV that correspond to your desired partition strategy.

The second benefit of creating partitions in an environment where most of the data does not change is that you only need to process the current partition, which has new data added or modified. You need to only process the currentMonth partition in the partition scheme to refresh the latest data changes within your UDM. The data volume to process is reduced and the process time will be significantly decreased compared to processing the entire UDM.

The third benefit of partitioning data is that you can set up different storage modes for each partition. In business scenarios where a certain amount of data is not changing and the data volume is huge, it is better to use MOLAP to increase query performance. In addition, if you need real-time access to your data for analysis you can create a small partition with the current month's data and set the storage mode for that partition as ROLAP. Analysis Services retrieves the data from the appropriate partitions and provides you the aggregated real-time data for your business analysis.

Yet another benefit of partitioning data is that you can create different aggregations (pre-calculated data cache for improved query performance) for maximum benefit. Creating aggregations for your UDM is covered in detail later in this chapter. You can design heavy aggregations for those partitions that are queried most (the current year data) to maximize query performance, and create less aggregations for old data that are queried less to save the server storage. Creating such aggregations not only saves storage space but also reduces processing times if the entire UDM is processed.

Finally, refreshing the data within a partition is much faster than refreshing the entire UDM. You do not have to apply incremental processing on all the partitions. You just have to do incremental processing on the partition whose data needs to be updated. During incremental processing of the current partition, a temporary partition is created and then merged into the existing partition, which could possibly result in data fragmentation. By refreshing the partition, the server will re-sort the data for optimized query performance.

Merging Partitions

If you have multiple partitions where data is used sparsely, merge the partitions so that data from each partition does not get aggregated every time a query is issued. Assume you have your measure group data partitioned by month for the year 2002. If every user's query is asking for the entire year's data, Analysis Services needs to retrieve the data from all the partitions and aggregate data within the server.

Having too many partitions could hurt query performance because the server needs to scan those partitions and aggregate data from them. Instead you can merge the data from all the partitions to form a single partition. Queries referring to 2002 will henceforth touch a single partition. If you have aggregations created at the year level then your queries can be instantaneous.

A common scenario for many Analysis Services users is to partition by time, and have a weekly or monthly schedule of updating the cube. This typically involves merging the most recent partition into the year-to-date partition, and creating a new partition for the next period. Sometimes SSIS (SQL Server Integration Services which you learn in Chapter 16) is used to control the flow of operations. This is another scenario where data from existing partitions need to be merged.

Consider the example reviewed in the "Partitions" section, where data was partitioned by time. If you want to merge the partitions to a single partition because queries are infrequent, you can do so using SMSS by following the steps below.

1. Deploy the sample Adventure Works DW project shipped with the product. The Adventure Works cube contains several measure groups. Connect to the Adventure Works DW database using SSMS.

2. Navigate through the cube and notice the four partitions under the Internet Sales measure group as shown in Figure 13-10.

3. Right-click the internet_sales_2003 partition and select Merge Partitions. Assume you want to merge the 2004 data into this partition.

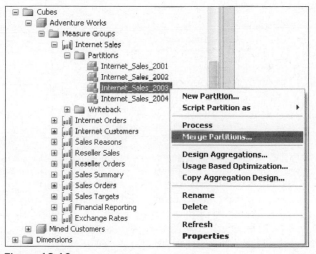

Figure 13-10

4. In the Merge partitions dialog, select Internet_Sales_2004, as shown in Figure 13-11, and click OK. You are done! You have now successfully merged 2004 partition data into the 2003 partition.

5. In the SSMS object browser, refresh the measure group object. The partition of internet_sales_2004 is gone because it was just merged to the internet_sales_2003 partition. You can see this in Figure 13-12. You can still query the data for 2004 and 2003 as before. The cube still contains the same data and all queries still return the same result.

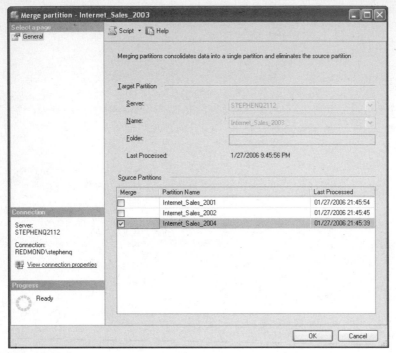

Figure 13-11

Figure 13-12

We expect your UDM to have several partitions for each of your measure groups, especially the ones that contain a large volume of fact data. We recommend you investigate the queries that are sent to your UDM and identify the requirements of your business users. One mechanism used to identify the queries sent to Analysis Services is SQL Server Profiler. You will learn about Profiling Analysis Services using SQL Server Profiler in this chapter. Most measure groups partitioned are data that map to time. This is the most logical and common scenario for most businesses. If after analyzing the queries you see that your user queries are targeted to specific partition(s), and the remaining partitions are infrequently queried or queries to those partitions retrieve data at a higher grain, we recommend you merge such partitions.

Optimizing ROLAP Partitions

Assume a large-scale UDM containing several partitions where all the partitions are ROLAP. In such a scenario, when a query comes in requesting data Analysis Services sends relational queries to each partition with appropriate conditions to retrieve the data. Analysis Services then aggregates the data retrieved from the relational data source and sends the results to the end user. However generating the queries for each partition, establishing connection to the data source and then retrieving results is an operation that takes a certain amount of time. Even if the data requested is for a single partition, Analysis Services will send queries to all the partitions, which is not essential. Most likely, data in various partitions has been partitioned based on a specific hierarchy. For example, data can be partitioned based on months. In such circumstances you can provide a hint to Analysis Services about the data contained in a ROLAP partition through a property of the partition called Slice. This property allows you to specify an MDX expression which indicates the slice on a hierarchy (a member or a group of members in that hierarchy) that uniquely identifies the data within the partition. When the Slice property is specified then Analysis Services sends ROLAP queries to partitions only if the MDX query requested is expected to retrieve results from those partitions. If the Slice property is not specified then by default Analysis Services assumes data can be contained in that partition for any MDX query.

Assume you have partitioned the data by time, 5 partitions for 5 years. Typically, most of the queries will involve only the current year. In this case there is no need to send 5 queries, of which 4 will return no data. By setting the slice property indicating that the 2001 partition contains data for year 2001, 2002 partition contains data for year 2002 and so on, you provide a hint to Analysis Services so that it can optimize the relational queries sent. The Slice property for a partition can be set in BIDS or SSMS. For example, if you need to set a specific partition's data for year 2004, you will provide the MDX expression for 2004 as [Date].[Calendar].[Calendar Year].&[2004]. By default the value for the slice property is set to null, which indicates to Analysis Services that this specific partition can contain data for all the queries. The following steps show how to set the slice property.

1. Deploy the sample Adventure Works DW project shipped with SQL Server 2005 and ensure the database is processed. Connect to the Adventure Works DW database using SSMS.

2. Navigate through the partitions of Internet Sales measure group. Change the storage mode for all the partitions to ROLAP.

3. Right click on the Internet_Sales_2001 partition object and select Properties. Alternatively, you can double-click the partition, which will bring up the property page of the partitions as shown in Figure 13-13.

4. Click the ellipses next to the Slice property. This launches the MDX editor, as shown in Figure 13-14.

5. Navigate through the Date dimension and select the member [Date].[Calendar].[Calendar Year].&[2001]. When you double-click this member, the MDX expression corresponding to it appears in the text box. Click Check to verify the MDX syntax and then click OK.

6. Similar to step 5, specify the slice property for the remaining partitions Internet_Sales_2002, Internet_Sales_2003 and Internet_Sales_2004 with corresponding members in the Date dimension for the years 2002, 2003, and 2004.

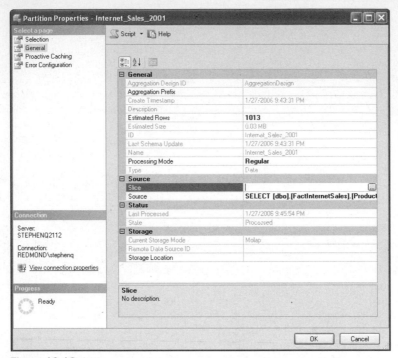

Figure 13-13

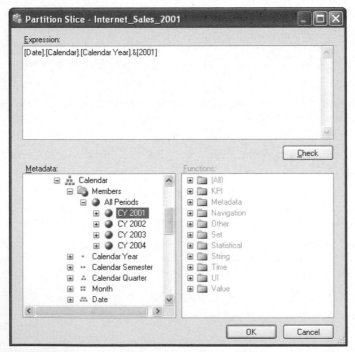

Figure 13-14

You have now successfully defined the slice for all the partitions in the Internet_Sales measure group of the Adventure Works cube. To verify that Analysis Services is able to utilize the slice information, you can send an MDX query that retrieves measures from the Internet_Sales measure group containing specific members from the [Date].[Calendar] hierarchy, such as year 2001. If you trace the queries sent to the SQL Server using SQL Profiler without setting the slice information, you will see that Analysis Services sends four queries to the relational server. After setting the slice information you can see that exactly one query is sent to the SQL Server.

An important factor to note is that Analysis Services does not validate your slice information for ROLAP partitions. Analysis Services just honors the slice property you have set, assuming you have the in-depth knowledge of your data. If you set an incorrect slice on a partition, you will get incorrect query results. For example, if you set the slice for partition Internet_Sales_2002 with a time member corresponding to 2001, a query requesting data for year 2002 will result in no data (assuming slice information is set for the remaining partitions correctly). The slice property is a directive to Analysis Services, and you need to be careful about setting the correct slice. The slice property is not needed for MOLAP partitions because Analysis Services is aware of the slice during processing, and hence optimizes the subqueries sent to partitions. Because Analysis Services is aware of the slice information for MOLAP partitions, if you set an incorrect slice for a specific partition and try to process the partition, the processing will result in errors.

You have learned various design techniques that can help you to optimize your UDM for better performance during processing and querying. In the next section you learn about other optimizations that will help you reduce processing time.

Optimize for Processing

To understand how to improve UDM processing performance you first need to understand the processing operation of Analysis Services. Analysis Services 2005 supports ROLAP and MOLAP storage modes for dimensions and ROLAP, MOLAP and HOLAP storage modes for partitions. Assume the data source is a relational database. Figure 13-15 shows the architecture of a regular processing operation when the storage mode for the dimensions and cubes is MOLAP. Analysis Services sends separate relational queries to the retrieve dimension and fact data. The relational data source reads records from its file storage for the queries and sends the records to Analysis Services. Analysis Services reads the data from the relational data source and stores it in a proprietary format for fast data access. During dimension processing Analysis Services sends separate queries to process each attribute of the dimension. Members from each attribute are stored indexed by Key and Name for fast data access. The related properties to the attribute are also indexed. If an attribute has a related attribute defined then the related attribute needs to be processed first before the attribute itself. Analysis Services processes attributes in parallel based on resource availability, parallelism specified and dependencies. The key attribute of the dimension is the last attribute processed since all the attributes are related to the key attribute. While processing the partitions Analysis Services reads fact data from the relational data source and stores it in proprietary format. Analysis Services then creates indexes to access the data efficiently. If aggregations are designed for the partitions then aggregations are built followed by indexes.

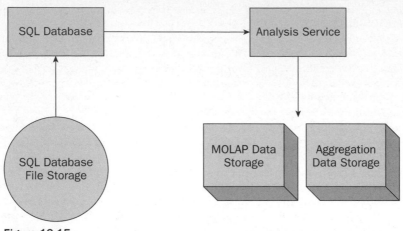

Figure 13-15

If the storage type is ROLAP, Analysis Services only needs to store the metadata in Analysis Services. There is no data transfer between the relational data source and the Analysis Services database, and there is no actual data storage on the Analysis Services side. Hence ROLAP processing is faster. Use of the ROLAP storage format, does impose a performance penalty at query time; query results will come slower when compared to MOLAP. This is due to the fact at query time data needs to be retrieved from the data source, aggregated within Analysis Services and then results returned to the end user.

When the storage type is HOLAP the source data resides in the data source while aggregations are calculated and stored on Analysis Services. HOLAP storage is typically used only when you primarily have space constraints on replicating the data on Analysis Services. HOLAP storage mode doesn't save much processing time as compared to MOLAP. Given the performance advantage of MOLAP data storage, we recommend using MOLAP storage for Analysis Services databases instead of HOLAP. For small and active partitions (current period data) we recommend use of ROLAP storage mode to get the most recent data.

You can have users querying the cube when you initiate processing. Analysis Services uses locks inside transactions to ensure atomic changes and consistent views of data. The lock is referred to as database (DB) commit lock. Usually everything just works and one does not need to even know about the DB commit lock. However for sophisticated usage scenarios, understanding this process can help explain system behavior that might otherwise seem anomalous. This can also help you to perform processing operations based on the load on the system.

During a query, the server takes a read DB commit lock. This ensures the database will not be deleted or modified during the query. During processing, a new version of the object (dimension, fact-table partition, etc.) is created. The original version on disk is not immediately overwritten though; a shadow copy is created. Once the new version has been successfully created, within the process transaction, a write DB commit lock is acquired. Then the new files automatically replace the old files, and the lock is released. The duration over which the lock is held is typically very small, perhaps less than 1 second. However, acquiring this lock requires waiting for current lock holders to relinquish their locks. Thus a long-running query can block the completion of a processing command.

The ForceCommitTimeout server property specifies the period of time a process command has to wait to acquire the DB commit lock. The default is 30000 milliseconds (30 seconds) and is specified in the configuration file \Program Files\Microsoft SQL Server\<MSSQL.x>\OLAP\Config\msmdsrv.ini. After the timeout all transactions holding the lock will be forced to fail. For the English version of Analysis Services the error message returned is "The operation has been cancelled." There are other scenarios under which this message will also be returned, but this is one cause to keep in mind when troubleshooting. Typically the holder of the read lock will be one or more long-running queries, and for the system as a whole, forcing them to fail is probably the better choice.

Lock chains can result when long running queries coexist with processing commands. While a process command is waiting for a long-running query, new queries must wait for the processing command to complete. Although the request for a new read lock is compatible with existing granted read locks, granting the new request could lead to starvation of the processing command, so locks are queued. The resulting behavior can appear to be a server hang even though it is not. You can see this behavior if you try to connect to Analysis Services using SSMS when you have a long running query along with a processing command which is waiting for the long running query to complete. This is due to the fact that SSMS sets a default database which requires a read DB commit lock. Here is a list of events creating a lock chain:

```
1. Long-running query acquires and holds read DB commit lock.
2. Process command completes and waits to acquire write DB commit
   lock.
3. New query waits to acquire read DB commit lock.
```

Having learnt the basic trade offs in terms of processing time and query performance benefits for the various storage modes supported by Analysis Services let us look at some of the techniques that help in optimizing processing.

Create Partitions to Speed Up Processing

We expect Analysis Services to be installed on a multi-processor machine to take advantage of multiple processors and have better performance. When a fact table is partitioned into multiple partitions within a measure group, due to the inherent parallelism in Analysis Services, the partitions are processed in parallel. You can also specify the parallelism to be used by Analysis Services through the processing option as discussed in Chapter 12. Hence having multiple partitions reduces the processing time for the measure group as compared to a single partition.

As discussed in the design optimization section, creating partitions can significantly improve processing performance during the typical daily, weekly, or monthly updates. Most often the partition corresponding to the most recent time period needs to be updated. Since a small subset of the data (most recent partition) is processed you speed up the processing time for the entire measure group.

We recommend you create multiple partitions for the measure groups whenever you have large volumes of data. Consistent with the *Microsoft SQL Server 2000 Analysis Services Operations Guide* by Carl Rabeler and Dave Wickert (http://www.microsoft.com/technet/prodtechnol/sql/2000/maintain/anservog .mspx), you should consider having partitions of size 5GB, or 20 million rows. Based on your business scenario, you might need to create partitions outside of that size profile.

Creating too many partitions can potentially can potentially hurt processing performance. Analysis Services processes objects in parallel based on your system resources. If all the partitions are processed in parallel they can be competing for resources. Furthermore the relational data source can also slow down processing performance if Analysis Services sends requests to retrieve data for all the partitions. Analysis Services allows you to control the number of objects to be processed in parallel (described later in this chapter). Make sure you design the right number of partitions based on user queries and process with a certain degree of parallelism.

Choose Small and Appropriate Data Types and Sizes

Choosing integers as keys for your tables helps improve processing and query performance. Using single integer keys (rather than strings or composite keys) results in faster processing time due to decreased size, decreased network usage, and the handling of keys internal to the relational data source, and Analysis Services can be done with simple native machine instructions. Analysis Services looks up the keys of dimension members while processing dimensions as well as cubes. The key lookup routines used by Analysis Services can run tens or hundreds of times faster for integer data types compared to other data types that are used as the key. In general, we recommend you set appropriate keys and or consider a design using integer surrogate keys in the relational data source in advance of building your UDM.

SQL Server and Analysis Services Installations

When you install SQL Server 2005, you can have SQL Server and Analysis Services installed on the same machine or a different machine. There are some trade-offs that you might want to consider for processing when you have UDMs retrieving data from the SQL Server. If you have both installations on the same machine, SQL Server and Analysis Services may compete for resources. You need to make sure you have sufficient processors and memory configurations on your system. Whenever your Analysis Services dimensions are large (millions of members) there will be an impact on processing speed. If SQL Server and Analysis Services are competing for memory, you might have significant paging of data to disk, which could slow down operations dramatically.

For 32-bit versions of Windows we recommend turning on the /3GB flag. By default each process running in Windows can access a maximum of 2GB. By turning on the /3GB flag, you allow the Analysis Services process to access up to 3GB of addressable space. This increases the accessible memory and facilitates large dimension processing and aggregation building. To enable the /3GB option, open your boot.ini file on your system drive and add the /3GB option as shown here, and then reboot the machine.

```
multi(0)disk(0)rdisk(0)partition(2)\WINNT="????" /3GB
```

In addition to turning on the /3GB option on a 32-bit machine, consider using a machine with a large amount of memory (e.g. 8GB) whenever you have SQL Server and Analysis Services installations on the same machine and your UDMs have large dimensions (on the order of millions of members). The additional memory on the 32-bit machine can be accessed by SQL Server 2005 through Address Windowing Extensions (AWE). Hence adding the additional memory helps ensure that both servers have sufficient memory resources to provide good performance. Another option is to use SQL Server and Analysis Services on 64-bit machines with larger memory.

If you do install SQL Server and Analysis Services on separate machines, they do not compete for resources, but you need to make sure you have a good high-speed network connection between the servers, such as gigabit Ethernet. Having good network connectivity helps reduce the network transfer time for queries returning large volumes of data. To stay legal, we recommend you check your licensing agreement for installing SQL Server and Analysis Services on separate machines.

Optimizing a Relational Data Source

Analysis Services 2005 has improved fact table data reading by sending the fact table scan query without joining dimension tables during MOLAP partition processing. In Analysis Services 2000, you had to set the dimension key uniqueness to eliminate the joins between the fact table and dimension table during the processing of the fact table. Analysis Services 2005 sends a table scan query similar to the following to get the fact data without the join and hence it is efficient as compared to Analysis Services 2000 by default.

```
SELECT [dbo_WB_Fact].[BudgetExpenseAmount] AS [dbo_WB_FactBudgetExpenseAmount0_0],
[dbo_WB_Fact].[EmployeeKey] AS [dbo_WB_FactEmployeeKey0_1],
[dbo_WB_Fact].[quarterkey] AS [dbo_WB_Factquarterkey0_2]
FROM
[dbo].[WB_Fact] AS [dbo_WB_Fact]
```

This query is a pure table scan query for the whole partition. It is unnecessary to put an index on the fact table because there are no joins involved with the dimension table.

However, if you do have ROLAP partitions set up, we recommend you have appropriate indexes created so that queries sent to the relational data source at query time return results faster because those will involve joins to dimension tables. If you trace the operations of Analysis Services with the help of SQL Profiler, you can identify the queries sent to your relational server. We recommend that you set up efficient indices for the queries targeted to your relational server for best performance when querying ROLAP partitions.

Avoid Excessive Aggregation Design

Aggregation design is a way to define aggregated data that needs to be created during processing of partitions. You learn more about aggregations later in this chapter. If you have the right aggregations created, it will help in query performance. However, having excessive aggregations for partitions will increase the processing time of the partitions. Analysis Services may need additional temporary files during the process and need to write more data onto the disk for each partition. As a general rule of thumb we recommend you create aggregations to improve performance by 10-30%. If you do need additional query performance improvements, we recommend you use usage-based aggregation design to create targeted aggregations based on the requests sent by the users accessing the cubes. You also have the choice of using different aggregations for each partition, which will help in removing unwanted aggregations for certain partitions and hence speed up cube processing time. We recommend designing more aggregations on heavily queried partitions, and using less aggregations for partitions rarely used. Ok, so perhaps we have a flair for the obvious — just be sure you do this!

Use Incremental Processing when Appropriate

Often, data changes in the relational data source. These changes could be due to new rows being added to existing tables or updates on existing rows. If you have set up the storage mode for dimensions and partitions as ROLAP, you will be retrieving the data from the relational data source for queries sent by users. In situations where the result set has been cached on Analysis Services due to a previous query, Analysis Services will not be fetching data from the relational database by default. You can force Analysis Services to always fetch data from the relational data source by using ROLAP (see Chapter 18 for more details). However, if the storage mode for all your cubes and dimensions is MOLAP, Analysis Services serves queries only from the processed MOLAP data that resides on Analysis Services. Future updates to relational tables will not be available to end users unless you update the MOLAP data on Analysis Services.

You have several ways of updating the data on Analysis Services. You can do a full process of the corresponding dimensions and/or cubes that need to be refreshed due to changes in the corresponding relational tables. There are several processing options to optimize your processing needs. Process Incremental and Process Add are options that help you process the dimensions and partitions so that they are updated with the new data on the relational data source as necessary. Not all the data in the partitions or dimensions gets updated during these operations; only data that changed since the last round of processing will be refreshed.

During an incremental process of partitions Analysis Services retrieves the new data from the relational data source and adds it to a temporary partition. Aggregations are then created for this new data, and finally the temporary partition is merged to the existing partition. As soon as the data is merged it is available for querying and you will see the new data reflected in user queries. Because Analysis Services only retrieves the new data added to relational tables, the incremental processing option for partitions helps you to process the partition quickly as compared to full process. However, if your partition is to be processed frequently due to data changes in the relational data source, we recommend you do a full process on that partition periodically (not often), because full processing will sort and optimize the data storage of multidimensional data. Similar to the defragment technique in file storage, sorting the data on disk will improve query performance.

Dimensions can be incrementally processed using the ProcessIncremental or ProcessAdd options. ProcessIncremental retrieves the data from the relational data source, compares the data to existing dimension members on Analysis Services, and then makes updates to existing dimension members if there are any changes. If there are new members, they are added to the dimension and this does not affect the partitions. However, if the dimension members are updated such that the relationship between attributes have changed (an employee's marital status changed from single to married) then the aggregations for the corresponding partitions will be dropped. The cube will still be available for querying but it can impact the performance of the queries which were using the dropped aggregations. ProcessIncremental takes more time than Full process of the same dimension because Analysis Services does the additional work of checking for updates for existing members; however, it provides you the flexibility of having the dimension available for querying and the cube does not have to be reprocessed. ProcessAdd is a new option in Analysis Services 2005 for processing dimensions. This option allows you to add new dimension members that have been added in the relational data source to existing processed dimensions. We recommend using the ProcessAdd option for dimensions whenever you have new members being added to the corresponding dimension tables in the relational data source. ProcessAdd for dimensions is useful in cases where new products are added to the products table on a periodic basis. You need to specify relational queries to the data source that will return the new rows that have been added since the last dimension update. The query to retrieve new data along with the data source and data source view elements is to be specified in the DDL along with the ProcessAdd called as out of line binding. Enclosed below is an example of using DDL using ProcessAdd with out of line binding.

```xml
<Batch xmlns="http://schemas.microsoft.com/analysisservices/2003/engine">
 <Parallel>
  <Process xmlns="http://schemas.microsoft.com/analysisservices/2003/engine">
   <Object>
    <DatabaseID>Adventure Works DW</DatabaseID>
    <DimensionID>Dim Customer</DimensionID>
   </Object>
   <Type>ProcessAdd</Type>
   <DataSourceView>
    <ID>Adventure Works DW</ID>
    <Name>Adventure Works DW</Name>
    <DataSourceID>Adventure Works DW</DataSourceID>
    <Schema>
     <xs:schema id="Adventure_x0020_Works_x0020_DW" xmlns=""
xmlns:xs="http://www.w3.org/2001/XMLSchema" xmlns:msdata="urn:schemas-microsoft-
com:xml-msdata" xmlns:msprop="urn:schemas-microsoft-com:xml-msprop">
      <xs:element name="Adventure_x0020_Works_x0020_DW" msdata:IsDataSet="true"
msdata:UseCurrentLocale="true">
       <xs:complexType>
        <xs:choice minOccurs="0" maxOccurs="unbounded">
         <xs:element name="dbo_DimProduct" msprop:FriendlyName="DimProduct"
msprop:DbSchemaName="dbo" msprop:DbTableName="DimProduct"
            msprop:QueryDefiniton ="SELECT
          * FROM DimProduct WHERE ProductKey &gt; 600"
            msprop:DbTableName="DimProduct"
            msprop:IsLogical="True"
            msprop:TableType="View">
          <xs:complexType>
           ... //Details of columns returned
          </xs:complexType>
         </xs:element>
        </xs:choice>
       </xs:complexType>
      </xs:element>
     </xs:schema>
    </Schema>
   </DataSourceView>
  </Process>
 </Parallel>
</Batch>
```

Parallelism during Processing

When compared to Analysis Services 2000, Analysis Services 2005 has improved processing behavior by using max parallelism to process independent components by default. If you have 16 partitions, all 16 partitions will be processed in parallel. Having too much parallelism can actually hurt performance through context switching and disk thrashing — happily, Analysis Services provides you with several options to control the amount of parallelism used for processing. Based on the complexity of the cube and the set of aggregations, we suggest you have two to three objects being processed per CPU.

You can control the amount of parallelism by changing certain server properties. For processing, the main server property impacting processing performance is CoordinatorExecutionMode. The server properties can be changed using the properties dialog from SQL Server Management Studio or in the config file msmsdsrv.ini located in the %System Drive%\Program Files\Microsoft SQL Server\ MSSQL.x\OLAP\Config folder. The CoordinatorExecutionMode server property sets the maximum parallelism allowed for a specific job, such as processing that needs to be executed on the server at a specific time. This property can have a positive or negative value. If the value is positive, the actual value is used and if the value is negative, it is multiplied by the number of processors and the absolute value of the result is used. For example, the default Analysis Services 2005 value is -4, which on a 4-processor machine indicates that the maximum parallelism to be used on the machine is 16 for each request. By setting this property you can avoid the server being overloaded with processing operations, perhaps to allow some resources for queries.

Another property, ThreadPool\Processing\MaxThreads, specifies the maximum number of threads in the processing thread pool. We recommend this not be used as a way to limit concurrency because internally the server often executes tasks by queuing other tasks and waiting for completion. The server is designed to be smart enough to know that more threads are needed to avoid deadlocking by exceeding MaxThreads.

When all the objects within a database are processed in parallel then Analysis Services sends queries to the data source for dimension as well as partition processing. Sometimes having too many connections and queries to the data source can increase processing time. You can limit the number of connections Analysis Services establishes with the data source. You can limit concurrent connections using the Data Source property "Maximum Number of Connections". This value can be altered from SQL Management Studio. See Figure 13-16.

Connection String	Provider=SQLNCLI.1;Data Source=Localhost;Persist Security Inf(
Query Timeout	00:00:00
Maximum Number of Connections	10
Isolation	ReadCommitted

Figure 13-16

You can specify the amount of parallelism for a specific processing operation along with the processing command. Follow the steps below to restrict the parallelism in the Processing Dialog while processing a database:

1. Open the sample Adventure Works DW project and deploy it to the Analysis Services instance.

2. Open SSMS and connect to the Analysis Services instance.

3. Navigate to Internet_Sales measure group for the Adventure Works cube in the Object browser window.

4. Right-click the measure group and choose Process to open the Process dialog shown in Figure 13-17.

5. Click the Change Settings button to open the settings dialog.

6. The settings dialog shown in Figure 13-18 allows you specify the amount of parallelism while processing the current object. Select the value 8 as shown in the figure and click OK.

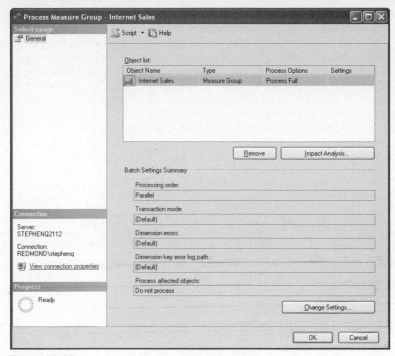

Figure 13-17

Figure 13-18

7. You learned in Chapter 12 that you can process the objects on an Analysis Services instance using the dialogs or through scripts. The Process dialog has the option to script the current settings to process the Internet_Sales measure group. Click the Script to New Window in the process dialog shown in Figure 13-17. A processing script is now opened within SSMS as shown below. Note that you could also use SQL Profiler to view the process command received by the server.

```xml
<Batch ProcessAffectedObjects="true"
xmlns="http://schemas.microsoft.com/analysisservices/2003/engine">
 <Parallel MaxParallel="8">
  <Process xmlns:xsd="http://www.w3.org/2001/XMLSchema"
xmlns:xsi="http://www.w3.org/2001/XMLSchema-instance">
   <Object>
    <DatabaseID>Adventure Works DW</DatabaseID>
    <CubeID>Adventure Works DW</CubeID>
    <MeasureGroupID>Fact Internet Sales 1</MeasureGroupID>
   </Object>
   <Type>ProcessFull</Type>
   <WriteBackTableCreation>UseExisting</WriteBackTableCreation>
  </Process>
 </Parallel>
</Batch>
```

In the processing script you can see the option MaxParallel=8, which instructs the Analysis Services instance to process a maximum of 8 objects in parallel.

Identify Resource Bottlenecks

Analysis Services processing and query performance requires well-configured hardware resources for best results. Processing performance requires sufficient memory, CPU speed, and good hard disk IO speed. These three play a significant role in getting the best performance. Analysis Services allows you to monitor resources used during operations of the server by way of perfmon counters. There are specific perfmon counters that show the memory utilization on the Analysis Services instance. You can monitor the server behavior during the processing operation via perfmon counters of the objects \\<machinename>\Processor, \\<machinename>\Memory, \\<machinename>\PhysicalDisk and specific counters provided by Analysis Services \\<machinename>\MSAS 2005: Processing, \\<machinename>\MSAS 2005: ProcIndexes, \\<machinename>\MSAS 2005: ProcAggregations, and \\<machinename>\ProcIndexes. After identifying the bottlenecks of the system, you can take appropriate action to relieve the server performance hot spots.

Some simple hardware additions, such as increasing server memory, adding more CPU, or using fast writing disks can potentially improve the system processing performance. As mentioned earlier, if you have memory over 3G for a 32-bit machine, you might consider using the /3-GB flag to allow Analysis Services to use memory over the 3GB limit as discussed earlier in this chapter. If memory is the main bottleneck we highly
recommend you to consider using 64-bit machines to increase the performance and capacity of your system, especially for cubes with large dimensions (>10 million dimension members).

In certain cases where the number of partitions is in the order of hundreds, processing partitions in parallel on a 32-bit machine can result in partitions competing among themselves for memory resource. In such circumstances processing can result in errors that system does not have sufficient memory. In such circumstances you can split the processing of the partitions by one of the following techniques.

1. Process fewer partitions at a time and stagger them to complete processing of all the partitions.

2. Use one of the techniques mentioned in the Parallelism during Processing section.

3. Instead of doing a full process of the partitions which includes processing data, indexes, and aggregations, split the processing as Process Data first for all partitions followed by Process Indexes.

4. By default the server property OLAP\ProcessPlan\MemoryLimit is set to 65 which means 65% of the available memory. If the /3GB flag is not enabled then Analysis Services determines this to be 65% of 2GB. If you are aware that you have more memory you can try increasing this value to 75 or 80.

Query Performance Improvement

The power of Analysis Services is its ability to provide fast query response time for decision makers who need to analyze data, draw conclusions, and make appropriate changes in business. As per OLAP Report (http://www.olapreport.com), OLAP is defined as Fast Analysis of Shared Multidimensional Information (FASMI). The word FAST actually means that system is able to delivery results to users in 5 seconds with very few queries that are complex might take more 20 seconds. We expect most of the business users to use business client tools that graphically represent that data from Analysis Services for easy interpretation and understanding. As an end user you would expect to see the data quickly (OLAPReport cites users typically wait for only 30 seconds as per an independent study in the Netherlands) to analyze and make decisions. Some of the common operations the client tools offer are drill down, drill up, and compare data year over year. Users do not have the time to wait hours for a response. Hence the queries sent to Analysis Services need to return data within seconds, at most in minutes. The query performance is pivotal to a successful Business Intelligence project deployment. A system that has very good performance will bring great business value to your system and company.

Even though Analysis Services supports storage modes MOLAP, ROLAP, and HOLAP, you obtain the best performance when your UDM storage mode is MOLAP. When you choose MOLAP storage, Analysis Services 2005 will store the dimension data and fact data in its own efficient, compact, and multidimensional structure format. Fact data are compressed and the size is approximately ten to thirty percent of the size in the relational database. In addition to its own efficient and compact data store, Analysis Services builds specialized dimension attribute indices for efficient data retrieval. The data is stored specifically in a multidimensional structure to best serve MDX query needs. If you use the ROLAP or HOLAP storage modes, queries to Analysis Services might have to fetch data from the relational data source at query time. Retrieving data from the relational data sources will significantly slow your query performance because you incur relational query processing time — the time needed to fetch the data over the network and then finally aggregating the data within Analysis Services.

Analysis Services 2005 tries to achieve the best of the OLAP and relational worlds. OLAP queries typically request aggregated data. For example, if you have sales information for products each day, a typical OLAP query might be to get the aggregated sales for the month or quarter or year. In such circumstances, every day's sales data needs to be aggregated for the entire year. If the users are requesting aggregated data on a single dimension, you will be able to do a simple sum in the relational database. However, OLAP queries are typically multidimensional queries, which need aggregated data across multiple dimensions with complex business logic calculations applied to each dimension. In order to improve the query performance, Analysis Services allows you to specify the multidimensional intersections for which data needs to be pre-aggregated so that queries requesting such data will be served instantaneously. Assume you have a database with a dimension called Products having a multi-level hierarchy Product Category⇨Product Sub Category⇨Product Name, a Time dimension having the hierarchy Year⇨Quarter⇨Month⇨Date, and a Geography dimension having a hierarchy Country⇨State⇨County⇨City. Fact data is typically at the lowest levels — sales of a specific product on a specific date at a specific city. For analysis you would request aggregated data of Sales at a city for a month for various product categories. You can have pre-aggregated data for the cross product of various levels in each hierarchy such as Quarter, State, and Year. In order to create the pre-aggregated data you need to specify the dimensions for which Analysis Services needs to pre-calculate the data. The pre-calculated data along with definitions are referred to as aggregations.

Understanding Aggregations

Analysis Services 2005 allows you to build pre-calculated subtotals for each partition of your cubes, and store them in either an OLAP data store or relational database based on the storage modes chosen for the partitions. Because most OLAP queries typically request aggregated data at various levels of dimension hierarchies, storing pre-aggregated data will help in getting the results to end users quickly. When you query for data at higher levels of hierarchies (other than the granularity level which is the level at which fact data is available), the server can directly fetch those aggregate numbers instead of bringing all related detailed fact data and aggregating them within the engine. In this section you learn to create aggregations for cubes using the Adventure Works sample database.

Using Adventure Works dimensions as an example, assume you have a measure group using the Date, Product, and Customer dimensions, and each dimension has hierarchies and levels as shown in the table below. Assume the granularity attribute for the dimensions Date, Products, and Customer are Date, Product Name, and Full Name, respectively. If you query the data for [Date].[2004].[Q3] and if there is no aggregated data stored in your OLAP database, the server needs to retrieve the lowest-level fact data for all dates in quarter Q3 of year 2004 for all products and all the customers in that State-Province. This can result in a large data scan on the OLAP fact data, followed by the server aggregating the data and returning the results to you.

Date Dimension		Products Dimension		Customer Dimension	
Year	4	Category	4	Country	6
Semester	8	SubCategory	37	State-Province	71
Quarter	16	Product Name	395	City	587
Month	48			Postal Code	646
Date	1461			Full Name	18484

Analysis Services 2005 provides wizards that help define the combinations of dimension hierarchies for which aggregated data needs to be created, either by analyzing the statistics of members at each level and/or based on the queries requested by users. Once the aggregations are defined you need to process the partitions so that Analysis Services creates the pre-aggregated data and stores them in the OLAP data store. In addition to the pre-aggregated data, Analysis Services also creates indexes to access the aggregated data, which speeds up data retrieval. Reviewing the preceding example, if the server has aggregations for levels Quarter, Subcategory, and State-Province of the user hierarchies in Date, Product, and Customer dimensions respectively, then a query for Quarter Q3 of year 2004 can be fulfilled right away from the aggregation. In this case, a fact scan is not needed and you receive the results instantaneously. Furthermore, queries requesting data for the levels above Quarter, Subcategory, and State-Province will also benefit from the aggregation. For example, if you query for Year, Subcategory, and State-Province, the server only needs to get the data for Quarter from the existing aggregations and aggregate a much smaller dataset than a huge fact table scan. Thus aggregations help in improving the query performance time of your MDX queries.

Storing aggregation values in the Analysis Services database is a typical tradeoff of database size and performance. Aggregation values will take disk space, and it will benefit query performance for queries sent to the server. In the example discussed in the preceding paragraph, if you count the permutations of all levels in the three dimensions you will see there are 74 combinations ($5*3*5 -1$ [fact table] = 74) to build aggregations. You might immediately have the following questions:

❑   Do I need to build aggregations for all the combinations? Will that be useful?

❑   Can I build a subset of the aggregations?

❑   What parameters will affect the choice of Analysis Services for aggregation design?

❑   How much disk space will these aggregations take?

❑   What percentage of optimization will I get based on the aggregations designed?

The estimated dimension members count of all the hierarchies in a dimension is an important metric to calculate the cost of storage for aggregations. For example, aggregation (Month, Subcategory, Postal Code) will potentially result in 12 million ($48*395*646 = 12,248,160$) cells to compute and store. However, not every cell will have data just as the fact data doesn't have all combinations for every dimension key. Because Analysis Services only stores data for coordinates that have fact values, the equation needs to be rectified by the partition fact count. Analysis Services assumes the data is of uniform distribution, and uses an algorithm to calculate the estimated aggregation cells for a specific aggregation. Analysis Services by default selects attributes from cube dimensions to be considered for aggregation. Analysis Services estimates the aggregation size and the benefit due to the aggregation for various combinations of attributes. Based on the aggregation disk size or percentage of optimization chosen by the user, Analysis Services stops iteration of calculating the optimized aggregation designs as soon as one of the criteria is met.

For query benefits, the lower the aggregation design, the more useful the aggregation, because all higher-level queries can benefit from the aggregation. However, the lower the aggregation design, the bigger the size of the aggregation data store and the longer the aggregation build time will be. It does not make sense to have aggregated cells with a size very close to the fact size; it won't save any disk scan time because the server will read almost the same amount of data from the disk. Therefore, building too many aggregations actually will not benefit query performance and sometimes might actually hurt it. Analysis Services, however, allows you to create aggregations up to 100%. As previously mentioned, we recommend you have aggregations where the estimated size is between 10% and 30% of the fact table size.

Creating Aggregations

Analysis Services allows you to specify the percentage of aggregation of the disk space to be used for creating aggregations. Analysis Services uses a complex algorithm to estimate the best aggregations based on the number of fact table and dimension members that will provide you the maximum benefit. The following steps show how to design aggregations for the Adventure Works sample Internet Sales partitions:

1. Open the Adventure Works DW sample project in BIDS.

2. Open the Adventure Works cube and switch to the Partitions tab.

3. Right-click the partition Internet_Sales_2001 under the Internet Sales measure group and select Design Aggregations... as shown in Figure 13-19.

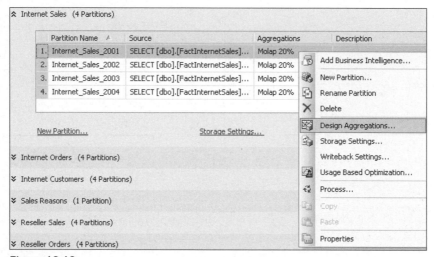

Figure 13-19

4. You will now be in the Aggregation design wizard. Click Next in the welcome screen.

5. You will see the Storage and Caching Options page of the wizard as shown in Figure 13-20. Select the option MOLAP partition to store fact data and aggregation data in Analysis Services multidimensional format. Click the Next button.

6. The Object Counts page allows you to retrieve the count of dimension members relevant to the current partition and the count of fact table rows as shown in Figure 13-21. At the top of the grid is the fact table count; Estimated Count is the total number of fact table rows for all partitions in the current measure group. The Partition Count contains the count of fact table rows for the current partition. This page also allows you to override the values for the current partition. Click the Count button. Analysis Services retrieves the count of dimensions members and the partition by sending queries to the relational database. Estimated Count is the count for the entire measure group and the partition count has the values for the current partition. If the values of the current partition will have different values in your production environment, you can enter the new counts in the Partition Count column. The count specified in the Object Counts page is used to calculate appropriate weights to design aggregations. Hence, make sure you provide the right counts. Otherwise you might end up with a suboptimal aggregation design.

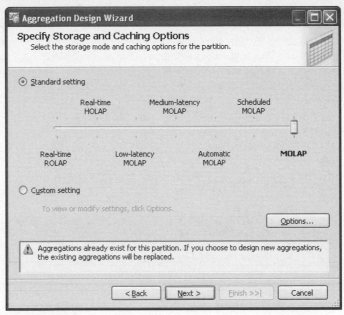

Figure 13-20

Figure 13-21

7. If you expand the customer dimension, you will find that all the attributes being considered for aggregation design are highlighted in bold font along with the estimated count of members as shown in Figure 13-22. For the partition count column, since the fact table only includes the granularity attribute (the customer key), that count is also available for Analysis Services to determine the aggregation design. You have the option to include or exclude attributes for consideration for aggregation design. By default, Analysis Services includes the key attributes for consideration during aggregation design. All the attributes that are levels of natural hierarchies are considered for aggregation design. If a user hierarchy is unnatural the topmost level is considered for aggregation design. The remaining levels of the unnatural hierarchy from the top most level are included for consideration if there is a one-to-many relationship from that level to the next level. As soon as there is no relationship between successive levels then the remaining levels below that level of the unnatural hierarchy are not considered during aggregation design. Click the Next button.

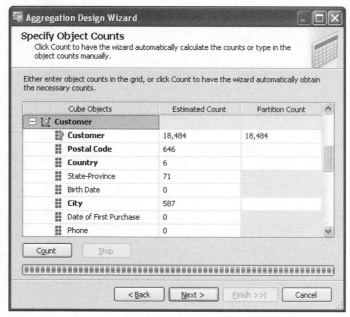

Figure 13-22

8. You are now in the Aggregation Options page, as shown in Figure 13-23. The engine gives you four possible options for how to design the aggregations:

❑ **Setting the storage limit for estimated aggregation data.** The system will look for the aggregation combinations whose total estimated size is within the user specified limit.

❑ **Performance gain setting.** You can choose a percentage of performance gain. The system will use the cost and performance gain algorithms to search for the best combinations that will fulfill the performance gain metric. The less the percentage is, the less aggregation will be built and the less queries will be answered through pre-calculation. We recommend you begin with 30% aggregations performance gain for most cubes.

❑ **User click stop option.** The system will start to analyze the aggregation design and design aggregations. The server will stop searching for more aggregation when the user click-stops or the performance gain reaches 100%

❑ **Do not design aggregations (0%).** The server will not design any aggregations for the current partition.

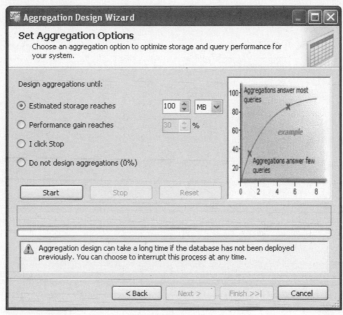

Figure 13-23

9. Choose the second option, Performance Gain Reaches, and set the number to 30%. Click the Start button to design the aggregation.

10. The server starts to analyze the aggregation design, and sends feedback on the aggregations being generated. The feedback is shown graphically in the Aggregation Options page as shown in Figure 13-24. The X-axis of the graph contains the amount of storage used and the Y-axis of the graph shows the percentage of performance gain. The status bar shows the number of aggregations that have been created during that time. Once the performance gain reaches the percentage you have specified (30%), the server stops designing further aggregations. You can see 32 aggregations have been created for 30% performance gain and the estimated storage is 38.6KB. Click the Next button.

11. In the final page of the aggregation wizard you have two choices to either deploy and process the partition or save the aggregation design and process later. Choose Save the Aggregations but Do Not Process Them and click the Finish button.

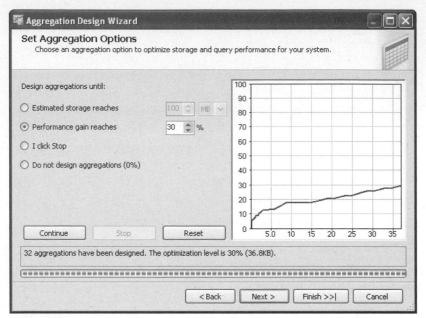

Figure 13-24

You have now successfully created aggregations for the partition Internet_Sales_2001 using the aggregation design wizard. To find out what partition aggregations have been created for this partition, you can either deploy the project followed by scripting from SSMS or open the file "Adventure works.Partitions" in your current project's directory in an XML editor. If you look at the partition Internet_Sales_2001 you will find the following definition, which indicates that the partition has an aggregation design defined and the aggregation design used has the id AggregationDesign.

```
<Partition dwd:design-time-name="d4f8812c-19a8-424f-8327-a3f332998400">
 <ID>Internet_Sales_2001</ID>
 <Name>Internet_Sales_2001</Name>
 <CreatedTimestamp>0001-01-01T08:00:00Z</CreatedTimestamp>
 <LastSchemaUpdate>0001-01-01T08:00:00Z</LastSchemaUpdate>
 ........
 <EstimatedRows>1013</EstimatedRows>
 <AggregationDesignID>AggregationDesign</AggregationDesignID>
</Partition>
```

You can find the aggregation designed by the server in the AggregationDesign section for the measure group "Internet Sales." Following is a section of the definition for the aggregation that has been designed. Each aggregation design can have one or more aggregations defined. The dimension section within Aggregations includes the estimated counts for dimension attributes. In the aggregation section, it lists the detailed aggregation design for each aggregation. The definitions for each aggregation contain the combination of the hierarchies that are to be included for aggregating the data. If a hierarchy has not been specified in the aggregation design, by default it is implied that the top-level member or the default member of that hierarchy is included.

```
<AggregationDesign dwd:design-time-name="53c7cd6c-e5af-4c9c-b714-00e33341f906">
 <ID>AggregationDesign</ID>
 <Name>AggregationDesign</Name>
 <CreatedTimestamp>2005-07-04T03:20:12Z</CreatedTimestamp>
 <LastSchemaUpdate>2005-07-04T03:20:12Z</LastSchemaUpdate>
 <EstimatedRows>1013</EstimatedRows>
 <Dimensions>
......
 </Dimensions>
 <Aggregations>
  <Aggregation dwd:design-time-name="530c0b42-9394-44fc-908e-df173dc4cd39">
   <ID>Aggregation 0</ID>
   <Name>Aggregation 0</Name>
   <Dimensions>
    <Dimension dwd:design-time-name="cb139092-5594-45dd-ae70-5def88daa6e2">
     <CubeDimensionID>Dim Promotion</CubeDimensionID>
    </Dimension>
    <Dimension dwd:design-time-name="e2f699b4-9f7d-440a-b65f-0d6cd66a4044">
     <CubeDimensionID>Dim Sales Territory</CubeDimensionID>
    </Dimension>
    <Dimension dwd:design-time-name="fc808e3c-4ccd-4d10-9235-5c4fbd0cb7e6">
     <CubeDimensionID>Internet Sales Order Details</CubeDimensionID>
    </Dimension>
    <Dimension dwd:design-time-name="550eebc4-a66f-4f11-8fd6-2314d4147742">
     <CubeDimensionID>Sales Reason</CubeDimensionID>
    </Dimension>
    <Dimension dwd:design-time-name="7b28dadd-e083-49c5-903d-159655a8abc4">
     <CubeDimensionID>Order Date Key - Dim Time</CubeDimensionID>
    </Dimension>
    <Dimension dwd:design-time-name="a49e1599-8bb5-4085-ad8f-6c6842d32d31">
     <CubeDimensionID>Ship Date Key - Dim Time</CubeDimensionID>
    </Dimension>
    <Dimension dwd:design-time-name="be96b4c4-d321-4778-9102-d1ff4e445189">
     <CubeDimensionID>Due Date Key - Dim Time</CubeDimensionID>
    </Dimension>
    <Dimension dwd:design-time-name="1e2832d3-effd-4ff5-8ee7-5b6fce141962">
     <CubeDimensionID>Dim Product</CubeDimensionID>
    </Dimension>
    <Dimension dwd:design-time-name="3bb92d6c-8460-482a-a4a2-62d3c6f1bda9">
     <CubeDimensionID>Dim Customer</CubeDimensionID>
     <Attributes>
      <Attribute dwd:design-time-name="25a43046-15f9-42c4-809a-34361ab90295">
       <AttributeID>Dbo Dim Geography - Country Region Name</AttributeID>
      </Attribute>
     </Attributes>
    </Dimension>
    <Dimension dwd:design-time-name="6bbce628-bf13-439a-9693-512e55b3a763">
     <CubeDimensionID>Dim Currency</CubeDimensionID>
    </Dimension>
    <Dimension dwd:design-time-name="fca71a9b-1792-4213-b4bf-2cab3726016e">
     <CubeDimensionID>Destination Currency</CubeDimensionID>
    </Dimension>
   </Dimensions>
  </Aggregation>
  ......
 </Aggregations>
```

Applying Aggregation Design

You have so far designed aggregations for a single partition. If all your partitions contain the same fact table data and characteristics in terms of dimension member distributions, you can design the same aggregations. You can select a group of partitions in the BIDS and then select design aggregations to design the same aggregation. Alternatively, Analysis Services 2005 allows you to apply an existing aggregation of a partition to other partitions in the same measure group. However, if you have some partitions that include fact records for an entire year and one partition holding current or last month's data, you would want to design separate aggregations to have the most optimal performance. To design the same aggregations for a group of partitions from BIDS follow the steps below.

1. Open the Adventure Works cube in BIDS and switch to the partitions tab. Select multiple partitions within the Internet Sales measure group. To do so hold the Ctrl key and then select the desired partitions using your mouse.

2. Right-click and choose Design Aggregations as shown in Figure 13-25 to bring up the design aggregation window.

3. Go through the same steps to design aggregations for the first partition. The wizard will automatically copy the aggregation design to other partitions.

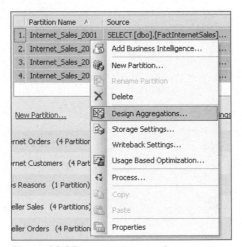

Figure 13-25

Applying aggregations designed for one partition to other partitions is considered a management operation and hence you need to use SSMS. To copy an existing aggregation from one partition to other partitions, perform the following steps:

1. Launch SSMS and connect to your Analysis Services instance.

2. Navigate to the Adventure Works cube in the object explorer.

3. In the measure groups folder, open the Internet Sales measure group, and open the partitions folder.

4. Right-click on Internet_Sales_2001 partition, and select Copy Aggregation Design as shown in Figure 13-26.

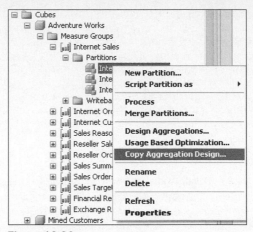

Figure 13-26

5. You will now see the Copy Aggregation Design wizard. You can choose to copy the aggregation design of the Internet_Sales_2001 partition to one or many partitions in this measure group. Select the partition for which you want to apply the same aggregation design as shown in Figure 13-27 and click OK.

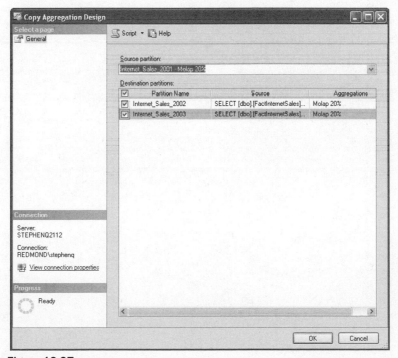

Figure 13-27

Analysis Services now applies all the aggregations designed for the Internet_Sales_2001 partition to all the partitions selected. Once all the partitions are applied with aggregation design, you need to process the partitions so that Analysis Services creates the aggregated data. You can later send a query that requests data for a specific level and analyze its performance. If aggregations have been built for the cells that have been requested then Analysis Services will serve the query from the aggregations. Based on the size of your cube and aggregations designed you can notice performance gain for queries touching the aggregations. Finally, you can use SQL Server Profiler to see if specific aggregations are getting hit (you will see this later in this chapter).

Usage-Based Aggregation Design

In addition to the Aggregation wizard, Analysis Services supports aggregation design based on the user queries sent to Analysis Services. Designing aggregations based on user queries is called usage-based optimization because aggregations are designed based on users' requests and making sure performance gains are achieved for those specific queries. In order for Analysis Services to analyze the queries and design aggregations, the queries served by Analysis Services need to be logged at a specific location. Analysis Services provides a way to log the queries in a relational table with specific parameters. Because this aggregation design technique is dependent on the usage pattern, it is more likely that Analysis Services can create more useful aggregations to increase performance of future queries. To create the user-based aggregation design, you first need to enable Analysis Services to log the queries sent to the server. Follow these steps to enable query logging and design aggregations based on a set of queries:

1. Launch SSMS and connect to Analysis Services.

2. Right-click the server and choose Properties. You will see the Analysis Server Properties window as shown in Figure 13-28.

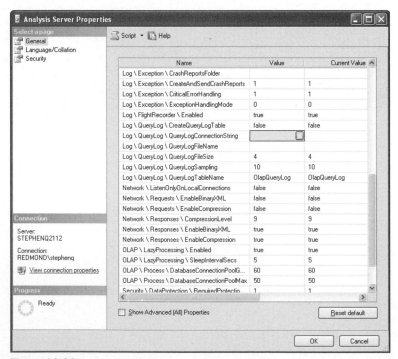

Figure 13-28

3. Set the "Log\QueryLog\QueryLogConnectionString" property so that it has a connection string pointing to a relational database where queries can be logged. To do so, click the ellipsis (...) to launch the connection string dialog.

4. You will see the connection manager dialog as shown in Figure 13-29, which you have used to specify data sources. Specify the connection details to your SQL Server that contains the sample relational database AdventureWorksDW. Click OK once you have specified the connection details.

Figure 13-29

5. The connection string will be copied as the value for the server property "Log\QueryLog \QueryLogConnectionString".

6. Define the server property Log\ Query Log\QueryLogTableName with a table name OLAPQueryLog.

7. Make sure the server property Log\Query Log\CreateQueryLogTable is set to true so that the query log table can be created by Analysis Services.

8. By default, the server logs a query for every 10 queries executed. You can change "Log\QueryLog\QueryLogSampling". Change it to 1 to log every query into the query log table.

9. Click OK to save the server properties.

10. Restart Analysis Services so that the new properties are set for Analysis Services and the query log table can be created on the relational database.

11. Connect to SQL Server and open AdventureWorksDW; you will find an OLAPQueryLog table has been created. The table definition is shown here:

```
CREATE TABLE [dbo].[OlapQueryLog](
  [MSOLAP_Database] [nvarchar](255) COLLATE SQL_Latin1_General_CP1_CI_AS NULL,
  [MSOLAP_ObjectPath] [nvarchar](4000) COLLATE SQL_Latin1_General_CP1_CI_AS NULL,
  [MSOLAP_User] [nvarchar](255) COLLATE SQL_Latin1_General_CP1_CI_AS NULL,
  [Dataset] [nvarchar](4000) COLLATE SQL_Latin1_General_CP1_CI_AS NULL,
  [StartTime] [datetime] NULL,
  [Duration] [bigint] NULL
) ON [PRIMARY]
```

12. In SQL Server Management Studio connect to your Analysis Services instance.

13. Right-click the Adventure Works cube and select Browse. Drag and drop measures into the data grid and drag and drop several dimensions. Perform some drill up and drill down to log some MDX queries into the query log.

14. Open a relational query window in SQL Server Management Studio and send the followng query:

```
SELECT [MSOLAP_Database]
    ,[MSOLAP_ObjectPath]
    ,[MSOLAP_User]
    ,[Dataset]
    ,[StartTime]
    ,[Duration]
FROM [AdventureWorksDW].[dbo].[OlapQueryLog]
```

You will find many records are logged in the OLAPQueryLog table. Analysis Services logs the username, time stamp, and the subcubes that are hit during the MDX query. The subcube definition is a sequence of 0s and 1s, which indicate which hierarchies are involved in the query.

15. In the Object Browser, right-click the Internet_Sales_2001 partition and choose Usage Based Optimization as shown in Figure 13-30.

16. You will see the Usage-Based Optimization Wizard. Click Next in the welcome screen. Choose Internet_Sales_2001 to modify aggregation settings as shown in Figure 13-31 and then click Next.

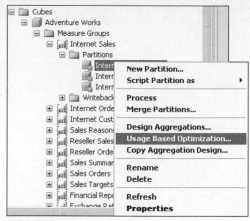

Figure 13-30

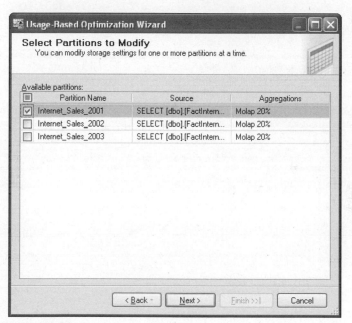

Figure 13-31

17. In the Query Criteria dialog you can select the queries based on time, users, or frequency and request those queries to be used for aggregation design as shown in Figure 13-32. In addition to that, this dialog also provides statistics of the queries that have been logged. You can specify a beginning and ending date to get specific queries running in a certain time period, or choose specific queries for a particular user or users, or the user can choose the latest percentage of queries. We will select all the queries logged so far to design aggregations. Do not make any selection in the Specify Query Criteria and click Next.

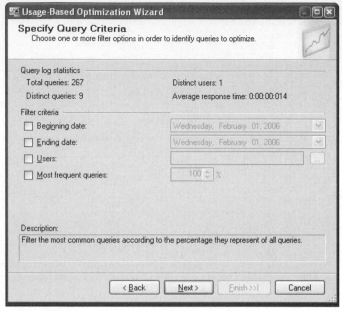

Figure 13-32

18. In the query list window (see Figure 13-33), Analysis Services provides information of all the queries requested by the users. Select all the queries and click Next.

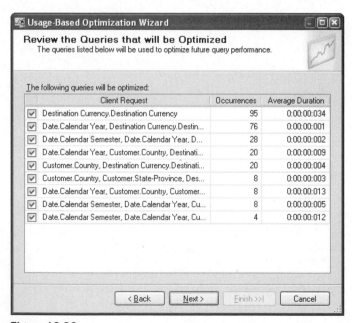

Figure 13-33

19. You will now see the storage design dialog that you saw during aggregation design. Select MOLAP storage and click Next.

20. In the object counts dialog, you do not have to update object counts since you did this during aggregation design. Click the Next button to proceed to the aggregations options page.

21. In the set design aggregation options, choose 30% performance gain and click the Start button to request aggregations be designed based on the queries selected. At this moment, Analysis Services explores the various aggregations that would benefit in improving the performance gain for the selected queries. If a specific aggregation would benefit a specific query, that aggregation is allocated more weight so that that aggregation can be chosen from all possible aggregations. Analysis Services does a breadth-first search to explore the search space. Hence, if you have a cube that has a large dimensionality, sometimes you might explore aggregations at a very low level (closer to the key) due to the queries and performance optimization that you have chosen. We recommend you look at the aggregations that are getting created in the script and if you are really interested in a specific aggregation being created, you can specify a higher performance gain (> 30%) that forces Analysis Services to expand the search space to deeper levels. Click the Next button after the aggregations have been designed.

22. On the process options page, select the Process Partitions Immediately check box and click Finish as shown in Figure 13-34. The new aggregations will be created and applied to the Internet_Sales_2001 partition.

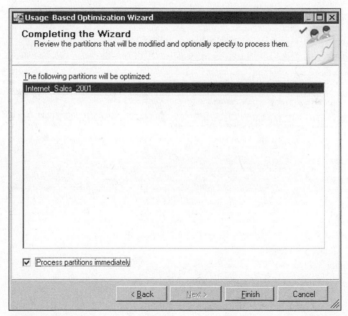

Figure 13-34

If you have existing aggregations at the start of design usage-based aggregation, Analysis Services doesn't take that existing aggregation design into consideration. You can design aggregations by writing your custom AMO program. You can download samples from this book's companion web site that show how to design aggregations using AMO.

Aggregation Design Options

So far you have learned to design aggregations using the Aggregation design wizard and the Usage Based Optimization wizard. In both wizards you have seen that some of the dimension attributes are being considered by Analysis Services for aggregations and some are not. The Aggregation design wizard considers certain hierarchies when designing aggregations based on the design of the hierarchies, as well as the properties of the dimensions and cube dimensions. In addition to that, the user can give hints to tell the aggregation designer to consider, include, or exclude hierarchies while designing aggregations.

Design Efficient Aggregations Using Hints

The aggregation design algorithm uses the partition fact data count and dimension-level member count to estimate the cost of aggregation design. Having an accurate fact data count and dimension-level member count is crucial for Analysis Services to find the aggregation designs that would yield the best performance. The fact table row count and level member count are metrics that are counted once at design time, stored in the Analysis Services metadata, and never changed afterwards. Therefore, it is important for the user to update the member counts and fact table counts for changing dimensions, and increasing rows in fact tables. You can click the Count button in the specify object counts window to get the newest counts for various objects.

Typically, partitions only contain a specific slice of the fact data. The member count for dimension attributes and the partition are by default the same. In the aggregation design wizard it is a good practice for you to provide Analysis Services the hint of accurate member count in the partition count column. In the Adventure Works DW sample, partitions contain data for each year so we recommend entering a value of 1 in the Fiscal Year column as shown in Figure 13-35. This helps Analysis Services use the value 1 instead of 4 to calculate the cost of the aggregation while including the Fiscal year attribute.

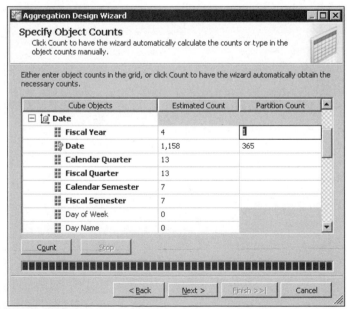

Figure 13-35

Relationships between Attributes

All the attributes within a dimension are related to the key attribute because there is a one-to-many relationship. When you establish a relationship between two attributes within a dimension, you can specify the type of relationship between these attributes. Two types of relationships are allowed in Analysis Services 2005, Rigid and Flexible, and they refer to the dimension attribute relationship changeability. Rigid relationships mean that there will be no change in the data value for this relationship. For example, if you have the relationship between City and State set to be rigid, it indicates that a specific city will always belong to only one state and the initial value will never change over time. Flexible relationships, however, mean that the values of the relationship can change over time. By default all the relationships between the attributes and the key attributes of the dimension are flexible. The relationship type determines how Analysis Services treats partition aggregation data when you choose to perform an incremental process of the partition. Assume a relationship between two attributes has been specified as rigid and the value changes for the attribute nonetheless. When an incremental process of the dimension is initiated Analysis Services will present an error that the data has changed for an attribute whose relationship has been specified as rigid.

You can set the relationship type between attributes in BIDS by doing the following:

1. Open the sample project Adventure Works DW.

2. Open the Customer dimension by double-clicking that dimension in Solution Explorer.

3. In the attributes pane, click the key attribute Customer. Click on the + sign to see all the attributes that are related to the key attribute.

4. Click any of the attributes under the key attribute such as Phone number. If you look at the properties window you will see a Relationship Type property as shown in Figure 13-36, which has the values Flexible and Rigid.

Figure 13-36

5. Expand the user hierarchy Customer Geography and click the Country attribute relationship as shown in Figure 13-37. In the properties window you will find that its relationship type is set as Rigid because a state's country won't change over time. On the other hand, click the customer address relationship and you will see it is set to Flexible because a customer's address can change over time.

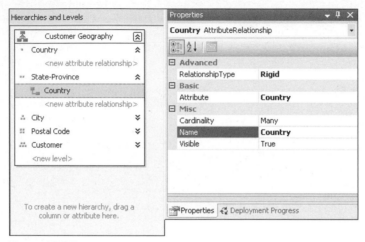

Figure 13-37

The aggregation design algorithm bases the aggregation being designed on the type of relationships between the attributes it's using, allowing you to classify aggregations as rigid or flexible. Rigid aggregations are aggregations that include attribute(s) that have a rigid relationship with the granularity attribute. Attributes from the remaining dimensions either need to be the All level or the lowest level. The aggregation created in the previous section that included Customer.Country, and all other dimensions where the other dimensions included the top level is an example of rigid aggregation. Flexible aggregations are aggregations that are built on one or more attributes with flexible relationship with the granularity attribute. An example of a flexible aggregation is an aggregation that uses Customer.Address attribute.

Rigid aggregations are updated when partitions are incrementally processed. If attributes that are part of rigid aggregations are incrementally processed then existing aggregations are not dropped. Analysis Services will keep the old aggregation data as such and create a temporary aggregation store for the newly coming data. Finally Analysis Services merges the temporary aggregation store with the old aggregation data within a transaction. Old aggregation will still be available for query access when aggregations are being processed. The aggregated data only gets rebuilt when the user chooses to do ProcessFull on the partition or cube.

Flexible aggregations are fully rebuilt whenever a cube and partition is incrementally processed. When attributes that are part of a flexible aggregation are incrementally processed then Analysis Services drops all the flexible aggregations, because the old aggregation data is not valid anymore due to dimension member changes. After dropping the flexible aggregations, Analysis Services recalculates those dropped aggregations. If you choose the option to create aggregations lazily (ProcessingMode property of a dimension), flexible aggregations are re-calculated as a background task. Users will still be able to query without aggregations; however, you might see that the queries are slow. Once the aggregations are rebuilt, future queries will be fast.

Properties Controlling Attributes and Aggregation Design

In addition to the dimension member count and partition member count, Analysis Services allows you to fine tune the aggregation design via a property called AllMemberAggregationUsage for Cube dimensions and an AggregationUsage property for CubeDimensionAttributes. Various values of these properties hint the aggregation design wizard to consider and include the attribute or dimension while designing aggregations. The following steps show you how to set the various values for these properties in BIDS:

1. Open the Adventure Works DW sample project.

2. Open the Adventure Works cube.

3. Click the cube dimension Customer in the Cube Designer as shown in Figure 13-38. You can see the associated properties in the properties pane, as shown in Figure 13-38.

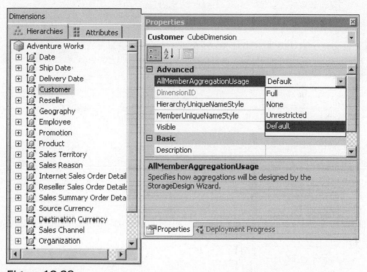

Figure 13-38

4. You will see the property AllMemberAggregationUsage. This property enables you to either include or exclude the "All Member" of the dimension while creating aggregations. Based on the value set for this property, Aggregation Design Wizard will consider this dimension while performing the design task. There are four choices for the AllMemberAggregationUsage property.

❑ **Full.** Always include the All member while creating aggregations.

❑ **None.** Never include the All member while creating aggregations.

❑ **Unrestricted.** Let Analysis Services consider the dimension during aggregation design, and it can choose to build or not build aggregation for all members of the dimension.

❑ **Default.** Same as unrestricted.

If most of your users query All member of this dimension, we recommend that you change the AllMemberAggregationUsage property to Full. This ensures that aggregations include the All member and that your user queries hit and benefit from the aggregations. If most of your users query this dimension at the detail level, we recommend you set it to None to avoid aggregation at the All level. There is no need to create aggregations at the All level because most of the queries will not hit the aggregation.

5. Leave the setting for the customer dimension as Default, and click the Attributes tab in the cube editor as shown in Figure 13-39. BIDS will now show all the cube dimensions with their cube dimension attributes. Click the country dimension to view its attributes.

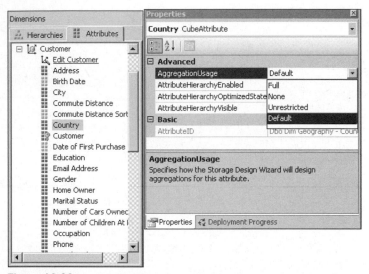

Figure 13-39

6. Click any of the cube dimension attributes. If you look at the properties window you will see the property AggregationUsage as shown in Figure 13-39. Similar to AllMemberAggregationUsage, the AggregationUsage property also has four possible values. They are Full, None, Unrestricted, and Default. These properties once again instruct the aggregation design algorithm to appropriately include or exclude a dimension attribute while designing aggregations. The meaning of the values are as follows:

❏ **Full.** Always include this attribute in any of the aggregation designs being considered while designing aggregations.

❏ **None.** Never include this attribute in any of the aggregation designs being considered while designing aggregations.

❏ **Unrestricted.** Analysis Services might consider this attribute during aggregation design as any other attribute.

❏ **Default.** Same as unrestricted.

If most of your users query the data by customer country, you can change the country attribute's AggregationUsage to Full. However, if you know your users rarely break down numbers for one attribute, you can turn it off by setting the property to None. You need to analyze your user's MDX queries using SQL Profiler (explained later in this chapter) and then set the appropriate values for these properties for various dimensions and attributes.

Yes, query performance can be improved by designing aggregations and fine tuning. However, your users might be generating MDX queries that are not optimal. Next you see a few ways to optimize MDX queries.

Optimizing MDX Queries

Most cubes are quite sparse. By sparse we mean that the cell corresponding to every tuple found in the cube does not have a value associated with it. For example, in the Adventure Works sample database if every coordinate has data for the Internet sales measure group, and assuming only the key attribute in each dimension then the total cells would be (Date) 1158 * Date (Ship Date) 1158 * Date (Delivery Date) 1158 * Customer (18484) * Promotion (16) * Product (606) * Sales Territory (11) * Sales Reason (10) * Source Currency (105) * Destination Currency (105), which is $3.37*10^{23}$ cells. This result increases when additional attributes are added from each dimension. Although most of the cells do not have any business meaning associated with them — for example, if delivery date is ahead of order date — they belong to cube space and can be queried by the users. Querying such cells results in a null value, which indicates that the data is not available for that cell coordinate.

The fact table rows represent the leaf-level cells for cubes. The fact table rows count is much less than possible cube space. The Analysis Services engine has many optimizations for improving query performance by utilizing the fact tables to limit the search space. The basic rule is that if a cube doesn't have calculations (such as calculated scripts, custom rollup, and custom members), the non-empty space of the cube is defined by fact table cells and their aggregations. Analysis Services allows users to write effective, optimized MDX queries to prevent empty cells from being returned. This is because those empty cells simply do not add value for business analysis. By limiting the search space, Analysis Services can find the results more quickly.

Analysis Services 2005 supports many ways for users to eliminate the cells containing null values in a query. The keyword NON EMPTY helps you to eliminate members along an axis whose cell values are null. The NON EMPTY keyword is used at the beginning of the axis statement in an MDX query as shown here:

```
SELECT Measures.Members on COLUMNS,
NON EMPTY Dimension.Hierarchy.Members on ROWS
From <CubeName>
```

The NON EMPTY keyword can be used on rows or columns (or any axis). Assume that if you execute the preceding query without the NON EMPTY keyword, you see the results shown in the following table.

	Measure 1	Measure 2	Measure 3	Measure 4
Member 1	Null	Null	Null	Null
Member 2	Value 1	Value 2	Value 3	Value 4
Member 3	Null	Null	Null	Null
Member 4	Value 5	Value 6	Value 7	Value 8
Member 5	Value 9	Value 10	Value 11	Value 12

If you execute the query with the NON EMPTY keyword, you will see the results shown in the following table. You can see that Member 1 and Member 3, which had null values for all the measures, have been removed from the results.

	Measure 1	Measure 2	Measure 3	Measure 4
Member 2	Value 1	Value 2	Value 3	Value 4
Member 4	Value 5	Value 6	Value 7	Value 8
Member 5	Value 9	Value 10	Value 11	Value 12

In addition to the NON EMPTY keyword that can be used on the axes, Analysis Services 2005 supports the functions NONEMPTY() and NONEMPTYCROSSJOIN() which you learned in Chapter 7. These functions take in a set as one of the parameters, filter all the tuples that contain a null cell value in the context of the default measure or the measure that is passed as another parameter, and return a set of non-empty tuples.

Analysis Services has an optimized and an un-optimized code path to identify non-empty data and return results to a user query. In the un-optimized method, Analysis Services will iterate over the entire region of the user query and evaluate cell values individually to see if the cell value is null. This is usually a slow operation for a large and sparse data query. The optimized method leverages much smaller searching space (fact table rows) to quickly discard the empty cells, and it is fast. The performance difference is significant for queries with large datasets. Under certain conditions, running the un-optimized code path might result in non-intuitive results. For example, the NonEmptyCrossJoin function enforces the optimized code path, but you should use this function very carefully when you are using calculated members because these might produce non-intuitive results, which is not what you are expecting. The NonEmptyCrossJoin function is being deprecated. If you use the NonEmpty function, Analysis Services decides to execute either the optimized or un-optimized code path based on the conditions and ensure correct results are returned. We recommend you use the key word NON EMPTY of the function NONEMPTY() to eliminate tuples containing null values in your results.

Analysis Services will try to use the optimized method anytime a non-empty query is sent to the server either using NON EMPTY key word or using NONEMPTY function. However, there are cases under which the server will default to the un-optimized code path whenever it is unable to identify an easy way to evaluate if the cells are empty. Such an unoptimized code path is usually taken when there are complex expressions for calculated members where the server is unable to identify the real measure that it needs to use to run the optimized code path. If you do know the real measures that will help in identifying whether or not the calculation will result in an empty value, you can specify the real measure to Analysis Services through the syntax NON EMPTY BEHAVIOR. This helps the server force the optimized code path even when there are complex calculation evaluations. You learn more about the NON EMPTY BEHAVIOR in the following sections.

Using Non-Empty to Eliminate Cells

In most cases, only results with non-empty cells are meaningful for end users. You should always use the NON EMPTY keyword in your MDX cellset and rowset queries whenever possible. Not only will it limit the size of the cellset returned, but there are additional optimization benefits that speed up your query execution time.

Following is an MDX query without the NON EMPTY keyword. Execute this query using SQL Server Management Studio against a deployed sample Adventure Works project.

```
Select [Customer].[Customer Geography].[Customer].members *
Descendants([Product].[Product Categories].[Category].&[3],[Product].[Product
Categories].[Product Name]) on 1,
{[Measures].[Internet Sales Amount]} on 0
from [Adventure Works]
```

You will see that the query returns 18,485 cells. This query took 12 seconds on a single proc server machine when we executed it. Now change the query to include the NON EMPTY keyword on both axes as shown here and execute the new query in SQL Server Management Studio.

```
Select NON EMPTY [Customer].[Customer Geography].[Customer].members *
Descendants([Product].[Product Categories].[Category].&[3],[Product].[Product
Categories].[Product Name]) on 1,
{[Measures].[Internet Sales Amount]} on 0
from [Adventure Works]
```

The query that includes the NON EMPTY keyword returns just 6,853 non-empty cells and it took only 3 seconds to execute. This clearly highlights for you the benefit of eliminating empty cells using NON EMPTY.

Using Non-Empty to Improve Performance for Filter and Sort

Many users apply filter conditions on a set or try to evaluate the top members from a set based on certain conditions using the Filter and TopCount functions, respectively, from a large cube space. In most cases, only non-empty member sets are needed in the filter and topcount functions. You can improve the performance dramatically by first using NONEMPTY() to find the non-empty sets using optimized algorithm, followed by the filter, sort, or topcount functions on a much smaller set. In the Adventure Works sample for example, if you want to get the top ten Customer, Product combinations to start a marketing campaign, your query will look like the following:

```
Select
TopCount([Customer].[Customer Geography].[Customer].members*
[Product].[Product Categories].[Product].members, 10 ,
    [Measures].[Internet Sales Amount]) on rows ,
[Measures].[Internet Sales Amount] on columns
from [Adventure Works]
```

Notice the above query contains a cross-join of all the customers and products (shown by the expression below). Whenever a cross-join is applied, the server sorts the result based on the order of the hierarchies.

```
([Customer].[Customer Geography].[Customer].members*[Product].[Product
Categories].[Product].members)
```

The cross-join of the customers and products dimension results in 18485 * 396 = 7,320,060 cells. Analysis Services now evaluates the top 10 cells out of the seven million cells to return the results for the preceding query. This query took around 101 seconds on the server machine and it consumed 1 CPU at 100% during the entire execution. Most of the cells of the cross-join were actually empty cells that need not have been part of the result of the cross-join. Not only did the server take the time in sorting these cells, but it also had to iterate through the seven million cells to determine the top 10 cells. The following query uses the NonEmtpyCrossJoin function that eliminates the empty cells.

```
Select
TopCount(NONEMPTYCROSSJOIN(
[Customer].[Customer Geography].[Customer].members*
[Product].[Product Categories].[Product].members,
{[Measures].[Internet Sales Amount]},1),10,
   [Measures].[Internet Sales Amount]) on rows ,
[Measures].[Internet Sales Amount] on columns
from [Adventure Works]
```

In the above query the NonEmptyCrossJoin function first eliminates all the empty cells, and hence the TopCount function only had to work on a smaller number of cells. The query took 3 seconds because of the optimization provided by the NonEmptyCrossjoin function. Only cells containing facts were sorted and the top 10 values were returned. The performance improvement is sometimes beyond comparison and both queries are returning the exact same results. The rule of thumb is that the fewer tuples or cells involved in calculations, the better the query performance. Because Analysis Services has an efficient algorithm to get non-empty sets, which are much smaller in most cases, the user should use NonEmpty whenever it is applicable and appropriate for the business requirement. You can use the NonEmptyCrossJoin function whenever you are aware that a real measure will be used by the server for Non-Empty evaluation, and use it with caution when you have calculated measures.

You can also use the HAVING clause that eliminates cells with null values as seen in Chapter 7.

Using Non-Empty Behavior to Improve Calculation Performance

If you query for cells that involve evaluation of complex calculations then the cells' emptiness (if the cell returns a null value) is not determined by fact table cells; each cell must be evaluated to return the correct results. Analysis Services provides you with a keyword called NON_EMPTY_BEHAVIOR, to instruct the server to use the optimized algorithm to determine cells' emptiness. The following query returns the Forecast sales by applying different rates:

```
WITH member [Measures].[ForecastSales] as
'iif([Measures].[Internet Sales Amount] >500 ,
[Measures].[Internet Sales Amount]*1.2,
[Measures].[Internet Sales Amount]*1.2)'
Select NON EMPTY [Customer].[Customer Geography].[Customer].members*
Descendants([Product].[Product Categories].[Category].&[3],[Product].[Product
Categories].[Product]) on 1 ,
NON EMPTY {[Measures].[ForecastSales]} on 0
from [Adventure Works]
```

Even though the above query uses NON EMPTY, you will find the server still takes around 12 seconds to execute it. This is because the optimized code path cannot be applied on complex calculated members. In the preceding query you have a calculated member that is multiplied by 1.2 and hence the server needs to evaluate the expression to identify if the corresponding cells are empty. Given the non-empty behavior for this measure, you can specify NON_EMPTY_BEHAVIOR for this member, and tie the calculated measure to a real fact measure. The server will use the optimized code path for the non-empty determination. Execute the following modified query that contains the NON_EMPTY_BEHAVIOR:

```
WITH member [Measures].[ForecastSales] as
'iif([Measures].[Internet Sales Amount] >500 ,
[Measures].[Internet Sales Amount]*1.2,
[Measures].[Internet Sales Amount]*1.2)',
 NON_EMPTY_BEHAVIOR = '[Measures].[Internet Sales Amount]'
Select NON EMPTY [Customer].[Customer Geography].[Customer].members*
Descendants([Product].[Product Categories].[Category].&[3],[Product].[Product
Categories].[Product]) on 1 ,
NON EMPTY {[Measures].[ForecastSales]} on 0
from [Adventure Works]
```

Did you notice the difference in how long this query took as compared to the original query? This is why we recommend applying the NON_EMPTY_BEHAVIOR for the calculated members whenever you are using complex calculations and you have a fact measure or a simple calculated member that is helpful in evaluating if a cell is empty. We have just illustrated a few important optimizations that will help you write optimized MDX queries. There are many more MDX optimizations that can be done. We recommend *MDX Solutions 2nd edition* by George Spofford, et al., (Wiley, 2006) which devotes an entire chapter to MDX optimization.

Scalability Optimizations

Scalability with respect to Analysis Services indicates how well Analysis Services handles parameter value increases for dimension sizes, number of dimensions, size of the cube, number of databases, and number of concurrent users — all of which affect server behavior. Analysis Services provides several scalability parameters, such as handling a large number of partitions or a dimension with a large number of members (>5 million). In this section you will learn about optimizations relevant specifically to scalability of Analysis Services.

For Analysis Services 2005 you can control the number of queries executed concurrently with the advanced configuration property ThreadPool\Query\MaxThreads. The default value 10 works well for most scenarios, but on a machine with many processors it should be increased, or for scenarios combining short-running queries with long-running queries there may be benefits from decreasing the value.

Configuring Server Configuration Properties

There are several configuration properties provided by Analysis Services with which to fine tune the server. The default values for these properties have been set for the most common scenarios. However for specific requirements you might have change these settings to achieve the best performance from Analysis Services. Microsoft recommends you change configuration settings only when working with Microsoft product support. Documentation of all the server configuration properties is expected to be released by Microsoft in 2006. Here we provide information on some of the configuration properties.

1. **Memory\Total Memory Limit:** The value for this property is between 0 and 100 since it is a percentage of the available memory. On a 4GB memory machine if you have not enabled the /3GB switch the msmdsrv.exe process will get 2 GB. Be aware that the total memory limit on the server should be 80% of the available memory since Analysis Services is expected to use the remaining 20%.

2. **Memory\Low Memory Limit:** Analysis Services contains a cleaner thread which reclaims memory from jobs that are idle or have lower priority. The cleaner thread constantly wakes up and reclaims memory based on the Low Memory Limit. The default value is 75%. As soon as the low memory limit crosses the 75% threshold then the cleaner thread requests existing jobs to shrink memory and starts to reclaim the memory. In certain instances while processing multiple partitions in parallel the cleaner thread might not be fast enough to wake up and reclaim memory. Due to this existing processing, jobs could fail. By lowering the Low Memory Limit you can make sure cleaner thread starts to reclaim memory earlier and hence all the processing jobs will complete.

3. **CoordinatorExecutionMode:** This property is used for parallelism of jobs and takes a negative or positive value. The value indicates the number of coordinator jobs that can be in parallel at a given point in time. If the value is negative then the number is multiplied by the number of processors on the machines. Having a high value can deteriorate performance since multiple threads are competing for resources. The default value is -4.

4. **ThreadPool\Query:** This node contains several properties such as minimum and maximum number of threads to be allocated for a query and the priority for these threads. The MinThreads property indicates the number of threads created for each query and the MaxThreads property indicates the number of maximum threads that will be allocated for a query. A query can be split into multiple jobs and these jobs can be executed in parallel. Based on the MaxThreads, Analysis Services will have all the jobs execute in parallel (assume there are no dependencies).

5. **ThreadPool\Processing:** Similar to ThreadPool\Query this node contains the same sub-properties. However, the properties are applicable for each process statement rather than the query.

6. **OLAP\ProcessPlan\MemoryLimit:** This value is represented as a percentage of available system memory. This value indicates the maximum amount of memory used for a specific processing job. As mentioned earlier in this chapter we recommend you increase this value up to the Total Memory Limit if you encounter out of memory errors while processing multiple partitions in parallel.

7. **OLAP\ProcessPlan\ForceMultiPass:** This holds a Boolean value (0 or 1). When Analysis Services is processing dimensions it processes all the attributes in parallel. While processing the key attribute it retrieves all the related properties. If the number of members in the dimension is large then the entire row might not fit in memory. Hence Analysis Services provides you a way to process this in multiple passes of having chunks of related attributes processed based on memory availability. By default this value is set to 0 and Analysis Services gets into ForceMultiPass code path whenever Analysis Services is under memory pressure. However if you do need to force Analysis Services to use the multi-pass algorithm then you need to set this property to 1.

8. Query\DefaultDrillthroughMaxRows: While performing drill-through on a specific cell the number of resulting rows can be quite large. This impacts the performance of drill-through. Most often users might look for a top 100 rows. While defining drill-through you can specify the number of rows to be returned. However if that option is not specified in the drill-through statement then the value specified for this property is used to restrict the number of rows returned.

Scale Out

If your cube contains a large number of partitions (thousands of partitions) then queries retrieving data from all the partitions might be slow. This is because Analysis Services needs to read the data from all the partitions and then needs to aggregate the data. For efficient data reads you need to have high speed disks optimized for reads. Keep in mind that the aggregation of the data from various partitions is a CPU intensive operation; you can certainly increase the number of processors on the machine to reduce latency. Another alternative provided by Analysis Services is to make the partitions remote so that multiple Analysis Services are involved in reading data from various partitions. This scale out solution helps in distributing the read and data aggregation on multiple Analysis Services and thereby reduces the overall query time. You do have the master Analysis Services which still needs to gather the data from various slave machines and then aggregate the final data to the end user. We recommend you perform cost benefit analysis where you calculate the total costs of all the Analysis Services machines and the benefit you would be getting from it — all before implementing a solution using remote partitions.

Scale up

For large databases where the queries are data intensive or the load on the system is quite heavy with several users you need to consider adding additional CPUs. Typically commodity machines for servers are 4 processors. Based on your system load consider increasing the number of processors. Your system might be bottlenecked by memory as well. Assuming you have a system with 4GB (maximum on 32-bit machine), by default each process can access up to 2GB of memory. We recommend you change the boot.ini file to enable the /3GB option so that Analysis Services can utilize maximum memory on the system. If your database is large (dimensions having greater than 10 million members) and the user load on your system high, consider moving to a 64-bit system and adding additional processors and memory.

Handling Large dimensions

Certain Analysis Services databases can contain very large dimensions. Analysis Services 2000 had limitations in handling very large dimensions. Analysis Services 2005 overcomes most of these limitations by loading parts of dimensions that are requested. For MOLAP dimensions you might reach the theoretical maximum of 32-bit systems. Based on our experience of working with certain customers with very large dimensions we have identified that you might reach the 32-bit system limit if you have dimensions containing memory in the range of around 10 to 15 million members along with several hundred attributes in the dimensions. Typically when you have customer or product dimension along with various properties of the customer you can encounter processing issues due to unavailability of system resources. You can certainly tweak certain server configuration properties to get the maximum from Analysis Services. However we recommend you to move to 64-bit systems if you have dimensions having more than ten million members. Another suggestion is to have very large dimensions as ROLAP dimensions. Consider the alternatives mentioned in this section while handling large dimensions.

Using Profiler to Analyze Performance

SQL Server Profiler is a tool to trace operations on SQL Server and Analysis Services. This is the first release in which you have the ability to trace operations on Analysis Services through the well-known Profiler. Analysis Services exposes the commands sent to it as well as internal operations that occur within the server through what are called Events. For example, you have Events such as Command Begin, Command End, Query Begin, and Query End. Each Event has several properties associated with it such as start time, end time, and user sending the query. These properties as exposed as Event columns. SQL Profiler requests these events and event column values through a trace command to the Server. Analysis Services periodically sends the events to the clients who have subscribed to a trace. SQL Profiler shows the events and event column values in a matrix, only some columns of which might be applicable. Only administrators on Analysis Services can trace Analysis Services events. To learn more about how to use profiler follow the steps below.

1. Make sure you are an administrator on Analysis Services. You can connect to Analysis Services through SSMS and use the Analysis Services server properties dialog to add users as administrators of Analysis Services.

2. Launch SQL Server Profiler from Start➪All Programs➪Microsoft SQL Server 2005➪ Performance Tools➪SQL Server Profiler.

3. You will now see the SQL Server Profiler application. Create a new trace by selecting File➪ New Trace.

4. You will see the Connect to Server dialog shown in Figure 13-40. Select the Server type as Analysis Services and type the machine name of your Analysis Services instance.

Figure 13-40

5. In the Trace properties dialog type the name of the trace as FirstTrace. SQL Profiler provides three templates of traces with pre-selected events to trace. Select the Standard template as shown in Figure 13-41.

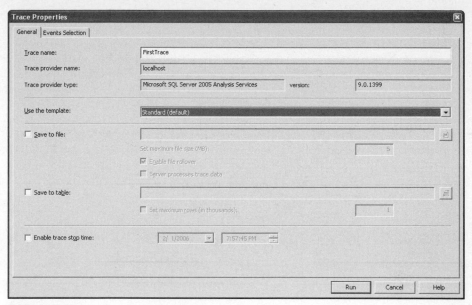

Figure 13-41

6. To see the various events and event columns selected for the standard template click on the Events Selection tab. You will see the various events and the event columns that have been selected for the standard template as shown in Figure 13-42. This page only shows the events that have been selected. To see all the events and event columns supported by Analysis Services you can click on the check boxes Show all events and Show all columns. Familiarize yourself with the various events and click Run.

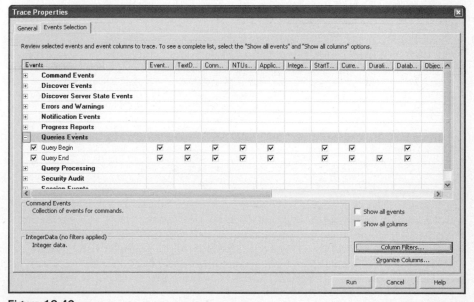

Figure 13-42

7. You will now be able to see the various event columns within Profiler. To see certain processing operations events open the Adventure Works DW sample project and deploy it to the Analysis Services instance. You can see the various events during the processing including the processing duration of each object as shown in Figure 13-43. This will help you to identify information such as dimension processing duration, duration of processing partitions, as well as overall processing time of the entire database. You can also see the relational queries sent to data source to retrieve data during processing for each object.

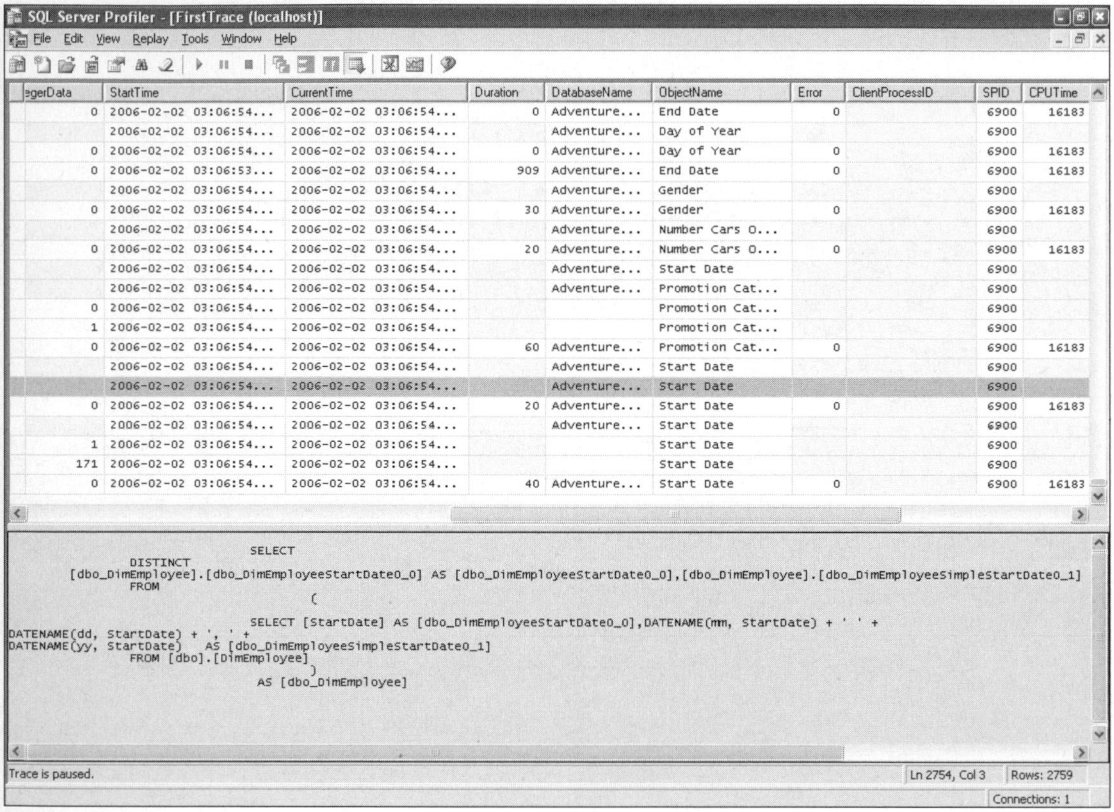

Figure 13-43

After the processing has completed for the Adventure Works cube send the following MDX query.

```
select {[Measures].[Sales Amount],[Measures].[Gross Profit]} on 0,
[Customer].[Customer Geography].members on 1
from [Adventure Works]
```

You can see the Query events in the SQL Profiler as shown in Figure 13-44 along with the duration. One of the information that would be interesting is to notice the subcubes accessed by this query and how long each subcube query took. The subcubes events indicate the internal part of the cubes that are utilized to retrieve data from disk. You can utilize the subcube information to build custom aggregations. Please refer to download samples of this chapter on building custom aggregations.

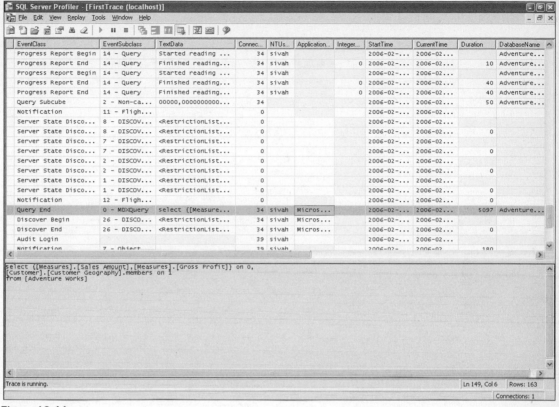

Figure 13-44

8. Assume you build aggregations using usage based optimization wizard. You would want to learn if the aggregations are being utilized. Analysis Services provides events to help you identify if the aggregations are hit. Create a new Trace and switch to the Events Selection tab. Check the box next to Show all events. Expand the events under the event class Query Processing. You can see the various events that are provided by Analysis Services as shown in Figure 13-45.

If you select the events under Query Processing and monitor the trace events you will be able to obtain information such as if Non Empty code path is being utilized, if MDX script is being evaluated, if data is retrieved from Aggregations or from existing cache. These events will help you identify more details about the queries sent by the users as well as total duration. You can later analyze the MDX queries, build usage based optimization for long running queries or try to optimize the long run MDX queries. As an administrator you definitely need to know a little bit about the internals of the server to fine tune it. We believe the ability to trace Analysis Services through SQL Profiler will help with that, so try it out.

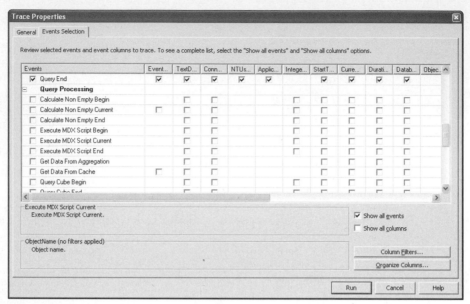

Figure 13-45

Summary

After reading this chapter, on hearing the very word *performance*, your head should swell with visions of highly performing, scalable systems, each optimized to fulfill its designated mission—never again will this word simply evoke images of entertainment provided by a theatrical group! To build a system that scales up and performs well, you have to consider high and low-level issues. At the high level, aggregation design forms the foundation for an optimally performing OLAP system; take the time to analyze the requirements of the application to get this step right. Another high-level consideration is the type of storage you choose for your system, be it MOLAP, HOLAP, or ROLAP. At lower levels there are many ways to optimize design, like avoiding the use of unnecessary attributes that are never used in customer queries. They can waste precious system data storage and slow down both processing performance and query performance. You learned other lower-level issues, about natural and unnatural hierarchies, and about how you should specify one-to-many relationships whenever possible for better query performance and reduced system data space requirements. You even dove down deep into tuning the Analysis Services instance by changing certain server properties. Finally, you learned how to tune query performance through use of aggregations and MDX query format optimization. And please, don't ignore this final important take-away, use the NonEmpty filter! In fact, use it unless there is a compelling reason not to (like empty cells don't exist in some data set). Finally you learned about tracing Analysis Services operations using SQL Server Profiler. We are confident you exploit the ability to collect Analysis Services traces using Profiler; further, that you will use the traces to enhance performance of the system.

14

Data Mining

Not everyone is well versed in the area of data mining, so this chapter starts straight away with what it is and what it is generally used for. So, without further ado... Data mining is the process of applying algorithms to data sets with the goal of exposing patterns in the data that would not otherwise be noticed. The reason such patterns would not otherwise be noticed owes to the complexity and volume of information within which the patterns are embedded. Another, less academic way to look at data mining is as a technology that can be used to answer questions like the following:

❏   When customers visit our corporate web site, what paths are they most likely to take when navigating through the site?

❏   When a $10 credit card transaction is processed at a gas station immediately followed by a $600 purchase on the same account from an electronics store in a different zip code, should a red flag be raised?

❏   For optimal sales revenue generation in a grocery store, which products should be placed in close proximity to one another?

To address these types of questions, and many others, turn to data mining technology. What is coming up in this chapter on data mining will teach you more about the types of questions that can be asked and answered in the real world by creating and using data mining applications. You look at each algorithm in detail, and then learn about mining models, which can be built on top of cubes (OLAP Mining Models) or on top of raw relational data (relational mining models).

The Data Mining Process

Wherever you look, people and businesses are collecting data, in some cases without even an obvious immediate purpose. Companies collect data for many purposes, including accounting, reporting, and marketing. Those companies with swelling data stores have executives with many more questions than answers; in this book you have seen how executives can use UDM based analysis to find the answers they need. This is typically a process in which you typically know what you are looking for and you can extract that information from your UDM. However there might be additional information in your data that can help you to make important business decisions which you are not aware of since you don't know what to look for. Data mining is the process of extracting interesting information from your data such as trends, clusters, and other patterns that can help you understand your data better. Data mining is accomplished through the use of statistical methods, as well as machine learning algorithms. The ultimate purpose of data mining includes the discovery of subtle relationships between data items. It can also entail the creation of predictive models. When data mining is successfully applied, rules and patterns previously unknown and potentially useful emerge from heaps of data.

You don't need a vintage coal-mining helmet with a lamp to begin the data mining process (but if you feel more comfortable wearing one, you can buy a used helmet off eBay). What really is required is a problem to solve with a very good understanding of the problem space; this isn't just an exploratory adventure. The main requirement would be to have the appropriate hardware to store the data to be analyzed and the analysis results. Then you would either need off-the-shelf data mining software, or if you are particularly knowledgeable, you can write your own software. In terms of hardware, you're going to need a machine for the storing data (typically relational databases that can store gigabytes or even terabytes of data) and a machine to develop and run your data mining application from. While those are normally two different machines, these functions can all reside on a single machine. We discuss data mining software in terms of data mining algorithms, infrastructure to use them, and data visualization tools for use in evaluating the results. Once you have the software and the required hardware you then need to have a good understanding of the data you are about to mine as well as the problem you are trying to solve. Having a good understanding of the data and the problem is a critical step before you start using the software to perform mining. You will learn more about understanding the problem space and data in subsequent sections.   Having the hardware and right software setup is a necessary pre-cursor to the data mining process. If data miners had to go through a pre-flight checklist like pilots and co-pilots do, it might look something like this:

Data Miner 1: "Ready to start pre-mine check."
Data Miner 2: "Ok, data store on-line with verified access?"
Data Miner 1: "Roger on the data store with access."
Data Miner 2: "Software loaded and ready to run?"
Data Miner 1: "Check."
Data Miner 2: "Data visualization tools; loaded and ready to run?"
Data Miner 1: "That's affirmative."
Data Miner 2: "Then we're ready to start, call it in."
Data Miner 1: "Sysadmin, sysadmin, this is miner 1, come in."
      {the static crackles over the voicom interop}
  Sysadmin: "This is Sysadmin, go ahead miner 1."
Data Miner 1: "Checklist complete, request clearance on server tango."
  Sysadmin: "Roger, miner 1, you are cleared for mining on tango. Over."

Once you have hardware and software requirements satisfied you then get into the process of building a model or representation of your data which helps you to visualize and understand information in your data better. Over time, through systematic efforts and by trial and error, several methodologies and guidelines emerged. Figure 14-1 shows the typical process of data mining divided into just five steps. First and foremost you need to understand the domain area and what your business needs. Once you have understood the domain area you then understand the data. You might run some initial statistics on the data to understand the data better. After understanding the data you create mining models and train the model with the input data. You need to analyze the mining models and validate the results from the models. Once you have built mining models to suit your business needs you deploy the models on to your production system. Your end users can consume the results from the model directly from the model or through applications that utilize the content from the model. You might have to go through this data mining life cycle periodically to meet the changing needs of your business or data or both.

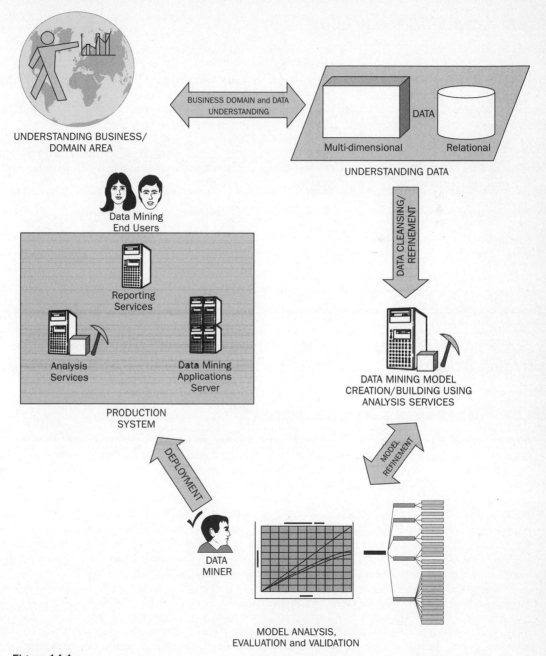

Figure 14-1

A great public resource on the data mining process (independent of specific data mining software products) is CRISP-DM (http://www.crisp-dm.org). CRISP-DM is a process guide that is available for download free. Yes, the process you see here maps roughly to the CRISP-DM process guide, but that would probably be true for any reasonable description of the data mining process.

Topic Area Understanding

Back in the last section, before Data Miner 1 begins to mine data he or she would first need to understand the data and then the problem space. Problem type and scope vary dramatically by subject area, from retail business, sales forecasts, and inventory management to logistics. Outside the realm of business there are data-mining-relevant science questions such as, "Some star has luminosity L, radiates brightly in the ultraviolet spectrum, and appears to have a small surface area. How hot is it likely to be?" If we have a reasonably sized database from which to train initially — more on what that means later — predictive data mining could uncover that the hotter the star, the shorter the wavelength peak in the star's spectrum and that the hottest stars peak in the ultraviolet area of the spectrum. You do need to have an idea about the topic or subject area and the problem you want to solve in order to identify non-intuitive relationships and patterns using data mining as a tool.

To accomplish the goal of your data mining project, you must understand what business you're in; moreover, what success means for your business in quantitative terms. By "understand the business" you have to sometimes ask the hard questions like does your company sell sugar water with flavoring? Or does it really sell an imagined lifestyle of fun, action, and perpetual happiness through the marketing of sugar water? What metrics can be used to measure gradients of success? For example, volumes of sales, market share ownership, or customer feedback scores? You as the person to mine your company's data or as a data mining consultant at a customer's site need to know as much information as possible about the customer and what they are trying to achieve so that you can interpret the results from data mining and make good recommendations. The bottom line is the company wants to improve profits earned. That can be accomplished by targeting the best sellers, adding value for customers (in the form of making suggestions based on customer usage patterns or detecting frauds against customer's credit cards) and loss reduction (by identifying processes which drain the business of funds unnecessarily).

Data: Understand It, Configure It

First off, you must know how to collect the data from disparate sources and then ensure the data description scheme (metadata) is integrated, consistent, and makes sense for all data to be used. It is a good idea at this point to explore the data by creating distributions, and running simple statistical tests. Though not required, it is not a bad idea to do so. It is critical that the data be clean and free of type mismatches; otherwise the algorithms might not extract important information, or if they do, possibly yield erroneous results. Other preparatory actions might be taken; for example, you might want to construct derived attributes, which are also called computed attributes or calculated columns. In order to verify the accuracy of the data mining algorithm results, the source data is often divided into training and testing data. We recommend splitting your source data; two-thirds for training purposes and the remaining one-third of the data for testing and verification of the algorithm results.

Understanding the data also involves understanding attributes of the data. For example if you are looking at customer data then name, gender, age, income, children, etc., are possible attributes of the customer. You need to have a good understanding of the values of the attributes that will best represent attributes to the data mining model you are about to create. For example, gender of a customer can typically have values Male, Female, or Unknown. There are only three possible values for the attribute gender. If you look at income of the customer, though, then the income can have a wide variance such as 0 to millions of dollars. These attributes need to be modeled appropriately for the chosen data mining algorithm to get the best results. The gender attribute would typically be modeled as a discrete attribute which means fixed number of values while the income would typically be modeled as continuous since there is a wide variation of the values for income. Understanding your data is critical.

Choose the Right Algorithm

Once you have a good understanding of your business, matching your needs to the data, you then need to choose the right data mining algorithm. A data mining algorithm is a technique or method by which data is analyzed and represented as patterns or rules which are typically called as data mining models. Choosing the right algorithm is not always easy. There might be several data mining algorithms that can solve your business problem. First, identify the algorithms that can solve your problem. The data mining model created by the algorithm is later analyzed to detect patterns or predict values for new data. Now, if you are aware of each data mining algorithm in depth you can potentially pick the right one. If not, identify the algorithms that can solve your problem and analyze results from each algorithm. Later in this chapter you will learn about various algorithms supported by Analysis Services 2005 and what class of problems they are helpful in solving. Fine tune the models of various algorithms and pick the most efficient one that provides you the maximum satisfaction for your business needs. Several techniques can be used to compare the results of several mining models, such as lift versus profit chart (you learn about these later in this chapter). Once you have compared and identified the right model, you can use the specific algorithm for more detailed analysis.

Train, Analyze, and Predict

With the data mining algorithm in hand, you now need to choose the data set to identify and analyze interesting information for your business. Data mining is used not only to analyze existing data, but also to predict characteristics of new data. Typically the data set to be analyzed will be divided into two — a training set and a validation set — usually in the ratio 2:1. The training data set is fed as input to the data mining algorithm. The algorithm analyzes the data and creates an object called a data mining model, which represents characteristics of the data set analyzed. You need to identify the right training data set to best represent your data. You also need to consider training data size because that will directly impact training time. Training of a model is also referred to as *model building* or *processing of a model* in this book. Once you have determined the training data set, you train the model with the chosen algorithm. Once you have the trained model, you can analyze it and have a better understanding of the training data set and see if that provides you useful information for your business.

Prediction is the process of predicting a value or values of a data set based on characteristics of the data set. For example, if you own a store and create a mining model of all your customers, you might classify them as Platinum, Gold, Silver, or Bronze membership based on several factors, such as salary, revenue they bring to your store, number of household members, and so on. Now, if a new member shops at your store you might be able to predict his or her membership based on salary, household members, and other factors. Once you have this information, you can send membership-relevant promotional coupons to the member to increase your sales.

In addition to analyzing your data using a mining model, you can perform prediction for new data sets by simply providing the new data set as input to the model and retrieving the prediction results. In order to determine the accuracy of the model, you could use the validation data set, predict values for the validation set, and compare the actual values with the predicted values. Based on the number of accurate predictions, you will know how good the model is. If the model is not providing prediction results as per your expectations, you might be able to tweak it by changing properties of the data mining algorithm or choosing the right attributes as inputs or choosing a different mining algorithm. You might have to periodically maintain the model based on additional information available to you — in this way, your model is trained well with the most up-to-date information and should yield optimal results.

Real-World Applications

Mapping theory to the real world is not always the most intuitive process imaginable. There are several successful data mining applications that have been deployed across various sectors. In this section you learn examples of real-world applications which use data mining technology.

Fraud Detection

Have you ever received a call from your credit card company asking whether you made a specific credit card purchase? Do you know why you received the call? Chances are very good that it was due to an anomaly detected in your credit card usage as part of the company's fraud detection effort. Typically, customer usage patterns on credit cards are quite consistent. When a credit card is stolen, the usage pattern changes drastically. In spite of increasingly advanced theft protection schemes, credit card companies still lose a lot of money due to theft. Because credit card fraud is roughly 10% higher on the internet than off, Visa introduced CISP (Cardholder Information Security Processing) in 2000 and MasterCard followed with its Site Data Protection Service (SDPS) in 2001. The CISP and SDPS only help in securing and validating the data and do not actually prevent the use of stolen credit cards. In order to detect anomalies and act immediately, credit card companies are now using data mining to detect unusual usage patterns of credit cards; and once such a pattern is detected, the customer is called to verify the legitimacy of certain purchases.

Increasing Profits in Retail

Now here is an example almost everyone can relate to. Have you shopped at Amazon (the online book seller) and seen a suggestion pop up that read something like this: "Customers who bought this book also bought the following" and then some list of pertinent books followed? Do you know how they do this? This is typically accomplished with the use of a data mining algorithm called "association rules." In order to boost sales, companies like Amazon use this algorithm to analyze the sales information of many customers. Based on your book buying behavior, Amazon uses the algorithm to predict what other books you would likely be interested in. From the list of books provided by the algorithm, they typically choose the top 5 books that have the highest likelihood of being purchased by the customer — then they suggest those books. Another example of where just such an algorithm is being used is in the area of DVD rentals.

Data Mining in the NBA

As many of you sports fans know, NBA coaches need to analyze opponent teams and adopt appropriate strategies for winning future games. Typically, the coach will look for key players on the opposing team and appropriately match up his own players to counter their strengths and expose their weaknesses. Relevant information can be from past games that have been analyzed and gleaned from other sources. The NBA is fast paced, and coaches need to adapt based on current game situations. For this purpose, they need to analyze information every quarter and often in real time.

NBA coaching staffs collect all the information on the players and points scored during a game and feed it into a data mining software application called Advanced Scout. With the help of this software, coaches are able to analyze patterns — when did the opponent score the most points, who were the players on our team, who was guarding the highest point scorer on the opposing team, where were the shots taken, and so on. With such information readily available, coaches adapt to the situation and make decisions that will help their team to win.

Yes, but how was Advanced Scout helpful, you ask? When the Orlando Magic NBA team was devastated in the first two games of the 1997 season finals, which was against the second-seed Miami Heat, the team's fans began to hang their heads in shame. Advanced Scout showed the Orlando Magic coaches something that none of them had previously recognized. When Brian Shaw and Darrell Armstrong were in the game, something was sparked within their teammate Penny Hardaway — the Magic's leading scorer at that time. Armstrong was provided more play-time and hence Hardaway was far more effective. The Orlando Magic went on to win the next two games and nearly caused the upset of the year. Fans everywhere rallied around the team and naysayers quickly replaced their doubts with season-ticket purchases for the following year.

Data Mining in Call Centers

Companies spend a lot of money on call center operations to meet customer needs. Customers use the toll-free number provided by the company and the company pays for each call based on the duration of the call. Typically, most calls target a few specific questions. For example, if the documentation for product setup was not sufficient, the call center might get calls with the same question or related questions on getting the product set up and configured properly.

Often the information obtained from customers is entered in the computer system for further analysis. With the help of Text Mining, the customers' questions can be analyzed and categorized. Most often you would end up identifying a set of questions that are due to a specific problem. Companies can use this information to create a FAQ site where they can post answers on how to solve the specific problem. Making the FAQ available and providing the answers to some of the common problems helps the company and the customers have a faster turnaround, saving both time and cost. In addition to this, the call center operators can be trained to use the information provided by Text Mining to easily nail down a solution to the problem posed by the customer. The duration of each call is reduced, thereby saving valuable cash for the company.

Data Mining Algorithms in Analysis Services 2005

Analysis Services 2005 provides you with nine data mining algorithms that you can utilize to solve various business problems. These algorithms can be broadly classified into five categories based on the nature of the business problem they can be applied to. They are

- ❑ Classification
- ❑ Regression
- ❑ Segmentation
- ❑ Sequence analysis
- ❑ Association

Classification data mining algorithms help solve business problems such as identifying the type of membership (Platinum, Gold, Silver, Bronze) a new customer should receive or whether the requested loan can be approved for a customer based on his or her attributes. Classification algorithms predict one or more discrete variables based on the attributes of the input data. Discrete variables are variables which contain a limited set of values. Some examples of discrete variables are Gender, Number of children in a house, and number of cars owned by a customer.

Regression algorithms are similar to classification algorithms; instead of predicting discrete attributes, however, they predict one or more continuous variables. Continuous variables are variables that can have many values. Examples of continuous variables are yearly income, age of a person, and commute distance to work. The algorithms belonging to the regression category should be provided with at least one input attribute that is of type continuous. For example, assume you want to predict the sale price of your house, a continuous value, and determine the profit you would make by selling the house. The price of the house would depend on several factors, such as square feet area (another continuous value), zip code, and house type (single family, condo, or town home), which are discrete variables. Hence regression algorithms are primarily suited for business problems where you have at least one continuous attribute as input and one or more attributes as predictable attributes.

Segmentation algorithms are probably the most widely used algorithms. Segmentation is the process of creating segments or groups of items based on the input attributes. Customer segmentation is one of the most common business applications, where stores and companies segment their customers based on the various input attributes. One of the most common uses of segmentation is to perform targeted mailing campaigns to those customers who are likely to make purchases. This reduces the mailing cost to all the customers, thereby maximizing the profit for the company.

Sequence analysis algorithms analyze and group input data based on a certain sequence of operations. For example, if you want to analyze the navigation patterns of Internet users (sequence and order of pages visited by a user on the internet) and group them based on their navigations, sequence analysis algorithms would be used. Based on the sequence of pages visited you can identify interests of people and provide appropriate information to the users as a service or show advertisements relevant to the users' preferences to increase sales of specific products. For example, if you navigate through pages of baby products on www.amazon.com, subsequent visits to Amazon pages might result in baby product-related advertisements. Similarly, sequence analysis is also used in genomic science to group a sequence of genes with similar sequences.

Association data mining algorithms help you to identify association in the data set. Typically these algorithms are used for performing market-basket analysis where association between various products purchased together are analyzed. Based on the analysis, associations between various products are identified and these help in the cross-selling of products together to boost sales. One famous data mining example highlights associations — customers buying diapers also bought beer, and the purchases occurred on Thursday/Friday. One of the reasons is that diapers often need replenishing and women request their husbands or significant others to buy them. Men often buy over the weekend, and hence these purchases were made together. Based on this association, supermarkets can have diapers and beer stocked adjacently, which helps boost the sales of beer.

Enclosed below are brief descriptions of the nine data mining algorithms supported in Analysis Services 2005. The description will give you an overview of the algorithm and scenarios where the algorithm can be utilized. We recommend you to refer to SQL Server Analysis Services documentation for details such as algorithm properties, their values, and various content types supported by the algorithm for input and predictable columns. Following these descriptions you will learn two data mining algorithms in detail by creating mining models using the data mining wizards.

Microsoft Decision Trees

Microsoft Decision Trees is a classification algorithm that is used for predictive modeling and analysis. A classification algorithm is an algorithm that selects the best possible outcome for an input data from a set of possible outcomes. An input data set called the *training data* that contains several attributes is provided as input to the algorithm. Usage of the attributes as either input or predictable are also provided to the algorithm. The classification algorithm analyzes the attributes of the input data and arrives at a distribution, which includes a combination of input attributes and their values that result in the value of the predictable column. Microsoft Decision Trees is helpful in predicting both discrete and continuous attributes. If the data type of the predictable attribute is continuous, the algorithm is called Microsoft Regression Trees and there are additional properties to control the behavior of the regression analysis.

Naïve Bayes

Naïve Bayes is another classification algorithm available in Analysis Services 2005 that is used for predictive analysis. The Naïve Bayes algorithm calculates the value of the predictable attribute based on the probabilities of the input attribute in the training data set. Naïve Bayes helps you to predict the outcome of the predictable attribute quickly because it assumes the input attribute is independent. Compared to the data mining algorithms in Analysis Services 2005, Naïve Bayes is computationally less intense for model creation.

Microsoft Clustering

The Microsoft Clustering algorithm is a segmentation algorithm that helps in grouping the sample data set into segments based on the characteristics. The clustering algorithm helps in identifying relationships existing within a specific data set. A typical example would be grouping store customers based on their characteristics of sales patterns. Based on this information you can classify the importance of certain customers to your bottom-line. The Microsoft Clustering algorithm is unique because it is a scalable algorithm that is not constrained by the size of the data set. Unlike the Decision Trees or Naïve Bayes algorithm, the Microsoft Clustering algorithm does not require you to specify a predictable attribute for building the model.

Sequence Clustering

As the name indicates, the Sequence Clustering algorithm helps in grouping sequences in the sample data. Similar to the clustering algorithm, the sequence clustering algorithm groups the data sets but based on the sequences instead of the attributes of the customers. An example of where Sequence Clustering would be used is to group the customers based on the navigation paths of the Web site they have visited. Based on the sequence, the customer can be prompted to go to a Web page that would be of interest.

Association Rules

The Microsoft Association algorithm is an algorithm that typically helps identify associations or relationships between products that are purchased. If you have shopped at Amazon.com you have likely noticed information "people who have purchased item one have also purchased item two." Identifying the association between products purchased is called market-basket analysis. The algorithm helps in analyzing products in a customer's shopping basket, and predicts other products the customer is likely to buy. That prediction is based on purchase co-occurrence of similar products by other customers. This algorithm is often used for cross-selling through product placement in the store.

Neural Networks (SSAS)

The Microsoft Neural Networks algorithm is a classification algorithm similar to Microsoft Decision Trees and calculates probabilities for each value of the predictable attribute, but it does so by creating internal classification and regression models that are iteratively improved based on the actual value. The algorithm has three layers (the input layer, an optional hidden layer, and an output layer) that are used to improve the prediction results. The actual value of a training case is compared to the predictable value and the error difference is fed back within the algorithm to improve the prediction results. Similar to the decision trees algorithm, the Neural Network algorithm is used for predicting discrete and continuous attributes. One of the main advantages of neural networks over the decision trees algorithm is that neural networks can handle complex as well as large amount of training data much more efficiently.

Time Series

The Microsoft Time Series algorithm is used in predictive analysis but is different from other predictive algorithms in Analysis Services 2005 because during prediction it does not take input columns to predict the predictable column value. Rather, it identifies trends in the input data and helps predict future values. A typical application of a time series algorithm is to predict the sales of a specific product based on the sales trend of the product in the past, along with the sales trend of a related product. Another example would be to predict stock prices of a company based on the stock price of another company. The Time Series algorithm is used for predicting continuous attributes.

Microsoft Linear Regression

Microsoft Linear Regression is a special case of Microsoft Decision Tree algorithm where you set an algorithm property so that the algorithm will never create a split there by ending up with a linear regression. The algorithm property MINIMUM_LEAF_CASES for the Microsoft Decision Tree will be set to a value greater than the number of input cases used to train the model. The linear regression algorithm will typically be used when you want to find the relationship between two continuous columns. The algorithm finds the equation of a line that best fits data representing the relationship between the input columns. Microsoft Linear Regression algorithm only supports input columns that have certain content type. The main content type typically used will be continuous. The algorithm does not support content types discrete or discretized. For more details on the content type supported by the algorithm please refer to product documentation.

Microsoft Logistic Regression

The Microsoft Logistic Regression is a variation of the Microsoft Neural Networks algorithm where the hidden layer is not present. The simplest form of logistic regression is to predict a column that has two states. The input columns can contain many states and can be of many content types (discrete, continuous, discretized, etc.). You can certainly model such a predictable column using linear regression but the linear regression might not restrict the values to the minimum and maximum values of the column. However, logistic regression is able to restrict the output values for the predictable column to the minimum and maximum values with the help of a S-shaped curve instead of the linear line which would have been created by a linear regression. In addition, logistic regression is able to predict columns of content type discrete or discretized and able to take input columns that are content type discrete or discretized.

Working with Mining Models

Analysis Services 2005 provides two types of mining models: the relational mining model and the OLAP mining model. Relational mining models are created directly from the relational data source and the OLAP Mining models are created from an existing cube or part of a cube. Use of the nine types of data mining algorithms are made within the context of relational or OLAP mining models. In this chapter you will learn both these models by creating mining models using a few algorithms and analyzing the results.

Relational Mining Model

The Adventure Works DW sample relational database has specific patterns to demonstrate various algorithms available in Analysis Services 2005. In this section you learn how to create and analyze a decision tree model and a clustering model. Obviously, you need to create a new mining model to explore and analyze the information. When you build a mining model, Analysis Services 2005 retrieves data from the data source and stores it in a proprietary format. When you do want to build several mining models from the data set, there will be redundant data stored on Analysis Services 2005. In order to share the data across several mining models, Analysis Services 2005 stores the information about the data that can be shared across several mining models under an object called Mining Structure. Internally the information read from relational data sources is stored as a cube in order to efficiently retrieve the data during mining model creation. The Mining structure stores data type of attributes metadata in the mining model, the corresponding column in the data source, and allows you to modify the certain data mining properties that are common across all of your mining models.

Have you received coupons in the mail? If you have a postal address, you have. Retail companies used to send coupons to all customers and even some who weren't customers. That was expensive and of less than optimal efficiency. In order to minimize cost and maximize profit, companies now use data mining to select targets for coupon or other special postal distributions. Based on certain attributes, retail companies can classify customers into several groups (Gold, Silver, or Bronze membership). By doing this they clearly identify unique characteristics of the group. From there, targeted mailing to those groups can be made instead of mailing to every address on file. This practice saves marketing money for the companies and they have a better probability of making sales.

The following steps show you how to solve the targeted mailing type problem by creating a relational mining model on top of the vTargetMail view in the Adventure Works DW database. To create a relational mining model, you first need a data source view containing the table(s) on top of which you want to build a mining model.

1. Create a new Analysis Services project DM2005Tutorial. Create a data source to the Adventure Works DW relational database

2. Create a DSV that includes the vTargetMail view in the Adventure Works DW.

   ❑ The vTargetMail is a view that retrieves information from the server tables in the Adventure Works DW database. The vTargetMail view contains information about customers who buy bicycles. Based on the information in the view, you can identify potential customers who are likely to buy bicycles. The vTargetMail view has been specifically designed to contain patterns that can be identified by the data mining algorithms. As the name of the view indicates, vTargetMail is used to demonstrate the usefulness of the data mining where the customers can be categorized based on their attributes, and targeted mails with discounts or attractions can be sent only to customers who are likely to buy bicycles.

3. Similar to the wizard that helped you to create cubes and dimensions, there is a wizard to create data mining structures. To create a relational mining model right-click the Mining Structures folder in the solution explorer and select New Mining Structures as shown in Figure 14-2.

Figure 14-2

4. The welcome page provides information on the data mining wizard. Click the Next button on the Welcome page.

5. You will now see the Select the Definition Method page as shown in Figure 14-3. This page allows you to create a mining model from a relational data source or from a cube. Select the "From existing relational database or data warehouse" radio button and then click Next.

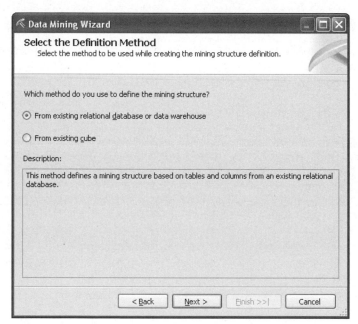

Figure 14-3

6. On the Select the Data Mining Technique page you can select the data mining technique to use for modeling. If you click the drop-down list box you can see all the algorithms available, as shown in Figure 14-4. Analysis Services also provides you the option of adding your own data mining technique. If you have added your custom data mining technique and exposed it you will see your data mining technique in this drop-down list box. Select the Microsoft Decision Trees algorithm and click Next.

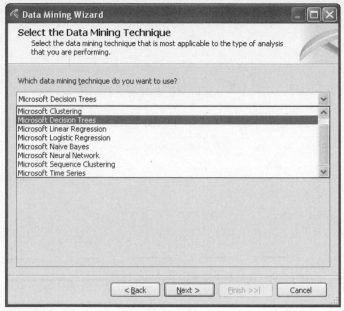

Figure 14-4

7. On the Select Data Source View page, select the DSV that contains vTargetMail (the DSV you created in Step 2) and click Next.

8. Of the multiple tables or views in your DSV, the Specify Table Type page allows you to select the table(s) upon which you create a mining model. The Specify Table Types page, as shown in Figure 14-5, shows two selections: Case (the primary table) and Nested. Certain algorithms are used for problems such as Market-basket analysis and the need to analyze data across multiple tables. In such cases you need to select certain table(s) as Nested tables. Typically there is a one-to-many relationship between the case and nested tables. Select the vTargetMail as a Case table and click Next.

9. On the Specify Training Data page of the wizard you need to select the columns from the source table(s) that are to be used in creation of mining models. In addition, you need to specify whether a specific column should be used as a key column, input column, or predictable column. If you specify a column as an input column, Analysis Services uses this column as an input to the mining model for determining patterns. If a specific column is marked as predictable, Analysis Services allows you to predict this column for a new data set based on the existing model if the input columns for the new data set are provided.

❑ In the current data set you want to predict if a customer is a potential buyer of bikes. The column BikeBuyer determines if an existing customer bought bikes before. Therefore, you need to mark this column as a predictable column. Once you have marked this column as predictable, you need to identify the potential factors that can influence a customer who buys bikes. If you think certain factors can influence a customer to buy bikes we recommend you select those columns as input columns. The wizard provides you a way to recommend columns as input columns by analyzing a sample data set. Click the Suggest button on the page and then click Next.

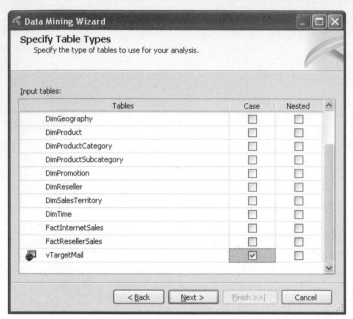

Figure 14-5

10. The wizard analyzes a sample of the data set and provides you the list of columns that are related to the selected predictable attribute BikeBuyer, as shown in Figure 14-6. The score column indicates how close an attribute is related to BikeBuyer column; a higher number indicates a stronger relationship. Stronger relationship can mean that a specific column can influence the chosen predictable column. Based on the score the wizard will auto select certain columns as input columns. You can deselect these attributes or select additional attributes that you think might influence a customer's decision on buying bikes. Click OK to Continue.

11. The selections you made in Suggest Related Columns page can now be seen in the Specify the Training Data page, as shown in Figure 14-7. Select the columns Age, Commute Distance, English Education, English Occupation, Gender, House Owner Flag, Marital Status, Number Cars Owned, Number Children At Home, Region, Total Children, and Yearly Income as input columns.

12. The selected columns along with their data types are shown in the Specify Columns' Content and Data Type page. As shown in Figure 14-8, the column Content Type indicates how each selected column will be used by Analysis Services while creating the mining model. You learn more about these content types while refining this model. For now, make all of the Continuous content types Discrete except Yearly Income. The relational data type of a column is mapped to the corresponding data type used within Analysis Services 2005 by the mining model wizard. Click Next.

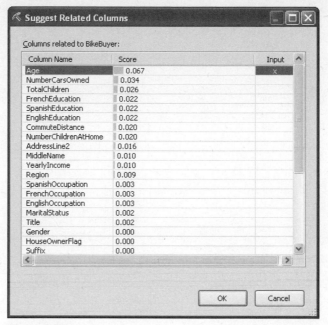

Figure 14-6

Figure 14-7

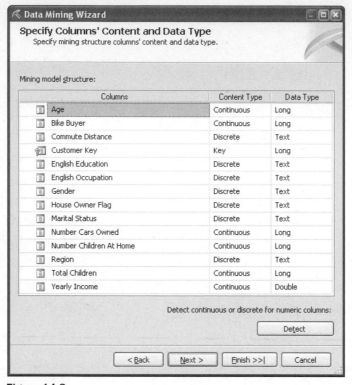

Figure 14-8

13. Similar to the completion pages of dimension and cube wizards, you can specify a name for the mining structure object. Enable the Allow Drill through option so that you have the ability to see additional details when you browse the Mining Model. Click Finish to create the mining model. Since each mining model is within a mining structure, Analysis Services automatically creates a mining structure with the same name as the mining model.

The mining structure object with a decision tree mining model can be seen in the mining model editor, as shown in Figure 14-9. The mining model editor contains five views: Mining Structure, Mining Models, Mining Model Viewer, Mining Accuracy Chart, and Mining Model Prediction. By default you will be in the Mining Structure tab. The mining structure view contains two panes. The DSV pane shows the tables part of the mining structure and allows you to perform the operations available within a DSV. The pane on the left shows the columns part of the mining structure in a tree view. You can delete existing columns or add columns to the mining structure by dragging and dropping them from the DSV. The properties of an attribute can be edited in the properties pane when the column is selected.

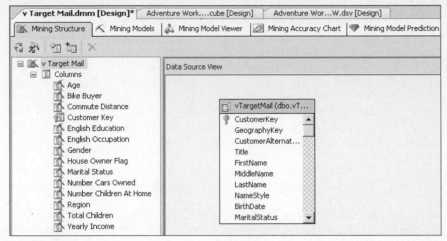

Figure 14-9

Figure 14-10 shows the Mining Models view. The mining models view shows the mining models in the current mining structure. You can have one or more mining models within each mining structure. The columns of the mining structure are by default inherited as columns of a mining model. Each column of a mining structure can be used for a specific purpose in a mining model. A column can be used as an input column or predictable-only column, input and predictable column, or need not be used in the mining model at all. These four usages of a mining structure column within a mining model are represented as Input, Predict only, Predict, and Ignore, respectively. These can be selected from the drop-down list box corresponding to a column and a mining model. You can add additional mining models within a mining structure by right-clicking in the mining models view and selecting New Mining Model. The mining structure wizard detects the content type of the mining model columns based on a sample of the data.

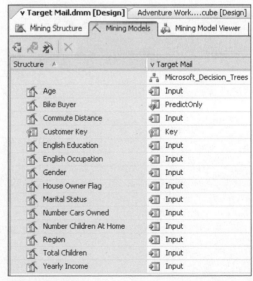

Figure 14-10

The mining model editor is used to make refinements to the mining model created by the mining model wizard. You will learn to make refinements in the mining model editor by making a few refinements to the decision tree mining model you have created now. You will make two refinements: change the content type for column Age and the usage of the Bike Buyer column. Age is a unique attribute that can be viewed as discrete, because the value is recorded as an integer between 0 and 100. If you have ever participated in a market survey you know they generally ask your age within a specific range rather than your exact age. Almost no adult likes to admit his or her age publicly, especially in the later years, so if you find yourself extremely reticent to mention your age, be worried. Be very worried. In this example you will model Age as a range rather than a discrete value. This content type is called Discretized. Discretized means that the values will be split across N number of ranges and any value of Age will be assigned the new value based on the range. The number of ranges is controlled by the property DiscretizationBucketCount. Based on the value set for DiscretizationBucketCount property, Analysis Services 2005 will identify the right ranges based on the minimum and maximum values of Age.

14. In the Mining Models view select the column Age under the column Structure. The properties for the Age column can be seen in the properties window as shown in Figure 14-11. Change the property content from Discrete to Discretized and the DiscretizationBucketCount to 10.

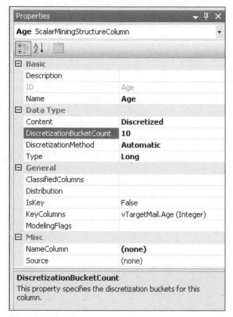

Figure 14-11

15. The Usage of the column Bike Buyer was initially set to Predict Only because this is what you selected in the wizard. Change the usage to Predict. The value Predict means that the Bike Buyer attribute will be used as an input as well as an output to the mining model. By choosing the Bike Buyer as an input column you are providing additional information to the mining model algorithm so that the model accurately represents the input data.

16. Having completed all the refinements to the decision tree model, you can now deploy this model to the server similar to the cube or dimension. Hit the F5 button to deploy the mining model.

Business Intelligence Development Studio sends the definition of the entire project you created to the server along with a process request. Once the database is processed, the BIDS switches the view to the Mining Model viewer as shown in Figure 14-12. The decision trees algorithm identifies the factors influencing customers to buy bikes and splits customers based on those factors and stores it within the model. The information stored in the model is better visualized using a tree structure. The mining model viewer represents the contents of the mining model in the form of a tree view which contains a series of nodes. The root of the tree starts with a single node that represents all the customers. Each node shows the percentage of customers (shown by the horizontal bar within the node) who have bought bikes based on the input set. Each node is split into multiple nodes based on the next most important factor that determines why a customer has bought a bike. The tree contains nodes at several levels from 1 to N based on the number of splits determined by the decision tree algorithm. Each node in the tree is associated to a specific level in the tree. The root node is at level 1 which is the top most level. The depth of the tree is measured by the number of splits or levels of the tree. In the mining model viewer you can make the selection to view the tree up to a specific level by selecting the option from Default Expansion or Show Level. Figure 14-12 shows nodes with the horizontal bar that is shaded with two colors. When you are using the product you will see these shaded regions of the horizontal bar in colors red, blue, or both. The mining legend window shows the legend for the colors in the horizontal bar or a node. If the legend window is not visible, right-click in the mining model viewer and select Show Legend.

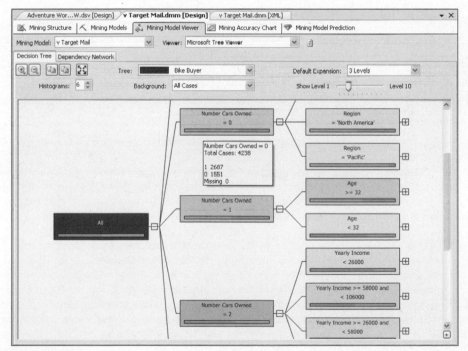

Figure 14-12

The legend in Figure 14-13 shows that blue (Value=0) indicates customers who are not bike buyers, red (Value=1) indicates the customers who have bought bikes, and white indicates customers for whom the BikeBuyer value is missing. Even though the underlying relational data source does not have a missing value for the BikeBuyer column, the algorithm does add a small percentage (0.03%) for the root node so that algorithm is not biased for certain prediction inputs. The split from a node at one level to nodes in the next level is based on a condition that is determined by an input column that influences the predictable attribute which is shown within the node such as Region=North America.

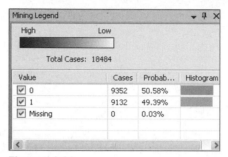

Figure 14-13

In the sample which you are analyzing, the most important factor that determines a customer buying a bike is the number of cars owned by the customer. The root node is split into five nodes based on the values for the number of cars owned (zero to four); three of these nodes are shown in Figure 14-12. A node with Number Cars Owned >=2 shows 40% of such customers are likely bike buyers. The next influencing factor for a customer to buy a bike is the customer's Yearly Income. You can traverse the tree from each node to identify the conditions that are likely to affect customers' decision to buy a bike. Based on the information available in the mining model, you can not only understand factors influencing the customers' decisions to buy bikes, but now you predict if a customer is a potential bike buyer based on his or her properties. Once you identify potential customers you can send targeted mails to customers who are potential buyers rather than all customers.

Once created, can your model predict accurately? If so, how accurate is it? How much trust can you place in the results of the model? To answer these questions the data mining editor has a view called the Mining Accuracy Chart, as shown in Figure 14-14. The Mining Accuracy Chart view contains three subviews that help you validate model accuracy. These are Column Mapping, Lift Chart, and Classification Matrix (see Figure 14-14). The column mapping view contains three sections that help you compare the accuracy of the model with a specific data set.

In order to compare the accuracy of a model that was created, often a subset of the input data set is set aside in the data mining process. The Column Mapping tab is used to select the input data set against which predication accuracy needs to be compared. You can filter the input data set for which you do want to compare the accuracy by specifying the filter conditions in the Filter the Input Used to Generate the Lift Chart section. The filtering can be applied in the second section of the Column Mapping tab. In the third section of the Column Mapping tab you have the option to do the accuracy comparison only on certain predicted values. For example, if you only want to compare the accuracy for all the customers who are buying bikes, you can select the predictable column Bike Buyer and the predicted value 1. This means that you are interested in identifying all the customers that the model has predicted as bike buyers and compare the original bike buyer value in the relational data source.

The mining model is used to predict the bike buyer value for each customer. If the predicted value is the same as the original value in the relational data source, it means the model has predicted the correct value. If not, the model has inaccurately predicted the Bike Buyer value for a customer.

To analyze the accuracy of the mining model, do the following:

1. In the Mining Accuracy Chart view click Select Case Table button for selecting the input table to identify the accuracy of the model built. Select the DSV containing the vTargetMail table; select the vTargetMail view and click OK.

The designer detects the column mappings between the mining model and the case table you have provided based on the name-matching criteria. Corresponding lines are created between the mining model and the case table; these lines are clearly displayed in Figure 14-14. If the mappings detected by the data mining editor are incorrect or mappings were not made by the data mining editor, you can make the correct mappings from the modify mappings dialog. The modify mappings dialog can be launched by right clicking within the data mining editor and selecting modify mappings.

2. In this example, you compare the accuracy of the decision tree model with the entire data set that was used to create the model. Therefore you do not apply any filters on the input data set.

3. In the third section of the Column Mapping tab leave the predict value blank so that all the predict values can be compared for accuracy.

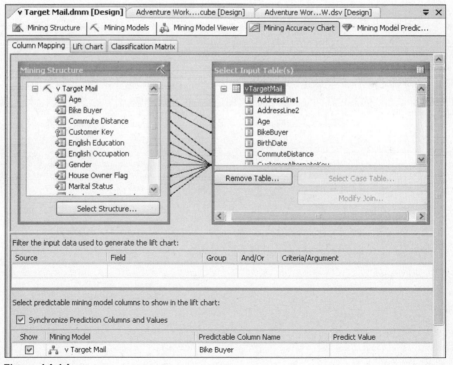

Figure 14-14

Analysis Services 2005 provides two ways to analyze the validity of the model. One of them is to show the validity graphically and another is to show the validation through actual numbers. To see the validity of the model graphically, select the Lift Chart sub-view within the Mining Accuracy Chart view. You will now see the graph with two lines as shown in Figure 14-15. The X-axis shows the percentage of data set used for prediction and the Y-axis shows the percentage of prediction correctness. You can see a legend window providing details on the two lines. If you created a perfect model that predicted all inputs correctly, the percentage correctness will always be 100%. This is represented by a blue line in the graph (the 45 degree line in Figure 14-15). In the current model the predictable attribute value can only have one of the two values: 0 or 1. Obviously you would want a model that predicts values very close to that of an ideal model. This graph gives you a visual way to easily compare the prediction correctness of the model as compared to an ideal model. The prediction correctness percentage of the model will be shown in a red line. You can see from Figure 14-15 that the prediction correctness of the model is not very close to that of an ideal model but is reasonably good since the prediction results are correct for 76% (population correct % for 100% of overall population) of the overall data set.

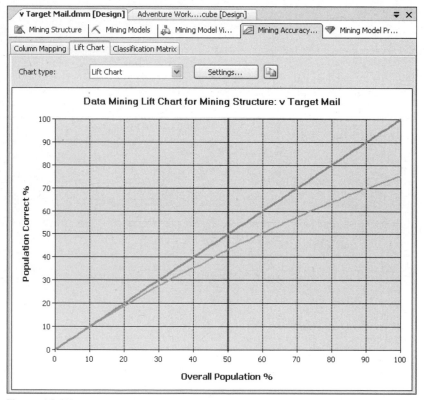

Figure 14-15

That's all well and good, but how is the lift chart calculated and visually represented? Analysis Services 2005 predicts the bike buyer attribute for every row in the input table. Each prediction also has a value called predict probability that provides a confidence value associated with the prediction. If you have a predict probability of 1.0, that means that the model believes the predicted value is always correct. If the predict probability for an input is 0.90, that means there is a 90% probability the predicted value is correct. After predicting the values for all the input rows, the results are ordered based on the predict probability. Now the predicted results are compared with the original value to calculate the prediction correctness percentage, and then they are plotted on a graph. The input data set is ordered based on the predict probability for the predicted value. This can be seen in the graph in Figure 14-15 where the lines indicating the current model and ideal model are nearly identical up to 10% of the population. The mining legend shows the score, population percentage, and predicts probability values for a specific population selection. Figure 14-15 shows that the population selection is 50%, which is indicated by a darker line. You can select a different population percentage by clicking the mouse on a specific population. When 100% of the data set is considered, the decision tree mining model is able to predict correct values for 76% of the data set correctly. This is indicated by the score value. For an ideal model this score value is 100%. The score for a model indicates the accuracy of the model and is in between 0 and 1. A higher score value means the model is more accurate and closer to an ideal model.

Two types of charts are provided by the Mining Accuracy Chart viewer to help in analysis of the mining model. You have learned about the lift chart. The second chart is called the profit chart. The profit chart helps you to analyze the potential profit your business would make based on four input parameters: number of samples, fixed cost incurred, cost per each row, and profit gained due to prediction. You will see the benefit of the profit chart only when there is a significant cost involved per sample. Select the chart type Profit Chart. Click on the Settings button to launch the profit chart settings dialog. Specify the Individual cost as 11, choose the remaining default values, and click OK. You will now see the profit chart as shown in Figure 14-16.

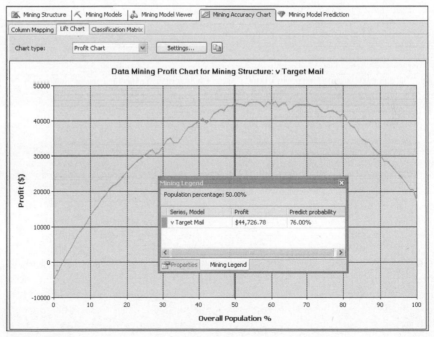

Figure 14-16

Analysis Services 2005 predicts the bike buyer column and calculates the profit based on the profit chart settings you have provided. Similar to the lift chart you can slide the gray vertical line. The mining legend shows the profit and predict probability values for the corresponding population percentage selected by the gray vertical line as shown in Figure 14-16. Similar to the lift chart, the predicted values are sorted based on prediction probability and then plotted on the graph. Therefore, the lower values of overall population percentage have higher prediction probability values. As you can see from the profit chart, the profit increases with increase in the sample size, reaches a maximum profit, and then drops down. If you send mail to the entire population, the net profit would be just less than $17,500. You want to get the maximum profit. The maximum profit you can obtain for the specified lift chart parameters is around $45,300. In order to maximize your profit you need to send mails only to customers who have a prediction probability greater than the prediction probability corresponding to the population percentage that has maximum profit. Thus the profit chart helps improve the profit of a business by saving the cost that would have been incurred for mailing to customers who are not potential buyers.

The third sub-view in the Mining Accuracy chart view is called the classification matrix. The classification matrix of the decision tree model on vTargetMail is shown in Figure 14-17. The classification matrix shows the original and predicted values for the predict attribute. In the decision tree model, the predictable values for bike buyer are 0 or 1. The matrix shows the actual and predicted values for all the specified input rows. As shown in Figure 14-17, the columns indicate the actual values while the rows indicate the predicted value. There are a total of 9,121 input rows that have the Bike buyer value 0. Of these, the model predicted 7,049 of them to be the correct value 0, while it predicted the remaining 2,072 rows incorrectly to value 1. Similarly the model predicted 7,060 of 9,363 input rows correctly to have a value of 1. This matrix provides you an overview of how good the predicted values are as compared to the actual values in a matrix format.

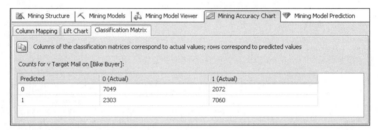

Figure 14-17

Having seen the accuracy of the model created by Analysis Services 2005, you can meaningfully start predicting the values using the model. The Mining Model Prediction view helps you in performing the predictions and store the results. Figure 14-18 shows the Mining Model Prediction view. Similar to the Mining Accuracy Chart view, you need to specify the case table that contains the input data for which you want to predict. Select the source table vTargetMail for which you will now predict the bike buyer value. In this view you can now select the columns from the input table that you want to be retrieved along with the predicted value(s). You can also apply certain data mining prediction functions or custom expressions on the predicted values to retrieve results such as top 10% of the customers or top 10 customers. The columns from the input table or applying certain data mining prediction functions can be selected in the lower half of the window pane as shown in Figure 14-18. Select the predicted column bike buyer from the model and the columns Customer key, first name, last name, and email address from the input table. You can select additional columns if you need to.

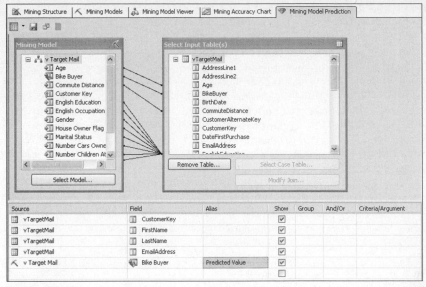

Figure 14-18

To see the prediction results, click the button that allows you to switch between the design or query or result view as shown in Figure 14-19. You will now see the results of the prediction as shown in Figure 14-19. You can specify constraints to the predicted value such as predicted value = 1 so that the results view only shows customers who are likely to buy bikes.

	FirstName	LastName	EmailAddress	Bike Buyer
	Jon	Yang	jon24@advent...	1
	Eugene	Huang	eugene10@adv...	1
11002	Ruben	Torres	ruben35@adve...	0
11003	Christy	Zhu	christy12@adv...	0
11004	Elizabeth	Johnson	elizabeth5@ad...	0
11005	Julio	Ruiz	julio1@adventu...	1
11006	Janet	Alvarez	janet9@advent...	1
11007	Marco	Mehta	marco14@adve...	0
11008	Rob	Verhoff	rob4@adventur...	0
11009	Shannon	Carlson	shannon38@ad...	0
11010	Jacquelyn	Suarez	jacquelyn20@a...	0
11011	Curtis	Lu	curtis9@advent...	0
11012	Lauren	Walker	lauren41@adve...	1
11013	Ian	Jenkins	ian47@adventu...	0
11014	Sydney	Bennett	sydney23@adv...	0
11015	Chloe	Young	chloe23@adve...	0
11016	Wyatt	Hill	wyatt32@adve...	0
11017	Shannon	Wang	shannon1@adv...	0
11018	Clarence	Rai	clarence32@ad...	1
11019	Luke	Lal	luke18@advent...	0

Figure 14-19

You were able to predict the bike buyer value for the input case table using the designer. The designer creates a query that retrieves the predicted data from Analysis Services. The query language used to retrieve predicted results from mining models is called DMX, which stands for Data Mining Extensions. The DMX language is specified in the OLEDB specification for data mining. The DMX language is similar to SQL and contains statements for data definition and data manipulation. The data definition language includes statements for model creation, and the data manipulation language contains statements for training the model, which includes inserting data into the model and retrieving prediction results from it. Just as SQL language has a SELECT statement to retrieve data from a relational database, DMX has a SELECT statement to retrieve data from mining models. The DMX SELECT statement has several variations based on the nature of the results being retrieved. For detailed information on the data definition language and data manipulation language for data mining, please refer to the documentation of Analysis Services 2005.

Click the icon that you used to switch between design and result view (shown in Figure 14-19) and select the Query option. You can see the following DMX query contained in the query window pane which is generated by the query designer to retrieve prediction results.

```
SELECT
  t.[CustomerKey],
  t.[FirstName],
  t.[LastName],
  t.[EmailAddress],
  [v Target Mail].[Bike Buyer] as [Predicted Value]
From
  [v Target Mail]
PREDICTION JOIN
  OPENQUERY([Adventure Works DW],
    'SELECT
      [CustomerKey],
      [FirstName],
      [LastName],
      [EmailAddress],
      [MaritalStatus],
      [Gender],
      [YearlyIncome],
      [TotalChildren],
      [NumberChildrenAtHome],
      [EnglishEducation],
      [EnglishOccupation],
      [HouseOwnerFlag],
      [NumberCarsOwned],
      [CommuteDistance],
      [Region],
      [Age],
      [BikeBuyer]
    FROM
      [dbo].[vTargetMail]
    ') AS t
  ON
    [v Target Mail].[Marital Status] = t.[MaritalStatus] AND
    [v Target Mail].[Gender] = t.[Gender] AND
    [v Target Mail].[Yearly Income] = t.[YearlyIncome] AND
    [v Target Mail].[Total Children] = t.[TotalChildren] AND
```

```
[v Target Mail].[Number Children At Home] = t.[NumberChildrenAtHome] AND
[v Target Mail].[English Education] = t.[EnglishEducation] AND
[v Target Mail].[English Occupation] = t.[EnglishOccupation] AND
[v Target Mail].[House Owner Flag] = t.[HouseOwnerFlag] AND
[v Target Mail].[Number Cars Owned] = t.[NumberCarsOwned] AND
[v Target Mail].[Commute Distance] = t.[CommuteDistance] AND
[v Target Mail].[Region] = t.[Region] AND
[v Target Mail].[Age] = t.[Age] AND
[v Target Mail].[Bike Buyer] = t.[BikeBuyer]
```

The preceding prediction query is one of the variations of the DMX SELECT query that has the following syntax:

```
SELECT [FLATTENED] [TOP <n>] <select expression list>
FROM <model> | <sub select> [NATURAL]
PREDICTION JOIN  <source data query>
[ON <join mapping list>]
[WHERE <condition expression>]
[ORDER BY <expression> [DESC|ASC]]
```

The input data for prediction is specified after the keywords PREDICTION JOIN. The <select expression list> contains the columns to be retrieved as part of the results and includes columns from the input/case table and the predicted columns which are specified after the SELECT keyword. The mining model used for prediction is specified after the FROM keyword. The mapping of columns from input data set to the mining model attributes is specified in the ON clause as seen in the preceding prediction query. The prediction query retrieves four columns from the input table along with the predicted column for each input row. Similar to executing MDX queries from SQL Server Management Studio, you can execute the preceding DMX query. You have only learned a simple DMX query in this example. Analysis Services 2005 tools help you to build the DMX query graphically, but if you are the kind of person who wants to write your DMX query this will be a good start. You can learn more about DMX and writing prediction query from Analysis Services 2005 documentation.

You can create multiple mining models within the same mining structure and they can use either the same or different mining algorithm. One would typically want to create a new mining model with the same algorithm if you want to see the accuracy of the existing mining model with a slight change in properties of the columns, such as disabling certain input columns or changing columns from PredictOnly to Predict. Alternatively, you can create a new mining model with a different mining algorithm and have the same attributes. A typical example would be to create a clustering or naïve bayes algorithm on a data set for which you have created a decision tree model. Next, learn to create a clustering algorithm on the same data set and analyze the results. Follow these steps to create a new clustering algorithm:

1. Switch to the mining model view in the mining model editor.

2. Right-click anywhere within the mining pane and select New Mining Model.

3. Select the mining algorithm Microsoft Clustering from the mining algorithm drop-down list and type in the name Clustering for the name of the mining model and click Ok.

A new clustering mining model with the name Clustering is created in the mining model view, as shown in Figure 14-20.

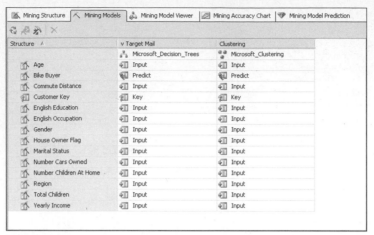

Figure 14-20

4. Deploy the project to the Analysis Services 2005 server for processing the Clustering mining model. The mining model editor switches to the mining model viewer view as soon as the server processes the clustering mining model. In the mining model viewer view, the default viewer shows the decision tree mining model. Click the mining model drop-down list and select Clustering, the name of the clustering mining model you have created (Figure 14-21).

You will now see the clustering mining model represented as several nodes with lines between these nodes as shown in Figure 14-21. By default the clustering mining model groups the customer into ten different clusters. The number of clusters to be generated can be changed from a property for the cluster mining model. Each cluster is shown as a node in the cluster viewer. The shade of the node is dependent upon the shading variable column and a specific state of the column that is shown in the viewer. Darker shading on the node indicates that the cluster favors a specific input column and vice versa. If there is a relationship (that is, similarity) between two clusters, that is indicated by a line connecting the two nodes. Similar to the shade of the color node, if the relationship is stronger between two nodes, it is indicated via a stronger line such as the relationship between clusters cluster5 and cluster6. You can move the slider on the left of the cluster diagram from All Links to Strongest Links. As you move the slider from All Links to Strongest Links you can see the weaker relationships between the clusters are not displayed. You can change the cluster name by right-clicking the cluster and selecting Rename. The cluster diagram helps you get an overall picture of the clusters, how the cluster is affected based on a specific column of the model that is used as the shading variable, as well as the relationship between clusters.

In Figure 14-21 the chosen column is population. Population is the name that is used in the mining model viewer for the entire data set used for training the mining model. You can select desired input columns of the mining model from drop-down for Shading Variable to see the effect of the column on the various clusters. When you choose a specific shading variable column you need to choose one of the states of the column to be used as the shading variable for the clusters.

For example if you choose the shading variable as Age, then you have several options as the state such as missing value, < 32, >=86 as shown in Figure 14-22. You can see that Cluster 7 has a darker shade indicating that cluster is predominantly populated with customers whose age is < 32. Overall the cluster diagram provides you the ability to analyze the various clusters, their characteristics, and relationship between clusters based on a specific column value for you to get a quick grasp of the cluster characteristics.

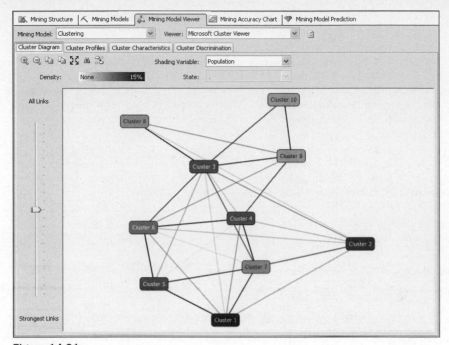

Figure 14-21

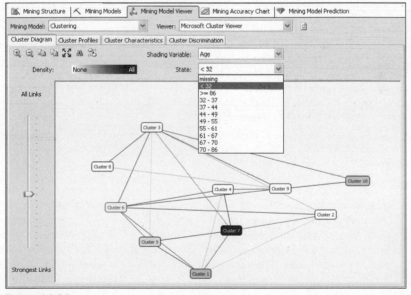

Figure 14-22

5. Once you have a good overview of the clusters from cluster diagram view the next step is to learn more about each cluster along with the distributions of various values for each column. Click on the Cluster Profile tab to learn more details about each cluster and various values for each column.

The cluster profiles view shows the relationship between the mining columns of the model and the clusters in a matrix format as shown in Figure 14-23. The intersection cell of a specific column and a cluster shows a histogram bar of the various values of the column that are part of the cluster. The size of each bar reflects the number of items used to train the model. If you hover over the histogram you will be able to see the size of each bar as shown in Figure 14-23. The number of histogram bars shown is controlled by the value set for histogram bars. The histogram bars are sorted based on the size and the first N bars (where N is the value set for Histogram bars) are shown. For example, for the age attribute, there are eleven groups shown in the legend. Because the histogram bars value is 4, the cluster viewer picks up the four most important buckets of the column age and shows how this column contributes toward the profile of a specific cluster.

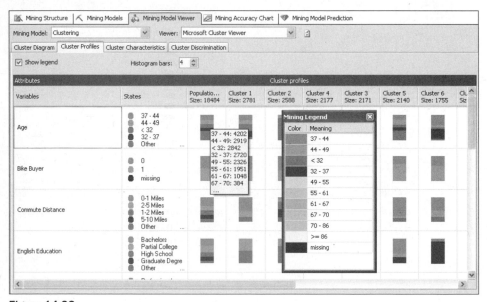

Figure 14-23

Each column has a histogram bar called missing value for the input records that do not have any value specified for that column during training. The columns that have a lot of states as compared to the number of states to be shown (number of states to be shown is controlled by the value set for histogram bars), then those columns have a histogram called Other which shows the value for all the histogram bars that are not shown explicitly. In the cluster diagram view for overall population you can see the strongest link is between clusters cluster5 and cluster6. This is due to the fact that the predict column Bike Buyer for these clusters has similar distribution for the values of Bike Buyer; this can be seen in Figure 14-23.

6. Click on the Cluster Characteristics tab to see the characteristics of a single cluster and how the various states of the input columns make up the cluster.

You will see the cluster characteristics of the entire data set as shown in Figure 14-24. You can view the characteristics of a specific cluster by selecting the cluster name from the drop-down list for Cluster. The probability associated with a specific value for an input column such as Number Cars Owned = 0 is calculated based on the number of input records having that specific value. The probability column shows the calculated probability for an input variable for the chosen cluster. If you hover over the bar in probability column you will see the corresponding probability value as shown in Figure 14-24.

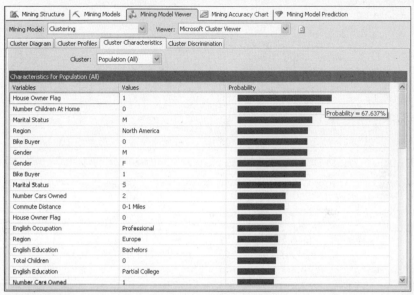

Figure 14-24

Once the clusters are formed one of the typical operations that one would want to find out is to compare the characteristics of two clusters to have a better understanding of each cluster; especially the clusters that are related. The data mining editor provides a way to compare the differences between clusters.

7. Click on the cluster discrimination tab to see the characteristics that distinguish a cluster from other clusters or another cluster. You will see the characteristics of cluster 1 and the complement of cluster 1. From the cluster diagram you can identify that the strongest relationship for the entire data set is between clusters cluster5 and cluster6. To compare the differences between these clusters select clusters 5 and 6 from the drop-down list next to Cluster 1 and Cluster 2 as shown in Figure 14-25.

In Figure 14-24 you learned the characteristics of a single cluster. In the cluster discrimination you will learn the states of an input column that favor one cluster over another. The states of the input columns indicate the differences between the two clusters and are ordered based on the importance of the difference the column contributes towards the clusters. The two columns on the right indicate which cluster the specific column value favors and the length indicates how strong the value influences the cluster as shown in Figure 14-25.

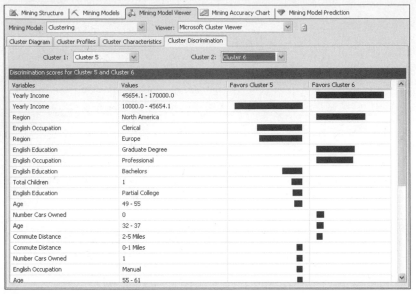

Figure 14-25

The cluster mining model you created can also be created using the mining model wizard. However, when you create a new mining model with the wizard, the wizard will automatically create a new mining structure and then create the mining model within this mining structure. Whenever you need to create multiple mining models for comparison we recommend you create one model using the wizard and the remaining models within the same mining structure using the data mining editor. The mining model wizard is self-explanatory and you can explore the creation of other mining models such as Microsoft Sequence Clustering, Microsoft Regression Trees, Neural Networks, and Sequence clustering using the data sets available in the Adventure Works DW sample relational database.

OLAP Mining Models

Certain types of business problems necessitate the use of aggregated data for analysis instead of individual input rows. For example, assume a customer buys several products from various stores. You might want to segment the customers not only by their individual attributes but also by the total amount they have spent in the stores. The mining model would require aggregated sales from the various purchases made by the customer, and include that amount as an input attribute to the clustering mining model. You can certainly add such a column to the customer table using a named query, but if the sales information table has billions of records, the aggregation by the relational data source will be slow. You should also consider maintainability of the mining model because you might want to process the models on a periodic basis. You indeed have a better solution than aggregating the data at the relational data source level. What better way to aggregate data than by creating a cube?

Because Analysis Services helps you create cubes as well as mining models, Analysis Services 2005 provides a way of creating mining models from cubes. Such mining models created on top of a cube are called OLAP mining models since the data source for the mining models is a cube and cubes contain OLAP data. Analysis Services 2005 also provides you the functionality of creating new cubes that include content from the created mining model along with the original cube which provides you the power and flexibility to analyze the cubes based on patterns discovered by the mining model. Such an analysis can further help you understand your data better and make better business decisions. You will create and analyze cubes containing mining model content in this section. You will use the AnalysisServices2005Tutorial you created earlier to create OLAP Mining Models in this chapter. When you download the samples for this book you will find the AnalysisServices2005Tutorial project under Chapter14 folder. To create an OLAP mining model, do the following:

1. Open the AnalysisServices2005Tutorial project. Deploy the entire project to your Analysis Services instance. In Solution Explorer, right-click the Mining Structures folder and select New Mining Structure... to launch the Data Mining Wizard.

2. In the Select the Definition Method page of the Data Mining Wizard, select the option From existing cube as shown in Figure 14-26 and click Next.

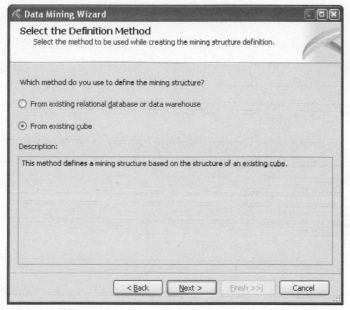

Figure 14-26

3. In the algorithm selection page, select the Microsoft Clustering algorithm as shown in Figure 14-27 and click Next.

4. You will now be in the Select the Source Cube Dimension page as shown in Figure 14-28. The Select the Source Cube Dimension page lists the cube dimensions within the database upon which a mining model can be created. You need to select the cube dimension that will be used as the case table for creating the mining model. Select the cube dimension Dim Customer and click Next.

5. In the Select Case Key page of the wizard select Dim Customer, the key of the dimension Dim Customer to be the key for the mining structure as shown in Figure 14-29. The Dim Customer attribute will also be used as the key for the mining model.

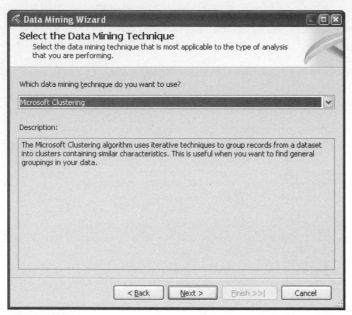

Figure 14-27

Figure 14-28

Figure 14-29

6. On the Select Case Level Columns page you need to select all the attributes that will be part of the mining model. Attributes that will be used as input or predictable should be selected on this page. Select the cube dimension attributes Commute Distance, English Education, English Occupation, Gender, House Owner Flag, Marital Status, Number Cars Owned, Number Children At Home, Total Children, and Yearly Income. Also, select the facts, Fact Internet Sales - Order Quantity, and Fact Internet Sales - Sales Amount of the measure group Fact Internet Sales as shown in Figure 14-30 and click Next.

7. On the Specify Mining Model Column Usage page you need to specify the input and predictable attributes. Make the input and predictable selections as shown in Figure 14-31 and then click Next.

8. On the Specify Columns' Content and Data Type page you can change the data type and content type for each attribute if needed. Both the content type and data type play an important role in the creation or training of the mining model. Accept the defaults and click Next.

9. You will now be in the Slice Source Cube page. The Slice Source Cube page provides you the functionality to slice the cube and build the mining model only on a specific part of the cube. You can specify the constraints for slicing the cube in this page similar to specifying filter conditions in the cube browser. You have the option to filter on dimensions other than the Dim Customer dimension, such as specific dates for Order date or specific categories or products. Select the default in this page and click Next.

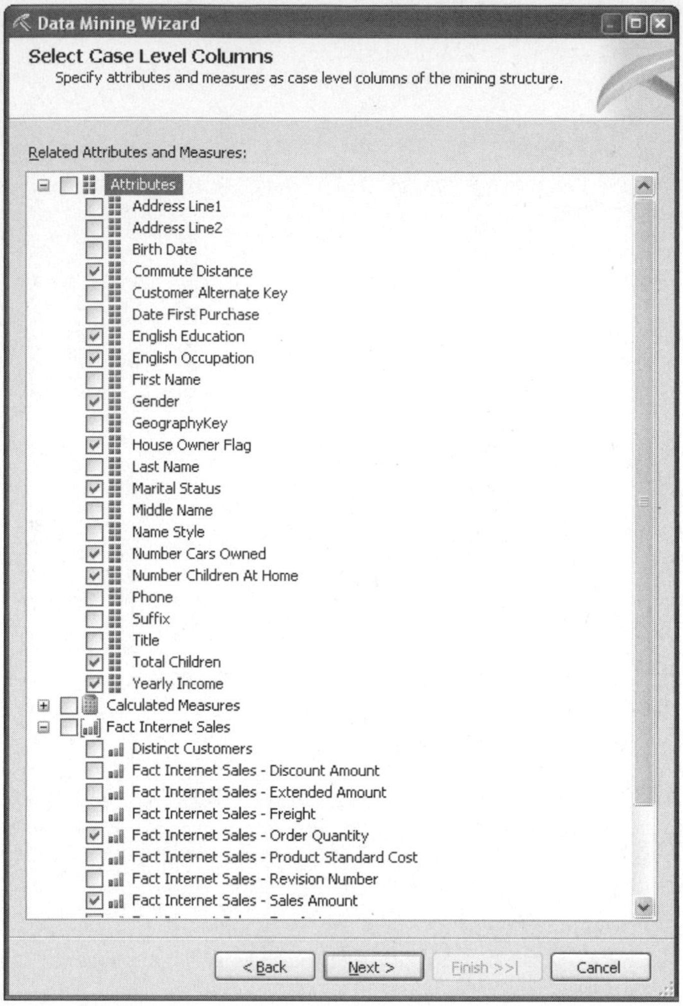

Figure 14-30

10. In the final page, specify the name for the mining structure as OLAPMiningStructure and for the mining Model as CustomerOLAPMiningModel as shown in Figure 14-32. You can analyze the mining model separately using the mining model viewer, but Analysis Services 2005 takes it one step further by allowing you to create a cube that will include the results of the mining model. In Analysis Services 2005 you can create a dimension from the results of the mining model and add this to the existing cube. The mining structure wizard facilitates the creation of the new cube that will include the existing cube and results of the mining model. Click the check boxes for Create Mining Model Dimension, Create Cube Using Mining Model Dimension, and Allow Drill Through as shown in Figure 14-32 and click Finish.

Figure 14-31

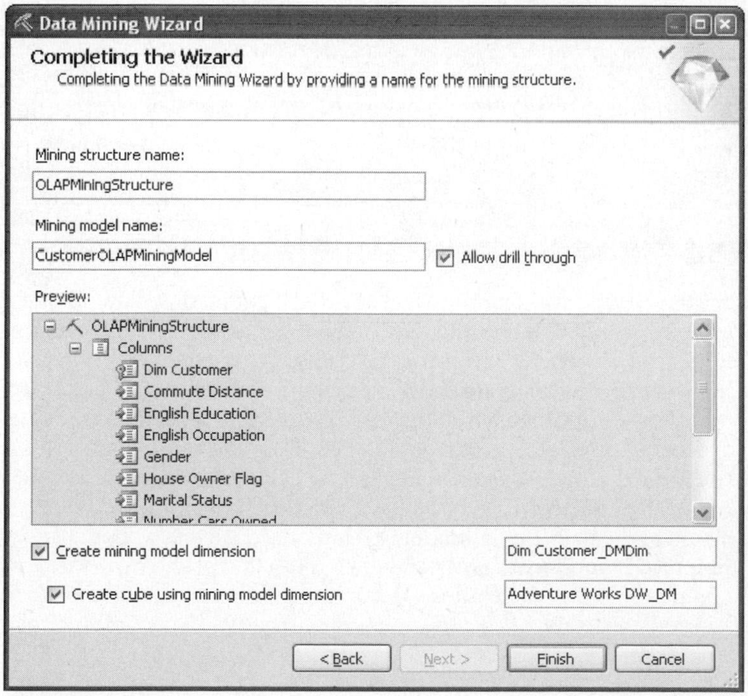

Figure 14-32

11. The OLAP Mining Model is created and you will now see it in the Mining model editor as shown in Figure 14-33. The input columns of the data mining structure are mapped to the corresponding cube dimension and measure group of the cube which is indicated by the line connecting the case level columns and fact internet sales within the DSV of the data mining editor. When the mining model is processed, the aggregated data of the measures is used instead of the individual transactions. Deploy the project to the server.

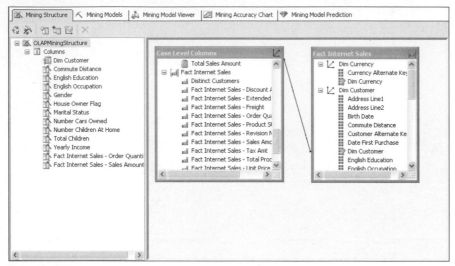

Figure 14-33

Once the processing is complete, the mining model editor switches to the mining model view where you can see the various clusters created based on the chosen attributes from the cube. There are 10 clusters created by default and you will find the strongest relationship between clusters cluster4 and cluster10. Similar to analyzing the relational mining model clusters, you can use the cluster profiles, cluster characteristics, and cluster discrimination tabs to learn more about the clusters created from the cube.

Analyzing the Cube with a Data Mining Dimension

When you created the OLAP Mining Model you selected creation of a data mining dimension and a cube in the data mining wizard. In order to create a new dimension and cube you need a DSV. Hence a DSV that includes a query to the OLAP mining model to retrieve the data from mining model is created. You will see a DSV called Dim Customer_DMDSV created under the DSV folder in the solution explorer. Next a dimension called [Dim Customer_DMDim] that includes attributes from the data mining model is created. Finally a cube called [Adventure Works DW_DM] is created that includes all the cube dimensions and measure groups of the Adventure Works DW cube but also includes the newly created data mining dimension [Dim Customer_DMDim]. In Chapter 9 you learnt the data mining relationship between a dimension and cube. The data mining relationship is defined between a dimension derived from a data mining model and a cube that contains it. The cube [Adventure Works DW_DM] that was created by the data mining wizard includes a data mining dimension. If you open the Dimension Usage tab of the [Adventure Works DW_DM] cube you will see there is a data mining relationship as shown in Figure 14-34.

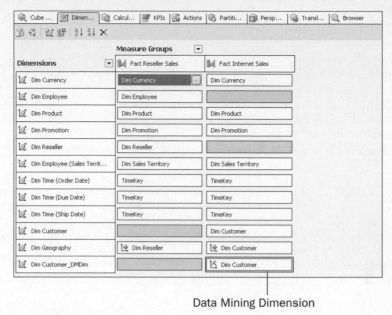

Data Mining Dimension

Figure 14-34

You can browse the [Adventure Works DW_DM] cube along with the data mining dimension to analyze the Internet sales you have obtained from various clusters as shown in Figure 14-35. How is this information useful? You can perform an analysis of the current sales with various clusters, and then perform a comparison of sales after the targeted mailing to analyze the sales and identify the effectiveness of the targeted mailing. Analysis Services thereby provides an integrated environment for creating mining models and cubes that help you with effective business analysis.

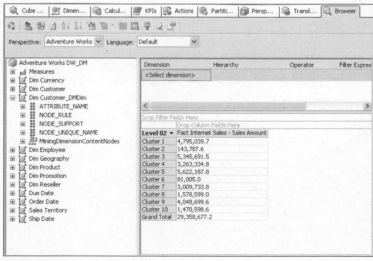

Figure 14-35

Summary

In this chapter you learned about data mining, what it is used for, and what is specific algorithms are available for use in Analysis Services 2005. The most important answer is to the question, "How does it help your business?" If you are now a step or two closer to that answer, you're doing great.

After learning the data mining algorithms in Analysis Services 2005, you drilled down on two, going step-by-step developing Microsoft Decision Trees and Microsoft Clustering Models using data from a relational data source. You also learned about OLAP mining models, where you essentially built a model on top of a cube. With the OLAP mining model you segmented the customers based on Internet Sales, and you were able to utilize the results of that mining model within a cube.

Aside from those off-the-shelf algorithms, Analysis Services 2005 provides a way to plug in your own data mining algorithm and/or data visualization capability (viewer). For details on this, please refer to the SQL Server 2005 product documentation. In a nutshell, you implement certain interfaces so that the server can utilize the results coming out of the algorithm you created. Once you have implemented your algorithm you can expose your data mining algorithm using the server properties. For an in-depth understanding of Data Mining in Analysis Services 2005, please refer to *Data Mining with SQL Server 2005* by Jamie MacLenan and ZhaoHui Tang (Wiley, 2005).

In the next chapter you will learn to analyze cube data from client tools other than the ones provided within the Analysis Services 2005. Microsoft Office products are tightly integrated with Analysis Services so you can analyze data from cubes. Microsoft Office products like Microsoft Excel, Microsoft Office web components, and Microsoft Data Analyzer all have the ability to retrieve and present data from Analysis Services in a way that is easy to interpret by users.

15

Analyzing Cubes using Office Client Components

We spent a good deal of time in this book exploring design and implementation options, but we haven't spent much time on the end-user experience — until now. In this chapter you learn about the many ways your aggregated data can be presented to the end user for their analysis. It is popular to use knife-wielding metaphors to represent the process of extracting information from a UDM; words like slice and dice are often applied. To slice cube data means to look at the data across some axis, such as a dimension member, and to dice data means to drill down on data by breaking it into smaller and smaller cubes. To put this all in more concrete terms, if you cut a potato longitudinally to make French fries, you are "slicing" the potato. Should you cut those strips into small cubes, you are "dicing" the potato (which, by the way, should fry up quite nicely with eggs sunny side up). Perhaps the word *chiffonade*, which is what one does to cabbage to make coleslaw, should be applied as well. (If you can think of what the chiffonade cut should mean in the context of business analysis, please alert the authors.)

In the sections that follow, typical usage scenarios in Excel using pivot tables are discussed. Not only will you find that you can connect to Analysis Services directly from Excel, you can even create offline cubes with any data in your spreadsheet which can be used for analysis without interaction with Analysis Services. When you have the feature set of Analysis Services complemented by the analytical tools in Excel, it makes for a great combination. With this feature set, you can analyze data; you can build reports off the data; not to mention build charts and graphs from any view you formulate. As a developer of business intelligence solutions, you will likely do much of your proof-of-concept browsing within BIDS, but the real consumers of your work will likely be browsing using Excel or Office Web Components, both of which include pivot table browsing functionality. All the examples mentioned in this Chapter use Office 2003 and Data Analyzer which is a client tool to analyze data from Analysis Services.

Microsoft Excel Pivot Tables

If you have been using Excel you might be familiar with the pivot table feature, especially considering that pivot tables date back to Excel Version 5. The pivot table feature in Excel is used to create reports for Excel users, which help them analyze data with ease. The pivot table feature can work on data stored in Excel or some other data source that can be accessed by Excel. The only requirement to use the pivot table in Excel with Analysis Services is that Excel should connect the Analysis Services instance. In such a case, Analysis Services becomes a data source for Excel. However there is a tight integration between Excel and Analysis Services. Excel is well aware of the Analysis Services models and objects and presents them effectively to the end users. As you might expect, creating a pivot table can be accomplished through the use of a wizard. The wizard has some smarts to it and even creates what it calculates to be the best resulting layout.

As for the capabilities of a pivot table, they are similar in nature to the cube browser seen in BIDS where you can drag and drop dimensions and measures to analyze the data. You can analyze data using Excel pivot tables in a similar fashion. Not only can you arrange data to best surface the information contained in it, but also the pivot table technology will sum the appropriate columns for you automatically. It is quite common for people to construct pivot tables to some planned configuration that is suited to act as a foundation for building charts and graphs. Charting and graphing capability comes with Excel off the shelf, so you don't need to buy any additional software to exploit a pivot table in this way.

> **Why is it called a pivot table? Why not call it what it really is, a digital fulcrum for tabulated compilations? Let's deconstruct the name: first, to "pivot" means to swivel and second, "table" refers to the form of representation for the data, in this case tabular with rows and columns. Therefore, the name suggests the user can swivel or pivot on data that is tabular in nature. In simplest possible terms, it is a way to display data such that seeing how different columns interact with each other is very easy to arrange and view.**

Creating a Pivot Table against Analysis Services Data

As you can see, the pivot table helps you to view multidimensional data in a two-dimensional nested tabular form. Normally, you will find that users only pivot on two or three dimensions at a time while engaged in data analysis. The reason for this is simple: if you add fourth and fifth dimensions to a pivot table, the results become so complex as to hinder understanding. The pivot table client component helps you visualize the interactions between dimensions, and if used properly will, in fact, facilitate insights about the nature of the results being analyzed. To create a pivot table using Analysis Services data as the source to populate the table, work through the following steps.

1. Deploy the Adventure Works sample project shipped along with Analysis Services 2005. It is available for install with SQL Server 2005 if you don't have it loaded already.

2. Launch Excel and create a new worksheet. Click the Data menu item and select Pivot table and Pivot Chart Report.... You will now see the Pivot Table and Pivot Chart Wizard, as shown in Figure 15-1.

You can create pivot tables from different data sources including data within an Excel sheet. In this example you will retrieve data from Analysis Services 2005. To specify the Analysis Server, select External data source and click Next.

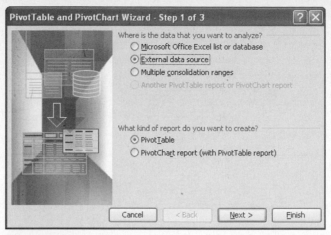

Figure 15-1

3. To specify the Analysis Server, click the Get Data... button as shown in Figure 15-2.

Figure 15-2

4. You are now in the Choose Data Source dialog. Click the OLAP Cubes tab as shown in Figure 15-3. If you have established connections to Analysis Services you will see those connections here. Double click on <New Data Source>.

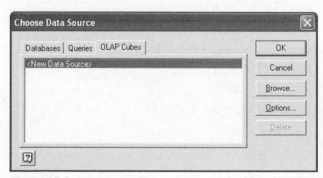

Figure 15-3

5. At the Create New Data Source dialog shown in Figure 15-4, provide a name for the data source you will establish (we recommend "AdventureWorks"). This is not the actual server name but a name that will be shown under OLAP Cubes tab. In the drop down list 2, select Microsoft OLE DB Provider for Analysis Services 9.0. Finally, click the Connect... button.

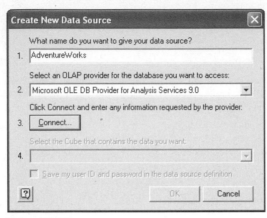

Figure 15-4

6. In the Multidimensional Connection 9.0 dialog you can either connect to an Analysis Services instance or connect to a file that contains data for a specific cube. You learn to create cube files later in this chapter. Provide the name of the Analysis Services as shown in Figure 15-5 and click Next.

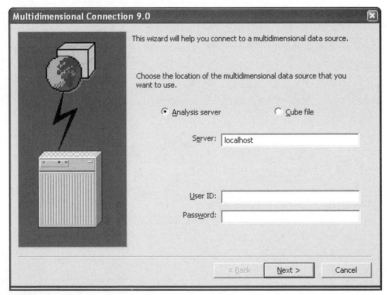

Figure 15-5

7. You will now see the list of databases available on the Analysis Services instance. Select the Adventure Works DW database as shown in Figure 15-6 and click Finish.

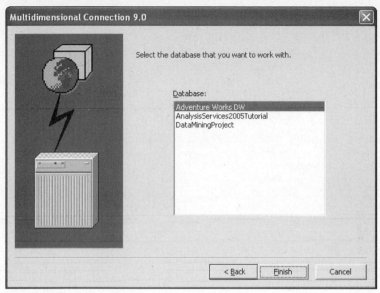

Figure 15-6

8. The wizard establishes a connection to the Analysis Services instance, retrieves the list of cubes available within the chosen database, and makes them available in the drop-down list box of the New Data Source dialog (see Figure 15-7). Select the Direct Sales cube and click OK.

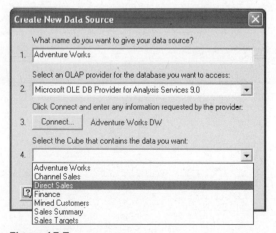

Figure 15-7

9. At this point the connection details for the database and cube are stored in a file named AdventureWorks.oqy, which is located under <DefaultDrive>:\Documents and Settings\<UserName>\Application Data\Microsoft\Queries. You can check out that file, just substitute the correct information for Default Drive and UserName appropriately for your configuration. If you open the .oqy file you find the connection details to the Analysis Server. The AdventureWorks.oqy file contains the following details:

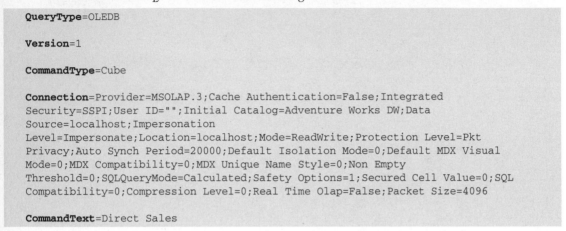

```
QueryType=OLEDB

Version=1

CommandType=Cube

Connection=Provider=MSOLAP.3;Cache Authentication=False;Integrated
Security=SSPI;User ID="";Initial Catalog=Adventure Works DW;Data
Source=localhost;Impersonation
Level=Impersonate;Location=localhost;Mode=ReadWrite;Protection Level=Pkt
Privacy;Auto Synch Period=20000;Default Isolation Mode=0;Default MDX Visual
Mode=0;MDX Compatibility=0;MDX Unique Name Style=0;Non Empty
Threshold=0;SQLQueryMode=Calculated;Safety Options=1;Secured Cell Value=0;SQL
Compatibility=0;Compression Level=0;Real Time Olap=False;Packet Size=4096

CommandText=Direct Sales
```

The details of the connection to Analysis Server are represented by the name Connection= and the CommandText contains the name of the cube or perspective you chose.

10. Click OK to dismiss Choose Data Source and then Next on the resulting page. What appears is the final step of the Pivot Table Wizard. You need to specify if you want the pivot table to be formed in a new worksheet or existing working sheet (the default value) at a specific location. Select the default value as shown in Figure 15-8 and click Finish.

Figure 15-8

You will now see the pivot table created within the existing worksheet as shown in Figure 15-9. There is a window called the Pivot Table that contains the various options that can be set for the pivot table. Another window called PivotTable Field List shows the list of hierarchies and measures from the selected cube, all of which is the data that can be analyzed. Finally you have the main pivot table, which contains an area for holding row fields, column fields, page fields, and data items. As with the cube browser, the data items can only hold the measure values. The row, column, and page area can only hold members of hierarchies.

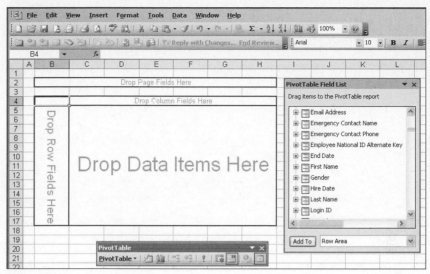

Figure 15-9

Each object shown in the PivotTable Field List that is collapsible or expandable (shown with a + sign) represents a hierarchy in the cube. If you expand the object you will be able to find out if it is an attribute hierarchy or a multilevel hierarchy. If you create a pivot table against Analysis Services 2000 data, you will see each dimension object is represented as an item in the pivot table list; by expanding the dimension you will see the level. There was exactly a one-to-one correspondence between the objects shown in PivotTable Field List to the dimensions in the cube if you used Analysis Services 2000. Analysis Services 2005, on the other hand, has introduced the notion of hierarchies (attribute and multilevel) within a dimension. Excel 2003 does not understand the notion of multiple hierarchies within a single dimension. It would have certainly been much easier for the user if the hierarchies grouped within the dimension were similar to the metadata pane in the cube browser. However, it does allow you to browse each of the hierarchies. In the cube browser you see the measures grouped based on the display folders. Excel 2003 does not understand display folders because this is a new feature, and hence shows all the measures available in the cube. The next version of Microsoft Office (Excel in particular) is expected to have improvements that will present the dimensions in Analysis Services 2005 in an efficient way. The new pivot table will allow users to more easily browse the dimensions and measures of Analysis Services 2005 cubes.

Figure 15-10 shows the two types of hierarchies in the Customer dimension; one is a multilevel hierarchy and another is an attribute hierarchy, which have been expanded in the list.

You can see the levels for each of these hierarchies. Attribute hierarchies can be easily identified because they are one level deep, whereas multilevels are almost always several levels deep. If there is a multilevel hierarchy with a single level, you can distinguish them easily because the name of the hierarchy and level are not the same. For example, an attribute hierarchy Customer will have the name of the hierarchy shown as Customer with the same level name, as shown in Figure 15-10. If there is a multilevel hierarchy created with a level called Customer, the name of the hierarchy itself could not therefore be called Customer.

Figure 15-10

One of the drawbacks of analyzing Analysis Services 2005 cube data using Excel 2003 is the inability to distinguish hierarchies in dimensions that have the same name. For example, if you have the dimensions employee and customer, each of these dimensions can have hierarchies with the name Name or Geography. If you are designing a cube for users analyzing data using Excel 2003, we recommend you take this into consideration and create names that have full qualification so that your users are not confused as to which hierarchy to select from the Pivot Table Field List.

Analyzing Data using Pivot Tables

Having created a pivot table against Analysis Services cube data, the next logical question is how is the pivot table helpful in analyzing this data? Assume you are interested in looking at the Sales of products to customers in various countries over time. The first step for analysis is to drag and drop the hierarchies and measures of interest to the appropriate rows, columns, pages, and data areas. To start, drag and drop the measure Internet Sales Amount to the field containing the instructions "Drop Data Items Here," which you'll see if you look back at Figure 15-9. The value that you'll see in cell C4, as shown in Figure 15-11, is the total Internet Sales Amount across all dimensions. The pivot table allows you to analyze data on a two-dimensional view based on rows and columns. When there are no hierarchy members specified in the row and column field's area, the default is to show the total value.

	A	B	C
1		Drop Page Fields Here	
2			
3		Internet Sales Amount	Total
4		Total	29358677.22

Figure 15-11

Let's start fresh, go ahead and remove the Internet Sales Amount by dragging and dropping back to the Pivot Table List. To analyze the product Sales based on customer's countries and various years drag and drop the Customer Geography hierarchy to the "Drop Column Fields Here" area and the Date.Fiscal hierarchy to the "Drop Row Fields Here" area. And finally, drop Internet Sales Amount back on the Drop Data Items Here area. You will now see the sales amounts for various fiscal years and customer countries as shown in Figure 15-12.

	Internet Sales Amount	Country						
	Fiscal Year	Australia	Canada	France	Germany	United Kingdom	United States	Grand Total
FY 2002		2568701.386	573100.9702	414245.316	513353.1742	550507.3268	2452176.071	7072084.244
FY 2003		2099585.429	305010.6919	633399.6983	593247.244	696594.9741	1434296.26	5762134.297
FY 2004		4383479.54	1088879.5	1592880.75	1784107.09	2140388.5	5483882.67	16473618.05
FY 2005		9234.23	10853.7	3491.95	3604.83	4221.41	19434.51	50840.63
Grand Total		9061000.584	1977844.862	2644017.714	2894312.338	3391712.211	9389789.511	29358677.22

Figure 15-12

The Pivot table provides you with an additional column and row that provide the subtotal along that specific row or column. To retrieve the data from Analysis Services, Excel sends the following MDX query:

```
SELECT NON EMPTY HIERARCHIZE(
            AddCalculatedMembers({
                DrillDownLevel({[Customer].[Customer Geography].[All Customers]})})))
            DIMENSION PROPERTIES PARENT_UNIQUE_NAME ON COLUMNS ,
NON EMPTY HIERARCHIZE(
            AddCalculatedMembers({
                DrillDownLevel({[Date].[Fiscal].[All Periods]})}))
            DIMENSION PROPERTIES PARENT_UNIQUE_NAME ON ROWS  FROM [Direct Sales]
WHERE ([Measures].[Internet Sales Amount])
```

Send the above query to Analysis Service instance using the MDX query editor in SQL Server Management Studio. When you execute the query you will see the results in the result pane of SSMS as shown in the following table.

	All Customers	Australia	Canada	France	Germany	United Kingdom	United States
All Periods	$29,358,677.22	$9,061,000.58	$1,977,844.86	$2,895,777.05	$2,894,312.44	$3,391,712,21	$9,389,789.51
FY 2002	$7,072,084,24	$2,568,701,39	$573,000.43	$414,777.09	$513,353,17	$550,507.33	$2,452,176.07
FY 2003	$5,762,134.30	$2,099,585.43	$$305,010.43	$593,347.78	$593,247.24	$696,594.97	$1,434,296.26
FY 2004	$16,473,618.05	$4,383,479.54	$1,800,344.54	$1,592,880.75	$1,796,888.04	$2,140,388.50	$5,483,882.67
FY 2005	$50,840.63	$9,234.23	$10,854.76	$3,491.22	$3,604.83	$4,221.41	$19,434.51

You can see that the results shown in SQL Server Management Studio are identical to the results you see in the Excel Pivot table, but the order in which the results are presented differ. The first row and first column of the results shown in the following table are the final rows and columns you see in the Pivot table, which correspond to the aggregated data corresponding to that specific member in the dimension based on the aggregation function specified for the measure. The members All Customers and All Periods shown in the table are actually the names of the All member specified in the respective dimensions.

Having seen the MDX generated by the pivot table, we are sure you are keen on understanding the query. Similar to the MDX queries you have learned so far, Excel generates a two-dimensional MDX query that requests data on the axes columns and rows in this example. For the dimension dropped on the columns of the Pivot table (Customer Geography), the following MDX expression is specified:

```
NON EMPTY       HIERARCHIZE(
                AddCalculatedMembers(
                {DrillDownLevel({[Customer].[Customer Geography].[All Customers]})}
                                )
                )
```

Let's start with the innermost function and work our way out. Whenever you drag and drop a specific hierarchy to the Pivot table, the member in the topmost level of that hierarchy is identified and used in the query. In the previous example, the All member in the Customer Geography hierarchy, All Customers, is used. The DrillDownLevel MDX function is a function that can take multiple parameters. The Syntax of the DrillDownLevel function is as follows:

```
DrillDownLevel(<Set>,{<Level>,<Index>}])
```

The first argument to the DrillDownLevel function is a Set. The second and third arguments are optional. The DrillDownLevel function returns the members of the specified Set (provided as the first argument) that are one level lower than the level of the members specified in the set. If the optional Level parameter is specified, the function returns members one level below the specified level. If the set contains tuples, the index is used to reference the dimension for which the drill down has to be applied. In the query we are currently examining, the members at the Country level of the hierarchy Customer Geography is returned. You could have retrieved the members by specifying the following MDX expression, but the DrilldownLevel function provides you with more options and is useful while drilling down to multiple levels, which is why Excel uses this function. We talk about drilling down to multiple levels later in this section.

```
{[Customer].[Customer Geography].[All Customers], [Customer].[Customer
Geography].[All Customers].children}
```

The result of the DrillDownLevel function is a set of members. By default during MDX evaluation the calculated members typically do not get included in the set. You would have to explicitly include them. While browsing the Pivot table Excel generates calculated members based on the user selections in the Pivot table. To make sure appropriate calculated members do get included in the result, we use the MDX function AddCalculatedMembers. Following is a simple illustration using the Measures dimension for you to understand the behavior of AddCalculatedMembers (you have learned that Measures is a special dimension within the cube).

```
select measures.[Sales Amount] on 0
from [Adventure Works]                  //Calculated measures not returned

select AddCalculatedMembers( measures.[Sales Amount]) on 0
from [Adventure Works]                  //Calculated measures are returned in result
```

In the code illustration the first MDX query only returns the result for the Sales Amount measure; however, the second MDX query returns the Sales Amount measure and all the calculated members in the measures dimension.

Finally, the result of the AddCalculateMembers function, a Set of members, is passed as an argument to the Hierarchize function. Hierarchize is an MDX function used for sorting the members in a set. The syntax is as follows:

```
Hierarchize (Set, [POST])
```

The Hierarchize function takes a Set and returns the members in the set after a sort. If the second parameter POST is not specified, the default sort ordering of the hierarchy is used to sort the members in the set. If the parameter POST is specified, the members are sorted based on the default ordering but the parent member will be at the end. This is illustrated by the following two MDX queries:

```
select Hierarchize(AddCalculatedMembers(
{DrillDownLevel({[Customer].[Customer Geography].[Country]})})) on 0,
Measures.[Internet Sales Amount] on 1
from [Adventure Works]                //MDX Query 1—Default sort ordering

select Hierarchize(AddCalculatedMembers(
{DrillDownLevel({[Customer].[Customer Geography].[Country]})}),POST) on 0,
Measures.[Internet Sales Amount] on 1
from [Adventure Works]                //MDX Query 2—Sort based on POST
```

The first MDX query uses the default sort ordering of the hierarchy and returns the members in Country and State levels in the format {<Country Member 1>, <State members for Country Member 1>, <Country Member 2>, <State members for Country Member 2> ...}. However, the second query that specified POST sorts the results as {<State members for Country Member 1>, <Country Member 1>, <State members for Country Member 2>,<Country Member 2>, ...} .

Hierarchize does not eliminate duplicate members.

You have learned about the first part of the MDX query and why these functions are used to retrieve the results. The keyword NON EMPTY is used to ensure empty values are eliminated in the results. To refresh your memory, here is the MDX query that is generated by Excel:

```
SELECT NON EMPTY HIERARCHIZE(
                AddCalculatedMembers(
                {DrillDownLevel({[Customer].[Customer Geography].[All Customers]})}
                )
                )
DIMENSION PROPERTIES PARENT_UNIQUE_NAME ON COLUMNS ,
NON EMPTY HIERARCHIZE(
        AddCalculatedMembers(
                {DrillDownLevel({[Date].[Fiscal].[All Periods]})}
        )
        )
DIMENSION PROPERTIES PARENT_UNIQUE_NAME ON ROWS
FROM [Direct Sales] WHERE ([Measures].[Sales Amount])
```

The members being retrieved for COLUMNS and the members retrieved for ROWS use the same approach to retrieval as members in the Date-Fiscal hierarchy. As you learned earlier in chapter 5 the member properties of dimensions members can be retrieved using Dimension Properties option on an axis. The MDX expression "Dimension Properties PARENT_UNIQUE_NAME" is used to retrieve the member property PARENT_UNIQUE_NAME; which, in turn, is returned for each member that can be used in subsequent MDX queries based on the user's actions in the Pivot table. Finally, the WHERE clause is used for not only retrieving the right measure used in the Pivot table but also restricting the multi-dimensional coordinate space so that the right values are being returned. Excel appropriately displays the result from the query within the Pivot table. Excel identifies the values for All members of each hierarchy and uses those values for subtotals along the row or column.

You have so far successfully created a pivot table and were able to analyze the Sales data for customers in various countries for various fiscal years. Assume you want to analyze the data for the United States. Because you are interested in the Sales data for customers in the United States, you are not interested in the customers from other countries. The most obvious thing is to restrict the data. To restrict the data for United States customers, click the drop-down arrow next to the hierarchy Country. You will see all the members of the Country hierarchy in Customers dimensions. The boxes next to each member act as toggle switches. If a tick mark is within the box that means the specific member is selected. To select or deselect all members, Excel provides you with a check box for (Show All). Click the box next to (Show All) to deselect all the members and then select the member United States, as shown in Figure 15-13. Click OK. You will now see the Sales data for United States for various years.

Figure 15-13

Excel generates the following MDX query when you restrict the data analysis to United States:

```
SELECT NON EMPTY HIERARCHIZE(
Except({AddCalculatedMembers(
Except(
  {AddCalculatedMembers(
        DrillDownLevel({{[Customer].[Customer Geography].[All Customers]}
                      )
                      )
    },
  {[Customer].[Customer Geography].[Country].&[United Kingdom],
  [Customer].[Customer Geography].[Country].&[Germany],
  [Customer].[Customer Geography].[Country].&[France],
  [Customer].[Customer Geography].[Country].&[Canada],
  [Customer].[Customer Geography].[Country].&[Australia]}
  )
  )},
  {[Customer].[Customer Geography].[Country].&[United Kingdom],
  [Customer].[Customer Geography].[Country].&[Germany],
```

```
   [Customer].[Customer Geography].[Country].&[France],
   [Customer].[Customer Geography].[Country].&[Canada],
   [Customer].[Customer Geography].[Country].&[Australia]}))
DIMENSION PROPERTIES PARENT_UNIQUE_NAME ON COLUMNS ,
NON EMPTY HIERARCHIZE(
AddCalculatedMembers({DrillDownLevel({
[Date].[Fiscal].[All Periods]})}))
DIMENSION PROPERTIES PARENT_UNIQUE_NAME ON ROWS  FROM [Direct Sales]
WHERE ([Measures].[Internet Sales Amount])
```

In this MDX query the MDX function Except is used to restrict the data to United States. The Except function takes two arguments, Set1 and Set2, and eliminates all the members in Set1 that are found in Set2. In the preceding example the AddCalculatedMembers function returns the members in the country level for Customer Geography hierarchy. This set is passed as the first parameter to the Except function. The second set is generated based on the user's de-selection of country members in the Pivot table (set containing members United Kingdom, Germany, France, Canada, and Australia). The Except function eliminates the members specified in the second set and returns only United States and the All Customers members in the result. You can view the Except function directly translating to a business question where the question would be "Show me the Sales amount for various years for customers in different countries except Australia, United Kingdom, Germany, France, and Canada." Except is one of the several MDX functions where the meaning of the word reflects its actions, so you will know exactly what the results of the function might be when it's performed. The Except function by default eliminates duplicate members in both sets before performing the operation. A third optional parameter can be used if you want to include the duplicates. You need to pass the value ALL as the third parameter if you want to retain the duplicate members in the result set. Figure 15-14 shows the results in the Pivot after you select the member United States.

Drop Page Fields Here		
Internet Sales Amount	Country ▼	
Fiscal Year ▼	United States	Grand Total
FY 2002	2452176.071	2452176.071
FY 2003	1434296.26	1434296.26
FY 2004	5483882.67	5483882.67
FY 2005	19434.51	19434.51
Grand Total	9389789.511	9389789.511

Figure 15-14

In Figure 15-14 you can see that the Sales Amount shown in Grand Total is identical to the value shown for the United States member. You know the Grand Total for each year should be the aggregate of the sales amount for all of the countries. Then how is Excel able to display the Grand Total value same as that for the member United States? By default Excel sets a specific connection property called VisualTotals while connecting to Analysis Services; this results in a request for Analysis Services to send the Grand Total reflecting aggregated data for only the members currently visible (here it is just the United States). You can change this property if you want to see the Grand Total reflect the Total Sales for a specific year. In the Pivot Table window click the icon "Include Hidden Items in Totals" as shown in Figure 15-15. You will now see the Grand Total value is the aggregate of all the countries as seen earlier in Figure 15-12.

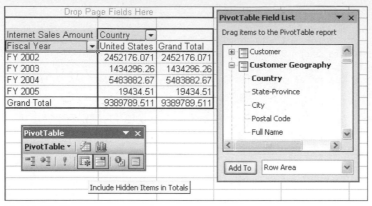

Figure 15-15

You have so far been analyzing the Sales data based on customers' geographic location and fiscal years. If you now want to analyze the data based on a certain class of products, you have two ways of doing this. Drag and drop the Product Categories hierarchy to the "Drop Page Field Here" area. Assume you want to analyze the sales data for bikes and bike accessories. Click the drop-down list next to Product Categories as shown in Figure 15-16. Click the Select multiple items check box and then select Accessories and Bikes. Click the OK button. You will now see the Sales amount in the pivot table reflecting the sales of only accessories and bikes. If you want to analyze individual members you can make the appropriate selections in the Product categories.

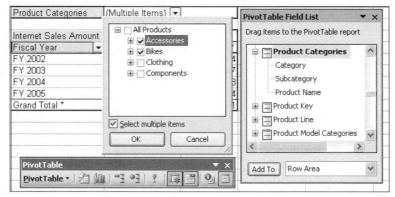

Figure 15-16

The second option to analyze the data for Accessories and Bikes is to drag and drop the Product Categories hierarchy to the rows adjacent to the Fiscal Year. When you had Product categories in the Page Fields area the pivot table showed the "All" members of the Product Categories hierarchy. However, while dropping the product categories on rows you will see the first level of the Product Categories hierarchy and its members will be visible in the pivot table. Figure 15-17 shows the results of the Pivot table.

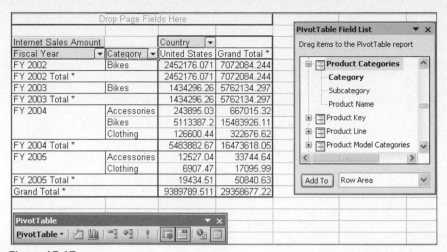

Figure 15-17

Whenever there are multiple hierarchies in rows or columns, the Pivot table creates an automatic grouping for each member in the hierarchy and creates a subtotal. In Figure 15-17 you can see a row showing the subtotal for each year. Because you wanted to analyze the data for Accessories and Bikes, you need to restrict the visible members. Select the drop-down list next to category, deselect the Show All checkbox, and then select the members Accessories and Bikes. You will now see the pivot table only showing the results of Accessories and Bikes as shown in Figure 15-18.

	A	B	C	D	E
1		Drop Page Fields Here			
2					
3		Internet Sales Amount		Country ▼	
4		Fiscal Year ▼	Category ▼	United States	Grand Total
5		FY 2002	Bikes	2452176.071	2452176.071
6		FY 2002 Total		2452176.071	2452176.071
7		FY 2003	Bikes	1434296.26	1434296.26
8		FY 2003 Total		1434296.26	1434296.26
9		FY 2004	Accessories	243895.03	243895.03
10			Bikes	5113387.2	5113387.2
11		FY 2004 Total		5357282.23	5357282.23
12		FY 2005	Accessories	12527.04	12527.04
13		FY 2005 Total		12527.04	12527.04
14		Grand Total		9256281.601	9256281.601

Figure 15-18

The MDX query generated by Excel to retrieve the results shown in Figure 15-18 is shown below.

```
SELECT NON EMPTY HIERARCHIZE(
    Except({
    AddCalculatedMembers(
        Except({
            AddCalculatedMembers(
```

```
                        DrillDownLevel({[Customer].[Customer Geography].[All
Customers]})))},
                {[Customer].[Customer Geography].[Country].&[United Kingdom],
                [Customer].[Customer Geography].[Country].&[Germany],
                [Customer].[Customer Geography].[Country].&[France],
                [Customer].[Customer Geography].[Country].&[Canada],
                [Customer].[Customer Geography].[Country].&[Australia]})))},
    {{[Customer].[Customer Geography].[Country].&[United Kingdom],
     [Customer].[Customer Geography].[Country].&[Germany],
     [Customer].[Customer Geography].[Country].&[France],
     [Customer].[Customer Geography].[Country].&[Canada],
     [Customer].[Customer Geography].[Country].&[Australia]}))
DIMENSION PROPERTIES PARENT_UNIQUE_NAME ON COLUMNS ,
NON EMPTY CROSSJOIN(
    HIERARCHIZE(
        AddCalculatedMembers({
           DrillDownLevel({[Date].[Fiscal].[All Periods]})})),
              HIERARCHIZE(
                Except({AddCalculatedMembers(
                Except({AddCalculatedMembers(
                    DrillDownLevel({[Product].[Product Categories].[All Products]})))}
                    ,
                    {[Product].[Product Categories].[Category].&[2],
                    [Product].[Product Categories].[Category].&[3]})))},
                {[Product].[Product Categories].[Category].&[2],
                [Product].[Product Categories].[Category].&[3]})))
DIMENSION PROPERTIES PARENT_UNIQUE_NAME ON ROWS
FROM [Direct Sales]
WHERE ([Measures].[Internet Sales Amount])
```

Excel generates an MDX query that uses Hierarchize, Except, and AddCalculatedMembers to restrict the members on the Product Categories Hierarchy. The MDX function CROSSJOIN is used to obtain a set containing a crossjoin of the members of the hierarchies Fiscal Year and Product Categories, which are subsequently displayed on rows.

Drilling Down to Detailed Data

So far you have used the pivot table to analyze data using the axes rows, columns, and pages; you have seen how to pivot on select members and view corresponding measure values. One of the key aspects of analyzing OLAP data is not only viewing the aggregated data, but also to drill down or up to view member details as needed. Follow the steps below to drill down to detail data in pivot tables.

1. Move the product categories hierarchy from the row axes to the page axes.

2. To drill down to details of the customer sales within the United States, double-click the United States member. You will now see that the level State-Province is shown in the column axes and you see all the states within United States as shown in Figure 15-19. You can also achieve drill down by selecting the United States member and then clicking on the Show Detail icon in the Pivot table toolbar as shown in Figure 15-20.

	A	B	C	D	E	F	G
1		Product	All Products ▾				
2							
3		Internet Sales Amount	Country ▾	State-Province			
4			United States				
5		Fiscal Year ▾	Alabama	Arizona	California	Florida	Georgia
6		FY 2002			1526344.2		
7		FY 2003		2071.42	804136.49	2854.41	782.99
8		FY 2004	2.29	32.60	3374621.67	4867.52	875.93
9		FY 2005	35.00		9155.30	38.98	
10		Grand Total	37.29	2104.02	5714257.69	7760.91	1658.92

Figure 15-19

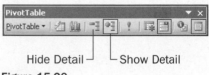

Hide Detail ⌐ ⌐ Show Detail

Figure 15-20

3. If you want to drill up from the current level you can once again double-click the member United States or click the member and then click the Hide Detail icon in the Pivot Table toolbar. You can choose certain members after the drill down in the pivot table. Select the drop-down list next to the Country level and select the members Alabama, Arizona, and California. You can drill down on members on each axes. On the row axes, drill down on Fiscal Year up to the Month level by double-clicking the first member in each level. Your Pivot table will show the sales amount for three states within the United States for various fiscal years, with detailed data for the months in the first quarter of fiscal year 2002 as shown in Figure 15-21.

	A	B	C	D	E	F	G	H	I
1	Product Categories	All Products ▾							
2									
3	Internet Sales Amount				Country ▾	State-Province			
4					United States			United States Total	Grand Total
5	Fiscal Year ▾	Fiscal Semester	Fiscal Quarter	Month	Alabama	Arizona	California		
6	FY 2002	H1 FY 2002	Q1 FY 2002	July 2001			69906.1446	69906.1446	69906.1446
7				August 2001			97476.6464	97476.6464	97476.6464
8				September 2001			114065.301	114065.301	114065.301
9			Q1 FY 2002 Total				281448.092	281448.092	281448.092
10			Q2 FY 2002				403897.8648	403897.8648	403897.8648
11		H1 FY 2002 Total					685345.9568	685345.9568	685345.9568
12		H2 FY 2002					840998.2752	840998.2752	840998.2752
13	FY 2002 Total						1526344.232	1526344.232	1526344.232
14	FY 2003					2071.4196	804136.4906	806207.9102	806207.9102
15	FY 2004				2.29	32.6	3374621.67	3374656.56	3374656.56
16	FY 2005				35		9155.3	9190.3	9190.3
17	Grand Total				37.29	2104.0196	5714257.693	5716399.002	5716399.002

Figure 15-21

4. Click the drop-down list next to the fiscal year. You will see the members of the Fiscal hierarchy as shown in Figure 15-22. The checkboxes act to enable or disable members. In addition, you can see a third option that contains two tick marks. These tick marks indicate that the member has not only been selected but the user has also drilled down to see the details of its children. If at least one of the children of a member in a hierarchy is made visible, you will see the double tick

mark for that member in this dialog. You can also use this dialog to drill down to the details of a member since the check box next to a member is actually a tri-stated option. The three options indicated by the check box are:

❑   Member not visible (no tick mark)

❑   Member is visible (single tick mark)

❑   Member is visible along with at least one of its children (two tick marks)

Figure 15-22

The MDX query generated to see the results shown in Figure 15-21 is quite long because the query needs to exclude all the states in the United States except Arizona, Alabama, and California. In order to understand the type of MDX query sent by Excel while drilling down to member details, we will use an example where you select all the countries in the column axes and apply drill down only for the first fiscal quarter of 2002. The following MDX query is sent to the Analysis Services to retrieve the results shown in Figure 15-21.

```
SELECT NON EMPTY HIERARCHIZE(
    AddCalculatedMembers({
        DrillDownLevel({[Customer].[Customer Geography].[All Customers]})}
            ) // AddCalculatedMembers
        ) //Hierarchize
DIMENSION PROPERTIES PARENT_UNIQUE_NAME ON COLUMNS ,
NON EMPTY HIERARCHIZE(
    AddCalculatedMembers(
        {DrillDownMember({{
            DrillDownMember({
                DrillDownLevel({[Date].[Fiscal].[All Periods]}
                            ) //DrillDownLevel
                            },
                    {[Date].[Fiscal].[Fiscal Year].&[2002]}) //DrillDownMember
                        }},
                {[Date].[Fiscal].[Fiscal Semester].&[2002]&[1]}
                ) //DrillDownMember
            }
        ) //AddCalculatedMembers
        ) //Hierarchize
```

```
DIMENSION PROPERTIES PARENT_UNIQUE_NAME ON ROWS
FROM [Direct Sales]
WHERE ([Measures].[Internet Sales Amount],
[Product].[Product Categories].[All Products])
```

There is a MDX function in the query called DrillDownMember. The function DrillDownMember takes two sets — Set1 and Set2 — as parameters and returns a set that contains the drill down of members in Set1 that are included in Set2. You can see that the innermost DrillDownMember is called with the sets DrillDownLevel({[Date].[Fiscal].[All Periods]})} and {[Date].[Fiscal].Fiscal Year].&[2002]}. The first parameter is another MDX function that returns all the members in the Year level. [Date].[Fiscal].Fiscal Year].&[2002] is one of the members in the first set and hence a drill down on this member will result in the members "H1 FY 2002" and "H2 FY 2002". Subsequent DrillDownMember functions drill down on the first half of fiscal year 2002 and the first quarter of fiscal year 2002. There is an optional third parameter for the DrillDownLevel MDX function which takes the flag RECURSIVE. This prompts a recursive drill down on members in Set1 based on the members in Set2. You can understand the behavior of the RECURSIVE flag by looking at the results of the following MDX queries:

```
select DrillDownMember({
                  DrillDownLevel( {[Date].[Fiscal].[All Periods]})
               },
               {[Date].[Fiscal].[Fiscal Year].&[2002],
                [Date].[Fiscal].[Fiscal Semester].&[2002]&[1],
                [Date].[Fiscal].[Fiscal Quarter].&[2002]&[1]}
               ,RECURSIVE) on 0
FROM [Sales Summary]
WHERE ([Measures].[Sales Amount], [Product].[Product Categories].[All])

select DrillDownMember({
                  DrillDownLevel( {[Date].[Fiscal].[All Periods]})
               },
               {[Date].[Fiscal].[Fiscal Year].&[2002],
                [Date].[Fiscal].[Fiscal Semester].&[2002]&[1],
                [Date].[Fiscal].[Fiscal Quarter].&[2002]&[1]}
               ) on 0
FROM [Sales Summary]
WHERE ([Measures].[Sales Amount], [Product].[Product Categories].[All])
```

Execute the above queries in SSMS to see the results of the queries. The first query returns all the months of the first quarter of fiscal year 2002, but the second query only returns the members in the semester level for the fiscal year 2002. You have now successfully learned to drill down to details in your pivot table report.

Viewing Multiple Measures with Your Pivot Table

So far you have been analyzing a single measure within your pivot table. As an executive making financial decisions, a user might need information concerning additional measures — for example, to analyze sales along with the initial targets or to analyze the budgeted cost versus actual cost. In the cube browser within BIDS you were able to select multiple measures. However, within a pivot table you cannot have more than one measure in the data area. In this section, you learn how to analyze multiple measures within a Pivot table.

Drill up to the fiscal year level on the fiscal hierarchy from the last example. Assume you want to see the quantity ordered along with the sales amount in your Pivot table. Drag and drop the measure Internet Order Count from the Pivot table field list into the data area. The pivot table now creates a new hierarchy called "Data" on the row axes, and adds the two measures Sales Amount and Order Count as members in this hierarchy. Corresponding values in the data area show the values for these measures. This is shown in Figure 15-23. You can select or deselect the members within the Data hierarchy. The Pivot table creates two Total rows along the row axes corresponding to the two measures Sales Amount and Order Count.

	A	B	C	D	E	F	G	H
1		Product	All Products					
2								
3				Country	State-Province			
4				United States			United States Total	Grand Total
5		Fiscal Year	Data	Alabama	Arizona	California		
6		FY 2002	Internet Sales Amount			1,526,344.23	1,526,344.23	1,526,344.23
7			Internet Order Count			478.00	478.00	478.00
8		FY 2003	Internet Sales Amount		2,071.42	804,136.49	806,207.91	806,207.91
9			Internet Order Count		1.00	489.00	490.00	490.00
10		FY 2004	Internet Sales Amount	2.29	32.60	3,374,621.67	3,374,656.56	3,374,656.56
11			Internet Order Count	1.00	1.00	4,315.00	4,317.00	4,317.00
12		FY 2005	Internet Sales Amount	35.00		9,155.30	9,190.30	9,190.30
13			Internet Order Count	1.00		184.00	185.00	185.00
14		Total Internet Sales Amount		37.29	2,104.02	5,714,257.69	5,716,399.00	5,716,399.00
15		Total Internet Order Count		2.00	2.00	5,466.00	5,470.00	5,470.00

Figure 15-23

Custom Grouping within a Pivot Table

If any word in the English language is overused, it is the word "cool" — but custom groupings are cool and must be described as such! When you analyze the results within Pivot table you might want to group certain members and analyze the data for those specific members. For example, if you have sales data for all the countries you might want to analyze the sales based on continents. If continent is not a level in the hierarchy then you might have to modify the cube design and add this information. Instead Pivot table helps you to group members and provide a name. It is important to know that Grouping functionality in Pivot Table is supported in SQL Server 2005 Service Pack 1 and beyond. Follow the steps below to create custom groups within pivot tables.

1. Create a Pivot Table by connecting to the Direct Sales cube in Adventure Works DW database.

2. Drag and drop Internet Sales Amount to the Data area, Customer Geography hierarchy to Rows, and Ship Date Calendar hierarchy to Columns.

3. You will see all the countries in the Customer Geography hierarchy in your pivot table. Assume you want to group the countries within the same continent. Multi-select France, Germany, and United Kingdom countries by holding the Ctrl key and selecting the members with the mouse. In the Pivot Table window select Pivot Table→Group and Show Detail→Group as shown in Figure 15-24. You can also group the members on a hierarchy by selecting the members, right click, and then select Group and Show Detail→Group.

4. The members France, Germany, and United Kingdom will be grouped together under a new member called Group 1 as shown in Figure 15-25. Sub Total for the member Group 1 is also created within the pivot table. Select members Canada and United States and Group them. You will now see countries Canada and United States are grouped under a member called Group 2. Australia is under a member called Other.

Internet Sales Amount	Calendar Year				
Country	CY 2001	CY 2002	CY 2003	CY 2004	Grand Total
Australia	1251388.081	2166222.532	3002149.051	2641240.92	9061000.584
Canada	143251.5374	618206.7698	507224.7649	709161.79	1977844.862
France	172716.0538	508909.9892	992681.6413	969710.03	2644017.714
Germany	219372.822	528003.5775	1021797.169	1125138.77	2894312.338
United Kingdom	280855.7094	583463.6463	1271712.795	1255680.06	3391712.211
United States	1038003.125	2172172.466	2721983.109	3457630.81	9389789.511
Grand Total	3105587.329	6576978.981	9517548.53	10158562.38	29358677.22

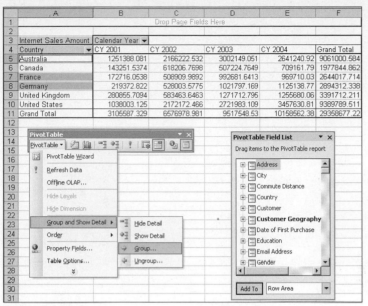

Figure 15-24

Internet Sales Amount		Calendar Year				
Customer Geography	Country	CY 2001	CY 2002	CY 2003	CY 2004	Grand Total
Group1	France	172716.0538	508909.9892	992681.6413	969710.03	2644017.714
	Germany	219372.822	528003.5775	1021797.169	1125138.77	2894312.338
	United Kingdom	280855.7094	583463.6463	1271712.795	1255680.06	3391712.211
Group1 Total		672944.5852	1620377.213	3286191.605	3350528.86	8930042.263
Group2	Canada	143251.5374	618206.7698	507224.7649	709161.79	1977844.862
	United States	1038003.125	2172172.466	2721983.109	3457630.81	9389789.511
Group2 Total		1181254.663	2790379.236	3229207.874	4166792.6	11367634.37
Other	Australia	1251388.081	2166222.532	3002149.051	2641240.92	9061000.584
Other Total		1251388.081	2166222.532	3002149.051	2641240.92	9061000.584
Grand Total		3105587.329	6576978.981	9517548.53	10158562.38	29358677.22

Figure 15-25

5. Click on the member Group 1 and rename it as Europe. Similarly rename Group 2 as North America and Other as Australia. Your pivot table should look like Figure 15-26. You can see that the totals for the groups are qualified by the new name you have provided.

Internet Sales Amount		Calendar Year				
Customer Geography	Country	CY 2001	CY 2002	CY 2003	CY 2004	Grand Total
Europe	France	172716.0538	508909.9892	992681.6413	969710.03	2644017.714
	Germany	219372.822	528003.5775	1021797.169	1125138.77	2894312.338
	United Kingdom	280855.7094	583463.6463	1271712.795	1255680.06	3391712.211
Europe Total		672944.5852	1620377.213	3286191.605	3350528.86	8930042.263
North America	Canada	143251.5374	618206.7698	507224.7649	709161.79	1977844.862
	United States	1038003.125	2172172.466	2721983.109	3457630.81	9389789.511
North America Total		1181254.663	2790379.236	3229207.874	4166792.6	11367634.37
Australia	Australia	1251388.081	2166222.532	3002149.051	2641240.92	9061000.584
Australia Total		1251388.081	2166222.532	3002149.051	2641240.92	9061000.584
Grand Total		3105587.329	6576978.981	9517548.53	10158562.38	29358677.22

Figure 15-26

Thus the grouping feature in Excel helps you to group members in a hierarchy and define a group name that makes it easy to analyze the data. Since the totals are created for the groups for the end user the group name will appear to be a level in the hierarchy which they can drill down or drill up. If you click on the drop-down list for Customer Geography you can see the new members created due to custom grouping along with the members in the Country level as shown in Figure 15-27. If you double-click on the group member you will see that the double-click acts as a toggle switch to hide or show details in the next level. For example if you double-click on Europe you will see the members France, Germany, and United Kingdom are hidden if they are visible and vice versa.

Figure 15-27

You can create a custom group of existing groups. For example you can group Europe and North America as Northern Hemisphere. Hence Grouping in Excel provides you the flexibility to do multiple levels of grouping which is really useful when there are several members in a hierarchy and you want to perform data analysis by grouping the members into several groups. You can ungroup a group of members by right-clicking on the group name and selecting Group and Show Detail→Ungroup.

It is important to know the limitations of grouping hierarchy members in Excel Pivot tables. You cannot group members of a parent-child hierarchy and hierarchies of ROLAP dimension using Excel Pivot tables. Having learnt to use various options in the pivot table for data analysis you will learn to present the data to end users as formatted reports in the next section.

Formatting Your Pivot Table Report

The Pivot table is one of the report formats in which data is shown to the end users. As with any reporting tool, you need the ability to format the report based on end-users' needs. The Pivot table provides you several formatting options; principally, you have the ability to format individual cell values in the data, row, or column areas because these are just cells in an Excel spread sheet. You have been analyzing the sales amount and you have not seen any kind of currency associated with the numbers in the data area. You can select all the cells in the data area, right-click, select Format Cells, and choose the currency formatting. Alternatively, you can right-click the cell Internet Sales Amount, select Format Cells, and select the Currency option in the Category list; any formatting changes here will be applied to all the cells in the data area. The formatting options available to any cell in Excel such as alignment, font, border, and patterns can be applied to the cells in the pivot table.

The Pivot table provides you additional formatting options as shown in Figure 15-28. To launch the Pivot Table Options page, click the Pivot table drop-down in the Pivot table toolbar and select Table Options. Most of these options are self-explanatory. You can enable or disable totals for rows and columns, center the labels of the members, and show different values in the report whenever empty cells are retrieved from Analysis Services. We leave the exercise of exploring these options and the impact on the report as an exercise for the reader.

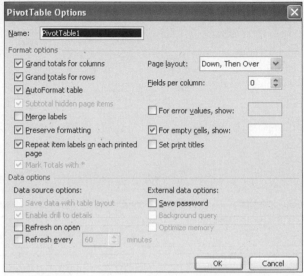

Figure 15-28

Excel Pivot tables provide you with various kinds of layouts for your report. Certain standard templates can be applied to your pivot table report that will enhance the look and feel for your end users. To select a specific template, click the drop-down Pivot table in the Pivot table toolbar and select Format Report. You will see the Auto format page shown in Figure 15-29.

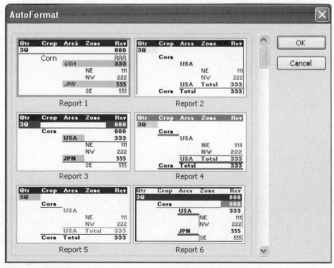

Figure 15-29

You can browse through the options in the auto format templates that are made available to you within Excel. If you choose a specific template, your existing Pivot table report is automatically formatted to the style chosen. Explore the various report and table options available in the auto format dialog so that you can present cool reports at no additional cost to your end users and look like a hero to your boss!

Creating Pivot Chart Reports

Reports generated through the Pivot table present the information in a way that is easily comprehensible to end users. However, there is an even better way to represent certain types of data to end users by using the Pivot charts feature. Charts are a good way to convey information to users, especially while comparing and analyzing data. Pivot charts allow you to represent the data within a pivot table in a graphical way to the end users with or without the actual numeric values. Pivot charts are always connected to a specific pivot table and the values within the pivot table. The following instructions show you how to create a pivot chart.

1. Create a pivot table to Adventure Works cube of Adventure Works DW database by creating a new connection. Drag and Drop Date.Fiscal on the row axes, the Customer Geography hierarchy on the column axes, the Product Categories hierarchy on the Page axes, and the Internet Sales Amount on the data area.

2. Click the drop-down Pivot table in the Pivot table toolbar and select Pivot Chart or click the chart icon in the Pivot table toolbar. A new data sheet is created in Excel that represents the data shown in the pivot table, as shown in Figure 15-30. You do have the pivot table toolbar available within the pivot chart. The hierarchy on rows is represented on the X-axis of the chart. The sales amount corresponding to a specific year is shown as a bar graph. The members of the customer geography hierarchy are represented as a legend, and the sales amount for various years for a specific country are shown in the same color. The Internet Sales Amount representing a specific year is shown in different colors proportional to the value for various countries. The total Internet Sales Amount indicated as a bar is the total Internet Sales Amount for a specific year. Similar to the drop-down for hierarchies on page axes in a pivot table, you can select specific product categories to analyze the Internet Sales Amount for a specific product or products. If you want to see the Internet Sales Amount based on countries rather than Fiscal Years, you can interchange the levels of the Country and Fiscal Year of the hierarchies Customer Geography and Date.Fiscal respectively. To do so you need to drag and drop Country from legend to X-axis and Fiscal Year from X-axis to legend. Any changes made within the pivot chart are automatically reflected in the pivot table.

3. If you want to drill down to details for a specific year, you need to click the Fiscal Year level and then click the show detail icon in the pivot table toolbar. You will now see the drill down data for the second level of the Date.Fiscal hierarchy as shown in Figure 15-31.

4. Pivot charts facilitate visualization of data in three dimensions. Click the chart wizard icon in the chart pivot table to select the chart type. Select the three-dimensional bar chart. You will now see the sales data in a three-dimensional view. Click Next in the Chart Wizard.

5. Some end users prefer to see the graphical representation of the data in the chart along with the numerical data embedded within the same report. The Pivot chart allows you to display the data within a table beneath the chart. In the Chart Wizard – Chart Options click the Data Table tab as shown in Figure 15-32 and select the option to "show the data table" to display the numeric values of the pivot table with the pivot chart; then click Finish.

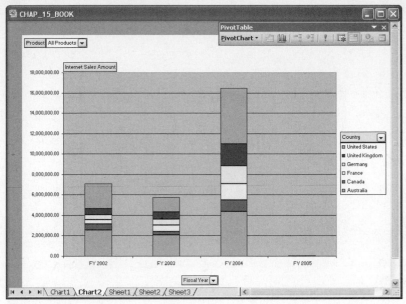

Figure 15-30

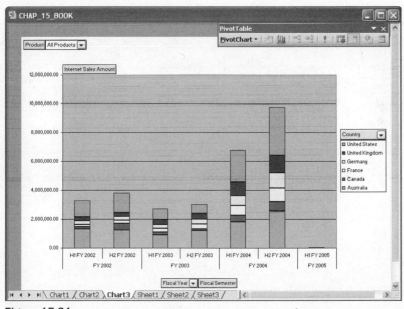

Figure 15-31

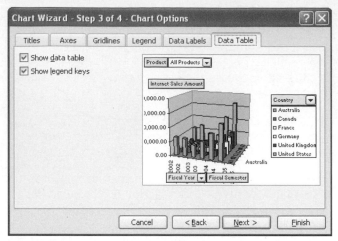

Figure 15-32

Typically, end users print the charts for meetings or use them in power presentations. In order to remove the axis information, click the Pivot table toolbar and under the Pivot Chart drop-down select menu item "Hide PivotChart Field Buttons". You will see the pivot chart containing a three-dimensional view of the sales data along with the pivot table as shown in Figure 15-33.

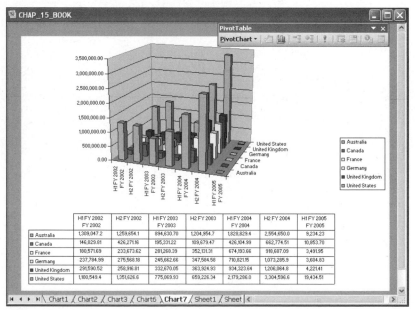

Figure 15-33

Creating Local Cubes from Excel

Being busy executives, many consumers of business intelligence information want to be able to access their cubes from the most remote of locations, like from business class aboard a Boeing 747. Yes, some people actually find themselves with a laptop and no Internet connection. Once you stop shivering from the very thought of not being connected to the internet, consider this alternative: you can create what are called local cubes for your customers. With these offline cubes you can distribute an analytic environment to someone sans a network connection. In other words, these customers do not need to have access to an Analysis Services instance to see the data. Local cubes can be created directly by sending the DDL of the database or using Excel. In this chapter you will learn to create local cubes from Excel 2003. Typically, local cubes are small sections of a server cube which are distributed to the end users to analyze the data offline. Customers using local cubes can do almost all of the operations associated with online analysis. However there are some restrictions that you need to be aware of while using local cubes.

The user creating a local cube from a server cube should have the ability to drill-through to the source data so that appropriate data can be retrieved from the server cube to form the local cube. Appropriate permissions to see the source-level data is specified using a role that has specific access permissions to the cubes and dimensions in a database. Though local cubes behave similarly to a server cube in functionality, there are certain restrictions. Local cubes in Analysis Services 2005 do not have the ability to execute stored procedures (.NET assemblies as well as COM DLLs). Hence if the server cube has a stored procedure that is called while querying the cube, you would not be able to send such queries against the local cube. Because the local cube is often a section of the server cube, some of the calculations in the MDX scripts might not be able to access tuples because they are not available in the local cube. These are some things for you to consider during creation of local cubes that might be distributed to end users. Creation of local cubes from server cubes is available in SQL Server 2005 RTM version. You need to at least have SQL Server 2005 Service Pack 1 in order to create local cubes through Excel. To create a local (or "offline") cube, follow the steps below.

1. Create a pivot table on the Direct Sales perspective of the sample Analysis Services database Adventure Works DW that includes the hierarchies Customer.[Customer Geography] on columns, Date.Fiscal on rows, Products.[Product Categories] on page, and the measure Internet Sales Amount on the data area. Recall that Page is just another dimension to pivot on.

2. Click the Pivot table drop-down in the pivot table toolbar and select Offline OLAP. You will see the dialog shown in Figure 15-34. Click the Create Offline Data File button.

Figure 15-34

3. Click the Next button in the welcome screen of the Create cube file dialog. You will now be in the level selection page where you choose the list of dimension hierarchies and the levels you want to be included in the offline cube file, as shown in Figure 15-35. In this dialog Excel shows

the hierarchies of all the dimensions. By default Excel selects the hierarchies that are included in the pivot table. You can alternately add additional dimensions to your local cubes if you or the end users using the local cube would need them to analyze the data. Select the hierarchies Customer Geography, Date Fiscal, Destination Currency, and Product Categories and click the Next button.

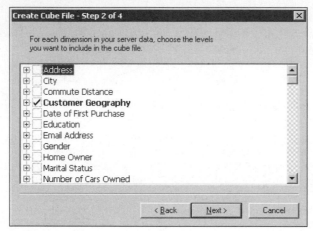

Figure 15-35

4. In the third page of the local cube wizard (see Figure 15-36) you can see the hierarchies that are part of the pivot table. Specific members can be selected for inclusion in the local cube, as opposed to using all of the members in the hierarchy. For example, if different employees are responsible for analyzing the data for various categories of products, you can restrict the data in the local cube for those specific products. At the time we are writing the book we believe there are still some more issues to be fixed in offline cubes. In Figure 15-36 you can notice that the top level of Customer Geography Countries is not available. Expand each level in this dialog and analyze the members selected by the wizard and click Next.

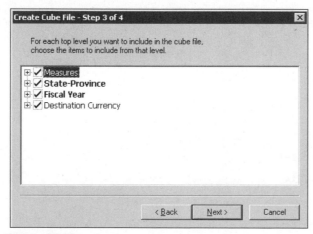

Figure 15-36

5. In the final page of the offline cube wizard shown in Figure 15-37, specify a file name to store the data and click the Finish button. At this point Excel sends a request to the Analysis Services instance to create a local cube using the OLEDB provider for Analysis Services.

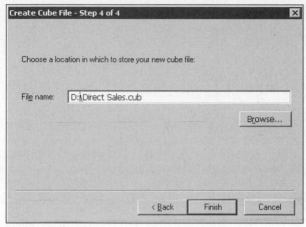

Create Cube File - Step 4 of 4

Choose a location in which to store your new cube file:

File name: D:\Direct Sales.cub

Browse...

< Back | Finish | Cancel

Figure 15-37

Shown below is the statement sent to Analysis Services instance to create an offline cube with your selections of measures and hierarchy levels. This statement can also be executed from SQL Server Management Studio.

```
CREATE GLOBAL CUBE [Direct Sales] STORAGE 'D:\Direct Sales.cub' FROM [Direct Sales]
(
  MEASURE [Direct Sales].[Internet Sales Amount],

  DIMENSION [Direct Sales].[Customer].[Customer Geography]
  (
          LEVEL [(All)],
          LEVEL [State-Province],
          LEVEL [City]
  ),
  DIMENSION [Direct Sales].[Date].[Fiscal]
  (
          LEVEL [(All)],
          LEVEL [Fiscal Year]
  ),
  DIMENSION [Direct Sales].[Product].[Product Categories]
  (
          LEVEL [(All)],
          LEVEL [Category]
  )

)
```

In the Offline OLAP Settings page (shown in Figure 15-38) select Offline OLAP and click OK. The operations including drill up and drill down, appropriate member selections, and so forth, all of which you did online, can also be performed offline. Once the offline cube (usually a subset of the server cube) is created, it can then be distributed to business decision-makers who do not need real-time access to the server cube.

Figure 15-38

As this Chapter is being written, the offline cubes are not yet completely functional. However, most of the steps mentioned above should be sufficient for you to create offline cubes. If there are any updates or instructions that need to be added to the content in the Offline cube section we will provide them through the download site for the book.

Office Web Component Pivot Table

To present Office data within web pages, Microsoft introduced a set of ActiveX controls called Office Web Components (OWC). The OWC Pivot tables are similar to Excel Pivot tables, but provide a slightly different range of functionality. We will use OWC Pivot tables shipped with Office 2003 for illustrations in this section along with Front Page 2003, which helps you to create web pages for your end users.

The OWC Pivot table provides end users the added flexibility to analyze data as compared to the Excel Pivot table, but has limited functionality with regards to formatting and reporting. With OWC Pivot tables you can easily identify the top or bottom values it provides you. There is a tight integration between Excel Pivot tables and OWC Pivot tables; they both provide the functionality of exporting data from one to another. There are two ways to create a web page using an OWC pivot table. The easiest way is to export an existing Excel pivot table. The following steps show you how to create an OWC pivot table from an existing pivot table:

1. Create an Excel pivot table with hierarchies and data in Excel. You can use the pivot table you created in the "Analyzing Data using Pivot Tables" section. Say, arranged like Figure 15-12.

2. In the File menu, select Save as Web Page. You will see the Save As dialog as shown in Figure 15-39. Assuming you have IIS (Internet Information Service) installed on your machine navigate to the folder Inetpub\wwwroot in your system directory. Click the Publish button to select the pivot table to publish.

3. In the Publish as Web Page screen, select the Pivot table as shown in Figure 15-40. Select Pivot Table under Choose option. Make sure the "Add interactivity with:" check box is enabled under Viewing options and select Pivottable functionality. This option enables you to manipulate the controls of the pivot table in the published web page. Type the file name so that the web page is published at the location shown in Figure 15-40. Click the Publish button.

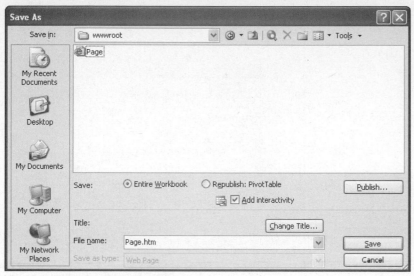

Figure 15-39

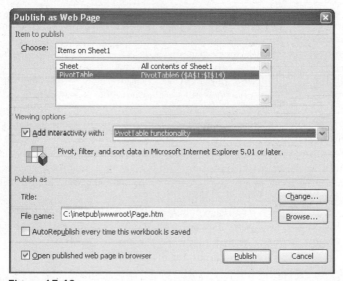

Figure 15-40

4. The OWC Pivot table within a web page will be opened in Internet Explorer. If your Internet Explorer settings disable ActiveX controls, the OWC Pivot table will be blocked, so you might have to enable ActiveX controls. Also, your internet browser settings might be set to block data being read from different domains. If you see an error within the OWC pivot table that data cannot be accessed across domains, enable the option in your Internet Explorer security settings as shown in Figure 15-41. If you have temporary blockers please enable them so that you can view the OWC Pivot table with the data within internet explorer.

Figure 15-41

5. Once you have enabled all the options, you will see the OWC pivot table with the data as shown in Figure 15-42. You can enable the pivot table field list and command options toolbars by clicking on the last two icons on the OWC Pivot table.

Similar to the Excel Pivot table you can drag and drop measures and dimensions across various axes. In the OWC Pivot table you will see the members along with a "+" next to them. You can click the "+" to drill down to the members at the next level, unlike the Excel pivot table where you will need to double-click on the member. You can do data sorting by clicking the ascending or descending icons in the toolbar of the OWC pivot table. You have the option of including or excluding subtotals or including hidden members in the total similar to Excel Pivot tables. If you right-click the level of a hierarchy you will see the various options available to you. Almost all the functionality available in the Excel Pivot table is also available in the OWC Pivot table. One of the important differences in the OWC Pivot table as compared to Excel Pivot table is the ability to see multiple measures in the data area. The OWC Pivot table extensively uses session calculations for retrieving the data to be displayed. It sends separate MDX queries for retrieving members to be displayed on each axes and the data area. MDX queries generated by OWC are not discussed in this section in detail for the sake of brevity.

6. The OWC Pivot table has an option to display the top N members in a hierarchy. Expand the sales for fiscal year 2002 to the day level. Right-click the Date level and select "Show Only the Top→5". The OWC Pivot table will send an MDX query to retrieve the top 5 members in this level based on the data selected. Figure 15-43 shows the results of the operation.

7. Additional functionality offered by the OWC Pivot table is the ability to hide certain levels of a hierarchy. If you only want to show the fiscal year and the month levels of the date.fiscal hierarchy, you can select each level and drag and drop them outside the pivot table. This will result in hiding the levels in your OWC pivot table. Figure 15-44 shows a pivot table that includes only the fiscal year and month levels.

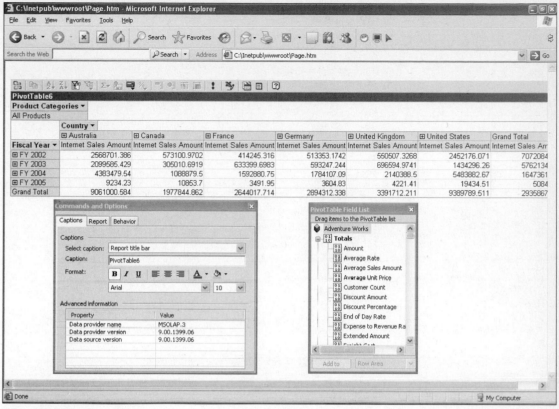

Figure 15-42

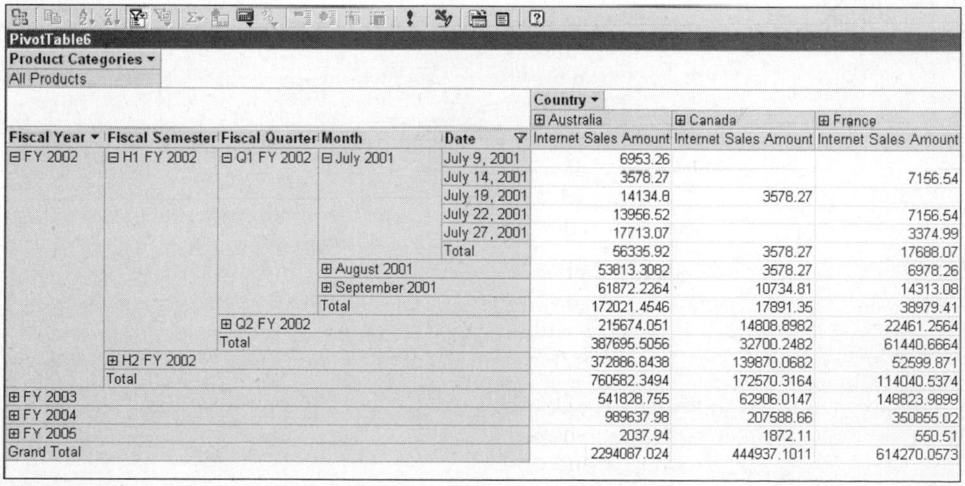

Figure 15-43

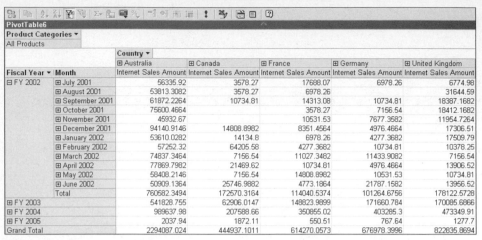

Figure 15-44

8. When you create the OWC Pivot table and publish the Web page you can specify multiple behavioral options which will impact the browsing experience for end users. The Behavior tab in the Command and Options dialog of the OWC Pivot table allows you to control expansion of items and expansion of details. Figure 15-45 shows the various options available to you.

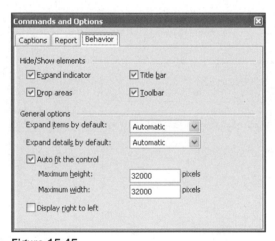

Figure 15-45

The second way to create an OWC Pivot table is to include the component within a web page. Microsoft's Front Page allows you to graphically design web pages. We will use Front Page 2003 to illustrate the creation of an OWC pivot table. The following steps show how to create an OWC Pivot table within a web page and retrieve data from Analysis Services 2005:

1. Launch Front Page 2003 and select New from the File menu. Create a new blank page.

2. From the Insert menu select Web Component. You will see the Insert Web Component dialog as shown in Figure 15-46. Select the spreadsheets and charts component type and choose the Office PivotTable control.

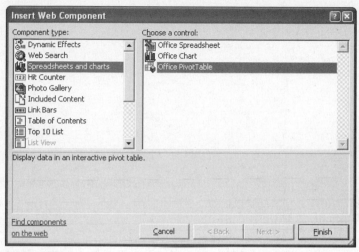

Figure 15-46

3. You will see the OWC pivot table that was shown in Figure 15-42 inserted into your html page, as shown in Figure 15-47.

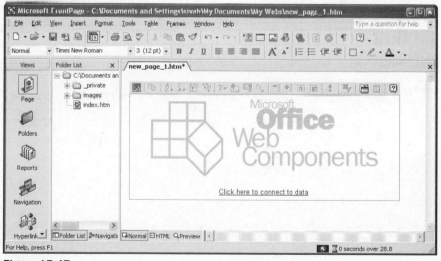

Figure 15-47

4. Click on the "Click here to connect to data" link. You will see the Commands and Options dialog shown in Figure 15-48.

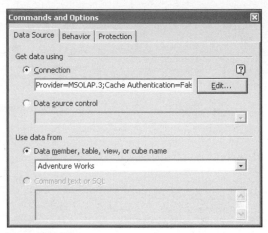

Figure 15-48

5. Click the Edit button to specify the connection details to Analysis Services 2005. You will now see the Select Data Source dialog. You will see the data source connection you established to the AdventureWorks database while working with Excel Pivot tables. You can select from one of the data sources available in this dialog or create a new data source connection to an Analysis Services database. Select the existing connection and click OK. In the commands and options dialog select the cube Adventure Works as shown in Figure 15-48. You can now close the commands and options dialog.

6. At this point you have established a connection to the Analysis Services database and you can now analyze data within the pivot table by dragging and dropping dimensions and measures from the pivot table field list. You can now create your OWC pivot layout with appropriate protection and publish this web page to your end users.

7. You have now learnt to create web pages that include OWC pivot tables that can be published on your IIS so that your end users can analyze data. In the next section you will look at another product from Microsoft called Data Analyzer that helps in analyzing data from Analysis Services.

Analyzing UDM Data using Microsoft Data Analyzer

Microsoft's Data Analyzer is a business intelligence client tool that allows you to analyze data graphically. With the help of charts, graphs, and easy navigation, Data Analyzer helps you to have a consolidated view on one screen so the user can better understand patterns of data and make business decisions. Data Analyzer provides the flexibility to configure various colors for showing data that help surface any anomalies in data quickly. The following steps show you how to analyze your UDM using Data Analyzer:

1. Launch Data Analyzer. You will see the Data Analyzer startup page, which allows you to create a new view or open an existing view as shown in Figure 15-49. Select the option to create a new view and click the OK button, and then click the Next button on the welcome page.

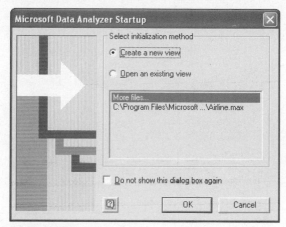

Figure 15-49

2. If you had already established connections you will see the connections in the view connections page. The view connections page (Figure 15-50) shows a clean slate to start with. Click the Add button to create a new connection to Analysis Services 2005.

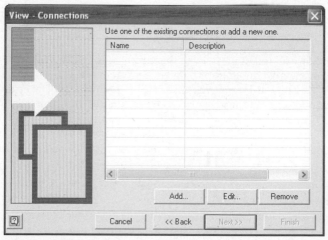

Figure 15-50

3. Data Analyzer allows you to connect to Analysis Services directly via TCP or over HTTP; it also allows you to analyze data from a local cube file. In the connection properties page specify the Analysis Services instance name next to Server as shown in Figure 15-51. The Advanced option allows you to specify special connection string properties and HTTP passwords. Specify a name for the connection and click the Connect button. Data Analyzer now retrieves the list of databases from the Analysis Services instance along with the cubes within each database. You can choose the database name from the Catalog drop-down list and the cube from the Cube drop-down list. After selecting the catalog and cube names as shown in Figure 15-51, click the OK button. In the View Connections dialog select the connection currently established and click the Next button.

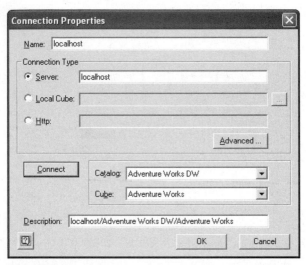

Figure 15-51

4. You now need to select the dimensions to be included in your view for data analysis. Data Analyzer shows all the hierarchies of the dimensions in the selected cube as shown in Figure 15-52. The hierarchy names are shown within parentheses after the dimension name. Select the hierarchies Customer Geography from Customer dimension, Date.Calendar from Data dimension, Departments, Organizations from Organization dimension, and Product Category from the Product dimension. You will notice that certain dimensions do not have the hierarchy name qualified along with dimension name. This occurs when the dimension contains only hierarchy that is visible. Click Next after you complete your hierarchy selections mentioned in step 4.

5. You now need to specify the measures that are to be included in your view along with display type. Data Analyzer supports two display types: bar and grid. The bar view provides the graphical representation, while the grid view provides the data similar to the pivot tables. In our opinion the bar view is more helpful in data analysis. Select the bar view as the display type. Select the length of the bar to indicate the Internet Sales Amount as shown in Figure 15-53. Whenever you are browsing the various members, the length of the bar is determined by the value of Internet Sales Amount. Click the Finish button after you have made the selections.

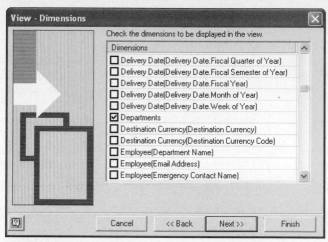

Figure 15-52

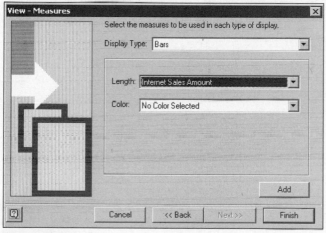

Figure 15-53

6. Data Analyzer now retrieves the data from the Analysis Services instance with the help of several MDX queries, and you will see a view in your Data Analyzer as shown in Figure 15-54. Members within a hierarchy are indicated using bars and the length of the bar is determined based on the Internet sales amount. You can see that United States has a bar that has the maximum length closely followed by Australia. This allows you to easily infer that Internet sales in the United States are at least three times the sales in Germany. The visual indication really helps the analysts to capture the information quickly. In addition to that you see the Internet Sales not only based on the customer's geography, but also on various other dimensions such as Calendar and Product category. If you click a specific member, United States, in a customer geography hierarchy you will notice that that member gets highlighted (Figure 15-55). In addition to that,

the length of the bars on other dimensions automatically changes because those bars now represent the data corresponding to the United States. Hover over the member United States to get the Internet Sales Amount as shown in Figure 15-55.

7. Data Analyzer allows you to drill down or drill up to the members in the next level. For example, if you want to see the sales within the United States you can double-click the bar for United States, or click the bar and then click the icon for drill down. If you hover over the icons on the left you will see the description of each icon. Once you drill down on United States you will see all the states in the United States and the bars representing the sales in corresponding states. You will also notice that the bars for other dimensions automatically get readjusted. You have the ability to hide members in a level or specify a filter condition to view appropriate data. For example, if you want to see the sales amount for the top N members or M percentile of the members you can do so by applying such a condition using the filter icon.

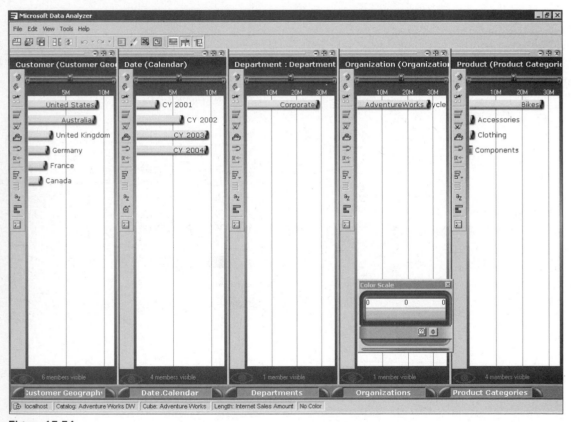

Figure 15-54

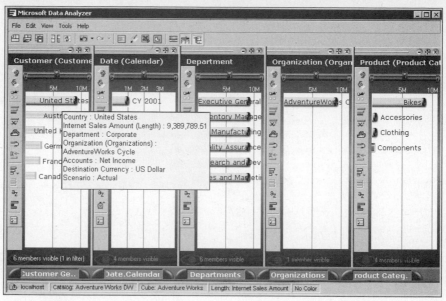

Figure 15-55

8. To drill down to the states within United States select the member United States and then double click on the member or click on the drill down icon. Launch the filter dialog by clicking on the filter by criteria icon. You will now see the filter dialog as shown in Figure 15-56. Specify filter condition to get the top five states in the United States that have the maximum Internet Sales Amount. Once you click in the Filter by Criteria dialog Data Analyzer now applies the filter and you will see the top 5 states in the United States as shown in Figure 15-57.

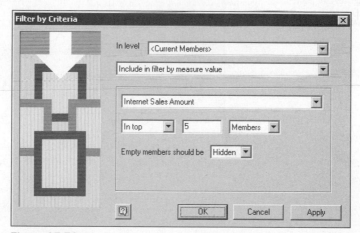

Figure 15-56

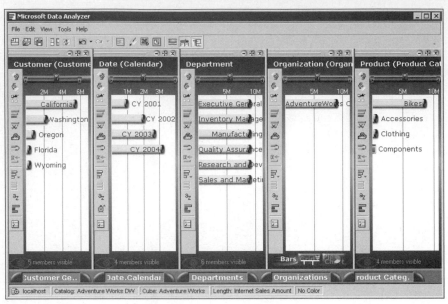

Figure 15-57

9. Data Analyzer provides you a way to visualize data in Bar View, Grid View, or Pie Chart View. For each of the dimensions. if there is not sufficient space to show the results in the Pie Chart view, Data Analyzer will default to Bar view. To see the effect of the Grid View and Pie Chart views close the windows showing hierarchies Organizations and Departments. Go to the Date (Calendar) hierarchy. Click on the Pie Chart view option at the bottom of the window. To do so, hover the mouse cursor over the "eye" (as shown in Figure 15-58) at the bottom left of the corresponding window. Similarly click on the Grid view for the Product (Product Categories Hierarchy). You will now see the data displayed in the Pie Chart view and Grid views as shown in Figure 15-58.

We have introduced you to some of the basic functionalities available in Data Analyzer. You have likely noticed the flexibility and power of analyzing data from within Data Analyzer from this brief overview. We recommend you refer to the product documentation for an in-depth understanding of the capabilities provided by Data Analyzer.

Data Analyzer dynamically creates MDX queries for each of the operations you perform in the view. Data Analyzer creates Sets and calculated members for querying the data. We have not detailed the MDX queries sent to the server because the Sets and calculated members have dynamically generated names that are lengthy, and because multiple MDX queries are sent to the Analysis Services for each user action. If we start explaining each MDX query sent by Data Analyzer, this book will grow to the size of a New York City phone book. We leave this as an exercise for the reader: to analyze the MDX queries and understand the mapping between the query and the value shown in the view. To identify the MDX query sent to the server, you can use SQL Profiler and create trace events. Please refer to Chapter 13 on how to create traces to Analysis Services.

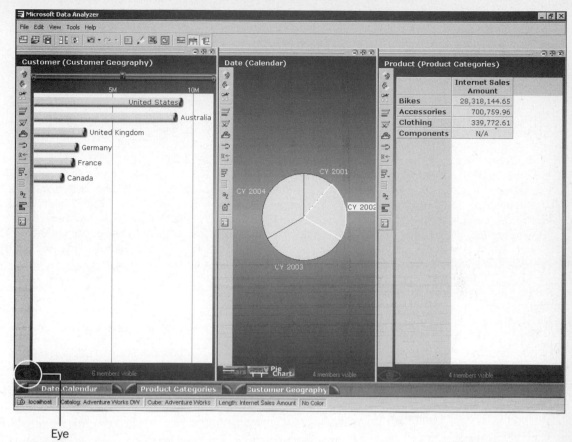

Eye

Figure 15-58

Use of correct terminology is critical in business intelligence; saying one thing when you mean another doesn't help matters. Drill down versus Drill-through is the poster child for inaccurate use of terminology. To drill down means to continue opening lower levels of dimension members, thereby "drilling" into lower levels of data granularity. Drill-through has a completely different meaning; to drill-through means to access the fact (detail) data corresponding to a cell in the cube which you learned in Chapter 9. Nobody who has dutifully read this book should ever confuse the two.

Summary

As a business intelligence application developer you will likely do your proof-of-concept browsing in BIDS, but in using the cubes you've built for them, your customers will actually do the slicing and dicing in Excel pivot tables or by using Office Web Components technology. Analysis Services and Excel together make a formidable business intelligence platform and there is no reason not to take advantage of that. Furthermore, there are very few business professionals who don't know Excel; it really is a nearly ubiquitous application. The next version of Excel provides you with additional capabilities that help in easy interpretation of data.

Nonetheless, there are tools from other companies that provide connectivity to and leverage from Analysis Services 2005, each with their own value-add proposition. This chapter was focused on Microsoft client services and tools, but there are other options available. Some of the commonly used client tools which we are aware of are from Panorama, Proclarity, and MIS AG. There are many more.

The offerings from Panorama are designed to complement the use of Office, SQL Server, Analysis Services, and Reporting Services. Central to their strategy is the NovaView Intelligence Server and the NovaView Development Tools. Proclarity offers a number of products in the business analytics space. They provide a Software Development Kit in support of the "Proclarity Analytics Family" of products. That SDK supports the building of custom business intelligence applications. Finally, MIS Plain is an Excel plug-in that provides a unique Excel analytics experience; not only does it articulate with Analysis Services 2005 as you would expect, it also makes use of the Reporting Services 2005 offering. For more information on these offerings, you can explore the relevant web sites:

1. http://www.panorama.com/

2. http://www.proclarity.com

3. http://www.misag.com/ca/jm/sfj/

16

Integration Services

SQL Server Integration Services (SSIS) 2005 is similar to what used to be called Data Transformation Services (or DTS for short) in SQL Server 2000. Like the names suggest, this service is all about integrating data from disparate data sources to a destination with the ability to apply transformations on the data based on business needs. Integration Services is really a collection of utilities, named tasks, and transforms that allow you to merge data from heterogeneous data sources to data destination(s), apply transformations to clean the data before loading them to data destinations, bulk load data to OLTP and OLAP systems, and automate administrative tasks on relational and OLAP databases and even do data mining. Integration Services is not just about data; it helps you to perform operations on files ranging from simple file search operations on disk to transferring files using FTP. It also allows you to write managed code and execute it as a script, and define and automate your complex business processes as nightly tasks. Finally, SSIS allows you to build your own custom tasks and transform components that can be added to the SSIS toolbox.

Integration Services is used extensively to operate on relational databases from data loading to automated administrative tasks. The reason Integration Services is so important to the Business Intelligence professional is simple; data is almost never clean or formatted quite the way you would like and the data almost always comes from heterogeneous data sources. It is imperative to get the data squared away and ready for processing, and Integration Services is one of the ways to accomplish that. Although these things are important parts of the story, they are not the whole story. If there is one thing you have learned working through this book, it is that there are multiple ways to accomplish most any given task. Integration Services adds a whole new operator to that equation! It provides the functionality to do a specific operation via different methods and you can choose the one that is most convenient for you.

Integration Services is based on the formation and use of packages. These packages are made up of connections and tasks; typically built in the user interface, but which could be written directly in XML (though that is not recommended as an approach). These can be reasonably divided into two parts — control flow elements and data flow components. Precedence constraints are what connect tasks in a control flow and define the criteria for progression through the package. Control flow elements take account of cases like; some tasks that fail should result in the termination of the whole package, while failure for another task might mean nothing more than a speed bump and the processing should continue. With data flow such distinctions can be implemented.

Creating an Integration Services Project

At this point, it may come as no surprise that a data source formulated for use in Integration Services isn't any different than a data source formulated for use with Analysis Services. Not only that, but data source views play the same role across both Integration Services and Analysis Services. A great benefit of having a common data source is to share it across multiple SSIS packages. Perhaps you recall from earlier in this book that data source views are similar to views in SQL Server. If you want to work with a limited set of tables, that is, a view in the relational world, you can emulate that using a data source view when creating SSIS packages. If you want to use the same table more than once for certain operations, you can create named queries, all of which utilize a shared data source connection in turn. You will learn more about these capabilities when creating a SSIS package.

Integration Services Task

In this chapter you learn specifically about Analysis Services–related tasks but you should know that there are 29 control flow items (most of which are tasks), plus another 11 maintenance plan tasks. Examples of commonly used tasks are the Send Mail Task, which is used to notify the administrator of job status; the Bulk Insert Task, which is used to insert data from flat files into tables at high speed; and the Data Flow Task, which contains a number of transforms internally — a container that helps to complete tasks like merging data and then sorting it, and so on. One capability of interest regarding the tasks is the product allows you to have multiple tasks in the designer that can be executed in parallel — more on that later this chapter.

Integration Services Transform

The process of populating data warehouses and data marts requires well-groomed data. Getting to well-groomed data requires the use of capabilities found in Data Flow Transformations. These Transforms can be used, for example, to sample, count, or merge data. Because there are 28 Transforms under Data Flow Transformations, there is no lack of tools you can use to make your data conform to whatever design you wish it to take.

In Chapter 1 you saw an example that included various representations of Microsoft such as MSFT, MS, Microsoft, and MSoft. These different representations from various source systems might cause some difficulties; there could be a strong business need to have a standard format and merge the relevant data. SSIS fuzzy look-up transformations help you in achieving the transformation by means of comparing the various Microsoft strings and deriving a standardized output MSFT. You can use the lookup transforms and do conditional split transforms, or write your own code to perform this operation using the script transform. This example demonstrates a typical data cleansing operation with SSIS transforms and multiple ways of achieving the end goal.

Creating Integration Services Packages for Analysis Services Operations

Integration Services is great for creating packages to accomplish administrative tasks on Analysis Services. Even more convenient is how these automated tasks can be performed on a periodic basis. Integration Services provides several tasks and transforms that help you in building packages in the uniform Business Intelligence IDE you have been working with in Analysis Services 2005. Tasks and transforms have been specifically designed for integration with Analysis Services.

Execute DDL Task

The Execute DDL task is used for sending a DDL script to Analysis Services. This task is typically used to accomplish administrative tasks like backup, restore, or sync operations that need to be performed on a periodic basis. You can also use this task to send process statements to Analysis Services for processing Analysis Services objects or include this task along with other Integration Services tasks to create a more generalized package; for example, dynamically creating a new partition in a cube by analyzing the fact data — and then processing that partition. To create a package that will backup your Analysis Services database on a periodic basis, do the following:

1. Open BIDS and load the AnalysisServices2005Tutorial project found under folder Chapter16Samples of the book's sample that can be downloaded from the Wrox Web site. Once you have loaded it, go ahead and deploy the project. This specific project has some additions to the ones you have created earlier, and hence make sure the full project is deployed.

2. While still in BIDS, create a new Integration Services project named IntegrationServicesTutorial by selecting File⇨New⇨Project and selecting Integration Services project. You will now be in the Integration Services project shown in Figure 16-1.

3. The solution explorer window shows four folders containing the following: Data Sources, Data Source Views, SSIS Packages, and Miscellaneous as shown in Figure 16-1. As with Analysis Services you can create connections to data sources and add them to a data source object. The main purpose of data sources is to share connections between multiple SSIS packages within a single project. Again, as with an Analysis Services project, DSVs help you create a subset of tables, views, named queries, and named calculations that can be used by SSIS packages rather than creating equivalent views on your relational backend. If you are designing a single SSIS package that uses a database too small to merit a view, you might not use the data source views. The properties window helps you to define properties of various objects. The primary objective of SSIS is to retrieve data from a source, perform some operations to transform the data, and store the data at a destination. Therefore we expect almost all the SSIS projects will have some form of connection object. Familiarize yourself with the various windows in the SSIS design surface and various windows. All the connections used in your SSIS package will be shown in the Connection Managers window thereby providing a consolidated view. If you right-click in the connection window you can see the various types of connections that SSIS supports. The main window, which is a graphical designer, is used to create SSIS packages. The SSIS Design window has four views: Control Flow, Data Flow, Event Handlers, and Package Explorer. You explore the use of these views in this chapter.

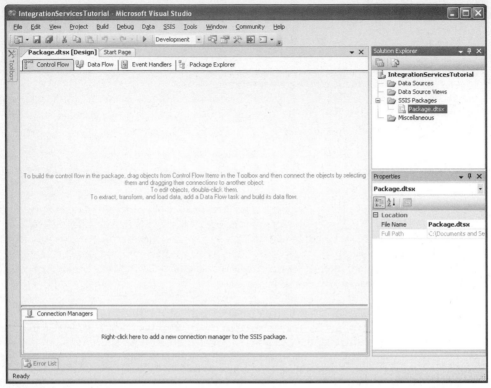

Figure 16-1

4. All the tasks and transforms provided by SSIS are represented within the toolbox window. To see the toolbox window, click View⇨Toolbox in the drop-down menu . The toolbox window can be docked by clicking the pin icon as shown in Figure 16-2. Drag and drop the SQL Server Analysis Services Execute DDL task to the Control Flow tab. You will now see the task in the window as shown in Figure 16-2. The SSIS designer in BIDS completes a validation on every task and transform in your package. Each task has a certain set of required properties and some optional properties. If the required properties are not specified, you will see a red "x" mark within the task. If the optional properties are not defined you will see a yellow "x" mark within the task. If any of the tasks or transforms within your package have a red "x" mark, that indicates that there is an error in your package and you will not be able to run the package without resolving the error. The Execute DDL task needs the connection details to Analysis Services and the DDL to execute. Because these properties have not been defined when you drag and drop the task in your editor, you will see a red "x" mark as shown in Figure 16-2.

5. One of the properties for the Execute DDL task is to specify the connection details to an Analysis Services database. To create a connection to the Analysis Services 2005 Tutorial database, right-click the Connection Managers window. You can see all the various types of connections SSIS supports as shown in Figure 16-3. Select "New Analysis Services Connection..."

Menu Pin   Red "x"

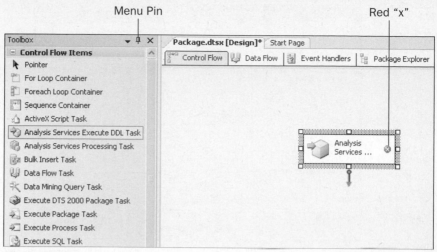

Figure 16-2

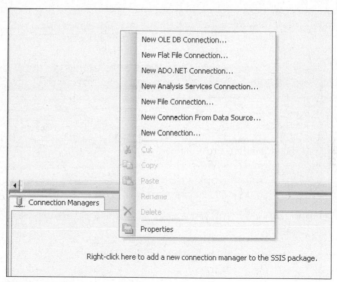

Figure 16-3

6. The Add Analysis Services Connection Manager dialog is launched as shown in Figure 16-4. You have the option of establishing a connection to an Analysis Server database or to an Analysis Services project within your solution. BIDS supports having multiple projects within the same solution. This means that you can have Analysis Services and Integration Services projects within the same solution. If you are building a SSIS package for the Analysis Services project within the same solution, you choose the second option. Select the first option and click Edit.

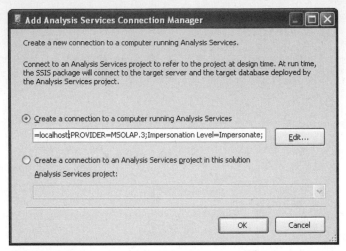

Figure 16-4

7.   In the Connection Manager dialog you can specify the connection details to your Analysis
      Services database such as server name, database name as shown in Figure 16-5. After you have
      specified the connection details, click OK to complete both dialogs.

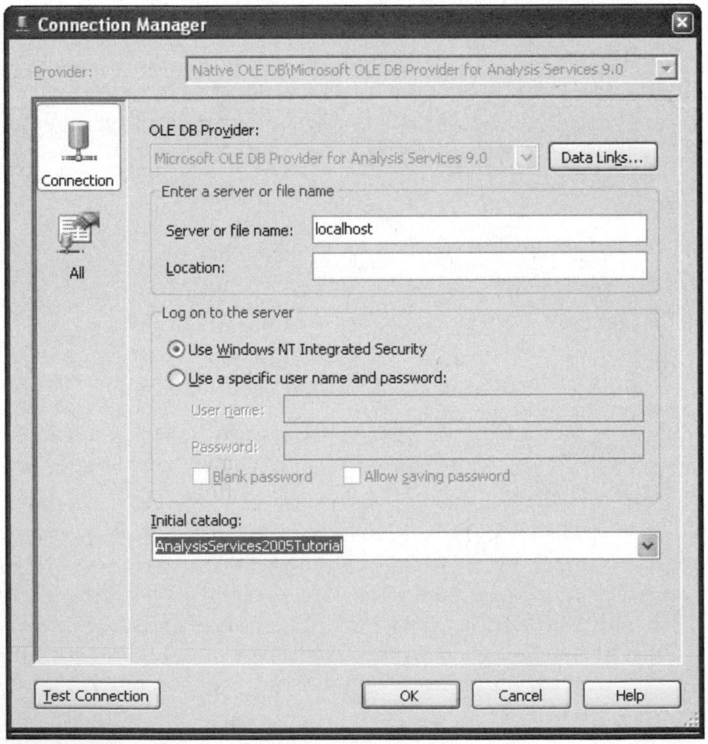

Figure 16-5

8. To specify properties needed by the Execute DDL task double-click the Execute DDL task object within the designer. You will see the Execute DDL task editor as shown in Figure 16-6.

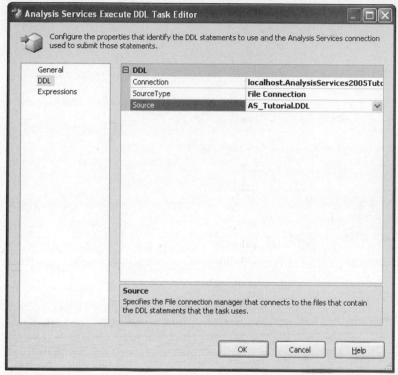

Figure 16-6

9. From the drop-down list for connection you can either create a new connection or select an existing connection. Select the Analysis Services connection you established in step 7. There are three ways of specifying the DDL to be executed.

- ❑ **Enter the DDL in a text box.** Whenever you know that your DDL is static and will not change you can use this option.

- ❑ **Specify a connection to the file.** This option is used whenever you have a file containing the DDL. This file can be static or dynamic in the sense that the DDL contents can be changed by another operation, such as a different SSIS task or an external program.

- ❑ **Specify the DDL using a variable in the SSIS package where the value of the variable is the actual DDL.** This option is used whenever the results from one task need to be used as an input to another task. The variable can be initialized during package execution, or the task setting the value for the variable needs to be executed before the Execute DDL task in the control flow.

10. Select the source type as File Connection. Select the drop-down list under Source and select New Connection. In the File Connection manager dialog, select the DDL file provided under the Chapter 16 directory on the Web site. The contents of the DDL are shown below. This DDL will take a backup of the Analysis Services 2005 Tutorial database.

```
<Backup xmlns="http://schemas.microsoft.com/analysisservices/2003/engine">
  <Object>
    <DatabaseID>AnalysisServices2005Tutorial</DatabaseID>
  </Object>
  <File>AnalysisServices2005Tutorial.abf</File>
</Backup>
```

11. Once you have specified all the properties for the Execute DDL Task editor as shown in Figure 16-6, click OK.

If you run the SSIS package you have created a backup of the Analysis Services 2005 Tutorial database will be created in Program Files\Microsoft SQL Server\MSSQL.2\OLAP\Backup. Backup is usually an operation scheduled for when the load on Analysis Services is minimal. Many companies do backup operations on a nightly basis, but if you are a multinational company or have customers using the database across the globe, you would have to factor in your customers' needs and take the backup at an appropriate time.

Regardless of when the package is run, you want to know whether the operation succeeded or failed. Obviously you can check the logs on Analysis Services or the logs of the SSIS package, but as an administrator one of the easiest ways is to send an e-mail about the results of the operation. To facilitate this operation, SSIS provides a task called the Send Mail Task. By specifying appropriate parameters to this task you can send an e-mail upon completion of a specific task or an entire SSIS package.

To add the send mail task to your SSIS package, drag and drop two instances of Send Mail Task to your designer. You will use one task to send an e-mail when the Execute DDL task succeeds and the other one to send mail when the Execute DDL task fails. Now that you have two send mail tasks in the Control Flow pane, it is time to connect the Execute DDL task to the send mail tasks. You can connect tasks in a control flow by clicking on the originating object (a downward facing green arrow will appear) and dragging the arrow end to the target object. Do that for the first Send Mail task. For the second Send Mail Task, just click the Execute DDL task again and you will see another green arrow appear as an output of the item. Drag the green arrow and connect it to the next Send Mail task. Your package should look like the one shown in Figure 16-7. That connecting line represents precedence constraint functionality; in fact, if you double-click the green line, the Precedence Constraint Editor will appear. The green lines indicate success and whenever the Execute DDL task completes successfully, execution continues with the task connected on the success line. To configure the second mail task to send e-mail on failure, double-click the connecting line.

12. You should see the precedence constraint editor as shown in Figure 16-8. The connecting line between the two tasks has several properties that are evaluated after the completion of the source task. You can specify an expression and/or constraint that can be evaluated after the completion of the task. The value property of the connecting line helps you to choose the constraint and determines whether the control will be transferred to the next task. The three options for the value property are success, failure, and completion. Change the value from Success to Failure. You can also configure the precedence control by right-clicking the connecting line between two tasks and selecting Success, Failure, or Completion. Click OK after you have completed specifying the constraint.

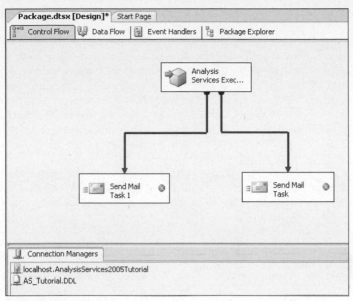

Figure 16-7

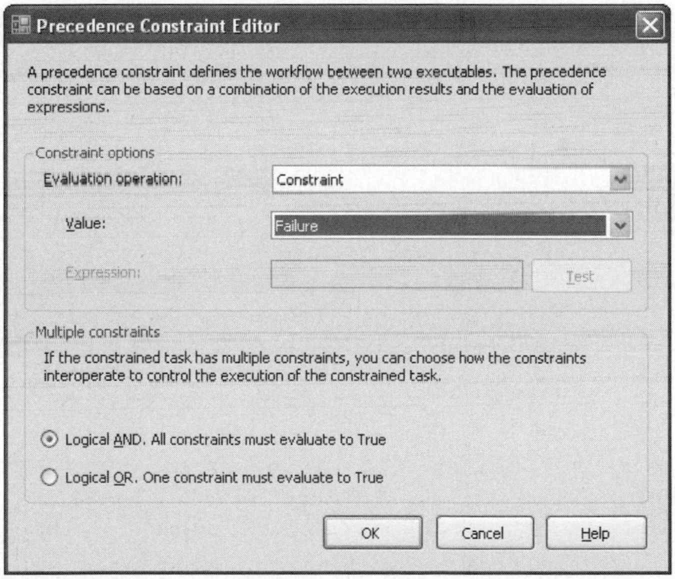

Figure 16-8

13. Double-click the Send Mail task to configure the properties of the task. You need to specify the mail server and details of the mail content in the properties of the Send Mail task. The Send Mail Task Editor is shown in Figure 16-9. Specify the details of the mail server by clicking the drop-down list of the SmtpConnection property. Your company should have a SmtpServer.

Contact your IT administrator to get details on the name of your SMTP server. Specify the e-mail address from which you want this mail to be sent, the people who need to receive the status of this package execution, and the content of the mail, as shown in Figure 16-9. Based on the Send Mail task you have chosen, provide the appropriate subject and message source. Figure 16-9 shows the contents of the Send Mail task that will be executed on successful completion of the Execute DDL task created in a previous step. Make sure the other send mail task properties are appropriately entered. Rename the Send Mail Tasks as Send Mail Success and Send Mail Failure by changing the name of the tasks as shown Figure 16-10. Appropriate naming makes the SSIS package easily readable and can be interpreted immediately by another person working on this task.

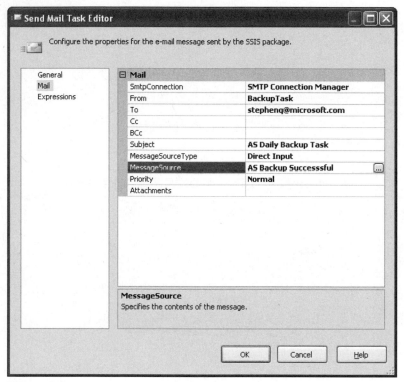

Figure 16-9

14. The SSIS package is now ready for execution. You can select Debug➪Start, hit the F5 key, or right-click the package name and select Deploy. The BIDS now starts the execution of the SSIS package. The BIDS will operate in the debugging environment, similar to debugging a program. You will first see the SQL Server Analysis Services Execute DDL task highlighted in yellow as shown in Figure 16-11, which indicates that the task is currently under execution. If the task completed successfully, the status of the task is shown in green, and if it failed the status is shown in red. You do have the ability to insert break points, and analyze variables used within tasks or transforms in the debug environment.

Once the entire package is completed, status on each of the tasks is shown; that is, the two tasks are shown in green having completed successfully.

Green Line   Red Line

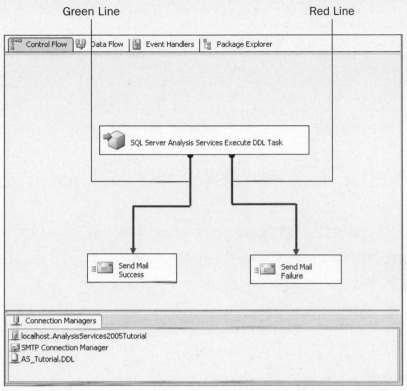

Figure 16-10

Back Color changes to yellow when the task is executing

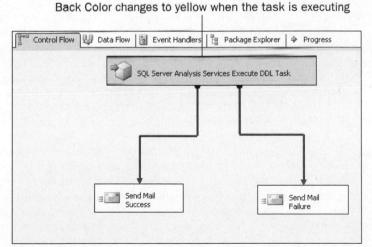

Figure 16-11

15. In the debug environment you can see detailed information for each task and the time taken by the task for completion in the Progress window. You can switch to the progress window when the package is being executed. The progress window gets updated when the control moves from one task to another. Figure 16-12 shows the progress report of the execution of the package. You can see that the DDL Execute task, which took a backup of an Analysis Services database, took 47 seconds to complete.

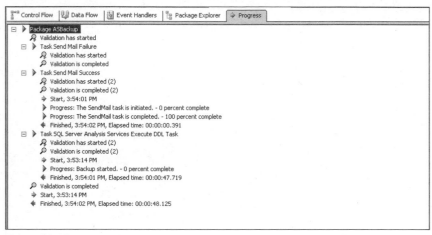

Figure 16-12

Processing an Analysis Services Object

SSIS provides a task for processing Analysis Services objects. You can process an entire Analysis Services database or choose a specific dimension or cube or even partitions for processing using the SSIS task called the SQL Server Analysis Services Processing task. The Analysis Services processing task is useful whenever you have changes in your relational data that need to get propagated to the cube. Often retail companies have new products added to their catalog every day, and the products table gets updated with the new products or changes in existing products as a daily batch process. Also, the daily sales data gets updated in the relational database as a nightly batch process. In order to propagate these changes to the cube for analysis, the dimensions and cubes need to be processed unless you have set the storage mode as ROLAP for dimensions and cubes. There are several considerations involved in determining frequency of processing. Should cubes be processed on a daily, weekly or monthly basis? The decision to process the Analysis Services objects is typically based upon the size of the dimensions and cubes, how often data changes on the relational database, and the frequency with which business analysts analyze the cube data. In most cases there are additions to the products table rather than updates, and hence an incremental process of the products table might be sufficient. If your fact table gets updated with daily transactional data in the same table, you have the option of creating new partitions in the cube on a daily/weekly basis or doing a full process of the cube. The Microsoft operations guide for Analysis Services suggests you have a new partition for every 20 million records or when the partition file reaches 5GB—in this way you can achieve optimal performance. How you partition your data is based on decisions that relate to your business needs. To create an Integration Services package that processes an Analysis Services Sales partition, do the following:

1. Right-click the SSIS Packages folder and select New SSIS Package. Name the package PartitionProcessing.

2. Similar to what we did in the Backup package earlier in this chapter; create a connection to the Analysis Services Tutorial 2005 database in Connection Managers.

3. Drag and drop the SQL Server Analysis Services Processing task and two Send Mail tasks into the SSIS designer. Configure one of the Send Mail tasks for success and another one for failure.

4. Double-click the SQL Server Analysis Services Processing task. This launches the Analysis Services Processing Task editor as shown in Figure 16-13. This dialog is similar to the Processing dialog of Analysis Services, which you learned about in previous chapters.

If you click the Change Settings button, the Change Settings dialog pops up as shown in Figure 16-14. The Change Settings dialog allows you to process the selected Analysis Services objects sequentially or in parallel. You can use the "Dimension key errors" tab to configure the processing options so that appropriate actions are taken when errors are encountered during the processing operation. The selected option will apply to all the Analysis Services objects chosen in the Analysis Services processing task editor. To add Analysis Services objects for processing, click the Add button on the Analysis Services Processing Task Editor (Figure 16-13).

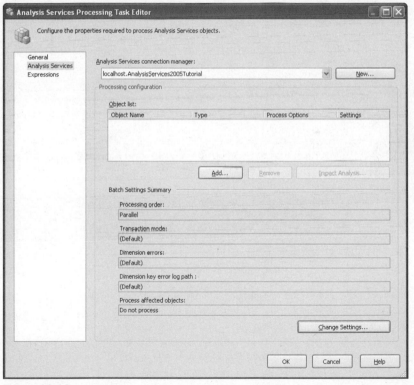

Figure 16-13

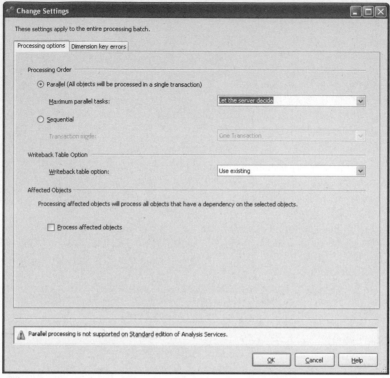

Figure 16-14

5. The Add SQL Server Analysis Services Object allows you to choose the object you want to process. Select the Fact Internet Sales Partition as shown in Figure 16-15 and click OK. Click OK again to dismiss the Task Editor dialog.

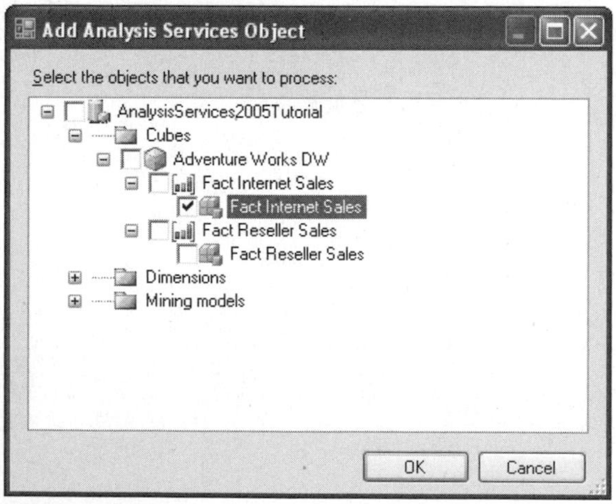

Figure 16-15

6. Press the F5 button on your keyboard to deploy the SSIS processing package and make sure it executes correctly. If everything has been specified correctly you will see successful completion of the SQL Server Analysis Services Processing task and the Send Mail Success tasks — also, these tasks will be highlighted in green indicating the successful execution. Of course you do need appropriate privileges on the Analysis Services instance to perform these operations.

Loading Data into an Analysis Services Partition

Typically, the data from the transactional source database (production system) is extracted, staged to some intermediate storage, and then undergoes transformations before being stored in a data warehouse (flat file or relational format). This data then needs to be propagated to the cube for analysis. Analysis Services has the ability to read data from various data sources from flat files to various relational databases. One way to add new fact data to the cube is to create new partitions that read data from the data sources. You can use SSIS's Script task to create a new DDL, execute the DDL using the Execute DDL task, and then process the partition using the Analysis Services processing task. You can create a package that will integrate all these tasks. Even though you can utilize these tasks to load fact data, it is not easy to load new dimension data to an existing dimension table. Therefore, SSIS provides an easy way to load new fact and dimension data into your current cube using SSIS transforms. The two transforms that help in loading such data are the partition processing transform and the dimension processing transform.

Many large retail stores still use flat files to extract data from the transactional systems. Your company probably does the same. Often the columns in the flat files do not contain clean data. During the staging process you clean the data and format it with appropriate IDs that match your cube in order to load the data into your cube. SSIS provides transformations to do lookups, get the correct ids, clean the data on the fly, and then load the data into your cube. In the following example you will be working with clean data that needs to be loaded from a flat file into one of the partitions of the AnalysisServices2005Tutorial cube:

1. Create a new SSIS package under the SSIS packages folder and name it PipelineDataLoad.

2. The SSIS task that helps you to read data, perform transforms, and then push the data into a destination is called the Data Flow task. Drag and drop the Data Flow task into your SSIS editor as shown in Figure 16-16 and name it Data Flow Partition Load.

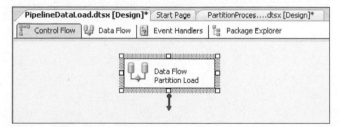

Figure 16-16

3. Double-click the Data Flow task. You will now be in the Data Flow view. The Toolbox window will show you the SSIS transforms available for use in the Data Flow view. The data flow transforms are categorized into three main areas, namely, data flow sources, data flow transformations, and data flow destinations. Data to be loaded into the partition of the Analysis Services 2005 Tutorial cube is provided as a flat file in the Chapter16Samples folder named AdventureWorksPartition3 Data.txt. To retrieve this data you need to use the Flat File Source transform. This data needs to be pushed to the partition in the Analysis Services2005Tutorial cube. Therefore, you need a Partition Processing transform. Drag and drop the Flat file source and Partition processing transforms from the Toolbox to the Data Flow editor and join them through the connector as shown in Figure 16-17.

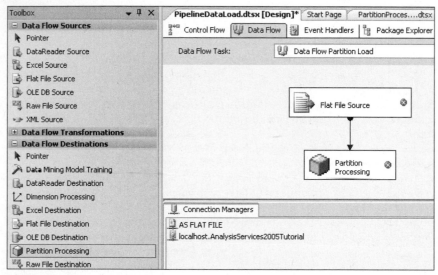

Figure 16-17

4. Double-click the Flat File Source transform to specify the connection to the flat file. You will now be in the Flat File Source Editor as shown in Figure 16-18. You need to specify the flat file using the Flat file connection manager. Click the New button.

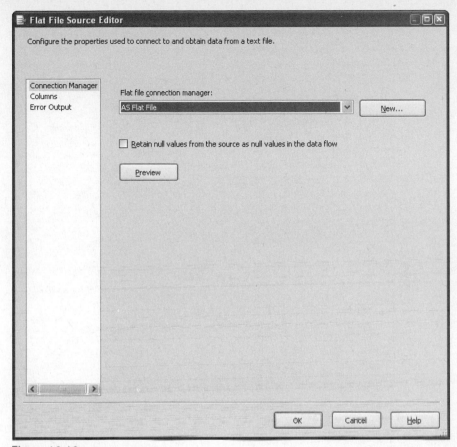

Figure 16-18

5. The flat file connection manger dialog as shown in Figure 16-19 now pops up. Click the Browse button and select the flat file AdventureWorksPartition3Data.txt which is available for download from the book web site. The dialog now parses the data in the flat file. You need to specify the type of delimiter used in the flat file to separate the columns. Click on the Columns and choose the delimiter as comma, see Figure 16-20. You also have the option to skip rows from the flat file if the first row or the first few rows indicate column headers. Click on the check box Column names in the first datarow. To see if the dialog is able to read the data from the flat file correctly based on the delimiter, click the columns property

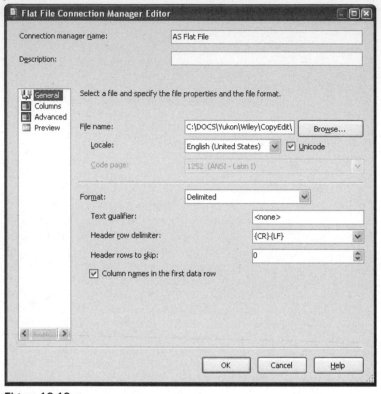

Figure 16-19

6. You will now see the data from the flat file organized as rows and columns as shown in Figure 16-20. After you have confirmed that the dialog is able to read the data in the flat file, click OK.

7. In the flat file editor dialog click on the Columns as shown in Figure 16-21. By default SSIS will use the column names to be the output column names. You can change the output column names in this dialog by editing the appropriate row. Leave the default names suggested by SSIS and click OK.

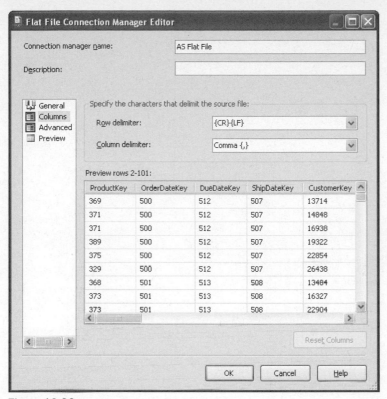

Figure 16-20

8. After configuring the flat file source, you need to specify the partition into which this data needs to be loaded. Click the partition processing transform in the SSIS data flow view editor. You can now see the partition processing connection editor as shown in Figure 16-22. Similar to the first two SSIS packages, you need to specify the connection to the database. Click the New button to specify the connection to AnalysisServices2005Tutorial database. You will now see the cubes and partitions within the database.

9. Select the partition under which the data needs to be loaded and specify the processing method that needs to be applied. If the data is new you typically need to use the Add (Incremental) option that processes the partition incrementally. Processing the partition incrementally means that the new data will be incrementally added to the cube while the current data is available for querying. Once the new data has been processed, the data is committed and it is available for querying. The incremental processing method's primary functionality is to serve the customer's queries even when the new data is being added to the partition. Analysis Services is able to accomplish this by cloning the existing version of the partition and adding data to that. Once the entire data has been processed in the new version of the partition, and when the original partition is free from any query locks, Analysis Services switches the versions and the new version containing the entire data set is now available for querying. Select the Fact Internet Sales Partition2 as the partition to add the data and Add (incremental) as the processing method as shown in Figure 16-22.

Figure 16-21

A more typical package using the partition processing transform will contain several lookup transforms to map the incoming dimension columns to the right id in the dimensions of the OLAP database. Once the correct ids for each dimension are obtained, retrieved dimension id columns are mapped to the partition processing columns to load the data.

10. Click on the Mappings as shown in Figure 16-23 to specify the right mappings from the columns from the flat file to the columns in the partition. The columns in the flat file have been specified to be the same names as the ones in the cube. Hence you will find it easy to map each column directly as shown in Figure 16-23. Make sure you mark all the columns correctly in this page. You can ignore the Dim Geography.Dim Geography destination column since Dim Geography is a reference dimension and hence the key for this dimension does not exist in the fact table. Click OK after completing all the mappings in the Partition Processing Destination Editor.

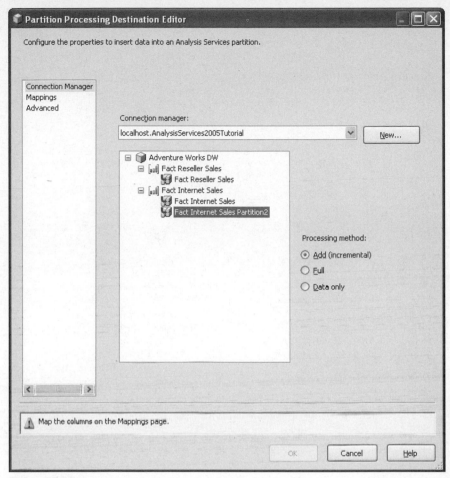

Figure 16-22

11. You have completed all the necessary settings in the SSIS package to load data into a partition. Hit the F5 key to test the execution of your SSIS package. You will see that the background colors of the two data flow transforms Flat File Source and Partition Processing are highlighted in yellow indicating that the SSIS package is being executed. Along the connector line between the two transforms you can notice the number of rows being processed. Figure 16-24 shows a snapshot of the SSIS package execution. After all the data has been loaded without errors you will see the background color of the two transforms turn to green indicating successful completion of the package. During this SSIS operation that does incremental processing, Analysis Services creates a new temporary partition, loads the data from flat file, and then merges the partition to Internet Sales Partition 2.

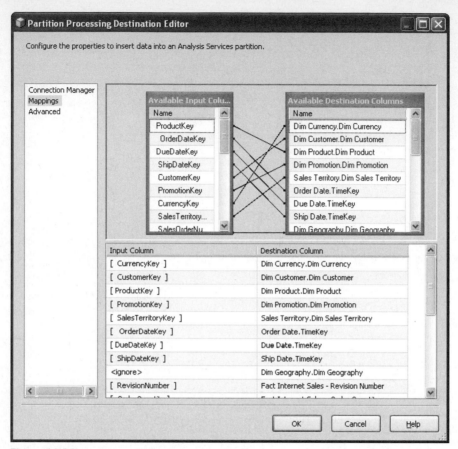

Figure 16-23

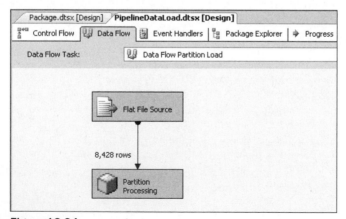

Figure 16-24

In the above data load example there was one-to-one mapping between the columns in the flat file and the measures and granularity attributes of the partitions, except for the reference dimension granularity attribute DimGeography. This was possible because all the measures in the partition directly mapped to the columns in the flat file. Assume you have a fact data column that was used twice in a measure group as two measures: one with sum as the aggregation function and another as count or distinct count as aggregation functions. Such a scenario is pretty common. In this scenario you will not be able to map the corresponding column from the flat file to the two measures since SSIS partition processing transform disallows a column from the source (in this example flat file) to be mapped to multiple destination columns that are part of the partition. If you ignore mappings even for a single destination column that is part of the partition, your data load will fail. You would need to either have additional column(s) in the source so that you can map those to the corresponding columns in the partition or use SSIS transform Copy Column to duplicate existing column(s) to serve as input to the partition processing transform. We recommend you modify the AdventureWorks2005Tutorial database to have a distinct count measure in Internet Sales partition and then create an SSIS package with Copy Column transform between flat file data source and partition processing transform to map the column from fact file to the distinct count measure.

You have successfully learned to create SSIS packages for performing administrative tasks on Analysis Services such as backup and processing. Other administrative tasks such as synchronization, restore, etc., can be performed using the tasks and transforms provided by SSIS. In addition to providing tasks and transforms for OLAP features, SSIS also provides tasks and transforms data mining to perform administrative tasks, as well as querying, which you learn in the next section.

Integration Services Tasks for Data Mining

SSIS 2005 provides tasks and transforms specifically targeted for Data Mining objects in Analysis Services 2005. With the Data Mining Query task you can query mining models and store the results in a destination like a relational database. One of the common uses of such a task is to predict a list of customers for a targeted marketing campaign. If the company wants to offer promotional discounts to targeted customers every month, they would predict if a new customer is valuable based on the customer's attributes, calculate an appropriate discount, and mail them a coupon. The data mining query transform is used when you want to manipulate the source data to the mining model or the output of the mining model in a better format. For examples and illustrations of Integration Services Tasks for Data Mining please refer to *Professional SQL Server 2005 Integration Services* by Brian Knight, et al. (Wiley, 2005).

Automating SSIS Packages

Integration Services works on a slightly different model compared to Analysis Services. With Analysis Services, you deploy projects to the server; not so with Integration Services. There are three ways to make a package available to Integration Services, first through SQL Server, second through the file system, and finally through the SSIS Package Store (which is a variant of the file system solution). Here we'll look at the file system approach. Specifically, from BIDS, you save off a package in the form of an XML file (a .dtsx file). You might be wondering why the extension dtsx. Well, as mentioned earlier SSIS was originally called DTS in SQL Server 2000 and hence the file extension starts with dts. You can see the source for a .dtsx by right clicking on a package in Solution Explorer and selecting View Code. After you check that out, do the following:

1. In BIDS Solution Explorer, right-click on one of your working packages and select File⇨Save <filename> As... and give the file a descriptive name. In this way you save off an XML version of the package to the file system. Next, open up SSMS and connect to Integration Services; open it in object explorer and right-click on Stored Packages. At this point you can select Import Package... as shown in Figure 16-25.

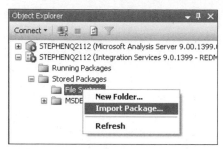

Figure 16-25

2. The Import Package dialog will appear and you should change Package location from SQL Server to File System. Then click the button associated with Package path to specify the dtsx file you want. If you just click on the Package name text entry box, it will fill in the package name for you. At this point, the dialog should look something like Figure 16-26.

Import Package	
Package location:	File System
Server:	
Authentication	
Authentication type:	Windows Authentication
User name:	
Password:	
Package path:	C:\IS_PACKAGES\PROCESSOR.dtsx
Import package as	
Package name:	PROCESSOR
Protection level:	
	OK Cancel Help

Figure 16-26

With the package in the Stored Packages area, you can easily run it by right-clicking the package name and selecting Run Package. What we really want to be able to do, however, is schedule to have our package run on a regular basis so we don't have to think about it. Scheduling SSIS packages to be run periodically can be accomplished by using the SQL Server Agent. The Agent is its own process which you can access by opening a connection to the Database Engine as shown in Figure 16-27.

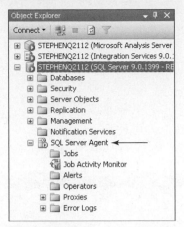

Figure 16-27

3.   To create a scheduled job, right-click on the Jobs folder and select New Job. Give it an appropriate name and description as shown in Figure 16-28.

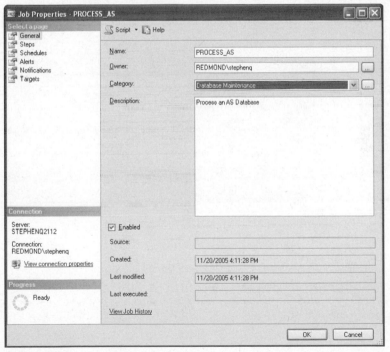

Figure 16-28

On the Select a page pane at the top click on Steps and then the New... button that appears at the bottom of the dialog. On the New Job Step page, name your step PROCESS_AS and under Type (type of operation) select SQL Server Integration Services Package as shown in Figure 16-29.

For Package source you need to select File system (since we will use the dtsx previously saved to the File system).

Click on the ellipsis button for Package and select the package you saved before. At this time, your New Job Step dialog should look something like the one in Figure 16-29. Click OK to continue; when you are asked if the On Success action is intended, click Yes.

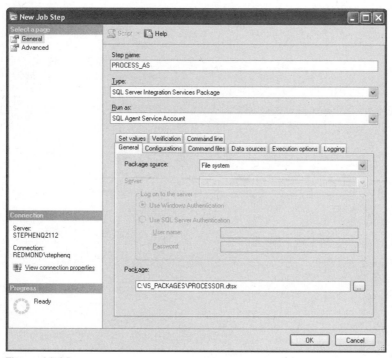

Figure 16-29

4. On the Select a page pane at the top right, click on Schedules and then the New... button that appears at the bottom of the dialog. The dialog that comes up now is the New Job Schedule dialog; it is here that you can schedule your package to be run on a recurring basis. For illustrative purposes, we'll select Schedule type: One time. Select today's date with a time of five minutes from now. After you have entered the details your Job Scheduler dialog should resemble Figure 16-30.

5. To see the job kicked off as scheduled, you only need to double-click on the Job Activity Monitor icon which is under the SQL Server Agent Folder in SSMS's Object Explorer. Once your job starts, you will see the Status change to Executing as shown in Figure 16-31.

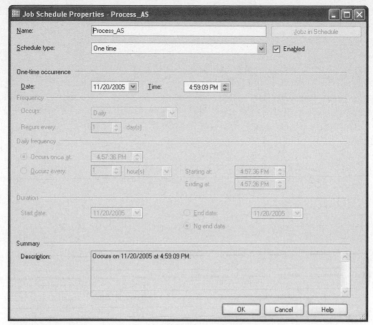

Figure 16-30

Figure 16-31

We're sure you can see the power of this approach. The ability to create packages chock full of administrative functions to manage your instance of Analysis Services — all scheduled to run on a recurring basis and send out emails based on success or failure. This is great stuff, especially for users who want to automate as much as possible and utilize their remaining time to learn and implement new things! We are confident you have gained sufficient knowledge of SSIS by now that you can create Analysis Services SSIS packages and schedule them. Make a habit of using SSIS when and where applicable for your business.

Summary

Integration Services provides the infrastructure for all sorts of automated tasks from data cleansing, data split to data merging. In this chapter you learned that a package must have a control flow and may also have data flows; the control flow is represented by tasks and containers, which are connected by precedence constraints. These precedence constraints determine the fate of a control flow after each step is completed. The precedence constraint can be an expression that leads to a success or failure condition, or the constraint can be set to "completion" without further consideration for continued control flow.

Finally, you learned how to import packages into Integration Services using SSMS and create scheduled jobs of packages using SQL Server Agent.

In the previous chapter summary, you were promised a wonderful synergy between Integration Services and Analysis Services, and from the section on "Creating Integration Services Packages for Analysis Services Operations" to "Automating SSIS packages," you got it! The fun is not over, because in the next chapter, you learn about yet another profound and cool form of product synergy. Only this time it is about integrating Business Intelligence with Reporting Services. There is some amazing stuff in store, like designing static and ad-hoc reports on top of UDM. Don't miss it!

Part IV
Scenarios

17

Reporting Services

Microsoft first introduced Reporting Services in January of 2004 under the title SQL Server 2000 Reporting Services. Since that time it has become an award-winning product (see *Intelligent Enterprise* Reader's Choice award for Ad Hoc Query & Reporting, 2004). More importantly, Reporting Services has become critical to many business intelligence suite implementations. Face it, reporting is the centerpiece for consumption of business intelligence information. Sure, doing the number crunching and actual decision-making are important and not reporting related per se, but you will want to cover all the bases and complete the job right. And to accomplish that you can even do better than just create tabular reports; you can create charts that show the results in a much more appealing and easy-to-understand fashion. Related to that is the ability to embed your own custom static graphics in your reports, like your company logo, for example. Some companies out there integrate seamlessly with Reporting Services to provide additional enhancements beyond those described here; one such company is Panorama Software (http://www.panorama.com/), whose products provide drag-and-drop placement of report objects in reports for use against Reporting Services.

Even after all the cool integration discussed in the Integration Services chapter, you will see that what you are about to read here is similarly cool, if not blatantly hip. Not only can reports be built by dragging and dropping data objects onto a canvas with SQL subsequently generated behind the scenes, but you can also drag and drop Analysis Services–specific objects, like dimensions and calculated members, onto that same canvas with MDX subsequently generated behind the scenes. Using the report designer you can design reports from relational as well as multidimensional databases. Indeed, you get to use a highly integrated business intelligence reporting infrastructure that requires little more than drag-and-drop techniques to create reports.

In an effort to realize the great techniques just discussed, you learn to do the following things in this chapter: how to create a report on top of a relational database, deploy that report to the reports server, and then browse it locally or over your corpnet. You learn to create a report using an Analysis Services database from the report wizard, and further enhance your Analysis Services reporting skills by creating calculated members and using specific properties within a report. You also learn to create charts in reports for better representation of data, how to manage reports from the Reports Server front end, and finally, how to build ad-hoc reports from a UDM using the report builder capability.

Report Designer

As the name suggests, the Report Designer is used to create the infrastructure of and layout for a report. The infrastructure first requires specification of one or more data sources. Data sources supported include anything accessible through the list of Providers shown in the Data Link Properties dialog (what you're used to seeing when creating data sources for other purposes). For the extraction of specific data, you have query builders that facilitate the query building process. This is built into Business Intelligence Development Studio and hosts a similar look and feel to Analysis Services and Integration Services projects. These tools enable the creation of tabular and matrix-based reports. In addition, charts are also supported. You can customize your report to span multiple pages based on conditionals and grouping; this capability supports readability as does the judicious use of fonts and colors. Note that less is often more when it comes to things like fonts and colors; the fewer variations displayed in a report, the more meaningful are those that are used. So, for best results, use the power of customization sparingly! If you are not already dizzy from wielding all this power, note that you can specify parametric reports and subreports. And the user can seamlessly navigate all these reports because you can provide clickable cells in the reports. Once you have defined your report, it can be previewed within the designer; only after you are pleased with the layout do you deploy the report to a report server.

Report Definition Language

Report Definition Language (RDL) is an XML-based language used to specify all the characteristics which make up a report; RDL is created in the Report Designer and manifests itself when a report is processed and viewed. When you create your report, all the definitions are in this form of XML. It is this definition that is deployed on to the server. If you are a reporting whiz, you might take to editing RDL files easily; all of the element definitions and appropriate XML Diagrams are described in Books On-Line. Beware that any malformed XML you feed the report server will likely have less than desirable consequences at runtime! The following table shows some sample report definition XML elements from Books On-Line:

Element	Parent	Description
Axis	CategoryAxis, ValueAxis	Defines properties for labels, titles, and gridlines on an axis.
DataCollectionName	Grouping	Contains the name of the data element of the collection containing all instances of the group in a report rendered using a data rendering extension, like the XML rendering extension.
Parameters	Drill-through, Subreport	Contains a list of parameters to pass to the report or control.
Visible	Axis, DataLabel, Legend	Indicates whether the item is displayed in the chart.

Report Wizard

There is no shame in using the Report Wizard. It is a time-saving device that simplifies the creation of the most basic reports; actually, you can get as sophisticated as you like in terms of query building because the Query Builder is covered in the wizard. Of course, you also have the option to create reports without use of the report wizard.

Report Server

As the name suggests; the Report Server "serves" reports to users. The manageability of the Report Server is provided through a web interface as well as through SSMS (SQL Server Management Studio). Some of the management tasks on Report Server include credentials definition which is needed by Report Server to retrieve data from the data source, to provide appropriate access to the reports for end users and to define report execution schedule. You can cache the results of a report on Report Server, which really comes in handy when the report takes a long time to run (a batch SQL query is used to do this).

Creating a Report on Relational Database

The Report Designer is used to design reports based on a relational database. The Report Designer provides the functionality to retrieve data from various data sources, design the actual report and, finally, deploy it. The report designer also allows you to preview the report before you deploy to the report server and provide subsequent access to various users. In this section you will be designing a report on Sales of products from the Adventure Works DW database. To design this report, perform the following steps:

1. Launch the BIDS and create a new Project.

2. In the Business Intelligence Projects Project Type, select Report Project and provide a new project name, as shown in Figure 17-1.

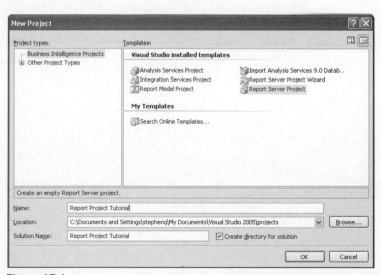

Figure 17-1

3. You will see two folders called Shared Data Sources and Reports in the Solution Explorer window. The Shared Data Sources folder is used to share data sources between multiple reports. Right-click the Reports folder and select Add New Report, as shown in Figure 17-2, to launch the Report Wizard.

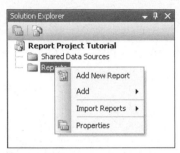

Figure 17-2

4. If you get the "Welcome" page, dismiss it. The first real page of the Report Wizard allows you to specify the data source. The default data source type is Microsoft SQL Server, as shown in Figure 17-3. Click Edit to specify the data source connection detail.

Figure 17-3

5. In this example you will be creating a report based on the Adventure Works DW relational database. Specify the connection details in the Connection Properties dialog as shown in Figure 17-4. Click OK once you have tested the connection to the data source using the Test Connection button.

Figure 17-4

6. Click Next to see the Report Wizard's "Design the Query" page; here you will form the query to retrieve data from the relational data source using a query builder. Click Query Builder to launch the Query Builder page.

7. The default query builder page is a generic query builder that can be used against any relational data source. Click the leftmost icon on the query builder page to switch over to a graphical designer user interface. This query builder has four panes as shown in Figure 17-5.

❑ Initially the Table organizer pane is empty. Right-click within this pane and select Add Table. You will see the list of tables available within the AdventureWorksDW database. Select the FactInternetSales, DimTime, DimProduct, and DimProductSubcategory tables and click Add. The query builder will retrieve the relationships between tables from the database and show them graphically in the Table Designer pane (see Figure 17-6). You can select the required columns from the table designer pane by clicking the check boxes adjacent to the columns. The designer in the Query pane will create appropriate SQL queries. You can edit the selections in the Column chooser pane or the query directly in the query pane. The query used for retrieving the sales information in Figure 17-5 is shown below. Enter the SQL query in the query designer.

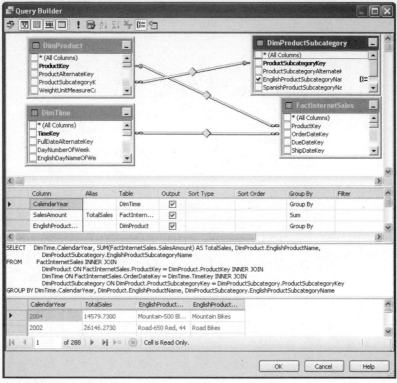

Figure 17-5

```
SELECT   DimTime.CalendarYear, SUM(FactInternetSales.SalesAmount) AS TotalSales,
     DimProduct.EnglishProductName,
     DimProductSubcategory.EnglishProductSubcategoryName
FROM   FactInternetSales INNER JOIN
     DimProduct ON FactInternetSales.ProductKey = DimProduct.ProductKey
     INNER JOIN
     DimTime ON FactInternetSales.OrderDateKey = DimTime.TimeKey INNER JOIN
     DimProductSubcategory ON DimProduct.ProductSubcategoryKey =
     DimProductSubcategory.ProductSubcategoryKey
GROUP BY  DimTime.CalendarYear,
     DimProduct.EnglishProductName,
     DimProductSubcategory.EnglishProductSubcategoryName
```

If you already have a SQL query from which you want to create your report, you can type the query in the query pane. The query designer will validate the query. If you click the exclamation (!) icon in the Query Builder page you can see the results of the query in the results pane near the bottom of Figure 17-5. Click OK after you have completed the query and click Next in the Report Wizard.

8. Next, you need to select the type of report to create; the two forms of report available are the tabular report and the matrix report. In the tabular report, the report contains the values in the row column format similar to the relational tables. The columns have a header corresponding to the column and each row contains the values. In the matrix report there are headers for rows

and columns and each cell in the report corresponds to a specific row and column. For example, you can have Time on rows and Cities on columns and the cells will indicate the sales amount of a product or a store for a given time and a city. Select the tabular report type and click Next.

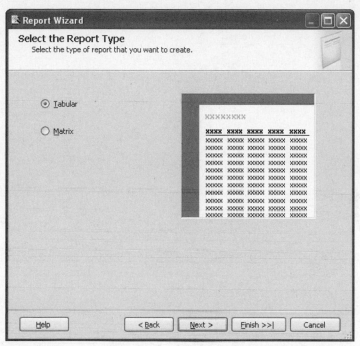

Figure 17-6

9. On the Design the Table page, you can choose the results from the data source to be shown in the report as well as how you want to show them. You can move the fields to one of the Page, Group, or Details panes. If you choose a specific field on the page, then for each value of that field a new page will be created that shows the fields in groups and details. A typical example would be to show the sales of products by each year or by each store. In this example you will be creating a report that creates a new page for the sales of products for each year. Select the CalendarYear field and click the Page button. Rows can be grouped based on a specific field. For example, sales of various sizes of televisions in a store can be grouped under a category called TVs. In this example you will be grouping the sales of products based on the subcategory name. Grouping helps you to organize reports for enhanced readability. Select the EnglishProductSubCategoryName and click the Group button. Typically there is a one-to-many relationship between a field in the group and the fields in the details. The fields in the group are shown exactly once in the report. Select the fields for the detail level reporting. Select the TotalSales and EngineProductName fields and click the Details button. Your Design the Table page should look like Figure 17-7. Click Next.

10. On the Choose the Table Layout page you can choose the layout of the report, specify the visual layout, and include subtotals for groups. The Enable Drilldown option, which allows you to drill down into the details of the report, can be enabled here too. Stepped and block report styles are quite similar; they only differ due to the values being housed in a block. If you click the options you can judge the visual impact of the final report. Select the desired options in the table layout page as shown in Figure 17-8 and click Next.

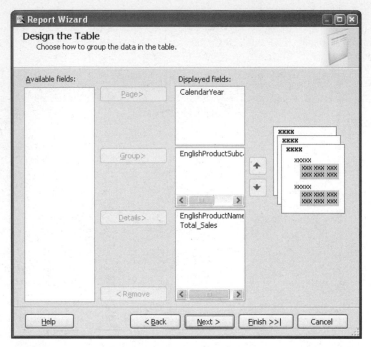

Figure 17-7

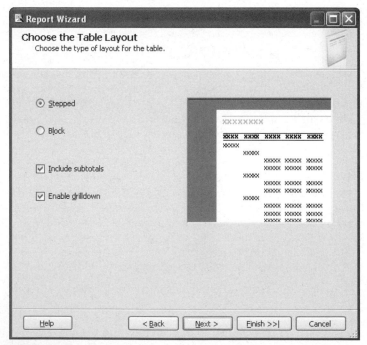

Figure 17-8

11. The next page of the Report Wizard provides you the option to choose predefined report styles or templates. When you select the specific option you can see a preview of the style within the pane on the right side. The slate style is shown in Figure 17-9. Select the template of your choice and click Next.

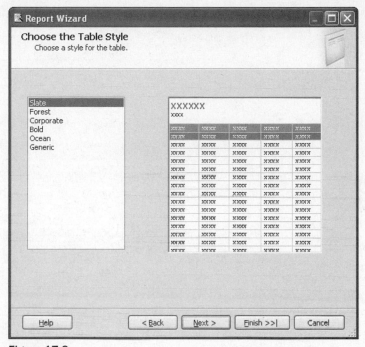

Figure 17-9

12. In the final page of the Report Wizard you can specify the name of your report. Enter the name AdventureWorksDWSalesRelationalReport and click Finish. You have now successfully created your first report using Reporting Services 2005.

The Report Wizard creates the RDL for the report you designed, and you will now be in the Report Designer as shown in Figure 17-10. The Report Editor has three tabs: Data, Layout, and Preview. The Data view is used for editing data sources or the query so that you can modify your report accordingly. The Layout view is the main view where you design your report. The Preview pane helps you to preview the report within the report designer with your current credentials. The list of report items available to build your report is within the Toolbox window. If you do not have the Toolbox window showing, just select the menu item "View" and click on "Toolbox" under that.

Now that you have created the report, you no doubt want to see a preview. Click the Preview tab to view the report you have created. Figure 17-11 shows the preview of the report you have created. This report spans multiple pages, one page for each Calendar Year. You have controls to move between various pages. Within each page you can see the product subcategories along with the sales information. Because the report is grouped and you selected the drilldown option, the default view of the report does not show all the details. You can click the + sign associated with a product subcategory to see the details of the total sales of that product category.

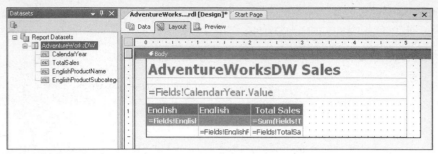

Figure 17-10

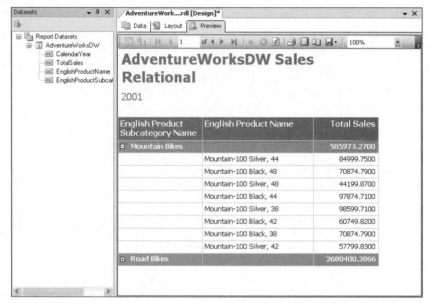

Figure 17-11

Creating Reports Based on a UDM

You have so far seen some capabilities provided by Reporting Services 2005 and how it can facilitate the creation of reports from a relational database. In Chapter 16 you learned the tight integration of Analysis Services with Integration Services that helps you load data into Analysis Services and perform administrative operations. By adding to those functions, Reporting Services 2005 provides you the ability to create reports from the UDM by which Microsoft's SQL Server 2005 provides a truly end-to-end business intelligence solution to the market. Designing reports from Analysis Services 2005 databases is actually similar to designing reports from a relational database using Reporting Services 2005.

In the event you have experience with Reporting Services 2000, you will be excited to know that Reporting Services 2005 contains both new features and extended capabilities associated with the original feature set.

In Reporting Services 2000, specifying an MDX query and using the OLEDB provider for Analysis Services to integrate cube-based data into your reports was about the extent of the integration between the two products. There are significant improvements on that model; you will find much tighter integration exists between Reporting Services 2005 and Analysis Services 2005. Specifically, the product now has an MDX query designer, which enables you to retrieve data from any UDM through the technique of drag and drop, without you actually having to understand and write MDX queries. Assuming you worked through this whole book, you already know some MDX, but in the event you are a shameless chapter surfer who started here, well, you're in luck.

Some other points more than merit mention here. In the 2000 version, you could only pass a single parameter to Analysis Services from a Report for dynamic report building. For example, you could send a single country name. Now, you can send a whole list of country names as parameters; this enhances what you can accomplish in terms of building dynamic reports. The ability to retrieve intrinsic properties for dimension members and cells is intact with 2005, not to mention accessing member and extended properties. You are sure to love this next one—Reporting Services 2005 takes advantage of aggregated data provided by Analysis Services! This helps increase performance of report processing—especially when there is a large amount of source detail-level data (like sales per store) and the report includes aggregations based on that (like sales per region.) There is much to like about the integration between Reporting Services and Analysis Services in this SQL Server 2005; report building directly off a UDM, for one, is awesome.

Designing Your Analysis Services Report

In this section you create a sales report from the UDM for AdventureWorks2005Tutorial using the Report Wizard. You later refine the report based on certain requirements surprisingly imposed by your boss at the last moment. At the end of this section you will be familiar with creating specialized reports on a UDM. The following steps will help you to build reports from Analysis Services by establishing a connection to Analysis Services, building the MDX query, and previewing the report. Follow the steps to create your Analysis Services reports:

1. Open the AdventureWorks2005Tutorial under Chapter17 and deploy it to your Analysis Services instance.

2. Right-click the Reports folder and select Add⇨New Item. Select the Report Wizard and click the Add button. If a Welcome to the Report Wizard page appears, click Next.

3. The first step in the Report Wizard is to provide the connection details to the data source. In the Data Source Wizard select the Microsoft SQL Server Analysis Services option for data source type, as shown in Figure 17-12. Then click Edit.

4. Click the Edit button in the Select Data Source page to launch the Connection Properties dialog. In the Connection Properties dialog enter the machine name of your Analysis Services instance, select the AdventureWorks2005Tutorial project as shown in Figure 17-13, and test your connection. Once your connection has been tested successfully, click OK.

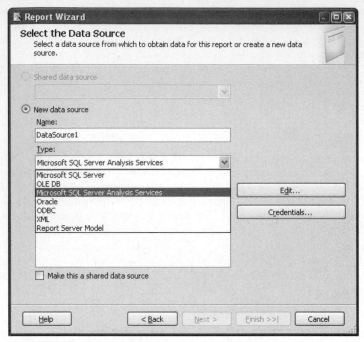

Figure 17-12

Figure 17-13

5. The next page of the Report Wizard is the Query Builder page. Click the Query Builder button to launch the MDX query builder shown in Figure 17-14. The MDX query builder contains a metadata pane where you can select a specific cube from the database and see the measures and dimensions of the cube. There is a pane in which you can specify calculated members that will be within the scope of the query sent to your Analysis Services instance. There is a filter pane to restrict data, and finally, there is a data pane where you can drag and drop the dimensions and measures that you want to include in your report.

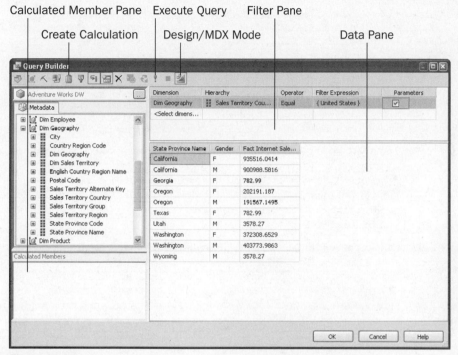

Figure 17-14

6. Drag and drop the measure Fact Internet Sales-Sales Amount from the metadata pane to the data pane. At this moment the MDX query builder creates the MDX query to retrieve the selected measure from the Analysis Services instance and shows the results in the data pane. Using the Report Wizard you will create a report of Internet sales of products in the U.S. along with the customer's gender information. Drag and drop the gender attribute hierarchy from the customer's dimension and the State Province Name attribute hierarchy from the geography dimension, which indicates the customer's geographical location. You will now see results set in the data pane. Because the UDM contains Internet sales information from various countries, you see the data for all the provinces of various countries.

7. To restrict the data to the provinces in the United States, drag and drop the Sales territory country attribute from the geography dimension to the filter pane. Similar to filtering data while browsing a UDM, set the filter expression equal to United States by selecting the United States member. You will see the Internet Sales from various provinces within the United States along

with the gender of the customer as shown in Figure 17-14. You can see the MDX query by switching from the graphical design view to the MDX query view by clicking on the Design/MDX icon shown in Figure 17-14.

❑ The MDX query generated by the query builder (which you can happily ignore if so inclined) is

```
SELECT NON EMPTY { [Measures].[Fact Internet Sales - Sales Amount] } ON COLUMNS,
 NON EMPTY { ([Dim Geography].[State Province Name].[State Province
Name].ALLMEMBERS
 * [Dim Customer].[Gender].[Gender].ALLMEMBERS ) }
DIMENSION PROPERTIES MEMBER_CAPTION, MEMBER_UNIQUE_NAME ON ROWS
FROM
( SELECT ( { [Dim Geography].[Sales Territory Country].&[United States] } )
ON COLUMNS
FROM [Adventure Works DW])
WHERE ( [Dim Geography].[Sales Territory Country].&[United States] )
CELL PROPERTIES VALUE, BACK_COLOR, FORE_COLOR,
FORMATTED_VALUE, FORMAT_STRING, FONT_NAME, FONT_SIZE, FONT_FLAGS
```

❑ The query generated by the MDX query builder within Report Designer is an MDX sub-select query, which you learned about in Chapter 7. The above query contains two MDX select queries. The inner SELECT query restricts the cube space based on the member [Dim Geography].[Sales Territory Country].[Sales Territory Country].&[United States], and the outer SELECT query retrieves the data within the cube space provided by the inner SELECT query.

❑ One important thing you should be aware of in the MDX query builder is that if you switch from the design view to the MDX view and make changes, at that point you are at risk of losing the original configuration built in the design view if you then return to the design view. Therefore, we do not recommend that particular action — if you want to return to the design view. In the design view as you drag and drop fields, the automatically generated MDX query is executed immediately and displays the results. If you know that your query is going to retrieve a large result set, you can turn off the autoexecute query mode using the icon in the toolbar or by right-clicking in the result pane and deselecting auto-execute mode. If you are an MDX expert, you might actually prefer to use the MDX view. In such a circumstance, switch to the MDX view, type in your MDX query, and then click Execute to ensure your query is correct and returns results expected by you. Click OK once you have selected the fields you need for the query.

8. The MDX query will now be shown in the Design the Query page, as shown in Figure 17-15. Click the Next button.

9. In the Select the Report type page select the Tabular report which is the default option and click Next.

10. In the Design the Table page you will see the three fields you selected in the MDX query builder. In this report you will group the sales of customers based on the provinces. Therefore, select the State_Province_Field and click on the Group button to move the field to the Group pane. Select the fields Customer Gender and Fact_Internet_Sales__Sales_Amount fields and click on the Details button to move the fields to the Details pane as shown in Figure 17-16.

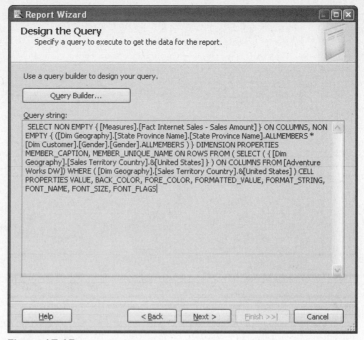

Figure 17-15

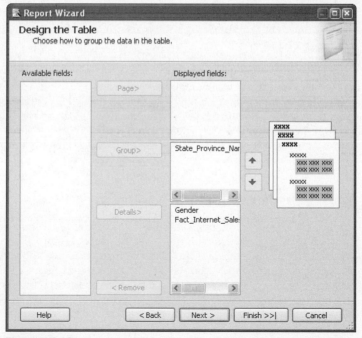

Figure 17-16

11. Similar to the relational report you created earlier, select Stepped layout in the next page. Select the option to have subtotals displayed as well as enable drilldown in this page as shown in Figure 17-17 and click the Finish button. In the Final page of the wizard, name the report AnalysisServicesSalesReport and click the Finish button.

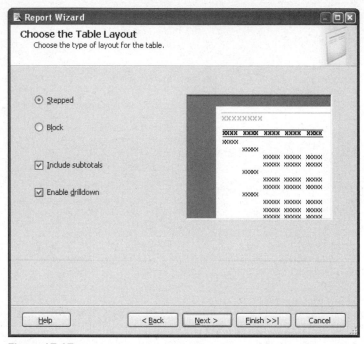

Figure 17-17

12. You will now be in the Layout view of the Report Designer. Click the various items in the layout such as the table and the grouping row within the table based on the State Province, and look at their properties to have a brief overview of how the Report Wizard created your layout. Once you have created your report, you will want to see the behavior of the report before you deploy it on to your Report server. To preview your report, click the Preview tab. You will now see a report as shown in Figure 17-18.

Enhancing Your Analysis Services Report

You have successfully created your first report on top of a UDM. This is a very basic report. The report you created in the previous section only includes the Fact Internet Sales information for the states within the U.S. and the genders of various customers. In this section you enhance your report by including the countries, and instead of sales information you will be creating a report that shows sales profits of each state for various years. Follow the steps below to enhance your report.

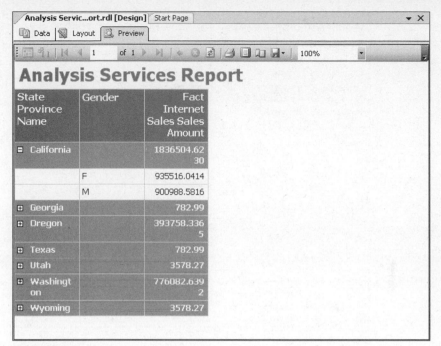

Figure 17-18

First you need to change the query that retrieves the results from your Analysis Service instance. To change the MDX query, switch from the Preview pane to the Data pane. The Data pane is nothing but the MDX query builder you saw in the Report Wizard. Since your new report needs to include the profit, you need to create a measure that will calculate the profit. The Adventure Works DW cube contains measures for Internet and Reseller sales along with the cost of the products sold over Internet and Reseller sales. You need to create calculated members in the cube to aggregate these data and then calculate the profit. Instead of creating these calculated measures within the cube, you know you can create calculated measures in an MDX query using the WITH MEMBER clause, which you learned in Chapter 3. The MDX query designer allows you to graphically specify these calculated members instead of writing the full MDX query. Creating the calculated members using the designer allows you to still work in the design mode.

1. To create a calculated measure Total Sales, click the calculator icon or right-click in the Calculated Members pane and select New. The Calculated Member Builder dialog shown in Figure 17-19 will be launched.

2. Type Total Sales Amount in the Name text box for the calculated measure. Drag and drop the Sales Amounts from Internet and Reseller Sales measure groups from the Metadata pane and add a plus (+) sign between these measures as shown in Figure 17-19. Click OK to create the calculated measure.

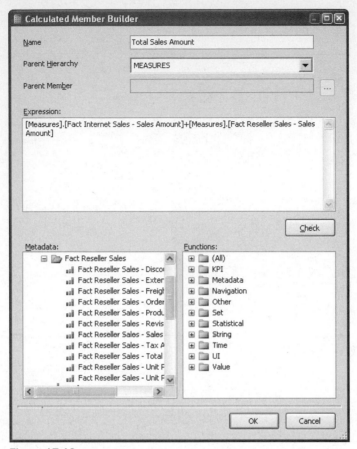

Figure 17-19

3. Create a calculated measure called Total Product Cost as the sum of the product costs of the Products sold via Internet and Reseller.

4. Create a calculated measure called Total Profit, which is the difference between the numerical values in the calculated measures Total Sales Amount and Total Product Cost. You will now see the three calculated measures in the calculated members' pane of the query builder as shown in Figure 17-20.

5. Remove the Internet sales amount measure from the result pane by dragging and dropping the field from Result pane to the Metadata pane or by selecting the field, right-clicking, and selecting Remove. Similarly remove the field Gender from the data pane. Drag and drop the calculated member Total Profit from the Calculated Members pane to the Result pane. Add the attribute hierarchy Sales Territory Country from the Geography dimension and Calendar Year hierarchy from the Order Date dimension to the data field as shown in Figure 17-21.

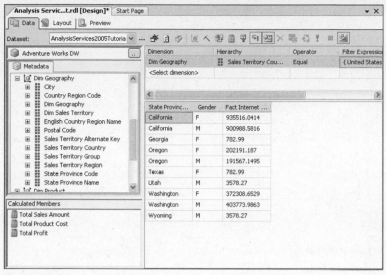

Figure 17-20

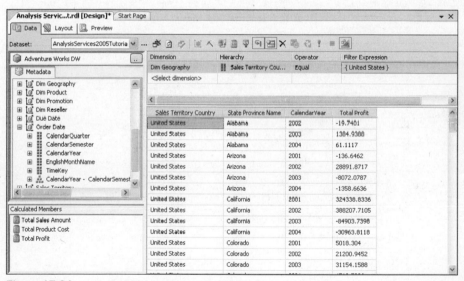

Figure 17-21

6. Click the filter Sales Territory Country and drop-down the filter expression list box. Select all the countries except N/A and Unknown from the list as shown in Figure 17-22.

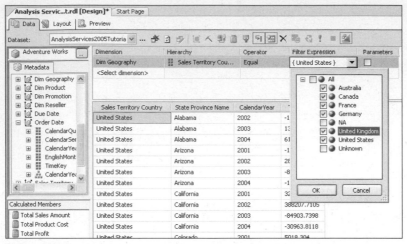

Figure 17-22

The Result pane now shows the Sales profit for various countries and provinces for all the years, as shown in Figure 17-23. Now you have all the data required for enhancing your report.

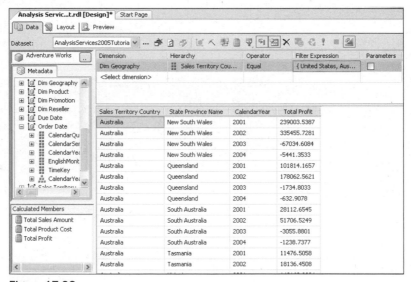

Figure 17-23

7.   Switch from the Data pane to the Layout pane. The Layout pane contains an object that includes the fields State Province Name, Gender, and Fact Internet sales as shown in Figure 17-24. This object is called a table. A table report item is used whenever you have multiple rows of data to show. Select the existing table object, right-click, and select delete to delete the table. You can see

the fields from the new Result pane in the Datasets pane as shown in Figure 17-24. You will use the new fields to re-design the report.

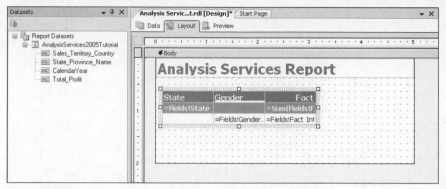

Figure 17-24

8. In your report you need the profits of each country to be seen on different pages. In order to design such a report you need a report item called List in your report designer layout. Click the toolbox window and drag and drop the report item List to your report designer layout below the title of the report as shown in Figure 17-25. If you cannot see the tool box window select Toolbox from the View menu item. You now need to select the field by which you want to group the details of the report. To select this field, click the properties window for the List report item and launch the dialog to select the grouping property of this list item. You will now see the dialog shown in Figure 17-26. Select the Country field.

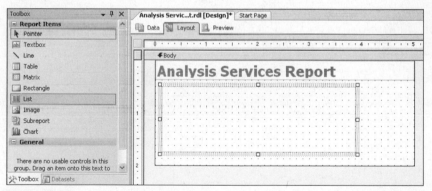

Figure 17-25

9. Next, drag and drop the Table report item within the List item. You want to group the yearly sales based on the states. To see a grouped report, right-click one of the rows of the table report item and select Insert Group. You will now see the Grouping and Sorting Properties dialog. Select the field State_Province_Name as the expression to Group on. Hide the table footer of the table report item by right-clicking and selecting Table footer which is a toggle switch. Drag and drop the State Province Name field to the group header row (after the table header row), first

column of the table. Drag and drop the fields Year and Total Profit to the second and third columns of the detail row within the table. Notice the titles of these fields will automatically be updated with appropriate names in the header. Drag and drop the Country as a text box on top of the table. Drag and drop Total Profit field to the last column in the group footer row. Your layout should now look similar to Figure 17-27.

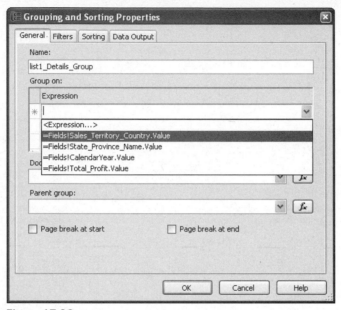

Figure 17-26

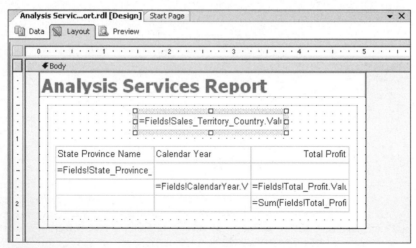

Figure 17-27

10. Click on the Preview tab to see the initial version of the report you have designed. You should see a report as shown in Figure 17-28. The report shows the profit report for a specific country in a single page which includes the states within the country along with profits for each year. The report also shows the aggregated profit for each state. You can switch to the profit report for the next country by selecting the next page or entering a specific page number as shown in Figure 17-28.

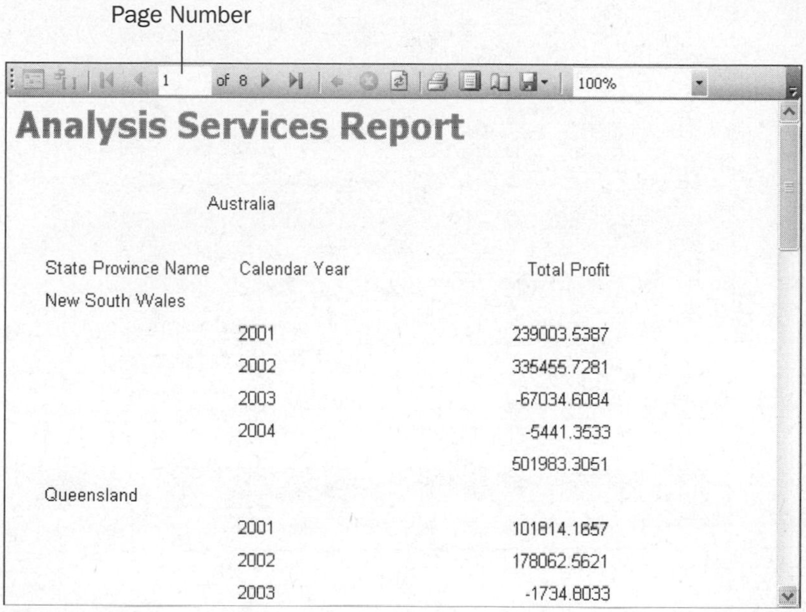

Page Number

Analysis Services Report

Australia

State Province Name	Calendar Year	Total Profit
New South Wales		
	2001	239003.5387
	2002	335455.7281
	2003	-67034.6084
	2004	-5441.3533
		501983.3051
Queensland		
	2001	101814.1657
	2002	178062.5621
	2003	-1734.8033

Figure 17-28

11. The report you just designed will not win any beauty contests nor is it particularly well formatted. You can beautify the report by making the headers bold, adding a background color, etc. Multi-select all the cells within the table by holding the Ctrl key down and then selecting each cell in the table. In the properties window change the border style to Solid; next select the BackgroundColor Silver. Select the header row and in the properties window change the Font property so that the Font Size is 12 pt and Font Weight is Bold. For the text box showing the Country change the property such that the BackgroundColor is Silver, the FontColor is Dark Red, FontSize is 12 pt and FontWeight is Solid. If you preview the report you will see a report similar to the one shown in Figure 17-29.

12. One of the key things in reports involving profit is the ability to easily distinguish the amount of profit. Typically in ledgers positive amounts are shown in black and negative amounts are shown in red. In this report we will modify the profit to be shown in green or red depending upon the profit amount. To specify appropriate colors to be displayed for profit select the cell corresponding to the profit in the layout mode. In the properties window set the property Color to be an expression. You will immediate see the Expression editor dialog. You can use VBA functions as part of the expressions. To check if the profit amount is positive or negative we will use the VBA function IIF. Set the expression for Color to check if the value for profit is greater than zero. If yes, the function will return the color green, or else the color red. Once you specify the expression your expression window should look like Figure 17-30. Click the OK button.

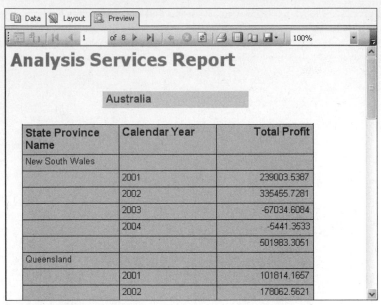

Figure 17-29

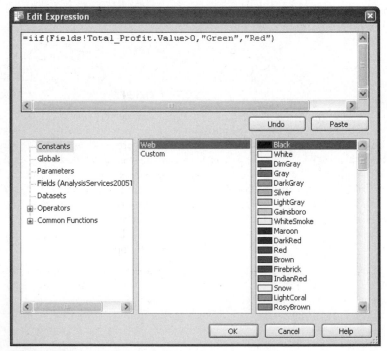

Figure 17-30

If you preview the report after setting the colors you will see a report as shown in Figure 17-31. You have seen some of the enhancements that can be made to your UDM reports using Report Designer. Next you will look at some of the new extensions in Reporting Services 2005 that have been specifically added to have a tighter integration with Analysis Services 2005.

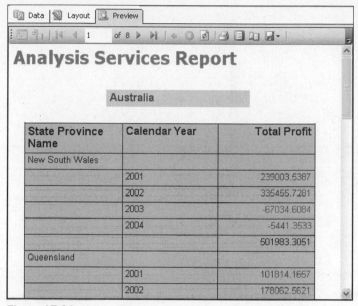

Figure 17-31

Enhancing Your Report using Extended Properties

The dimension members and cells in Analysis Services have certain specific properties associated with them. These properties can be retrieved from the Analysis Server along with the query result. There are certain properties from Analysis Services that get mapped on to properties in Reporting Services. These are called predefined properties and are accessed within reports as Fields!FieldName.PropertyName. Predefined properties in Reporting Services are Value, UniqueName, IsMissing, BackgroundColor, Color, FontFamily, FontSize, FontWeight, FontStyle, TextDecoration, FormattedValue, LevelNumber, and ParentUniqueName. Extended properties are additional properties that are returned from Analysis Services. Since these properties are not returned as fields, you cannot drag and drop from the field list to your report layout. Reporting Services 2005 provides functionality to access these values in a unique way and include them in the report. You can access the extended properties in one of the following formats.

❑ Fields!FieldName!PropertyName

❑ Fields!FieldName("PropertyName")

❑ Fields!FieldName.Properties("PropertyName")

To see an example of how extended properties can be used in your reports you will now enhance the report in the previous section by using the extended property FORMAT_STRING that is returned by Analysis Services for the measure Total Profit. Switch to the Layout mode in Report Designer and select the cell showing the Total Profit in the report. Select the property Format for this cell and set its value as an expression. In the Expression dialog enter the value =Fields!Total_Profit!FORMAT_STRING. Save the report and switch to the preview mode. You will see a report where the profit values are formatted based on the format string that is retrieved from Analysis Services as shown in Figure 17-32. Using the extended properties you will be able to retrieve and use the member properties for dimension members and cell properties for cells that are not part of the predefined reporting services properties.

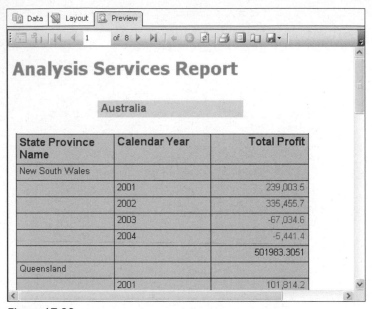

Figure 17-32

Custom Aggregates

When you create reports that contain groups, then most likely you have subtotals for the group members. For example, if you have sales for various years and products then you might want to view the sales for each year which needs to be aggregated. Reporting Services provides you a set of aggregation functions such as sum, count, distinct count, etc. For a detailed list of the aggregation functions supported by Reporting Services 2005 please refer to the product's documentation. In addition to these aggregate functions, it supports custom aggregates supported by data providers. If a data provider such as Analysis Services supports custom aggregates then Reporting Services has the ability to retrieve that data for the aggregate rows by the aggregate function called Aggregate. Custom Aggregates are also referred to as Server Aggregates.

Examples of custom aggregates in Analysis Services 2005 are semi-additive measures which use aggregate functions such as ByAccouunt, FirstNonEmpty, LastNonEmpty, FirstChild, LastChild, AverageofChildren, None. Some of the custom aggregate functions supported by Analysis Services 2005 are also supported by Reporting Services 2005. However we recommend you use custom aggregates for improved performance; in this way Reporting Services does not have to calculate the aggregate once again, for that was already done by Analysis Services. In this section you create a report that uses customer custom aggregate function to retrieve semi-additive measures from Analysis Services 2005. Follow the steps below to generate a custom aggregate report.

1. Add a new report item to the Reporting Services project you used in the last section called CustomAggregate.rdl.

2. Switch to the Data tab and create a new connection to the database AnalysisServices2005Tutorial.

3. The measure Fact Internet Sales – Unit Price in the cube AdventureWorksDW is a semi-additive measure with aggregate function FirstNonEmpty. Drag and drop this measure from the Metadata pane to the Result pane. Drag and drop the hierarchy Products from the Product dimension and Calendar Year hierarchy from the Order Date dimension. Your Result pane should now include columns Calendar Year, the two levels of the Products hierarchy Model Name and Product Name, and the measure Fact Internet Sales – Unit Price as shown in Figure 17-33.

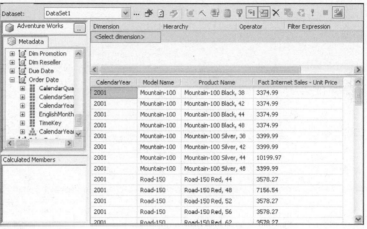

Figure 17-33

4. Switch to the Layout tab to design your report. Add a list report item with Grouping/Sorting option as Calendar Year similar to the report you designed in the previous section. Add a table item within the list item. Right-click on one of the rows and select Insert Group to add a new group within the table. In the Grouping/Sorting dialog select Model Name and disable group header. Disable the table footer by right-clicking on a row and selecting Table footer. Drag and drop Model Name to the group footer row as shown in Figure 17-34. Drag and drop Product Name and Fact Internet Sales – Unit Price fields to the second and third columns in the detail row as shown in Figure 17-34. Drag and drop Fact Internet Sales – Unit Price to the last column of the group footer row as shown in Figure 17-34. You will notice that Report Designer automatically adds the aggregate function Sum for the measure Fact Internet Sales – Unit Price as shown in Figure 17-34. Drag and drop the Calendar Year field above the table and change BackgroundColor, Color, and FontWeight for table header and group footer rows as shown in Figure 17-34.

5. Change the Aggregate function in the group footer row from Sum to Aggregate so that Reporting Services uses the custom aggregate from Analysis Services. When you change the aggregate function to Aggregate then report designer modifies the MDX query to retrieve the aggregated data from Analysis Services. If you switch to the Data tab you will see additional rows are being returned in the Result pane that contain null values for Product Name as shown in Figure 17-35. Reporting Services detects these rows with null values for Product Name as the aggregate rows and appropriately renders the report.

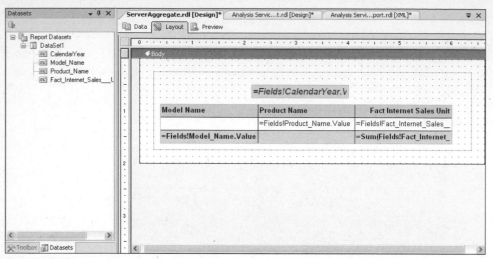

Figure 17-34

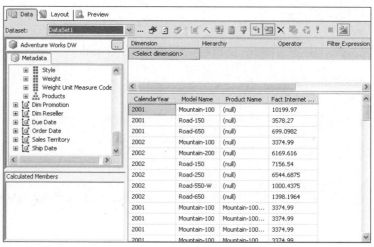

Figure 17-35

6. Click on the Preview tab to see the report. You will see the report shown in Figure 17-36 where the aggregated data for the various Model Names are retrieved from Analysis Services rather than being calculated by Reporting Services.

Custom aggregates, as mentioned earlier are useful to create reports that need the aggregated data from Analysis Services. You definitely need to use custom aggregates when the aggregate function is not supported by Reporting Services. In addition to that we recommend you use custom aggregates whenever you need aggregated data from Analysis Services because you will see performance benefits, especially when the report retrieves a large set of members from Analysis Services.

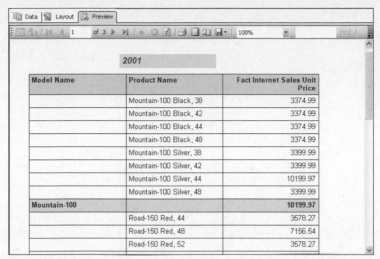

Figure 17-36

Deploying Your Report

Using BIDS you have learned to design and preview the reports. However when the reports need to be accessed by the end users, then you need to deploy the reports to a centralized location. This centralized location contains the Report Server which can render the reports to the end users. Access to the functionality of the Report Server is provided through the Report Server Web Service which uses SOAP (Simple Object Access Protocol) over HTTP and exposes interfaces for report execution and report management. When you install Reporting Services, SQL Server 2005 setup sets up a web interface to the report server. You can access your reports and perform management operations through `http://<machinename>/reports`. In addition to this interface you can perform management operations through SQL Server Management Studio. In this section you will learn to deploy and access reports.

To deploy the reports you designed in the previous section you need to set the location of your report server. Right-click on the solution Report Project Tutorial in solution explorer and select properties. You will see the Property dialog shown in Figure 17-37. Specify `http://localhost/reportserver` for TargetServerURL also shown in Figure 17-37. Deploy the reports by right-clicking on the solution and selecting deploy.

If there were any errors in deployment then you will see the errors in the BIDS Output window. To make sure your reports can be accessed, open internet explorer and go to the URL `http://localhost/reports`. You will see the reports under the folder Report Project Tutorial. When you select the Analysis Services Report, the report server renders the report and you will see the report as shown in Figure 17-38. Reporting Services allows you to export the report in various formats. If you want to export this report, select the desired format such as PDF, CSV, Excel, etc., and then click Export.

Once the reports are deployed to your report server, the next important task is to manage (group, setup security permissions, delivering options) the reports through the web interface or through SQL Server Management Studio which you will learn in the next section.

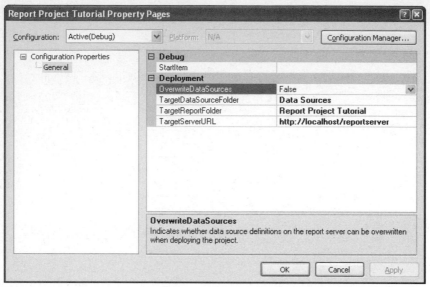

Figure 17-37

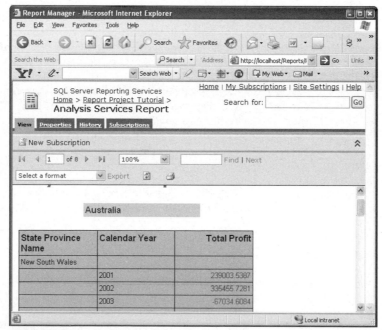

Figure 17-38

Managing Your Analysis Services Reports

Most likely you are the administrator on your machine and you are able to design, deploy, and view reports on your machines. However you do not want to provide administrative privileges to all your users. If you are a Report Server administrator then you would need to provide the appropriate access to your report designers who build and deploy reports as compared to the end users who consume the reports. You can also provide certain administrative privileges to certain users on your Report Server machine. Managing your Report Server by itself can be a separate chapter since it is so vast and is not covered completely in this section. However in this section you will learn a few basic operations of management including defining security permissions on how the reports have to be rendered, as well as creating permissions to end users to view reports which are specifically targeted towards reports built on top of Analysis Services databases. Finally, you will learn to automate reports so that they can be delivered to end users on a periodic basis.

Security and Report Execution

First and foremost you need to define the right permissions under which Reporting Services should retrieve the data from Analysis Services. In order to define the permissions click on the Properties tab of a report as shown in Figure 17-39. You will see the options General, Data Sources, Execution, History, and Security. The General tab provides information about the report such as the user who create the report along with the date and time when it was created or accessed. The Data Sources tab allows you to specify specific credentials under which Report Server should retrieve data from the data source. The Analysis Services Report shown in Figure 17-39 has a custom data source connecting to the AnalysisServices2005Tutorial. When the report is deployed from BIDS the default setting for Report Server connection to Analysis Services is Windows Integrated Security. You can modify this setting to one of the remaining three options. In general the users of the Analysis Services Report need not have access to query data from the database AnalysisServices2005Tutorial. In such circumstances you would need to choose the option Credential stored securely in the report server and provide a valid domain username and password which has access to query data from an Analysis Services instance. We recommend the use of this option compared to other options if you want to ensure that your users can view the report without appropriate permissions set on your Analysis Services database. If you want to provide access to users whose security is managed only through Analysis Services instance then choose the option Credentials supplied by the user running the report. Specify the right permissions and then click on the Execution tab.

The Execution tab shows the various ways in which the report can be rendered on the report server (see Figure 17-40). You can have the report run at the time when users access the report or schedule the report to be run every 30 minutes or specific time interval. In this way data is cached on your report server ensuring the reports are rendered immediately. If you do want the most recent data then you should not cache the report. The query to retrieve data from the data provider (in this example it is Analysis Services) can take a long time. You do have the option of specifying snapshots at which this specific report or additional reports get rendered and stored on the report server using the option Render the report from a report execution snapshot. Report server provides you certain options in report execution to limit the amount of time the report server should wait to retrieve the data. The last option under Report Execution Timeout is to define a specific timeout value. Use the default settings for report Execution and then click on the Security tab.

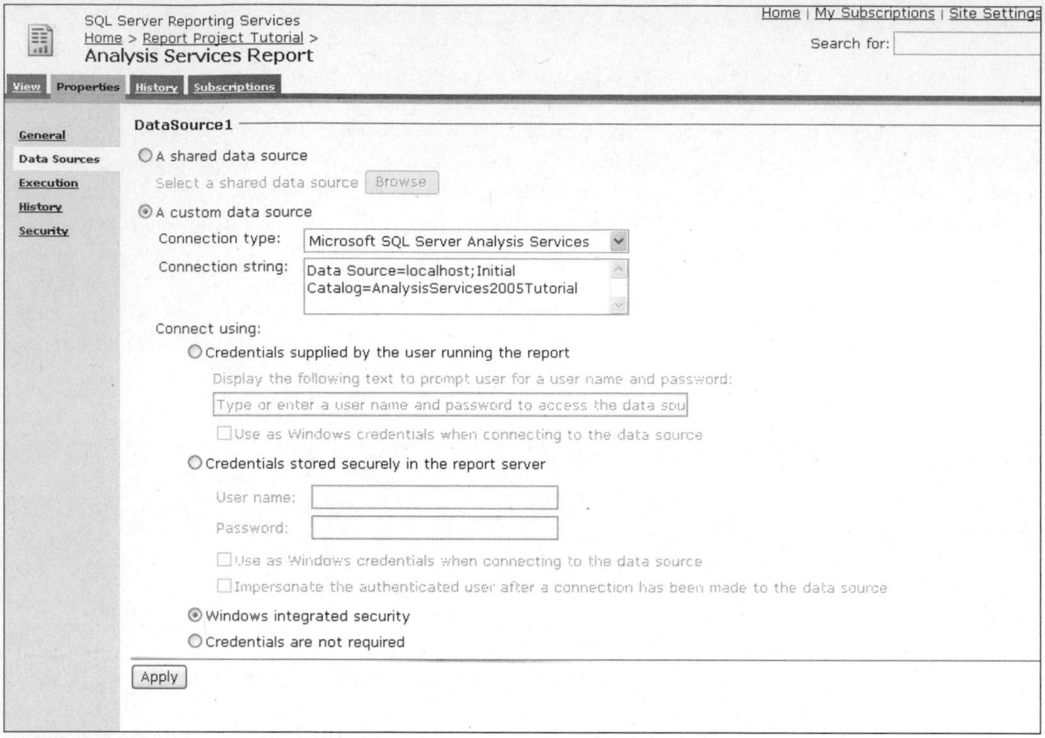

Figure 17-39

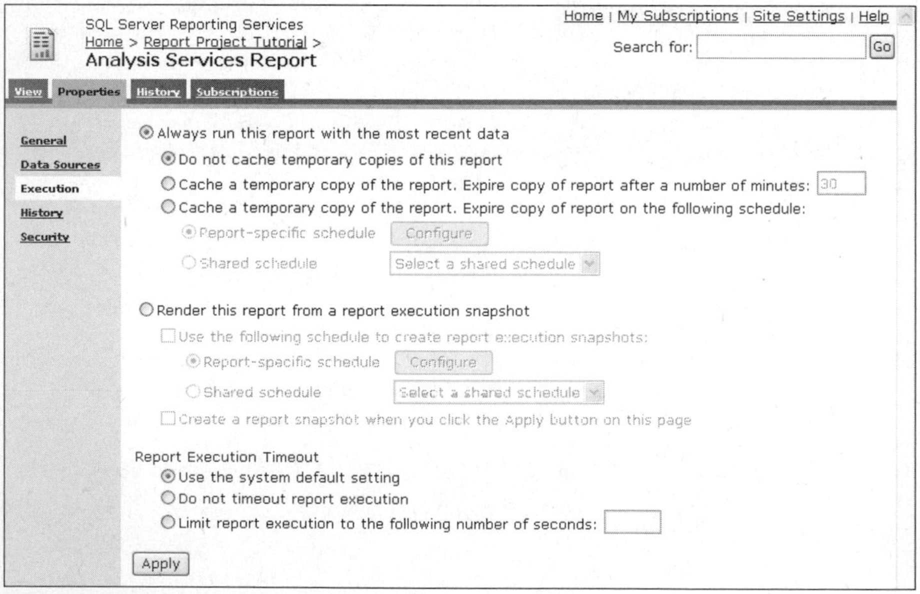

Figure 17-40

The Security tab provides you the option of specifying security to the end users accessing the report. You can add new users and provide access to specific roles from Content Manager who has administrative rights to just viewing reports. Figure 17-41 shows the default security settings for the reports.

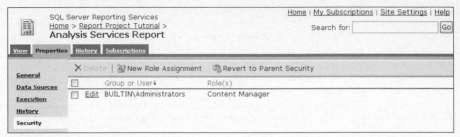

Figure 17-41

If you want to add a new user and provide specific permissions for the user then click on New Role Assignment. You will now be in the New Role Assignment page as shown in Figure 17-42. Specify the domain username or a group next to Group or user name. You next need to select the predefined roles on your report server such as Browser, Content Manager, etc. If you want to see what type of tasks a specific role can accomplish, click on the role. You also have the ability to define new roles and select specific tasks by clicking on the New Role button. Once you have chosen the roles for the user then click OK. You will now be in the default Security page which lists all the users or groups who have specific access permissions for the report.

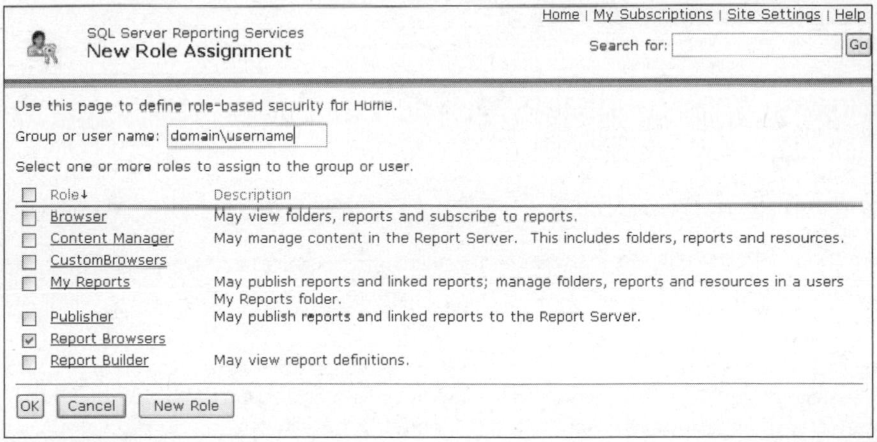

Figure 17-42

You have successfully learned to specify credentials under which Report Server needs to connect to your Analysis Services instance, report execution parameters, and finally provide access to your end users. You can perform all the management operations available through the web interface through SQL Server Management Studio by connecting to your Report Server.

Automating Your Reports

Your end users can access reports through the web interface. In addition to this, Reporting Services 2005 provides you certain ways of delivering the reports to end users through a file server or email. In order to deliver reports at periodic intervals you need to setup report subscriptions. Click on the My Subscription tab for a specific report. You will now be in the subscriptions page where you can define a regular subscription or data driven subscription. Click on the New Subscription button and you will see the subscription page as shown in Figure 17-43.

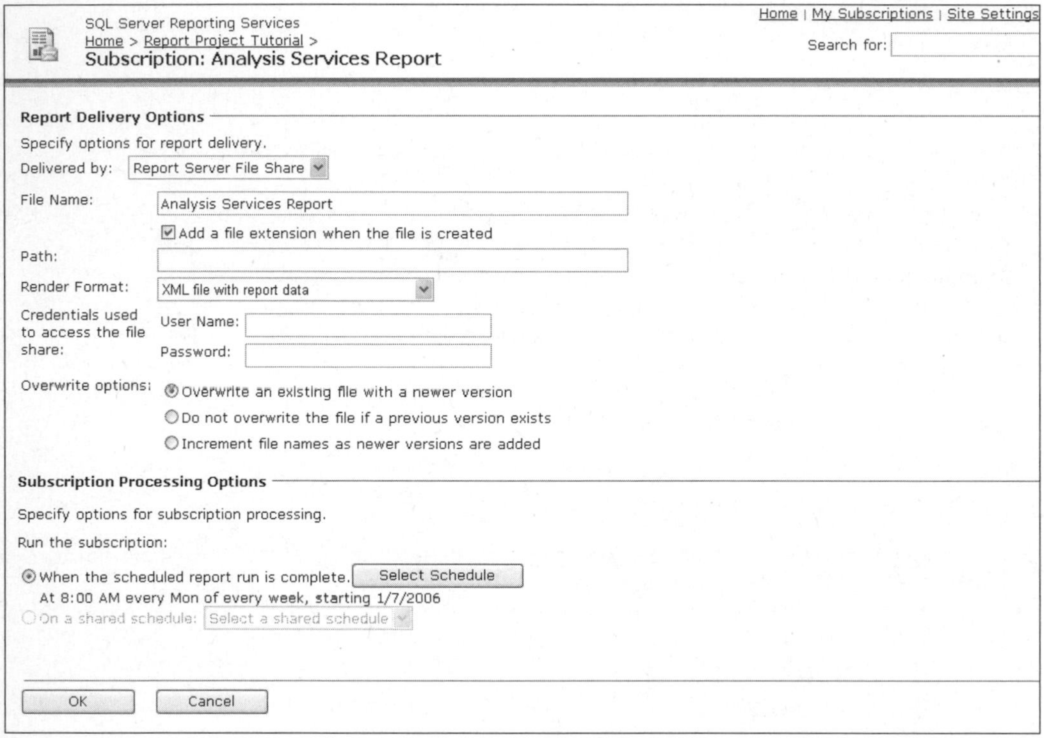

Figure 17-43

The subscription page allows you to choose a specific subscription type. Reporting Services 2005 supports two types of subscription delivery — email and file share. You can build your own subscription delivery mechanisms through the extensions provided by the Reporting Services platform. In the subscription page select the Report File Share delivery as shown in Figure 17-43. You now need to choose a format for the report (PDF, Excel, CSV, etc.), specify the path where the report needs to be delivered and credentials to access the file share where the report needs to be delivered. Once you specify the options for report file share delivery you need to specify when the report needs to be delivered. The report can be delivered based on a schedule that you define in the subscription page of a shared schedule that was already defined. Once you specify the delivery options click OK. The report is then scheduled to be run using SQL Agent and hence you need to have SQL Agent running on your machine. Reports will be delivered to the file share based on the defined schedule and the end users can access the reports from that file share.

The second delivery option is to deliver the reports via email. You need to setup your mail server configurations on your report server and enable the email delivery option. Refer to products documentation on setting up the email delivery option on your report server. Once the email delivery option is enabled you can choose this option and specify the email addresses for the TO, CC, and BCC lines along with the delivery schedule.

Ad-Hoc Reports using Report Builder

You have so far learned to create reports using Report Designer from relational and multi-dimensional databases. However these reports are pre-defined and often business users want to modify reports to better understand the data. Business users are most likely not used to understanding the underlying data sources and the query languages to retrieve data and design their reports. Most of them do understand entities and relationships between entities since they analyze data. Reporting Services 2005 provides Report Builder for the business users to explore the business data in a timely way and to make effective decisions. Report Builder exposes the business data through a model called report model and translates users' actions into appropriate queries to retrieve the underlying data source.

Report Builder is a Winforms application that is accessed from the Report Server for centralized management. Users can create reports using Report Builder through simple drag and drop of entities that are exposed through the report model. The reports generated by Report Builder are published to Report Server using the Report Definition Language (RDL).

Report Model

A report model is a metadata description of data objects and the relationships between the data in the underlying data source. Report models expose the data objects and relationships from the data sources as entities and relationships logically grouped together. Also, note that the entities and relationships are easier to understand than the underlying data source objects for business users. A report designer or a report server administrator would typically create a report model using a report model project in BIDS or SSMS and deploy it to the Report Server. These report models can then be accessed through the Report Builder application by business users.

You can create report models from relational and multi-dimensional databases. The report model consists of three objects — the semantic model, the physical model, and the mapping between the semantic model and physical model. The semantic model is the end users' view of the data which is defined using the Semantic Model Description Language (SMDL). The physical model is the physical representation of the objects such as cubes, dimension, levels, measures, etc. The mapping between the semantic model and physical model is used by Report Builder to translate users' actions into appropriate queries to the data source.

A Report Model project is created using BIDS when you need to create a report model from a relational data source. You need to create a data source, data source view, and then finally using the Report Model Wizard you create the report models. The generated model is then deployed to the Report Server. To create report models from Analysis Services data source you create a data source on the Report Server using SSMS and then generate a report model.

In this chapter you will create a report model from an Analysis Services UDM. Each UDM from Analysis Services is translated to a single report model. You will not be able to edit the report models generated from Analysis Services. Follow the steps below to generate a report model from the AdventureWorksDW UDM in the AnalysisServices2005Tutorial multi-dimensional database.

1. Open SSMS and create a connection to the Report Server as shown in Figure 17-44.

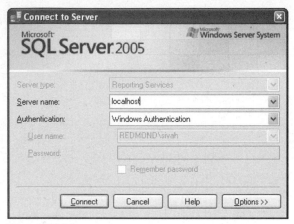

Figure 17-44

2. Right click on the Data Sources folder on your report server and select New Data Source. You will now see the Data Sources dialog. Provide the name AnalysisServices2005Tutorial and click on Connection to specify the connection details. Select the Data source type as Microsoft SQL Server Analysis Services. This dialog lacks the ability to launch the Connection Manger dialog to specify the connection parameters. You can obtain the connection to an Analysis Services database by creating a data source in Analysis Services project or Report Designer project. Type the connection string as "Provider=MSOLAP.3;Data Source=localhost;Integrated Security= SSPI;Initial Catalog=AnalysisServices2005Tutorial" as shown in Figure 17-45. Finally you need to specify the credentials under which Report Server needs to connect to the Analysis Services database. Select the Windows integrated security for the credentials and click OK.

3. Right-click on the Analysis Services data source created in step 2 and select Generate model as shown in Figure 17-46.

4. You will now be in the Generate Model dialog as shown in Figure 17-47. Provide a name for the report model to be generated and if needed, you can change the path where the report model needs to be generated and then click OK.

The report model AnalysisServices2005TutorialModel is now generated under the Data Sources folder. You have now successfully created a report model from AnalysisServices2005Tutorial database. In the next section you will learn to create reports using the Report Builder application.

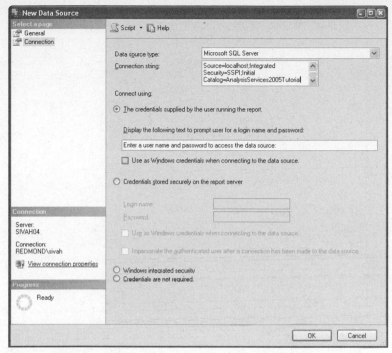

Figure 17-45

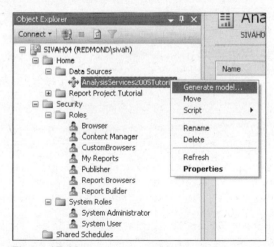

Figure 17-46

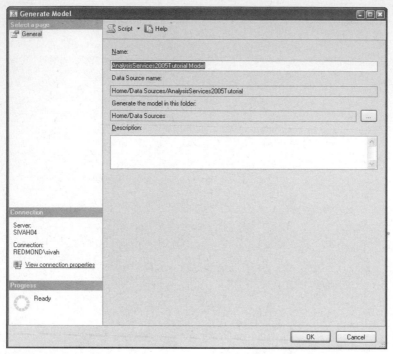

Figure 17-47

Ad-hoc Reports

Once the report models are available on the Report Server, users can create ad-hoc reports using the Report Builder application. Report Builder represents the report model as entities and relationships and makes it easy for business users to generate ad-hoc reports. Follow the steps below to create a report using Report Builder application.

1. Using internet explorer go to the report server interface at http://localhost/reports. Launch the Report Builder application by clicking on the button Report Builder.

2. The Report Builder application is downloaded on your machine and launched. You now need to choose the report model as a data source. Select the AdventureWorksDW as the data source, tabular report for report layout as shown in Figure 17-48, and click OK.

You will now see the various entities in the data source as well as the fields for the selected entity on the left side. On the right side you can see the design surface to create a report as shown in Figure 17-49. On the top you can see a tool bar containing buttons to operations on a report such as design, run, filtering, open, and save reports, and another tool bar for formatting the reports.

Assume you want to create an ad-hoc report to analyze the customer internet sales in various territories based on the number of cars owned. Enter the title of the report as "Sales Territory and Cars Owned by Customers". Select the entity Dim Geography in the explorer window. Drag and drop the field Sales Territory on the design surface.

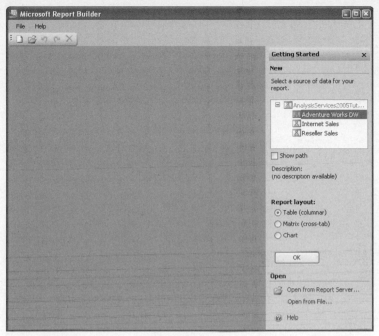

Figure 17-48

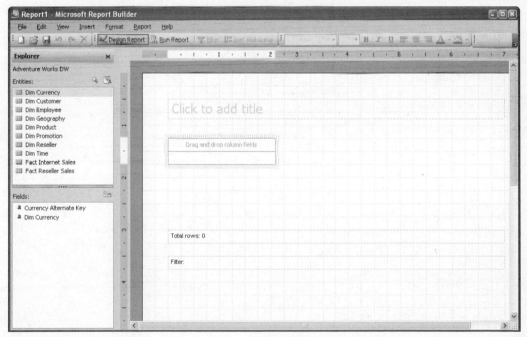

Figure 17-49

Your explorer view now contains the entity Dim Geography and the related entities Fact Internet Sales and Fact Reseller Sales. If you click on the Fact Internet Sales you will see all the related entities.

Since you need to analyze the sales based on the number of cars owned by customers, click on the Customers entity under Fact Internet Sales. Drag and drop the field Number Cars Owned to the design surface. Click on the entity Fact Internet Sales and drag and drop the fields Distinct Customers and Fact Internet Sales – Sales Amount on to the design surface. Your Report Builder will now look like Figure 17-50.

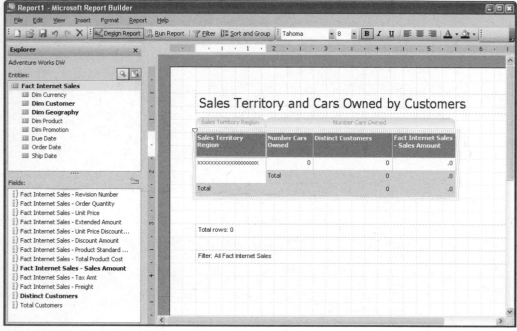

Figure 17-50

3. You have now designed an ad-hoc report which should just have taken you a few minutes and you didn't have to write any SQL query or change properties. You can see how easy it is for end users to create an ad-hoc report that is needed by them. To preview the report click on the button Run Report. You will now see the report as shown in Figure 17-51.

4. Once you have reviewed the report you can save the report on the Report Server. Click on the Save icon on the tool bar to save the report. In the Save As Report dialog enter the report name as Sales Territory and Cars Owned as shown in Figure 17-52.

In this section you have learned about creating report models and later generating ad-hoc reports using the Report Builder. There are several features in the Report Builder application that help you to filter, sort, and group the data in the report which are not covered in this section. We recommend you explore these features to refine your reports.

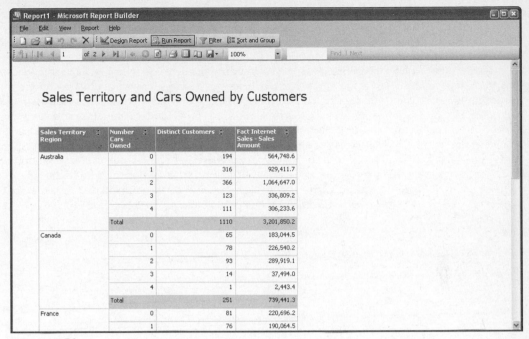

Figure 17-51

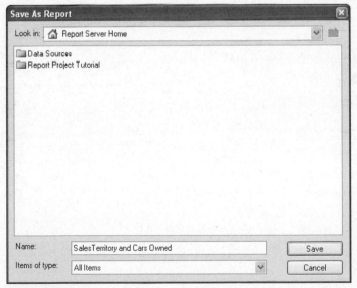

Figure 17-52

Summary

In this chapter you discovered that Integration Services isn't the only stellar example of product feature integration for enterprise business intelligence software. Indeed, Microsoft's Reporting Services provides an awesome platform to round out the business intelligence lifecycle. Specifically, this chapter covered three scenarios; first, there was an introduction to Reporting Services by way of building a report on a relational database. Then, you created a report on top of a UDM, which showed some of the great integrated features of Reporting Services such as drag-and-drop-based query generation and retrieving dimension and cell properties for inclusion in a report. You learned some of the key enhancements in Reporting Services 2005 such as custom aggregates, retrieving extended properties, and the ability to manage report servers and setup security for your reports. Finally, you learned to create a report model from Analysis Services database and to generate ad-hoc reports using the Report Builder application. If you need an in depth understanding of Reporting Services 2005 we recommend you read the book *Professional SQL Server 2005 Reporting Services* by Paul Turley, et al. (Wiley, March 2006).

18

Designing Real-Time Cubes

So, you're ready to go real-time with your cubes? Or perhaps you would be if only you knew what real-time cubes were? We define real-time cubes as cubes that are configured for automatic data updates on a time scale that makes them appear to be working in real time. This can be profoundly useful for certain types of analytical applications. First, consider an application for which real-time cubes would not be useful: An application designed to create profit projections and economic analysis of harvesting an old growth forest (a renewable resource) — that would require updates, say, every five years or so to reflect macroeconomic trends. There is a much more exciting application that would exploit real-time techniques. Consider a case such that your cube is directly built against your transactional data that is has several transactions per second which need to be updated in your UDM so that users can query the data real time. With the use of real-time streaming stock quotes of your company and results of a business analysis could be fed into a digital dashboard for viewing results. Ok, it is an unlikely example, but you get the idea. Such a dashboard might house multiple Key Performance Indicators (KPIs), clearly indicating the performance of target metrics with changes in color or graphics displays based on the data. Attaching the real-time stock quote stream to analyze the constantly changing cube and/or dimensions can be done through a dot net stored assembly. All this is possible in Analysis Services 2005 due to the flexibility of the Universal Dimension Model (UDM).

What does real-time mean to you or your business? Does it mean the ability to query the cube at any time? Does it mean you have the most up-to-date data in your cube? If you think of "most up-to-date data," what does that mean to you? Perhaps it means something like the previous quarter's data or previous month's data or perhaps it is a weekly or daily data. There are cases where even seconds count, as with the stock-related example. The question of how soon does the data needs to be available in the UDM is what you need to think about when you are designing a real-time cube. The daily transactional data in most retail companies arrives at the data warehouse nightly or on a weekly basis. Typically these companies have a nightly job that loads the new data to your cube through an incremental process.

If your company is multi-national, the concept of a nightly job (which is typically considered a batch process) is not nightly at all — due to the many time zones involved. Assume your company had offices in the USA and you were loading new data during the night. If your company expanded to include data-generating offices in Asia and those employees needed to access the cubes, you would need to make sure the UDM was available for querying throughout the day and night while giving consistently correct data. Some companies can find the right sweet spot of time needed to upload the data while users do not access the cube; and do the data load then. What if your transactional data arrives at regular intervals during the day and the end users of the cube need access to the data instantaneously? Then you would have to design a special way to meet the needs of your users. Analysis Services 2005 allows you to address these very sorts of challenges. You simply need to choose the right method based on your requirements.

By now, you are very familiar with MOLAP, HOLAP, and ROLAP storage modes; they can be crossed with varying methods of data update for both fact and dimension data through a technique called *proactive caching*. With the proactive caching technique you can count on getting the real-time data with MOLAP performance through the use of cache technology. In addition, proactive caching provides you the ability to manage any changes that occur to the source transactional data being propagated to the end user through the UDM (that is where the real-time part comes in). It is important to understand that proactive caching itself does not provide real-time capability; it is a feature that helps you manage your real-time business needs. This chapter provides you with some thoughts on which approach to take in which case and why. We have divided this chapter into three general scenarios to explain proactive caching and how it is useful for designing real time cube. They are long latency scenario for those times when quick updates are not required; an average latency scenario for those periodic, non-time-critical updates; and finally, the low latency scenario for the most demanding of users.

Proactive Caching

Traditionally, OLAP refers to fast access of aggregate or summarized data, with the source data retrieved from a relational data warehouse and stored in a storage format called MOLAP (Multidimensional OLAP). Relational databases are nonetheless really helpful for detail-level data and also helpful for reporting. You learned that MOLAP storage is optimal and provides the best performance while ROLAP storage provides instant access to the latest data but does not have the same performance as that of MOLAP storage. Proactive caching is an important feature addition in Analysis Services 2005 because it aids the UDM to deliver the best of relational and OLAP worlds, most importantly real time data access with near MOLAP performance. Proactive caching helps UDM to achieve real time data by providing controls that help in data propagation from the source data to the UDM which is then available for users queries. When appropriate proactive caching properties are set then Analysis Services starts building a new MOLAP cache when data in the underlying data source changes. Analysis Services serves users from the existing MOLAP cache. As soon as the new MOLAP cache is rebuilt then all the users are served from the new MOLAP cache and start seeing the new data. You see the use of this concept in action throughout this chapter.

As mentioned earlier, the UDM merges the relational and OLAP worlds. We consider proactive caching to be a management feature that helps the administrator or database designer to specify certain settings that help to achieve real-time data access based on customer needs. Proactive caching can be applied to both partitions and dimensions. Figure 18-1, 18-2 and 18-3 you can see details of how this feature works. Figure 18-1 shows an UDM which has proactive caching enabled. Analysis Services 2005 creates a MOLAP cache of the UDM on Analysis Services 2005 from which users query for information. When there are updates to the relational database that affects the UDM data then that information is notified to Analysis Services which is shown in Figure 18-2. If proactive caching has been enabled on the UDM, there is a background thread within Analysis Services 2005 which we refer to as the Proactive Caching Management. This thread controls operations within Analysis Services based on certain parameters to ensure the customers get the real-time data access requested as shown in Figure 18-3.

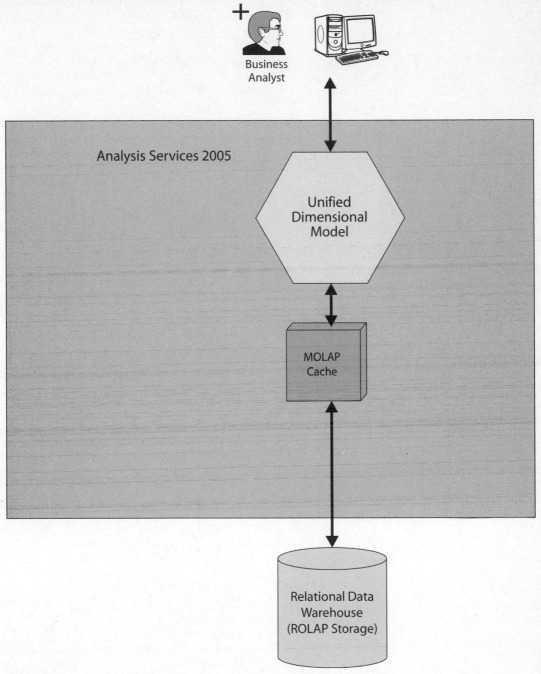

Figure 18-1

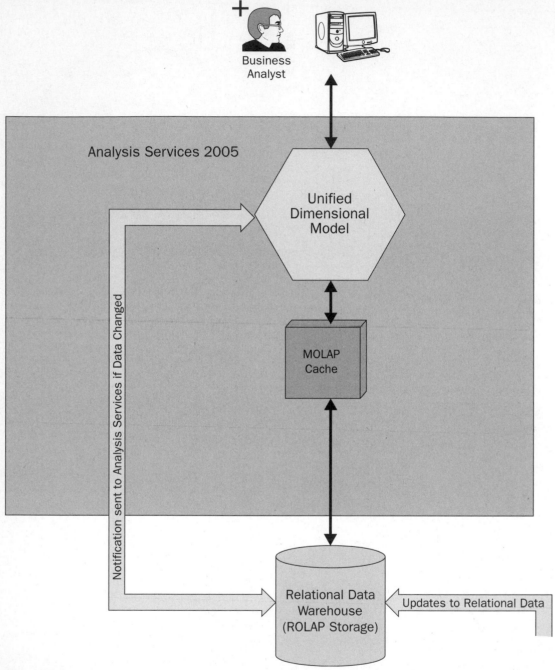

Figure 18-2

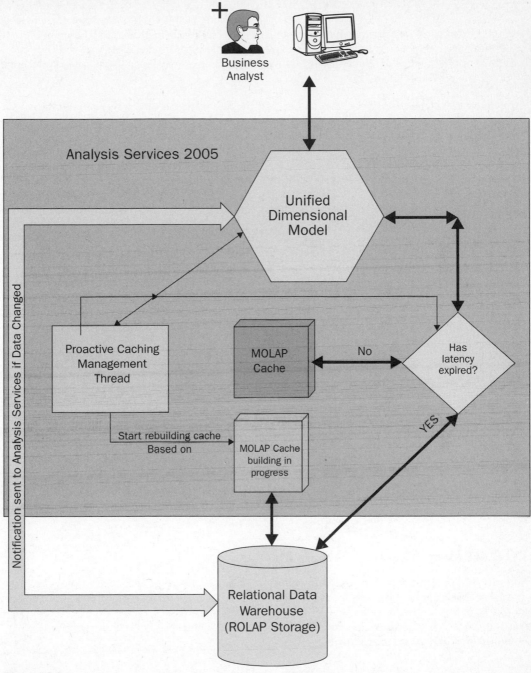

Figure 18-3

The typical configuration which we predict users would use is to have the MOLAP storage mode for the UDM with proactive caching enabled which is shown in Figure 18-3. If users are sending queries to your cube, there is an existing MOLAP cache of the UDM on your server. If a user sends a query, data is

641

retrieved from this MOLAP cache. The proactive caching thread looks for changes in the relational data warehouse based on certain mechanisms, which you see later in this chapter. As soon as there is a data change made known to the proactive caching management thread, the thread itself then initiates rebuilding of a new MOLAP cache and clears the existing MOLAP cache. Note that you can set properties that control the time at which the current MOLAP cache gets cleared and the time at which the new MOLAP cache needs to be rebuilt.

Any query that comes to Analysis Services is first checked to see if it can be served with the existing MOLAP cache. If the current cache is valid based on proactive caching settings, results are retrieved from that. If the current cache is not valid, that means a new cache is being rebuilt. Because Analysis Services does not know how long it will take to rebuild the cache, it will then directly go to the relational data warehouse to retrieve the data. Analysis Services creates SQL queries to retrieve the correct data. The SQL queries generated by Analysis Services are optimized to efficiently retrieve data from the relational data warehouse. Any calculation that cannot be done in the relational data warehouse is then computed within Analysis Services after retrieving the data, and the results are returned to the user.

Keep in mind that there might be slight performance degradation during the time data is being retrieved from a relational data source; this is likely due to involvement of query translation as well as network activity—nonetheless, users get the real-time data. If the users do not mind getting the data from the existing cache and they only want to see the refreshed data with good performance, they can set a proactive caching property called *latency*, which is the time up to which the current MOLAP cache will be valid even after the notification of change in data in the relational data warehouse. Setting the latency (inactivity time interval) close to the rebuilding time helps in getting MOLAP-level performance—keep in mind that a slight delay in the real-time data to users is to be expected.

Fortunately for the users, MOLAP cache building is done as a background thread and assigned a low priority. This means that if queries are submitted to Analysis Services databases, the queries will be given higher priority than the background proactive caching thread. If at any time during this rebuild process the user initiates a process that will change the data in the cube—for example, by re-processing the cube or doing a writeback to the cube—the background proactive caching thread to rebuild the MOLAP cache will be cancelled. Similarly, if Analysis Services receives another notification of a data change, the MOLAP cache rebuilding process will be cancelled unless you have explicitly specified not to do so through a proactive caching property. It is important for you as an administrator or database designer to be aware of this behavior so that you can make sure the proactive caching properties are set with desired values based on your business requirements.

Proactive Caching at Work

In order to demonstrate how proactive caching works, this section also uses the sample Adventure Works Analysis Services project that comes with the product. The sample is located in the directory within your SQL Server installation (%SystemDrive%$\Program Files\Microsoft SQL Server\90\Tools\Samples\AdventureWorks Analysis Services Project\Enterprise). To understand proactive caching functionality, do the following:

1. Open the sample "Adventure Works" Analysis Services project. This Analysis Services project contains a cube called Adventure Works that has several measure groups and dimensions. The measure group ResellerSales retrieves the data from the relational table FactResellerSales. The data from the FactResellerSales table has been partitioned within Analysis Services so that the ResellerSales measure group has four partitions, one for each year. You will see the behavior of proactive caching by adding rows to the last partition of the FactResellerSales measure group.

2. Click the Partitions tab of the Adventure Works cube and expand the ResellerSales measure group. You will see the four partitions of the ResellerSales measure group as shown in Figure 18-4. If you click in the Source column for year 2004, you will be able to see the SQL query that restricts the data for that year (OrderDateKey > 915 and OrderDateKey < 1280).

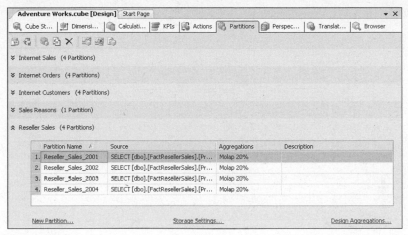

Figure 18-4

From here, we'll delete some rows from the ResellerSales table and do a bulk insert of these rows to see the behavior of proactive caching.

3. Open SQL Server Management Studio and execute the following query to your relational database Adventure Works DW. You will see 3004 rows are retrieved. Select the entire results set and right-click within the results pane to save the results in a text file. Name the file AdventureWorksFactResellerSales.CSV.

```
SELECT *              FROM [dbo].[FactResellerSales]
WHERE OrderDateKey >= '1050' AND OrderDateKey <= '1280'
```

4. Execute the following SQL statement to delete the rows from the table:

```
DELETE   FROM [dbo].[FactResellerSales]
WHERE OrderDateKey >= '1050' AND OrderDateKey <= '1280'
```

5. Deploy the Adventure Works project to your Analysis Services instance. Connect to your Analysis Services instance using SQL Server Management Studio and execute the following MDX query. You will see the results as shown in Figure 18-5.

```
SELECT [Measures].[Reseller Sales Amount] ON 0,
NON EMPTY [Geography].[Country].MEMBERS ON 1
FROM [Adventure Works]
```

6. Now you need to set the proactive caching settings for the ResellerSales partition so that changes in source data are automatically detected by Analysis Services and you get real-time data while querying the UDM. Connect to the Analysis Services instance in the Object explorer from SSMS. Navigate to the Reseller_Sales_2004 partition as shown in Figure 18-5. Right-click the partition and select Properties.

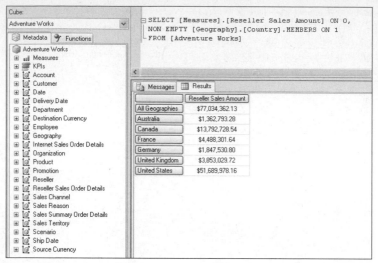

Figure 18-5

7. You will see the properties page for the partition. Select the proactive caching page as shown in Figure 18-6. You will see the various storage options for the partitions from Real-time ROLAP to MOLAP. In order to have this partition as MOLAP as well as enable proactive caching, you need automatic MOLAP; also you do need to set some additional proactive caching properties. Click the Custom setting radio button, then click on the Options button at the bottom right of the dialog.

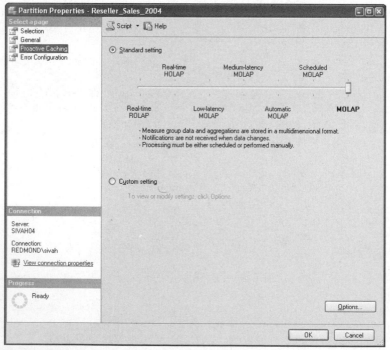

Figure 18-6

8. You will see the Storage options dialog as shown in Figure 18-7. Enable proactive caching for the selected partition by clicking on the check box next to Enable proactive caching. Set the Latency to zero seconds, and select the option Bring Online Immediately. This ensures that you do see the updated results immediately. By default the silence interval and silence override interval are at 10 minutes. This means that the MOLAP cache will start rebuilding after 10 seconds of the notification of data change. Now you need to inform Analysis Services on the method of detecting change in the relational data source. Click the Notifications tab.

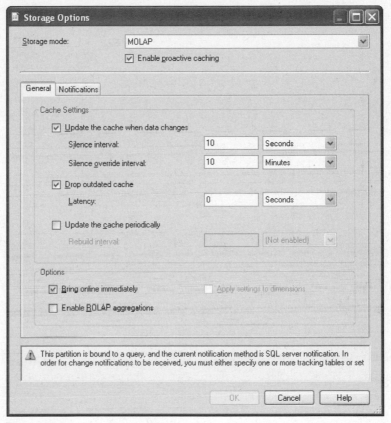

Figure 18-7

9. Select the SQL Server option and specify the tracking table as FactResellerSales as shown in Figure 18-8. This is a unique option specific to Microsoft SQL Server. The Analysis Services instance is able to detect changes in the data with the help of SQL Server notification. This is not available with other relational databases. You would have to choose the second option of specifying a query that will result in a value that indicates the change in data for other data sources. Click OK to accept changes made in the dialog.

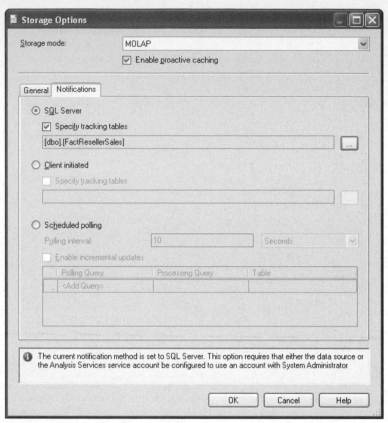

Figure 18-8

10. You have now set up proactive caching successfully for the Reseller partition. To see the results, you just have to load the rows you deleted from the FactResellerSales table in step 4. Execute the following bulk insert SQL query to your relational database. Make sure you use the correct path!

```
BULK INSERT dbo.FactResellerSales
FROM 'C:\Chapter18\AdventureWorksFactResellerSales.csv'
WITH
(
        FIELDTERMINATOR =',',
        ROWTERMINATOR = '\n',
        FIRE_TRIGGERS
)
```

11. The preceding statement adds 3004 rows to the FactResellerSales table. Now you need to verify if you are able to see the real-time data by querying the UDM AdventureWorksDW. Go to the MDX query editor and execute the MDX query from step 5. You will see that the Reseller Sales for all the countries are higher than their original value, as shown in Figure 18-9. This is due to the 3004 new rows added to the FactResellerSales table. At the moment the MDX query is executed, the new MOLAP cache is not rebuilt. Therefore, Analysis Services retrieves the data for the 2004 partition from the relational data source, aggregates the data along with the data from the remaining three MOLAP partitions, and provides you the results.

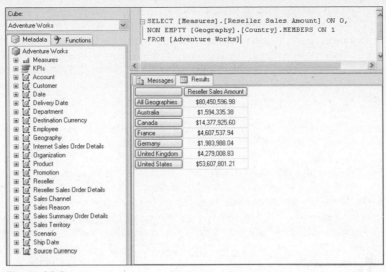

Figure 18-9

You have now successfully been able to set the proactive caching option for a partition using the SQL Server notification option and are able to see real-time results. Similarly, you can manage other partitions and dimensions with proactive caching based on the real-time needs of your business users. Having learned about the basics of the proactive caching feature and how it works, now you can look at important scenarios where this feature would be useful for your business.

Long Latency Scenario

Assume you own a small company that is selling a key set of products which are essentially static in nature; the base list of products just doesn't change. New products may be added to the list, but the original set of products remains the same. In this scenario, several of your products are sold each day and the sales data arrives at your data warehouse sometime after normal business hours. Further, your company is headquartered in the United States. The business analysts on your team want to see sales data no later than the next working day following the actual sale. In this scenario, assume incremental processing of your cube takes a relatively small amount of time (just 1–2 hours), which can be completed before start of the next business day. It is also assumed that data updates (information about new products added into the system) in your relational databases arrive within a reasonable time.

The traditional approach to solving the outlined scenario would be to have the dimension storage as MOLAP and doing an incremental update of dimensions after relational data update is completed. This approach is computation intensive and is a fairly costly operation. Following that dimension data update, an incremental process of the relevant measure groups is required, and once that completes, the consumers of the cube can browse the results. This approach has advantages. Indeed, this approach is good whenever your relational data updates occur regularly at a specific time interval and you have sufficient time to update the cubes to appropriate users. Several existing Analysis Services users in the retail space use this solution. Data typically arrives during the night and the cubes are processed nightly for use the next business day.

As with the traditional approach, you can do an incremental process of dimensions and measure groups. Or for the sake of completeness, and given the time, you could even do a full process of the entire cube. Again, these things typically take place during the night so time is not often a constraint. You could use SQL Server 2005 Integration Services to create a package to do this job as seen in Chapter 15. Alternatively, you can use the proactive caching feature. There are two basic methods (with multiple variations) within proactive caching that can be used to initiate data updates. They are query-based method and the time-based method; the method you choose will depend on your needs.

One of the solutions for the long latency scenario is to use proactive caching feature in Analysis Services 2005. In the proactive caching solution, you set proactive caching to kick in as soon as the data changes using the option scheduled MOLAP. For the schedule MOLAP option you need to specify a query that is to be run at scheduled time intervals to determine if there has been a change to the source data. Here is how it works: the first time Analysis Services sends the specified query to the relational data source, it collects and stores the response. That stored response provides a baseline against which subsequent query results can be compared. When a subsequent query returns a result set that does not match the baseline, it is presumed there has been a data update and proactive caching will start the process of incremental update. Depending on the other proactive caching settings such as latency the cache will be updated. The latency setting is a property associated with proactive caching; specifically, it tells Analysis Services how long to wait between cache updates. This is what provides that real-time feeling to the end user.

Figure 18-10 shows the proactive caching option where you specify a polling query that will detect the change in source data. This could be as simple as a count of rows in the relational table or as complex as a hash value of the entire result set. For the long latency scenario you would need to click on the Enable incremental updates option so that dimension and partitions are processed incrementally only with the data that has been added. If this option is enabled, Analysis Services processes the dimension or partition object by sending a Process Add statement. If you do not specify this option, Analysis Services will automatically send a Process update statement to the dimension or the cube partitions. Process updates on dimensions could be expensive based on the size of the dimensions and the partitions and aggregations built for the partitions. For tradeoffs on which processing option (process update or process add) would be good for your cube, please refer to the performance chapter (Chapter 13) in this book. After specifying the polling query, you need to specify the processing query that will retrieve appropriate data from the relational data source for processing.

> Here is a handy proactive caching technique that can be applied to dimensions by which your incremental processing query is optimized. First, you specify the polling query. The results of the polling query can be used as parameters to the incremental processing query. For example, if you have SELECT max(product_id) from Products — let's say initially it returns 100 — then 50 products are added. When the polling query is subsequently run, you would get 150. These two parameters can then be used to create the incremental processing query as
>
> ```
> SELECT * from Products where product_id>COALESCE(?,0) And
> product_id <=COALESCE(?,-1)
> ```
>
> In this way, the processing query only returns those rows that were added since last data change. This technique can be a real timesaver if your Products table is the size of, say, Wal-Mart's or Amazon.

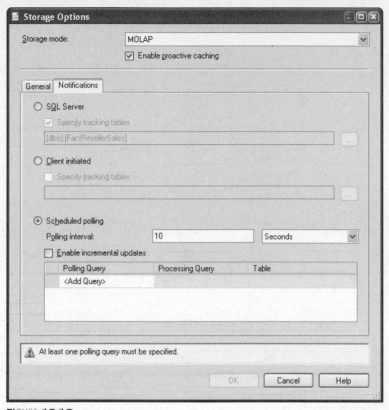

Figure 18-10

Proactive Caching Using Timed Updates

The second method of proactive caching is to have the dimension and partition data updated periodically. While this approach could hardly be considered sophisticated, there is no doubt it gets the job done and doesn't take much in the way of setup. Here is how it works: You set proactive caching to update any new source data and itself (the cache) at a predetermined time. For example, if you want to set the update at "24 hours since last process," you set a proactive caching property which ensures the MOLAP cache is rebuilt every 24 hours. In the long latency scenario you would typically not set the latency property since you want the new data to be available as soon as the MOLAP cache is rebuilt. You need to specify the option of when to rebuild the cache using the option "Update the cache periodically" as shown in Figure 18-11. This option ensures that the MOLAP cache is rebuilt every 24 hours. However you should be aware that the cache update occurs 24 hours after the previous update. For example, on the first day if the processing started at 12 midnight and it took 30 minutes for the cache to be updated then on the second day the cache update will start at 12:30am instead of 12 midnight. It would have been nice to have the update cache to happen at the same time each day. Probably we will get this in future releases. However you can implement this functionality using SQL Server Integration Services as seen in Chapter 16. You might have to reset the proactive caching property periodically to keep it aligned with your business needs so that the most up to date data is available for your end users. The configuration you setup using for updating cache periodically is also referred to as scheduled MOLAP since the cache update is scheduled. If you click OK in the screen shown in 18-11 you will be in partition's properties pane where you will see the scheduled MOLAP option selected as shown in Figure 18-12.

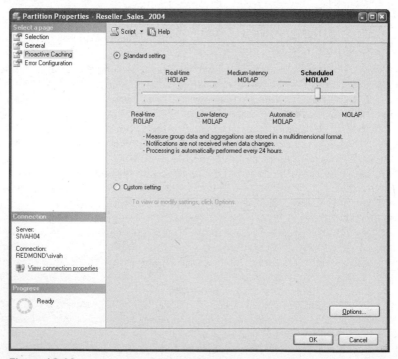

Figure 18-11

Figure 18-12

Average Latency Scenario

For the average latency scenario, assume you are running a large retail business intelligence implementation with several hundred product-related data changes being added overnight, every night. These additions come in the form of stocking and pricing changes. Actual sales information arrives in your data warehouse periodically and your users really want to see the data under reasonable real-time conditions. For this case, assume updates are available every two hours or so and your cube typically takes about an hour to process. However your users are willing to see old data for up to four hours. Assume the data partition itself is not large (say, less than 5 GB) for this scenario.

Proactive Caching with MOLAP Storage Option

Let's say you have built the cube, and dimensions are updated nightly using incremental processing. Incremental processing is good whenever you want the current dimensions to be used by customers, because incremental processing can take place in the background and not prevent customers from querying the data.

The case for which it makes sense to use Proactive Caching with the MOLAP storage option is when you need to update the sales information (or other information) into the measure groups on a periodic basis so that users see near real-time data without any performance degradation. In this case, the data arrives in your data warehouse in the form of a bulk load from your relational transactional database. Further, let's say that incremental processing of your cube is faster than the time required for a bulk load to your data warehouse. You can set up proactive caching for the average latency scenario to be medium latency MOLAP as shown in Figure 18-13 so that as soon as a notification arrives, Analysis Services automatically starts building the new MOLAP cache. Since your users are willing to wait to get the old data for up to four hours the proactive caching property called latency is set to 4 hours. If the new MOLAP cache is not built in 4 hours since the last data change then Analysis Services switches to ROLAP mode to retrieve data from the relational data source. As soon as the new MOLAP cache is completed Analysis Services will serve the users from the new MOLAP cache. Typically in this scenario you would want to specify the latency time interval to be much higher than the incremental processing time for the partitions. If the incremental processing takes much longer than the latency, you might experience occasional degradation in performance because the Analysis Services's existing MOLAP cache is outdated and Analysis Services needs to fetch the results from the relational data source.

Latency simply refers to the amount of time you want the system to wait before unceremoniously dumping an existing MOLAP cache that is used to serve users. The SilenceInterval indicates that no less than the specified period must elapse before initiating the rebuilding of a new MOLAP cache upon data change. SilenceOverrideInterval is a little trickier to get your head around, but by no means daunting. If SilenceInterval is reset time and again due to frequent data changes then the MOLAP cache never gets rebuilt fully and gets dumped often whenever data changes. There is some limit to our patience since users will always see performance degradation from the time Analysis Services switches to fetching the data from the relational data source after the specified latency time. To overcome this issue SilenceOverride Interval property ensures that it stops resetting the silence interval for future data changes till the existing MOLAP cache is rebuilt fully.

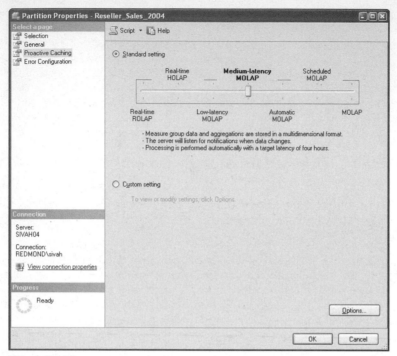

Figure 18-13

Normally you know how frequently updates are occurring to your relational data source. Based on that information you can specify the SilenceInterval. On certain occasions there might be frequent data changes that result in the Silence interval timer being reset, and this can potentially lead to not rebuilding the MOLAP cache. That's when SilenceOverrideInterval comes in handy. Think of SilenceOverrideInterval as simply your way of saying, "I don't care if the update notifications keep coming, I want to do an update no longer than, say, every sixty seconds." So, even though SilenceInterval keeps on ticking away the seconds, SilenceOverrideInterval will override it if SilenceInterval overstays its welcome—and that is just what happens in Figure 18-14. You can see how SO (SilenceOverrideInterval) times out and a rebuild of the MOLAP cache is kicked off. Typically, if the SilenceInterval is specified in the order of seconds, your SilenceInterval override would be specified in minutes so that your MOLAP cache is not too long outdated. Figure 18-14 shows a graphical timeline representation of events occurring due to proactive caching being enabled, but is demonstrated using smaller time intervals for SilenceInterval and SilenceOverrideInterval rather than typical values. Once the cache is rebuilt, the normal process of proactive caching using the SilenceInterval during future notifications will be handled by Analysis Services.

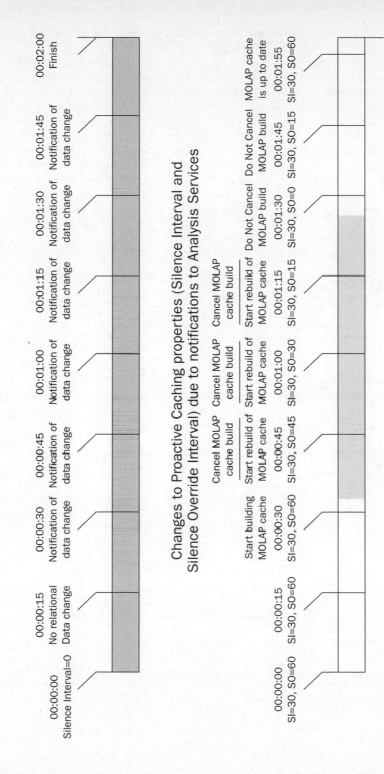

Notification of Events To Analysis Services

| 00:00:00
Silence Interval=0 | 00:00:15
No relational
Data change | 00:00:30
Notification of
data change | 00:00:45
Notification of
data change | 00:01:00
Notification of
data change | 00:01:15
Notification of
data change | 00:01:30
Notification of
data change | 00:01:45
Notification of
data change | 00:02:00
Finish |

Changes to Proactive Caching properties (Silence Interval and
Silence Override Interval) due to notifications to Analysis Services

| | Start building
MOLAP cache | Cancel MOLAP
cache build | Start rebuild of
MOLAP cache | Cancel MOLAP
cache build | Start rebuild of
MOLAP cache | Do Not Cancel
MOLAP build | Do Not Cancel
MOLAP build | MOLAP cache
is up to date |
| 00:00:00
SI=30, SO=60 | 00:00:15
SI=30, SO=60 | 00:00:30
SI=30, SO=60 | 00:00:45
SI=30, SO=45 | 00:01:00
SI=30, SO=30 | 00:01:15
SI=30, SO=15 | 00:01:30
SI=30, SO=0 | 00:01:45
SI=30, SO=15 | 00:01:55
SI=30, SO=60 |

Figure 18-14

For the average latency scenario example explained here we recommend you customize the medium-latency MOLAP default settings so that you set the SilenceInterval, SilenceOverrideInterval and Latency as shown in Figure 18-15. Latency is pretty straight forward based on requirement and you set it to 4 hours. SilenceInterval is set to 10 seconds so that the MOLAP cache rebuilding starts in 10 seconds. The processing of the partition takes approximately 2 hours. If there are multiple data updates within the first two hours you want to make sure the SilenceOverrideInterval kicks in and stops frequent cache updates and by the time of the 4 hour time limit you do have a new MOLAP cache ready for users to query. There might be some times where you have frequent data updates on relational database and your MOLAP rebuilding has not completed but latency has expired. During that time all requests will be served by retrieving results from the data source. You need to ensure this time period is as small as possible so that users perceive the data is real-time and with very good performance (due to MOLAP cache).

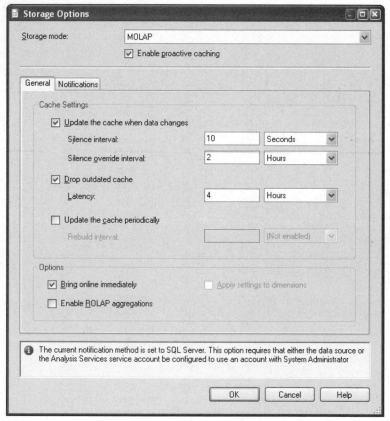

Figure 18-15

Analysis Services serves data to users with the help of a cache. If the data in the relational data warehouse changed, the cache needs to be updated (that is, rebuilt). It takes some amount of time to rebuild the cache. Latency is one of the proactive caching properties that allows you to control serving your customers from an old MOLAP cache for a certain period of time; or to instantaneously serve the customers with the latest data. If your users are concerned about getting the most up-to-date data, you would set the property called Latency to zero. This informs the Analysis Services that users are interested in the latest data and the existing MOLAP cache needs to be cleared. Because the new MOLAP cache might take some time to be rebuilt, you want to take steps to keep the results coming to the users. During the time the MOLAP cache is being rebuilt, Analysis Services fetches the data from the relational data warehouse. Even though you do get the most up-to-date data, you might see slight performance degradation because Analysis Services needs to retrieve the data from the relational data warehouse.

As soon as the MOLAP cache is rebuilt, Analysis Services starts serving the customers with the new MOLAP cache and you will start seeing your original query response times. If you want the users to continue using the existing cache while a new cache is generated based on new data, you can specify the time that it would take for rebuilding the MOLAP cache as latency. For example, if it takes 15 minutes to rebuild your MOLAP cache, you can specify the latency as 15 minutes. By specifying this, the current users would be receiving slightly old data for 15 minutes but at the MOLAP performance level. As soon as the MOLAP cache is rebuilt, Analysis Services starts serving all the customers using the new MOLAP cache and they would instantaneously see the new data. The trade-off here is how current the data is versus query performance.This is a key configuration and one we expect many will apply if they want to see near real-time data but with MOLAP performance. In this scenario, customers need to be willing to wait for a certain period of time for data to be propagated through the UDM.

We do not recommend this solution for dimensions (changes to existing dimension members) because occasionally you might end up in a state where you would have to query the data from the relational data source. This is not a problem, but when the dimension storage mode switches from MOLAP to ROLAP, it is considered a structural change by Analysis Services, which means that the partitions have to be rebuilt. This can potentially have a significant performance impact and clients might have to reconnect to query the UDM. However, if your business needs demand this and your users always establish a new connection to send queries, you can still use the settings for dimensions.

No Latency Scenario

In this short latency scenario you are in charge of an eCommerce site that provides customers' links to the most up-to-date products on the Web, which when sold, provide you a commission. Your Internet affiliates are adding additional products to your catalog electronically and at this point you are at 2.3 million product SKUs and the number is rising. Meanwhile, your partition data is changing frequently, and you have large numbers of members in the product dimensions. What does a BI apps developer do?

Real-Time ROLAP Storage Option

The recommended solution here would be to set up the measure group and dimension data (which are frequently changing) to be in ROLAP mode so that data is automatically retrieved from the relational data store as needed by the user. Working in this way does not come without a price; indeed, although it is definitely a useful storage mode, the performance of ROLAP mode is much slower than the MOLAP equivalent. In general we would always recommend a MOLAP solution for large dimensions, but if your dimension members are constantly changing and these changes need to be reflected immediately to end users, the ROLAP would be a better option. This is because the data is being retrieved directly from your relational data source, which often requires over-the-net communication. Yes, you could go with HOLAP, but performance depends largely on your aggregated data and how frequently it is impacted due to changes in the data.

Just setting the storage mode to ROLAP is not sufficient. Analysis Services caches data and if there is a change in your relational data warehouse, this might need to be immediately reflected in your users' queries. If you definitely need real-time, as in no latency updates, you need to specify REAL-TIME ROLAP, which amounts to setting up proactive caching on ROLAP partitions or dimensions. Under this configuration, on a change in the source data, Analysis Services immediately drops the cache and gets the data from the relational data warehouse. Figure 18-16 shows the selection for REAL TIME ROLAP in the proactive caching dialog. If you click on the options button you can see the proactive caching properties setup so that latency is 0 and you bring the new data online immediately as shown in Figure 18-17.

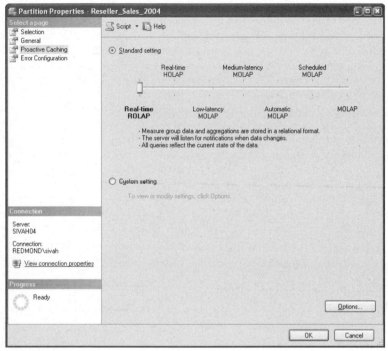

Figure 18-16

Billions and Billions of Records

The American astronomer Carl Sagan seemed fond of pondering the number of stars in a galaxy or cluster of galaxies; well, these days it is not a stretch to have similarly mind-boggling numbers of records in your transactional repositories. For reference, the Milky Way contains about 200 billion stars. Anyway, you don't have to ponder how to deal with them because we have a recommended solution for you right here. If you have a large number of fact data (on the order of billions of rows), ask yourself if the dimension data does not change much as compared to the fact data that changes regularly. If this is the case, building the cache might take a disproportionate amount of time since the dimension and fact data needs to be updated. Typically you will have the fact data split across hundreds of partitions. However if the fact data is changing frequently, and if you do need real-time access of the data, then the cache needs to updated frequently and needs to be merged with existing partitions for the new fact data and Analysis Services needs to aggregate the data from multiple partitions to the end users.

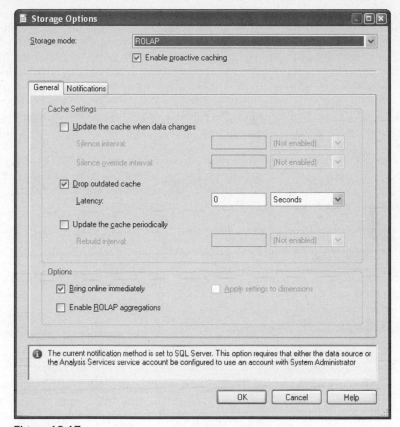

Figure 18-17

The way to approach this type of case is to store historical data (data that does not changes) using the MOLAP storage method and store current data (which can be defined as hours, days, or weeks) in ROLAP mode. Then set proactive caching to operate on the ROLAP partition only. In this way you will get fast access to fact data from the MOLAP store even when there are changes being processed on the ROLAP partition. We recommend this solution whenever you have very large amount of fact data with new fact data arriving periodically and which you need to see in real-time.

> **Even if you have a MOLAP cube specified, if you still want real-time data you should use the connection string property called Real Time OLAP and set it to True while connecting to Analysis Services. This will help provide you the most up-to-date data from the relational data source.**

Summary

Now you really are ready to go real-time with your cubes! To let you in on one of the arcane secrets of "real-time" anything — there is no such thing as real-time in computing, unless you plan to violate the cosmic speed limit (about 186,000 miles per second). There are varying degrees of latency, however, the shortest of which appear instantaneous to the user. Your job as an architect of Business Intelligence solutions is to design your application in such a way as to satisfy the needs of your users. That often means application of these techniques with particular attention paid to keeping the production system online and available during specified hours.

In this chapter you read about three real-world scenarios with one or more recommended solutions for each. These scenarios addressed solutions to long, average, and no latency requirements. A key takeaway here is that you should remain calm in the face of massive amounts of source data; there are ways to contend with it. If you get it right, your users will remain blissfully ignorant of the challenges you faced in keeping up the illusion of real-time data presentation. Indeed, your business decision makers using the system won't know (or care) how the system is implemented, they'll know, "...it just works and has amazingly up-to-date data." That is where you want to be.

19

Securing Your Data in Analysis Services

Your data has value, and as with any item of value it must be protected from outside threats. Security is the set of techniques used to provide you that protection. Indeed, security is an important consideration in the area of business intelligence. Think about it — the very keys to your company's profitability can be surfaced through your data and analytical applications. Just as you secure your personal belongings in a safe place, like a safe deposit box, you must secure your corporate data and applications. In the real word, a safe deposit box has a lock on it requiring a key for entry; only people to whom you give access (provide the key) can actually open the secured object. These concepts map directly onto Analysis Services security. Analysis Services provides you ways to protect your data so that you can restrict access to only those users who are authorized.

The environment within which you are working has a significant impact on the security precautions you should take. In general, if a server is running within the confines of a firewall it helps mitigate the external threats posed and provides increased protection. Disabling unused services/features that can potentially be exploited by hackers is yet another way to reduce risk. Running servers under least-privilege accounts like the network service account also helps ensure your system will not be compromised. Analysis Services provides you the ability to enable or disable various features and run under least privilege accounts on the system as seen in Chapter 12. In addition to these techniques, you learnt additional core security features in Analysis Services that restrict access to unauthorized users (in Chapters 9 and 12.)

In this chapter you learn about the security features in Analysis Services that allow the administrator to define access permissions such as read or write to objects in Analysis Services, followed by restricting access to sensitive data only to those who are allowed to access the data. Restricting access to cube and dimension data is done by specifying MDX expressions that define if the member or cell can be viewed by the user. What better way to learn how to restrict the data than a real world scenario? You learn the functionality of restricting dimension and cell data by means of two scenarios.

Securing Your Source Data

You need to ensure your source data is not compromised through Analysis Services. Analysis Services 2005 provides you with several authentication mechanisms to ensure your source data is retrieved securely by Analysis Services. To retrieve data either at processing time or at query time, an Analysis Services instance needs to connect to data sources based on the storage options (MOLAP or ROLAP) specified for the dimensions and cubes within the database. In order to connect to the relational data source and retrieve the data, the Analysis Services instance needs appropriate credentials.

Analysis Services 2000 supported integrated security as the main authentication mechanism to the data source. The drawback with integrated security is that the Analysis Services 2000 instance used the credentials of the service startup account to connect to the data source. One of the main limitations of Analysis Services 2000 is that you need to provide access to the service startup account for each data source used within databases of an Analysis Services instance, and that can be a little tiresome. If the data source provided username and password options as with Microsoft's SQL Server or Oracle then you were able to specify those in connection strings to the data source. Analysis Services 2005 overcomes this deficiency by providing additional control and flexibility over Analysis Services instances connecting to relational data sources as seen in Chapters 2 and 4.

As with Analysis Services 2000, when you establish a connection to the data source you can specify an authentication mechanism provided by the data source. For example, if you choose Microsoft's SQL Server you have the choice of either choosing Windows authentication or SQL Server authentication as shown in Figure 19-1. Instead of connecting to the data source as the service startup account as in Analysis Services 2000, Analysis Services 2005 provides four options to connect to data sources as shown in Figure 19-2. Once a data source has been created, you can then specify the credentials under which you want the Analysis Services instance to retrieve data. The Impersonation Information tab in the Data Source Designer page shown in Figure 19-2 provides you the flexibility to specify the impersonation option suited for your database. Whenever Analysis Services 2005 instance connects to the data source, Analysis Services uses the impersonation information specified in the data source.

The default selection in the Impersonation Information page is "Use the service account" as in Analysis Services 2000. If this option is chosen, then Analysis Services 2005 impersonates as the Windows account used as the services startup account for Analysis Services instance to connect to the specified data source. When the option "Use specific username and password" is chosen then you need to specify a valid Windows credential account username and password. The Windows username is specified as <domainname>\<username>. This option overcomes the limitation of Analysis Services 2000. You can now have different Windows accounts having access to various data sources within a single database or across Analysis Services databases. If a specific account has access in the data source, then that account can just be specified in the Impersonation tab and you do not have to provide data source access to the service startup account of Analysis Services. It is recommended that the service startup account of Analysis Services be a low privileged account such as network service in order to reduce the attack surface on your system. In such circumstances the network service will typically not have access to your data sources. You can certainly provide data source access to Analysis Services by providing access to the network service account under which Analysis Services is running and choose the service account option for Impersonation Information. However, we recommend you use the "Use specific username and password" with Analysis Services running under a low privilege account to have a more secure environment. However you do need to be aware that whenever the password of the Windows account expires you would need to update the passwords in data sources, which can be done through a custom AMO program if needed. The third option in the Impersonation Information page is "Use the credentials of the current user". This specific option is selected primarily for issuing open rowset queries which are used during data mining querying and for processing objects that have out of line bindings (the object to be processed retrieves data through a query or a table dynamically at the time of processing through the process command). The last impersonation option is "Default". When the Default impersonation is selected, then the impersonation information is obtained from the impersonation information of the database object which also has the same four options. If the impersonation information is Default even for the database object, then the service startup account is used for impersonation while retrieving data for processing Analysis Services objects, server synchronization, and ROLAP queries, and uses Impersonate Current User option for data mining open rowset queries and out of line binding data sources.

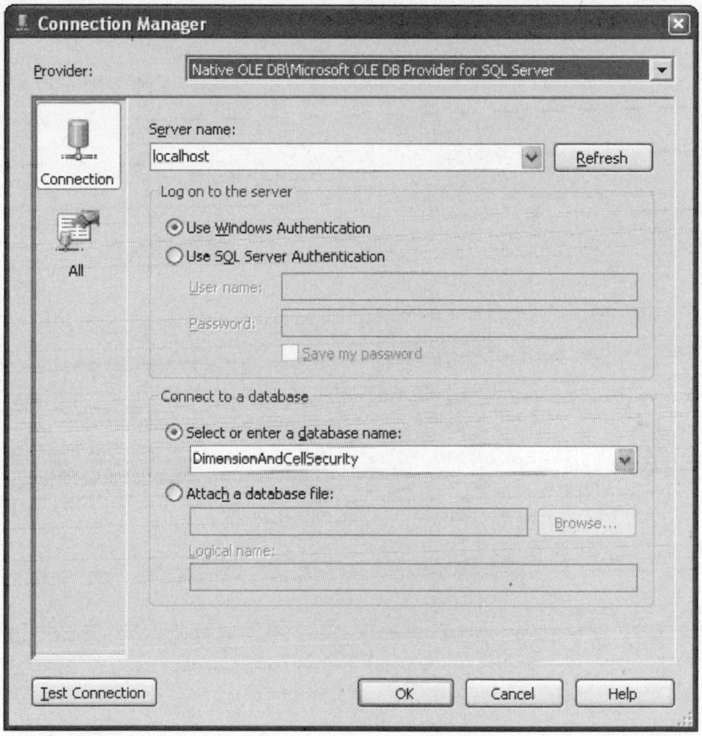

Figure 19-1

You have learned the various impersonation modes that can be set on data source object in Analysis Services 2005 databases along with the recommended option to ensure source data exposed through Analysis Services is secure. You next learn to secure your dimension and cube data appropriately for your end users.

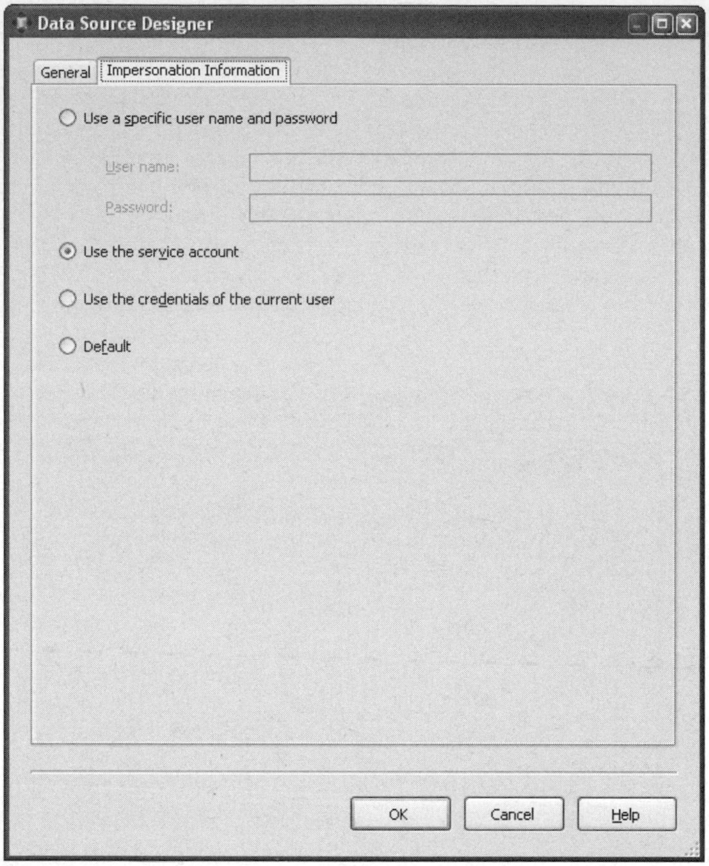

Figure 19-2

Securing Your Dimension Data

Often in business you have to restrict data access from certain sets of users. You might have to restrict whole members of a dimension or just cell values. Restricting access to members of a dimension to users is called dimension security. Restricting access to cell values from users is called cell security. You learn more about securing dimension members in this section, followed by restricting access to cell values in the following section with the help of a business scenario.

Dimension security helps you to restrict access to members of a dimension for your Analysis Services database users based on your business needs. For example, you can have a dimension account that could have members such as accounts payable, accounts receivable, and materials inventory for your company. You might want to restrict user access such that certain users can see only the account types that they are authorized to work with. For example, the personnel working in the accounts payable department should only be able to see the members under accounts payable and should not be able to see all the accounts under accounts receivable or materials inventory. Here is another example: If your company is selling products in various cities, you might want to restrict access to sales employees so that they can only see the data for which they are responsible on a city-by-city basis.

Analysis Services provides security restrictions on objects using an object called "role" as seen in Chapter 9. You can define roles in your database and then restrict permissions to certain members or cells based on those roles. There are several techniques to model security based on the user, and you learn those techniques in this section. A user or a group of users is typically part of a specific role, and all the users in a role will have the same level of security. A user can be part of one or more roles. An Analysis Services instance identifies a user based on the Windows login credentials. When a user connects to an Analysis Services instance, the server iterates through various roles within the server to determine the roles the user is part of. Based on the list of roles a user belongs to, Analysis Services establishes appropriate security restrictions specified in those roles. If a user is part of multiple roles, Analysis Services provides access to a union of all the roles the user is part of. The important thing to know about this union is that if two roles give contradicting indications for user access of some object, access will be allowed. So, this is not a process that tends to upset users. If you have a group of users whose security constraints keep changing dynamically, you do have design alternatives by which you can specify security dynamically. That this is called dynamic security should come as no surprise. You will see the use of dynamic security in the following business scenarios; you will also see the various approaches of securing dimensions that have been mentioned.

Scenario using Dimension Security

Business Problem definition: You are the data warehouse designer for the sales team in your company. You have sales representatives in certain states in the U.S. and each sales representative is responsible for sales within that state. The sales representatives report to regional managers who might also be responsible for sales in a state, and the regional managers report to the U.S. sales manager. The sales representatives can see the sales information of their state. The managers can see the sales information specific to them, as well as the data of the sales representatives reporting to them. You need to design a sales cube so that all the preceding security restrictions are applied to the users when they browse the cube.

We have generated data specifically for this scenario so that it will help you understand the various design techniques that can be applied. This data set contains a list of employees in a company along with several months' worth of sales data; there is also a geography table that contains a list of states. Follow these instructions to restore the relational database from which you will create a cube:

1. Copy the file DimensionandCellSecurity.bak to the back up folder of your Microsoft SQL Server.

2. Connect to the relational SQL Server in SQL Server Management Studio. Right-click the databases folder and select Restore. You will see the SQL Server Restore dialog as shown in Figure 19-3.

3. Select the "From device" option. Click on the ... button and specify the entire path to the relational database back up. You will now see the various databases within the back up file listed below "Select the backup sets to restore".

4. Select the database "DimensionandCellSecurity-Full Database Backup" to restore as shown in Figure 19-3. Select the "To database" drop-down box and select DimensionAndCellSecurity as shown in Figure 19-3. Click the Options page in the Restore Database dialog and make sure the path for restoring the back up for the database and log files are specified correctly as shown in Figure 19-4. Once you have verified this, click the OK button. The database will be successfully restored on your machine.

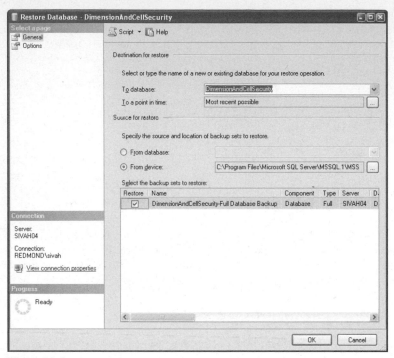

Figure 19-3

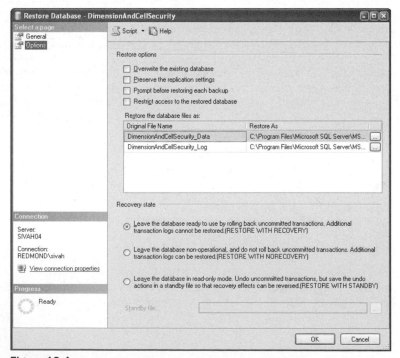

Figure 19-4

5. In order to demonstrate the dimension and cell security, you need users on a domain. To keep it simple you will create local users on your current machine. Run the batch file runuserscript.bat that is provided in the Chapter 19 samples. You will now see that 15 users are added to your machine.

6. Some of the recommended solutions would need to detect the username along with domain name. The Employee table within the DimensionAndCellSecurity database has two columns called employee login and manager login. You have already created the login names for the users in the Employee table in step 5. You need to update the domain name in these columns to your machine name. To get the machine name of your system, open a command prompt and type hostname. Open the employee table by right-clicking it in SQL Server Management Studio and selecting Open Table. You will now have all the rows of the Employee table, as shown in Figure 19-5. Update the login, manager login, and access rights columns by replacing domain with your machine name (You can see that some of the login and manager logins for a few rows are updated with domain name as sivah04.)

You are now ready to create a cube and restrict users to view sales information only for the states for which they are allowed to see the information.

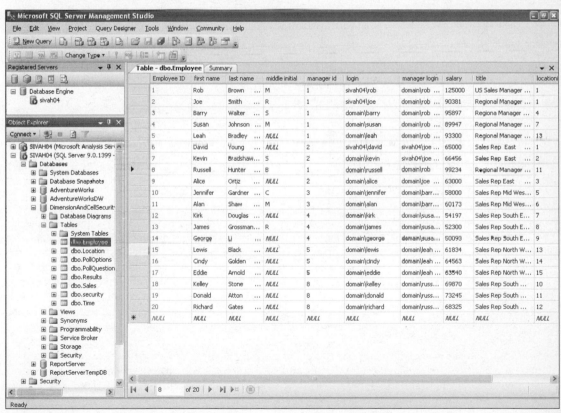

Figure 19-5

7. You need to build a cube from the relational data source. Figure 19-6 shows the UDM of the data warehouse. There is one measure group called Sales that contains the Sales information. The dimensions are Employee, Location, and Time. You can create the UDM yourself using the auto-build option of the cube wizard and select the Sales, Employee, Location, and Time tables from the data source. Alternatively you can use the Analysis Services project DimensionSecurity provided with Chapter 19. The manager-employee relationship in the employee dimension is modeled as a parent-child hierarchy. All the remaining attributes in the employee dimension are only used as member properties for the employee and the corresponding attribute hierarchies are made invisible.

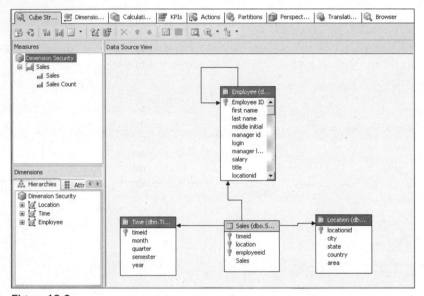

Figure 19-6

Once you have created your UDM, the next step is to define security to restrict the data being seen from the users based on their location. The roles object in Analysis Services allows you to restrict data access based on the login of a user. The roles object contains a collection called membership which you learned in Chapter 12. You can add a user or a group of users to this membership collection. The security restrictions applied in this role will be applied to all the users in the membership collection. In this business problem you need to limit access to the sales representatives so that they can only see the sales information relevant to their state or their direct reports. You will learn several solutions to restrict the dimension member access along with their merits and de-merits.

Restricting a user to see only certain members of the dimension Location automatically restricts the user from seeing the sales information for that location. Location is a dimension and applying security or restrictions to users to certain members of a dimension is therefore called dimension security. If a user is part of more than one role, Analysis Services restricts the user to just a union of the roles the user is member of. For example, if a user is a member of Role1 where you have restricted the users to see location New York, and the user is also a member of Role2 where you have restricted the users of Role2 to location New Jersey, the user can see both these locations when he connects to Analysis Services. If Role1 had security restrictions for a user that does not allow you to see the dimension member New York and Role2 had security restrictions the same user in a way you are able to see the member New York, then the Analysis Services allows the user to access and retrieve the dimension member New York.

Now you will see the various design techniques concerning role definition and what the trade-offs are of those design techniques. Some of the techniques mentioned below are from the dynamic security presentations by Dave Wickert, Program Manager, Microsoft Corporation. These design techniques have been modified for Analysis Services 2005.

The User-Role Approach

One approach is to restrict location access by defining the list of locations a user can see. In order to do this you need to create a role for each user and define the restrictions so that user can only have access to members of specific states. In the example below you will create roles for the users David and Robert. The following instructions show how to solve the problem definition by creating roles for each user:

1. To create a new role for the Sales UDM, right-click the Roles folder and select New Role. A new role is created with the name Role and you will now see the roles designer. Right-click on the Role.role in solution explorer and rename it to David.role. You will be prompted with a dialog box asking you if the object name needs to be changed. Click the Yes option. The roles designer has several views, as shown in Figure 19-7. In the General view you can define administrative tasks on the cube, such as process permissions or permission to read definition of the objects in the database. You can also give full control at the database level, which means the users have full control to edit objects within this database.

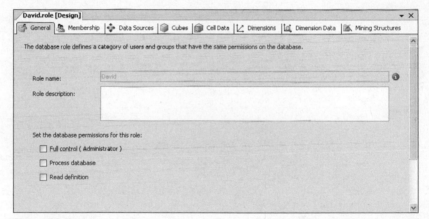

Figure 19-7

2. Click the Membership tab in the roles designer. Click the Add button to add a user to this role, and add the user David. You already created a user account for David earlier in this section. David's login account will be <machinename>\David, where machine name is the name of the machine you are working on. When you click the Add button you will see a dialog where you can enter the domainname\loginname. Enter your machine name followed by "\David" in this dialog and then click OK. You will now see that the user David has been added to the role Role as shown in Figure 19-8.

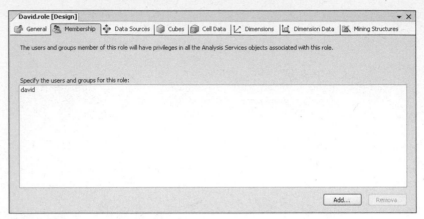

Figure 19-8

3. The next step is to provide access to the cubes and dimensions in the database. Click the Cubes view. You will now see the list of cubes within the database. You can see your UDM Dimension Security. From the drop-down list box under Access, select Read access to the UDM as shown in Figure 19-9. By selecting this access type you have allowed users in this role the ability to read the data in the cube. In addition to providing access to the cube, you can also provide access to the users to drill-through to detail data or to process the cube in this pane. Leave the Local Cube/ Drillthrough Access option to None.

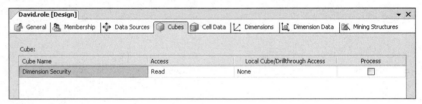

Figure 19-9

4. After providing access to the cube, you can provide access to the database dimensions as well as the cube dimensions in the Dimensions View, as shown in Figure 19-10. The Select Dimension Set option allows you to choose the database dimensions or the cube dimensions. The default view shows all the dimensions in the database. Similar to providing access to the cube, you can provide Read or Read/Write access to each of the dimensions. If you specify Read definition, users have the ability to send discover statements to see the metadata information associated with the dimension. For the database dimension objects you can specify administrative tasks of read definition and processing, but for the cube dimension objects you can only specify access to read or read/write. You have the option to inherit the permissions specified for database dimensions by selecting the inherit check box next to the cube dimension. You can override the permissions set for database dimensions for cube dimensions by deselecting the checkbox under inherit column and then selecting appropriate permissions from the Access column. This is helpful whenever you have a dimension that is shared across multiple cubes within the database and users of a specific role only have specific permissions to dimensions within a specific cube. Provide Read access to all three dimensions as shown in Figure 19-10.

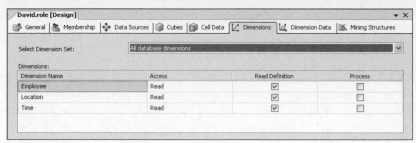

Figure 19-10

5. Click the Dimension Data tab to restrict the members that can be seen by the current role. Specifically, you are restricting access to the user David. Because David is responsible for New York City, he should only be able to see sales information pertaining to New York City. In order to specify this you need to select the dimension Location from the Dimension drop-down list. Select the attribute hierarchy City from the Attribute Hierarchy drop-down list and then select the member New York, as shown in Figure 19-11. The selection of the city New York restricts the users of the role from seeing other cities when they access the dimension Location. If you have complex business logic concerning access to members of a hierarchy, you can implement your logic using MDX expressions in the Advanced tab.

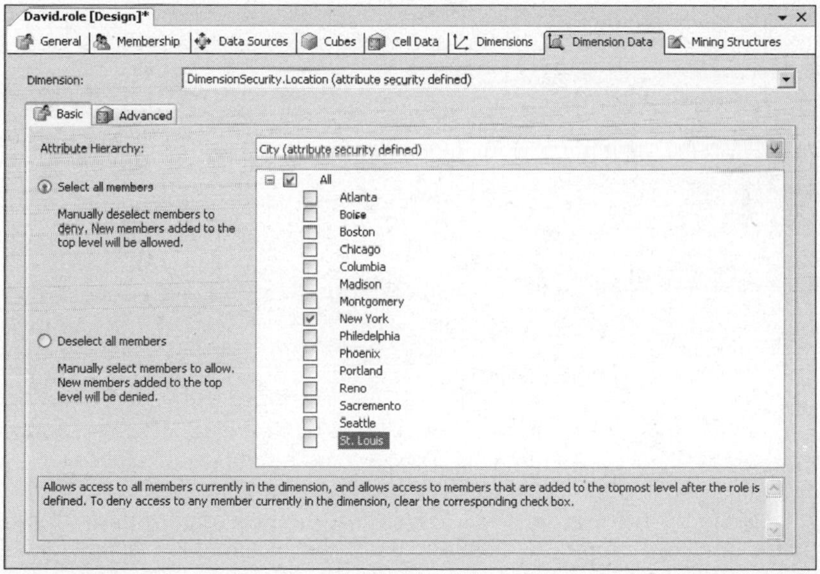

Figure 19-11

If you click the Advanced tab, you will see three sections: Allowed member set, Denied member set, and Default member, as shown in Figure 19-12. You will see that the Denied member set shows all the members of the City hierarchy, except New York, that were not selected in the Basic tab. Analysis Services interprets all members not in the Denied member set to automatically be included in the Allowed member set. That's the reason why you do not see the member

New York in the Allowed member set. You can include your business logic to select the members that are to be allowed or denied for this specific role. The MDX expressions should result in a set of members of the current hierarchy in the Allowed member set and Denied member set. The result of the MDX expression specified in the default member pane should be a single member from the current hierarchy.

An empty set for **Allowed member set** (shown in Figure 19-12) indicates all the members of the current role have access to the members of the current hierarchy. An empty set in the **Denied member set** indicates there are no restrictions applied. {} is not the same as an empty set. Having {} in the **Allowed member set** simply disallows the role members to see any member.

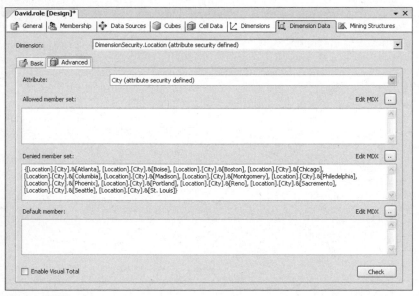

Figure 19-12

6. Similar to restricting access to New York City using the Basic tab in the Dimension data, restrict access for the hierarchies Area, State, Country, and Location so that the user David can only see members relevant to New York City such as East Area, New York State, USA, and the location id 1, which represents New York City. You need to select the appropriate attribute hierarchy from the drop-down list box. You can now test the security you have defined for user David.

7. Open the Dimension Security cube and switch to the Browser pane. By default, if you select Sales and the hierarchy Geography you will be able to see the sales information for all the cities. Click on the Change User icon as shown in Figure 19-13. You will now have a dialog where you can select the role you have created. Select the role David as shown in Figure 19-14 and click OK.

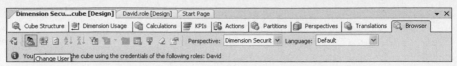

Figure 19-13

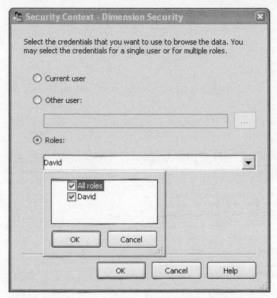

Figure 19-14

8. Drag and drop the sales measure and the Geography hierarchy of the Location dimension into the cube browser as shown in Figure 19-15. As you can see, the user David can only see results for the member New York; his access to the sales information is restricted to that and the totals. However the Totals for the State, Area, and Country do not match the value for city New York. This is due to the fact that sales for other cities are included in the totals.

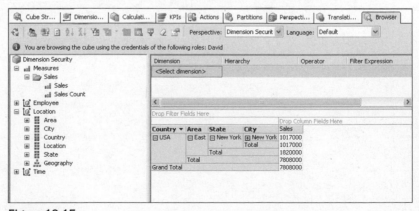

Figure 19-15

9. You can define security permissions on roles so that the totals returned by Analysis Services are calculated for the visible members rather than all the members in the dimension. Open the role David and switch to the Dimension Data tab. Select the cube dimension Location and the hierarchy Area. Switch to the Advanced security definition tab and enable the check box Enable Visual Total as shown in Figure 19-16. Similarly enable the check box for the hierarchies City, Location, and State, and deploy the project to your Analysis Services instance so that new security definitions are updated on the server.

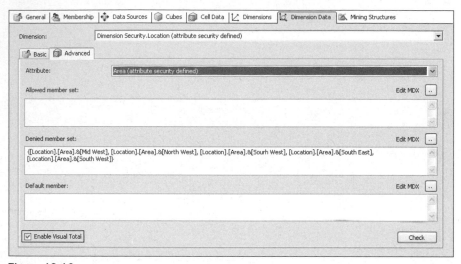

Figure 19-16

If you return to the cube browser and refresh the connection you will see that user David can see the sales information for the city New York and all the totals now match the sales of the city New York as shown in Figure 19-17. By enabling visual totals while defining dimensions security you have ensured that the role David can only see aggregated data for cities that can be accessed by users of the role David.

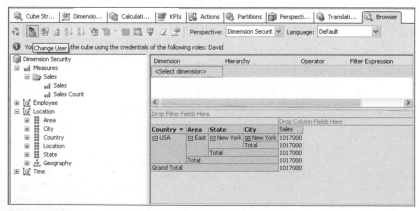

Figure 19-17

10. You need to define security for all the users of the cube. The goal of security definition is that the regional sales managers should be able to see results for all the cities of just their direct reports while the U.S. Sales manager can see the entire set of cities. Just as you specified security on Location dimension for the role David, we recommend you repeat the process to create a role for each user and provide access to the cities that can be accessed by the user. In this way you can restrict data access to users of the cube using the dimension security feature of Analysis Services.

11. In order to restrict the user David to only see sales data relevant to him, you should restrict him from seeing other employee members in the employee dimension. The employee dimension has a parent-child hierarchy called Manager Id. Select the Employee dimension and the Attribute hierarchy Manager Id as shown in the Dimension Data tab. Select the member David Young and the members parents Joe Smith, Rob Brown, and All from the Manager Id hierarchy as shown in Figure 19-18. You have now restricted the user David to have appropriate permissions on employee dimension.

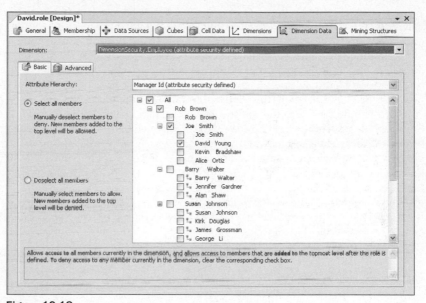

Figure 19-18

12. The role David was restricted so that members of role David can only see the dimension member David and its parents under the parent-child hierarchy Manager Id. In order to make sure David truly can only see data relevant to himself, verify it once again using the cube browser. Drag and drop the Employee⇨Manager Id from the metadata browser to the column area of the OWC in the cube browser. You will now only see the user David. However, you can see that the users of role David can also see the totals of David's managers Joe Smith and Rob Brown as shown in Figure 19-19. This is due to the security definition unique to parent-child hierarchy. In order to make sure David only sees the sales amount sold by him, you might be thinking you can enable visual totals for the Manager Id hierarchy — though Analysis Services 2005 does not actually support enabling visual totals for parent-child hierarchies. Hence you would need to restrict access to the fact data of Joe Smith and Rob Brown using cell security which you will learn about later in this chapter.

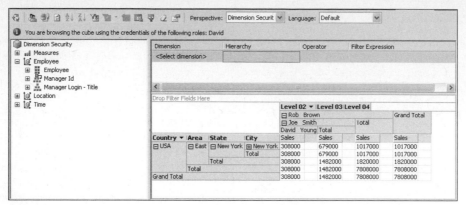

Figure 19-19

13. Each hierarchy has a default member that can be specified using the properties of the hierarchy or by using an MDX script. When you define dimension security, the default member of a hierarchy might be restricted to the users of a role. The roles designer allows you to specify the default member for hierarchies in a dimension for a specific role. In order to specify the default member for a hierarchy, you can either enter the member name in the Default member pane or use the Edit MDX button. In the Dimension Data tab of the roles designer click on the Advanced tab. Click the Edit MDX button for the Default member pane. You will now see the MDX Builder dialog as shown in Figure 19-20. Click the member you want to set as the default member for the hierarchy chosen; New York for the hierarchy State in the Location dimension. If you double-click the member name, the unique name of the member will be shown in the Expression pane. Once the MDX expression is entered in the Expression pane you can click the Check button to make sure your chosen MDX expression is correct. Click the OK button. You will see the default member expression is the roles designer. Specify the default member for the remaining hierarchies for which you have applied dimension security. Deploy the changes to your Analysis Services instance.

14. To verify your default member setting, you can run SQL Server Management Studio as a specific user who is part of the role you have created. Go to Program Files⇨Microsoft SQL Server 2005⇨SQL Server Management Studio. Right-click on SQL Server Management Studio and select Run As. Enter one of the local users who is part of the role, such as <yourmachinname>\ David, and enter the password for the user as shown in Figure 19-21.

15. Open the MDX query editor in SQL Server Management Studio. Select the Dimension Security database. If you send the following MDX query by substituting for dimension, hierarchy, and cube name, you should see the results for the default member you specified in the role as shown in Figure 19-22. If a user belongs to more than one role, the default member for the first role in the roles collection is chosen as the default member for the hierarchy.

```
SELECT <Dimension>.<Hierarchy>.Defaultmember on 0
From <CubeName>
```

The user-role approach is suited to business scenarios where you have a limited set of users and their security permissions do not change frequently. Typically, when the permissions for users are static, this approach will be sufficient to suit your business need and is easy to implement and maintain.

Figure 19-20

Figure 19-21

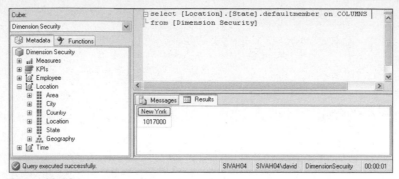

Figure 19-22

The Access-Role Approach

In the user-role approach, you solved the business problem of restricting data access for certain employees in the company. You created a role for each employee in the company and provided appropriate restrictions. Under that design, if new employees are joining the company, the administrator of the cube needs to create a new role for every new salesperson and appropriately provide the restrictions. Similarly, if employees are leaving or changing roles, such as a salesperson promoted to sales manager, you would have to appropriately update the dimension security within the cube. There are two design alternatives from which you can choose to accommodate changes of this nature, which you will learn in this section.

You can create roles based on cities rather than the users. In this design alternative you add all the users who have the right to access specific cities to the role of a specific city. If your company had 100 employees selling into 10 different cities, you would create 10 roles and assign users to those roles — as opposed to creating 100 roles with cities assigned to each. This design leaves open the question of how to go about restricting the employee name in the employee dimension. Assuming the employee have an account of the format <domain name>\<login name> then you can restrict the employee access using an MDX expression that uses the MDX function "username" as shown below.

```
FILTER(employee.employee.MEMBERS,
instr(employee.employee.CURRENTMEMBER.NAME,
right(USERNAME,len(USERNAME)- instr(USERNAME,"\"))))
```

In this dimension security scenario, the logins of each employee match the first name of the employee. The employee parent-child hierarchy in the employee dimension has been modeled in a way that the employee's full name is the named column for the hierarchy. Therefore, while browsing the employee hierarchy you see the full name of the users. If you check the name in the login and match it with the appropriate employee name, you will automatically get the employee member for the user who has logged in. The preceding MDX expression completes the operation of identifying the employee member for the corresponding login using the MDX function username. The username MDX function returns the <domainname>\<loginname>. Finally, the third line in the MDX expression extracts the loginname. This loginname is used in the condition of the Filter MDX function to iterate through all the members of the employee hierarchy and extract the member(s) where the employee name contains the login name.

To extract the login name from the employee name, the VBA function "Instr" is used. The result of the MDX expression is the correct employee member name. Most companies do not have login names that match exactly to the first name or last name of the employees. In such a case you would need to form a complex MDX expression that will return the correct employee member for the Allowed set. You will see an example of a complex MDX expression in this chapter under the Securing your Cube Data section.

To test the preceding solution you can go to the cube browser and bring up the user of interest as shown in Figure 19-23. Analysis Services now impersonates the user account specified in the Other User option to access the cube data. Security restrictions are applied to the user based on the roles that user is part of. You can now browse the dimensions and cell values in the cube browser to ensure your security restrictions were applied correctly.

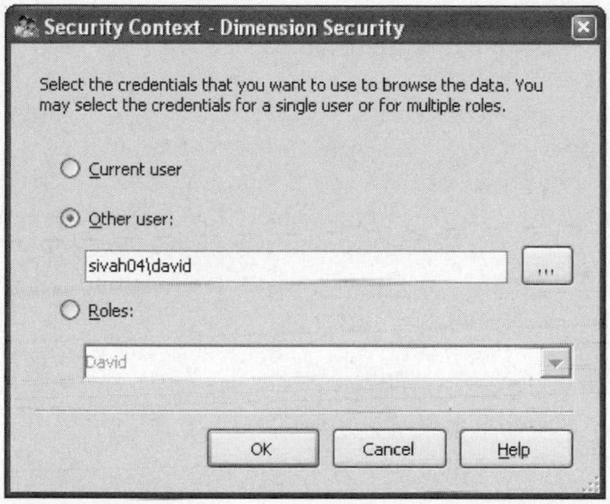

Figure 19-23

If your business needs are such that data access restrictions to users are reasonably static but the number of users is large as compared to the data members in the dimension, the access-role approach might be best suited for your business problem. If your business needs are such that the security restrictions of users change due to modification of roles or location, then you need a solution where you can dynamically add or remove users. We recommend the approach of creating windows user groups and adding the users to those windows groups. The windows groups will actually be added to the membership of a role rather than the users themselves. For the current scenario, you would create a windows group for each city. If the employees move from one location to another, they can easily be removed or added to the appropriate city group. In this way, you do not have to make changes to the roles in Analysis Services. This solution is feasible because Analysis Services leverages windows authentication to authenticate users, and users' permissions keep changing through windows security groups, and Analysis Services is able to handle the security restrictions dynamically. However, in this technique you still need to maintain a role for each windows group. Therefore your Analysis Services database can potentially have several roles that are equivalent to the number of members in the dimension. If you only want to have one role that provides you the ability to restrict data for all users dynamically, you have three different techniques which are explained in subsequent sections. Restricting dimension data access using one role for several users whose data access permissions change periodically is called dynamic dimension security.

The Member Property Approach

One of the ways to provide access to locations for employees is to have a column in the relational data source that contains the list of employees who have access to that location. When you need to modify user access to a location, you can either restrict them or provide access by updating the list of users who have access in the relational column. You might be wondering how this translates into defining the security in Analysis Services dynamically — when a list in the relational data source must be maintained. Actually, it is quite simple with the help of an MDX expression.

First, you need to make sure the relational column in the dimension table is added as an attribute hierarchy in the dimension. You do not necessarily need to browse this attribute, but you need to make this attribute a member property for the attribute hierarchies for which you need to apply dimension security. Create or open an existing relational table called "Location" from within SQL Server Management Studio. Just as you changed domain names in the Employee table, replace all instances of the name domain\username in the column Access to your local machine name\username. If you have created your own Analysis Services project from the relational data source, you will have the Access attribute in the Location dimension. If you are working with the sample project Dimension Security, you will notice that the column access does not exist in the DSV. Go to the DSV designer, right-click and select Refresh. You will now see the prompt that a new column has been added to the table. Click OK to add the column to the DSV. In the dimension editor for Location dimension, drag and drop the column access to the attributes pane to create an attribute hierarchy. Specify the access attribute as a member property for the remaining attribute hierarchies Area, City, State, and Country as shown in Figure 19-24. By default the access attribute is a member property of the key attribute "Location." If you do not want your users to browse this attribute, you can disable the attribute hierarchy Access by changing its AttributeHierarchyEnabled property to false.

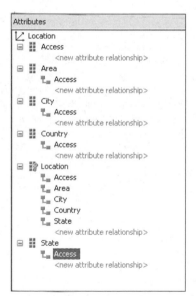

Figure 19-24

The next step is to create the MDX expression in a single role that will define dynamic security for all the users. Once again, you need the MDX function username. Create a new role. Add all the users who need access to the cube to the membership collection of the role. Once you have provided read access to the cube and the dimensions, go to the Advanced tab of the Dimension Data pane. Select the dimension Location and hierarchy City. Enter the following MDX expression for the Allowed set:

```
Filter(Location.City.City.members,
Instr(Location.City.currentmember.properties("Access"),
USERNAME))
```

This expression filters the list of cities that can be accessed by the current user. Member property Access for each city is checked to see if the current user has access using the VBA function Instr. The expression Location.City.currentmember.properties("Access") returns a string that contains the login names of all the users who have access to the current city. The user name function returns the string containing the login name of the current user. The Instr VBA function searches for the occurrence of the current user in the member property. If there is a match, the Instr function returns a positive number and the Filter expression uses that as an indication the condition is true, and therefore the current city can be accessed by the current user. Thus the Filter function is used to retrieve a set of cities that can be viewed by the current user. The Analysis Services project modeling the business problem using the Member property approach is provided with Chapter 19 and is called DimensionSecuritywithMemberProperties. You can test the preceding expression by deploying the current role to the Analysis Services instance and then browsing the cube using a specific user as shown in Figure 19-23.

The member property approach is one of the three dynamic security approaches recommended in this chapter. This is easy to implement and the cost of maintenance (updates of permissions to users in the relational table) is typically low because only a single column gets updated for security changes. One of the advantages of the Member Property approach over the previous approaches is that you have a single role to mainatin. However, the important trade-off in this approach is that whenever you change the security restrictions for the users, the dimension needs to be processed to reflect the changes in the database, thereby restricting the right dimension members. Based on your business requirements you can enable proactive caching on the dimension so that the dimension is processed automatically without intervention from an admin. If your dimension has a large number of members and if you need security changes to be in effect immediately, you might have performance implications because Analysis Services would have to use the dimension in ROLAP mode till the time MOLAP cache gets updated. Based on the size of the dimension members and your business need, you can choose to implement this approach.

The Security Measure Group Approach

In this approach dimension security is modeled using a fact table. A relational table will hold the access permissions of users for the dimension members. If a user has permission for a specific location, that is indicated by a row containing the username, the location, and another column containing a value 1, which indicates the user has permissions to the location. A value of 0 indicates that the user does not have permissions. Ah, something simple! Now you really want to learn this approach, right?

The fact table containing the dimension security restrictions is added as a measure group to the existing cube. The relational column that contains the value of 0 or 1 is the measure that will be used for modeling dimension security. An MDX expression using the measure from the security measure group is used to restrict the dimension members to authorized users. Follow the steps below to model the measure group approach for restricting access to users.

1. Use the Analysis Services project you used in any of the approaches discussed earlier and delete all existing roles. In the DSV designer, right-click and select Add/Remove Tables. Select Table Security and click OK. Mark the employeeid and locationid as key for the security table and make appropriate joins to the dimension and employee tables in the DSV.

2. Open the cube Dimension Security and click the Cube Structure tab. Right-click the cube name in the Measures pane and select New Measure Group. Select the security table from the DSV.

The Analysis Services cube designer automatically adds a new measure group called security and creates two new measures, as shown in Figure 19-25. The Analysis Services tools automatically define the right relationships between the existing dimensions based on the joins specified in the DSV. If you click on the Dimension Usage tab you will see the details of the dimension types and the granularity attributes. Deploy the new cube structure to your Analysis Services instance.

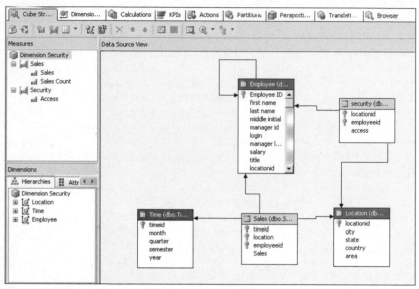

Figure 19-25

3. Create a new role, add all the users who need to access the Dimension Security cube, and provide read access to the cube and dimensions in the database.

4. Go to the Dimension Data tab in the roles designer and select the Advanced option.

5. Select the dimension Location and hierarchy City. Enter the following MDX expression for the Allowed set:

```
FILTER(Location.city.city.MEMBERS,
(FILTER(Employee.Employee.MEMBERS,
instr(Employee.Employee.CURRENTMEMBER.NAME,
right(USERNAME,len(USERNAME)- instr(USERNAME,"\")))).ITEM(0),
measures.access)=1)
```

In the above expression, the login of the current user is retrieved using the username MDX function. The inner filter expression iterates through all the members of the employee dimension and retrieves the set of members who have the name same as the login name. Because there is a one-to-one relationship between users and logins, the inner filter condition results in a set with one member. The returned set cannot be used directly to form a tuple in the conditional expression. There are several ways of forming the condition expression using the outer filter function to retrieve the list of cities accessible by the current user. In the preceding MDX expression, you can retrieve a single tuple of the inner filter function using .ITEM(0). You then have to check if the current user has access to the location. In order to do so, the outer filter function is used, which checks for a value of 1 for each tuple. The resulting set from the outer filter function is the set of cities for which the current user has access. Thus you form an MDX expression that secures the location for each user.

6. Similar to the MDX expression used in step 5, you need to form an MDX expression with the remaining attribute hierarchies Area, Location, State, and Country in the Location dimension, and set the allowed member set for each hierarchy.

7. To restrict the access to members of the employee dimension, you use the MDX expression shown below which uses the login of the user and restricts access to members in the Employee parent-child hierarchy in the Employee dimension.

```
FILTER(Employee.Employee.MEMBERS,
instr(Employee.Employee.CURRENTMEMBER.NAME,
right(USERNAME,len(USERNAME)- instr(USERNAME,"\"))))
```

8. Once you have completed specifying dimension security for each hierarchy, you can deploy the project to the Analysis Services instance. The Analysis Services project modeling dimension security scenario using a fact table is provided under Chapter 19 samples and is called DimensionSecuritywithSecureMG.

9. Using the cube browser's change user option you can verify the dimension security restrictions you have applied in the measure group approach.

The security measure group approach is an extension of the member property approach. Similar to member property approach, you can implement this approach fairly quickly and maintenance is also fairly low cost. You do need to process the security measure group whenever there are security changes and you need the security permissions to take effect immediately. This approach has a lower performance impact as compared to member property approach because only the specific measure group needs to be updated. If you have proactive caching set on this measure group, retrieving the data from this measure group would be fast even if you have a very large number of members in the dimension for which security has been updated. Once the security information is cached on Analysis Services, you do not have a dependency on the relational data source.

The External Function Approach

The member property approach and the secure measure group approach require appropriate dimensions and measure group processing to keep abreast of changes. You can certainly setup proactive caching on the dimension and measure group so that changes to security are immediately reflected. However, processing does involve some cost. The external function approach alleviates the problems of processing and ensures that only the most up-to-date security restrictions are applied to the users.

In the external function approach you write a UDF or a .NET stored procedure that will retrieve the list of locations the current user is authorized to access. For example, the stored procedure can return the list of cities or states or area that a specific user can access as an MDX set. This set is then defined in the Allowed member set as the dimension security restrictions for the current user. Analysis Services exposes the security permissions for .NET stored procedures which restricts the stored procedures access on specific resources such as accessing a network or creating a new file. The security permission provides an extra level of code security so that your Analysis Services is more reliable. There are no such security permissions that can be defined for COM UDFs and you need to trust the programmer has written good quality code. In addition to that you have the option of using the ADOMD server object model in your .NET stored procedure to perform custom business logic which is not available if you code a

COM UDF. You still need to maintain a relational table that provides information on a user's access to locations via a column. In this example you will use the security table that was used in the measure group approach. Since the security table only contains ids of employees and location you will need to make joins to employee and location tables in the relational database to retrieve the right location members. However you can create a new table that will have the list of locations for employees based on the login information. Such a table will probably have the columns login name, city, state, country, location id and access where the column access has values 1 or 0 that indicate if the user has access or not to the specified location.

The .NET stored procedure either needs to return a string that contains the list of locations or an MDX Set of locations. The string needs to contain the unique name of the locations separated by a comma so that you can be converted to a set using StrtoSet MDX function. This function in a .NET store procedure or a UDF allows you to get an MDX set of members that need to be allowed or denied for the users of the current role. Your .NET stored procedure alternatively can return an MDX set using ADOMD server object model that can be directly used in the Allowed members or Denied member sets for dimension security restrictions. In order to create the set of members, your .NET stored procedure needs to identify the member(s) from Analysis Services based on the security restrictions defined in the relational database.

In this dimension security you will create a .NET stored procedure that returns a string containing the unique names of the locations accessible for the current user. The stored procedure will take two arguments, login and location, which are strings. For the login of the current user you can directly pass the MDX function username. The location argument will be the column name of the attribute hierarchy for which you need to retrieve the list of members accessible by the current user. What follows is the pseudo-code for translation into a function in your favorite .NET language

```
Public string getAllowedSet(string login, string location)
{
        1. Connect to your relational data source database
        2. Form the SQL query using the login and location to retrieve
           the members that can be accessed by the users
        3. Iterate through the result set and form the output string so that the
           members are returned in the unique name format.
}
```

The stored procedure first needs to connect to the relational database and send the following query.

```
select <location>
from employee, location, [security]
where employee.[login]= '<login>' and
employee.[employee id] = [security].employeeid and
location.locationid = [security].locationid
```

The words within <> are the parameters passed to the stored procedure. There is a potential for SQL injection attacks with the following query. We recommend use of a parameterized SQL query, which will help you to prevent a breach of security. The stored procedure retrieves the results from the query and forms the output string, which needs to be of the following format.

```
{[Location].<location>.<location>.&[<resultvalue1>],
[Location].<location>.<location>.&[<resultvalue2>],
[Location].<location>.<location>.&[<resultvalue3>],...}
```

The unique name for a member is represented as [Dimension].<Hierarchy>.<Level>.&[MemberName]. For attribute hierarchies the Hierarchy name and Level name will be the same. If the key column and named column for an attribute hierarchy are the same, the member in an attribute hierarchy can be referenced as [Dimension].[AttributeHierarchyName][AttributeHierarchyName].&[MemberName]. Follow the same approach to build a string that will represent the set of members for the members of a hierarchy in the location dimension. The values resultvalue1, resultvalue2, and so on are the results from the SQL query which you need to iterate to form the output of the function. You need to add appropriate error handling to your stored procedure. Once you have compiled your stored procedure, add the stored procedure to the assembly collection of the database with the appropriate impersonation mode and Permission Set. This stored procedure will require an external access permission because it needs to access an external resource (the relational database).

Create a new role and add all the employees' logins to the membership collection. Then specify read access to the cube and dimensions. Assuming the name of the assembly that contains the getAllowedSet function is SecurityMemberSet, specify the following MDX expression for the Allowed member set.

```
StrtoSet(SecurityMemberSet.SecurityMemberSet.getAllowedSet(USERNAME, "City"))
```

Test the security restriction using the cube browser and change to one of the local users and verify the current user is only able to see the locations for which he has been given access.

The external function approach provides maximum flexibility in terms of design approaches. Also, you do not have the overhead of processing a measure group or dimension whenever there are changes to security restrictions. Security restrictions are always immediate because they are queried directly from the relational database each time; hence, you need to make sure the relational server is up and running all the time. Implementing this involves some amount of coding and proper error handling, but it should be worth spending the time up front to implement this type of solution.

Securing your Cube Data

Restricting access to certain cell values of the cube for users is referred to as cell security. For example, in the case of confidential information like employee salaries, you can allow your employees to browse information about other employees such as number of years in the company, title, phone number, address, and login information, but restrict salary information. Because you want the information viewable by the person's manager, you need to control access at the cell value level rather than for whole dimension members.

Similar to dimension security, Analysis Services allows you to specify permission to cells using the roles. Access to cell values in a cube is restricted through an MDX expression that can be defined similar to dimension security. The MDX expression needs to evaluate to true or false. You can specify read and write permissions for cells in a cube. When a query is sent to the Analysis Services instance, the cells that are part of that query result are evaluated and returned. Whenever a cell is being evaluated, Analysis Services checks the permissions set for the cell. If the permission is set, it evaluates the condition to see if the user has access to the cell. If the user is allowed to view the cell, that cell value would be returned as part of the result. If the user does not have access to that specific cell, an appropriate message will be returned to the user.

Scenario using Cell Security

Business Scenario definition: You are the director of the company and you want to take a satisfaction survey or poll of your employees. Employees can only view results of the survey they have filled in. However, managers can view the aggregated results of the poll results if and only if they have more than two direct reports. Managers cannot see individual responses of their direct reports because this is a confidential survey. As an administrator you need to implement a UDM in Analysis Services 2005 so that you give appropriate security restrictions to the users to see the results.

You will use the same Dimension and Cell security relational database. This database contains tables that have the questions of the poll and the results from the employees. The following steps show how to create the right UDM and then apply cell security restrictions for the employees.

1. Create a data source to the relational database Dimension and Cell security relational data source.

2. Create a data source view that includes all the tables from the data source. Remove the security table from the DSV because this is primarily used only for defining dynamic dimension security. Create the joins between the tables as shown in Figure 19-26. Browse the tables Poll Questions, Poll Options, and Results so that you get a good understanding of the scenario. You will notice there are 25 Poll questions with responses from each employee stored in the Results table. Create a calculated column in the employee table so that you have a column called Full name — this will contain a string concatenation of Firstname and LastName. Enter the name for the calculation as Name and enter [First Name] + [Last Name] in the expression.

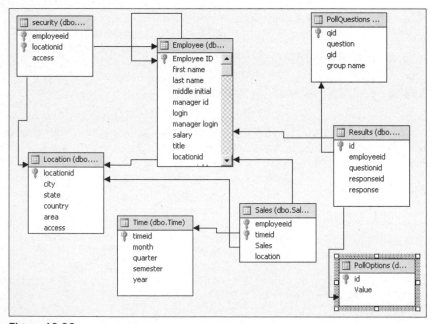

Figure 19-26

3. Run the intellicube wizard to create the cube. You will now have the UDM as shown in Figure 19-27.

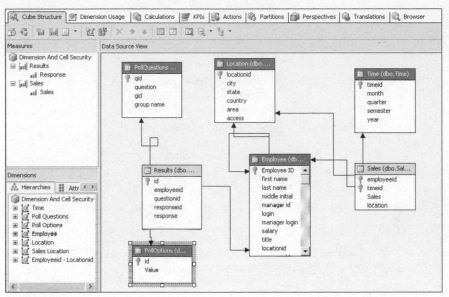

Figure 19-27

4. Delete the count measures created by the intellicube wizard for both the measure groups because they are not needed for analysis in this scenario. The response measure contains a value corresponding to response whether the employee agrees or disagrees to the question. Make the AggregationFunction (a property of the measure) for the response measure as Count instead of Sum since we want to analyze how many users agreed or disagreed to the poll questions.

5. Open the Employee dimension editor and rename the key attribute from Employee to Employee id. Then rename the parent attribute hierarchy as Employee so that you can browse the employee hierarchy. Make the named column for the key attribute of the employee dimension point to the named column Name so that when you browse the parent-child hierarchy you see the names of the employees instead of the ids.

6. In this business example, managers are also involved in the survey. You need a way to distinguish the responses of the manager against the responses of the aggregated results of the direct reports. In order to distinguish the results, set the MembersWithDataCaption property of the parent attribute to " (* data)" as shown in Figure 19-28.

7. Having created the UDM, you now need to define security restrictions for the cells as per the business requirement. Similar to dimension security, create a new role in the database, add all the employees to the membership collection, and provide read access to the cube and the dimensions in the database. Click the Cell Data tab. Click the drop-down list box for the Cube and select the cube Dimension and Cell Security as shown in Figure 19-29.

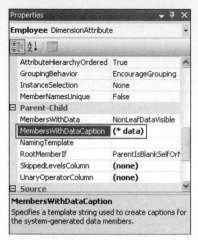

Figure 19-28

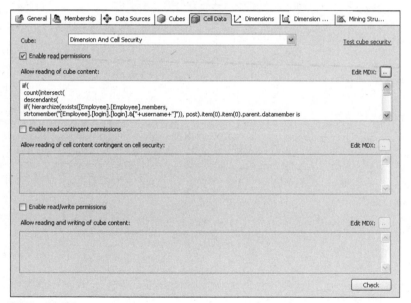

Figure 19-29

The three panes shown in Figure 19-29 help you define the MDX expression for securing the cells. The MDX expression specified here needs to evaluate to either true or false, and this expression gets evaluated for each cell. You need to be careful in specifying the right MDX expression so that you secure the cell values correctly. You can define read permission, read-contingent permission, and read/write permission to the cells. The read and read/write permissions are intuitive as to what the behavior is. If the MDX expression evaluates to true, either read or read/write access for that specific cell is provided to the current user accessing the cell. If an expression is specified for read-contingent permission then the cells specified as viewable by the MDX expression are viewable under two conditions. If those cells are not derived from other cells then they are viewable based on the MDX expression. If those cells are derived from other cells in the cube then those cells are viewable only if that cell and all the cells from which it is derived from are viewable.

8. Following is the MDX expression that needs to be entered in the Enable read permissions pane to meet the business requirement of allowing employees to view their individual responses and managers to see the aggregated response of the poll questions whenever they have more than two direct reports. In the dimension security section, we mentioned that we will demonstrate a complex MDX expression to retrieve the employee name based on the login. The following MDX expression is a generic MDX expression and does not depend on the login name to be the users name.

```
iif(
count(intersect(
descendants(
iif( hierarchize(exists([Employee].[Employee].members,
strtomember("[Employee].[login].[login].&["+username+"]")),
post).item(0).item(0).parent.datamember is

 hierarchize(exists([Employee].[Employee].members,
 strtomember("[Employee].[login].[login].&["+username+"]")), post).item(0).item(0),

 hierarchize(exists([Employee].[Employee].members,
 strtomember("[Employee].[login].[login].&["+username+"]")),
post).item(0).item(0).parent,

 hierarchize(exists([Employee].[Employee].members,
 strtomember("[Employee].[login].[login].&["+username+"]")), post).item(0).item(0))

).item(0)
, employee.employee.currentmember)) > 2    // Condition Check


(count(employee.employee.currentmember.children) > 2
and
count(intersect(
descendants(
iif( hierarchize(exists([Employee].[Employee].members,
strtomember("[Employee].[login].[login].&["+username+"]")),
post).item(0).item(0).parent.datamember is

 hierarchize(exists([Employee].[Employee].members,
 strtomember("[Employee].[login].[login].&["+username+"]")), post).item(0).item(0),

 hierarchize(exists([Employee].[Employee].members,
 strtomember("[Employee].[login].[login].&["+username+"]")),
post).item(0).item(0).parent,

 hierarchize(exists([Employee].[Employee].members,
 strtomember("[Employee].[login].[login].&["+username+"]")), post).item(0).item(0))

).item(0)
```

```
, employee.employee.currentmember))

    > 0 ) or
(strcomp(employee.employee.currentmember.properties("login"),username) =0),
// Value 1

( count(intersect(
descendants(
iif( hierarchize(exists([Employee].[Employee].members,
strtomember("[Employee].[login].[login].&["+username+"]")),
post).item(0).item(0).parent.datamember is

hierarchize(exists([Employee].[Employee].members,
strtomember("[Employee].[login].[login].&["+username+"]")), post).item(0).item(0),

hierarchize(exists([Employee].[Employee].members,
strtomember("[Employee].[login].[login].&["+username+"]")),
post).item(0).item(0).parent,

hierarchize(exists([Employee].[Employee].members,
strtomember("[Employee].[login].[login].&["+username+"]")), post).item(0).item(0))

).item(0)
, employee.employee.currentmember))

    > 0 ) or (strcomp(employee.employee.currentmember.properties("login"),username)
=0)
) // Value 2
```

The above MDX expression can be broken up into three different parts for easier understanding. First, the MDX expression checks if the current user logged in is a manager. If the user is a manager with more than two direct reports, then value 1 expression is evaluated. If the user is a regular employee, then value 2 expression is evaluated. This is done using the IIF statement. The following MDX expression is used to identify if the current user is a manager with more than two direct reports:

```
count(intersect(
descendants(
// Check if current employee is a manager
iif( hierarchize(exists([Employee].[Employee].members,
strtomember("[Employee].[login].[login].&["+username+"]")),
post).item(0).item(0).parent.datamember is

hierarchize(exists([Employee].[Employee].members,
strtomember("[Employee].[login].[login].&["+username+"]")), post).item(0).item(0),
// End of check if current employee is manager

hierarchize(exists([Employee].[Employee].members,
strtomember("[Employee].[login].[login].&["+username+"]")),
post).item(0).item(0).parent,

hierarchize(exists([Employee].[Employee].members,
strtomember("[Employee].[login].[login].&["+username+"]")), post).item(0).item(0))
).item(0)
, employee.employee.currentmember)) > 2
```

The Username function is used to retrieve the current user's login. With the help of StrToMember function and appropriate string concatenation the corresponding member in Login hierarchy is identified. The MDX function Exists is used to identify the intersection of the Employee hierarchy with the member in the login hierarchy for the current user. The result of the Exists function is a set that will contain the employee's name and all his parents. In order to retrieve the employee's name, we use the Hierarchize MDX function with the parameter Post so all the members in the set are ordered in a hierarchical order so that the employee name is the first item in the set. We then retrieve the first item of the set using .ITEM(0).ITEM(0) to retrieve the employee's name. In a parent-child hierarchy, if a member is a parent and also has data values (manager having sales quotas), the same employee name is used to represent the real member as the one that will have the aggregated values. However, these employee names will be at different levels in the parent-child hierarchy, which helps in distinguishing its own data value from the aggregated value for that member. This is shown in Figure 19-30 for the employee Rob Brown.

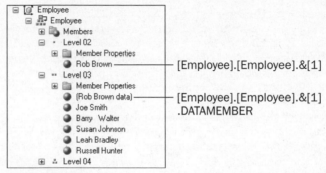

Figure 19-30

To check if the current member is a manager or not, we use the .parent.datamember function and compare it against another MDX expression that just gives the employee name. This MDX expression for evaluating if the current user is a manager is enclosed within comments in the above MDX expression. Based on the evaluation, the correct employee name is identified and we check if the employee has more than two direct reports using the MDX function Descendants.

Once a member has been identified as a manger having more than two direct reports, the IIF function chooses the following expression as the expression for evaluation:

```
(count(employee.employee.currentmember.children) > 2  // Check 1
and
count(intersect(
descendants(
iif( hierarchize(exists([Employee].[Employee].members,
strtomember("[Employee].[login].[login].&["+username+"]")),
post).item(0).item(0).parent.datamember is

hierarchize(exists([Employee].[Employee].members,
strtomember("[Employee].[login].[login].&["+username+"]")), post).item(0).item(0),

hierarchize(exists([Employee].[Employee].members,
strtomember("[Employee].[login].[login].&["+username+"]")),
post).item(0).item(0).parent,

hierarchize(exists([Employee].[Employee].members,
```

```
    strtomember("[Employee].[login].[login].&["+username+"]")), post).item(0).item(0))

    ).item(0)
    , employee.employee.currentmember))

        > 0 )   // Check 2
    or
    (strcomp(employee.employee.currentmember.properties("login"),username) =0)
    // Check 3
```

In this expression two checks are performed to give access to the cells for the employee. The first conditional check (Check 1 AND Check 2) is for providing access to the aggregated cell for the managers, which involves checking if the employee corresponding to the current cell has more than two direct reports followed by the second condition (Check 3), which is an OR condition to allow access to the cells of the employee themselves. The second check (Check 3) is a simple check to match the employee with the login name because login is a member property for the employee attribute. The first condition has two conditional checks, Check 1 and Check 2, which are combined by a logical AND. By default parent members can see the cell values of their descendants (Check 2). In order to make sure individual cell values are not seen by managers, rather just the aggregated cell values can be seen, the additional conditional check (Check 1) is done in the preceding expression.

If the first argument of the IIF function evaluates to false, the result of the third argument of the IIF function will be the result of the function. The third argument is basically the MDX expression to allow regular employees or managers with less than or equal to two direct reports to see their individual responses of the Poll.

You may have grasped the entire MDX cell security expression that solves the business problem by now. You can verify the results of your expression using the cube browser and choosing a specific user or by sending queries from SQL Server Management Studio as a specific user. Launch SQL Server Management Studio using the Run As command with the user Rob. Send the following query to an instance of Analysis Services:

```
SELECT [Measures].[Response] ON 0,
{DESCENDANTS([Employee].[Employee].[Level 02].&[1])}*
[Poll Options].[Value].MEMBERS ON 1
FROM [Dimension And Cell Security]
```

You will see results for the query with certain cell values showing #N/A, as you can see in Figure 19-31.

If you click the cell with #N/A you will see a message that the cell has been secured, as shown in Figure 19-32. You have now successfully solved the business problem of securing the poll results so that managers can only see the aggregated results if they have more than two direct reports.

Writing an MDX expression like the one shown in this example is not trivial. Even an expert MDX developer is bound to make some mistakes. We recommend you execute sections of your MDX expression as MDX queries or create MDX expressions as calculated members (especially in the cases where the MDX expression contains .currentmember), and then ensure the results of the MDX expressions are correct. Once you have validated your MDX expressions, you will be able to successfully define cell security and verify that cell security is applied correctly.

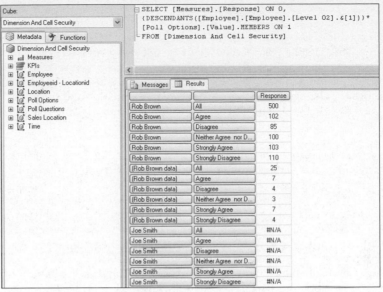

Figure 19-31

Figure 19-32

Summary

Just because you're paranoid doesn't mean they're not out to get you! That should be your mantra as you ponder the possibilities in the security space. In this chapter, you have seen many possible approaches to keeping your data secure. You learned about applying permissions to your relational data sources to help keep them secure, and about how you can restrict access to data in your Analysis Services databases using one of two types of restriction — dimension security and cell security. You learned the techniques of applying dimension security, like how to define roles and how to manage security in a dynamic business environment. Further, you learned about the relevant design choices and how they can be implemented in a real business scenario. You learned how to apply cell security to restrict data at the cell level for certain defined roles at your company. That technique can prevent members of the targeted roles from seeing confidential information. With all that information and the samples demonstrated in this chapter, you should have a good grasp of the techniques and challenges associated with security in Analysis Services.

It was our goal with this book to get you to learn through hands-on work which started as early as Chapter 2. Our other goal was to get you to learn through interaction with sample scenarios, of which there were two, "real-time OLAP" and "dimensions and cell security." We sincerely hope that these goals to engage you for a more powerful learning experience were realized. Less critical, but still important, was the need to impart our sense of possibility and excitement about the powerful user interface and complete SQL Server Business Intelligence stack. Like any software system, it has its strengths and weaknesses, but taken as a whole, the strengths far out-weigh the weaknesses. What you can accomplish using this environment is nothing less than profound. Decide what you want to accomplish and then figure out how to do it using the appropriate tools — chances are very good the system will accommodate your plans. Where possible we threw in some business education — knowing all the while it would not be comprehensive — just to stimulate your appetite for business knowledge. We strongly encourage you to follow up on that aspect of your education moving forward.

We hope you enjoyed this book and learned a lot from it. Please do email any comments about the book to us, positive or negative. We plan to upload additional samples and/or white papers on the web site associated with this book based on requests from readers, so don't be shy. Please do check the book's web site periodically.

MDX Function and Operator Reference

This appendix is a detailed reference to the functions and operators of standard MDX, and extensions as implemented in Microsoft's Analysis Services 2000 and 2005. The main body of the appendix lists the functions and operators in alphabetical order, along with any arguments and the result's data type. We have included a pair of indexes at the beginning to help you navigate.

Index to Functions

We have found that two different types of indexes are useful for looking up a function or operator: by name and by return type.

Alphabetical Index

Return Type Index

The functions are all listed here by return type:

Number

Predict(): 769

.Properties(): 769

.PropertyName: 770

Rank: 771

RollupChildren(): 772

StdDev(): 776

StdDevP(): 776

StDev(): 776

StDevP(): 776

StrToValue(): 779

Sum(): 779

.Value: 787

Var(): 787

Variance(): 787

VarianceP(): 787

VarP(): 787

String

CalculationPassValue(): 711

CASE: 712

CoalesceEmpty(): 713

CustomData: 719

Generate(): 738

Iif(): 740

LookupCube(): 754

MemberToStr(): 756

.Name: 758

.Properties(): 769

.PropertyName: 770

SetToStr(): 774

TupleToStr(): 783

.UniqueName: 784

UserName: 786

Logical

And: 707

Is: 742

IsAncestor(): 743

IsEmpty(): 743

IsGeneration(): 744

IsLeaf(): 745

IsSibling(): 584

NOT: 760

Or: 761

XOR: 794

Member

Tuple

Set

Dimension, Hierarchy, and Level

The following functions return references to dimensions, hierarchies, or levels:

Miscellaneous

Call: 711

Error(): 734

Scope: 774

SetToArray(): 774

Basic Operators

This section lists the basic operators for manipulating strings, numbers, and logical conditions.

Value Operators

Table A-1 lists the basic operators. A *ValueExpr* can be either numeric or string, but it must be the same type on both sides of the operator. An *ObjectExpr* can refer to any metadata object or to NULL.

Expressions can be grouped with parentheses () to make the ordering of operations clear.

Table A.1   List of Operators

OPERATOR	RESULTS IN
NumericExpr + NumericExpr	Addition
NumericExpr - NumericExpr	Subtraction
*NumericExpr * NumericExpr*	Multiplication
NumericExpr / NumericExpr	Division
- NumericExpr	Unary negation
StringExpr + StringExpr	String concatenation (Microsoft extension)
ValueExpr < ValueExpr	Less than
ValueExpr > ValueExpr	Greater than
ValueExpr <= ValueExpr	Less than or equal to
ValueExpr >= ValueExpr	Greater than or equal to

Table A-1 *(continued)*

OPERATOR	RESULTS IN
ValueExpr <> *ValueExpr*	Not equal to
ValueExpr = *ValueExpr*	Equal to
BooleanExpr **AND** *BooleanExpr*	True if both expressions are true, false otherwise.
BooleanExpr **OR** *BooleanExpr*	True if either expression is true.
NOT *BooleanExpr*	True if expression is not true, false otherwise.
BooleanExpr **XOR** *BooleanExpr*	True if either of the expressions is true but not both of them, and false otherwise.
MemberExpr **IS** *MemberExpr*	True if the two member expressions evaluate to the same member. This is an extension to OLE DB for OLAP that both Microsoft and Hyperion implement. Note that *NULL* may be used in AS2000 and AS2005 to test if the other member reference is not valid.
ObjectExpr **IS** *ObjectExpr*	True if the two object expressions refer to the same object, and false otherwise. Any reference to a nonexistent object will return true when combined with NULL, as in Time.[All Time].Parent.Level IS Null. (Microsoft extension to OLE DB for OLAP).
SetExpr1 + *SetExpr2*	Set union, preserving duplicates as sequence (like { *SetExpr1*, *SetExpr2* }; see below; Microsoft extension).
SetExpr1 - *SetExpr2*	Set difference (Microsoft extension).
-*SetExpr*	Complement of *SetExpr* (Microsoft extension). The *SetExpr* must consist only of members from one level of one hierarchy-dimension. Returns all members of that level except those appearing in *SetExpr*.
SetExpr1 * *SetExpr1*	Cartesian product of sets; see *CrossJoin()* (Microsoft extension).
Existing *set_expression*	Evaluates *set_expression* within the current member context. If the existence of the set's members or tuples depends on the current member context (in all dimensions other than those of the *set_expression*), the returned set will reflect the context

Constructing Tuples

```
( member [, member . . .] )
```

Tuples can be explicitly constructed by listing members from one or more dimensions, enclosed within parentheses and separated by commas. If only one dimension is present in the tuple, the parentheses can be omitted as well. Any member specification will work, not just explicitly named members. For example, the following examples are all tuple specifications:

```
[Time].[1997]
([Time].[1997])
([Time].[1997], [Customer].[All Customers])
([Time].[1997], {[Customer].Members}.Item (0))
```

Note that when a function requires that a tuple be one of its arguments within parentheses, the parentheses must be placed around the tuple as well as used to enclose the argument list for the function. For example, the following would be a correct tuple specification to be passed to TupleToStr():

```
TupleToStr( ([Time].[1997], [Customer].[All Customers]) )
```

Trying to create an empty tuple with () will result in a syntax error. In Analysis Services 2005, you can create an essentially empty tuple with null member references. For example (null, null) specifies an empty tuple.

Constructing Sets

```
{ tuple or set  [, tuple or set  . . . ] }
```

Sets can be explicitly constructed by enclosing one or more tuples or sets with the same dimensionality within curly braces, "{" and "}". Each tuple or set specification must be separated from the next by a comma. For example, the following are all sets:

```
{ [Time].[1997] }
{ ([Time].[1997], [Customer].[All Customers]) }
{ [Time].[All Time], [Time].[Year].Members,
  { [Time].[Quarter].Members } }
```

The first two are sets of one tuple each, and the last one is a set composed of one member and two sets, in order. Note that in the last example, one set is syntactically inside the other, and the inner one is also enclosed in curly braces. This is not required, and it does not affect the interpretation in any way. Although an empty set is not usually of much practical use, it may be created with an empty pair of curly braces: {}

```
member : member
```

This operator constructs a set from two members and uses the two members as endpoints. The two members must be on the same level; if they are not, a parse error will occur. If you use the database ordering of the members in the dimension, all members between the endpoints will be included. It is not an error for the two members to be the same (that is, {[Time].[2006] : [Time].[2006]}).

In Microsoft Analysis Services 2005, and 2000, if the member on the right-hand side of the colon is earlier in the database ordering than the member on the left, a range is constructed from the member on the right to the member on the left (as though the members were flipped around the colon; the set will be in dimension order). In AS2005, if only one member is invalid and the other is valid, a range is constructed from the valid member to the end of the level. An invalid left-hand member creates a range from the first member in the level, and an invalid right-hand member creates a range to the last member in the level. In AS2000, if either of the members is invalid, a parse error occurs.

See also: MemberRange()

Function and Operator Reference

A

AddCalculatedMembers(*set***)**   Returns: set
Extension: AS2000, AS2005

By default, when a set of members is specified using a function that retrieves a set based on metadata (such as .Members, .Children, Descendants(), and so on), only base members are returned, even though calculated members may be within that range. The AddCalculatedMembers()

function adds in all of the calculated members that are siblings of the members specified within the *set*. Each calculated member that was not already in the set is added in database order after its last sibling member in the *set*. The *set* is limited to only one dimension. Note that this function adds all calculated members defined, whether they were defined by CREATE MEMBER at the server or at the client, or in the query through WITH MEMBER.

See also: .AllMembers, StripCalculatedMembers()

Aggregate(*set* **[,** *numeric value expression***])** Returns: number
Standard

This function aggregates the cells formed by the set according to the default aggregation operator for any measures in context. If a numeric value expression is provided, then this function sums the expression's set of values over the cells. In the event that the cells are of a base measure, the aggregation function specified for the measure is used. In AS2000, if the aggregation functions of the measure are COUNT, MIN, or MAX, then COUNT, MIN, or MAX, respectively, is the aggregation operation used; otherwise, the aggregation operation used is summation. In AS2005, the list of intrinsic measure aggregation functions with which the Aggregate() function will work is much longer, including:

Sum

AverageOfChildren

ByAccount

Count

FirstChild

FirstNonEmpty

LastChild

LastNonEmpty

Max

Min

DistinctCount

Aggregate() will not aggregate measures whose aggregation function is None, however.

NOTE Although you may specify an expression to be evaluated by this function, this function does not work if you use calculated members as its inputs. (If a calculated member "M" has a higher SOLVE_ORDER than a calculated member on a different dimension that is performing the Aggregate(), then "M" will use the results of the aggregating member.)

This comes in handy when you have a set of different measures with different aggregation rules that are all being queried for. Calculated members performing period-to-date aggregations as well as aggregations on other dimensions will often be best constructed out of this operator. (Essentially, this is the implicit operation carried out within Analysis Services's hierarchies.) Consider the following calculated member:

```
CREATE MEMBER [Time].[MonthsOf2006ToDate] AS
'Aggregate ( {[Time].[Jan 2006] : [Time].[May 2006]} )'
```

When combined with a summing measure, this member will yield the sum of its values over the range of January through May 2006. When combined with a measure aggregating by MAX, this member will yield the MAX of its values over that same time period.

NOTE In Analysis Services 2000, measures aggregated by DISTINCT COUNT cannot be aggregated by this function. This is fixed in Analysis Services 2005.

See also: Sum(), Count(), Min(), Max(), Avg(), DistinctCount()

dimension.**AllMembers**

hierarchy.**AllMembers**   Returns: set

level.**AllMembers**

All return: set

All are extensions: AS2000, AS2005

Generally, the .AllMembers functions are semantically equivalent to Add-CalculatedMembers(Scope.Members), but they provide a more intuitive syntax. Although the Microsoft documentation only refers to .AllMembers for dimensions and levels, we note that in the case of multiple hierarchies on a dimension, you can only use this against one hierarchy.

The only case where .AllMembers and AddCalculatedMembers() differ is when no members are visible in the scope of [Dimension].Members, [Hierarchy].Members, or [Level].Members. This can occur on the measures dimension if all measures are hidden in a cube.

The following two statements will generally return the same set:

```
[Measures].AllMembers
AddCalculatedMembers([Measures].Members)
```

See also: AddCalculatedMembers(), StripCalculatedMembers()

Ancestor(*member, level***)   Returns: member**
Standard

Ancestor(*member, distance***)   Returns: member**
Extension: AS2005, AS2000

This function finds the source *member*'s ancestor at the target *level* or *distance*. If the target level is the level of the source member, then the source member is returned. If a distance number is specified, it is the number of hierarchical steps above the member. A distance of 0 will return the source member. The behavior of Ancestor() is shown in Figure A-1.

See also: Descendants(), .Children

Ancestors(*member, level***)   Returns: set**
Standard.

Ancestors(*member, distance***)   Returns: set**
Standard.

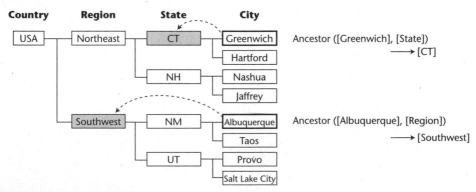

Figure A-1   Behavior of Ancestor().

The standard and Microsoft implementations of this function find the set of ancestors for the source *member* at the target *level*. If the database supports multiple parents for a single member in a hierarchy, then this function may return multiple members. Other databases (like Microsoft Analysis Services) will return a set of one member. If the target *level* is the level of the source *member*, then the source member is returned as a set.

The target level can be expressed either by name as a string expression or by distance as a numeric expression where 1 represents a parent, 2 represents a grandparent, and so on. Using 0 as a distance will return the member itself.

Note that although this function in theory may return multiple ancestors, the ancestors must be from the same hierarchy and the same level.

See also: Ancestor(), Ascendants(), Descendants(), .Children

expr1 **AND** *expr2*   Returns: Boolean
Standard

The AND operator returns true if both *expr1* and *expr2* are true, and false otherwise. In Microsoft Analysis Services, if *expr1* is false, then *expr2* is not evaluated (there is no need to; the result is guaranteed to be false); this may be relevant when *expr2* could have side effects or is costly to evaluate.

Ascendants(*member***)**   Returns: set
Extension: AS2005, AS2000

This function returns the full set of ancestors for the given member all the way up to the root of the hierarchy or dimension. The ancestors are ordered from the bottom up, so that parents follow children. The given member is included in the set. It is very useful in queries when you want to include all higher level totals for a given member or set of members. The behavior of Ascendants() is shown in Figure A-2.

Note that the order of the resulting set must be changed by using Hierarchize() to get a top-down ordered set before being used in conjunction with any of the drill-related or VisualTotals() functions.

See also: Ancestor(), Ancestors(), Descendants(), .Children

Avg(*set* [, *numeric expression*])   Returns: number
Standard

This function takes the average of the nonempty values found across
cells related to the *set*. If a numeric expression is supplied, then its values
are averaged across the cells in the set. Note that the average is formed
out of the sum of the cells divided by the count of the nonempty cells. If
you want to take the average over all cells, treating empty as zero, then
you can either create a numeric value expression that converts missing
to zero, or you can take the Sum() over the set divided by the Count() of
the set, including empty cells.

See also: Aggregate(), Sum(), Count(), Min(), Max()

Axis(*Axis number*)   Returns: set
Extension: AS2005, AS2000

This function returns the set of members or tuples that are included on a
specified axis. Axis(0) returns the column tuples, Axis(1) returns the row
members, and so on. This function is likely to be used most often in
client applications when building queries. The following example uses
Axis() in conjunction with Generate() and TopCount() to select the top
two stores for each of the four quarters of 2006. Note that this statement
will return results for all selected stores for each of the four quarters:

```
SELECT
Generate(
  Axis (1),
  TopCount(
    [Store].[Store Name].Members,
    2,
    ([Measures].[Amount],
     Axis(1).Current)
  ),
  ALL
) on 0,
{[Time].[2006].Children} on 1
FROM Sales
```

You can use this set as the source for various set-related functions, such
as .Count, Extract(), Distinct(), Except(), and so on. The .Item() function
can be used as well. To use this function to select the top two stores
based on the first member in the set down the rows, you would write
the following:

```
SELECT
TopCount(
  [Store].[Store Name].Members,
  2,
  ([Measures].[Amount],
   Axis(1).Item(0))
) on 0,
{[Time].[2006].Children} on 1
FROM Sales
```

Regardless of which dimensions were involved in the rows, the query would work fine (so long as [Store] is not in the rows!).

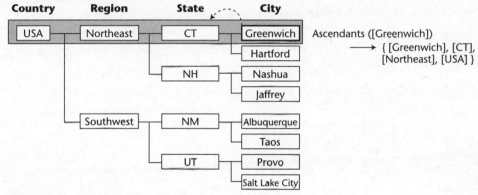

Figure A-2   Behavior of Ascendants().

However, the execution of a query (building the axes and calculating cell values) does not provide a context on its own for iterating over the tuples in the set. For example, the following results in an error with the message stating that .Current cannot be used in this context:

```
WITH
MEMBER [Measures].[Disp] AS
'[Measures].[Unit Sales]',
FORE_COLOR = 'iif (Axis(1).Current.Item(0).Level.Ordinal > 1, 0, 5)'
SELECT
{ [Time].[Quarter].members } on 0,
{ Ascendants ([Customers].[Name].&[2659]) } on 1
FROM Sales
WHERE   [Measures].[Disp]
CELL PROPERTIES FORMATTED_VALUE, FORE_COLOR
```

This can be explained by the fact that the filter is always evaluated first. However, the following will also fail with the same error:

```
WITH
MEMBER [Measures].[Disp] AS
'[Measures].[Unit Sales]',
FORE_COLOR = 'iif (Axis(1).Current.Item(0).Level.Ordinal .> 1, 0, 5)'
SELECT
{ CrossJoin (
    [Time].[Quarter].members,
    { [Measures].[Disp] }
) } on 0,
{ Ascendants ([Customers].[Name].&[2659]) } on 1
FROM Sales
CELL PROPERTIES FORMATTED_VALUE, FORE_COLOR
```

B

BottomCount(set, index **[,** numeric expression**])**   Returns: set
Standard

See the description for TopCount()

BottomPercent(set, percentage, numeric expression**)**   Returns: set
Standard

See the description for TopPercent()

BottomSum(set, value, numeric expression**)**   Returns: set
Standard

See the description for TopSum()

C

Calculate   Returns: null
Extension: AS2005

Aggregates the cell values within a cube according to the defined behavior. Before Calculate statement is applied contents of non-leaf cells are null.

CalculationCurrentPass()   Returns: number (integer)
Extension: AS2005, AS2000

This returns the current pass number for which the expression is being calculated. Typically, this will be used with iif() to pick out a particular expression based on the pass number. The lowest pass number is 0. Calculated cells begin calculations with pass 1.

See also: CalculationPassValue(), iif()

CalculationPassValue (*numeric expression*, *pass number* [, *flag*]) Returns: number
Extension: AS2005, AS2000

CalculationPassValue (*string expression*, *pass number* [, *flag*]) Returns: string
Extension: AS2005, AS2000

This function evaluates the given expression at the calculation pass identified by pass number and returns the value to the current calculation pass. If the flag is specified, it may be one of the following:

FLAG	DESCRIPTION
ABSOLUTE	The pass number is the absolute number of a pass (starting from zero). If you refer to a pass number that is higher than the currently executing pass, you will begin invoking the higher numbered pass for the cells that are referenced in the expression if they have not already executed that pass.
RELATIVE	This indicates to take the value from the pass that was pass number passes later. A negative pass number will refer to an earlier pass, and a positive pass number will invoke a later pass. A pass number that would refer to a pass earlier than pass 0 will silently cause a reference to pass 0.

Note that in AS2005, passes for session-scoped cell calculations (created by CREATE CELL CALCULATION) and those for query-scoped cell calculations (created by WITH CELL CALCULATION) are separated, so that query, session and global passes (from MDX scripts) cannot refer to calculations in each other.

See also: CalculationCurrentPass(), iif()

Call UDF-Name ([*arguments*]) Returns: Void or rowset
Extension: AS2005, AS2000

This function executes a registered external function that does not return anything (that is, a procedure in Visual Basic). Data can be passed to the function as if it were any other external function. In AS2005, Call can return either nothing or a rowset. In AS2000, the Call itself will return an empty cell value. Unlike other MDX functions and operators, this one cannot be combined with any other operators or functions; when used in an expression, the sole contents of the expression will be the Call invocation. Here's an example:

```
Call MailMsgToUser (
  [Employee].CurrentMember.Properties ("Email Address"),
  "Look at department" + [Department].CurrentMember.Name
)
```

CASE

```
CASE reference-expression WHEN test1 THEN result1
    [ ... WHEN testN THEN resultN ]
    [ ELSE DefaultResult ]
  END
```

Returns number, string, member, tuple, set, level, hierarchy, array (all AS2005 only)

Standard (except AS2000)

```
CASE WHEN textExpr1 THEN result1
    [ ... WHEN testExprN THEN resultN ]
    [ ELSE DefaultResult ]
  END
```

Returns number, string, member, tuple, set, level, hierarchy, array (all AS2005 only)

Standard (except AS2000)

This operator provides a multiway conditional test for values to return. It is similar to the iif() function, but can handle more conditions. The different implementations provide different capabilities.

The *expression* in the first form can be either a numeric expression or a string expression, and each *test* must the same type (numeric or string). Each *test* from *test1* through *testN* is evaluated in sequence until the result of a test is equal to the *reference-expression*. When that happens, the corresponding *result* following the THEN clause is returned. If no *test* expression is equal to *reference-expression*, then the *DefaultResult*, if any, is returned. If none is specified, then the result of the function is NULL.

In the second form of CASE, each *testExpr* is evaluated as a Boolean expression in sequence until one evaluates as true. The *result* expression of the corresponding THEN clause is returned. If no *testExpr* evaluates to true, then the *DefaultResult*, if any, is returned. If none is specified, then the result of the function is NULL.

In AS2005, the type of result from any THEN clause can be different from that of any other THEN clause. A single CASE operator could return strings, numbers, and/or any of the other types listed depending on the *reference-expression* and/or *test* expressions. When no test evaluates to true and there is no default clause, a NULL is returned.

AS2005 allows the CASE expression to serve as an axis expression or as the input to other functions that use sets, such as Avg() or Generate(). For AS2005, since CASE can return most MDX objects, you can write expressions such as the following, which uses the CASE construct to pick an attribute dimension whose members end up in a named set [ASet]:

```
WITH SET [ASet] AS
CASE
WHEN condition1 THEN [Customer].[Region]
WHEN condition2 THEN [Customer].[State]
ELSE [Customer].[City]
END.Members
...
```

See also: *CoalesceEmpty(), iif()*

member.**Children**   Returns: set
Standard

This function returns the children of the given member. *member*.Children is equivalent to {*member*.FirstChild : *member*.LastChild}. As you might expect, if you apply *member*.Children to a leaf member, the result is no members (an empty set). Figure A-3 illustrates the behavior of the .Children function.

See also: *Ancestor(), Descendants(),.Parent, .Siblings*

ClosingPeriod ([*level* [, *member*]]**)**   Returns: member
Standard

See description of *OpeningPeriod()*

CoalesceEmpty (*value expression* [, *value expression* ...]**)**   Returns: number or string
Standard

This function evaluates the first *value expression* listed. If it is not NULL, then the value of that expression is returned. If it is NULL, then the second *value expression* is evaluated and it is returned if it is not NULL. Each subsequent expression, if present, is evaluated in turn; if the last one is NULL, the entire operator returns NULL.

CoalesceEmpty() can either take all number-valued expressions and return a number or it can take all string-valued expressions and return a string.

See also: iif(), IsEmpty(), CASE

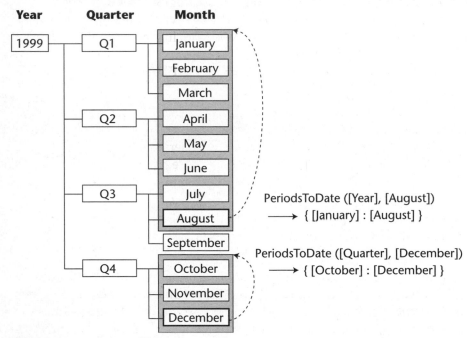

Figure A-3 member.Children.

Correlation (*set, y numeric value expression* [*, x numeric value expression*])
Standard

This function calculates a correlation coefficient between x-y pairs of values. The *y numeric expression* is evaluated over the set to get the y values for each pair. If the *x numeric expression* is present, then it is evaluated over the set. Otherwise, the cells formed by the set are evaluated within the current context, and their values are used as the x values. The formula for the correlation coefficient is as follows:

$$\frac{n\sum_{i=1}^{n}x_iy_i-\sum_{i=1}^{n}x_i\sum_{i=1}^{n}y_i}{\sqrt{n\sum_{i=1}^{n}x_i^2-\left(\sum_{i=1}^{n}x_i\right)^2}\sqrt{n\sum_{i=1}^{n}y_i^2-\left(\sum_{i=1}^{n}y_i^2\right)^2}}$$

If either the y or the x *numeric expression* is a logical or text value, or if the value is NULL, then that tuple and its related values are not included in the correlation. Zero values for y and x are included.

Count(*set* **[, INCLUDEEMPTY | EXCLUDEEMPTY])**   Returns: number (integer)
Extension: AS2005, AS2000

This function counts the cells in the range formed by the *set* (as opposed to counting the tuples in the set). In Analysis Services, without the INCLUDEEMPTY flag, only nonempty cells are counted; with the flag, all cells are counted. INCLUDEEMPTY is the default.

See also: .Count, Sum(), Avg(), DistinctCount(), NonEmptyCount()

*Dimension.***Count**   Returns: number (integer)
Extension: AS2005, AS2000

This function counts the number of dimensions in a cube. For AS2005 it returns the total number of hierarchies within the cube.

*Levels.***Count**   Returns: number (integer)
Extension: AS2005, AS2000

This function count returns the number of levels in a dimension on hierarchy including [All] level.

*Set.***Count**   Returns: number (integer)
Extension: AS2005, AS2000

This function counts the tuples present in *Set*. It is equivalent to `Count (Set, INCLUDEEMPTY)` but is syntactically simpler.

See also: Rank(), Count(), Avg(), Set.Item()

Tuple.**Count**   Returns: number (integer)
Extension: AS2005, AS2000

This function counts the dimensions present in *Tuple*.

See also: Tuple.*Item()*

Cousin(*member, ancestor_member*)   Returns: member
Standard

This function returns the member that has the same relative position under a specified ancestor member as the initial member specified. The Cousin() function is best understood by walking through its algorithm. Figure A-4 shows the behavior of the Cousin() function. From the *member*'s level to the *ancestor_member*'s level, Cousin() tracks which sibling it is related to under its ancestor at that level. [March 2001] is the third child of the first child of [2001]. The same path is then followed from the ancestor member down to the level of *member*. [March 2002] is the third child of the first child of [2002]. Because of the straightforwardness of this algorithm, it works best when you can guarantee the same number of descendants under each ancestor. For example, it is likely that years, quarters, and months or days, hours, and minutes can be used with Cousin(), because each of these levels has a fixed relationship within itself. However, a cousin of January 31 in February will not exist because February will not have a thirty-first day.

See also: ParallelPeriod(), PeriodsToDate()

Covariance(*set, y numeric expression* [*, x numeric expression*])   Returns: number
Standard (9)

CovarianceN(*set, y numeric expression* [*, x numeric expression*])   Returns: number
Standard

Covariance() calculates the population covariance and uses the biased population formula (dividing by the number of x-y pairs). CovarianceN() calculates the sample covariance and uses the unbiased population formula (dividing by the number of x-y pairs minus 1). If either the *y* or the *x numeric value expression* is a logical or text value, or if the value is NULL, then that tuple and its related values are not included in the correlation. Zero values for y and x are included.

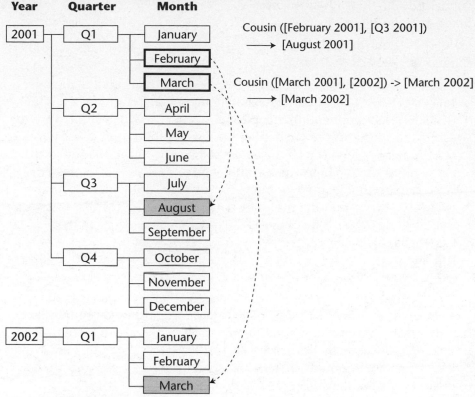

Figure A-4   Cousin() function.

These functions calculate the statistical covariance across x-y pairs of values. The *y numeric expression* is evaluated over the set to get the y values for each pair. If the *x numeric expression is present*, then it is evaluated over the set. Otherwise, the cells formed by the *set* are evaluated within the current context, and their values are used as the x values. The biased population formula for covariance is as follows:

$$\sqrt{\frac{\sum_{i=1}^{n}(\bar{x}-x_i)^2}{n}}$$

CrossJoin(*set1*, *set2*)   Returns: set
Standard (additional behavior in AS2005)

set1 * *set2*   Returns: set
Extension: AS2005, AS2000

These functions return a set forming the Cartesian product of the two sets (except for a Microsoft extension to the semantics noted below). The two sets must represent different dimensions; you will get an error if the same dimension appears in both of them. CrossJoin() only takes two sets as arguments. However, because it takes two sets as input and returns a set as its output, you may nest multiple calls to CrossJoin() to take the Cartesian product of three or more dimensions. Following the same rules used for composing tuples by hand, the order of the dimensions in the resulting tuples is the same as the order of dimensions in the set arguments. Using an asterisk between two sets, as with {set1 * set2}, is a Microsoft-specific synonym for CrossJoin(). The expression set1 * set2 * set3 is the same as CrossJoin(set1, CrossJoin(set2, set3)).

In Analysis Services 2005, if the two sets are composed of tuples from the same base dimension but different attribute hierarchy-dimensions, then only the combinations of tuples that actually exist in the underlying dimension are returned. There is no way to produce tuples that do not have corresponding entries in underlying tables.

See also: Extract(), Generate(), Distinct(), NonEmptyCrossJoin()

Set.**Current**   Returns: tuple
Standard

This function returns the current tuple from a set within an iteration over the set. *set*.Current is only valid while there actually is an iteration occurring over the set. It returns a full tuple from the set. The set needs to be named, and can be either a set alias or a named set.

See also: .CurrentMember, .CurrentTuple, Generate()

dimension[**.CurrentMember**]   Returns: member
Standard

This function returns the current member in that dimension. "Current" is relative to the context that the calculation is taking place in. That context may be the axis of a query being executed or a Generate() function within that query. We indicate that .CurrentMember is optional. The default operator applied to a dimension is .CurrentMember.

Note that the MDX specification states that .CurrentMember may be applied to any set to return the current tuple. Analysis Services restricts the application of this operator to a set that has a single dimension, which will then return a single member. The .Current operator is applied to an arbitrary set to retrieve a tuple.

In Analysis Service 2005, keep in mind that the current member of an attribute dimension is influenced by the "current" members of other related attribute dimensions and the underlying base dimension.

See also: .Current, .CurrentOrdinal

*set.***CurrentOrdinal**   Returns: number
Extension: AS2005

This function returns the current iteration number within a context that iterates over *set*. The Filter() and Generate() functions provide an appropriate iteration context. Functions like Sum() and Order() do not. The *set* must be an alias name — it cannot be a named set.

See also:. Current, .Current Tuple, .CurrentMember

CustomData   Returns: string
Extension: AS2005

This function returns the current value of the CustomData connection property. If this property was not set, then the function returns NULL. This can be used to pass in one arbitrary configuration setting to be used by MDX functions.

See also: UserName, Call()

D

*Member.***DataMember**   Returns: member
Extension: AS2005, AS2000

This function returns the system-generated data input member associated with a member (as opposed to the input data). In AS2000 this function generally applies to parent-child dimensions where data is input at the parent level and also calculated by aggregating the parent's children. In AS2005, you can use this on any hierarchy. The following example produces both the input individual salary and the aggregated organizational salary for each employee:

```
WITH MEMBER [Measures].[Individual Salary] AS
'([Employees].CurrentMember.DataMember, [Measures].[Salary])'
SELECT
{ [Employees].Members } on columns,
{ [Measures].[Salary], [Measures].[Individual Salary] } on rows
FROM HRCube
```

Note that when using the UPDATE CUBE command, the .DataMember function enables you to write data to the actual member, as opposed to the member's leaf descendants.

dimension.**DefaultMember**
Standard

hierarchy.**DefaultMember**
Standard

Each of these returns the default member for the *dimension* or *hierarchy*. If the dimension has an All level and member, then the default member is the All member. If the dimension does not have an All member, then an arbitrary member from its top level will be the default member. Microsoft Analysis Services also allows you to override these defaults at the server or through their ALTER CUBE UPDATE DIMENSION command.

See also: .CurrentMember

Descendants (*member*, [*level* [, *desc_flag*]])
Standard

Descendants (*member*, *distance* [, *desc_flag*])
Standard

This function returns a set of descendants of the given member using the indicated level, or numeric distance from the specified member's level, as a reference point. The desc_flag parameter is used to pick from the many possible sets of descendants. If no level or desc_flag is provided, then the member and all of its descendants are returned. Figures A-5 through A-12 illustrate the behavior of the Descendants() operator. The flags are:

SELF	SELF_AND_AFTER
AFTER	SELF_AND_BEFORE
BEFORE	SELF_BEFORE_AFTER
BEFORE_AND_AFTER	LEAVES

SELF

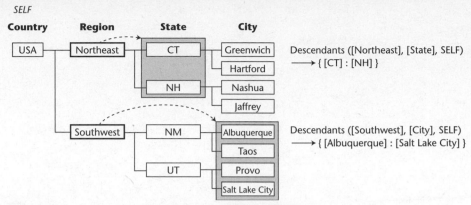

Descendants ([Northeast], [State], SELF)
⟶ { [CT] : [NH] }

Descendants ([Southwest], [City], SELF)
⟶ { [Albuquerque] : [Salt Lake City] }

Figure A-5 Behavior of descendants() with SELF FLAG.

AFTER

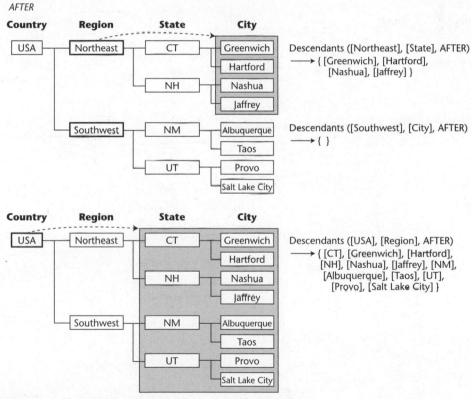

Descendants ([Northeast], [State], AFTER)
⟶ { [Greenwich], [Hartford],
      [Nashua], [Jaffrey] }

Descendants ([Southwest], [City], AFTER)
⟶ { }

Descendants ([USA], [Region], AFTER)
⟶ { [CT], [Greenwich], [Hartford],
      [NH], [Nashua], [Jaffrey], [NM],
      [Albuquerque], [Taos], [UT],
      [Provo], [Salt Lake City] }

Figure A-6 Behavior of descendants() with AFTER flag.

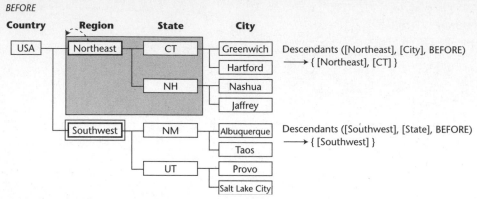

Figure A-7 Behavior of descendants() with BEFORE flag.

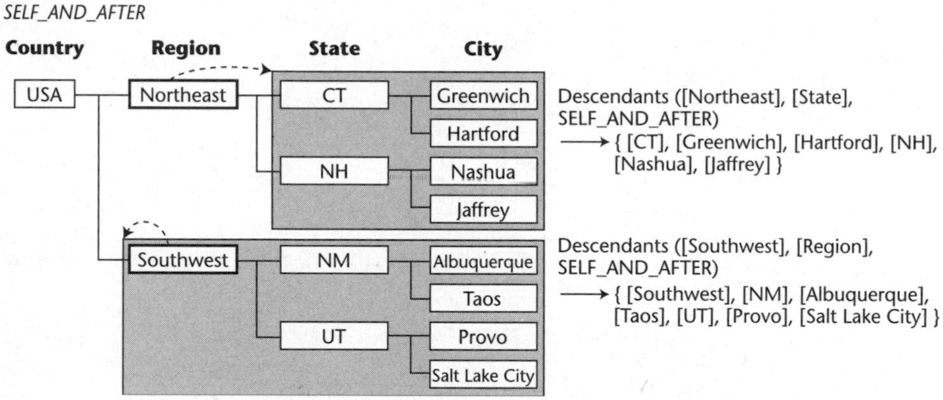

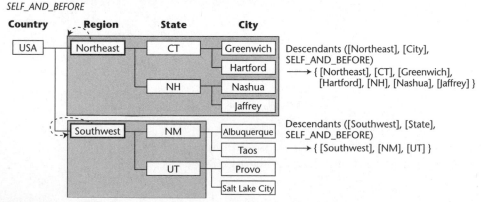

Figure A-8 Behavior of descendants() with SELF_AND_AFTER flag.

SELF_AND_BEFORE

Descendants ([Northeast], [City], SELF_AND_BEFORE) ⟶ { [Northeast], [CT], [Greenwich], [Hartford], [NH], [Nashua], [Jaffrey] }

Descendants ([Southwest], [State], SELF_AND_BEFORE) ⟶ { [Southwest], [NM], [UT] }

Figure A-9 Behavior of descendants()with SELF_AND_BEFORE flag.

BEFORE_AND_AFTER

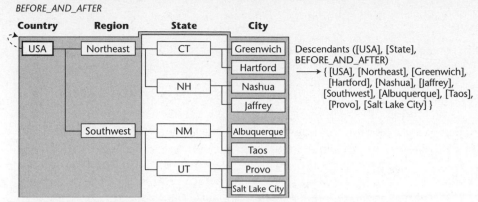

Figure A-10   Behavior of descendants() with BEFORE_AND_AFTER flags.

SELF_BEFORE_AFTER

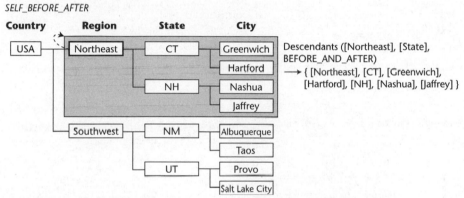

Figure A-11   Behavior of descendants() with SELF_BEFORE_AFTER flags.

SELF refers to the level listed as the second argument and means to take the members at that level. AFTER refers to the level or levels that appear below the level listed as the second argument. BEFORE refers to the level or levels that appear above the level listed and below the member given as the first argument. The BEFORE_AND_AFTER, SELF_AND_AFTER, SELF_AND_BEFORE, and SELF_BEFORE_AFTER flags combine these basic options, as shown in Figures A-5 through A-12.

The LEAVES flag is used in conjunction with a depth number and is intended for use with ragged and parent-child hierarchies. If a depth number is specified without LEAVES, then only members that are at that depth are returned. If a depth number is specified with LEAVES, then any leaf members encountered up to that depth are retained. In Analysis Services, you can request leaf-level members regardless of their depth by leaving the depth argument empty. The following would perform that:

```
Descendants (
  [Accounts].CurrentMember,
  ,   /* empty */
  LEAVES
)
```

In Essbase, you don't need to use LEAVES, since you can request leaf-level members by referring to the dimension's level 0 (remember that in Essbase, levels refer to heights while generations refer to depths). The following would retrieve leaf-level members in Essbase:

```
Descendants (
  [Accounts].CurrentMember,
  [Accounts].Levels (0)
  /* LEAVES is optional at this point */
)
```

If no flag is specified, the default behavior is SELF.

See also: Ancestor(), Ancestors(), Ascendants(), .Children

Hierarchy.**Dimension**   Returns: dimension
Extension: AS2005, AS2000

This function returns the dimension that the hierarchy is in. Because Microsoft Analysis Services 2000 and, to some degree, 2005 semantically treat different hierarchies as different dimensions, this function is essentially a "no-op" in those products.

Level.**Dimension**   Returns: dimension
Extension: AS2005, AS2000

The function returns the dimension that contains Level.

Member.**Dimension**   Returns: dimension
Extension: AS2005, AS2000

This function returns the dimension that contains Member.

Dimensions(*numeric expression***)**   Returns: dimension
Extension: AS2005, AS2000

This function returns the dimension whose zero-based position within the cube is *numeric expression*. Note that the Measures dimension is always Dimensions(0), while the order of the other dimensions depends on the order in which they were added to the cube when it was being constructed (and/or modified).

Dimensions(*string expression***)**   Returns: dimension
Extension: AS2005, AS2000

This function returns the dimension whose name is given by string expression.

See also: Dimension.*Name*

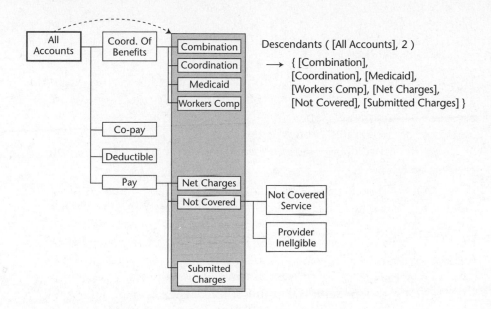

Descendants ([All Accounts], 2)

⟶ { [Combination],
    [Coordination], [Medicaid],
    [Workers Comp], [Net Charges],
    [Not Covered], [Submitted Charges] }

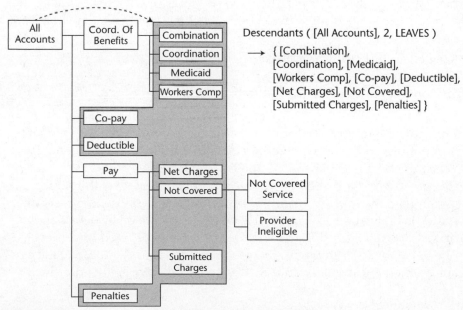

Descendants ([All Accounts], 2, LEAVES)

⟶ { [Combination],
    [Coordination], [Medicaid],
    [Workers Comp], [Co-pay], [Deductible],
    [Net Charges], [Not Covered],
    [Submitted Charges], [Penalties] }

Figure A-12   Behavior of Descendants() with LEAVES flag.

Distinct(*set***)**   Returns: set
Standard

This function removes any duplicates from the *set*. The first instance of each tuple is retained in the order in which it appears.

See also: DistinctCount(), Except(), Extract()

DistinctCount(*set***)**   Returns: number (integer)
Extension: AS2005, AS2000

This function counts the distinct, nonempty tuples in a set. It is equivalent to Count (Distinct (set), EXCLUDEEMPTY). Only a measure can use this function. If you define a calculation on another dimension that uses DistinctCount(), you will get a syntax error. (If you want this functionality on another dimension, you can use the equivalent Count(...) expression.)

When this function is used to calculate a cell, the distinct tuples in *set* are determined, and the nonempty cells formed by intersecting those tuples with the current member in every other dimension are counted. This function can be used to simulate the DistinctCount measure aggregation type in Analysis Services, but its strength is when you want the distinct count along only a subset of cube dimensions (one or two), when you are limiting the scope within the dimensions, when you are taking the distinct count at aggregate members in one or more of the dimensions, or when one or more dimensions involve a calculated member. Remember that the DistinctCount aggregation is handled to some degree by the server during cube aggregation, while this function is calculated at client query time.

See also: Distinct(), Count(), .Count

DrillDownLevel(*set* **[,** *level***])**   Returns: set
Standard

This function returns a set resulting from a particular drill-down operation performed by the function. *Set* can be of arbitrary dimensionality. When the *level* argument is specified, all members or tuples in *set* that are in *level* are drilled down into the next lowest level (if there is one). When the *level* argument is not specified, only those members or tuples that are at the lowest level in the first dimension of the *set* are drilled down into, and they are drilled down into the next lower level. The behavior of DrillDownLevel() is shown in Figure A-13. All children are inserted immediately after their parents; otherwise, the order is preserved. If *level* is specified, but there is no member at *level* in the *set*, then the given set is returned without modification.

In Essbase, the *layer* can be a generation or level specification.

> **NOTE** If one or more children of a member to be drilled down into immediately follows a parent in set, then that parent will not be drilled down into.

DrillDownLevel(*set,* , *index***)**   Returns: set
Extension: AS2005, AS2000

This variation is a Microsoft – specific extension to DrillDownLevel(). It enables the dimension to be drilled down into by leaving the level field empty and providing a zero-based dimension index to specify which dimension should be drilled down into. This is really only useful when *set* has tuples with more than one dimension. The first dimension to drill down into is at index 0, the second dimension is at index 1, and so on. As with the rules for the standard version of DrillDownLevel(), tuples containing the lowest level members of that dimension are drilled down into.

> **NOTE** If one or more children of a member to be drilled down into immediately follows a parent in set, then that parent will not be drilled down into.

DrillDownLevelBottom(*set, index* [*,*[*level*] [*, numeric expression*]]**)**   Returns: set
Standard

Similarly to DrillDownLevel() and DrillDownLevelTop(), this function drills down through all members in the *set* that are at the specified *level*, if the *level* is provided (or the lowest *level* of members that are present in the *set* if *level* is not provided). However, instead of returning all children, this function returns only the bottom *index* members or tuples. The *set* can be of arbitrary dimensionality. The ranking is determined through the *numeric expression*, if one is provided, or through the values of cells found in the default context when the set is evaluated, if the *numeric expression* is left out. Figure A-14 illustrates the behavior of DrillDownLevelBottom().

> **NOTE** If one or more children of a member to be drilled down on immediately follows a parent in the set, then that parent will not be drilled down into.

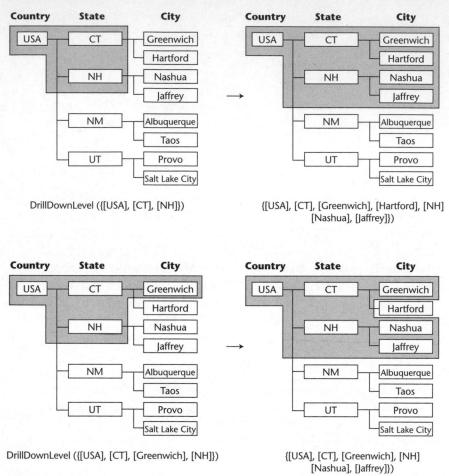

DrillDownLevel ({[USA], [CT], [NH]})

{[USA], [CT], [Greenwich], [Hartford], [NH]
[Nashua], [Jaffrey]})

DrillDownLevel ({[USA], [CT], [Greenwich], [NH]})

{[USA], [CT], [Greenwich], [NH]
[Nashua], [Jaffrey]})

Figure A-13 DrillDownLevel().

DrillDownLevelTop(*set*, *index* [, [*level*] [, *numeric expression*]]) Returns: set
Standard

Similarly to DrillDownLevel() and DrillDownLevelBottom(), this function drills down all members in *set* that are at the specified *level*, if the *level* is provided (or the lowest level of members that are present in the *set* if *level* is not provided). However, instead of returning all children, this function returns only the top *index* members or tuples. The set can be of arbitrary dimensionality. The ranking is determined through the *numeric expression*, if one is provided, or through the values of cells found in the default context when the set is evaluated, if the numeric value expression is left out. Figure A-15 illustrates the behavior of DrillDown-LevelTop(). As with DrillDownLevel(), if a member at *level* is immediately followed by one of its children, it will not be drilled down on.

NOTE If one or more children of a member to be drilled down into immediately follows a parent in set, then that parent will not be drilled down into.

DrillDownMember(*set1***,** *set2* **[, RECURSIVE])**   Returns: set
Standard

This function returns a set that is formed by drilling down one level on
each member in *set1* that is present in *set2*. *Set1* can be of arbitrary
dimensionality; *set2* must be of only one dimension. The ability of *set1* to
consist of more than one dimension is an extension to the OLE DB for
OLAP specification.

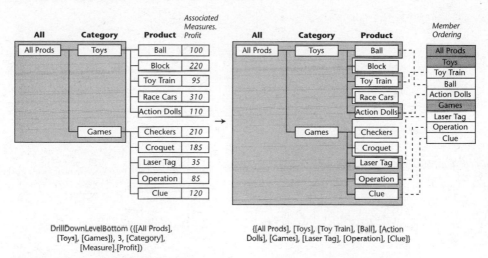

DrillDownLevelBottom ({[All Prods],
[Toys], [Games]}, 3, [Category],
[Measure].[Profit])

{[All Prods], [Toys], [Toy Train], [Ball], [Action
Dolls], [Games], [Laser Tag], [Operation], [Clue]}

Figure A-14   DrillDownLevelBottom().

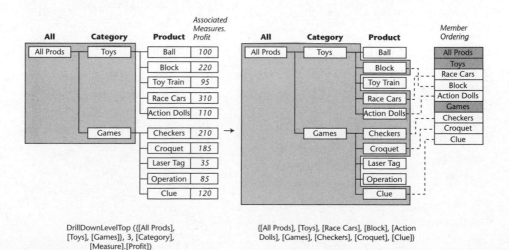

DrillDownLevelTop ({[All Prods],
[Toys], [Games]}, 3, [Category],
[Measure].[Profit])

{[All Prods], [Toys], [Race Cars], [Block], [Action
Dolls], [Games], [Checkers], [Croquet], [Clue]}

Figure A-15   DrillDownLevelTop().

If *set1* contains tuples, this function will return a set that is formed by drilling down each tuple in *set1* that has a matching member from *set2* in it. If RECURSIVE is not specified, then only one pass through *set1* is performed, matching each member or tuple with each member in *set2*. If RECURSIVE is specified, then the set resulting from the first pass is again matched with each member in *set2*, and so on until no more members in the set being constructed are found in *set2*. Figure A-16 illustrates the behavior of DrillDownMember().

NOTE If one or more children of a member to be drilled down into immediately follows a parent in set, then that parent will not be drilled down into.

See also: DrillUpMember()

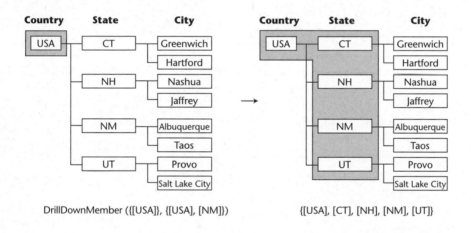

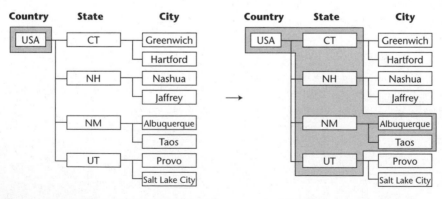

Figure A-16 DrillDownMember().

DrillDownMemberBottom(*set1*, *set2*, *index* [, *numeric expression*][, **RECURSIVE]))**   Returns: set
Standard

Much like DrillDownMember(), this function returns a set that is formed by drilling down one level on each member in *set1* that is present in *set2*. However, it returns the bottom *index* children for a parent rather than all children. *Set1* can be of arbitrary dimensionality; *set2* must be of only one dimension.

If *set1* contains tuples, this will return a set that is formed by drilling down each tuple in *set1* that has a matching member from *set2* in it. If RECURSIVE is not specified, then only one pass through *set1* is performed, matching each member or tuple with each member in *set2*. If RECURSIVE is specified, then the set that results from the first pass is again matched with each member in *set2*, and so on until no more members in the set being constructed are found in *set2*. At each step of drilling, the bottom *index* child members or tuples are returned instead of all children. The ranking is based on the *numeric expression*, if specified; otherwise, values from the set of children are evaluated in the current context, and those results are used. Figure A-17 illustrates the behavior of DrillDownMemberBottom().

DrillDownMemberTop(*set1*, *set2*, *index* [, *numeric expression*][, **RECURSIVE]))**   Returns: set
Standard

Like DrillDownMember(), this function returns a set that is formed by drilling down one level on each member in *set1* that is present in *set2*. However, it returns the top *index* children for a parent rather than all children. *Set1* can be of arbitrary dimensionality; *set2* must be of only one dimension.

If *set1* contains tuples, this will return a set formed by drilling down each tuple in *set1* that has a matching member from *set2* in it. If RECURSIVE is not specified, then only one pass through *set1* is performed, matching each member or tuple with each member in *set2*. If RECURSIVE is specified, then the set that results from the first pass is again matched with each member in *set2*, and so on until no more members in the set being constructed are found in *set2*. At each step of drilling, the top *index* child members or tuples are returned instead of all children. The ranking is based on the *numeric expression*, if specified; otherwise, values from the set of children are evaluated in the current context, and those results are used. Figure A-18 illustrates the behavior of DrillDown-MemberTop().

DrillUpLevel (*set* [, *level*])   Returns: set
Standard

This function strips away all members in the set that are below the given *level*. (In Essbase, either a generation or level may be used.) If the *level* is not provided, then it is assumed to be one level higher in the hierarchy than the level of the lowest level member(s) in the set (the lowest-level members in the set are removed). Figure A-19 illustrates the behavior of DrillUpLevel(). A set returned by DrillDownMember() or DrillDown-Level() will be suitable for cleanly drilling up with this function.

See also: DrillDownLevel(),DrillDownByLayer(),DrillUpByLayer(),

DrillUpMember (*set1*, *set2*)   Returns: set
Standard

This step strips away members in *set1* that are descendants of members in *set2*. Figure A-20 illustrates the behavior of DrillUpMember(). *Set1* can contain tuples of arbitrary dimensionality; *set2* must contain only members of one dimension.

Note that only descendants that are immediately after the ancestor member in *set2* are stripped away. If an ancestor member specified in *set2* is not present in *set1*, any descendants will remain. Descendants that precede the ancestor or that appear after another member that is not a descendant has intervened will not be stripped away. A set returned by DrillDownMember() or DrillDownLevel() will be suitable for drilling up cleanly with this function. Figure A-20 illustrates the behavior of DrillUpMember().

See also: DrillDownMember()

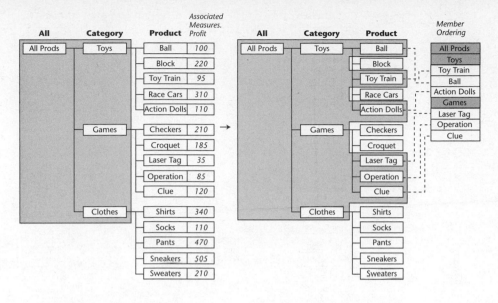

DrillDownMemberBottom ({[All Prods],
[Toys], [Games], [Clothes]} , { [Toys], [Games] },3,
[Measures].[Profit])

{ [All Prods], [Toys], [Toy Train], [Ball], [Action
Dolls], [Games], [Laser Tag], [Operation], [Clue] }

Figure A-17   DrillDownMemberBottom().

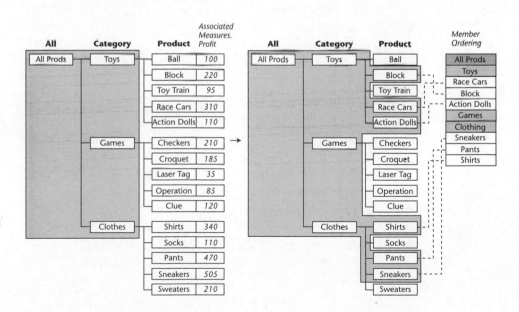

DrillDownMemberTop ({ [All Prods],
[Toys], [Games], [Clothes]} , { [Toys], [Games] }, 3,
[Measures].[Profit])

{ [All Prods], [Toys], [Race Cars], [Block], [Action
Dolls], [Clothing], [Sneakers], [Pants], [Shirts] }

Figure A-18   DrillDownMemberTop().

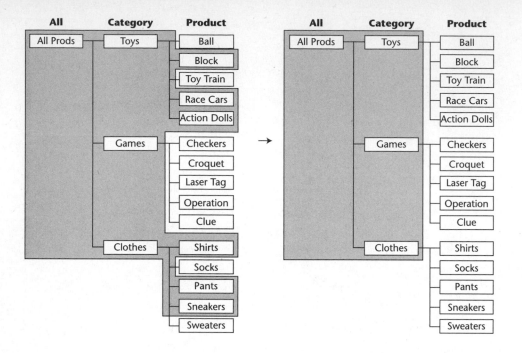

DrillUpLevel ({ [All Prods],
[Toys], [Race Cars], [Block], [Action Dolls],
[Clothing], [Sneakers], [Pants], [Shirts] }, [Category])

{ [All Prods], [Toys], [Games], [Clothes] }

Figure A-19   DrillUpLevel().

E

Error([*string_expr*])   Returns: (no return)
Extension: AS2005

The Error() function raises an error. This will propagate to callers; if an
error occurs for evaluating a cell that is an input to a function like Filter()
or Order() in an axis or slicer, the query will not successfully execute. If
the error occurs while calculating a result cell, then the client will receive
an error result when retrieving that cell's value. It may be possible to
detect and work around the error with the IsError() function that is part
of VBA and .Net, although this may not work correctly until service
pack 1 of AS 2005.

Except(*set1***,** *set2* **[, ALL])**   Returns: set
Standard

set1 – set2   Returns: set
Extension: AS2005, AS2000

The Except() function removes all elements from *set1* that also exist in *set2*. The ALL flag controls whether duplicates are retained or eliminated. When ALL is specified, duplicates in *set1* are retained, though any tuples matching them in *set2* are discarded. When ALL is not specified, no duplicates are returned. The members returned are determined by the order in which they appear in *set1*.

See also: Union(), Intersect(),and the unary – (complement) operator for sets

Microsoft Analysis Services also provides "-" as an alternate way of specifying Except(). Duplicates are removed from the resulting set. The expression `Set1- Set2` is equivalent to `Except (Set1, Set2)`.

See also: Union(), Intersect(), and the unary – (complement) operator for sets

Existing *set*   Returns: set
Extension: AS2005

This function applies the attribute relationships in effect in the current context to restrict the tuples in *set*. For example, if the [Product].[Ship Weight] current context consists of the member [12], then Existing [Product].[SKU].Members will return only those [SKU] members associated with the ship weight [12]. The current context may contain multiple members for each related attribute (for example, due to a set in the slicer or in a defined subcube), in which case the set will be restricted to tuples which are associated with at least one of the members in context.

See also: Exists

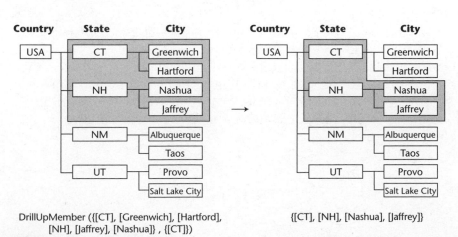

DrillUpMember ({[CT], [Greenwich], [Hartford], [NH], [Jaffrey], [Nashua]} , {[CT]})

{[CT], [NH], [Nashua], [Jaffrey]}

Figure A-20   DrillUpMember().

Exists (*set1*, *set2* [*, measure_group_name*]**)**   Returns: set
Extension: AS2005

Returns all tuples in *set1* which exist with respect to the tuples in *set2*. *Set1* and *set2* may or may not include related attribute hierarchy-dimensions. When the optional *measure_group_name* is provided, it uses existence of fact records for the measure group as the basis for relating members. members when *set1* and *set2* contain tuples from different dimensions (not just different hierarchy-dimensions). In this case, it is similar to NonEmpty(). If all measures in the measure group are NULL in a fact table row, Exists() will consider the relationship to exist, whereas if a fact table row doesn't exist at all, it will consider the relationship to not exist. This is different from NonEmpty(), which requires at least one non-NULL measure value to exist for non-emptiness to be established.

See also: CrossJoin(), Extract(), NonEmpty()

Extract (*set*, *dimension*[*, dimension* . . .]**)**   Returns: set
Standard

This function behaves as an opposite to the CrossJoin() function. The resulting set consists of tuples from the extracted dimension elements. For each tuple in the given *set*, the members of the dimensions listed in the arguments are extracted into new tuples. Since this could result in a great deal of redundancy, this function always removes duplicates from its results.

See also: CrossJoin(), Generate()

F

Filter (*set*, *search condition***)**   Returns: set
Standard

Filter returns those tuples of set for which the search condition (a logical expression) is true. If none are true, an empty set is returned. The tuples in the resulting set follow the same order in which they appeared in the original set. Note that the search condition must be phrased as a Boolean expression; you cannot use the assumption that a nonzero numerical result means "true" and a zero numerical result means "false."

See also: iif(), CoalesceEmpty()

member.**FirstChild**   Returns: member
Standard

member.**LastChild**   Returns: member
Standard

These functions return the first child or last child of the *member* according to the database ordering of the child members. Their behavior is illustrated in Figure A-21.

See also: .FirstSibling, .LastSibling, .Children, .Siblings

member.**FirstSibling**   Returns: member
Standard

member.**LastSibling**   Returns: member
Standard

Figure A-22 shows the behavior of the .FirstSibling and .LastSibling operators. The first child of a parent is its own first sibling, and the last child is its own last sibling. If no parent exists, then the first member in that level is the first sibling and the last member in the level is the last sibling. For example, the All or root member of a dimension is its own first and last sibling. In a dimension without an All level, the first member of the top level is the first sibling of all members at that level, and the last member of the top level is the last sibling of all members at that level.

See also: .Siblings, .FirstChild, .LastChild

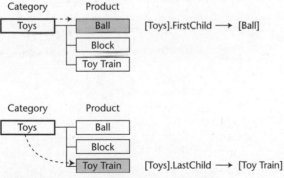

Figure A-21   .FirstChild and .LastChild.

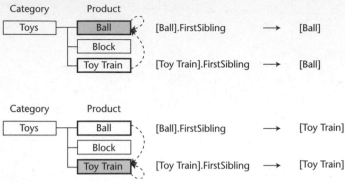

Figure A-22   .FirstSibling and .LastSibling.

G

Generate(*set1***,** *set2* **[, ALL])**   Returns: set
Standard

Generate(*set***,** *string expression***,** [*delimiter*])   Returns: string
Extension: AS2005, AS2000

The set version of Generate() iterates over each tuple in *set1*, and for each element in *set1*, it puts every element specified by *set2* into the result set. The dimensionality of the result set is the dimensionality of *set2*. If ALL is specified, then duplicate result tuples are retained. If ALL is not specified, duplicates after the first are removed. *Set1* and *set2* may be composed of completely different dimensionality, or they may be composed of exactly the same dimensionality. When *set2* is a relatively static set of members, this function behaves much like CrossJoin(). Generate() gains its iterative power when *set2* is an expression that depends on the current member or tuple in *set1*.

The string version of this function iterates over each tuple in the set specified as the first argument, evaluates the string expression for the current member of the set, and returns the concatenated result, optionally with a delimiter. For example, the following generates an HTML table of member names:

```
"<table><tr><td>"
+ Generate (
  [Product].[ByCategory].CurrentMember.Children,
  [Product].[ByCategory].CurrentMember.Name,
  "</tr></td><tr><td>"
) + "</tr></td></table>"
```

See also: CrossJoin(), Extract()

H

Head (*Set* **[***, Count***])**   Returns: set
Extension: AS2005, AS2000

This function returns a set of the first *Count* elements from the given *set*. The order of elements in the given set is preserved. If *Count* is omitted, the number of elements returned is 1. If *Count* is less than 1, an empty set is returned. If the value of the *Count* is greater than the number of tuples in the set, the original set is returned.

See also: Tail(), Subset(), Rank(), .Item()

Hierarchize (*set***)**   Returns: set
Standard

Hierarchize (*set***, POST)**   Returns: set
Extension: AS2005, AS2000

Hierarchize() returns the set that it is given after it puts all the members in each dimension of *set* into hierarchical order. By default, within each level, members are put into their database ordering, top down. Children are sorted to immediately follow after their parents. The optional POST keyword returns the members in bottom-up rather than top-down order; that is, the children precede their parents. When the tuples are composed of more than one dimension, they are sorted primarily on the first dimension, then on the second dimension, and so on. Any duplicate tuples are retained.

In Analysis Services, Hierarchize() is similar to sorting on the members' internal ID property.

See also: Order(), Ascendants(), Ancestor(), .Parent

level.**Hierarchy**   Returns: hierarchy
Standard

This function returns the hierarchy that contains the level. Because Analysis Services semantically treats different hierarchies as different dimensions, this function is essentially equivalent to *Level*.Dimension.

member.**Hierarchy**   Returns: hierarchy
Standard

This function returns the hierarchy that contains the member. Because Analysis Services semantically treats different hierarchies as different dimensions, this function is essentially equivalent to *Member*.Dimension.

I

dimension.**Ignore**   Returns: member
Extension: AS2000

When used in an expression, .Ignore fixes the member of *dimension* at the current one in the context and prevents any further recursion along that dimension. In recursive calculations, sometimes a cell reference will end up being circular. For example, the level-wide custom rollup expression

```
IIf (IsLeaf ([Accounts].CurrentMember),
  [Accounts].CurrentMember,
  RollupChildren ( [Accounts].CurrentMember,
    Accounts.CurrentMember.Properties ("UNARY_OPERATOR") )
)
```

becomes recursive at leaf levels, because the evaluation of the [Accounts].CurrentMember at the leaf level will still result in another cycle through the whole iif() clause. Modifying the expression to

```
IIf (IsLeaf ([Accounts].CurrentMember),
  [Accounts].Ignore,
  RollupChildren ( [Accounts].CurrentMember,
    Accounts.CurrentMember.Properties ("UNARY_OPERATOR") )
)
```

fixes the problem; no more recursion will take place on the Account dimension.

Iif (*search_condition*, *true_part*, *false_part***)**   Returns: number, string, member, tuple, level, hierarchy, array (all only in AS2005)

The standard version of the `iif()` function can either take numerical expressions for the true part and the false part and return a number, or it can take string expressions for the true part and the false part and return a string. Analysis Services 2005 extends this to allow the parts to have separate types, and for the results to be almost any MDX object (numeric and string values, members, sets, tuples, levels, hierarchies, dimensions and arrays). be numeric or string separately from each other.

AS2005 allows you to return sets an hence, you can write expressions like the following:

```
SELECT IIF( condition, set1, set2) on axis(0) ...

Avg (
  iif ( condition, LastPeriods (3), LastPeriods(4)),
 [Measures].[Units]
)
```

AS2005 allows iif() to return other kinds of things as well. For example, you can select the members from a level determined dynamically with the following:

```
SELECT
IIF (condition,
  [Customer].[Customer].[Region],
  [Customer].[Customer].[State]
).Members on axis(1) ...
```

This function evaluates *search_condition*, which can be any value expression in AS 2005 and any logical or numeric expression in AS 2000. If the result is true, or at least nonzero in Analysis Services, then the *true_part* expression is evaluated and returned. If the result is not true, then the *false_part* expression is evaluated and returned. The standard version of the iif() function can either take numerical expressions for the true part and the false part and return a number, or it can take string expressions for the true part and the false part and return a string. Microsoft extends this to allow the parts to be numeric or string separately from each other.

Note that when the search condition contains a logical expression that involves comparison operations, since NULL cells compare as equal to zero with any comparison operator, the result of the search condition cannot be NULL. However, either the *true_part* or the *false_part* may evaluate to NULL, in which case NULL will be the result when that condition is met.

See also: CoalesceEmpty(), Filter(), CASE

Intersect(set1, set2 [,ALL])   Returns:
Standard

The ALL flag controls whether duplicates are retained or eliminated. When ALL is not specified, only the unique tuples appearing in *set1* that also appear in *set2* are returned. When ALL is specified, then duplicated tuples in *set1* that appear anywhere in *set2* are returned. If duplicates of a tuple occur in *set2*, only the duplicates that exist in *set1* will end up in the resulting set. The members are returned in the order in which they appear in *set1*. For example, the expression

```
Intersect (
  {[Customer].[AZ].[Phoenix], [Customer].[AZ].[Scottsdale],
    [Customer].[KS].[Pittsburg], [Customer].[AZ].[Phoenix]},
  {[Customer].[NM].[Albuquerque], [Customer].[AZ].[Phoenix],
    [Customer].[AZ].[Scottsdale], [Customer].[AZ].[Phoenix]},
)
```

yields the following set:

```
{ [Customer].[AZ].[Phoenix], [Customer].[AZ].[Scottsdale] }
```

The expression

```
Intersect (
  {[Customer].[AZ].[Phoenix], [Customer].[AZ].[Scottsdale],
    [Customer].[KS].[Pittsburg], [Customer].[AZ].[Phoenix]},
  {[Customer].[NM].[Albuquerque], [Customer].[AZ].[Phoenix],
    [Customer].[AZ].[Scottsdale], [Customer].[AZ].[Phoenix]},
    , ALL
)
```

yields the following set:

```
{ [Customer].[AZ].[Phoenix], [Customer].[AZ].[Scottsdale],
  [Customer].[AZ].[Phoenix]}
```

object1 **IS** *object2*   Returns: boolean
Extension AS2005, AS2000

The Is operator is used to determine if two objects are equivalent. For example, the expression

```
[Customers].CurrentMember
  IS [All Customers].[Canada].[BC].[Vancouver]
```

will only return TRUE when the current customer member in the context is Vancouver, BC. In Analysis Services, you can compare objects of any kind, and you can compare objects with NULL as well to see if they exist. For example, if the first month in the Time dimension is [Jan 2000], then the following two expressions will return TRUE:

```
[Jan 2000].PrevMember IS NULL
[Jan 2000].Level IS [Time].[Month]
```

See also: IsEmpty(), IsValid()

IsAncestor (*AncestorMember*, *StartingMember*)   Returns: boolean
Extension: AS2005, AS2000

This function returns true if the *AncestorMember* is indeed a proper
ancestor of *StartingMember*, and false otherwise. No error is returned if
the two members are from different dimensions (just false).

See also: IsChild(), IsGeneration, IsSibling(), IsLeaf(), iif(), Is, .Ordinal

IsEmpty(*ValueExpression***)**   Returns: boolean
Standard

This function returns true if the *ValueExpression* is NULL, and false otherwise. Note that in Analysis Services, if the *ValueExpression* is a tuple
instead of a simple member reference, then it must be enclosed by
parentheses to distinguish the use of parentheses for tuple construction
from parentheses for delimiting the argument to IsEmpty(), as in:

```
IsEmpty ( ([Measures].[Units], [Time].PrevMember) )
```

Also, in Analysis Services, note that IsEmpty() will return false if a
property reference is not valid for the member (like IsEmpty
([Time].CurrentMember.Properties("Mailing Address")).
More generally, in AS 2005, it will return false if evaluation of
ValueExpression raises an error.

See also: iif(), IS, IsValid(), Error()

IsGeneration(*member*, *generation_number***)**   Returns: boolean
Extension: AS2005, AS2000

*(Analysis Services and Essbase implement different semantics for this function,
although the syntax is the same.)*

In Analysis Services, this function returns true if the *member* is *generation_
number* steps from the leaf level, and false otherwise. The definition of a
generation is as follows: The leaf level is considered to be generation 0.
For every non-leaf member, the generation number is 1 plus the range of
generation numbers from all of the children of its parent. In an irregular
hierarchy, this means that a member may belong to more than one generation. For example, the generation numbers for a simple hierarchy are
shown in Figure A-23.

In the case of a ragged level-based dimension, the generations are counted from the visible members. If a leaf member has a hidden parent and a visible grandparent, for example, the visible grandparent will be considered to be generation 1.

The expression IsGeneration ([Account].CurrentMember, 0) is equivalent to IsLeaf ([Account].CurrentMember).

See also: IsAncestor, IsSibling(), IsLeaf(), IsLevel() iif(), IS, .Ordinal

IsLeaf (*Member***)** Returns: Boolean
Extension: AS2005, AS2000

This function returns true if the *Member* is a leaf member in its dimension, whether the dimension is a parent-child dimension or a regular dimension.

In the case of a ragged level-based dimension, a member is considered to be a leaf member if it has no visible children.

Essbase accomplishes the same thing with IsLevel().

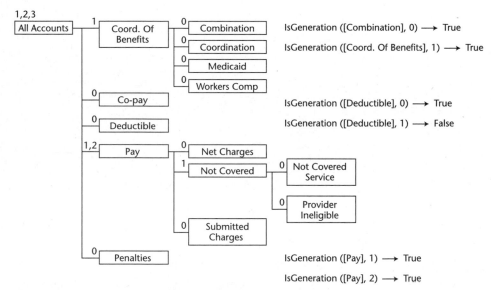

Figure A-23 Microsoft Implementation of IsGeneration().

IsSibling(*Member1***, ***Member2***)**   Returns: boolean
Extension: AS2005, AS2000

This function returns true if the *Member1* is a sibling of *Member2*. In
Analysis Services, IsSibling() considers a member to be a sibling of
itself.

In Analysis Services, in a ragged, level-based dimension, the sibling relationship is determined by the visibility of members. If a parent has one
hidden child and one visible child, and the hidden child has a visible
child, the two visible children will be considered as siblings.

See also: IsAncestor, IsLeaf(), IsGeneration(), iif(), IS, .Ordinal

*tuple***[.Item](***index***)**   Returns: member
Standard: AS2005, AS2000, Essbase

This function returns the member at the index position within the tuple.
The index is based at 0. For example, (`[Product].[Jackets]`,
`[Time].[2006]).Item (0)` is [Product].[Jackets], and `([Product]`
`.[Jackets], [Time].[2006]).Item (1) is [Time].[2006]`.
We indicate that Item() is optional because it is the default operator. The
following are equivalent:

```
Tuple(index)
Tuple.Item(index)
```

*set***[.Item](***index***)**   Returns: tuple
Standard

*set***[.Item](***string expression***[,***string expression*** ...])**   Returns: tuple
Standard

The first variation of the .Item() operator returns the tuple at the index
position within the set. The index is based at 0. For example, consider:

```
{ [Time].[1996], [Time].[1997] }.Item (0) is [Time].[1996]
{ [Time].[1996], [Time].[1997] }.Item (1) is [Time].[1997]
```

The second variation returns the first tuple in the set whose name is
matched by the string expressions. When using the string form, you can
use either one string or more than one string. If you use one string, it
must contain a complete tuple specification. If you use more than one
string, then the number of strings must match the number of dimensions, but each string will identify only one member from one dimension. In either case, the order of dimensions listed in the string(s) must

match the order of dimensions in the set. If some member from the strings is not found in the metadata when the expression is parsed, then a parse error results. If the member is found in the metadata, but not in any tuple in the set, then an empty tuple is returned. For example, the following two item specifications are identical:

```
Crossjoin ([Time].[Year].members, _[Customer].[State].Members).Item(
"[1997]", "[FL]")
Crossjoin ([Time].[Year].members, _[Customer].[State].Members).Item(
"([1997], [FL])")
```

Note that in the tuple specifications, member expressions can be used as well as named members. For example, the following are also equivalent to the two-item specifications just given:

```
Crossjoin (
   [Time].[Year].members,
   [Customer].[State].Members
).Item( "[1998].lag(1)", "[FL]")
Crossjoin (
   [Time].[Year].members,
   [Customer].[State].Members).Item( "([1997].[Q1].Parent, [FL])")
```

We indicate that .Item() is optional because it is the default operator. The following are equivalent:

```
Set(index)
Set.Item(index)
```

Remember: If you are trying to use Rank() to pick out an index for Item(), that Rank returns a 1-based index, and you will need to subtract 1 from it to use it with Item().

K

KPICurrentTimeMember (*KPI_name***)**   Returns: member
Extension: AS2005

This function returns the time member associated with the KPI named *KPI_name*. The *KPI_Name* is a string expression.

KPIGoal (*KPI_name*)   Returns: member
Extension: AS2005

This function returns the member that calculates the value of the goal for the KPI named *KPI_name*. The *KPI_Name* is a string expression.

KPIStatus (*KPI_name*)   Returns: member
Extension: AS2005

This function returns the member that calculates status value associated with the KPI named *KPI_name*. To conform to the conventions used in constructing the KPI graphic images, you should try to have this function return a value that is the KPIStatusValue() result somehow normalized between -1 and 1, although there is no technical requirement that you do so. The *KPI_Name* is a string expression.

KPITrend (*KPI_name*)   Returns: member
Extension: AS2005

This function returns the member that calculates a trend value associated with the KPI named *KPI_name*. To conform to the conventions used in constructing the KPI graphic images, you should try to have this function return a value normalized between -1 and 1, although there is no technical requirement that you do so. The *KPI_Name* is a string expression.

KPIValue (*KPI_name*)   Returns: member
Extension: AS2005

This function returns the member that calculates the value of the KPI named *KPI_name*. The *KPI_Name* is a string expression.

KPIWeight (*KPI_name*)   Returns: member
Extension: AS2005

This function returns the number that calculates weighting of the contribution of the KPI named *KPI_name* to its parent KPI. To conform to the conventions used in constructing the KPI graphic images, you should try to have this function return a value normalized between -1 and 1, although there is no other technical requirement that you do so. The *KPI_Name* is a string expression.

L

member.**Lag**(*index*)   Returns: member
Standard

.Lead() returns the member that is *index* number of members after the source member along the same level, and .Lag() returns the member that is *index* number of members before the source member on the same level. .Lead(0) and .Lag(0) each result in the source member itself. Lagging by a negative amount is the same as leading by the positive quantity and vice versa. Figure A-24 shows examples of .Lead() and .Lag().

member.**LastChild**   Returns: member
Standard

See definition for .FirstChild

LastPeriods(*index* [, *member*])   Returns: set
Standard

This function returns the set of *index* periods from member back to the member lagging by *index*-1 from member. This is almost equivalent to

```
{ member.LAG(index - 1) : member }.
```

If member is not specified, then it defaults to the current member of the Time-typed dimension in the cube. If the index is a negative number, then the range goes forward from the member to *index* −1 members instead of backward. If *index* is 0, then an empty set is returned (which makes it slightly different from using .Lag()). If member is omitted, and no dimension in the cube is marked as being Time-typed, the statement will be parsed and execute without error. However, when a client attempts to retrieve a cell calculated in part by the LastPeriods() function, a cell error will occur.

The behavior of LastPeriods() is shown in Figure A-25.

See also: OpeningPeriod(), ClosingPeriod(), .Lag(), .Lead()

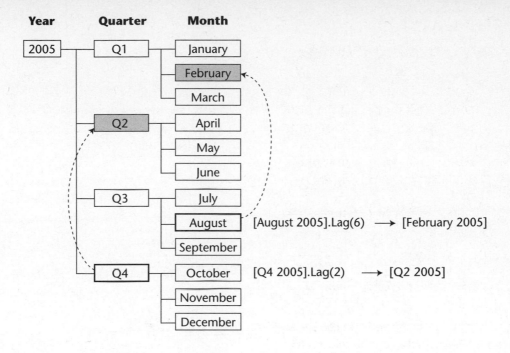

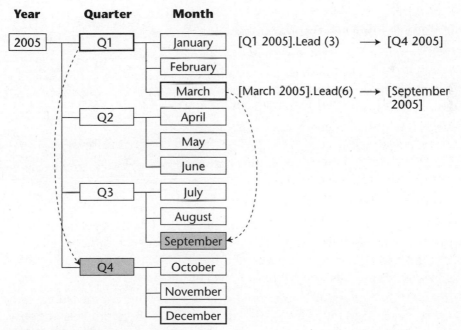

Figure A-24 .Lag() and .Lead().

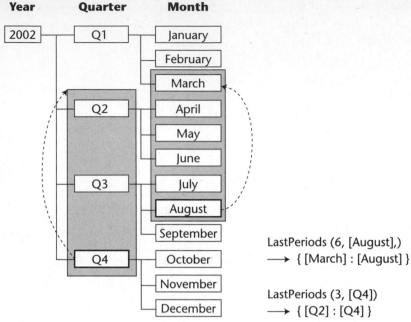

Figure A-25   Behavior of LastPeriods().

member.**LastSibling**   Returns: member
Standard

> *See definition for .FirstSibling*

member.**Lead**(index)   Returns: member
Standard

> *See definition for .Lag()*

Leaves ()   Returns: set

Leaves (*dimension*)   Returns: set

This function returns a set of the cross-join of the lowest level of all attribute hierarchies in the dimension. This includes the dimension's key attribute and all leaf-level attributes. If the *dimension* is omitted, the leaf level space is a set for the entire leaf level of the cube (!).

Note that the Leaves() function cannot be used if different measure groups in scope in the cube use the dimension at different levels of granularity (including if some are dimensioned by it and some do not). You can select from a subcube that only includes measures from a suitable measure group or groups.

While you can use this function in any MDX expression, it is most likely to be useful as part of specifying subcubes either in an MDX script or in a query or session subcube.

See also: MeasureGroupMeasures(), Root()

member.**Level**   Returns: level
Standard

This function returns a member's level.

Levels (*string expression***)**   Returns: level
Extension: AS2005, AS2000

This function returns the level whose name is given by string expression. It is typically used with user-defined functions (UDFs) that return a name. The string expression can be any expression that results in a level reference. For example, the string "[Time].[Year]" will result in the year level of the Time dimension. However, the string "[Time].Levels(1)" in a Time dimension where the year level is the first one down from the root level will also result in the year level. (See the following description for the Dimension.Levels() function as well.)

Dimension.**Levels (***numeric expression***)**   Returns: level
Standard

This function returns the dimension level specified by numeric expression. Note that in Analysis Services, the number is zero-based, starting at the root level, while in Essbase the number is one-based starting at the leaf level.

For example, in Analysis Services, if the levels of the [Time] dimension are [All], [Year], and [Month], then [Time].Levels(0) returns the [Time].[All] level, and [Time].Levels(2) returns the [Time].[Month] level. In Analysis Services, you can obtain the number of levels in the dimension with *Dimension*.Levels.Count, which lets you refer to the leaf level by the expression *Dimension*.Levels (*Dimension*.Levels.Count).

LinkMember(*member***,** *dimension***)**   Returns: member
Extension: AS2005, AS2000

The LinkMember() function is used to reference a member in one hierarchy based on a member from another related hierarchy. The hierarchies may either be from the same dimension (where a dimension has multiple hierarchies) or from different dimensions. (Remember that different hierarchies are different dimensions in Microsoft OLAP/Analysis Services.) The members are matched by key rather than by name, so members with the same key but with different names will be linked. For example, the expression

```
Hierarchize(
   Ascendants(
      Linkmember([Time].[Calendar].[Jan 1 1999],[Time].[Fiscal])
))
```

will return the ascendants in the fiscal hierarchy for the calendar hierarchy member [Jan 1 1999].

LinRegIntercept(*set***,** *y numeric expression* **[,** *x numeric expression*]**)**   Returns: number
Standard

This function returns the intercept of the linear regression line calculated from the given data points (where the regression line intersects 0). For the linear equation $y = ax + b$, which will be determined over some set of y and x, the values of the *y numeric expression* are evaluated over the set to get the y values. If the *x numeric expression* is present, then it is evaluated over the set to get the values of the x axis. Otherwise, the cells formed by the set are evaluated within the current context and their values are used as the x values. Empty cells and cells containing text or logical values are not included in the calculation, but cells with zero values are included.

Once the linear regression line has been calculated, this function returns the x-intercept of the line (represented by b in the equation $y = ax + b$).

See also the other LinRegXXX functions.

LinRegPoint(*x slice numeric expression***,** *set***,** *y numeric expression* **[,** *x numeric expression*]**)**   Returns: number
Standard

This function returns the value of the calculated linear regression line $y = ax + b$ for a particular value of x. For the linear equation $y = ax + b$, which will be determined from a set of y and x values, the values of the *y numeric expression* are evaluated to get the y values. If the *x numeric expression* is present, then it is evaluated over the *set* to get the values of the x axis. Otherwise, the cells formed by the *set* are evaluated within the current context and their values are used as the x values. Empty cells

and cells containing text or logical values are not included in the calculation, but cells with zero values are included.

Once the linear regression line has been calculated, the value of $y = ax + b$
is calculated for the value given in the *x slice numeric expression* and is
returned.

LinRegR2(*set*, *y numeric expression* **[**, *x numeric expression***])**   Returns: number
Standard

This function returns the statistical R^2 variance of the given data points
to the linear regression line calculated from them. For the linear equation
$y = ax + b$, which will be determined over some set of y and x, the values
of the *y numeric expression* are evaluated to get the y values. If the *x
numeric expression* is present, then it is evaluated over the *set* to get the
values of the x axis. Otherwise, the cells formed by the *set* are evaluated
within the current context and their values are used as the x values.
Empty cells and cells containing text or logical values are not included in
the calculation, but cells with zero values are included.

Once the linear regression line has been calculated, this function returns
the statistical R^2 variance between the points on it and the given points.

See also the other LinRegXXX functions.

LinRegSlope(*set* **[**, *y numeric expression* **[**, *x numeric expression***])**   Returns:
number
Standard

This function returns the slope of the linear regression line calculated
from the given data points. For the linear equation $y = ax + b$, which will
be determined over some set of y and x, the values of the *y numeric
expression* are evaluated to get the y values. If the *x numeric expression* is
present, then it is evaluated over the *set* to get the values of the x axis.
Otherwise, the cells formed by the *set* are evaluated within the current
context and their values are used as the x values. Empty cells and cells
containing text or logical values are not included in the calculation, but
cells with zero values are included.

Once the linear regression line has been calculated, this function returns
the slope of the line (represented by a in the equation $y = ax + b$).

See also the other LinRegXXX functions.

LinRegVariance(*set***, ***y numeric expression*** [, ***x numeric expression***])   Returns: number**
Standard

This function returns the variance of fit of the calculated linear regression line to the actual points given for it. For the linear equation y = ax + b, which will be determined over some set of y and x, the values of the *y numeric expression* are evaluated to get the y values. If the *x numeric expression* is present, then it is evaluated over the *set* to get the values of the x axis. Otherwise, the cells formed by the *set* are evaluated within the current context and their values are used as the x values. Empty cells and cells containing text or logical values are not included in the calculation, but cells with zero values are included.

Once the linear regression line has been calculated, this function returns the statistical variance between its points and the given points.

See also the other LinRegXXX functions.

LookupCube(*cube_string***, ***numeric_expression***)   Returns: number**
Extension: AS2005, AS2000

LookupCube(*cube_string***, ***string_expression***)   Returns: string**
Extension: AS2005, AS2000

LookupCube() can be used to retrieve a single value from another cube. This function can look up values from a regular cube or a virtual cube. The expression can also reference calculated members within the designated cube. The function is most likely to be used as part of a calculated member or custom rollup expression, although care must be taken to ensure that the result is as expected, because LookupCube() returns only a single value and does not respect the context of the current query. This means that any necessary current members need to be placed in the numeric expression or string expression. For example, the following calculated member only makes sense if we are looking at the All level on the other dimensions:

```
WITH MEMBER [Measures].[Store Net Sales] AS
'[Measures].[Store Sales] - LookupCube("Budget","[Account].[Total
Expense]")'
```

The following will include time and product dimensions from the sales cube:

```
WITH MEMBER [Measures].[Store Net Sales] AS
'[Measures].[Store Sales] - LookupCube("Budget",
  "([Account].[Total Expense]," + [Time].CurrentMember.UniqueName +
","
  + [Product].CurrentMember.UniqueName + ")"
)'
```

See also: StrToVal()

M

Max(*set* **[,** *numeric expression***])**   Returns: number
Standard

This function returns the maximum value found across the cells of the set. If a numeric expression is supplied, then the function finds the maximum of its nonempty values across the set. Note that in Analysis Services, a positive number divided by zero will cause an erroneous value that will be reported as the maximum.

See also: Min(), Median()

MeasureGroupMeasures (*string_expression***)**   Returns: set
Extension: AS2005

This function returns the set of measures contained in the measure group named by *string_expression*. Note that the name should be exactly as specified when designing the cube, e.g. "Sales" or "Currency Rates", not "[Sales]" or "[Currency Rates]".

See also: .Members, .AllMembers

Median(set **[,** numeric expression**])**   Returns: number
Standard

This function returns the median value found across the cells of the set. If a numeric expression is supplied, then the function finds the median of its values across the set.

See also: Min(), Max()

dimension.**Members**   Returns: set
Standard

hierarchy.**Members**   Returns: set
Standard (not in Essbase 9)

level.**Members**   Returns: set
Standard

> Each of the variations of the .Members function returns the set of all members within the scope of the given metadata object in the database's default order. Figure A-26 shows the scope of the members operator. Dimension.Members, shown in Figure A-26a, returns the members of the entire dimension and includes the All member of the hierarchy if present. Because in OLAP/Analysis Services a hierarchy is implemented as a dimension, the Hierarchy.Members function is also shown. Level.Members, shown in Figure A-26b, selects all members in the specified level.
>
> *See also: .AllMembers, MeasureGroupMeasures(), AddCalculatedMembers(), StripCalculatedMembers()*

Members(*string expression***)**   Returns: member
Extension: AS2005, AS2000

> This function returns the member whose name is given by *string expression*. (Yes, it only returns a single member, even though its name is plural.) The most common use for this function is to take a string from a user-defined function (UDF) that identifies a member and convert it to a member. For example, consider a UDF named UDF_GetMySalesTerritory on the client that returned the member name for the user's sales territory. Given this UDF, the following expression,

```
([Measures].[Sales], Members ( UDF_GetMySalesTerritory() ) )
```

> would refer to the sales value for that user's sales territory.
>
> *See also: StrToMember(), StrToTuple(), StrToSet(), .Name, .UniqueName*

MemberToStr (*member***)**   Returns: string
Standard

> This function returns the unique name of a member. In Analysis Services, the MDX Compatibility and MDX Unique Name Style connection parameters will determine the format of the name generated. This is identical in function to .UniqueName.
>
> *See also: Member.UniqueName*

Min (*set* [, numeric *expression*])   Returns: number
Standard

This function returns the minimum value found across the cells of the set. If a numeric expression is supplied, then the function finds the minimum of its values across the set. Note that in Analysis Services, a negative number divided by zero will cause an erroneous value that will be reported as the minimum.

See also: Max(), Median()

DIMENSION.Members
HIERARCHY.Members

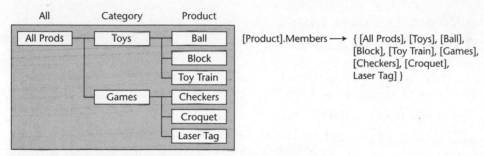

Figure A-26a   Members selected by .Members operator.

LEVEL.Members

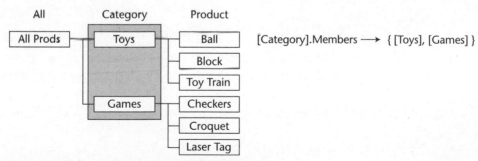

Figure A-26b   Members selected by Level.Members

MTD ([*member*])   Returns: set
Standard

MTD() is the equivalent of PeriodsToDate() with the level set to Month. If member is not specified, it defaults to the current member of the Time-typed dimension. If no Time-typed dimension is in the cube, or if it does not have a level tagged as Month, then an error results.

See also: PeriodsToDate(), YTD(), QTD(), WTD()

N

dimension.**Name**   Returns: string
Extension: AS2005, AS2000

This function returns the name of the dimension.

See also: .UniqueName, Dimensions()

hierarchy.**Name**   Returns: string
Extension: AS2005, AS2000

This function returns the name of the hierarchy.

See also: .UniqueName

level.**Name**   Returns: string
Extension: AS2005, AS2000

This function returns the name of the level.

See also: .UniqueName, .Ordinal, Levels()

member.**Name**   Returns: string
Extension: AS2005, AS2000

This function returns the name of the member. (Essbase uses the predefined member property *member*.[MEMBER_NAME] to achieve the same effect.)

See also: StrToMember(), StrToTuple(), StrToSet(), TupleToStr(), .UniqueName

NameToSet (*membername*)   Returns: set (of one member)
Extension: AS2005, AS2000

This function returns a set containing one member specified by the member name. If no member can be found with this name, then the set is returned empty (and it cannot be identified with .Dimension). The contents of *membername* must be only a member name or unique name. It cannot be a member expression, as StrToSet() would allow.

See also: Member.UniqueName, StrToSet(), StrToMember()

member.**NextMember**   Returns: member
Standard

See description of .PrevMember

NonEmpty (*set1* [, *context_set*])   Returns: set
Extension: AS2005

This function returns the tuples of *set1* that are non-empty across the tuples of *context_set*. Non-emptiness is a characteristic of cells, not tuples. The measure(s) to use in determining whether or not a tuple is "empty" are found in one of the sets. If the *context_set* is omitted, the current context of all current members from all dimensions not part of *set1* is used. Even if context_set is provided, the current context of all attributes is present, whether or not they explicitly participate in either of the sets.

See also: NonEmptyCrossJoin(), Filter(), Count(), NonEmptyCount(), IsEmpty()

NonEmptyCrossJoin (*set1*, *set2* [,*set3* . . .] [, *set-count*])   Returns: set
Extension: AS2005, AS2000

This function returns the nonempty cross-join of two or more sets. It is based on data actually present in fact tables. This means that it filters out all tuples involving calculated members.

Note that while this function is supported in Analysis Services 2005, Microsoft is recommending that you use NonEmpty instead.

Nonemptiness is a characteristic of cells as opposed to tuples. NonEmptyCrossJoin() takes a different approach to specifying the cells than the other functions that deal with empty/nonempty cells associated with tuples. If the set-count is present, then the number specified for it will be used as the number of sets (starting at *set1*) to actually cross-join. The remaining sets listed will be used to form the slices used to find the cells that are nonempty. (Any dimensions not listed will have their current member used to determine cells.)

If the *set-count* parameter is provided, then only that number of sets (in the order that they appear) will contribute tuples to the resulting set. The remaining sets will provide the context or add members for consideration in the nonemptiness. The other sets may have only one member, or they may have multiple members. If they have multiple members, it is possible that more than one contributes to result tuples. Only the distinct tuples from the dimensions listed in the first *set-count* sets will be returned, though.

Note that if a measure field is NULL in the underlying fact table, Analysis Services 2000 will treat the measure as zero, so the associated tuple will show up in the nonempty set (unless all measures in the row are NULL). Analysis Services 2005 allows measures to be NULLable, however, so the tuple won't show up unless there actually was a value for it in the underlying table.

Note that NonEmptyCrossJoin() always eliminates duplicate tuples, and ignores all calculations by calculated members, cell calculations, MDX scripts, and so on. This makes it less useful than NonEmpty() for determining true non-emptiness of a set of tuples, so in general NonEmpty() seems preferable.

See also: CrossJoin(), Extract(), Except(), Union(), Intersect()

NOT *expr*   Returns: Boolean
Standard

The NOT operator returns false if *expr* is true, and false otherwise.

O

OpeningPeriod ([*level* [, *member*]]**)**   Returns: member
Standard

ClosingPeriod ([*level* [, *member*]]**)**   Returns: member
Standard

The OpeningPeriod() and ClosingPeriod() functions are essentially first-descendant and last-descendant operators that are intended primarily to be used with the Time dimension, though they may be used with any dimension. The OpeningPeriod function returns the first member among the descendants of member at level. For example, `Opening-Period(Month, [1991])` returns [January, 1991]. If no member is specified, then the default is the current member of the Time-type dimension in that cube. If no level is specified, then it is the level immediately below that of member. `OpeningPeriod (level, member)` is equivalent to `Descendants(member, level).Item(0)`. Closing-Period() is very similar, only it returns the last descendant instead of the first descendant. Opening-Period() and ClosingPeriod() are illustrated in Figure A-27.

If member is omitted, and no dimension in the cube is marked as being Time-typed, the statement will parse and execute without error. However, when a client attempts to retrieve a cell calculated in part by the OpeningPeriod() or ClosingPeriod() function, a NULL member reference will occur in Analysis Services.

See also: PeriodsToDate(), ParallelPeriod(), Is

expr1 **OR** *expr2*   Returns: Boolean
Standard

The OR operator returns true if either *expr1* is true or *expr2* is true. In Analysis Services, if *expr1* evaluates to true, then *expr2* is not evaluated (because the result is already guaranteed to be true).

See also: AND, NOT, XOR, iif(), Filter()

Order (*set*, {*string_expression* | *numeric_expression*} **[,ASC | DESC | BASC | BDESC])**   Returns: set
Standard

Order() returns the set that it is given after it sorts it based on the given expression. If a numeric or string value expression is provided, then that is used to sort the tuples; otherwise, the values of the cells in context are used. This function also takes an optional flag to indicate how to sort. The default ordering is ASC (ascending without breaking the hierarchy).

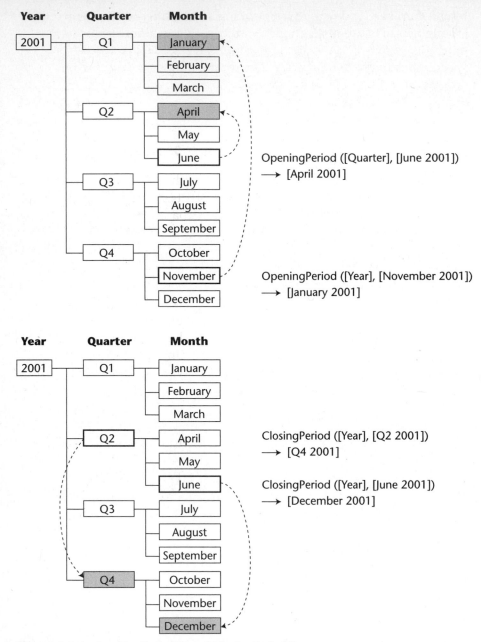

Figure A-27 OpeningPeriod() and ClosingPeriod().

Order() has two modes for sorting: breaking hierarchy and preserving hierarchy. The BASC and BDESC options break the hierarchy, while ASC and DESC do not. When the hierarchy is broken, the values associated with each tuple in the set are treated as peers, and the set is ordered only by the values. When the hierarchy is preserved, a more complex order-ing algorithm is used, which can lead to very useful results.

Note that there is no explicit way to sort a set based on more than one criterion. For example, if you want to sort a set based primarily on a string member property and secondarily on a numerical value, no good way is available for specifying this.

Preserving Hierarchy: Set Containing One Dimension

When the set consists only of one dimension's worth of members, sorting and preserving the hierarchy orders each parent before its children. At each level of members from the top down, the children of each parent are sorted relative to each other. For example, the product hierarchy for a fictional fishcake manu-facturer is shown in Figure A-28 and the units shipped per product are shown in Figure A-29. Ordering these members while preserving the hierarchy would give us the orderings shown in Figure A-30.

Also, an extra sophistication in the sorting process is not immediately evi-dent. Let us imagine that the category-level members [Standard], [Premium], and [Diet] were not part of the set being queried, while the ProductName members still were. Therefore, the category-level [Units] value does not come directly into play when the set is ordered. However, when sorting without breaking hierarchy, the [Units] value is still calculated at each parent member when Microsoft OLAP Services is trying to figure out how to order the groups of children relative to their cousins.

For example, suppose that the following set of product names was ordered by Units: {[Product].[Briny Deep], [Product].[Anglers Choice], [Product].[Ancient Mariner], [Product].[Gobi Crab Cakes], [Product].[Thin Fins]}. The ordering shown in Figure A-31 would be returned.

Category	Product Name
Premium	Ancient Mariner
Premium	Gobi Crab Cakes
Premium	Moby Dick
Premium	Neptunes Glory
Diet	Silver Scales
Diet	Thin Fins
Standard	Anglers Choice
Standard	Briny Deep
Standard	Gill Thrill
Standard	Mako Steak-o

Figure A-28   Sample product hierarchy.

Product	Units
Ancient Mariner	221,871
Gobi Crab Cakes	223,351
Moby Dick	200,745
Neptunes Glory	210,745
Premium	856,274
Silver Scales	425,604
Thin Fins	434,482
Diet	860,086
Anglers Choice	207,662
Briny Deep	201,443
Gill Thrill	209,962
Mako Steak-o	215,521
Standard	834,588

Figure A-29 Units shipped in hierarchy.

ASC

Product	Units
Standard	834,588
Briny Deep	201,443
Anglers Choice	207,662
Gill Thrill	209,962
Mako Steak-o	215,521
Premium	856,274
Moby Dick	200,745
Neptunes Glory	210,745
Ancient Mariner	221,871
Gobi Crab Cakes	223,351
Diet	860,086
Silver Scales	425,604
Thin Fins	434,482

DESC

Product	Units
Diet	860,086
Thin Fins	434,482
Silver Scales	425,604
Premium	856,274
Gobi Crab Cakes	223,351
Ancient Mariner	221,871
Neptunes Glory	210,745
Moby Dick	200,745
Standard	834,588
Mako Steak-o	215,521
Gill Thrill	209,962
Anglers Choice	207,662
Briny Deep	201,443

Figure A-30 Hierarchy preserved in ordering.

ASC

Product	Units	Parent's Units
Briny Deep	201,443	834,588
Anglers Choice	207,662	
Ancient Mariner	221,871	856,274
Gobi Crab Cakes	223,351	
Thin Fins	434,482	860,086

DESC

Product	Units	Parent's Units
Thin Fins	434,482	860,086
Gobi Crab Cakes	223,351	
Ancient Mariner	221,871	856,274
Anglers Choice	207,662	
Briny Deep	201,443	834,588

Figure A-31 Hierarchy preserved when ordering a set without parents.

Preserving Hierarchy: Set Containing Multiple Dimensions

When the set consists of multiple dimensions, the tuples are sorted so that the hierarchical ordering of the first dimension in the tuples is the primary ordering. According to this ordering, within each member of the first dimension, the members of the second dimension are sorted. Within each ([member from dim 1], [member from dim 2]) tuple, the members of the third dimension are sorted, and so on. For example, let's expand the example to include some customers and time periods and order the cross-join of

```
{ [Product].[Briny Deep], [Product].[Anglers Choice],  [Product].[Mako
Steak-o] }
```

with

```
{ [Time].[Quarter 2], [Time].[Quarter 3] }
```

with

```
{ [Customer].[Supernaturalizes Food Service], [Customer].[Hanover
Distributors], [Customer].[Subcommittees Anticipates Farms] }.
```

The ordering and values shown in Figure A-32 will appear. The products are arranged in order of decreasing quantity over year and customer parent. For each product, the quarters are arranged in order of decreasing quantity based on that product and customer parent. For each (Product, Time) tuple, the customers are arranged in order of decreasing quantity. Where tuples are tied (at the blank cells), the original ordering of the tuples is retained rather than the dimension's ordering (which was alphabetical).

See also: Hierarchize()

Level.**Ordinal**   Returns: number (integer)
Standard

This function returns the index of the level in the cube. The root level of a cube is number 0, the next level down (if there is one) is number 1, and so on. This is typically used in conjunction with IIF() to test whether a cell being calculated is at, above, or below a certain level in the cube (for example, below the All level or below the Quarter level). In Analysis Services, you can obtain the number of levels in the dimension with `Dimension.Levels.Count`.

See also: Is, .Name, Dimension.Levels(), Levels()

			Qty.
Mako Steak-o	Quarter 2	Subcommittee Anticipation Farms	199.00
		Supernatural Food Service	87.00
		Hanover Distributions	64.00
	Quarter 3	Hanover Distributions	185.00
		Supernatural Food Service	151.00
		Subcommittee Anticipation Farms	105.00
Anglers Choice	Quarter 3	Hanover Distributions	181.00
		Supernatural Food Service	179.00
		Subcommittee Anticipation Farms	
	Quarter 2	Supernatural Food Service	127.00
		Hanover Distributions	73.00
		Subcommittee Anticipation Farms	
Briny Deep	Quarter 3	Subcommittee Anticipation Farms	213.00
		Supernatural Food Service	
		Hanover Distributions	
	Quarter 2	Subcommittee Anticipation Farms	204.00
		Supernatural Food Service	
		Hanover Distributions	

Figure A-32   Hierarchy preserved when ordering a set with multiple dimensions.

P

ParallelPeriod ([*level* **[,** *index* **[,** *member***]]])**   Returns: set
Standard

This function is similar to the Cousin() function. It takes the ancestor of member at level (call it "ancestor"), then it takes the sibling of ancestor that lags by index (call it "in-law"), and it returns the cousin of member among the descendants of in-law. Figure A-33 illustrates the process of finding the parallel period. `ParallelPeriod (level, index, member)` is equivalent to `Cousin (member, Ancestor (Member, Level).Lag(index)`.

See also: Cousin(), OpeningPeriod(), ClosingPeriod(), Is

member.Parent
Standard

This function returns the source member's parent member, if it has one. The behavior of Parent() is shown in Figure A-34.

See also: Ancestor(), Ascendants(), IsAncestor(), IsGeneration()

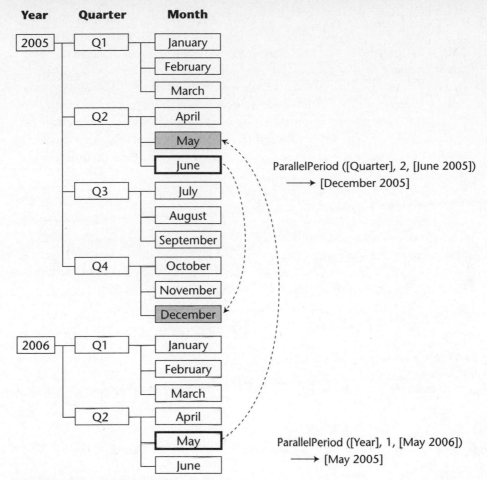

ParallelPeriod ([Quarter], 2, [June 2005])
⟶ [December 2005]

ParallelPeriod ([Year], 1, [May 2006])
⟶ [May 2005]

Figure A-33   ParallelPeriod() operator.

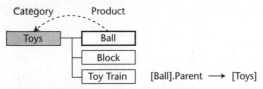

[Ball].Parent ⟶ [Toys]

Figure A-34   Behavior of .Parent.

PeriodsToDate ([*level* [, *member*]])   Returns: set
Standard

This function returns a set of members at the same level as *member*, starting at the first descendant under *member*'s ancestor at *level* and ending at *member*. If neither *level* nor *member* is specified, then the default member is the current member of the cube's Time-typed dimension, and *level* is the parent level of that member. If the *level* is specified but the *member* is not, then the dimension is inferred from the level, and the current member on that dimension is used. The function is identical to the following:

```
{ Descendants (Ancestor(member, level), member.Level).Item (0)
 : member }
```

If member is omitted, and no dimension in the cube is marked as being Time-typed, the statement will be parsed and execute without error. However, when a client attempts to retrieve a cell calculated in part by the PeriodsToDate() function, a cell error will occur.

The behavior of PeriodsToDate() is shown in Figure A-35.

See also: .Siblings, OpeningPeriod()

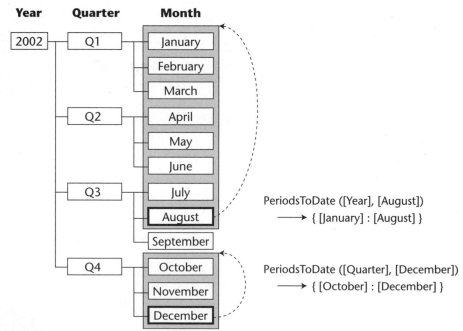

Figure A-35   Behavior of PeriodsToDate().

Predict (*mining_model_name, numeric_mining_expression***)**   Returns: Number
Extension: AS2005, AS2000

Predict() evaluates the given numeric_mining_expression against the data-mining model identified by mining_model_name. The actual syntax of the numeric_mining_expression is not part of MDX, but part of Microsoft's OLE DB for Data Mining specification.

*member.***PrevMember**
Standard

*member.***NextMember**
Standard

.PrevMember gives the previous member along the level implied by the member, while .NextMember gives the next member along the level implied by the member. Figure A-36 shows examples of .PrevMember and .NextMember. Note that these functions return the next or the previous member within the same level regardless of whether the new member shares the same parent or not.

See also: OpeningPeriod(), ClosingPeriod(), Is

member.**Properties(**property name**)** Returns: string
Standard

*member.***Properties(***property name***, TYPED)** Returns: various
Extension: AS2005

Returns the value of the named property at the member. The property name can be a string expression. If it is, the name expression is evaluated cell by cell every time the property reference is.

Even though Analysis Services 2000 and 2005 support member properties in a variety of data types, the return value of the .Properties() function is coerced to be a string unless you include the TYPED flag. Then, the property value is returned in its internal data type.

In Analysis Services, every member has associated properties named CAPTION, NAME, ID, and KEY.

See also: .PropertyName, .MemberValue, StrToMember(), StrToSet(), StrToTuple(), StrToValue(), Members(), Dimensions(), Levels()

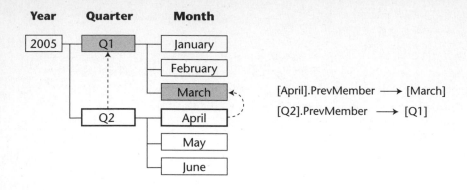

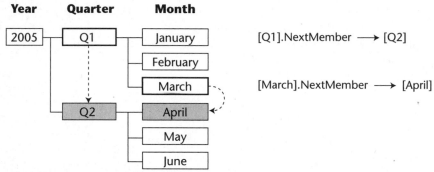

Figure A-36   NextMember and .PrevMember.

*member.**PropertyName*** Returns: string, number, boolean
Standard (except AS2000, AS2005)

In Essbase, a property value associated with a member is referenced by
member.PropertyName, where the name of the property is literally placed
in the MDX. For example, the following retrieves the ClubStatus property value for the current Customer member:

```
[Customer].CurrentMember.[ClubStatus]
```

Since the syntax for this kind of property reference is similar to the syntax for a number of functions, you should always use delimited names
(in []) for property names.

*See also: .Properties(), .MemberValue, StrToMember(), StrToSet(), StrToTu-
ple(), StrToValue(), Members(), Dimensions(), Levels()*

Q

QTD ([*member*])   Returns: set
Standard

QTD() is the equivalent of PeriodsToDate() with the level set to Quarter. If member is not specified, it defaults to the current member of the Time-typed dimension. If no Time-typed dimension is in the cube, or if one is in the cube without a level tagged as Quarter, then an error results.

See also: PeriodsToDate(), YTD(), MTD(), WTD()

R

Rank(*tuple, set*)   Returns: number (integer)
Standard

Rank(*tuple, set, numeric_expression*)   Returns: number (integer)
Extension: AS2005, AS2000

This function returns the (one-based) index of the *tuple* in the *set*. If the *tuple* is not found in the set, Rank() returns 0.

If the optional numeric expression is provided, then it is evaluated for tuple. In AS2005, when this expression is found, the given ordering of the set is ignored. Instead, AS2005 puts the tuples of the set in ascending order according to *numeric_expression*, and returns the tied rank number according to that numbering. In AS2000, the numeric expression is evaluated for the neighbors of *tuple* in the ordering of the set as it is passed to Rank(). If two or more tuples share the same value in the set, then the rank number returned is the tied rank. Note that if the set is not sorted by the same numeric expression, then the rank numbers will reflect the (possibly tied) rank according to the set as it is actually sorted.

MEMBER	SALES	UNITS
Leather Jackets	100	5
Leather Pants	120	4
Leather Gloves	150	200
Leather Bags	150	16
Leather Skirts	200	4

Consider the following examples against a simple set of numbers:

Against this set of tuples (which we will call Set1) and associated values, the following is true:

Rank (`[Product].[Leather Pants]`, Set1) is 2.

Rank (`[Product].[Leather Bags]`, Set1, `[Measures]`
`.[Sales]`) is 3 (tied with leather gloves).

Rank (`[Product].[Leather Skirts]`, Set1, `[Measures]`
`.[Units]`) is 5 in AS2000 (the tie with leather pants is not noticed). In AS2005, it is 1 (tied for first place when sorted in ascending order).

Note that the .Item() and Subset() functions use a zero-based index; the rank of Set.Item(0) is 1.

See also: .Item(), Subset(), Head(), Tail()

RollupChildren(*member***,** *string expression***)**   Returns: number
Extension: AS2005, AS2000

This function is used to return the value generated by rolling up the children of a specified parent member using the specified unary operator. The string expression is evaluated once per child of member. You can use a constant string value for the expression, as well as a string value that changes with each member. The first (or only) unary operator may be one of +, -, ~, or a number, while subsequent operators may be one of +, -, *, /, ~ or a number. When a number is used, it is a weighting value; the effect is to multiply the cell value related to the child member by the number, and add it to the accumulating rollup value. Frequently, a reference to a member property ([Dimension].CurrentMember.Properties ("Some Property")) will be the string expression. You may also use a string expression based on a property. For example, the following expression will create the positive sum of all children that would ordinarily be subtracted from the sum:

```
iif ([Accounts].CurrentMember.Properties ("UNARY_OPERATOR") <> "-",
   "~",
   "-"
)
```

This function could be used, for example, in a budgeting application where there may be more than one way to roll up the Accounts dimension, and perhaps some costs are ignored in the alternate rollup. You could create a member property "alternate operators" to hold the operators of this alternate rollup. The following expression would return the results of this alternate rollup (note that the current member is evaluated once per child of [Account].[Net Profit]):

```
RollupChildren([Account].[Net Profit],
        [Account].CurrentMember.Properties("ALTERNATE_OPERATORS") )
```

Note that if you use this function as a custom rollup operator (for example, in a local cube), you may need to use it in conjunction with an iif() test and the .Ignore function to avoid infinite recursion at leaf-level members.

See also: Sum()

Root ()   Returns tuple
Extension: AS2005

Root (*dimension***)**   Returns tuple
Extension: AS2005

Root (*tuple***)**   Returns tuple
Extension: AS2005

The Root() function returns a tuple of the root attribute-dimension members for each attribute hierarchy in the scope. If an attribute dimension does not have an All member, then the default member is included instead. It may return an empty or null tuple, as described below.

If the argument is a dimension, then all the related attribute dimensions/ hierarchies for that dimension are included. In this case, it does not matter whether you pick the overall dimension (for example, [Product]) or a hierarchy within the dimension (for example, [Product].[ByCategory] or [Product].[Ship Weight]).

If the argument is a tuple, then the result tuple contains the original members and all of the root members for the other attribute hierarchies in the respective dimensions. Note that the result tuple puts the members in a server-defined order, not the dimension order of members in the tuple. For example, you may have a tuple such as

```
( [Product].[Shipweight].[12],
  [Time].[YQMD].[Oct, 2005] )
```

but if Time appears before Product in the order of dimensions in the cube designer, the time components of the result tuple will appear first. However, the Shipweight member will be [12] and the YQMD hierarchy member will be [Oct, 2005]. The tuple can contain a member from different attribute hierarchies of a single logical dimension, like [Time] or [Product], but if the members do not have a corresponding tuple in the dimension, the result tuple is null. If they do, each of the members is retained in the tuple.

If this function is called with no argument, a tuple composed of the root members for each hierarchy is returned.

Note that this function can be used anywhere, not just in MDX scripts.

See also: Leaves()

S

Scope
Extension: AS2005

Scope is an MDX Scripting statement that defines a subcube, within which the actions of other statements is limited. The general syntax is:

```
Scope subcube ;
   statement1 ; [ ... statementN ; ]
End Scope ;
```

SetToArray(*set* [, *set* ...][, *numeric or string expression*])
Standard

The SetToArray() function creates an array as a COM Variant type that holds an array of values. The only use for this function in OLAP and Analysis Services is to pass the constructed array to an external function that is defined as taking an array.

The constructed array will hold values of only one type (which might be, for example, long integer, single float, double float, or string). That type is determined by the type of the first value that is actually placed into the array. The dimensionality of the array that is created is determined by the number of sets that appear as arguments to SetToArray(). If the optional numeric or string expression is provided, it is evaluated over the cross-join of the sets, and the values are placed in the array. If the numeric or string expression is not provided, then the cross-join of the sets is evaluated in the current context, and the results obtained are placed in the array.

SetToStr(*set*)   Returns: string
Standard

This function constructs a string from a set. It will frequently be used to transfer a set to an external function that knows how to parse the string, even though the string is syntactically suitable for OLAP Services to parse into a set. OLAP Services constructs the string as follows: The first character is { and the last character is }. Between the braces, each tuple is listed in order. A comma and a space separate each tuple from the next name. If the set contains only one dimension, then each member is listed using its unique name. If the set contains more than one dimension, then each tuple begins with an open parenthesis ["("] and ends with a closing parenthesis, ")". The unique name of the member from each dimension is listed in the order of the dimensions in the set, separated by a comma and a space. For example, in a Time dimension that has three years, the expression

```
SetToStr ([Time].[Year].Members)
```

would yield the following string:

```
"{[Time].[All Times].[1998], [Time].[All Times].[1999], [Time].[All
Times].[2000]}"
```

Moreover, the expression

```
SetToStr ( {([Time].[1998], [Customer].[Northeast]), ([Time].[1999],
[Customer].[Southwest])} )
```

yields the following string:

```
"{([Time].[All Times].[1998], [Customer].[All Customers].[Northeast]),
([Time].[All Times].[1999], [Customer].[All Customers].[Southwest])}".
```

Fairly large strings (greater than 16K) will take significant time to create, and the first release of OLAP Services was released with problems that led to the truncation of strings. The further down the hierarchy the members are, the longer and more numerous their unique names are likely to be. So, you may need to perform your own performance evaluations when using this function.

The style of the unique names generated into the string by this function will be affected by the MDX Unique Name Style and MDX Compatibility settings.

See also: Generate(), StrToValue(), StrToSet(), StrToMember(), LookupCube()

Member.**Siblings**   Returns: set
Extension: AS2005, AS2000

This function returns the set of metadata siblings of a specified member in the database's default order. The resulting set includes the specified member itself. It does not include calculated members. Figure A-37 diagrams the selection of .Siblings.

See also: .Children, .FirstSibling, .LastSibling

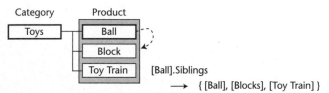

Figure A-37   Diagram of .Siblings.

StdDev(*set* [, *numeric value expression*])   Returns: number
Standard

StdDevP(*set* [, *numeric value expression*])   Returns: number
Extension: AS2005, AS2000, Essbase

StDev(*set* [, *numeric value expression*])   Returns: number
Extension: AS2005, AS2000

StDevP(*set* [, *numeric value expression*])   Returns: number
Extension: AS2005, AS2000

These functions return the standard deviation of a numeric expression evaluated over a set. If the numeric value expression is not supplied, these functions evaluate the set within the current context to determine the values to use. The formula for obtaining the standard deviation is as follows:

$$\sqrt{\frac{\sum_{i=1}^{n}(\bar{x}-x_i)^2}{n}}$$

StDev() calculates the sample standard deviation and uses the unbiased formula for population (dividing by n - 1 instead of n). On the other hand, StDevP() calculates the population standard deviation and uses the biased formula (dividing by n). StdDev() and StdDevP() are aliases of StDev() and StDevP(), respectively.

StripCalculatedMembers(*set*)   Returns: set
Extension: AS2005, AS2000

The StripCalculatedMembers() function returns the members of *set* after removing all the calculated members. The set is limited to only one dimension. Note that this function removes all calculated members defined, whether they were defined by CREATE MEMBER at the server or at the client, or in the query through WITH MEMBER.

See also: AddCalculatedMembers(), .AllMembers

StrToMember (*string_expression*)   Returns: member
Standard

StrToMember (*string_expression*, **CONSTRAINED**)   Returns: member
Extension: AS2005

This function refers to a member identified by the *string_expression*. This will frequently be used along with external functions to convert a string returned by the external function to a member reference within the query. The string expression can be dynamic as well as a fixed string. When the CONSTRAINED flag is omitted, the expression can resolve to an MDX expression that evaluates to a member as well as just the name of a member When the CONSTRAINED flag is present, the *string_expression* can still be a string expression instead of a literal string, but when the string is evaluated, it must be a qualified or unqualified member name, or else the evaluation results in an error. If the error occurs in evaluating a slicer or axis, the query execution will stop. If the error occurs in evaluating a result cell, the cell will have an error result.

See also: Members(), StrToTuple(), StrToSet(), .Properties(), IsError()

StrToSet(*string_expression*)   Returns: set
Standard

StrToSet (*string_expression*, **CONSTRAINED**)   Returns: set
Extension: AS2005

This function constructs a set from a *string expression*. This will frequently be used to transfer a set specification returned by a UDF back to the MDX statement. When the CONSTRAINED flag is omitted, the string must be a syntactically valid MDX set specification relative to the cube in whose context it is executed. For example, the set of all years in a Time dimension that has three year-level members could be created by passing either of the following strings into StrToSet:

```
"{[Time].[All Times].[2004], [Time].[All Times].[2005],
  [Time].[All Times].[2006]}"
"[Time].[Year].Members"
```

When the CONSTRAINED flag is provided, the string expression must contain either a valid MDX tuple composed of named members, or a set of tuples composed of named members and enclosed by {}. Of the two examples above, the first would be allowed with the CONSTRAINED flag while the second one would not. If the error occurs in evaluating a slicer or axis, the query execution will stop. If the error occurs in evaluating a result cell, the cell will have an error result.

See also: StrToTuple, SetToStr(), TupleToStr(), Members(), .Properties(), .Name, .UniqueName, IsError()

StrToTuple (*string_expression***)** Returns: tuple
Standard

StrToTuple (*string_expression***, CONSTRAINED)** Returns: tuple
Extension: AS2005

This function constructs a tuple from a string expression. This will frequently be used to transfer a tuple specification that is returned by an external function back to the MDX statement. The string must be a syntactically valid MDX tuple specification relative to the cube in whose context it is executed. When the CONSTRAINED flag is omitted, the *string_expression* can contain any MDX expression that results in a tuple. For example, the following two strings would give identical results in the customer dimension, where [AZ] is a child of [Southwest], in that both would result in the Southwest region member:

```
"([Customer].[Southwest],[Time].[2006])"
"([Customer].[AZ].Parent,[Time].[2006])"
```

When the CONSTRAINED flag is provided, the string expression must contain valid MDX tuple composed of named members, or else an error will result. Of the two examples above, the first would be allowed with the CONSTRAINED flag while the second one would not. If the error occurs in evaluating a slicer or axis, the query execution will stop. If the error occurs in evaluating a result cell, the cell will have an error result.

See also: StrToSet(), SetToStr(), TupleToStr(), Members(), .Properties(), .Name, .UniqueName, IsError()

StrToValue (*string expression***)**   Returns: number or string
Extension: AS2005, AS2000

StrToValue (*string_expression***, CONSTRAINED)**   Returns: number or string
Extension: AS2005

This function takes the results of an arbitrary string expression and evaluates it as an MDX expression in the current context of the cube or query. The string expression can be dynamic as well as a fixed string. When the CONSTRAINED flag is omitted, the MDX expression can be arbitrarily complicated so long as it returns a single cell value. When the CONSTRAINED flag is provided, the string expression must contain only a constant value, or else an error will result. If the error occurs in evaluating a slicer or axis, the query execution will stop. If the error occurs in evaluating a result cell, the cell will have an error result.

See also: StrToSet, SetToStr(), TupleToStr(), Members(), .Properties(), .Name, .UniqueName

Subset (*set***, ***start* **[, ***count***])**   Returns: set
Extension: AS2005, AS2000

This function returns up to *count* elements from *set*, starting at *start*. The start index is zero-based: the first element in the set is at index 0, and the last is at one less than the number of tuples in the set. If *count* is not specified or is greater than the number of elements in the set following *Start*, all elements from *Start* to the end of the set are returned. If *count* is less than 1, then an empty set is returned.

See also: Head(), Tail(), Index(), .Count, Count(), Rank()

Sum (*set* **[, ***numeric value expression***])**   Returns: number
Standard

This function returns the sum of values found across all tuples in the *set*. If *numeric value expression* is supplied, then it is evaluated across *set* and its results are summed; otherwise, *set* is evaluated in the current context and the results are summed.

See also: Aggregate(), Avg(), Count(), .Count, Min(), Max()

T

Tail(*set* [, *count*])   Returns: set
Extension: AS2005, AS2000

This function returns a set of the last *count* elements from the given *set*. The order of elements in the given *set* is preserved. If *count* is omitted, the number of elements returned is 1. If count is less than 1, an empty set is returned. If the value of the count is greater than the number of tuples in the set, the original set is returned.

See also: Subset(), Head(),Index(), .Count, Count(), Rank()

This   Returns: subcube

This function returns the currently specified scope in an MDX script. May be assigned to or have properties set for it.

See also: .CurrentMember

ToggleDrillState (*set1*, *set2* [, **RECURSIVE**])   Returns: set
Standard

This function returns a set in which those members or tuples in *set1* that are drilled up are drilled down and those members or tuples in *set1* that are drilled down are drilled up. This function combines the operations of DrillUpMember() and DrillDownMember(). *Set1* can contain tuples of arbitrary dimensionality; *set2* must contain only members of one dimension. A member or tuple in *set1* is considered drilled down if it has any descendant immediately following it and is considered drilled up otherwise. When a member is found without a descendant immediately after it, DrillDownMember() will be applied to it, with the RECURSIVE flag if the RECURSIVE is present.

See also: DrillDownMember(), DrillUpMember()

TopCount (*set*, *index* [, *numeric expression*])   Returns: set
Standard

BottomCount (*set*, *index* [, *numeric expression*])   Returns: set
Standard

TopCount() returns the top *index* items found after sorting the *set*. The *set* is sorted on the *numeric expression* (if one is supplied). If there is no *numeric expression*, the cells found in the evaluation context are used. The Bottom-Count() function is similar to TopCount(), except that it returns the bottom index items. TopCount() returns elements ordered from largest to smallest in terms of the cells or expression used; BottomCount() returns them ordered from smallest to largest. Any duplicate tuples are retained during sorting, and those that make the cutoff are retained.

These functions always break the hierarchy. If members from multiple levels are combined in the set, then they are all treated as peers. If duplicate values exist for some of the cells in set, these functions may pick an arbitrary set. For example, suppose the set of values (when sorted) is as follows.

FRUIT	VALUE
Strawberries	12
Cantaloupes	10
Peaches	8
Apples	8
Kiwis	8
Bananas	4

In this case, selecting the top three or bottom two fruits based on values will cause an arbitrary choice to be made at the value of 8. The results are functionally equivalent to Head(Order(*set, numeric value expression,* BDESC), *index*) and Head(Order(*set, numeric value expression,* BASC), *index*).

Note that Essbase always removes tuples from the set whose numeric expression is NULL. If you want them included at some position, use CoalesceEmpty() in the numeric expression to convert the NULL to some value.

See also: TopSum(), BottomSum(), TopPercent(), BottomPercent()

TopPercent(*set, percentage, numeric expression***)**   Returns: set
Standard

BottomPercent(*set, percentage, numeric expression***)**   Returns: set
Standard

TopPercent() returns the top percentage tuples of set, based on numeric expression if specified. The cells or expression are summed over the set, and the top set of elements whose cumulative total of the numeric expression is at least percentage is returned. Percentage is a numeric expression. For example, using the sorted set of fruits and values, TopPercent(fruit, 50, Value) will result in {Strawberries, Cantaloupes}. Strawberries is 24 percent of the total, Cantaloupes 1 Strawberries is 44 percent of the total, and Peaches would push the set over the 50 percent limit to 56 percent.

BottomPercent() behaves similarly, except that it returns the bottom set of elements whose cumulative total from the bottom is less than the specified percentage. TopPercent() returns elements ordered from largest to smallest in terms of the cells or expression used; BottomPercent() returns them ordered from smallest to largest.

The percentage is specified from 0 to 100 (not 0 to 1.0). These functions always break the hierarchy. Like TopCount() and BottomCount(), they may pick an arbitrary cutoff when some cells have the same values. Any duplicate tuples are retained during sorting, and those that make the cutoff are retained. Note that these functions do not have anything to do with taking tuples in the top or bottom percentile ranges according to the statistical definition of percentiles.

Note that Essbase always removes tuples from the set whose numeric expression is NULL. If you want them included at some position, use CoalesceEmpty() in the numeric expression to convert the NULL to some value.

See also: TopCount(), BottomCount(), TopSum(), BottomSum()

TopSum(*set, value, numeric expression***)**   Returns: set
Standard

BottomSum (*set, value, numeric expression***)**   Returns: set
Standard

TopSum() returns the subset of set, after sorting it, such that the sum of the cells (or numeric value expression, if supplied) is at least value. This function always breaks the hierarchy. For example, given the sorted set of fruits and values, TopSum(fruit, 24, value) would return {Strawberries, Cantaloupes}. Strawberries' 12 is less than 24, and Strawberries 1 Cantaloupes is 22, while adding Peach's 8 to the 22 would push it over the limit of 24 to 30. The BottomSum() function behaves similarly, except that it returns the bottom set of elements whose cumulative total from the bottom is less than the specified value. TopSum() returns elements ordered from largest to smallest in terms of the cells or expression used; BottomSum() returns them ordered from smallest to largest.

These functions always break the hierarchy. Like TopCount() and BottomCount(), they may pick an arbitrary cutoff when some cells have the same values. Any duplicate tuples are retained during sorting, and those that make the cutoff are retained.

Note that Essbase always removes tuples from the set whose numeric expression is NULL. If you want them included at some position, use CoalesceEmpty() in the numeric expression to convert the NULL to some value.

See also: TopCount(), BottomCount(), TopPercent(), BottomPercent()

TupleToStr(*tuple***)**   Returns: string
Standard

This function constructs a string from a tuple. This will frequently be used to transfer a tuple specification to an external function. If the tuple contains only one dimension, the unique name for its member is placed in the string. (In this use, it is identical to Member.UniqueName.) If the tuple contains more than one dimension, Analysis Services constructs the string as follows. The string begins with an open parenthesis ["("] and ends with a closed parenthesis ["("]. In between the parentheses, the member's unique name is placed in the string for each dimension in the order they follow in the tuple. Each member is separated by a comma and a space. For example, the expression

```
TupleToStr ( (Time.[1997], Customer.[AZ]) )
```

which uses names that are not quite the members' unique names, might return the following string:

```
"([Time].[All Times].[1997], [Customer].[All
Customers].[Southwest].[AZ])"
```

If the tuple is a result of an invalid member reference, then the resulting string is empty (instead of an error result).

The style of name generated depends on the MDX Unique Name Style and MDX Compatibility settings.

See also: SetToStr(), StrToTuple(), .Name, .UniqueName, StrToMember(), Members(), StrToValue(), LookupCube()

U

Union(*set1*, *set2* **[, ALL])**   Returns: set
Standard

set1 + set2   Returns: set
Extension: AS2005, AS2000

This function returns the union of the two sets. The ALL flag controls whether duplicates are retained or eliminated; by default, they are eliminated. When duplicates of each tuple are eliminated, the first instance of each tuple is retained according to the order in which it appears. The effect of this function is that *set2* is appended to *set1*, and then all copies of each tuple are removed after the first instance of that tuple in the appended version. When duplicates are retained, any duplicates in the *set1* are retained, and any additional copies in *set2* are also retained. The effect of the union is that *set2* is appended to *set1*. For example, the expression

```
Union (
    { [Customer].[AZ].[Phoenix], [Customer].[AZ].[Scottsdale],
      [Customer].[KS].[Pittsburg], [Customer].[AZ].[Phoenix] },
    { [Customer].[NM].[Albuquerque], [Customer].[AZ].[Phoenix],
      [Customer].[AZ].[Scottsdale], [Customer].[AZ].[Phoenix]
)
```

yields the following set:

```
  { [Customer].[AZ].[Phoenix], [Customer].[AZ].[Scottsdale],
    [Customer].[KS].[Pittsburg], [Customer].[NM].[Albuquerque] }
```

The expression

```
Union (
  { [Customer].[AZ].[Phoenix], [Customer].[AZ].[Scottsdale],
    [Customer].[KS].[Pittsburg], [Customer].[AZ].[Phoenix] },
  { [Customer].[NM].[Albuquerque], [Customer].[AZ].[Phoenix],
  [Customer].[AZ].[Scottsdale], [Customer].[AZ].[Phoenix] }
  , ALL
)
```

yields the following set:

```
  { [Customer].[AZ].[Phoenix], [Customer].[AZ].[Scottsdale],
  [Customer].[KS].[Pittsburg], [Customer].[AZ].[Phoenix],
  [Customer].[NM].[Albuquerque], [Customer].[AZ].[Phoenix],
  [Customer].[AZ].[Scottsdale], [Customer].[AZ].[Phoenix] }
```

Microsoft OLAP Services and Analysis Services also provide + as an alternate way of specifying Union(). Duplicates are removed from the resulting set. The expression `Set1 + Set2 + Set3` is equivalent to `Union (Set1, Union (Set2, Set3))`.

See also: Intersect(), Except(), {}

Dimension.**UniqueName**   Returns: string
Extension: AS2005, AS2000

This function returns the unique name of a dimension. In Microsoft's OLAP products, this does not include the name of the cube.

See also: .Name

Level.**UniqueName**   Returns: string
Extension: AS2005, AS2000

This function returns the unique name of a level. In Microsoft's OLAP products, this does not include the name of the cube. It will be either [Dimension].[Level] or [Dimension].[Hierarchy].[Level], depending on the structure of the dimension.

See also: .Name, Levels()

Member.**UniqueName**   Returns: string
Extension: AS2005, AS2000

This function returns the unique name of a member. In Microsoft's OLAP products, this does not include the name of the cube, and the results are dependent on the MDX Unique Name Style connection property or the equivalent server-side setting.

See also: StrToMember(), StrToTuple(), StrToSet(),TupleToStr(), .Name

member.**UnknownMember**   Returns: member
Extension: AS2005

This function returns the member created by AS2005 for handling "unknown hierarchy" conditions in fact data. Unknown members can be created at one of the following levels:

- The top level, in attribute hierarchies that cannot be aggregated
- The level beneath the (All) level for natural hierarchies
- Any level (for other hierarchies)

If the unknown member is requested for a member, then the child of the given *member* that is an "unknown member" is returned. If the unknown member does not exist under the given *member*, a NULL member reference is returned.

See also: .CurrentMember, .DefaultMember

Unorder()   Returns: set
Extension: AS2005

This function relaxes MDX-specified ordering from the tuples or members of a set. Generally speaking, this function is a hint for optimization of a set operation. For example, a set that is input to NonEmpty(), Top-Count() or Order() may not have any need to have the sequence of input tuples preserved. (For functions that sort the input sets, like TopCount() and Order(), this is because the stable sorting requirement becomes relaxed.) Therefore, `NonEmpty (Unorder (set))` may run more quickly than `NonEmpty (set)`. Note that AS2005 automatically attempts to perform this optimization for functions like Sum(), Aggregate(), so you may not notice any performance gain attempting to aggregated Unorder()'d sets.

UserName   Returns: string
Extension: AS2005, AS2000

This function returns the username of the user executing the function. The name is returned in Domain\Name format. For example, if user Lisa in the domain ITCMAIN invokes a calculation that uses this function, it will return "ITCMAIN\Lisa".

See also: CustomData

V

ValidMeasure (*tuple***)**   Returns: tuple
Extension: AS2005, AS2000

This function returns the value of the measure specified by the tuple where the measure has been projected to a meaningful intersection in a virtual cube. When a virtual cube joins two or more regular cubes that have different dimensionality, all base data values in the virtual cube are found at the ALL levels of each dimension that is not shared by all cubes. You can always reference these base data cells by explicitly qualifying the measure reference to the ALL level of each dimension (for example, ([Measures].[Employee Count], [Product].[All Products], [Customer].[All Customers])). This function is a convenience because you do not need to explicitly reference all of the dimensions that are not relevant to the measure.

The tuple may contain members from any dimensions of the virtual cube (and it does not need to have a measure in it). Any members for noncommon dimensions for the measure are projected to the ALL member. Any members for dimensions that are in common are used to locate the value returned. The function can be used with regular cubes, but in that case it does nothing to change the location of reference for the measure.

Note that you need an extra set of parentheses to define the tuple if it contains more than one member

```
ValidMeasure ( ([Measures].[Qty Purchased], [Time].PrevMember) )
```

instead of

```
ValidMeasure ( [Measures].[Qty Purchased], [Time].PrevMember )
```

In AS2005, keep in mind that setting the IgnoreUnrelatedDimensions option on a measure group will turn on an automatic ValidMeasure behavior, which obviates the need for this function

measure[**.Value**]   Returns: number or string
Standard (except AS2000)

The .Value operator returns the value of the specified measure at the location formed by the current members of all other dimensions in context. We show this operator as optional because it is the default operator on a measure in a calculation or query context. If you leave it off, you get the value of the measure anyway because the default interpretation of a measure is to take its value. This operator exists simply as a specific counterpart to the other functions that return aspects of a member, such as .Name (which would return the name of the measure).

Var(*set* [, *numeric value expression*])   Returns: number
Standard

Variance(*set* [, *numeric value expression*])   Returns: number
Extension: AS2005, AS2000

VarianceP(*set* [, *numeric value expression*])   Returns: number
Extension: AS2005, AS2000

VarP(*set* [, *numeric value expression*])   Returns: number
Extension: AS2005, AS2000

These functions return the variance of a numeric expression evaluated over a set. If the numeric expression is not supplied, these functions evaluate the set within the current context to determine the values to use. The formula for obtaining the variance is

$$\frac{\sum_{i=1}^{n}(\bar{x} - x_i)^2}{n}$$

Var() calculates the sample variance and uses the unbiased population formula (dividing by n – 1), while VarP() calculates the population variance and uses the biased formula (dividing by n). Variance() and VarianceP() are aliases of Var() and VarP(), respectively.

See also: Stdev(), StdevP()

VisualTotals (*set*, *pattern***) Returns set**
Extension: AS2005, AS2000

The function accepts a *set* that can contain members at any level from within one dimension. (The set can only include members from one dimension.) Typically, the *set* contains members with some ancestor/descendant relationship. For the set that is returned, aggregate data values for the ancestor data values are calculated as aggregates of the children or descendants provided in the *set* instead of using all children from the dimension. (When the *set* corresponds to children visible in the GUI, the parents are totaled according to the visible members, which is the origin of the "visual totals" name). The *pattern* is a string that is used to identify visual-total members "visually" totaled members are identified in the results using this pattern string. Wherever an asterisk appears in the string, the name (the simple name, not the unique name) of that parent member is inserted. A double asterisk (**) causes an asterisk character to appear in the name.

NOTE While this function exists in both AS 2005 and AS 2000, its behavior has changed substantially between the releases. In AS2005, the function works with all measure aggregation types, in contrast with AS2000 in which it did not work with DISTINCT COUNT measures. We will describe the AS 2005 behavior first and then the AS 2000 behavior.

In Analysis Services 2005, VisualTotals() effectively redefines the parent members listed in the set to have only children/descendants as they appear in the set, changing the display caption of the parent members to match the naming pattern as well. This affects all uses of the members in the entire query, not just within the set. In terms of calculations, it is similar to, but not the same as defining a subcube consisting of just the lowest-level members in the *set*.

Consider the following query, whose results are shown in Figure A-38:

```
WITH
SET [VT1] AS
VisualTotals (
  { [Product].[ByCategory].[Category].&[2],
    {[Product].[ByCategory].[Subcategory].&[12],
     [Product].[ByCategory].[Subcategory].&[15]}
  },
  "(total *)"
)
SELECT
{ [Measures].[Unit Sales], [Measures].[Dollar Sales]} on 0,
{  [VT1],
   [Product].[ByCategory].[Category].&[2],
   [Product].[ByCategory].[Family].&[1]  }
} on 1
FROM [Sales]
```

	Unit Sales	Dollar Sales
(total Outdoor Gear)	13,505	$346,008.44
Inflatable Boats	4,625	$199,377.93
Multi-Tools, Knives	8,880	$226,631.05
(total Outdoor Gear)	13,505	$346,008.44
Outdoor & Sporting	256,691	$6,493,322.31

Figure A-38   Results of VisualTotals() in AS 2005.

You can see that the first three rows represent the VT1 set, which includes two product subcategories and their Outdoor Gear parent. The fourth row was a request for the Outdoor Gear member outside of the VisualTotals(), but it returns the same value as the VisualTotals() result since the member has been redefined for the whole query. The last row is a request for the Outdoor & Sporting member which is the parent of Outdoor Gear. Its aggregates include only the visible Outdoor Gear values, but also all the values from the siblings of Outdoor Gear. Unlike a subcube, VisualTotals() does not effectively make members invisible, but it does change the set of children/descendants that contribute to an ancestor.

This global impact has a slightly surprising effect. Consider the following query, whose results are shown in Figure A-39:

```
WITH
SET [VT1] AS
VisualTotals (
   { [Product].[ByCategory].[Category].&[2],
     { [Product].[ByCategory].[Subcategory].&[12],
       [Product].[ByCategory].[Subcategory].&[15] }
   },
   "(total *)"
)
SET [VT2] AS
VisualTotals (
   { [Product].[ByCategory].[Category].&[2],
     { [Product].[ByCategory].[Subcategory].&[9],
       [Product].[ByCategory].[Subcategory].&[12] }
   },
   "(total *)"
)
SELECT
{ [Measures].[Unit Sales], [Measures].[Dollar Sales]} on 0,
{  [VT1], [VT2] } on 1
FROM [Sales]
```

	Unit Sales	Dollar Sales
(total Outdoor Gear)	14,536	$385,402.15
Inflatable Boats	4,625	$199,377.93
Multi-Tools, Knives	8,880	$226,631.05
(total Outdoor Gear)	14,536	$385,402.15
Coolers	9,911	$266,024.76
Inflatable Boats	4,625	$119,377.93

Figure A-39 Results of two VisualTotals() using same parent member.

You can see two different VisualTotals() calls, with the same parent member in each. This results in that member appearing twice in the query result. The aggregated values are calculated by the second call's set.

Note that placement of members is more flexible in AS2005 than in AS2000. In particular, you can have visual totals parents following their children instead of only preceding them, which enables more display requirements to be fulfilled.

In Analysis Services 2000, VisualTotals() returns a set that includes dynamically created calculated members that total up the given descendants for an ancestor. When a parent member is followed by one or more of its children in the given set, or an ancestor by one or more of its descendants, the function replaces that parent or ancestor member with a synthesized member that totals the values taken only from the children or descendants that follow it in the set. The name of the synthesized member is formed from the pattern given in the pattern argument. The order of the appearance of members is important; a parent that is to be replaced by a synthetic visual total must appear immediately before its children. The sets created by the `DrillDownXXX` functions are likely to fit `VisualTotal()`'s member ordering requirements.

The synthesized members are named using the text from the pattern string, per the rules described earlier. Consider the following Visual-Totals() expression, which contains numerous parents and ancestors (its results are shown in Figure A-40).

```
WITH
MEMBER [Measures].[AvgPrice] AS '[Measures].[Total] /
[Measures].[Qty]', FORMAT_STRING = '#.00000'
SET [Rowset] AS 'VisualTotals (
{
[Time].[All Time].[2001].[Q1, 2001],
[Time].[All Time].[2001],
[Time].[All Time].[2001].[Q1, 2001].[January],
[Time].[All Time].[2001].[Q1, 2001].[February],
[Time].[All Time].[2001].[Q2, 2001],
[Time].[All Time].[2001].[Q2, 2001].[May],
[Time].[All Time].[2001].[Q2, 2001].[June],
[Time].[All Time].[2001].[Q1, 2001],
[Time].[All Time].[2001].[Q2, 2001],
[Time].[All Time],
[Time].[All Time].[2001].[Q1, 2001].[January].[Jan 01, 1998],
[Time].[All Time].[2001].[Q1, 2001].[January].[Jan 02, 1998]
}
, "vt *")'
SELECT
{ {[Measures].[Qty],  [Measures].[Total],  [Measures].[AvgPrice} } on
axis(0),
{ [Time].[All Time].[2001].[Quarter 1], [Rowset]
} on axis(1)
FROM cakes03
```

This highlights some of the useful aspects of VisualTotals() and also some of its quirks, which you will need to be aware of. Looking at the [vt All Time] member toward the bottom of the report, the All Time total is simply the sum of the two day-level members following it, and a similar look at [vt Q2, 2001] shows that it is the sum of the two Q2 months following it. Looking at the Qty measure for [vt 2001], the value 1,186,056 is the sum of values found for January, February, [vt Quarter 2], [Quarter 1], and [Quarter 2]. In other words, [vt Quarter 2] was not double-counted with [May] and [June]. You do need to be careful in how you place descendants, however. [Quarter 1] and [Quarter 2] are included in the total without regard to the fact that their descendants have already been incorporated into the total.

	Qty	Total	Average Price
Quarter 1	1,811,965.00	44,166,000.00	24.37464
vt 2001	5,965,904.00	133,988,515.00	22.45905
January	620,829.00	16,343,870.00	26.32588
February	572,194.00	13,863,990.00	24.26447
vt Quarter 2	1,186,056.00	23,660,064.00	19.94852
May	614,945.00	12,267,870.00	19.94954
June	571,111.00	11,392,190.00	19.94743
Quarter 1	1,811,965.00	44,166,000.00	24.37464
Quarter 2	1,774,860.00	35,934,600.00	20.24644
vt All Time	39,239.00	1,220,641.20	31.10786
Jan 01, 2001	16,127.00	492,969.90	30.56799
Jan 01, 2001	23,112.00	727,671.30	31.48457

Figure A-40   Sample results from VisualTotals().

The bottom three rows of the VisualTotals() expression just presented show that VisualTotals() can work against ancestors and descendants of arbitrary depth. The [All Time] member is the higher level member in the dimension, while each day is at the leaf level. If you observe the values for the [AvgPrice] measure in the query, you can see that it is calculated after the visual totals, despite the fact that it is at solve order precedence 0. The VisualTotals() aggregation is documented to be at solve order –4096, so calculated member definitions will ordinarily override VisualTotals() synthetic aggregates. Meanwhile, VisualTotals() synthetic aggregates should be calculated from the results of custom rollups, because they are at solve order -5119.

Note that the synthetic members in the set returned by VisualTotals() are almost fully equivalent to calculated members created by other means. They cannot exist outside of a set as a calculated member, so they will not appear as metadata items through OLE DB for OLAP. They can be part of a set held in a CREATE SET statement and are treated as another calculated member by StripCalculatedMembers(). They can be filtered by name and unique name. They cannot, however, be referenced by a tuple reference in a formula because they are not entered into Microsoft Analysis Services's internal list of metadata objects.

W

WTD([*member*])   Returns: set
Standard

WTD() is the equivalent of PeriodsToDate() with the level set to Week. If *member* is not specified, it defaults to the current member of the Time-typed dimension. If no Time-typed dimension exists in the cube, or if it does not have a level tagged as Week, then a parser error results.

See also: PeriodsToDate(), QTD(), MTD(), YTD()

X

expr1 **XOR** *expr2*   Returns: Boolean
Standard

The result of this operator is true if only either *expr1* or *expr2* is true, and false if they both are true or both false. Both expressions must be evaluated in order to determine this.

Y

YTD([*member*])   Returns: set
Standard

YTD() is the equivalent of PeriodsToDate() with the level set to Year. If member is not specified, it defaults to the current member of the Time-typed dimension. If no Time-typed dimension exists in the cube, or if it does not have a level tagged as Year, then a parser error results.

See also: PeriodsToDate(), QTD(), MTD(), WTD()

Index

Index

D